lonely planet

Costa Rica

Arenal & the Northern Lowlands p221

Northwestern Costa Rica p176

Península de Nicoya p264

Central Valley & the Highlands p98

Caribbean Coast p137

San José p53

Central Pacific Coast p315

Southern Costa Rica & Península de Osa p364

Cassandra Brooklyn, Marco Ferrarese, Sarah Gilbert, Christa Jimenez, Anna Kaminski, Elizabeth Lavis, Marisa Megan Paska

CONTENTS

Plan Your Trip

The Guide

Ocelot, La Paz Waterfall Gardens (p112)

Volcán Arenal (p226)

FROM LEFT: ERIC MIDDELKOOP/SHUTTERSTOCK, PHOTO ©TAN YILMAZ/GETTY IMAGES, FRANCESCO RICCARDO IACOMINO/ GETTY IMAGES, VERNNY/SHUTTERSTOCK

Catarata Río Fortuna (p226)

Toolkit

Storybook

Ceviche (marinated seafood)

DAVE STAMBOULIS/ALAMY

El Chorro Waterfall (p308)

COSTA RICA

THE JOURNEY BEGINS HERE

Costa Rica is intoxicating, from the technicolor flowers and deeply saturated sunsets of the Central Pacific to the fresh-scented Orosí Valley dotted with charming coffee plantations and smoldering volcanoes. This vibrant realness and rawness hooked me on my first trip to Puerto Viejo in 2017, and I haven't been able or really wanted to shake it since. Costa Rica's vast natural wealth manifests itself in the gnarly waves of Witch's Rock and Montezuma's pale-pink clandestine beaches. It's evident in the biodiversity of Parque Nacional Tortuguero and Parque Nacional Manuel Antonio, as well as in the glittering bioluminescence of Bahía de Paquera. The country is also accessible – nobody can own the beach, and you'll see mega resorts scooted inland from the surf, leaving a public stretch of sand for all to enjoy. Costa Rica's inclusivity, warmth and phenomenal flora and fauna keep me coming back and deepen my delight every time.

Elizabeth Lavis

www.elizabethlavis.site

Elizabeth is an avid mountain climber and traveler with bylines in Lonely Planet, National Geographic, Wired for Adventure and HuffPost. She lives in Tbilisi, Georgia, with her boyfriend and two amazing rescue cats. She wrote the Península de Nicoya and Central Valley & the Highlands chapters.

My favorite experience is hiking to the very top of **El Chorro Waterfall** (p308) in Montezuma and looking out over Playa Cocolito and the Pacific Ocean.

WHO GOES WHERE

Our writers and experts choose the places which, for them, define Costa Rica.

CRIS YOUNG/SHUTTERSTOCK

I find the **Caribbean Coast** (p137) utterly beguiling: some of the best white-water rafting; sensitively conducted turtle tours; superb hikes in patches of jungle sufficiently remote and blissfully visitor-free... You may find yourself breakfasting while monkeys chitter overhead, touring an organic farm or pounding cacao beans with the Bribrí people to turn it into the freshest chocolate of your life.

Anna Kaminski

@anna.cohen.kaminski

Anna is a travel writer who covers adventure, culture and cuisine. She wrote the Caribbean Coast chapter.

ARKADIJ SCHELL/SHUTTERSTOCK

San José is so often left off itineraries and it was only on subsequent visits to Costa Rica that I became well acquainted with the big city. Its vibrant, pulsing culture and rapidly growing culinary and coffee scenes are undeniable and exciting to witness. While sipping tea and iced chocolate at places like **Modo** (p82) cafe, the lives of locals and the spirit of the city unfolded before me.

Cassandra Brooklyn

@escapingnewyork

Cassandra is a New York-based freelance writer. She wrote the San José chapter.

HARRY COLLINS PHOTOGRAPHY/SHUTTERSTOCK

The cloud forest is a feast for the senses at any time; a primeval, mystical place with its swirling mists and luxuriant greenery. The first time I went to the **Reserva Curi-Cancha** (p185) in Monteverde, I was lucky enough to spot not one, not two, but three resplendent quetzals (pictured above) in all their colorful glory. The sight of these extraordinary birds made the experience particularly special.

Sarah Gilbert

@SarahGTravels

Sarah is a globe-trotting freelance writer and photographer specializing in culture and wild nature. A long-time traveler to Central America, she wrote the Northwestern Costa Rica chapter.

FRANK GOMA SHUTTERSTOCK

On my right, pelicans dove into the waves to catch fish; on my left, a troop of spider monkeys stopped in their tracks to observe me from above. Couples of scarlet macaws kept zooming overhead, squawking loudly. As I continued walking, amazed, from Playa Pan Dulce to Backwash Beach, I even stumbled upon a group of capuchin monkeys. When I arrived at the beach, a dolphin jumped out of the sea. My first walk on **Playa Matapalo** (p348) was the best free safari I ever had in Costa Rica.

Marco Ferrarese

marcoferrarese.com

Marco is a Malaysia-based author and journalist. He wrote the Southern Costa Rica & Península de Osa chapter.

DUARTE DELLAROLE/SHUTTERSTOCK

The waterfalls of Costa Rica's Central Pacific Coast are genuinely breathtaking. **Nauyaca** (p346) is one of the gems, and although it's quite well known, the crowds do nothing to detract from its splendor. There are plenty of falls around the area that aren't known at all, so it's worth exploring if you want to escape the hordes, or simply head to the smaller swimming holes like Pozo Azul in Dominicalito.

Marisa Megan Paska

@_marisamegan

Marisa writes about travel, culture and conservation whenever she's not out surfing. She wrote the Central Pacific Coast chapter.

JOHN COLETTI/GETTY IMAGES

The **Río Sarapiquí** (p250) is a defining symbol of Costa Rica's unwavering commitment to sustainable tourism. As mysterious as it is majestic, the mighty river houses swimming holes, white-water rapids, hidden birding spots and waterfalls galore. Here, visitors and locals convene to enjoy nature's stunning handiwork while also reminding them to protect Mother Earth's most valuable resource – herself.

Christa Jimenez

puravidamoms.com

Christa is a Costa Rica travel writer specializing in family travel. She wrote the Arenal & the Northern Lowlands chapter.

Volcán Arenal & La Fortuna
Soak in volcano views and healing water (p226)
Monteverde & Santa Elena
Fly through the cloud-forest canopy (p182)
Nosara
Find your peace and surf big waves (p287)
Montezuma
Find a clandestine beach and ocean waterfall (p304)
Parque Nacional Manuel Antonio
Spy sloths, iguanas and monkeys (p334)
Rivas
NICARAGUA
Lago de Nicaragua
Islas Solentiname
Peñas Blancas
La Cruz
Santa Cecilia
Bahía Salinas
Golfo de Santa Elena
Volcán Orosí
Cuajiniquil
Parque Nacional Guanacaste
Upala
Los Chiles
Refugio de Vida Silvestre Caño Negro
Islas Murciélagos
Parque Nacional Santa Rosa
Volcán Rincón de la Vieja
Parque Nacional Rincón de la Vieja
Río Frío
Refugio de Vida Silvestre Maquenque
Bijagua
Volcán Tenorio
San Rafael
Golfo de Papagayo
Volcán Miravalles
Río San Carlos
Río Tempisque
Liberia
Parque Nacional Volcán Tenorio
Nuevo Arenal
Volcán Arenal
El Coco
Boca Arenal
Sardinal
Bagaces
Tilarán
Laguna de Arenal
La Fortuna
Pital
Potrero
Parque Nacional Palo Verde
Cañas
Parque Nacional Volcán Arenal
Huacas
Santa Elena
Ciudad Quesada
Aguas Zarcas
Tamarindo
Santa Cruz
Puerto Humo
Las Juntas
Volcán Porvenir
Paraíso
Nicoya
Isla Chira
Manzanillo
San Ramón
Puntarenas
Barranca
Alajuela
Nosara
Jicaral
Isla San Lucas
Esparza
Atenas
Ciudad Colón
Orotina
Sámara
Carrillo
Golfo de Nicoya
Paquera
Santiago de Puriscal
Tárcoles
Santa Teresa
Montezuma
Jacó
Reserva Natural Cabo Blanco
Parrita
PACIFIC OCEAN
0 100 km
0 50 miles

Río Sarapiquí
Tackle river rapids and see abundant birdlife (p248)
Parque Nacional Tortuguero
Glide through canals spotting turtles and manatees (p145)
San José
Immerse yourself in art, culture and history (p53)
Monumento Nacional Guayabo
Explore the relics of an ancient civilization (p133)
Puerto Viejo de Talamanca
Live it up in a surfing paradise (p163)
Parque Nacional Corcovado
Discover abundant wildlife and dense rainforest (p390)
Bahía Drake
Spot mega pods of dolphins and whales (p392)
San Juan River
Refugio Nacional de Vida Silvestre Barra del Colorado
Río Sarapiquí
Tortuguero
Puerto Viejo de Sarapiquí
Parque Nacional Tortuguero
Cariari
Parismina
Caribbean Sea
Río Sucio
Guápiles
Guácimo
Volcán Barva
Parque Nacional Braulio Carrillo
Siquirres
Batán
Heredia
Volcán Irazú
Volcán Turrialba
Puerto Limón
SAN JOSÉ
Cartago
Turrialba
Río Pacuare
Parque Nacional Barbilla
Paraíso
San Ignacio de Acosta
Orosí
Parque Nacional Tapantí-Macizo Cerro de la Muerte
Cahuita
Puerto Viejo de Talamanca
San Marcos
Bribrí
Manzanillo
Parque Nacional Chirripó
Río Telira
Providencia de Dota
Sixaola
Cerro de la Muerte
Quepos
Río Savegre
Rivas
Cerro Chirripó
Cerro Durika
Parque Nacional Manuel Antonio
Matapalo
San Isidro de El General
Cerro Kamuk
Dominical
Buenos Aires
Parque Internacional La Amistad
Uvita
Río General
Ojochal
Cerro Pittier
Palmar Norte
Boruca
Potrero Grande
Bahía de Coronado
Ciudad Cortes
Río Grande de Terraba
PANAMA
Sierpe
San Vito
Sabalito
Volcán
Isla del Caño
Bahía Drake
Parque Nacional Piedras Blancas
Agua Buena
Río Claro
Agujitas
La Palma
Neily
Parque Nacional Corcovado
Golfo Dulce
Paso Canoas
La Concepción
Puerto Jiménez
Carate
Matapalo
Pavones
Puerto Armuelles
Golfo de Chiriquí

WILD CREATURES

Costa Rica harbors an incredible diversity of wildlife, from the fearsome crocodiles of the Río Tárcoles to the jewel-bright hummingbirds of Los Santos in the Península de Osa. You can view these magnificent creatures in the wild or learn about the conservation efforts of organizations committed to protecting vulnerable animals. Whether you take a dedicated wildlife tour, or just keep your eyes peeled as you're out and about, you'll encounter critters of all shapes and sizes.

FROM LEFT: FRANCIS WONG/500PX, KOEN'S PHOTOGRAPHY/SHUTTERSTOCK, EMMA SHAW/LONELY PLANET

Go with a Guide

Wild animals can be notoriously difficult to spot, but a good guide can help you peep at high-up or elusive creatures through powerful spotting scopes.

Remember They're Wild

Although wild animals might look cuddly, they are not tame creatures or pets. Don't feed or try to touch them and give them a respectful berth.

Building the Bridge

Development has taken its toll on a lot of wild spaces in Costa Rica, so many conservation organizations are building bridges for the safe passage of wildlife.

Sloth, Parque Nacional Manuel Antonio (p334)

BEST WILDLIFE-WATCHING EXPERIENCES

Look for elusive anteaters, squirrel monkeys and Baird's tapir (pictured left) in the lush jungle setting of ❶ **Parque Nacional Corcovado** (p309).

Learn about conversation and creating safe habitats for jungle creatures at ❷ **Sibu Wildlife Sanctuary** (p290) near Nosara.

Catch a glimpse of shy sloths, iguanas (pictured far left) and white-faced monkeys in ❸ **Parque Nacional Manuel Antonio** (p334).

Hike through ❹ **Parque Nacional Braulio Carrillo** (p153) for a chance to see spiders, howler monkeys and fabulous tropical birds.

Spot humpback whales and dolphins in ❺ **Parque Nacional Marino Ballena** (p352) on the sunny Central Pacific Coast.

Reserva Biológica Bosque Nuboso Monteverde (p182)

MISTY MAGIC

Pull yourself away from Costa Rica's sunny shores and you'll find misty landscapes thick with lush foliage and bursting with animal life. In these tropical cloud forests, hanging bridges take you deep into the heart of the mist-shrouded wonder. Monteverde is the most impressive, but there are smaller ones in the Central Valley and in the south of the country.

Temperature Drop

The cloud forest can get considerably cooler than the rest of Costa Rica, so plan to bring several layers if you're headed this way.

Bird Guides

Cloud forests are homes to creatures like the resplendent quetzal and three-wattled bellbird, and a good guide can help you spot them.

BEST CLOUD FOREST EXPERIENCES

Explore the ethereal ❶ **Monteverde** (p182), the country's biggest cloud forest that's teeming with animal and bird life.

Hike the trails of ❷ **Santa Elena** (p188) cloud forest, full of fantastic wildlife and tons of birds including the resplendent quetzal.

Get a taste of the misty magic in ❸ **Bajos del Toro** (p111), a tiny and less touristy cloud-forest town in the Central Valley.

Look for the mythical quetzal in the cloud forests of ❹ **Parque Nacional Los Quetzales** (p373) in the southern Los Santos region.

Head to ❺ **Finca Modelo** (p190) for adrenaline-pumping ziplining through the cloud forests of northwestern Costa Rica.

ADRENALINE RUSH

From the mighty rapids of the Río Sarapiquí to the misty canopy of Monteverde, there's no shortage of heart-pounding adventures in Costa Rica. You'll find challenging rapids, rainforest ziplines and plenty of biking and hiking designed to let you see the raw side of the country. If you're in the mood for adventure sports, you've come to the right place.

FROM LEFT: NATURE'S CHARM/SHUTTERSTOCK, PAFNUTI/SHUTTERSTOCK

Wear the Right Gear

Whether you're zipping through the skies or taking on the rapids, it's important to wear the right gear. Pack light layers, waterproof clothes and proper shoes.

Know Your Rapids

Class I – calm, flat, family-friendly

Class II – a little rougher, fine for novices

Class III – intermediate

Class IV – challenging

Class V – difficult, not suitable for children

Rafting Safety

No matter how many times you've rafted, it's a good idea to pay attention to the safety briefing and wear protective gear in case you topple out of the boat.

BEST ADVENTURE SPORT EXPERIENCES

Take on the challenging rapids of the ❶ **Río Sarapiquí** (p248) and, if you're feeling brave, check out the wild rapids near San Miguel.

Cruise through the canopy of ❷ **Manuel Antonio** (p334) then enjoy a hearty trek through the national park and beach.

Ride the family-friendly Class II and III white-water rapids of the Central Pacific Coast's ❸ **Río Savegre** (p333).

Enjoy epic rafting on the Class III and IV rapids of the ❹ **Río Pacuare** (p154; pictured left) on the Caribbean Coast.

Test your wits and skills zooming over the frothing rapids of the ❺ **Río Reventazón** (p127) near Lago de Cachí.

VOLCANO POWER

The Cordillera de Guanacaste and Cordillera Central mountain ranges are lined with fiery giants that steam and sputter, infusing the earth with healing hot springs and inviting the courageous to climb their craters and peaks. From Arenal, which dominates the skyline in La Fortuna, to the sky-high Volcán Irazú in the Central Valley, you'll be amazed by the plethora of peaks with majestic views, perfect for a day of adventure.

FROM LEFT: JAKUB MACULEWICZ/SHUTTERSTOCK, ESTEBAN ALEJANDRO/SHUTTERSTOCK, POVFPV/SHUTTERSTOCK

Mind the Altitude

Volcán Irazú is a breathtaking 3432m above sea level, so the altitude can be next-level challenging. Stay hydrated and listen to your body.

Active Volcanoes

An 'active' volcano is one with a recent history of eruptions. Costa Rica's five active volcanoes are Poás (pictured), Arenal, Rincón de la Vieja, Irazú and Turrialba.

Hot Springs

Most 'hot springs' are actually artificial pools with volcano-heated water pumped in. Only a few places have natural pools in geothermal rivers or springs.

Volcán Irazú (p132)

BEST VOLCANO EXPERIENCES

Peer into the impressive caldera at ❶ **Parque Nacional Volcán Poás** (p109) and visit the turquoise lake.

Hike to the summit of ❷ **Volcán Irazú** (p132) to get a glimpse of the shimmering crater lake.

Take a soothing dip in the volcano-heated pools in the shadow of epic ❸ **Volcán Arenal** (p238).

Combine water and fire in one day by visiting ❹ **Volcán Tenorio** (p194) and nearby Río Celeste.

Witness live volcanic activity at Sector Las Pailas of ❺ **Parque Nacional Rincón de la Vieja** (p207).

JAKUB MACULEWICZ/SHUTTERSTOCK

La Paz Waterfall Gardens (p112)

FAB FALLS

Secretive jungle waterfalls, cutting through the forest green and tumbling over the rocks, are a sight to behold – you'll find them from the Península de Nicoya to the deep rainforests on the Caribbean side. These fab cascades combine the adventure of hiking with the soothing payoff of a cool dip in a refreshing waterfall pool.

Jump with Caution

Some waterfall pools are perfect for plunging but others have rocky or shallow bottoms, so always mind the safety signage.

Celestial Sight

Arguably, Catarata Río Celeste is the country's most beautiful waterfall due to its dreamy color, but swimming is prohibited in this true-blue beauty.

BEST WATERFALL EXPERIENCES

Visit Montezuma's trifecta of falls right outside the town core, or venture to ❶ **El Chorro** (p306), a river-to-ocean waterfall.

Lounge in the lower pool and explore the upper falls at ❷ **Nauyaca Waterfalls** (p346) on the Central Pacific Coast.

Go on a canyoneering expedition to discover the glorious ❸ **La Leona Waterfall** (p210) in Curubandé.

Swim under three different rainforest falls – known as ❹ **Naguala Falls** (p400)– along the Río Agujitas.

Marvel at the five scenic cascades in the Central Valley's ❺ **La Paz Waterfall Gardens** (p109).

SEA TURTLES

It's nothing short of magical to see a tiny sea turtle take its first tentative steps towards the great ocean or watch an olive ridley slog out of the roiling sea to lay her eggs on the beach. To witness any part of this annual process is to peek into a fascinating aspect of the natural world.

FROM LEFT: SUSAN M JACKSON/SHUTTERSTOCK, KRYSSIA CAMPOS/GETTY IMAGES

The Arribada is Sudden

The specific *arribada* (turtle nestings) dates are hard to pin down – you might find out a day or two before one. Make time in your schedule for it.

Red Lights

If you're attending the *arribada* at night, only red lights are allowed. Sea turtles depend on moonlight to find their natal beaches.

Look But Don't Touch

Do not interact with the turtles, touch them or impede their journey to or from the sea in any way.

BEST TURTLE-VIEWING EXPERIENCES

Witness the amazing arrival of hundreds of nesting olive ridley turtles at ❶ **Playa Ostional** (p293) near Nosara.

Watch olive ridley, hawksbill and Pacific black turtles at ❷ **Playa Matapalo** (p346) near Dominical.

Join the turtle patrol in the tiny fishing village of ❸ **Parismina** (p146) to help protect nesting sea turtles.

Marvel at the massive leatherbacks that nest at ❹ **Playa Langosta** (p283) near Parque Nacional Marino Las Baulas.

Sail the canals of ❺ **Parque Nacional Tortuguero** (p142), where four different species of turtles nest on the beaches.

SWEET BREAKS

Costa Rica's 1300km of coastline makes it an ideal spot for hitting the surf. Whether you're looking for gentle, beginner-friendly waves or want to take on the monsters near Witch's Rock or Salsa Brava, you'll find all you're looking for a few steps from the sandy shore. There's a thriving surf culture, complete with expert instructors and schools, and ample opportunities to connect with the ocean and enjoy the most heart-pounding water sport around.

FROM LEFT: ANGELA N PERRYMAN/SHUTTERSTOCK, MARCEL HAMONIC/SHUTTERSTOCK, GROGL/SHUTTERSTOCK

Surf Pacífico

The Central Pacific Coast and Península de Nicoya (pictured) enjoy big, consistent waves from May to October. The dry season is better for beginners.

Surf Caribe

Visit the Caribbean Coast from November to May, and you'll enjoy massive waves and a fabulous vibe. For expert-only surf, head to Salsa Brava (pictured).

Respect Your Limits

Surf's up for the taking, but it's best not to get in over your head. Be realistic and respect your limits before you hit the water.

Jacó (p320)

BEST SURFING EXPERIENCES

Combine beginner surfing with some next-level partying in ❶ **Jacó** (p320) on the Central Pacific Coast.

Catch some serious swells at ❷ **Playa Guiones** (p287) and soak up the chill atmosphere of Nosara.

Road-trip through ❸ **Santa Teresa's** (p298) bevy of blissful beaches on the Península de Nicoya.

Surf great waves and enjoy the authentic Tico ambiance at ❹ **Playa Dominical** (p343).

Take on ❺ **Salsa Brava** (p163), the notoriously tough surf spot near Puerto Viejo de Talamanca.

Museo del Oro Precolombino (p64)

INDIGENOUS CULTURE

Costa Rica's indigenous groups make up 2.4% of the population, and tourists can respectfully visit and learn about their way of life. There are traces of ancient civilizations throughout the country, including the Huetar on the Pacific Coast and the Quepoa around Manuel Antonio. The Bribrí and Cabécar are found on the Caribbean side, and the Maleku in the north.

Respect is Key

While tourists are welcomed into indigenous areas, it's important to be respectful and avoid taking unwanted photos or interfering in private daily life.

Archaeological Sites

The Central Valley's Monumento Nacional Guayabo and the Península de Osa's Finca 6 are major archaeological sites whose mysteries haven't been fully unlocked.

BEST INDIGENOUS CULTURE EXPERIENCES

Explore the ❶ **Parque Nacional Barbilla** (p155) with an indigenous Cabécar hiking guide.

Paddle a dugout canoe to ❷ **Reserva Indígena Yorkín** (p161) for a taste of Bribrí culture.

Spend a week with the Brörán and Boruca people in ❸ **Térraba** (p386).

Visit ❹ **Parque Nacional Carara** (p326), known as the 'River of Lizards' in the Huetar language.

Admire priceless artifacts at the ❺ **Museo del Oro Precolombino** (p64) in San José.

LOCAL FLAVORS

From hearty *gallo pinto* (rice and beans) to shots of *guaro* (sugarcane firewater), Costa Rica's food culture is bold and flavorful. On the Caribbean Coast, taste savory or sweet *patís* (Caribbean empanadas); inland, sample intensely flavored coffee, chocolate and local cheese. There's an impressive variety of tropical fruits at every weekend market, ready to savor.

FROM LEFT: BRYCE JACKSON/SHUTTERSTOCK, LUISGSII03/SHUTTERSTOCK

Stop by the Soda

These small, family-run restaurants serve typical Costa Rican food at very affordable prices. Stop by for *gallo pinto* (rice and beans; pictured) or a *casado* (set meal).

Chili Guaro

Every beach bar has its own version of *chili guaro* (pictured) – a fiery concoction that will have you reeling if you're not careful.

The Freshest Fruits

Enjoy the bounty of Costa Rica's tropical climate in the form of mangos, pineapples, bananas and papayas.

BEST FOOD & DRINK EXPERIENCES

Taste the spicy goodness of Creole and Caribbean cooking in ❶ **Puerto Limón's** (p149) Old Town.

Head to ❷ **Ojochal** (p360) on the Central Pacific Coast for a taste of high-end cuisine with a jungle view.

Discover the country's most elevated cuisine in the bistros of ❸ **Barrio Escalante** (p86) in San José.

Stop by ❹ **Tamarindo's** (p281) weekly night market and food-truck garden for fabulous eats.

Sample local favorites such as ❺ **Turrialba's** (p130) famous cheese in the Central Valley.

LIFE IN THE TREETOPS

Set back from the shimmering waves of Costa Rica's beautiful beaches is the emerald rainforest, which covers some 59% of the country and offers ample opportunities for exploring hidden waterfalls, zipping through the trees or simply admiring the wildlife. Conservation efforts in places like the Central Pacific Coast are aimed at preserving this green treasure – learn about how to do your part, all while getting in a rigorous hike in this pristine environment.

A Trio of Forests

There are three types of forest in Costa Rica: tropical rainforest (pictured), tropical cloud forest and tropical dry forest.

Mighty Ceiba

The tallest tree in the rainforest is usually the ceiba tree (also called the kapok). The tallest specimens tower more than 60m high.

Cautious Hiking

The rainforests provide fabulous hiking opportunities, but it's important to respect the signage and know your physical limits when heading into the wilderness.

Ziplining, Montezuma Waterfalls (p304)

BEST TREETOP EXPERIENCES

Visit the ❶ **Rainmaker** (p339) conservation project on the Central Pacific Coast, tackling the suspension bridges and hiking trails.

Climb the observation tower in ❷ **Santa Elena's** (p182) cloud-forest reserve for a view over four volcanoes.

Sleep in a treehouse, surrounded by the sights and sounds of the rainforest, at ❸ **Maquenque Eco Lodge** (p253) in Boca Tapada.

Ascend the ❹ **Nature Observatorio** (p169) near Puerto Viejo de Talamanca for an incredible lookout over the Caribbean Sea.

Speed on a zipline through ❺ **Montezuma's** (p304) impressive canopy for bird's-eye views of the mighty falls.

HECTOR SEGURA/SHUTTERSTOCK

Juan Santamaría monument, Alajuela (p104)

BYGONE DAYS

Historical sites may not be high on your list of places to go and things to see in Costa Rica, but history buffs will be surprised and delighted by this little country's rich and diverse story – from pre-Columbian archaeology to colonial architecture to battles to protect and preserve an independent Costa Rica.

Colonial Costa Rica

The historic centers of San José and Cartago contain the country's best examples of colonial architecture and history.

Independent Costa Rica

Costa Rica (along with the rest of Central America) gained its independence in 1821, with Spain's defeat in the Mexican War of Independence.

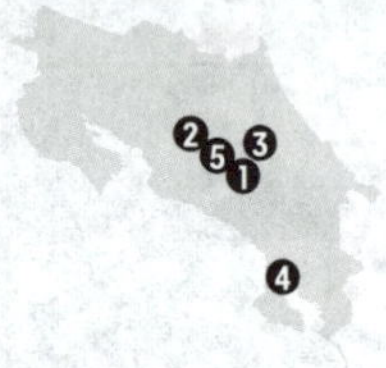

BEST HISTORY EXPERIENCES

Pay homage to legendary *La Negrita* (Black Virgin) and admire *Costa Rica Victoriosa* in ❶ **Cartago** (p114).

Learn about the legacy of Juan Santamaría, the poor drummer boy turned national hero, in ❷ **Alajuela** (p104).

Discover the remains of an ancient city at the ❸ **Monumento Nacional Guayabo** (p133) near Turrialba.

Investigate the mysterious stone spheres and ❹ **Finca 6** (p402) on the Península de Osa.

Visit the ❺ **Museo Nacional de Costa Rica** (p59) in San José for a comprehensive overview of the country's history.

EARTHY GOODNESS

Central Valley is Costa Rica's breadbasket, with vast coffee plantations, tasty local products and family-friendly farm tours. The country's prize fruit, banana, was once exploited on the Caribbean Coast and in places like Sarapiquí. Today, you can visit sustainable family-run *fincas* (farms) and try the fruits of the land in a responsible way.

Turrialba Cheese

Turrialba is famous for its *queso fresco*, a semi-hard cheese with a mild taste that's ideal on bread or paired with fruit.

Coffee Aplenty

You'll find many farms where you can stroll amongst the coffee plants and learn about cultivating and harvesting Costa Rica's main crop.

A Sweet Treat

Costa Rican chocolate is absolutely next-level, and you can hop on a tasty chocolate tour near Heredia or in Sarapiquí.

BEST FARM EXPERIENCES

Visit the famous ❶ **Britt Coffee** (p121; pictured left) outside Heredia and gain a whole new appreciation for your morning brew.

Spend a day around ❷ **Sarapiquí** (p248) and learn how *palmito* (heart of palm), chocolate and pineapple are produced.

Learn all about cacao and its sacred history from the Bröran people on a tour at ❸ **El Descanso Térraba** (p387).

Take a delicious and educational bean-to-bar cacao tour at an organic farm in ❹ **Río Celeste** (p198).

Spend the night at ❺ **Hacienda Orosí** (p128), visit a family-friendly animal farm, take a coffee tour and enjoy the hot springs.

REGIONS & CITIES

Find the places that tick all your boxes.

Arenal & the Northern Lowlands

FROM FARMS TO FORESTS

Dominated by Volcán Arenal and encompassing La Fortuna with its endless font of healing mineral water, this region is rich in rainforests, bubbling volcanoes and agricultural land where you can sample some of Costa Rica's finest fruits. Take a trek, then treat yourself to a volcanic soak in paradise.

p221

Northwestern Costa Rica

ECOTOURISM AND ADVENTURE

From the misty cloud forests of Monteverde to the sparkling waters of Río Celeste, this region is bursting with fantastic natural landscapes, wildlife and the less-explored beach breaks of Santa Rosa. It speaks to the adventurous heart of travelers who prefer natural diversity and something a bit out of the box.

p176

Arenal & the Northern Lowlands p221

Northwestern Costa Rica p176

Península de Nicoya p264

Península de Nicoya

WIDE GOLDEN BEACHES AND FABULOUS SURF

The sunny shores of the Península de Nicoya beckon surfers from all around the globe and shelter caches of turtle eggs until the tiny creatures are ready to take to the waves. Head south for the waters of Bahía de Paquera, where you can swim in balmy seas.

p264

Central Pacific Coast

SURF, WATERFALLS AND WILDLIFE GALORE

The small but mighty Central Pacific Coast is full of unexpected treasures and finds, from the foodie hub of Ojochal to jungle-backed beaches perfect for surfing on glassy waves. See humpback whales, shy sloths, white-faced capuchin monkeys and ruby-colored macaws thriving on this biodiverse coastline.

p315

Central Valley & the Highlands

COSTA RICA'S BEATING AGRICULTURAL HEART

Slow down and savor every moment in Costa Rica's fertile crescent, full of sprawling coffee farms and laced with hiking and cycling trails. This region is also steeped in history, from the streets of Cartago to the archaeological treasures just beyond Turrialba and the verdant Orosí Valley.

p98

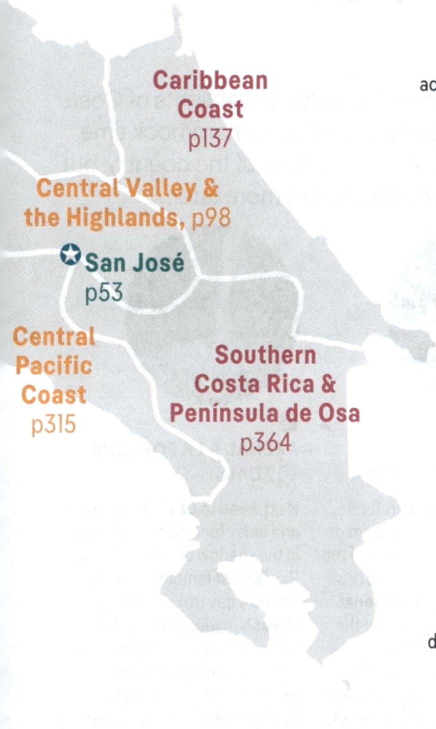

San José

COSTA RICA'S COSMOPOLITAN CAPITAL

Peek beneath the gritty veneer of Costa Rica's capital and you'll find a joyfully chaotic, artistic and sophisticated city full of fabulous museums, culture and nightlife. With so many neighborhoods to explore and surprises around every corner, San José is all you could want from a cosmopolitan adventure and more.

p53

Caribbean Coast p137
Central Valley & the Highlands, p98
San José p53
Central Pacific Coast p315
Southern Costa Rica & Península de Osa p364

Caribbean Coast

JUNGLE BEACHES, SPICY FOODS, DIVERSE CULTURES

Visit the coast less traveled and you'll find achingly beautiful beaches, excellent snorkeling and diving, and some of the country's best wildlife. El Caribe is a gift to those who love spicy cuisine, pairing Caribbean flavors with traditional Costa Rican dishes in a fabulous fusion that reflects the region's uniqueness.

p137

Southern Costa Rica & Península de Osa

UNMATCHED BIODIVERSITY AND ANCESTRAL ROOTS

The remote and rewarding southern part of Costa Rica has pristine natural wonders, fascinating archaeological mysteries and abundant wildlife. Journey through its microclimates and enjoy nature in its most dazzling form in the waters of Bahía Drake and the tropical fjords of Puerto Jiménez.

p364

MANAMANA/SHUTTERSTOCK

Parque Nacional Manuel Antonio (p334)

ITINERARIES

Costa Rica Highlights Reel

Allow: 9 days **Distance:** 800km

If you have just over a week, you can check out all the highlights of Costa Rica and still enjoy balmy days on the beach and some hammock time under the stars. This itinerary will give you a true taste of the country, but don't be surprised if you want to return and explore more later.

1

SAN JOSÉ 1 DAY

Juan Santamaría International Airport is only half an hour by bus or car from **San José** (p53), making this underestimated capital the ideal place to start your journey. Spend your first day exploring great museums and tempt your tastebuds in Barrio Escalante for a memorable evening meal. San José also has some tremendous shopping for every budget.

2

PARQUE NACIONAL TORTUGUERO 1 DAY

Head back to the airport for a half-hour flight to Tortuguero or, if you feel like seeing more of the countryside, rent a car and drive to El Caribe. **Parque Nacional Tortuguero** (p145), outside the small village of Tortuguero, is beautifully biodiverse – it's home to sea turtles (pictured), crocodiles, sloths and monkeys, and you can sail through the park's canals.

3

ARENAL & LA FORTUNA 2 DAYS

Next, head to **La Fortuna** (p226) and enjoy fantastic hot springs in the shadow of Arenal, Costa Rica's most famous volcano. Spend a day trekking the region's myriad trails and visiting La Fortuna waterfall (pictured) before relaxing in healing mineral water. On the second day, try some white-water rafting on the Río Sarapiquí for a taste of the rainforest.

FROM LEFT: GUAYO FUENTES/SHUTTERSTOCK, JARNO GONZALEZ ZARRAONANDIA/SHUTTERSTOCK, PAVEL TVRDY/SHUTTERSTOCK

4

MONTEVERDE & SANTA ELENA ⏱1 DAY

Drive to the misty cloud forest of Costa Rica's green giant, **Monteverde** (p182), where you can tackle sky-high monkey bridges (pictured), zipline through the forest canopy and discover hidden waterfalls. You can choose between plenty of hiking and coffee tours on offer in this region, or tap into your inner child with some tree climbing.

5

PARQUE NACIONAL MANUEL ANTONIO ⏱2 DAYS

The longest stage of this trip is also the most scenic as you head to **Parque Nacional Manuel Antonio** (p334) on the Central Pacific Coast. Admire the jungle and sea views on your way there, then spend two days exploring one of the country's best parks for spotting wildlife like sloths and monkeys (pictured), and snorkeling on a gorgeous beach.

6

MONTEZUMA ⏱2 DAYS

Drive back up the coast to Puntarenas, where you'll catch a ferry across the Golfo de Nicoya to **Montezuma** (p304). This artistic and nature-oriented town offers jungle waterfalls including El Chorro, which plunges straight into the sea, a friendly community and the option of a day tour to Paquera to see the bioluminescence. Fly home from Liberia airport, a four-hour drive north.

FROM LEFT: INTREEGUE PHOTOGRAPHY/SHUTTERSTOCK, WIRESTOCK CREATORS/SHUTTERSTOCK, TRAVELVIEWY/SHUTTERSTOCK

JORGE A. RUSSELL/SHUTTERSTOCK

Jacó (p320)

ITINERARIES

Pacific Surf Spectacular

Allow: 10 days **Distance:** 335km

The Pacific Coast is the delight of surfers, with kilometers of blissful beaches that stretch from the Central Pacific Coast up to the Península de Nicoya. Surf the big waves of Nosara, then soothe your soul with some restorative yoga, visit turtle-nesting beaches or hit up epic party towns like Jacó and Tamarindo.

FROM LEFT: MAX HERMAN/SHUTTERSTOCK, N K/SHUTTERSTOCK, STEFAN NEUMANN/SHUTTERSTOCK

1

TAMARINDO 2 DAYS

Fly into Liberia airport and hit the road for **Tamarindo** (p278). This surf party town has breezy, beginner waves, fun nightlife and access to Parque Nacional Marino Las Baulas, where you can chill out on the pristine Playa Grande and spot leatherback turtles at Playa Langosta.

Detour: *Drive north to* **Playa Conchal** *(p284) to see the white-shell beach before heading south to Nosara.* *3 hours*

2

NOSARA 1 DAY

Drive down the coast towards Guanacaste Province's hub of all things surf and yoga – **Nosara** (p287). You'll find generously sized waves on Playa Guiones and a lovely almond-tree-lined beach ideal for watching the sunset. At nearby Playa Ostional, olive ridley turtles lay their eggs during the mass *arribada*. Find your peace with a five-star yoga class or hike in the lush jungle.

3

SÁMARA 1 DAY

The family-friendly, cheerful and kooky town of **Sámara** (p291) is just half an hour down the coast, but the journey may take longer during the rainy season. You'll find regular beginner to intermediate waves here, and a fun vibe that's a nice mix of locals and travelers. There's a variety of accommodations, and great nightlife for those who want to partake.

4 SANTA TERESA 2 DAYS

Santa Teresa (p299) is one of the top destinations on the peninsula for those looking to surf the big waves. Intermediate waves await in Playa Santa Teresa, but you can find some gentler giants in nearby Playa Hermosa. If you're really up for a challenge, check out Suck Rock.

Detour: *Rent an ATV and head into the jungle to visit* **Montezuma** *(p304).* *5 hours*

5 JACÓ 2 DAYS

Head to Paquera, east of Santa Teresa, and hop on the ferry to Puntarenas. Once there, drive down the coast to **Jacó** (p320), the Central Pacific's premier surf and party town, with beginner swells and thriving nightlife. Visit nearby Playa Hermosa (not the same as the previous one) for a bigger challenge and the chance to watch a surf competition.

6 DOMINICAL 2 DAYS

Down the coast from Jacó, **Dominical** (p342) is an ideal spot to end your surf adventure in Costa Rica. You'll find fun, accessible waves in both Dominical and Dominicalito, gorgeous waterfalls nearby, abundant nature and stunning sunsets. On the last day, drive three hours to the Juan Santamaría International Airport to take your flight home.

FROM LEFT: JUAN JOSE JACINTO/SHUTTERSTOCK, JORGE A. RUSSELL/SHUTTERSTOCK, GIANFRANCO VIVI/SHUTTERSTOCK

Parque Nacional Cahuita (p157)

ITINERARIES

El Caribe Adventure

Allow: 6 days **Distance:** 520km

You can explore Costa Rica's relaxed and charming Caribbean Coast over just six days. You'll travel from San José to Parque Nacional Tortuguero for astounding wildlife, visit the chill Parque Nacional Cahuita for snorkeling and hiking, and finish at Puerto Viejo de Talamanca for fabulous beaches and a bit of partying.

1

SAN JOSÉ 2 DAYS

Start in vibrant **San José** (p53), checking out the arts scene, eating excellent dining and getting a feel for the country's *pura vida* ethos. If you have time, just north of the capital in Alajuela you can learn about Juan Santamaría, Costa Rica's national hero.

***Detour:** Stop by the **Britt Coffee Tour** (p121) near Heredia and sample what this region is famous for. 15 mins*

2

PARQUE NACIONAL TORTUGUERO 1 DAY

Drive east through Costa Rica's gorgeous Central Valley towards the Caribbean Coast. Along the way, you'll enjoy bucolic farmland scenery and get a glimpse of rural Costa Rica before arriving at Tortuguero for a visit to **Parque Nacional Tortuguero** (p145), a national park crisscrossed by canals and teeming with wildlife.

3

PARQUE NACIONAL CAHUITA 1 DAY

Hit the road again and head down the pristine Caribbean Coast to the village of Cahuita, the home of calypso music legend Walter Ferguson as well as the gateway to **Parque Nacional Cahuita** (p157), where you can enjoy some world-class hiking and snorkeling in the clear waters.

FROM LEFT: RAINER LESNIEWSKI/SHUTTERSTOCK, JULEN ARABAOLAZA/SHUTTERSTOCK, DUDAREV MIKHAILN/SHUTTERSTOCK

NICARAGUA
0 50 km
0 25 miles
Río San Juan
Refugio Nacional de Vida Silvestre Barra del Colorado
Tortuguero
2 Parque Nacional Tortuguero
Río Toro
Zona Protectora La Selva
Volcán Platanar
Laguna Hule
Volcán Barva
2h30min-3h
Guácimo
Río Parismina
Caribbean Sea
Guápiles
Britt Coffee Tour
Alajuela
15min
Heredia
SAN JOSÉ
1
START
Volcán Irazú
Siquirres
3h50min
Batán
Parque Nacional Barbilla
Puerto Limón
Cartago
Turrialba
Cachí
Tucurrique
Paraíso
Orosí
Zona Protectora Cuenca del Río Banano
Parque Nacional Cahuita
Puerto Viejo de Talamanca
Cahuita
3
4
20-30min
Bribri
Manzanillo
END
Sixaola
Zona Protectora Caraigres
San Marcos
Cerro Las Vueltas
Cerro de la Muerte
Zona Protectora Cuenca del Río Tuis
Reserva Biológica Hitoy Cerere
Río Telire
Cerro Chirripó
Parque Internacional La Amistad
Río Savegre
Páramo
Reserva Forestal Los Santos
Río Chirripó
Parque Nacional Chirripó
Cerro Durika
Cerro Kamuk
PANAMA
Río Teribe
Río Changuinola
Parque Internacional La Amistad
Bahía de Coronado
Parque Nacional Marino Ballena
Isla Ballena
Río General
Cerro Pittier

4

PUERTO VIEJO DE TALAMANCA ⏱ 2 DAYS

Only half an hour from laid-back Cahuita, **Puerto Viejo de Talamanca** (p163) is a surfer party hot spot with wonderful food, tons of great live-music venues and beach upon beach to choose from. Surf Salsa Brava if you're feeling brave, and spend some time cycling around this happening town.

NATALIA KUZMINA/SHUTTERSTOCK

Keel-billed toucan, Parque Nacional Cahuita (p157)

ABOVE: MATYAS REHAK/SHUTTERSTOCK

ESDELVAL/SHUTTERSTOCK

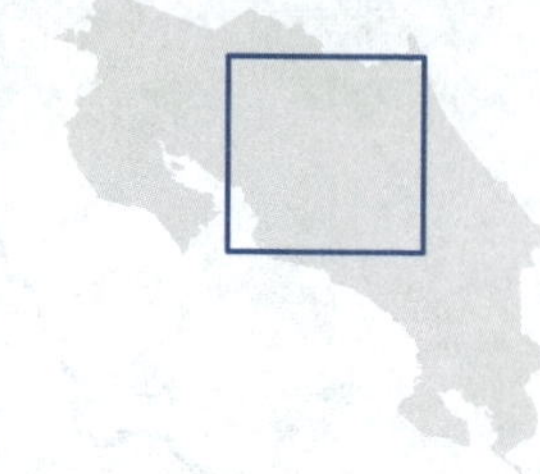

Volcán Arenal (p231)

ITINERARIES

Volcanoes & History Tour

Allow: 5 days **Distance:** 335km

The often-overlooked Central Valley region of Costa Rica is home to magnificent volcanoes, healing thermal hot springs and plenty of history. You'll get to combine it all, then marvel at the most impressive volcano of them all, Volcán Arenal, on this five-day tour.

1

ALAJUELA 1 DAY

Every visitor to Juan Santamaría International Airport starts their journey in **Alajuela** (p104) – it's just that many of them don't know it. Alajuela is the hometown of the airport's famous namesake, who stood up to the *filibusteros* and kept Costa Rica free. Learn about the country's proud history in this charming town.

2

PARQUE NACIONAL VOLCÁN POÁS 1 DAY

Volcán Poás (p109) is a fantastic example of a stratovolcano with a turquoise-colored crater lake and hummingbirds flittering everywhere. Arrive early, as the volcano closes in the early afternoon, and spend the night at nearby El Silencio Lodge & Spa.

Detour: *Visit* **La Paz Waterfall Gardens** *(p112), one of the most beautiful cascades in the Central Valley.* *20 mins*

3

OROSÍ VALLEY 1 DAY

Drive into the heart of Costa Rica to **Orosí Valley** (p122), dotted with coffee farms and brimming with hiking opportunities and lovely hot springs. Spend the night under a clear, star-filled sky in one of the valley's tiny towns and reach peak restoration.

Detour: *Visit the* **Ruinas de Ujarrás** *(p119), a colonial-era church with a mysterious past.* *30 mins*

FROM LEFT: GIANFRANCO VIVI/SHUTTERSTOCK, MATTEO COLOMBO/GETTY IMAGES, PELOY (ALLAN H.M.)/WIKIMEDIA/CC BY-SA 3.0

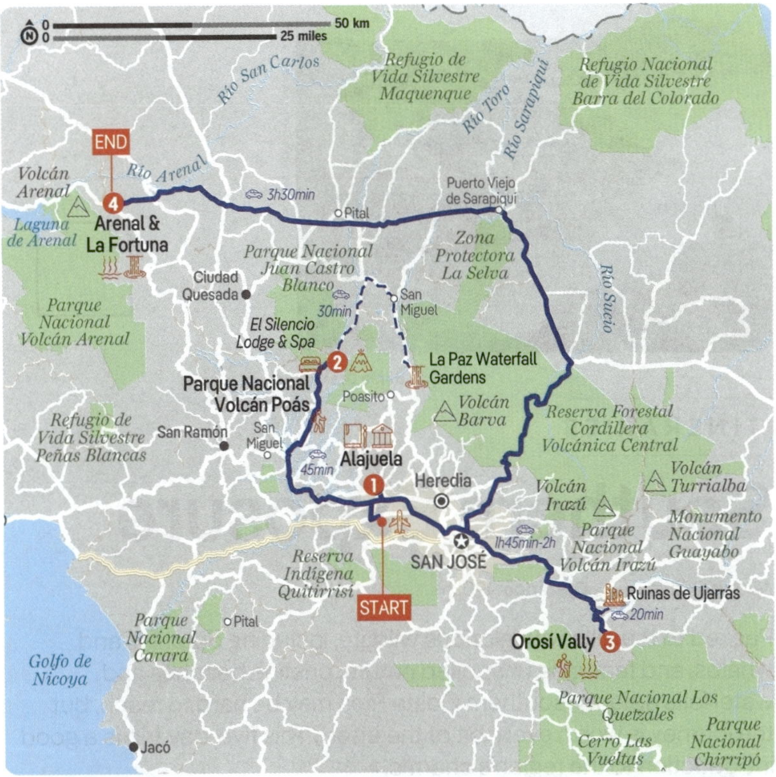

0 50 km
0 25 miles
Río San Carlos
Refugio de Vida Silvestre Maquenque
Refugio Nacional de Vida Silvestre Barra del Colorado
Río Toro
Río Sarapiquí
END
Volcán Arenal
Río Arenal
3h30min
Puerto Viejo de Sarapiquí
4 Arenal & La Fortuna
Laguna de Arenal
Pital
Zona Protectora La Selva
Parque Nacional Juan Castro Blanco
Ciudad Quesada
Río Sucio
San Miguel
30min
Parque Nacional Volcán Arenal
El Silencio Lodge & Spa
2
La Paz Waterfall Gardens
Parque Nacional Volcán Poás
Poasito
Volcán Barva
Reserva Forestal Cordillera Volcánica Central
Refugio de Vida Silvestre Peñas Blancas
San Ramón
San Miguel
45min
Alajuela
Volcán Irazú
Volcán Turrialba
1
Heredia
Parque Nacional Volcán Irazú
1h45min-2h
Monumento Nacional Guayabo
SAN JOSÉ
Reserva Indígena Quitirrisí
START
Ruinas de Ujarrás
20min
Parque Nacional Carara
Pital
Orosí Vally 3
Golfo de Nicoya
Parque Nacional Los Quetzales
Parque Nacional Chirripó
Cerro Las Vueltas
Jacó

4

ARENAL & LA FORTUNA

2 DAYS

The journey to **Volcán Arenal and La Fortuna** (p226) from the Orosí Valley leads through some of the most beautiful countryside in Costa Rica and offers spectacular hiking, plenty of opportunities to luxuriate in volcanic hot springs, and waterfalls galore. You can choose your own adventure: soaking and relaxing, hiking and exploring, or a bit of both.

Catarata de Río Celeste (p194), La Fortuna

FROM LEFT: JENARI/SHUTTERSTOCK, CHRISPICTURES/SHUTTERSTOCK

STEFAN NEUMANN/SHUTTERSTOCK

Bahía Drake

ITINERARIES

Southern Exposure

Allow: 5 days **Distance:** 190km

Packed to the gills with glorious wildlife, including dolphins and whales, and featuring unspoiled nature, pristine beaches and waterfalls aplenty, southern Costa Rica may be hard to reach, but the journey is worth every bit of the effort. This five-day trip is a good introduction to the region's charms.

1

DOMINICAL 1 DAY

Start with the jungle-backed beaches of **Dominical** (p342), the gateway to the country's south. This small beach town retains an authentic Tico atmosphere, has top surfing and offers a glimpse of the wildlife you can expect to see further south.

Detour: *If you have the time, head to Uvita and* **Parque Nacional Marino Ballena** *(p354). 20 mins*

2

SIERPE 1 DAY

Southeast of Dominical, the small town of **Sierpe** (p399) is the jumping-off point for Bahía Drake, one of the most impressive wildlife-spotting destinations in the country. Marvel at the mysterious pre-Columbian Diquís spheres of Finca 6 (pictured), go on a boat tour through the mangroves of the Río Sierpe and enjoy the sleepy, beachy vibe.

3

BAHÍA DRAKE 2 DAYS

If you do one thing in the southern part of the country, make it visiting **Bahía Drake** (p392). This bay is where you can find huge pods of dolphins and migrating humpback whales, monkeys skittering around on the beaches and clear, tanzanite-colored water full of fabulous sea creatures. Spend two days in this pristine paradise.

FROM LEFT: MIHAI-BOGDAN LAZAR/SHUTTERSTOCK, CRAIG SPROUT/SHUTTERSTOCK, TANGUY DE SAINT-CYR/SHUTTERSTOCK

San Gerardo de Rivas
Quepos
Rivas
Río Talari
Río Teliri
Parque Internacional La Amistad
Parque Nacional Manuel Antonio
START
San Isidro de El General
Río Chirripó
Parque Nacional Chirripó
Cerro Durika
Dominical 1
Uvita
20min
Parque Nacional Marino Ballena
1h25min
Isla Ballena
Ojochal
Río General
Río Cato Brus
Bahía de Coronado
Ciudad Cortes
Palmar Norte
Palmar Sur
Sierpe 2
PACIFIC OCEAN
Isla Violin
1h
Reserva Forestal Golfo Dulce
Laguna Sierpe
Isla del Caño
Bahía Drake 3
Drake
1h30min
Rincón
Parque Nacional Piedras Blancas
La Palma
Golfo Dulce
Península de Osa
Puerto Jiménez 4
Laguna Corcovado
Parque Nacional Corcovado
Bahía de Pavon
END
0 20 km
0 10 miles

4

PUERTO JIMÉNEZ ⏱1 DAY

Finish your journey in tranquil **Puerto Jiménez** (p404) on the Golfo Dulce, a tropical fjord with wonderful snorkeling opportunities. You'll see sharks, humpback whales, tropical fish and dolphins in these waters, and enjoy the transcendental sparkle of bioluminescence during a sunset kayak tour.

Humpback whales, Bahía Drake (p392)

FROM LEFT: HOLGER LEUE/GETTY IMAGES, AGA PRZYBYLSKA/SHUTTERSTOCK

WHEN TO GO

Whether you opt for rainy, dry or shoulder season, Costa Rica is a fantastic year-round destination.

December to April is Costa Rica's high season, with bright blue skies, balmy days and the best surfing on the Península de Nicoya. You'll find consistent, big waves and excellent surfing conditions. While the coasts dry up in November, the country's interior can still experience substantial showers until the beginning of the year.

The low (rainy) season starts on the Caribbean Coast in May and lasts through November, and on the Pacific Coast from April to December. While you'll have to contend with torrential rains and tricky road conditions, including closures due to mudslides, prices drop during the low season, and you'll have your pick of accommodations at great prices. Plus, Costa Rica does experience a 'mini summer' or 'little high season' between July and August, so you could actually get lucky with the weather if you plan right.

I LIVE HERE

SUMMER IN GUANACASTE

Jason Quirós works for his family business, Paradise Travel, and is based in Río Cuarto, Alajuela Province.

I work in tourism transportation, and as a local person who's been to many places in Costa Rica, my favorite beaches are in Guanacaste Province and I like to swim in the rivers and seas of that area. I prefer the summer months because they're better for enjoying activities like fishing and visiting volcanoes.

Playa Guiones (p287)

FROM LEFT: STOCK PHOTOS 2000/SHUTTERSTOCK, LINDSAY FENDT/ALAMY

SURF'S UP IN GUANACASTE

Guanacaste is the driest part of the country and you can find good surf year-round. The waves are best between April and July, when you'll find serious swells in places like Nosara and Santa Teresa.

Weather Through the Year

JANUARY	**FEBRUARY**	**MARCH**	**APRIL**	**MAY**	**JUNE**
Ave. daytime max: **25°C (77°F)**	Ave. daytime max: **26°C (78.8°F)**	Ave. daytime max: **26°C (78.8°F)**	Ave. daytime max: **27°C (80.6°F)**	Ave. daytime max: **26°C (78.8°F)**	Ave. daytime max: **26°C (78.8°F)**
Ave. rainfall: **8mm**	Ave. rainfall: **10mm**	Ave. rainfall: **13mm**	Ave. rainfall: **81mm**	Ave. rainfall: **267mm**	Ave. rainfall: **279mm**

BRILLIANT BIOLUMINESCENCE

If you want to swim, kayak or simply gaze upon the sparkling bioluminescence surrounding Costa Rica's shores, the best time is from May to November. You can also see phenomenal bioluminescence in Bahía de Paquera in December.

The Main Events

Uvita's wildly popular **Envision Festival** (p356) is a 10-day celebration of musical, cultural and spiritual events, concerts and workshops. **March**

Semana Santa (Holy Week) is a country-wide celebration. San José (p77) sees street processions reenacting Christ's crucifixion. **March/April**

The **Festival Flores de la Diáspora Africana** (p149) celebrates Afro-Caribbean culture in Puerto Limón and around the Caribbean Coast (plus San José). **August**

Costa Rica marks **Independence Day** (p106) with parades and parties. The main event is the 'Freedom Torch' relay from Guatemala to Cartago. **September**

I LIVE HERE

RAINY SEASON IN LA FORTUNA

Pedro Badilla Berrocal is a travel planner and advisor in La Fortuna.

These past few years, the dry and rainy seasons haven't differed so much, and it's raining more in various areas. In La Fortuna, we're supposed to have a dry season in February, but it rains moderately in the mornings or afternoons, and sometimes storms arrive. I don't mind. Even though the dry season is generally better for tourism, I like the rainy season because the whole region is green, fresh and alive.

Envision Festival (p356)

Local Festivities

Cahuita comes alive with concerts and dancing to honour the King of Calypso with the **Walter Ferguson International Calypso Festival** (p358). **July**

Catholic pilgrims make the spiritual journey on foot from San José to Cartago to pay homage to *La Negrita* during the annual **Romería** (p115) **August**

In Uvita, the **Festival de Ballenas y Delfines** (p353) features boat tours, live music, art displays and food as well as beach cleanups. **September**

At the Boruca community's **Fiesta de los Diablitos** (p387), participants don intricate masks to re-enact the battle with Spanish invaders. **December/January**

TRADE WINDS OF THE CARIBBEAN

The Caribbean Coast has a unique, wetter microclimate. Trade winds keep the humid and rainy weather consistent, although things do dry out a bit from November to May – a month earlier than the dry season on the Pacific Coast.

JULY	AUGUST	SEPTEMBER	OCTOBER	NOVEMBER	DECEMBER
Ave. daytime max: **27°C (80.6°F)**	Ave. daytime max: **27°C (80.6°F)**	Ave. daytime max: **27°C (80.6°F)**	Ave. daytime max: **27°C (80.6°F)**	Ave. daytime max: **26°C (78.8°F)**	Ave. daytime max: **26°C (78.8°F)**
Ave. rainfall: **183mm**	Ave. rainfall: **277mm**	Ave. rainfall: **356mm**	Ave. rainfall: **330mm**	Ave. rainfall: **135mm**	Ave. rainfall: **33mm**

FROM LEFT: MB PHOTOGRAPHY/GETTY IMAGES, CINEMATIC/ALAMY

Hiker on Arenal 1968 trail (p231)

GET PREPARED FOR COSTA RICA

Useful things to load in your bag, your ears and your brain.

Clothes

Beach gear and water shoes Bring swimwear, quick-drying clothes and cover-ups for the beach, plus closed-toe water shoes to scramble up rocky beaches and waterfalls or ford a river or stream.

Light layers The cloud forests and Central Valley can get comparably cooler than the beaches, so bring some light layers to keep you warm at night and in higher-elevation areas.

Hiking boots If you plan on doing any treks, you'll need proper shoes with good tread and ankle support. Costa Rica can get very muddy, and some of the terrain is tricky.

Manners

Hot-button topics Costa Rica is predominantly Catholic and many people are religious. Avoid criticizing the church or religion.

Tico time Costa Ricans tend to have a flexible sense of time, so patience and going with the flow will serve you well.

Tipping culture While tips are not obligatory, they are appreciated, especially in more tourist-oriented areas.

Umbrella and rain gear Showers happen even during the drier season, so pack a portable umbrella and a lightweight rain jacket that can double as a coat if needed.

READ

Monkeys Are Made of Chocolate (Jack Ewing; 2005) A dive into the southwestern Costa Rican rainforest and its biodiversity.

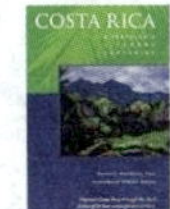

Costa Rica: A Traveler's Literary Companion (Barbara Ras; 1994) Twenty-six short stories from 20 Costa Rican authors.

The Quetzal and the Macaw (David Rains Wallace; 1992) A look at sustainability, ecotourism and conservation in Costa Rica.

Bananas: How the United Fruit Company Shaped the World (Peter Chapman; 2007) The exploitative history of bananas in Costa Rica.

Words

¡Pura vida! literally means 'pure life,' the unofficial ethos of Costa Rica; it can be a greeting or an expression of agreement or appreciation, and it comes with a sense that all is right in the here and now

Tico/Tica means 'Costa Rican' (m/f)

¡Buenas! is a universal greeting that can be used at any time of day; it's short for *buenos días* (good morning), *buenas tardes* (good afternoon) or *buenas noches* (good evening)

Chao is the most common 'goodbye'

Adiós is a more formal 'goodbye,' usually for an extended absence; confusingly, it can also mean 'hi' when used as a quick greeting between two people in passing

Hasta luego means 'See you later'

Usted is the polite version of 'you,' often used in Costa Rica rather than the more informal *tú*

Por favor means 'Please'

Gracias means 'Thank you'

Perdón means 'Excuse me' as in 'I'm sorry'

Disculpe means 'Excuse me' (to get somebody's attention)

Con permiso means 'Excuse me' (if trying to get by somebody)

Con gusto is the equivalent of 'You're welcome'

¿Cuánto cuesta? means 'How much does it cost?'

La cuenta, por favor means 'The check/bill, please'

¿Dónde está...? means 'Where is...?'

¿Habla inglés? means 'Do you speak English?'

Yo no entiendo means 'I don't understand'

WATCH

Jurassic Park (Steven Spielberg; 1993) Speculated to be set on Isla del Coco, Costa Rica's most remote and biodiverse island.

The Blue Butterfly (Léa Pool; 2004; pictured) The true story of a terminally ill boy who dreams of seeing a blue morpho butterfly.

Caribe (Esteban Ramírez; 2004) A struggle to save a banana plantation and forbidden love, set in El Caribe.

A Bold Peace (Matthew Eddy, Michael Dreiling; 2016) How Costa Rica disbanded its military to focus on social reform and conservation.

Land of Ashes (Sofía Quirós Ubeda; 2019) A story about life, death and familial love and responsibility.

LISTEN

King of Calypso Limonense – The Legendary Tape Recordings, Vols 1 & 2 (Walter Ferguson; 2020) Top tracks from Cahuita's King of Calypso.

Chúcaro (Cocofunka; 2015) An eclectic reggae and rock vibe with a socially aware message.

Pasaje Abierto (Edín Solís; 2017) Gorgeous and chill instrumental tracks with clever guitar work.

Luna Nueva (Debi Nova; 2010) A fun blend of pop and Tico rhythms with inspired lyrics and catchy beats.

BARRY VINCENT/ALAMY

***Ceviche* (marinated seafood)**

THE FOOD SCENE

Fresh, local ingredients and a focus on hearty fare and fruits of the sea meet international cuisine throughout Costa Rica.

Visit any *soda* (cheap eatery) from Puerto Viejo de Talamanca to Playas del Coco, and enjoy a generous serving of perfectly seasoned rice and beans paired with eggs, plantains, meat, seafood or salad, depending on the time of day. This stick-to-your-ribs fare is a staple of Costa Rican cuisine and, when drizzled with a little Lizano sauce, is the stuff of unadulterated culinary bliss. It's also a dish that varies by region. For example, the rice and beans on the Caribbean Coast are prepared with coconut milk and a uniquely delicious mix of savory, spicy and sweet. You'll also find the freshest, sweetest fruits like massive papayas and sunny pineapples in every market – the perfect midday snack or light pre-surf breakfast. While Costa Rica has deep ties to its culinary roots, it's not afraid to play with fusion flavors and showcase fine dining in places like San José or the tiny Central Pacific town of Ojochal, where haute cuisine is found tucked in the jungle.

Savor It All at the Soda

Every city, town and tiny village has at least one *soda,* or authentic, local Tico restaurant where you can literally get a taste of the country. *Gallo pinto* (Spanish for 'spotted rooster') is the first meal of the day – a portion of rice, beans and eggs that sometimes comes with plantains, avocado, cheese or sour cream and will more than satisfy your early hunger pangs. *Sodas* generally serve the eggs fried or scrambled, but you can make special requests for sunny-side-up

Best Costa Rican Dishes

GALLO PINTO
Red or black beans and seasoned rice.

EMPANADAS
Small pastries filled with cheese or meat.

CASADO
Rice and beans, fish or meat, and salad.

CEVICHE
Raw fish 'cooked' in citrus juice and generally served with chips.

or poached in some places. You can generally find breakfast deals that pair your *gallo pinto* with a cup of coffee for a few thousand colones – a steal when you consider how much food you get.

Lunch is *casado* (Spanish for 'married man'), a set meal that includes the same seasoned rice and beans with salad, chicken, meat or fish. *Sopa negra*, or black-bean soup, and *olla de carne* (beef stew) are also integral Costa Rican dishes offered at many *sodas*.

Vegetarian Fare

With rice and beans being the country's staple dish, vegetarians will always have a go-to meal that is certain to satisfy. If you're vegan, simply swap out the eggs for avocado or plantains at breakfast and request a veggie *casado* for lunch. These meals generally come with an extra serving of vegetables in addition to the salad, rice and beans. You can also find reliable vegetarian and vegan restaurants in virtually every popular tourist town.

Street & Beach Treats

Street eats, food trucks and tiny markets selling *empanadas* (turnovers stuffed with meat or cheese), grilled corn and churros are some of the best places to grab a quick and tasty bite. Beach food is another favorite find, usually composed of a mixture of *ceviche* (seafood marinated in lemon or lime juice) and tortilla chips, and best enjoyed when accompanied by an epic sunset view. Plus, you'll save cash and get to try a variety of glorious foods.

FROM LEFT: JUAN ROBALLO/SHUTTERSTOCK, CARVERMOSTARDI/ALAMY

Casado (set meal)

Caribeans chocolate (p170)

FOOD & DRINK FESTIVALS

San Isidro Fiestas (February) A week-long agricultural festival, with produce competitions, farm animals, cattle drives, live music and lots of food.

Fiestas del Maíz (October) See the crowning of a corn queen, admire corn-husk fashions and cheer on traditional *balsa* boat races in Upala.

Puerto Viejo Chocolate Festival (October) A weekend of sweet workshops, cooking classes and chocolate tastings in Puerto Viejo de Talamanca and Puerto Viejo de Sarapiquí.

Feria Nacional de Pejibaye (October) A week-long celebration in Tucurrique dedicated to eating (and drinking) the peach-palm fruit. (Hint: Ticos like it with a dollop of mayonnaise.)

Melcoches de Natilla Festival (December) An annual event dedicated to this traditional Costa Rican candy, held on the Feast of the Immaculate Conception in San Ramón.

TAMALES
Steamed corn pastry, meat and vegetables in plantain leaves.

RONDÓN
Seafood gumbo with plenty of spice and coconut milk from the Caribbean.

SOPA NEGRA
Rich black-bean soup and rice.

LIZANO SAUCE
Costa Rica's favorite condiment developed in 1920, perfect for seasoning anything.

Specialties

Snacks & Street Food

Patacones Deep-fried plantains, often accompanying *ceviche* or guacamole.
Chicharón Fried pork belly, used in dishes like *chifrijo* (rice and pinto beans with fried pork) and *vigorón*.
Vigorón A salad of shredded cabbage, boiled plantains and *chicharón*.

Sweet Treats

Cajeta de coco A sweet and sticky coconut cookie.
Tres leches Sponge cake soaked in sweet milk and topped with cream.
Melcoches de natilla Traditional candy made from sour cream and sugar.

Tropical Fruits

Caimito (star apple) Looks like an apple on the outside and a star on the inside, with a sweet, creamy flesh.
Carambola (star fruit)
Cas (sour guava) Tart cousin of the guava, used mainly for juice.
Guanabana (soursop)
Guayabá (guava)
Jocote (Spanish plum)

***Chicharón* (fried pork belly)**

Maracuyá (passion fruit)
Palmito (heart of palm)
Mamón chino (rambutan)

Holiday Fare

Tamales Corn pastry, stuffed with meat and wrapped in steamed plantain leaves. Traditionally made for Christmas.
Empanadas de chiverre A flour *empanada* filled with sweet *chiverre* squash, made for Easter.
Queque seco Light pound cake served at Easter.
Pozole Stew made from pork, hominy and bell peppers. Often prepared for religious holidays.

MEALS OF A LIFETIME

Gingerbread Hotel & Restaurant (p245) In Nuevo Arenal, Chef Eyal will wine, dine and delight you with divine fusion fare and endless merrymaking.
Calle 33 Mercadito (p86) Overload your senses in this upscale food hall in San José where you can enjoy flavors from around the world.
Jalapas Restaurant (p246) Sample local innovations and tropical cocktails with incredible views over volcanoes and plains, near La Fortuna.
San Lucas Treetop Dining Experience (p191) A multicourse eating extravaganza in a fantastic glass cube in the sky in Santa Elena.
Exotica (p360) Journey to the tiny village of Ojochal for unexpectedly excellent nouveau-French dining in a jungle paradise.

THE YEAR IN FOOD

JANUARY TO FEBRUARY

The beginning of the year is an excellent time to enjoy avocado, tangerine, pineapple and tree tomato. It's also the start of watermelon season, which runs through April.

MARCH TO JUNE

The zenith of watermelon season, and the start of mango season – you'll find fragrant and fresh fruits everywhere. You can also enjoy good passion fruit and cantaloupe during this time of year.

JULY TO OCTOBER

Seasonal favorites during these months include rambutan, star fruit and guava. This is also the time to taste jocote (pictured): try it with a pinch of salt.

NOVEMBER TO DECEMBER

Savor pineapple and passion fruit at this time of year, and if you're keen, enjoy them with a fresh cup of coffee as it's peak coffee-harvesting season in Costa Rica.

TOP: CESARASF/SHUTTERSTOCK; FROM LEFT: JORGE A. RUSSELL/SHUTTERSTOCK, PATDU PHOTOGRAPHY/SHUTTERSTOCK, RUI VALE SOUSA/SHUTTERSTOCK, ERIK COX PHOTOGRAPHY/SHUTTERSTOCK

CRIS YOUNG/SHUTTERSTOCK

Pipas (green coconuts)

HOW TO... Quench Your Thirst

Costa Rica's most popular alcoholic drink is *cerveza* (beer; aka *birra* locally), and there are several national brands. Imperial is the most popular – either for its smooth flavor or for the ubiquitous merchandise emblazoned with the eagle-crest logo.

After beer, the poison of choice is *guaro,* which is a colorless alcohol (most similar to aguardiente) distilled from sugarcane and usually consumed as a sour or by the shot, oftentimes with hot sauce and lime juice. This spicy concoction is called a *chili guaro,* and in the last few years it has become a staple in San José and certain beach towns. *Guaro* goes down mighty easily but leaves one hell of a hangover.

If you'd prefer to avoid the alcohol (and the hangover), however, Costa Rica has some incredibly tasty non-alcoholic options to keep your thirst at bay.

Batidos

For a refresher, nothing beats *batidos* – fresh fruit shakes made either *al agua* (with water) or *con leche* (with milk). The array of available tropical fruit can be intoxicating and includes mango, papaya, *piña* (pineapple), *sandía* (watermelon), *melón* (cantaloupe), *mora* (blackberry), *carambola* (starfruit), *cas* (sour guava), *guanabana* (soursop) and *tamarindo* (fruit of the tamarind tree).

Pipas

Pipas are green coconuts that have had their tops hacked off with a machete and then been spiked with a straw for drinking the coconut water inside – super refreshing when you're wilting in the tropical heat.

Agua Dulce

If you're lucky enough to find it, *agua dulce* is sugarcane water, a slightly grassy, sweet juice that's been pressed through a heavy-duty, hand-cranked mill.

Agua de Sapo

On the Caribbean coast, look for *agua de sapo* (literally 'toad water'), a beautiful lemonade laced with fresh ginger juice and *tapa de dulce* (brown sugar).

Coffee

Although not necessarily the most refreshing of drinks, coffee is probably the most popular beverage in the country, and wherever you go, someone is likely to offer you a *cafecito.* Traditionally, it is served strong and mixed with hot milk to taste, also known as *café con leche.* Purists can get *café negro* (black coffee); if you want a little milk, ask for *leche al lado* (milk on the side).

TOP TIP(PLE)

As in most of Central America, the local rums are inexpensive and worthwhile, especially the Ron Centenario, which recently shot to international fame. And at the risk of alienating the most patriotic of Ticos, it would be remiss not to mention the arguably tastier Flor de Caña from Nicaragua (pause for rotten tomatoes). The most popular rum-based tipple is a *cuba libre* (rum and cola), which hits the spot on a hot, sticky day, especially when served with a fresh splash of lime.

FROM LEFT: JORGE A. RUSSELL/SHUTTERSTOCK, ISTOCK/GETTY IMAGES

Surfing

THE OUTDOORS

If the great outdoors is beckoning you, Costa Rica is the ideal place to answer that call, with a bevy of brilliant activites to enjoy.

To call Costa Rica a nature lover's paradise is a dramatic understatement. The country's lush landscape and shimmering coastal waters offer every sort of outdoor adventure for a wide range of skill levels. Surf the impressive waves on both the Pacific and Caribbean coasts, trek through the vast expanses of forest, or strap on your scuba or snorkeling gear and dive beneath the waves to explore a whole new world.

Surfing

Surfers flock to Costa Rica to test their mettle on the big Pacific and Caribbean waves. You can find varsity-level adventures, like Salsa Brava on the Caribbean side or Suck Rock and Witch's Rock on thePacific's Península de Nicoya. Head to Nosara and Santa Teresa for gargantuan waves and achingly beautiful beaches, or the party towns of Jacó and Tamarindo for more beginner-friendly swells and a fun backpacker vibe. You can also pick up surfing lessons and attend surf camp virtually anywhere on the coast.

Two big bodies of water flank Costa Rica, so the surf is always up, but conditions change depending on the time of year you want to head out. The Caribbean Coast sees the big beasts from November to May, while you'll find the largest waves on the Central Pacific Coast between May and October.

More Outdoor Fun

KITESURFING
Head to the remote northwest of Costa Rica for **Playa Copal** (p216) in Bahía Salinas for the best kitesurfing in the country.

MOUNTAIN BIKING
Bike from Paraíso to **Lago de Cachí** (p126) for a fun and challenging loop through the Central Valley.

SEA KAYAKING
Kayak from Sámara to **Isla Chora** (p292), or challenge yourself with sea kayaking in the watery caves of **Playa Ventanas** (p360).

FAMILY ADVENTURES

Zip through the forest canopy in the cloud forest reserves of Santa Elena and **Monteverde** (p185) or in **La Fortuna** (p2330).

Learn to surf the gentler waves in places like **Jacó** (p322) on the Central Pacific Coast or **Tamarindo** (p278) on the Península de Nicoya.

Watch sea turtles nesting in **Parque Nacional Tortuguero** (p142) and **Playa Ostional** (p293) during the annual turtle *arribada*.

Tour a coffee farm in **Orosí Valley** (p129) and stroll through the coffee fields, learning every step in the process.

Go horse riding or hike to the **Nauyaca Waterfalls** (p347) near Dominical, enjoying a swim as a reward.

Hike to a volcanic crater in **Parque Nacional Volcán Póas** (p109) and peek into the belly of the stratovolcano.

Snorkeling

The blue waters of Costa Rica are rife with spectacular undersea life. Get under the waves with your snorkeling equipment and you'll see tropical fish, manta rays, sharks, octopuses and even the elusive sea turtle or two. Places like the Península de Osa's Golfo Dulce, one of only four tropical fjords on the planet, is a fabulous place to see dolphins, sea turtles and humpback whales. A little bit further up the coast, Uvita is one of the Central Pacific Coast's best places for snorkeling, thanks to Parque Nacional Marino Ballena, where you can see marine life swimming amongst the coral reefs.

On the Pacific side, Islas Murciélagos (Bat Islands) are a fantastic place to spot octopuses, sea turtles and nurse sharks during the rainy season. Parque Nacional Cahuita has one of the biggest coral reefs on the planet and half-day snorkeling tours on which you can see it all.

BEST SPOTS

For the best outdoor spots and routes, see map on p48

Hiking, Nauyaca Waterfalls (p346)

Hiking & Trekking

From the Orosí Valley to Montezuma on the Península de Nicoya, Costa Rica is packed with trails for all ages, needs and skill levels. Protected spaces like Parque Nacional Manuel Antonio have paved, accessible main walkways and more difficult hikes branching off them, and most jungle waterfalls require at least a bit of hiking to get to. Costa Rica's trails are predominately well maintained and thoroughly marked, and you're bound to spy ample wildlife along the way.

If you crave even more of a challenge, you can embark on a multiday hike, like El Camino de Costa Rica which spans 280km and connects the two coasts. Always abide by safe trekking practices – let someone know where you're going and be realistic about your ability level.

BOULDERING & ROCK CLIMBING
Check out **Escalada Cachí** (p127) near the Cachí Dam for epic rock climbing and rappeling.

WHITE-WATER RAFTING
Ride the thrilling rapids of Río Celeste (p196), Río Reventazón (p131) and Río Pacuare (p154).

WATERFALL TREKS
Discover off-the-beaten-path waterfalls on intense jungle hikes at places like **Playa Cocolito** (p306) in Montezuma.

SCUBA DIVING
Enjoy fantastic diving near Costa Rica's islands including **Isla del Caño** (p392), **Islas Murciélagos** (p215) and **Isla Tortuga** (p302).

Surfing

1. Puerto Viejo de Talamanca (p163)
2. Tamarindo (p279)
3. Nosara (p287)
4. Santa Teresa (p298)
5. Jacó (p322)
6. Dominical (p342)
7. Cabo Matapalo (p411)

White-Water Rafting & Tubing

1. Río Pacuare (p131)
2. Río Sarapiquí (p248)
3. Río Tenorio (p201)
4. Río Colorado (p210)
5. Río Celeste (p196)

Walking/Hiking

1. El Camino de Costa Rica (p147)
2. Parque Nacional Cahuita (p157)
3. Reserva Biológica Bosque Nuboso Monteverde (p187)
4. Parque Nacional Volcán Tenorio (p194)
5. Cerro Chirripó (p380)
6. Parque Nacional Corcovado (p390)
7. Orosí Valley (p124)

ACTION AREAS

Where to find Costa Rica's best outdoor activities.

COSTA RICA

THE GUIDE

Chapters in this section are organized by hubs and their surrounding areas. We see the hub as your base in the destination, where you'll find unique experiences, local insights, insider tips and expert recommendations. It's also your gateway to the surrounding area, where you'll see what and how much you can do from there.

Reserva Biológica Bosque Nuboso Monteverde (p182)

JAKUB MACULEWICZ/SHUTTERSTOCK

For places to stay in San José, see p97

JOSHUA TEN BRINK/SHUTTERSTOCK

Above: Escazú (p89); Right: Plaza de la Cultura (p64)

Researched by
Cassandra Brooklyn

San José

COSTA RICA'S COSMOPOLITAN HEART

Look beyond its gritty veneer and you'll find a capital rich in history, culture and civic achievement.

In the middle of San José stands a a plaque dedicated to the city's first *ermita* (hermitage), built in 1737. Back then, distant Cartago was still the capital of Costa Rica, and no one could have imagined that this tiny settlement would gradually grow into a sprawling city of 340,000 people. Those Spanish colonists would stare in awe at the high-rises and plazas that make up modern Chepe, as San José is affectionately known. The *ermita* is long gone, replaced by a clothing store called Scaglietti, but a layered history is still written on the city's facades.

Far from the toucans and ziplines that Costa Rica is famous for, San José is a dense and bustling city, the country's cultural (and geographic) center. Stroll down the pedestrian mall of Avenida Central, and you'll see the full diversity of the nation's people on display, plus a good number of travelers. San José doesn't have sweeping skylines or attractive bodies of water, and the city takes some time to appreciate. But here you'll find the biggest museums, the most dynamic art scene and the most thrilling nightlife Costa Rica has to offer. Music fans will find a decent concert almost any night of the week, from songwriters in corner bars to rockstars in sold-out auditoriums.

As the nation's capital, San José has also been the unlikely stage for groundbreaking social experiments. It was here that the short-lived civil war ended, and President Figueres Ferrer disbanded the military in 1949. It was also here that racial segregation ended the following year, allowing Afro-Caribbean people to move freely about the country. Same-sex marriage was legalized in 2020, a major stride for this deeply Catholic nation. Meanwhile, the Universidad de Costa Rica is the country's hub for higher learning and political discourse.

The city can be rough around the edges, but civic pride is everywhere in San José, and the streets frequently flood with parades, festivals and peaceful protests. Then there's the food, with offerings from around the world. If you've had your fill of rice and beans, San José has got you covered: sample Indian, Chinese and Pan-Latin eateries, plus upscale dining that strives to reinvent *comida típica* (traditional food).

INTREEGUE PHOTOGRAPHY/SHUTTERSTOCK

THE MAIN AREAS

FROM THE AIRPORT

The moment you step through customs you'll meet taxi drivers offering you rides into the city – or order an Uber and head upstairs to find it. There's a bus stop on the main road directly in front of the airport – express buses to San José stop here every few minutes.

HEREDIA
BARREAL
Río Virilla
Río Torres
Aeropuerto Tobías Bolaños
PAVAS
El Mestizo Mercado Gastronómico
Avenida Escazú
SANTA ANA
Escazú & Santa Ana
p89
SAN RAFAEL DE ESCAZÚ
ESCAZÚ
SAN ANTONIO DE ESCAZÚ

WALK

Most *chepes*, or *josefinos*, walk a great deal, and the city has several pedestrian malls that cut through downtown. For short distances, hoofing it through the narrow one-way streets is often just as expedient as driving.

Find Your Way

San José is a quilt of *pueblos* (villages) and *barrios* (neighborhoods) that blend together over hilly terrain. As the crow flies, no destination is far from where you are. With a little patience and a trustworthy *taxista* (cabby), you should be able to get anywhere in the city within a half-hour.

PUEBLA
SANTO DOMINGO
Río Virilla
SAN JUAN
SAN VINCENTE DE MORAVIA
GUADALUPE
SABANILLA
LA URUCA

La Sabana & Around
p72

SABANA NORTE
MÉXICO
Parque Metropolitano La Sabana
Estadio Nacional
Museo de Arte Costarricense
SABANA SUR
Mercado Central
Teatro Nacional
Museo del Oro Precolombino
Museo del Jade
Feria Verde de Aranjuez
Calle 33
Antigua Aduana

Barrio Escalante, Los Yoses & San Pedro
p79

SAN PEDRO
LOURDES
LOS YOSES
LA GRANJA

Downtown San José
p58

Río Tiribí
HATILLO
Río Maria Aguilar
ZAPOTE
Parque Recreativo La Paz
SAN SEBASTIÁN
CURRIDABAT
SAN FRANCISCO
ALAJUELITA

BUS

San José's intricate bus system connects the entire Central Valley. Buses are usually safe and fast, though routes can be tricky to figure out and signage is limited. The bus terminal downtown isn't the safest place to be at night, so if you arrive late, it's best to hail a taxi instead of walking.

TAXI

The most dependable cab is the *taxi rojo* (red taxi). These scarlet cabs cruise through San José at all times of day and night, and it's easy to flag one down. Just make sure it has a visible *maria*, or meter. Though not fully legal here, Uber is immensely popular.

Plan Your Days

The capital's metropolitan area is a big pill to swallow, and it's easy to get overwhelmed. Our advice: start in the middle and work your way outward, one neighborhood at a time.

Museo del Jade (p58)

Day 1

Morning

- Start at the **Plaza de la Cultura** (p64) and make your way down **Avenida Central** (p66). Grab a traditional breakfast at the **Mercado Central** (p65), then double-back for a visit to the **Teatro Nacional** (p63).

Afternoon

- Stop into **La Mancha** for a dose of caffeine and a pastry. Dedicate an hour to the **Museo del Jade** (p58) and learn about pre-Columbian peoples. Head to your hotel for a siesta – between the heat and the crowds, your first day will be tiring.

Evening

- Try some live music at a local venue, perhaps **El Observatorio** (p71), **StarView CR** (p71) or **Amón Solar** (p71). Afterward, order a *zarpe* (nightcap), or several, at one of the busy bars in **Barrio La California** (p71).

You'll Also Want to...

Find your way through the labyrinth of San José's suburbs in search of history, gastronomy and a surprising amount of ecotourism.

TRY THE BEER

Sample local craft beers at one of many local gastropubs such as **Costa Rica Beer Factory** (p87) in Escalante, where you can use the beer to wash down a great meal.

WATCH THE SOCCER

On **fútbol** game days, every TV and car radio will play the match, and victories are celebrated in the street. To watch (and perhaps join) a live game, head to La Sabana park.

HIKE THE MOUNTAINS

Ramble through the mountain roads and rural paths above Escazú and Santa Ana, including the **Tres Cruces Trail** (p95).

Day 2

Morning

● Head over to **Soda Tapia** (p75) for a heaping breakfast or an early *casado* (set meal), then enjoy a morning walk in **Parque Metropolitano La Sabana** (p75).

Afternoon

● Browse the exhibits at the free **Museo de Arte Costarricense** (p78), then make your way to **Franco Nunciatura** (p76) for lunch, coffee and people-watching on the patio.

Evening

● Grab some gourmet ice cream at **Corazón Contento Pastelería** (p76) and an afternoon cocktail and appetizers at **Bardo Natural Winebar** (p76) before heading to **El Social Sabana** (p76) for traditional bites and karaoke.

Day 3

Morning

● Make your way over to **Hacienda La Chimba** (p96) in Santa Ana to hike through the hills on the scenic Mantra Trail.

Afternoon

● Head into Escazú and treat yourself to a decadent lunch at **Taj Mahal** (p91) or **La Cascada** (p91). Amble around **Avenida Escazú** (p89) and window-shop for fancy knickknacks. Consider catching a matinee at **Nova Cinemas** (p91), or maybe just a treat at one of the local eateries.

Evening

● Cab or bus it over to **Calle 33** (p79) in Barrio Escalante for dinner at a bistro, then drinks at one of the many trendy bars.

GO SHOPPING

Retail is everywhere, from the souk-like **Mercado Municipal de Artesanías** (p68) to the massive **Multiplaza Escazú** (p91) where you'll find everything under the sun.

USE ALT TRANSPORT

Hop a morning **train** (p85) to San Pedro for some wonderful walking, or find yourself a bike and pedal around town with the **ChepeCletas** (p88).

SEE WILDLIFE

Support local naturalists by visiting the **Refugio Animal de Costa Rica** (p95) in Santa Ana and see fauna up close.

BRING THE KIDS

Visit the magical **Museo de los Niños** (p62) or the **Butterfly Kingdom Mariposario** (p94) in Escazú, among other kid-friendly venues.

Downtown San José

HUSTLE, BUSTLE AND SO MANY MUSEUMS

GETTING AROUND

Downtown San José is a densely populated area with lots of attractions located within a small space. Walking is the best way to get around, but, as a rule, the sidewalks are narrow, uneven and end abruptly. Rain gutters cut deep into the pavement, and litter is a persistent problem, so you'll want sturdy sandals or sneakers to negotiate these streets.

There's one thing you'll find in San José that you rarely find anywhere else in Costa Rica: crowds. Downtown is the nation's only equivalent to a big city, and it rises to the occasion: thousands of people throng these streets every day; the biggest businesses are headquartered here; and Ticos come to find specialty goods and services unavailable in their rural *pueblos*.

A big draw of central San José is its wealth of cultural institutions, including museums and historical landmarks designed as much for residents as for tourists. With so many exhibitions, a visitor could spend days learning the cultural heritage of Costa Ricans, from the ancient carvings of the Museo del Jade to symphonic performances.

Downtown is also a magnet for bargain hunters. An army of hawkers wander between the shoulder-to-shoulder storefronts selling everything from lollipops to cell-phone cases. The lively atmosphere can overwhelm newcomers, so it's best to travel light and keep your wits about you.

TOP TIP

During the pandemic, parts of the country (like San José) instituted contactless payment, so most businesses here accept credit cards, Apple Pay or Google Wallet. That said, you'll likely need cash for three things: food stalls, craft markets and tipping the hotel and restaurant staff and the person watching your car. Many businesses also accept US dollars but they may charge you more in that case.

A Deep-Dive into Indigenous Life

A collection of pre-Columbian jade

The **Museo del Jade** *(museodeljade.grupoins.com; adult/student/child US$11/5/2)* is a wonderful, immersive, five-story experience where you're treated to room after room of jade sculptures, sacred artifacts and dioramas of indigenous peoples doing daily tasks. An atmospheric sound design and interactive screens bring the pre-Columbian world to life, transfixing even the youngest visitor. In the second half of its title is *la cultura precolombina* (pre-Columbian culture), and the curators take this mission to heart. The Jade Museum doesn't shy away from topics like sexuality and ritual warfare, and each exhibit represents the most current archaeological findings. While most of the pieces are displayed under glass, one panel

Museo Nacional de Costa Rica

invites visitors to touch its stone surface, demonstrating the many textures of a single carving.

Stroll the Urban Jungle

Walking tour with a local

San José isn't easy to appreciate, or even digest. That's why local enthusiasts founded the **San José Free Walking Tour** *(sanjosewalking.com)*, which pairs informed Tico guides with curious visitors. Begun in 2017, the tour takes participants on 2½-hour promenades around the city – earn the confusing layout of San José with a resident who knows these blocks intimately. There is nothing more Costa Rican than ditching the tour bus and getting outside; by morning's end, you may find that the urban jungle is nearly as compelling as the actual rainforest. While technically these tours are free, don't forget to tip your guide generously.

A Powerful Monument to Civic Achievement

Explore the National Museum of Costa Rica

The bright yellow walls and medieval turrets of the **Museo Nacional de Costa Rica** *(museocostarica.go.cr; adult/student US$7/5)* are a welcome sight in the often dreary of San José, and the

continued on p62

THE HEART OF THE CITY

Alex González, a tour guide for ChepeCletas, shares what he loves about downtown San José.

The capital's center gets a bad rap that really is undeserved. While some travelers only associate it with commotion and big buildings, it is so much more. Downtown San José is the home of the city's culture, history and culinary scenes. It is the center of economic and social movement, so is a snapshot of the city itself. There are so many fascinating markets here selling incredible traditional food, but there are also newer restaurants pushing the limits of modern Costa Rican cuisine. Don't visit this country without spending some time in downtown San José.

EATING & DRINKING IN DOWNTOWN SAN JOSÉ: OUR PICKS

Café Rojo: Sunny, leafy space with outdoor seating that's popular with vegetarians and work-from-home types. *noon-8:30pm Mon-Fri, from 10am Sat & Sun* $$

El Frontón: *Empanada* (turnover stuffed with meat or cheese) chain with locations around the city. *hours vary* $

Soda Vegetariana SUSBIDA: Chinese meets Costa Rican cuisine, offering daily meat-free noodles, soup and *casado* (set meal) specials. *11:30am-4pm Mon-Sat* $

Buchón Cantina: Elevated Costa Rican and fusion cuisine and an extensive drinks menu in a traditional home turned restaurant. *5pm-midnight Tue-Sat* $$$

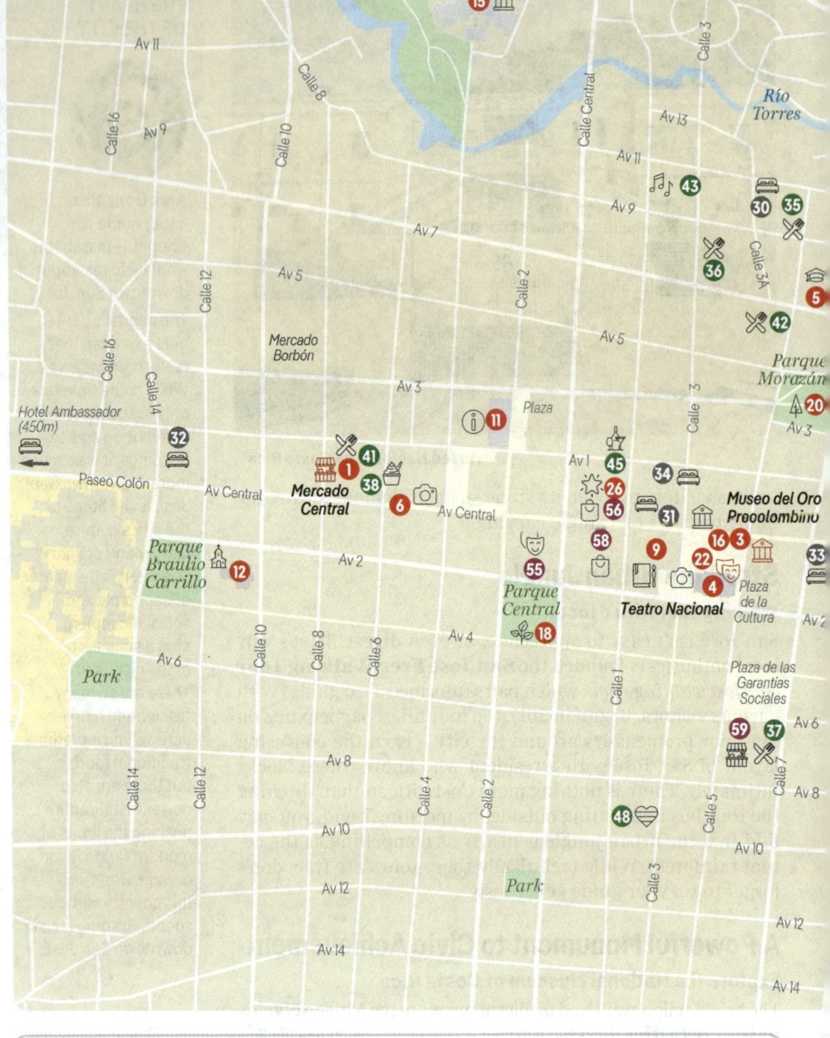

HIGHLIGHTS

1 Mercado Central
2 Museo del Jade
3 Museo del Oro Precolombino
4 Teatro Nacional

SIGHTS

5 Alianza Francesa
6 Avenida Central
7 Barrio Amón
8 Barrio California
9 Centro de Patrimonio Cultural
10 Centro Nacional de la Cultura
11 Edificio de Correos
12 Iglesia de la Merced
13 Jardín de Mariposas
14 Monumento Nacional
15 Museo de los Niños & Galería Nacional
16 Museo de Numismática
17 Museo Nacional de Costa Rica
18 Parque Braulio Carrillo
19 Parque España
20 Parque Morazán
21 Parque Nacional
22 Plaza de la Cultura
23 Plaza de la Democracia
24 Plaza de las Artes
25 TEOR/éTica

ACTIVITIES

26 San José Free Walking Tour

SLEEPING

27 Costa Rica Backpackers
28 Hostel Shakti
29 Hotel Colonial
30 Hotel Dunn Inn
31 Hotel El Maragato
32 Hotel Novo
33 Hotel Presidente

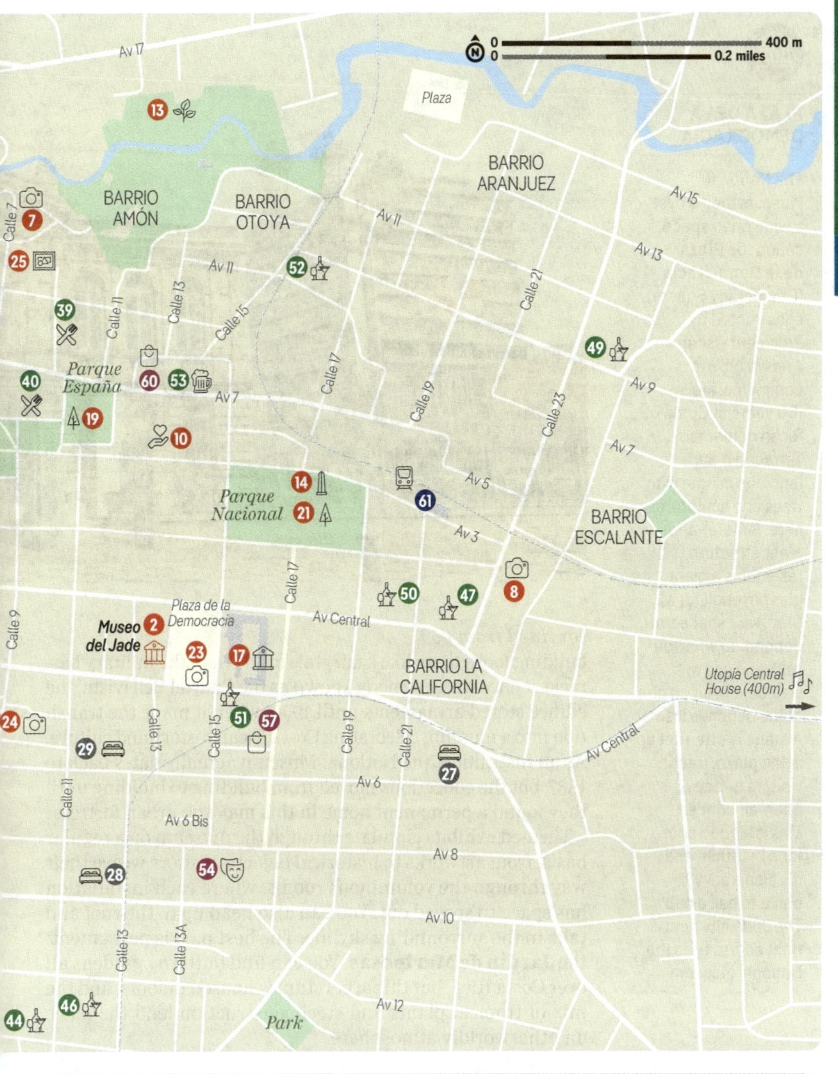

34 Urban Green Hotel & Suites	**42** Soda Vegetariana SUSBIDA	**49** La Buenos Aires	**SHOPPING**
EATING	**DRINKING & NIGHTLIFE**	**50** La Concha de la Lora	**56** Casa de Cacao
35 Alma de Amón	**43** Amón Solar	**51** Lunix Club	**57** Chietón Morén
36 Café Rojo	**44** Bar El 13	**52** StarView CR	**58** Librería Internacional
37 El Frontón	**45** Bombóm	**53** Stiefel	**59** Mercado Municipal de Artesanías
38 Lolo Mora	**46** Buchón Cantina	**ENTERTAINMENT**	**60** Tienda eÑe
39 October Six Café Bistro	**47** El Observatorio	**54** Teatro el Triciclo	**TRANSPORT**
40 Restaurante La Criollita	**48** La Avispa	**55** Teatro Popular Melico Salazar	**61** Estación del Ferrocarril al Atlántico
41 Soda Tala 1			

PLAZA DE LA DEMOCRACIA

The National Museum looms over a wide open space called the **Plaza de la Democracia** (Democracy Square), constructed by President Óscar Arias in 1989 to commemorate 100 years of Costa Rican democracy. Terraced brick landings mingle with trees and sculptures here. A metal-and-glass structure resembles a giant glass eyeball (or a *Star Wars* spacecraft, depending who you ask), and you are welcome to sit on one of the benches inside. A stage is often set up in the plaza, treating visitors to free open-air concerts. This is a good spot for a breather, and it's also a savvy place to hail a cab. The Jade Museum is right across from the National Musuem.

contined from p59

building looks more like a fairytale castle than the military barracks it once was. Formerly known as the Cuartel Bellavista, the edifice stored armaments until 1950, when it made the transition into a museum celebrating Costa Rican history and culture. As an institution, the National Museum actually dates back to 1887, but the collections moved from building to building until they found a permanent home in this majestic urban fortress.

Themed exhibits circulate through the museum on a regular basis, from artworks to historical objects. Visitors weave their way through the voluminous rooms, where each installation has space to spread out. You can also head up to the roof and take in the surrounding skyline. The best part is permanent: the **Jardín de Mariposas**. You can find butterfly gardens all over Costa Rica, but this arboretum is housed indoors, and the mix of tropical plants and steel construction lend the place an otherworldly atmosphere.

The Castle for Kids

A dream museum for children

Standing atop a hill, the **Museo de los Niños** *(museocr.org/ninos; adult/child US$4.50/4)* looks like a children's museum imagined by an actual child. The high walls are painted canary-yellow, and two towers stand around a central gate. Even the windows look like Arabian keyholes. Naturally, its nickname is 'El Castillo' (The Castle).

For its first 70 years, this compound served as a penitentiary, but in 1991 Costa Rica converted all those cells into playful installations and interactive games. The place does triple duty

LEONID ANDRONOV/SHUTTERSTOCK

Teatro Nacional

as auditorium and science museum, complete with full-scale dinosaur replicas.

Adults may enjoy the included **Galería Nacional**, which consists of 14 rooms with rotating art.

Costa Rica's Most Historic Stage

Admire the Teatro Nacional

When it first opened in 1897, the **Teatro Nacional** *(teatro nacional.go.cr)* was the domain of *damas* (ladies) in bustles and *caballeros* (gentlemen) in top hats, who often watched lavish productions from European-style box seats. Operas have been staged here, along with symphonies, ballets and plays. A fresco of flying angels is painted over the circular ceiling, punctuated by a majestic chandelier. Truly, the National Theater is the paragon of San José's public spaces.

The building is easy to explore. Visitors mosey through the lobby and museum all day, and in the afternoons you can step into the grand auditorium. The theater has a storied past, from its very first performance (of Goethe's *Faust*) to a 1991 earthquake that cracked one of its marble pillars. It remains as active as ever, holding performances large and small for audiences of up to 1140 people. You can buy tickets at the new booth on the north side of the building, including for actor-led tours of the building *(adult/child US$7/free)*, which is the only way to access areas beyond the lobby. Tours take place hourly from 9am to 4pm.

There's also an elegant bistro, **Alma de Café**, inside the theater, which serves Britt cappuccinos and pastries in a lavish Victorian setting.

TIP THE GUACHIMÁN

You'll see them everywhere on the streets of San José: men, usually older, wearing reflective vests and hanging out on curbs. Their quasi-official role is known as a *guachimán* (pronounced 'watch-ee-mahn'), and yes, you pay them to watch your car. Nearly every block has its own *guachimán*, who helps you park in a space and plays traffic cop to passing vehicles. This tip-based service usually merits a dollar or so. Drivers have a love-hate relationship with the *guachimanes*, but they can be helpful, and you're wise to keep a pocketful of loose change if you are driving around the city.

PLAZA DE LA CULTURA

San José's anchor point is the **Plaza de la Cultura** (Culture Square), an open space flanked by the Teatro Nacional, the historic Gran Hotel Costa Rica and a stately fountain and decorative clock. This massive construction project was completed in 1982, with mixed results. The plaza itself is an underwhelming concrete expanse, a magnet for pigeons and hawkers, and usually packed with locals slurping ice-cream cones and admiring the wide gamut of San José street life. But it's also a natural launchpad for exploring the downtown area, and it often serves as a stage for outdoor events.

Postal Grandeur

The nation's most unlikely post office

Sending a letter in Costa Rica has always been unusual, given the near-total lack of street addresses, a fact that makes the **Edificio de Correos** (Post Office Building) all the more impressive. Completed in 1917, this pillared Edwardian masterpiece looks like the set for a costume drama and looms over a buzzing plaza. The post office is a point of architectural pride, and it singlehandedly introduced Costa Rica to the telegraph system. All these years later, it's still a dependable place to dispatch a postcard. Stamp collectors may also want to swing by, as the post office sometimes sells limited-edition stamps.

Gold's Legacy

Explore the Pre-Columbian Gold Museum

The **Museo del Oro Precolombino** (*museosdelbancocentral.org; adult/student US$17/13)*) is actually three museums in one, all cleverly constructed beneath the Plaza de la Cultura. The formal name of the trio is the Museos del Banco Central (Central Bank Museums), but most people go for the Pre-Columbian Gold Museum and refer to the entire complex as such. The unassuming entrance leads you three stories beneath the street. The first museum explores the history of indigenous communities and the importance of gold in their lives, including how they used it as a material and not simply as the status symbol we now consider it to be.

Detailed maps illustrate the migrations of prehistoric peoples and how, thousands of years ago, they settled into the mountains and valleys of the isthmus. Glass cases display gold jewelry, decorations and spiritual totems. You could easily spend several hours here but if you're short on time, head toward the yellow placards, which display notable information (compared with the white placards).

In the middle level, you'll find an avant-garde art gallery with rotating exhibits, as well as the **Museo de Numismática**, which relates the history of Costa Rican currency. See how coins and paper bills evolved over time, as well as the country's first money-printing machine.

A Place of Respite in the City

Stroll the National Park

The **Parque Nacional** is one of several green spaces on the eastern side of downtown, along with **Parque España** and **Parque Morazán**. This one happens to be the largest, with well-groomed trees and walking paths, plus a collection of statues of famous personages. The most iconic is the 1953 **Monumento Nacional** (National Monument), an unusual depiction of soldiers defeating North American invaders during the Filibuster War. Taken together, all these parks are a decent place to escape the racket of downtown traffic.

IMAGEBROKER.COM/ALAMY

Mercado Central

A Historic Marketplace

Shop and eat at the Mercado Central

Customers have shopped in the **Mercado Central** (Central Market) since the 1880s, picking through fruit baskets and haggling over prices. This historic building is a labyrinth of 200 stalls, where you can buy groceries, pick up souvenirs or even grab a cheap breakfast at one of the many *sodas* (eateries serving a counter lunch). Some vendors coax visitors into their shops and hold out individual wares, but most will accept a polite '*No, gracias.*' Compared with other souvenir shops, bargains abound here.

Mercado Central is a great place to find traditional fare like tamales, seafood soups, *chorreada* (corn pancakes) and *tortillas aliñadas* (tortillas with cheese mixed into them). **Soda Tala 1** is a great stall for some of these homemade dishes, while the oldest ice-cream shop in the country, **Lolo Mora**, is where to head for a scoop of spiced frozen goodness.

The main entrance is located on Avenida Central and welcomes you with a colorful, hand-painted sign over the doorway. The low-lit depths of the Central Market are a welcome shelter from the sun, and you may find some relief after all the avenida's clamor. While you can certainly explore on your own, proper tours are quite fascinating and help you navigate the seemingly never-ending maze of stalls.

Traces of San José's Chinatown

Eat Asian at the Plaza de las Artes

You may wonder why they call it the **Plaza de las Artes** (Square of the Arts), given how empty this square seems to be. You'll find a few statues here, including one of John Lennon sitting on a bench, as well as a cryptic sculpture of concentric steel circles. The most compelling landmark is its Chinese-style

HIGHLIGHTS OF AVENIDA CENTRAL

Avenida Central tends to overwhelm, but there are some diamonds in the rough.

Centro de Património Cultural: This antique government building often opens its doors for special functions. Outside, artists peddle their paintings and jewelry in the building's shade.

Sculptures: The bronze statue *La Chola* depicts a mixed-race woman. It's one of several sculptures you'll pass along the avenue.

Street performers: Avenida Central is the best place in town to appreciate San José's street performers – you'll find dancers, singers and musicians, plus artists selling their work.

Casa de Cacao: Located in the Steinvorth Building, this chocolate shop offers cacao workshops.

Librería Internacional: This bookstore is the largest in town, making it a great place to pick up reads from local and international authors.

FRANCISCO SOSA/GETTY IMAGES

Decorated house, Barrio Amón

gateway, which was once the entrance to San José's Barrio Chino (Chinatown); a handful of Chinese restaurants are the only vestige of that old neighborhood, but you'll find great Asian food and bubble tea here.

A Distillery Turned Arts Center

Get your culture fix at CENAC

An imperious stone gate greets visitors at the **Centro Nacional de la Cultura** *(si.cultura.cr)*, but from the street, it's hard to tell what lies within. The National Culture Center, better known as CENAC, is a cluster of different buildings, packed with art exhibitions and cultural events. The free **Museo de Arte y Diseño Contemporáneo** (Museum of Contemporary Art and Design) features photography, painting and more, while the **Teatro 1887** hosts a range of Spanish-language performing arts.

CENAC's 19th-century walls make it look like a fort or monastery, and you'd never guess that the site formerly housed the National Distillery.

A Bastion of French Culture

Check what's on at Alianza Francesa

The **Alianza Francesa** *(alianzafrancesacostarica.com)* occupies an attractive bungalow on a quiet intersection in Barrio Amón. It's best known for hosting French classes, and if you have some time to spare and want to improve your language skills, you can almost certainly find someone to chat with. First opened in 1984, this branch is one of 800 Alliance Française offices around the world, bringing with it a vast network of teachers and professionals. This institution goes well beyond the call of duty, offering seasonal exhibitions and programming, from art exhibits to film screenings and lectures by visiting scholars. There's also a small cafe, giving you a handy excuse to step inside and order a coffee and French pastry.

Hoof it Through Chepe's Epicenter

Stroll the Avenida Central

The epicenter of San José is **Avenida Central**, a 10-block pedestrian corridor that skewers the city's commercial district. An extension is being built further east to provide easier pedestrian access for locals. This avenue roils with activity from dawn to midnight, and visitors run a disorienting gamut from hawkers to panhandlers. Storefronts are jammed together, interrupted only by busy cross-streets, where crowds play chicken with passing trucks and taxis. The avenue opens into the Plaza de la Cultura, the symbolic heart of the city. A stroll down Avenida Central thrills and frustrates; it's a natural starting point for all first-timers, who often get their fill and never come back.

A Homey Neighborhood

Exploring Barrio Amón

Just north of downtown San José, the land curves into a gentle hill, and as you descend into **Barrio Amón**, the noise quiets and traffic peters out. The further you go, the prettier the neighborhood becomes: houses decorated with trees and vines, walls covered in murals and tiles, and so many old houses repurposed as modern businesses.

Spend enough time in Barrio Amón, and you'll stumble into its many culinary nooks. **Café Rojo** (*caferojo.net*; p59) is tucked into a stately green house and serves coffee and lunches to local hipsters. **October Six Café Bistro** has a stone facade and sidewalk seating fit for Paris, with cappuccino to match. **Alma de Amón** *(facebook.com/almadeamon)* interprets standbys like flan and tacos in sophisticated new ways in its pop art–infused dining room.

One of Amón's best surprises is **TEOR/éTica** *(teoretica.org)*, an old corner building painted with a new mural every few months. The gallery's tagline is *arte y pensamiento* (art and thought), and artists build installations in each room that address social concerns such as feminism, migration and identity.

While you're there, don't miss Barrio Amón's best-known landmarks, the Alianza Francesa (p66) cultural center and Amón Solar (p71), which hosts live music events.

ATLANTIC RAIL STATION

At first glance, the **Estación del Ferrocarril al Atlántico** *(incofer.go.cr)* is an adorable one-story building in Barrio La California, where little has changed since it received its first passengers in 1908. It's a remarkable example of tropical architecture, with swirling art nouveau–inspired beams and elaborate stonework along the roofline. An antique locomotive outside reminds visitors just how long this historical train station has been in operation, and the terminal is still active, with commuter trains departing for destinations all across the Central Valley. The lobby isn't very big, but all train lines meet at Atlántico, making it Costa Rica's equivalent of New York City's Grand Central.

DRINKING IN DOWNTOWN SAN JOSÉ: CLASSIC & CONTEMPORARY

Restaurante La Criollita: This beloved restaurant has white tablecloths, framed paintings and a lively little bar. *6:30am-7pm Mon-Fri, to 5pm Sat*

Stiefel: Craft beer served with typical bar food like chicken fingers. *noon-11pm Sun-Wed, to midnight Thu, to 1am Fri & Sat*

La Buenos Aires: Old-school pub with an L-shaped bar and fashionable crowd. Located across from Parroquia Santa Teresita. *11am-midnight*

Buchón Cantina (p59): High ceilings and colorful tiled floors, plus an extensive cocktail/mocktail menu. *5pm-midnight Tue-Sat*

A CHURCH & BUS STOP ALL IN ONE

'La Merced' refers to Iglesia Nuestra Señora de la Merced (Our Lady of Mercy Church), but it's also a popular bus stop on the western side of downtown. The white church rises into a sharp crimson steeple and has been well maintained since 1894. La Merced watches over Parque Braulio Carrillo, a small square full of noise and activity. The church serves as a handy reference point, as it also lends its name to the surrounding barrio.

La Merced is the smartest place to board a bus to Escazú and Santa Ana; departures take place every few minutes.

Seek Souvenirs on the Streets

Shopping in San José

San José is crammed with little stores, and travelers will bypass many of them. But if you're looking for mementos, you'll get the most bang for your buck at the **Mercado Municipal de Artesanías** *(Municipal Craft Market; facebook.com/mercadoartesanias.sj)*. Brace yourself: the merchants here are hungry for customers, and as you work your way down the narrow aisles of this indoor bazaar, you'll encounter one eager salesperson after another. There's plenty of mass-market decor and crockery with 'Pura Vida' stamped on the side, but many of these wares are truly artisanal making this a great place to load up on gifts.

Search among the vendors of the Mercado Central (p65) and you'll find lots of similar goodies, along with hats and T-shirts. You can also visit the gift shop at the Museo del Oro Precolombino (p64) and find remarkable deals on local and indigenous artwork, such as beaded necklaces and hand-tooled water-gourds.

Two standalone stores worth checking out are **Tienda eÑe** *(facebook.com/esquina13y7)*, a stylish boutique specializing in Costa Rican–made designs, and **Chietón Morén** *(en.chietonmoren.org)*, which sources masks, clothing and handicrafts directly from indigenous communities and sends the full profit back to the artisans.

Art After Dark

Tour free exhibitions all evening

The **Art City Tour** *(artcitytour.gamcultural.com)* is basically a giant, citywide open house for cultural institutions, and anyone can join in. You can ride designated buses for free, and participants are encouraged to cycle or walk from site to site as well. The event takes place sporadically throughout the year and is organized by GAM Cultural, which stands for 'Gran Área Metropolitana' and endeavors to enrich urban living through the arts.

Thousands of people turn out for the tours, and streets teem with artists, students and families who might not otherwise come out at night. They trickle through museums and galleries, which often synchronize exhibition openings with Art City Tour dates. Joining this after-dark event is a budget-friendly way to see San José at its very best.

Granted, the odds of an Art City Tour taking place during your visit to the capital are slim, unless you're planning to stay for a while. Not to worry: all the institutions on this circuit are open during the week, and many are free to enter. Just as valuable as the event itself are the GAM Cultural social media pages, which actively post about local venues and showings. Art City Tours are held roughly every quarter so if this event is of particular interest to you, try to plan your trip around it.

A STROLL THROUGH DOWNTOWN

Discover some of the city's best museums and signature bites with this walking tour of the center.

START	END	LENGTH
Iglesia de la Merced	Barrio La California	1.8km; 1 hr

Begin your urban exploration atthe stunning 1 **Iglesia de la Merced** (p68).

Head north and over a block to make your way down 2 **Avenida Central** (p67), the city's main shopping corridor. Pop into the 3 **Mercado Central** (p65) to fuel up on typical soups, stews, *empanadas* (stuffed turnovers) and snacks like the *ceviche*-topped chips referred to as *caldosa*. You'll find them all over the market but Isla del Coco stand makes an especially tasty batch. If you're feeling overwhelmed by the market, head to Cafe El Único, which is on the west side of the market with an entrance on Calle 8.

As you make your way down the main avenue, keep your eyes open for murals, bronze statues and temporary art installations – and your ears open for street musicians. To pick up an English-language book, perhaps a recent novel by a Costa Rican author, visit 4 **Librería Internacional** (p66), the largest bookstore downtown.

Find respite in 5 **Parque Nacional** (p64), one of the prettiest parks in the city, full of shady trees and exotic plants. It's the perfect place to take a breather and reflect on the day's experiences.

End at 6 **Barrio La California** (p71), where you can take your time exploring the various bars and nightclubs along Calle 21.

The 1953 Monumento Nacional in **Parque Nacional** depicts the Central American nations driving out North American filibusters.

The **Museo Nacional** is housed in the building where, in 1949, President José Figueres Ferrer abolished the country's military.

Barrio La California is a proper, albeit small, neighborhood, but when locals refer to it, they're talking about a few blocks of bars along Calle 21.

A PROGRESSIVE TICO PLAYLIST

Young Ticos can argue for days about their favorite bands, but here's a sampler of streamable local artists.

Las Robertas: This woman-fronted grunge group harmonizes over heavy guitars, with mostly English vocals.

Gandhi: These alt-rockers have mixed rock and Latin sounds since 1993 and even opened for Sting and Aerosmith.

Sonámbulo Psicotropical: Their trippy, fast-paced jam-sessions are an awesome blend of rock, big-band and reggae.

Niño Koi: The four-man Niño Koi is known for brooding instrumental pieces and punchy samples.

Malpaís: Costa Rican fusion blending traditional folk and rhythm with jazz and rock.

A Night at the Theater

Catch a show in San José

The performing arts in San José are well hidden, and you could visit the city many times without ever thinking of it as a 'theater town.' Companies are scattered across downtown, and the vast majority of their productions are staged in Spanish for a Tico audience. But if you want to practice your language skills in a creative setting, the city has a number of playhouses.

The **Teatro Popular Melico Salazar** *(teatromelico.go.cr)* stands only a block from the Plaza de la Cultura, and its 1040-seat auditorium hosts symphonies, dance ensembles and theatrical works. Teatro 1887 and Dance Theatre are both components of the CENAC (p66) arts complex only a short walk away, and they regularly put on small and experimental productions.

Located inside the Antigua Aduana (p81) in Barrio Escalante, the **Compañía Nacional de Teatro** (National Theatre Company) is a program of the Teatro Popular Melico Salazar. Not to be confused with the Teatro Nacional (p63), this professional company produces a range of plays, from Shakespeare to contemporary dramas and Costa Rican premieres.

For something more playful, try **Teatro el Triciclo** *(teatroeltriciclo.com)* on Avenida 8, which specializes in comedies and farces. Triciclo is one of many black-box theaters designed for crowd-pleasing, Spanish-language entertainment.

MIROSLAV DENES/SHUTTERSTOCK

Teatro Popular Melico Salazar

Rock On

Catch live bands in San José

Salsa music is the Costa Rican standby, and many radios are tuned to danceable Latin love songs. But *josefinos* tend to have more eclectic tastes: North American and European rock bands are huge here, and superstar vocalists from around the world make regular stops in San José. Better yet, the capital is garnering a well-earned reputation for indie bands.

A popular nook for live music is **Barrio La California**, a thumping party district on the edge of downtown. DJs perform all night around here, and partygoers bar-hop from one venue to another. Mid-week starts heating up at **La Concha de la Lora** *(facebook.com/laconchalora)* with reggaetón, Latin and soca music. Come the weekend, try **El Observatorio** *(elobservatorio.tv)*, a brick-walled showroom with a sculpture of giant eyeballs hanging over a central stage. This place has a diehard following, and every band that plays here is worth the ticket price.

Amón Solar *(facebook.com/amonsolarcr)* has drawn music fans to Barrio Amón for several years. The pillared building looks like a tropical mansion, and the spacious interior is great for dancing and socializing. The venue hosts live jazz on Tuesdays and regular salsa nights. On the edge of Barrio Amón is **StarView CR** *(facebook.com/starviewcr)*, which is also housed in an antique building but feels more like a '90s grunge bar.

The pride of Escalante is **Utopía Central House** *(facebook.com/utopia.crc)*, a combination of restaurant, cocktail lounge and multimedia performance venue. On any given night you might find electronic music DJs, fire-jugglers or both.

LGBTIQ+ HANGOUTS IN DOWNTOWN SAN JOSÉ

In San José, most LGBTIQ+ hangouts are frequented by locals (and travelers) of all sexual persuasions – they just happen to be especially welcoming to the queer crowd.

La Avispa: 'The Wasp' is a big gay and lesbian nightclub with two tiers of seating, great cocktails and a packed dance floor.

Bar El 13: This popular entertainment venue is covered in experimental art. Look for the rooftop unicorn.

Lunix Club: Literally located on the train tracks, this small venue hosts karaoke, DJs and special events.

Bombóm: Lively queer bar and party venue located on the 3rd floor of the Steinvorth building.

La Sabana & Around

SPORTY GREEN SPACE

GETTING AROUND

Though highways and several main roads also cut through the west side of La Sabana, only allowing pedestrians a few access points to cross over, in general the neighborhood is quite walkable. Parking can be competitive, but hundreds of buses pass through here daily, so public transportation and taxis are great ways to get around if your destination isn't within walking distance.

TOP TIP

La Sabana is usually known for higher-end and international cuisine than affordable local food. Traditional Tico fare can be found at El Social and Soda Tapia, but the area is experiencing a mini culinary revolution with creative new establishments. Most of these are on the west side of the neighborhood, which also tends to be greener, quieter and more walkable.

In a metropolis as hilly and cluttered as San José, Parque Metropolitano La Sabana is a breath of fresh air. Covering nearly 1 sq km, it's the largest urban park within city limits and once served as the country's first international airport.

Today La Sabana is the capital's recreational nerve center, welcoming everyone from joggers and casual walkers to volleyball players and pickup football enthusiasts. Meanwhile, the Estadio Nacional draws massive crowdsfor everything from La Sele football matches to world-class concerts.

La Sabana is also the name of the surrounding area, where modernist high-rises mingle with fast-food restaurants. Two major highways converge on its eastern edge, and the park serves as a kind of gateway to downtown San José. Several embassies are located here, making the neighborhood a crossroads for diplomats too.

Escape the noise by strolling the quieter side-streets, which offer a range of hotels and international eateries. Many travelers spend their first few nights here to orient themselves.

Soccer Fever

Catch a game at Estadio Nacional

The **Estadio Nacional** *(facebook.com/EstadioNCR)* is the crown jewel of Costa Rican athletics, and it's generally considered the most cutting-edge stadium in Central America. Two canopies arc over the stadium like wings, and they're visible from miles away. The stands can seat more than 35,000 spectators, and events routinely sell out. It's also fairly new, completed in 2011. Curiously, the stadium was a gift from the People's Republic of China.

The National Stadium is busy year-round with large-scale events. Marathons have begun and ended on the field and major performers like Paul McCartney and Shakira have performed

HIGHLIGHTS
1 Estadio Nacional
2 Museo de Arte Costarricense
3 Parque Metropolitano La Sabana

SIGHTS
4 Gimnasio Nacional
5 Lago de la Sabana
6 Museo de Ciencias Naturales La Salle

SLEEPING
7 Apartotel La Sabana
8 Capital Hostel de Ciudad
9 Casa Colón
10 Casa Jardín de Mango
11 Del Cafetal
12 Hotel Ecological Innovation
13 Palma Real

EATING
14 Cloud Bar & Restaurant
15 El Social Sabana
16 Franco Nunciatura
17 Le Bistrot de Paris
18 Soda Tapia

DRINKING & NIGHTLIFE
19 Central Pub

ENTERTAINMENT
20 Sala Garbo

TRANSPORT
21 Tica Bus

THE FUTURE OF LAGO DE LA SABANA

La Sabana's pond was a beautiful addition to the park, reflecting the leafy surroundings on its surface. There isn't much standing water in San José, so the Lago de La Sabana was a rare opportunity to sit near its banks and have yourself a picnic or even go out paddleboating on the lake. These days, the water levels are so low that there are rarely more than a few large puddles scattered around the lake, but one can hope a strong rainy season will return the lake to its former glory. The city does hope to restore it in the future, but such a project – if it goes through – could be years away.

PANDORA PICTURES/SHUTTERSTOCK

Estadio Nacional (p72)

on its stage. It's hosted the FIFA Women's World Cup and the Copa Centroamericana, along with scads of regional tournaments. There's a century-old rivalry between the Heredia and Alajuela soccer clubs meaning game days here are intense.

Above all, the stadium is home turf for La Sele, Costa Rica's national football team. During FIFA games, the stands are awash in tricolor jerseys, and the atmosphere around La Sabana is frenetic, with flag-waving crowds and honking horns. You don't have to see a La Sele match in person – every television in the country will be playing the *partido* (match). Tickets usually start at around US$20, making it an irresistible treat for football fans – and a crash course in Costa Rican pride.

Dine in the Clouds

Meal with a view

If you're looking for food with a fantastic backdrop, the **Cloud Bar & Restaurant** occupies an upper floor of the local Hilton and overlooks the Estadio Nacional. Reflecting the name, the Cloud's interior is bright white, and the surfaces warp and flow, much like a tuft of cumulus. The south wall is made of plate-glass, providing one of the best views in the city, especially during a soccer match. Main courses from the rotating menu are artfully presented and layered with flavors, in keeping with Hilton's reputation for excellence.

From Rodeos to Gymnastics

Watch indoor sports at the Gimnasio Nacional

Basketball, cricket, taekwondo – it all happens in the **Gimnasio Nacional** *(concrc.org)*. This building doesn't look like much on the outside, but within there's a polished court and seating for 4000 people. The stadium's rounded shape was originally intended for rodeos, and many *vaqueros* (cowboys) faced off with horses and bulls here in the 1960s. Today, this is a modern facility that keeps sports fans entertained in any season. The building is often left open to visitors, and you never know what kind of event you'll stumble upon. One day it might be a gymnastics competition, the next a graduation ceremony.

Old-School Tico Dining

An iconic diner for carbo-loading

After a walk around the park, there's no better way to reward yourself than with a big plate of *casado* (set meal). **Soda Tapia** *(facebook.com/sodatapia)* stands on the eastern edge of La Sabana and beckons hungry visitors with its enormous red awning. Opened in 1965, the place is a local favorite, and the dining room has the cozy booths and checkered tile walls of an old-school diner. There's lots of shaded outdoor seating, and tables are usually packed with Tico families chowing down on *gallo pinto* and enormous burgers. The menu features just about every variation of *comida típica* (traditional food) there is, making it a great place to sample. No visit would be complete without dessert; Soda Tapia serves decadent scoops of ice cream with fresh fruit.

Parque Metropolitano La Sabana

Soccer fields and more

You have your choice of several public soccer fields in **Parque Metropolitano La Sabana**, assuming you can find an empty one. On a sunny day, pickup games take place from dawn till dusk, and locals divide into teams and make good use of the well-maintained goals. Most of these matches are informal and played in street clothes. It's usually easy to join in; if there's one sport that can always use another player, it's *fútbol*.

While soccer may be Costa Rica's most obsessive pastime, Parque Metropolitano La Sabana offers space for other sports as well. There's a volleyball court on the eastern side, along with several basketball courts and rollerblading tracks. In the southwest corner, you'll find two baseball fields and a separate one for softball. A boathouse by the lake sometimes rents out small paddleboats, although this depends on water depth (which tends to be low to non-existent these days). Among the football fields, there's a dedicated space for rugby. Finally, in the north-central section, there's a small playground for the kiddos to run around. The grassy expanses lend themselves to many other activities as well, such as Frisbees and kite-flying.

Runners will rejoice at the sight of La Sabana's race track. This oval track is public, always open and popular for sprints or laps. Inside this loop is a separate track for inline skating. Inside *that* track is a multipurpose court, most often used for football.

THE ROOTS OF TÍO CONEJO

The mascot of La Sabana's Parque Diversiones is Tío Conejo (Uncle Rabbit), a rascal and trickster. Like Br'er Rabbit, Tío Conejo originated in African and indigenous folklore and is well known throughout Central America. The character became even more popular thanks to Carmen Lyra, one of Costa Rica's most respected authors, who retold many Tío Conejo tales in her seminal book from 1920, *Cuentos de mi tía Panchita* (Tales of My Aunt Panchita). So when you see a busker approach in a giant rabbit costume, know that it's part of a rich literary tradition and make sure you snap a selfie with Uncle Rabbit.

LA SABANA AIRPORT

La Sabana remained open land until 1930, when the flat terrain was transformed into a runway. For 44 years, anyone flying into Costa Rica would touch down at La Sabana International Airport. Demand increased, as did the size of passenger jets, and the airport was replaced by the much bigger Juan Santamaría International Airport in Alajuela. La Sabana reopened as a public park in 1977, to the relief of *josefinos* in need of a green space to enjoy.

To the untrained eye, no remnants of the former airport remain, but take a close look at the Museo de Arte Costarricense (p78) at the eastern edge of the park, where the former airport's control tower has been immortalized, quite literally towering above the rest of the museum.

It's no secret that long-distance jogs are a challenge in San José, given all the cracked sidewalks and irrigation trenches, and while La Sabana's track is nothing to write home about, it'll spare you the sprained ankles and treacherous intersections of the rest of the city.

For a fuller experience, many people prefer to jog the full perimeter of La Sabana, or else wind their way through the park on the web of walking paths.

Get Your Thrills at Parque Diversiones

An old-fashioned amusement park

The 'Bocaracá' is your classic roller-coaster. For a few tense seconds, you're treated to glorious views of the San José suburbs, then you fly down a yellow track, flip upside-down and careen around corners at impossible angles while fellow riders scream all around you. Fittingly, *bocaracá* means 'eyelash viper' – one of the most venomous snakes in Central America.

Many of the rides at **Parque Diversiones** *(parquediversiones.com; US$5)* have cheeky nomenclature: 'Pacuare' is an outfit-soaking raft ride, just as the Río Pacuare is famous for white-water rafting. 'Splash Caribe' refers to the Caribbean. Other rides bear classic titles, like the 'Tornado,' the 'Boomerang' or 'La Torre' (The Tower), where you submit to 40m of free fall. The rides are well built and legitimately thrilling, earning the place its name, 'Fun Park.'

Parque Diversiones feels far from the city, but it's only a 10-minute drive from La Sabana. What's more, the park was founded in 1981 as a fundraising tool for the city's renowned Children's Hospital, located on Paseo Colón. This park is a favorite among local Ticos, and if you have a spare afternoon in the city, it really can be a great diversion, though don't expect the sort of thrills you'd get at Six Flags.

La Sabana's Hidden Nooks

Explore around Paseo Colón

San José has a red carpet, and its name is Paseo Colón. Named after Christopher Columbus (Colón in Spanish), this mile-long boulevard leads visitors from La Sabana into the city proper. Viewed from afar, the trees and wide sidewalks make for an inviting cityscape.

At street level, the picture isn't so pretty. Ranks of office buildings and fast-food restaurants line up on either side, and the biggest landmark is the Children's Hospital. Travelers

EATING IN LA SABANA: OUR PICKS

Franco Nunciatura: Spacious, sunny cafe with outdoor seating. Daily brunch-style menu. *7am-9pm Tue-Fri, 8am-9pm Sat, 8am-7pm Sun, 7am-7pm Mon* $$

El Social Sabana: Popular modern canteen serving traditional dishes like *chifrijo* (rice, beans and fried pork). *Noon-4am Mon-Thu, 4pm-5am Fri & Sat, to 8pm Sun* $$

Corazón Contento Pastelería: Meticulously prepared gourmet ice cream using all parts of the fruit. *noon-5:30pm Fri, 11am-6:30pm Sat & Sun* $$

Bardo Natural Winebar: Natural-wine bar pairing wine and cocktails with elevated appetizers in a relaxed setting. *4-11pm Tue-Sat* $$

MV/ALAMY

Tyrannosaurus rex skeleton, Museo de Ciencias Naturales La Salle

rarely stop on this road except to pick up a car from any of several rental services.

But Paseo Colón does have its charms. **Sala Garbo** *(salagarbo.com)* is a funky movie theater that screens a grab-bag of indie films, and patrons can also score dinner and a drink in its on-site pub, Shakespeare.

There's also **Central Pub**, a hip little bar near La Sabana, where you'll find inventive cocktails and live music in the London Room, which you access through the pub.

For French flair, **Le Bistrot de Paris** *(facebook.com/lebistrotdepariscr)* is an expectedly atmospheric locale serving coffee and pastries. Vintage posters are hung above white-cloth tables, transporting you to the Left Bank.

The most eye-catching facade is **Casa Colón**, a guesthouse with a knightly tower and Spanish-style architecture. Rooms are reasonable and put you a quick walk from Avenida Central.

Tica Bus *(ticabus.com)*, which was formerly located downtown, is now located near Paseo Colón and is the place to buy bus tickets for destinations across Central America.

PARADES OF PASEO COLÓN

The city routinely blocks off Paseo Colón for holiday parades. Here are some to look out for.

Día de la Independencia: Ticos celebrate their independence from Spain on September 15, and the city comes alive with marching bands and waving of the Costa Rican flag.

Semana Santa: During Holy Week, the processions are a dramatic reenactment of Christ's crucifixion. Actors perform major scenes in the streets of San José.

Festival de la Luz: In anticipation of Christmas, light-encrusted parade floats make their way past La Sabana, along with costumed buskers.

Pride Parade: Each June, thousands march to celebrate gay rights in this colorful, musical spectacular, typically starting in the park and heading east along Paseo Colón.

Meet the T-Rex

A general-interest science museum

It's hard to envision 65,000 specimens – until you step into **Museo de Ciencias Naturales La Salle** *(museolasalle.ed.cr; adult/child US$5/4)*, where the rooms and corridors are all lined with glass cases. Tucked into a government complex on the southwestern corner of La Sabana, this museum contains a treasure trove of environmental artifacts, from minerals to mammals. Thousands of fossils and stones hail from all over the world, including eons-old trilobites. Elaborate dioramas showcase both the diversity of species and the fine art of taxidermy. Although many parts of the collection come from Costa Rica, the museum is global and timeless in scope, including

THE RISE OF SAN JOSÉ

Villanueva de la Boca del Monte del Valle de Abra – as San José was first known – wasn't founded until 1737. For much of the colonial period, it played second fiddle to Cartago and remained a backwater for decades, though it became a stop in the tobacco-trading route during the late 18th century. Following independence in 1821, San José emerged as the capital in 1823. Despite its new status, the city remained a quiet agricultural center into the 20th century. In the 1940s, parts of it served as a battlefield in the civil war of 1948. The rest of the 20th century saw the expansion of the city from diminutive coffee-trading outpost to sprawling urban center. Today, the greater metro population stands at over 2 million.

SALVADOR AZNAR/SHUTTERSTOCK

Museo de Arte Costarricense

a full-scale skeleton of a T-Rex. Most impressive of all is the authentic stone sphere standing outside the front door.

Art in a Historic Setting

Tour the Museum of Costa Rican Art

Housed partly in what formerly served as the airport control tower, the free **Museo de Arte Costarricense** *(mac.go.cr)* makes for a quick but worthwhile visit. Temporary exhibits occupy the lower level while the museum's main attraction is upstairs.

'Salón Dorado' means 'Golden Room,' and the moment you step inside, you'll wonder how such a place is possible. The walls are made of dark wood, and every inch has been painstakingly carved into landscapes and human forms. Scene by scene, the pictorial walls tell the story of Costa Rica, from the arrival of the conquistadors to early farming and the rise of towns. The room was once a meeting place for diplomats; today, these 150 sq metres of engraved wood are available for all to see.

The Golden Room is just one of the magical alcoves you'll find in the museum, which stands at the eastern entrance of Parque Metropolitano La Sabana. This elegant building is constructed in traditional Spanish style, with bleached white walls and tile roofs, and it's hard to believe that it once served as an airport terminal. The interior is no less striking, with a vaulted ceiling and wraparound mezzanine. Art exhibits rotate through the galleries, most of them representing a Costa Rican artist or social movement in the country's history.

Once you've spent time browsing the artworks on the walls, head outside for a stroll in the sculpture garden, where you'll find artwork by Jiménez Deredia, the only Costa Rican to have a sculpture displayed in the Vatican.

Barrio Escalante, Los Yoses & San Pedro

YOUTHFUL NEIGHBORHOODS, GASTRONOMY AND NIGHTLIFE

The moment you cross the wide street of Ismael Murillo, the mood changes. You leave the teeming inner city and step into a mellow suburb of well-ordered blocks, with young professionals strolling the level sidewalks. Barrio Escalante, the most pleasant neighborhood in San José, lies to the east of downtown but feels totally different and much hipper.

The district blends with Los Yoses and San Pedro, and from a fast-moving *taxi rojo* they're hard to tell apart. San Pedro is home to the Universidad de Costa Rica, and the streets around its main campus are packed with fun restaurants and rambunctious nightlife. Los Yoses is a cozy residential neighborhood with a surprising number of pubs and eateries tucked into its thoroughfares.

Together, these barrios form a dynamic corridor for young Ticos in search of education, entertainment and a trendy place to live. And given Escalante's rising prices, many businesses are moving to the more affordable Los Yoses.

GETTING AROUND

Escalante is a quiet, walkable neighborhood where just about everything is a few blocks away. It's about 20 to 25 minutes' walk from downtown but there are fewer cars, and the streets and sidewalks are in better condition, making it perfect to get around on foot or by bicycle. Crossing over into Los Yoses, the topography becomes a bit more undulating. Here, you'll find small hills and some cracked sidewalks, yet the area remains walkable.

TOP TIP

If you're staying in the city and don't know where to rest your head, consider Barrio Escalante or Los Yoses. These neighborhoods are centrally located, and accommodations run the gamut from darling hostels to luxury apartments. For restful nights, both serve as a quiet place to retreat after a long day of exploring.

The Center of the Action

Explore Calle 33

Barrio Escalante has become a nightlife hotspot in recent years, drawing international attention. Nearly every street has some kind of dining option, but the main drag is **Calle 33**, which strings together about six blocks of bars and eateries. There's a lot to see here, and you could spend multiple evenings making your way down the row, testing out food and libations. In the middle of the action is **Fresh Market**, an exceptional Costa Rican grocery chain. If you're staying in Barrio Escalante, Fresh Market is the ideal place to pick up supplies.

Calle 33 is also within a few blocks of numerous hotels and guesthouses, making it convenient to walk, or stumble, back to your accommodations.

HIGHLIGHTS
1 Antigua Aduana
2 Calle 33
3 Feria Verde de Aranjuez

SIGHTS
4 Barrio California
5 Calle de la Amargura
6 Casa de Cuño
7 Centro Cultural Costarricense-Norteamericano
8 Museo Calderón Guardia
9 Museo de Insectos
10 Parque Francia
11 Parque John F Kennedy
12 Parroquia Santa Teresita
13 Sendero

ACTIVITIES
14 Boliche Dent
15 Universidad de Costa Rica

SLEEPING
16 BEE Suites
17 Chillout Hostel
18 Hostel Finca Escalante
19 Hotel 1492
20 Hotel Le Bergerac
21 Lost in Costa Rica Hostel
22 URBN Escalante

EATING
23 Apotecario
24 Árbol de Seda
25 Cafeoteca
26 Calle 33 Mercadito
27 Club Alemán
28 El Buho
29 Franco Escalante
30 Fresh Market
31 Huacamole
32 Indian Palace
33 Isolina
34 Jardin de Lolita
35 Kilka
36 Modo
37 Sikwa

DRINKING & NIGHTLIFE
38 Costa Rica Beer Factory
39 La Buenos Aires
40 Wilk

ENTERTAINMENT
41 Cine Magaly

TRANSPORT
42 Estación del Ferrocarril al Atlántico

Art in an Industrial Setting

A shipping house turned arts center

The brick walls of the **Antigua Aduana** stretch across a full block, and you might guess from its row of enormous doors that the complex was an Industrial Age factory. Not so; the name translates as 'Old Customs House,' and it was here that imported goods were processed and properly taxed. Completed in 1888, the architecture of the Antigua Aduana shows many Victorian flourishes, such as decorative masonry and flower-shaped windows above the former loading docks.

Today, the building is used for an endless variety of large-scale events, from cultural exhibitions to craft markets and concerts. If an occasion calls for lots of space and thousands of visitors, the Antigua Aduana is a likely host, and it's hard to predict what you'll find when you pass through the main entrance.

The building also marks the western edge of Barrio Escalante, standing like a wall between this neighborhood and downtown San José. Out front lies a broad cobblestone sidewalk and a busy street, easy landmarks for getting your bearings or meeting up with friends.

Just behind stands the **Casa de Cuño** (Stamp House), a modernist glass structure with a black framework. This building serves much the same function as the Antigua Aduana, but the transparent walls and I-beam construction exude an edgier atmosphere. Design festivals and fashion shows rotate in the Casa de Cuño's two-level interior. The building is situated on a brick plaza, where patrons tend to cluster before and after events.

Honoring a Revered Statesman

Visit a former president's residence

Before he became president of Costa Rica in 1940, Dr Rafael Calderón Guardia was a successful physician. Today, he is remembered as an important reformer and advocate for the working class, among other achievements. The free-to-visit **Museo Calderón Guardia** *(mcj.go.cr)* is based in his former residence, a glamorous columned mansion in Barrio Escalante. The museum hosts a wide range of gallery shows and lectures. On permanent display are ephemera from the former president's life, including personal possessions, archival photographs and a robust library.

AN IDIOSYNCRATIC RESIDENTIAL TOWER

Go big or go home – that was the thinking behind **URBN Escalante**, a 29-story apartment complex looming over Avenida 1, which opened its doors in 2019. There is nothing like it in San José: URBN is a monolith of brutalist concrete, far taller than any nearby building, and contains 186 residential units. It's well known for its rooftop pool, trippy communal spaces and the best view in town.

An architectural curiosity, URBN is also filled with Airbnb rentals, and the building has become a de facto hotel. Most residents live here full-time, but the lobby is always busy with luggage-dragging foreigners. It also has its own restaurant, MANTRA, at the top. There's an intercom on Calle 27A.

EATING IN BARRIO ESCALANTE: BRUNCH & BEYOND

Franco Escalante: Regular breakfasts are transformed into artful dishes layered in flavor. Sit outside in a garden-like environment. *hours vary* $$

Apotecario: A dining room festooned with plants and vines, plus masterful mains for brunch and dinner. *11:30am-10pm Mon-Wed, 9am-11pm Thu-Sat, to 8pm Sun* $$

Isolina: Creative food that is carefully prepared and smartly served, alongside a wine selection and a range of cocktails. *hours vary* $$$

Sikwa: Elevated indigenous cuisine, such as the multi-course 'ancestral tasting menu' and *cichleme* (blue-corn-and-ginger drink). *6-10pm Tue-Sat* $$$

ESCALANTE'S COFFEE CRAZE

Maria Elena Rivera is a barista and co-owner of Modo cafe. *@modocafecr*

Escalante is not just a destination for foodies but for coffee lovers too. There are so many great coffee shops here, all within a few blocks of each other, and each one offers their own appeal.

Franco (p81) is a coffee shop but it also has good food and is known for amazing weekend brunches. Cafeoteca (p86) puts an equal emphasis on coffee and food; they also offer information about their coffee so there's some interactive education there. **Kilka** has interesting coffees in a beautiful space and they also prepare unique coffee mocktails. At my cafe, **Modo**, it's hard to recommend a specific drink because we're always changing our menu. That said, our espressos and filtered coffee is always good.

LEONID ANDRONOV/ALAMY

Parroquia Santa Teresita

A Local Place of Worship

Peek inside Parroquia Santa Teresita

The massive red dome of the **Parroquia Santa Teresita** is one of Barrio Escalante's most familiar landmarks, but this formidable basilica looks much older than it is: Santa Teresita held its first service in 1941. The church has crisp white walls, inside and out, and aside from some pillars and molding, the choir's curved ceiling is almost entirely free of ornament. Art enthusiasts will appreciate the stained-glass windows and rooftop statue of the Virgin Mary.

A Taste of Bavaria in Los Yoses

Have a beer at Club Alemán

You don't have to be a member to hang out at the **Club Alemán** (German Club), never mind German. Yes, the place is popular among expats and Central European travelers, especially during relevant FIFA matches, and you can probably practice some Deutsch with staff. But at its heart, the club is a cozy Biergarten serving lots of (what else?) beer. The walls are decked with sentimental photographs and there's both indoor and outdoor seating. The food is meaty and well prepared. And come fall, there's no better place in Costa Rica to celebrate Oktoberfest.

EATING IN BARRIO ESCALANTE: VEGETARIAN FOOD

Árbol de Seda: Relaxed breakfast, brunch and dinner that are mostly international with a few local dishes. *9am-10pm Fri & Sat, to 5pm Sun, Tue-Thu* **$$**

Huacamole: Vegan fast food meets health food in an unpretentious space decorated with muralled walls. *noon-9pm Mon-Fri, to 6pm Sat & Sun* **$$**

Indian Palace: Though not fully vegetarian, this Indian restaurant has a meat-free menu of dosas, salads, soups and fried starters. *11am-10pm* **$$**

El Buho: Sunny eatery serving vegan, vegetarian and gluten-free treats, from eggplant croquettes and stir-fries to mushroom casseroles. *11:30am-6pm Tue-Thu* **$$**

Promoting Tico–US Ties

North American culture in San José

Put simply, the **Centro Cultural Costarricense–Norteamericano** *(CCCN; centrocultural.cr)* is a school for learning English as a second language. But the center also functions as a safe space for Ticos to learn about their friendly superpower to the north. The **Eugene O'Neill Theater** hosts a variety of live lectures and performances, and CCCN is the one place in Costa Rica where viewers can watch a live simulcast of the Metropolitan Opera in New York City. Visit the website or drop in to learn about the CCCN's cultural calendar. You can't miss its imposing headquarters: the facade is colored red, white and blue.

Be a Student for a Day

A college campus with open doors

The main entrance to the **Universidad de Costa Rica** *(ucr.ac.cr)* is called El Pretil (The Forecourt), a broad walkway where students take breaks between classes. Bolted to the wall is a gigantic sculpture of a sunflower, which welcomes visitors to the campus. On some nearby steps, you'll find the bronze statues of three students laughing aloud. El Pretil sets the tone for all of UCR's main campus: upbeat, welcoming and open to the public. Visitors can stroll past academic buildings in sheltered walkways or grab a snack at one of the cafes, but the real attraction here is the resident sloth that can sometimes be spotted lazing around in the greenery. The biology department has its own butterfly garden, and the **Planetario** *(Planetarium; planetario.ucr.ac.cr; US$6.5)* is only a few blocks away.

An Entomologist's Dream

Inspect the specimens at the Insect Museum

Scientists estimate that 5000 species of insects live in Costa Rica, more than 1000 of which are butterflies, so it's only natural that the University of Costa Rica would have its own **Museo de Insectos** *(facebook.com/insectosucr; adult/child US$3/1.50)*. If you have a interest in entomology, the glass cases full of six-legged specimens are a great way to kill an hour in San Pedro. The term 'insect' is used loosely; the museum displays arachnids as well, including a gigantic spider puppet suspended from the ceiling.

A Night at the Movies

Catch a flick at Cine Magaly

Costa Rica has plenty of movie theaters, but **Cine Magaly** *(cinemagaly.com)* is a true cinema, in the tradition of old-school art houses. The marquee shines like a beacon in the night for culture seekers, and its single screen is busy with classic, indie and international films. Stairs lead up from Calle 23 to a box office and modest entrance; you'd never guess from the outside how voluminous its auditorium is.

PARQUE JOHN F KENNEDY

In the middle of San Pedro's bustling commercial strip, **Parque John F Kennedy** is a quiet oasis. Little paths are lined with manicured hedges, and in the center stands a neoclassical gazebo, known locally as the Quiosco (Kiosk). **Parroquia San Pedro Apóstol** (St Peter's Apostle Parish) is a simple, cream-colored church that stands on the park's eastern side. President Kennedy's 1963 visit to Costa Rica isn't a major entry in his biography, but it was important enough to Costa Ricans to name this green space after him. On Sundays, the park comes alive with a popular farmers market.

FILM FESTIVALS OF SAN JOSÉ

Festival Internacional de Cine: This mega-festival takes place in June and usually has screening locations and workshops all across the country.

Shnit Short Film Festival: Started in Switzerland in 2003, Shnit plays in several countries, including Costa Rica. Look out for this 12-day festival at Cine Magaly (p83) in October.

La Filmoteca Short Film Fest: This film festival is still in its infancy, but it's one of many great events to take place at the Sala Garbo (p77) cinema.

Festival de Cine Europeo: One of the most anticipated cine events in the country draws crowds each June and July to see movies submitted by embassies from across Europe.

LEONID ANDRONOV/SHUTTERSTOCK

Estación del Ferrocarril al Atlántico

The fact that Cine Magaly even exists is something of a miracle. The cinema first opened in 1979, when it screened the Costa Rican premiere of *The Turning Point*. Many similar places in San José have shuttered over the years, but in 2012, Cine Magaly doubled down and became the go-to movie theater for independent film and several festivals. The variety here is refreshing: one night you may find a Hollywood blockbuster, the next, a micro-budget Spanish-language drama.

In the same building is **Kubrick**, a bistro serving craft beers and upmarket pub food. Filmmakers from around the world are known to eat here before watching their flicks on the big screen, and it's a great place to chat with fellow bohemians. No matter what movie you plan to catch, Kubrick and Magaly make a great pairing.

Feel-Good Dining in the Barrio

Escalante's trendy food hall

Jardín de Lolita *(jardindelolita.com)* describes itself as a 'gastronomic community,' and that feel-good vibe pervades everything about the place, from the festive lights strung up over repurposed shipping containers to the picnic-table seating. Pick from about 10 different eateries serving a smorgasbord of trendy foods, from burgers and pizza to tacos and ice cream.

The food hall has a sister location in Bogotá, Colombia, and the parent company is deeply interested in urban living and sustainable practices. Art lovers should also head across the street to **Sendero**, a cultural center that features photo and art exhibits.

A Classic Tico Pub Night

Hang out at La Buenos Aires

La Buenos Aires is your classic corner pub, where locals congregate for food and beverages. It nearly closed permanently during the pandemic but it was brought back to life when purchased by a former congresswoman. The new ownership conserved the traditional atmosphere of the space while ushering in a younger vibe. The L-shaped bar is long and full of stools, but the place quickly fills up come nightfall, and conversation is lively. Despite its namesake and some old photographs on the walls, any hint of Argentine influence is subtle. La Buenos Aires is located across from Parroquia Santa Teresita, and the place has a long history of wedding after-parties. The neighborhood may have blossomed with bars and restaurants in recent years, but La Buenos Aires remains a fixture of barrio nightlife, with affordable beer and *cantina* (canteen) food.

Ride the Rails

Cross the valley by train

The Central Valley is the one place in Costa Rica where you can hop on a train. What's more, it's a great way to visit several major cities across 32 stations.

For a taste of the commuter rail, visit the Estación del Ferrocarril al Atlántico (p67) in Barrio California and purchase a ticket in the well-preserved station house. Trains run in the early mornings and afternoons, carrying Ticos to work and back. Head to the UCR station in San Pedro, where you'll be within eyeshot of the University of Costa Rica campus. It will cost you about US$1.50, same as it would to ride to the last station, Cartago.

Most train cars are fairly new and available seats are usually plentiful. The cars wobble over old rails and the whistle is deafening, but the train bypasses the gridlocked traffic of Los Yoses and offers unique views of the urban landscape.

And there's no reason to stop there. The Atlantic Rail Station is a hub for several different lines, which continue to Cartago, Alajuela and Heredia. The train is cheap and moves quickly but because it's mostly used to get commuters in and out of the city during the work week, the schedule is limited midday and doesn't run on the weekends.

Bowling for All

Have some fun at Boliche Dent

Not only is **Boliche Dent** *(bolichecostarica.com/boliche-dent)* the only real bowling alley in San José, it's also the largest in Costa Rica, with a total of 14 lanes. The inclusive atmosphere is perfect for families, and Boliche takes pride in being wheelchair-accessible. Unlike the cheap beer you might find at lesser alleys, Boliche Dent mixes tropical iced cocktails fit for the beach. The snack bar serves burgers, tacos and *chifrijo*,

PARTYING IN CALLE DE LA AMARGURA

Calle de la Amargura translates as 'Street of Bitterness,' though mostly good times are to be had along this four-block stretch of San Pedro. Locals know 'La Calle' as the barrio's main party district, where students converge to socialize and blow off steam after class. Once the sun sets, the loud neon lights switch on, and violet-hued nightclubs fill up with partygoers. While La Calle still draws crowds from the nearby university, it's no longer the nightlife hub it used to be and most locals (and travelers) prefer to party in Barrio La California (p71). Still, if you're in the area, it's worth a visit.

making it a decent place for your bowling team to grab dinner. If the alley's busy, as it often is, kill some time with a round of foosball or pool.

Dent's unremarkable gray facade is easy to miss in the daytime, but just look for the overhanging Pepsi sign on Calle 37. Prices start from US$35 per pair for an hour of bowling plus shoe rentals and drinks.

FRESH FARMERS MARKETS

Eco-conscious shoppers and lovers of fresh produce should check out the Saturday Feria in **Sámara** (p261) and Dominical's **Eco Feria** (p345).

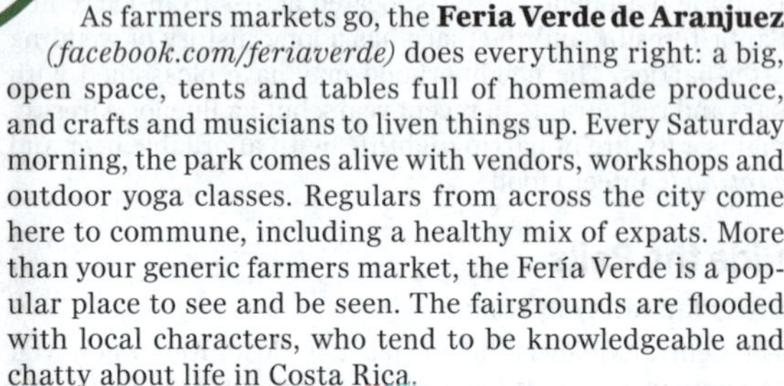

A Green Market for the New Millennium

Shop local at Feria Verde

As farmers markets go, the **Feria Verde de Aranjuez** *(facebook.com/feriaverde)* does everything right: a big, open space, tents and tables full of homemade produce, and crafts and musicians to liven things up. Every Saturday morning, the park comes alive with vendors, workshops and outdoor yoga classes. Regulars from across the city come here to commune, including a healthy mix of expats. More than your generic farmers market, the Fería Verde is a popular place to see and be seen. The fairgrounds are flooded with local characters, who tend to be knowledgeable and chatty about life in Costa Rica.

The market takes place in Parque Polideportivo de Aranjuez (Aranjuez Multi-Sport Park), which is technically in the next neighborhood over from Barrio Escalante. Aranjuez is mostly known for its massive medical campus, Rafael Angel Calderón Guardia Hospital, which makes the area busy but unimportant to travelers. Aranjuez is easy to reach on foot or by taxi, and you'll find the same kind of crowd at the Fería that you'll find on Calle 33: young urbanites and graying hippies who love to shop local.

THE JUNGLE TRAIN

Hard as it is to believe, railroads have shaped much of Costa Rican history. For 20 years, laborers toiled in the rainforest to build a continuous freight line from San José to the Caribbean Coast. Thousands of workers arrived from China, followed by thousands more from Jamaica. Many of these workers and their families settled in Costa Rica, dramatically enriching the nation's ethnic profile. After years of earthquakes and landslides, the line was largely replaced by modern highways. But urban segments live on, as do the descendants of the immigrants who built them. You can learn more about the Jungle Train in Turrialba (p131), a major stop on the line back in the 1880s.

Unleash Your Inner Foodie

Bistro-hopping in Barrio Escalante

You could eat every meal in Barrio Escalante for weeks and still find something new and delicious to try. It wasn't always this way; the neighborhood has only blossomed into an epicurean hotspot in recent years, to the astonishment of lifelong residents. These aren't just cool restaurants that travelers might enjoy, but sophisticated cafes and bistros aimed at true foodies.

One of the early locations was **Cafeoteca** *(facebook.com/cafeotecacoffee)*, formerly known as Kalú. This spacious ranch house has white walls and a generous atrium, giving it the atmosphere of a divine greenhouse. Several nearby cafes also specialize in gourmet Costa Rican coffee brewed in French presses and Chemex vessels.

Around the corner, the **Calle 33 Mercadito** food hall holds numerous different kitchens under one roof. You can order just about anything from ramen and burgers to soups and tacos, then sit down anywhere in this funky cafeteria. The open-seating environment makes Calle 33 a great spot for groups with diverse paletes.

EZEQUIEL BECERRA/GETTY IMAGES

Sikwa

True fine dining comes in the form of **Isolina** (*isolina restaurante.com*; p81), an elegant option known as much for its wine as for its international cuisine, and **Sikwa** (*sikwacostarica.com*; p81), which elevates indigenous culture and cuisine.

You will never hear the term 'gastropub' as often as you do in Barrio Escalante, and *cerveza artesanal* (craft beer) has become a local specialty. The most ostentatious is **Costa Rica Beer Factory** *(costaricabeerfactory.com)*, an enormous Biergarten located in the middle of Calle 33. Another popular choice is **Wilk** *(facebook.com/wilk.cr)*, a bar with a slacker vibe, multiple brews and an entire wall covered floor-to-ceiling in beer bottles.

San José by Pedal Power

Conquer the streets on two wheels

Until recently, riding a bicycle in San José was almost unthinkable. The streets are hilly and potholed, and Ticos have long seen cyclists as low-class or in the way.

But the city has experimented with *ciclovías* (bike lanes) in recent years, creating a network of painted routes that help cyclists safely navigate these garbled streets. The system is poorly mapped and hard to follow, but you can technically pedal from Parque Metropolitano La Sabana to San Pedro along secondary roads and rarely have to face off with cars. If you've brought a bike to Costa Rica and plan to tour anyway, the *ciclovía* is a smart way to warm up.

The best segments are in Barrio Escalante, where the streets are already level and calm, and cyclists can ride from one hotspot to the next with relative ease. A few corners even have bike racks for locking up your ride. Downtown, on the other hand, the *ciclovías* are often so crowded with pedestrians that they are impractical to ride through.

Only experienced urban riders should chance riding in San José, and we recommend tough tires and decent suspension.

PARQUE FRANCIA

Shaped like a diamond at a four-way intersection, **Parque Francia** is a cute little park on the western side of Barrio Escalante. A monument commemorates the French Revolution, but most locals know it as a reference point for directions and a peaceful place to linger. You'll find people here 24/7 – it's a favorite spot for local youth to hang out at night and cause harmless mischief – so it tends to be a safe space and great for people-watching any time of day. If you need to get the blood flowing, the well-maintained park also has a number of outdoor exercise machines. Should you visit in December, look out for the traditional Christmas concert.

WHY I LOVE BARRIO ESCALANTE

Robert Isenberg, Lonely Planet writer

I remember the first time I grabbed a craft beer in Barrio Escalante. I also remember my first ramen bowl here, and my first evening promenade. Each visit, I saw more signs, more pedestrians. All of a sudden, the barrio had visibly transformed. 'This isn't just a nice place to live,' I thought. 'It's a destination.'

Most travelers treat San José as a necessary stop on their way to somewhere better, but Barrio Escalante is chipping away at that expectation. This community is legitimately fun to visit. The hotels are comfortable, the food is diverse and delicious, and the atmosphere is lively. This is the enclave that San José has needed for decades, and at last, it's here. With luck, more neighborhoods will follow suit.

CHEPECLETAS

A ChepeCletas tour

But if you have the stamina and reflexes to give it a go, a bike can be way faster than a bus, taxi or two legs.

Explore Chepe Like a Local

Hit the streets with ChepeCletas

The name **ChepeCletas** *(chepecletas.com; tours US$39-53)* is a clever portmanteau of 'Chepe,' the nickname for San José, and *bicicletas*. This group has encouraged safe cycling and organized community rides since 2010. Up until the pandemic, they organized free weekly rides where police officers cordoned off streets to escort the two-wheeled caravan. Though the weekly rides are no more, ChepeCletas now arranges a free annual ride each May that attracts up to 500 cyclists.

The ChepeCletas also created **Chepe Tours**, which leads tourists through town by bike or on foot. The routes are based on different themes such as coffee, *cantinas*, food markets and history, and they tend to mostly attract travelers.

ChepeCletas also offers regular themed walking tours geared at locals to help them discover the hidden gems in their own backyard. While these affordable tours are held in Spanish, an English-speaking guide is available if you let them know in advance that you plan to attend. Unlike their other tours (and those offered by other companies) which tend to mostly attract visitors, these neighborhood walks offer the rare social opportunity to explore the city and exchange cultural experiences with native *costarricenses*.

Escazú & Santa Ana

FASHIONABLE SUBURBS

No neighborhood in Costa Rica has commercialized as rapidly as Escazú, the hillside area to the west of San José. Its main artery bombards you with ritzy restaurants, massive box stores and affluent gated communities. Many expats have settled here, earning it the cheeky nickname 'Gringolandia.'

But Escazú is really three historic towns mashed together, and the higher up the mountain you venture, the more traditional it becomes. In Escazú's old town, San Antonio, shops crowd around a central square overlooked by a red-steepled church. Ascend the steep slopes for epic views of the valley below.

Just beyond Escazú lies its smaller cousin, Santa Ana, aka 'Valley of the Sun.' It has its share of luxury condos and upscale restaurants, along with traces of a tight-knit community, like the weekly farmers market and handsome 19th-century church. Santa Ana is traditionally known for its potters, while its growing number of restaurants and food halls is enriching San José's gastronomy scene.

GETTING AROUND

Many buses run through Escazú and Santa Ana, mostly along busy Ruta 121. But these barrios were designed for private cars, and whole chunks of Escazú are dead-spots for hailing taxis. Note that Google Maps can get confused here, rerouting you on a 90-minute walk through its outskirts because it doesn't recognize the pedestrian path parallel to the highway. There are walkways cutting through many of the businesses, offices and medical facilities near Avenida Escazú, so you can easily get around on foot, though you may have to poke around to find unmarked walkways.

Shopping for the Jet Set

Window-shop on Avenida Escazú

You'll want to smarten up before visiting **Avenida Escazú** *(avenidaescazu.com)*, because this place is *posh*. The sparkling high-rises contain major retail outlets, like a Lego store and Banana Republic, and you'd be excused for thinking you've stepped into an outdoor mall in Beverly Hills. Avenida Escazú exists in a kind of bourgeois bubble, where fine dining stands side-by-side with high-end fashion and furniture stores. This has become a colony of luxury lofts, whose well-to-do residents need never venture beyond their cushy two hectares.

Yet the avenue is also open and walkable, and bike lanes have been painted into the flawless asphalt. In a suburb well known for its gated communities, Avenida Escazú is a mixed-use development that feels accessible to all, and visitors are welcome to window-shop to their hearts' content. Yes, there

TOP TIP

Weekends are especially lively in Escazú and the top restaurants fill up quickly, so be sure to make reservations in advance.

HIGHLIGHTS
1 Avenida Escazú
2 El Mestizo Mercado Gastronómico

SIGHTS
3 Butterfly Kingdom Mariposario
4 Casa Negra
5 D'Art Galería y Enmarcado
6 Galería de Antigüedades
7 La Marquetería
8 Parroquia San Antonio de Padua
9 Parroquia Santa Ana
10 Refugio Animal de Costa Rica
11 Vida del Arte

ACTIVITIES
12 Hacienda La Chimba
13 Valle Escondido

SLEEPING
14 AC Hotel Escazú
15 Alta Hotel
16 Aparthotel & Suites Villas del Río
17 Casa 41
18 Hotel Partal Colonial

EATING
19 Casona de Laly
20 Container Platz
21 Kololo Ramen
22 La Cascada
23 Maxis by Ricky
24 Taj Mahal

DRINKING & NIGHTLIFE
25 Hooligan's
26 Jazz Café
27 Pocket Food & Drinks
28 Stiefel Pub

ENTERTAINMENT
29 Grand Casino Escazú
30 Nova Cinemas

SHOPPING
see 9 Fería del Agricultor
31 Multiplaza Escazú

are plenty of international restaurant chains, but Tico restaurateurs have also made their mark with inventive dining.

The area is home to **Nova Cinemas** *(novacinemas.cr)*, the largest and most sophisticated cineplex in the country. Pick from seven theaters playing all the biggest Hollywood films, usually with Spanish subtitles, or get the immersive experience in Nova's IMAX theater.

Mall Life, Tico-Style

The ultimate Central American mall

The shopping mall is alive and well in Costa Rica, where e-commerce holds little sway and locals always seek an air-conditioned place to hang out. **Multiplaza Escazú** *(multiplaza.com/escazu)* is the reigning champion of Costa Rican malls – the concourses sparkle, the 365 stores are mostly upmarket chains and the food court is vast and varied. More than two million shoppers come here every year.

Foreign visitors may wonder what all the fuss is about. You'll find the same H&M and Victoria's Secret in any US or European city. But there are a few highlights that cater to the traveler: the Columbia Sportswear store sells top-of-the-line equipment, and it's a smart place to 'gear up' before a rainforest expedition. Several optical stores *(ópticas)* are available to replace eyeglasses. Visit the iCon store to repair or upgrade your Apple product. In short, if you're looking for first-world fixes, Multiplaza is a dependable destination.

The Multiplaza brand is based in El Salvador, but outposts are dotted across Central America, including a second Costa Rican location in Curridabat.

Have a Feast in Escazú

Wallet-friendly dining at El Mestizo

While Escazú may be best known for high-end dining, it's still possible to find more affordable fare. The new **El Mestizo Mercado Gastronómico** *(plazatempo.com)* food court in Plaza Tempo (roughly halfway between Avenida Escazú and the Multiplaza mall) is not just more wallet-friendly, but downright delicious. Choose between Caribbean, Peruvian, Argentine, Spanish, Mexican and more, then grab a seat at private or communal tables. Though the food comes quickly, make no mistake: this is not fast food. Rather, freshly prepared meals are served in real dishes and consumed with proper silverware, which is no surprise in posh Escazú.

PARQUE CENTRAL

Escazú's **Parque Central** looks like many town squares in Costa Rica, with the usual fountain, gazebo and concrete football court. A church, Iglesia San Miguel Arcángel, watches over the square with its cylindrical tower. It's a peaceful place, and it's also the symbolic heart of Escazú's more traditional downtown. Far above the glitz and sprawl of Ruta 121, Central Park is surrounded by small shops, modest houses and the Palacio Municipal (City Hall). For setting out on foot, there is no better place to start exploring this quaint hillside neighborhood. Drivers can usually find street parking or try the lot on the northern side.

EATING IN ESCAZÚ: OUR PICKS

La Cascada: This famed steakhouse has turned cuts of meat into works of art since the 1960s. *11:30am-10pm* **$$$**

Taj Mahal: The decor hints at the famous Indian palace. It serves the most decadent curries in Costa Rica. *11am-10pm* **$$$**

Kololo Ramen: Excellent Japanese and Korean noodles and soups in a trendy restaurant in Plaza Tempo. *11:30am-3:30pm & 5:30-9pm Tue-Sat, noon-5pm Sun* **$$**

Maxis by Ricky: Relaxed Caribbean restaurant in Santa Ana. Bob Marley paintings and reggae complement the oxtail and curry. *11:45am-11pm Mon-Sat, to 9pm Sun* **$$**

THE WITCHES OF ESCAZÚ

The official mascot of Escazú is La Bruja (The Witch), and you'll find references to her everywhere. There are restaurants called La Posada de las Brujas (The Witches' Pub) and La Bruja Marina (The Sea Witch). A former football club was known as Las Brujas, and a well-known shopping area is Plaza Brujas.

Witches are major characters in Escazú's folklore, but the Catholic Church's hunt for magic-wielding evil-doers was taken very seriously during the colonial period. Historical records and ghost stories tend to intertwine, and it's hard to tell fact from fiction. But the witches won in the end: there's even one pictured on Escazú's official emblem, with the words, 'Ciudad de las Brujas' (City of Witches).

ARII805/SHUTTERSTOCK

Parroquia San Antonio de Padua

Try Your Luck

Visit the nation's biggest casino

If you airlifted an entire entertainment complex out of Nevada and dropped it into Costa Rica, it would probably look like the **Grand Casino Escazú** *(casinoescazu.com)*. The halls ping and bleep with 120 machines. A half-dozen varieties of table games are in play at any given moment. There's a walk-up 'sportsbook' window for placing bets, and the **Poker Room**, with US$100 buy-in, lures high rollers from all over the world. Gambling is alive and well in Costa Rica, and the Grand Casino is its decadent core.

But like so many luxury casinos, this place has plenty of other pleasures. Start at **Joker's Sports Bar**, where you can grab a drink and a club sandwich before hitting the slots. Head up to club level for breakfast, a plate of sushi or a cocktail. The crowning stroke is **Burning Rooftop**, an indoor-outdoor lounge with creative lighting and a sweeping view of Escazú. The Grand Casino is symbiotic with the Sheraton next door, where guests usually stay. You're also likely to stumble into an event or two, from big-band performances to whiskey tastings.

Explore Your Creative Side

Join a craft workshop

Many artists have refined their skills in Santa Ana, and now it can be your turn. **Casa Negra** *(facebook.com/casanegracr)*

DRINKING IN ESCAZÚ: FUN NIGHTS OUT

Jazz Café: State-of-the-art performance venue hosting top musicians; note that admission doesn't include drinks. *6pm-midnight*

Stiefel Pub: This second location of the San José gastropub serves superlative beers in a youthful setting. *4-11pm Sun-Thu, to 1am Fri & Sat*

Hooligan's: Your classic sports bar, with buffalo wings, buckets of beer and global sports on TV. *noon-10pm Sun & Mon, to 11pm Tue & Wed, to midnight Thu-Sat*

Pocket Food & Drinks: Creative and over-the-top cocktails and *bocas* (appetizers). Reservations recommended. *4pm-midnight Mon-Fri, from 1pm Sat*

is an art gallery that showcases local crafts, and you're more than welcome to browse the prints and carvings on display. But you can also join a workshop in Casa Negra's studio, where a creative professional will guide you through the basics of ceramic sculpting or experimental photography. The schedule changes regularly, but the place is well suited to a traveler's schedule, thanks to its many one-day tutorials.

The Best of Tico Cuisine

Traditional canteen dining in Escazú

Order the *chifrijo* (rice and pinto beans with fried pork) or the *olla de carne* (beef stew) and sip a *michelada* cocktail (beer, lime juice, spices and chili peppers) – **Casona de Laly** excels at all of them. This peach-colored *cantina* in Escazú is the quintessential Tico dining experience, and you may struggle to pick a single dish from the exhaustive menu. The restaurant has expanded to San Pedro and Curridabat as well, but the original venue in Escazú remains the best, with its rustic tables and strung-up lights. If you try only one traditional restaurant in the Central Valley, this should be it.

Mingle with the Farmers

Santa Ana's farmers market

A lot has changed in Santa Ana in recent years, but the **Feria del Agricultor** continues to ground the town in its agrarian roots. Each Sunday morning, area farmers set up their tents in front of the **Parroquia Santa Ana**, and customers fill the streets in search of fresh fruits and vegetables. The market is most popular with townsfolk, but you can also find gift-worthy jewelry and ornaments made by local craftspeople. If you plan to do some shopping, just remember that Tico farmers tend to be cash-only so crisp bills may be more useful here than credit cards.

Industrial-Chic Communal Dining

The gastronomic experiment of Container Platz

Imagine if a whole bunch of food trucks were transferred to brightly painted shipping containers. Now imagine that the containers are stacked on top of each other like building blocks. Add some fun signage, a few potted plants, and you've got **Container Platz** *(facebook.com/containerplatz),* a colorful *plaza gastronómica* in Santa Ana. Patrons can choose from over a dozen different options, with specialties as diverse as burgers, Venezuelan arepas and sushi. The communal venue has been feeding and entertaining guests since 2017.

Diners can order from any combination of restaurants and sit at any of the polished picnic tables. Container Platz is pet-friendly, and fellow diners will often bring their leashed dogs along for dinner. It's also become one of the best spots in town for music, from live bands to DJs to karaoke nights. The building is located in the northeast corner of downtown Santa Ana, a quick walk from the bus line and recognizable to any *taxista* (cabbie). So feel free to order one more bottle of Bavaria for the road.

SAN ANTONIO VIEWS

San Antonio is technically part of Escazú, but this village is much higher up the mountain and more old-fashioned in character. The beige walls and twin red steeples of **Parroquia San Antonio de Padua** stand on scenic grounds with an adjacent rose garden, but the real glory of this site is the view: the church really does appear to watch benevolently over the Central Valley. Across from the church lie a football field, playground equipment and open lawn. This area is often busy with games and picnickers, and the church draws a strong congregation. A highlight is the Easter celebration, when it stages elaborate Passion pageants.

SANTA ANA'S SPIRITUAL ANCHOR

St Francis would have approved of the **Parroquia Santa Ana**, an understated stone structure in the very center of its town. The church has two bell towers and three main doorways, but the stained-glass windows are understated and the ceiling is assembled from simple wood beams. Services have been held here since the 1880s, although the architecture looks far older. A pleasant little park surrounds the church, and you can feel like you're miles away from the hustle and diesel fumes of Santa Ana.

IRINA CALVO/FLICKR/CC BY-SA 2.0 DEED

Turtles, Refugio Animal de Costa Rica

Antiquing, Tico-Style

Browse the Antiques Gallery

Even from the outside, the **Galería de Antigüedades** *(facebook.com/antiguedades.santa.ana)* in Santa Ana looks like a throwback to the past: terracotta roofs slope over plaster walls and mullioned windows. 'Antiquing' isn't as popular a pastime as it is in other countries, so the Galería is a rare chance to browse household decor from bygone times.

Many of the items are familiar, like steamer trunks and stove-heated clothes irons, but you'll find a lot of stock with a Tico twist: vintage machetes, local concert posters and even church pews. This place also has its own cafeteria, where you can sip coffee straight from the *chorreador* (Costa Rican coffee maker).

Up Close with Butterflies

An insectarium for the whole family

Up close, the wings of the blue morpho butterfly look like they're made of blue-tinted glass. Most of us would never get an intimate look at the blue morpho, but **Butterfly Kingdom Mariposario** *(en.butterflykingdom.net; adult/child US$7/5)* is full of the species, among many other Costa Rican natives. This lovely little *mariposario* (butterfly garden) in Escazú opened in 2011, with the intention of creating a 'spa for the soul.' Calling the little urban farm a 'kingdom' might be a little grand, but the *mariposario* has become a major attraction in Escazú, especially for children and school groups. A two-hour tour (9am to 11am) includes lectures, simple crafting and the chance to see larvae at different stages of metamorphosis. Butterfly Kingdom takes pride in being family-friendly and wheelchair-accessible.

Hit the Trails of 'Hidden Valley'

An all-ages bike park

Narrow paths zigzag across the gravel landscape of **Valle Escondido** *(facebook.com/valle.escondido506; admission US$6, parking US$2)*, then disappear into the grass and trees. As the fat tires of your mountain bike roll down single-track, you feel like you're miles away from civilization. This is fitting, because Valley Escondido translates as 'hidden valley.'

But this versatile adventure park is located in the middle of Santa Ana's sprawl, and you're never far from a high-end housing development. For a small fee, cyclists can pedal over rugged terrain, practice their jumps and skids and generally free themselves from the noisy city. Sponsored by bike manufacturer Cannondale, the park is designed for all ages and abilities. Rookies can take classes with experienced bikers, and even young children can hit the trails.

You *do* have to bring your own bike, but most courses don't require a souped-up MTB, just a sturdy set of tires and a helmet. Once you're finished for the day, you can pick from scores of restaurants in Santa Ana to replenish your calories.

ART GALLERIES IN ESCAZÚ

La Marquetería: The name translates as 'frame shop,' and while this place is indeed best known for its high-quality frames, you'll find a range of local and international artworks on display as well. It's right on Ruta 121.

D'Art Galería y Enmarcado: This two-story art gallery displays paintings and sculptures; it also doubles as a framery. D'Art is conveniently located next to Multiplaza.

Vida del Arte: A hip little gallery that's home to themed exhibitions and also serves as a design shop. You'll find it in the El Cortijo shopping plaza.

Wildlife in the City

A refuge for wild animals

The **Refugio Animal de Costa Rica** *(refugioanimalcr.com; adult/child US$30/15)* was formerly known as the Refugio Herpetológico, because it specialized in snakes and other reptiles. The organization has since expanded its repertoire to include primates, sloths and tropical birds. Unlike a more traditional zoo, the Refugio Animal only takes specimens that were injured, abandoned or are otherwise incapable of living in the wild. Here, you'll get an up-close view of animals that don't like to be seen. A trained naturalist will explain in detail the peculiarities of each species. This family-friendly sanctuary is located on the winding and scenic Calle Vieja between Escazú and Santa Ana and offers guided tours that take about 90 minutes.

Conquer the Mountains

Scaling the Cerros de Escazú

Escazú stands at the foot of several mountains and you can't help but feel their presence. If the creased green ledges call to you, there's good news: you can explore the Cerros de Escazú for days, by car or on foot. These escarpments are well developed – houses crowd along the steep roads for miles – but after a while, civilization gives way to trees and paths. Note that while the hiking is excellent, it can be easy to get lost so it's always wise to go with a guide.

The ultimate local hike is the **Tres Cruces Trail**, a 5km scramble along the mountains' crest. The trailhead is located just past the Valle Azúl restaurant, and true to its name, the trail takes you to three physical crosses, each marking a different stage of the route. The final monument is **La Cruz**

THE PLAZA CRAZE

Escazú's main drag is jammed with retailers, but instead of stand-alone buildings, you'll find that many of these stores are stacked inside 'plazas.' Plazas are generally two stories, with outdoor walkways and a dedicated parking area.

Also known as a 'Centro Comercial,' they function much like strip malls but aim to keep it classy, with jaunty names such as **Atlantis Plaza** and **Central Comercial La Paco**. Because Costa Rica doesn't bother with street addresses, a particular store may be hard to find. Locals may not know a particular business, but they almost always know the plaza, which makes giving directions easier.

REBECA BOLANOS/SHUTTERSTOCK

Hacienda La Chimba

de Alajuelita, a skeletal steel crucifix that rises 36m from the ground and has been a revered landmark since 1936. The trail is famous for its heart-stopping views of the valley, but be aware that it's steep and often muddy, depending on the season. This is no walk for rookies, and even experienced hikers may wheeze at nearly 2100m above sea level.

Ground Yourself at La Chimba

Santa Ana's dynamic coffee farm

The simplest way to experience **Hacienda La Chimba** *(lachimbacr.com)* is to hike the **Mantra Trail**. This 9km path winds its way through the hillside coffee fields where workers are actively picking beans. The route is well marked with eccentric monuments, such as a giant Buddha statue and a sculpture of a butterfly. One lookout point offers a unique view of the Central Valley, and the trail concludes with **La Mano de Mantra**, a gigantic wicker sculpture in the shape of a human hand. The rolling hills of La Chimba lie only a short distance from the commercial district of Santa Ana, but the estate feels like an isolated sylvan sanctuary. While the monuments are popular for social-media posing, you can find quieter trails if you hike a bit further and there are also ziplines and ropes courses. Note that trails can become muddy and slippery if it's been raining.

The hacienda was established as a coffee farm in 1970, but the property is now packed with activities. You could easily spend a full day ziplining through the canopy, navigating the high-ropes course and taking the 'Coffee Experience' tour. La Chimba recreates the atmosphere of a 1920s plantation; the tour concludes with a tasting of locally cultivated brews. Polish off your visit with dinner at **La Burra Restaurante**, then an ice cream at the *gelatería* across the path.

Places We Love to Stay

$ Budget $$ Midrange $$$ Top End

Downtown San José

MAP p60

Costa Rica Backpackers $ The classic hostel experience, with simple rooms and a grassy communal space.

Hostel Shakti $ A cheerful hostel with fun wall paintings, balconies and bunk beds. Located near the old Chinatown.

Hotel El Maragato $ Overlooking the Plaza de la Cultura, with budget-friendly bunk beds and private rooms.

Hotel Presidente $$ Popular rooftop cocktail bar, exposed-brick lobby and rooms with balconies.

Hotel Dunn Inn $$ This converted mansion in Barrio Amón is full of vintage charm and modern pop art.

Hotel Novo $$ The beige and boxy structure has pleasant rooms and private balconies. Easy access to downtown.

Hotel Ambassador $$ Great location on Paseo Colón. This big, clean hotel has a conference room and restaurant.

Hotel Colonial $$ Pillared architecture and a lovely pool make the Colonial a great option. Near the Plaza de la Cultura.

Urban Green Hotel & Suites $$ In the heart of downtown, Urban Green has a spa and pristine, modernist rooms.

La Sabana & Around

MAP p73

Casa Jardín de Mango $ A boutique hotel as charming as its 'mango garden' name. Variety of rooms and a cozy yard out back.

Del Cafetal $ Simple rooms in an attractive building, plus its own grocery store. Great price.

Apartotel La Sabana $$ Super-comfy apartments a block from the park. Spotless modern lodgings and pool.

Palma Real $$ Excellent rooms of all types, including suites with whirlpool baths. Banquet room and small casino.

Capital Hostel de Ciudad $$ This unremarkable ranch house has a smile-inducing interior design. The nice rooms are a bargain.

Hotel Ecological Innovation $$ Cryptic name, but there's a pleasant pool and game room. Two-story, motel-like layout.

Barrio Escalante, Los Yoses & San Pedro

MAP p80

Lost in Costa Rica Hostel $ Lost? Maybe. But with a fire pit, chill spaces and a pool table. This is a backpacker favorite.

Chillout Hostel $ Casual vibe and trippy artwork make this a comfy crash pad in Barrio Escalante.

Hostel Finca Escalante $$ With its tile roof, this place looks like an old, rural farmhouse. The location is unbeatable.

Hotel Le Bergerac $$ Los Yoses hotel that offers old-world charm, a tiny bar and a leafy patio.

BEE Suites Escalante $$ Towering above Barrio Escalante, with spotless rooms, a rooftop deck and fitness center.

Hotel 1492 $$ Plaster walls and thoughtful furnishings give this B&B class. Rooms are a bargain.

Escazú & Santa Ana

MAP p90

Aparthotel & Suites Villas del Río $$ These homey units feel like actual Escazú residences. Amenities include pool, business center and playground.

Hotel Partal Colonial $$ Economical pricing and a great location in San Rafael de Escazú. Simple rooms, pool and restaurant.

AC Hotel Escazú $$ Marriott chain hotel smack-dab in the middle of Avenida Escazú, where locals flock for Sunday brunch.

Hotel Vista Canyon Inn $$ Beyond Santa Ana, a quiet getaway that does, in fact, overlook a gaping canyon.

Casa 41 $$$ A boutique hotel with meticulous interior design and painstakingly crafted meals.

Fogo $$$ The height of Escazú luxury, Fogo is a mountaintop resort in a Greek Revival complex.

Alta Hotel $$$ This hotel's perfect positioning yields gorgeous views of Santa Ana. Crisp design and pool.

Researched by
Elizabeth Lavis

Central Valley & the Highlands

COSTA RICA'S BEATING AGRICULTURAL HEART

Explore the history and culture of Costa Rica's heartland, where local communities thrive in the shadow of stratovolcanoes.

All travelers to Costa Rica land in the Central Valley, it's just that most of them don't realize the rich and historic ground they've laid boots on before heading off to the coasts. Stay for a while and breathe in the fresh air of the Orosí Valley, stroll through the local markets of Alajuela and Cartago, and learn about the national hero of Costa Rica, a poor drummer boy who defeated the *filibusteros*.

The Central Valley is full of ruins, mysterious archaeological sites hidden in the jungle, churches with incredible lore associated with their precious relics, and hiking and cycling paths that snake over hills, into valleys and across human-made dams. Take a road trip through the western part of the Alajuela province, where you'll find tiny cloud-forest towns, artistic villages and gorgeous gardens bursting with bamboo and orchids. Relax in natural hot springs, see how coffee is grown and harvested, and discover how much better a cup tastes once you know the history.

The Central Valley is perfect for slowing your roll a bit, lounging in a hammock and gazing at an impossibly clear night sky on a balmy evening. It's an excellent place to take some Spanish lessons, live with a local family and experience a true slice of the culture too. Those with a yen for nature and traditions shouldn't miss out on one of Costa Rica's most overlooked regions.

MARDOZ/SHUTTERSTOCK

THE MAIN AREAS

ALAJUELA
Hometown of Costa Rica's national hero. p104

CARTAGO
Ruins and sacred churches. p113

OROSÍ VALLEY
Healing soaks and restorative hikes. p122

TURRIALBA
Mysterious ruins and Jungle Train. p130

For places to stay in Central Valley & the Highlands, see p135

PABLO QUESADA/GETTY IMAGES

Left: Escalada Cachí (p127); Above: Orosí Valley (p122)

Alajuela, p104
The birthplace of national hero Juan Santamaría, and modern-day home of La Liga soccer team and some of the Central Valley's best shopping.

BUS

Buses connect most of the towns in the Central Valley, although the further out you get, the fewer there are likely to be. Many towns have at least one main stop in the center, but it's not always marked. The fare is US$1 and the drivers prefer smaller bills.

CAR

A solid, 4WD car is your best bet for getting around the Central Valley, and it will give you the freedom to head off the path and explore areas not serviced by buses. You can also keep to a more robust and fast-paced schedule with a car.

TRAIN

You can take the morning or afternoon train between Alajuela, Cartago, Heredia and San José – an easy and enjoyable way to get around. Landslides or other significant weather events occasionally stop the trains from running, so have a backup if you're traveling in the rainy season.

Find Your Way

You'll need a private car or a driver to see the Central Valley properly, as the buses can only get you so far and there's a lot of off-the-grid sightseeing to do. You can also cycle through quite a bit of it, especially near the Cachí Dam.

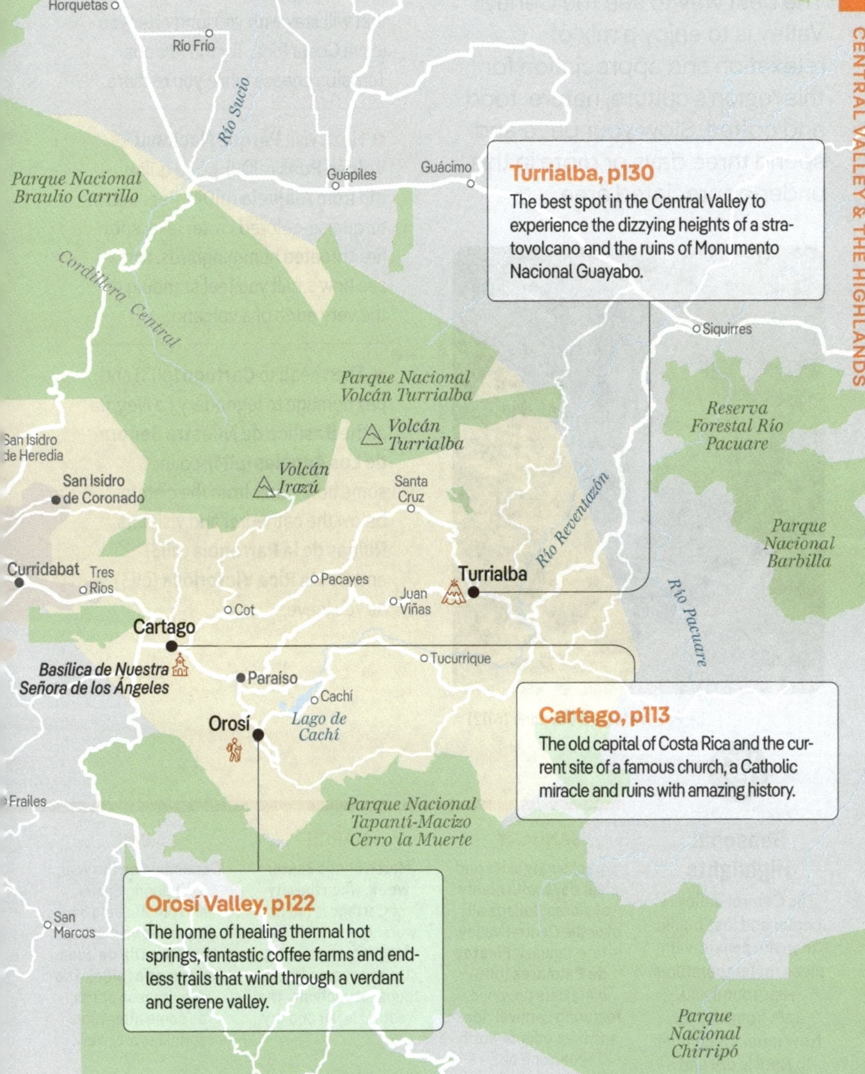

Turrialba, p130

The best spot in the Central Valley to experience the dizzying heights of a stratovolcano and the ruins of Monumento Nacional Guayabo.

Cartago, p113

The old capital of Costa Rica and the current site of a famous church, a Catholic miracle and ruins with amazing history.

Orosí Valley, p122

The home of healing thermal hot springs, fantastic coffee farms and endless trails that wind through a verdant and serene valley.

Plan Your Time

The best way to see the Central Valley is to enjoy a mix of relaxation and appreciation for this region's culture, nature, food and coffee. Slow your pace and spend three days or more in this under-appreciated area.

XENIA_PHOTOGRAPHY/SHUTTERSTOCK

La Paz Waterfall Gardens (p112)

Highlights in a Hurry

- Head to **Turrialba** (p130) to marvel at the mysterious **Monumento Nacional Guayabo** (p133). The origin of these structures is an enduring mystery that will stay with you long after you leave Costa Rica. Try the famous Turrialba cheese while you're there.

- Next, visit **Parque Nacional Volcán Poás** (p109), just a quick trip from **Alajuela** (p104). Peer into a turquoise-colored crater lake, spot fire-throated hummingbirds, and see how small you feel standing at the very edge of a volcano.

- Then head to **Cartago** (p113) and pay homage to legendary *La Negrita* at the **Basílica de Nuestra Señora de Los Ángeles** (p114), collect some holy water from the cistern below the cathedral and visit **Las Ruinas de la Parroquia** (p113) and **Costa Rica Victoriosa** (p113) as you leave.

Seasonal Highlights

The Central Valley is cooler and less humid than the coasts, with pleasant temperatures year-round and rain from May to November. December to April is dry and a lovely time to visit.

JANUARY

Expect sunny skies and clear days, with plenty of vibrant foliage all over the Central Valley. In late January, **Fiestas de Palmares** (p110) in Alajuela province, featuring carnival rides and fireworks, is worth checking out.

MARCH

March brings **Easter week**, when the city of Cartago is full of worshipers. You'll find bigger crowds in the city and at many major tourist attractions. The weather is fair and dry.

APRIL

Depending on the year, visit during Easter, and put Alajuela on your must-visit list on April 11 for **Día de Juan Santamaría** (p106). The rainy season starts, so some afternoon sprinkles are likely.

Three Days of Hiking & Cycling

- Start your first day in the **Orosí Valley** (p122) with hikes to **Happy Hammock Bridge** (p123), **Catarata de Nano** (p124) and the **Swimming Hole** (p124) before resting your bones and stretching your muscles in the thermal baths.

- On the second day, go to **Cachí Dam** (p126) for some cycling around the lake. Make sure you stop by the **Casa del Soñador** (p127) to see the whimsical woodwork and grab some snacks at the top of the dam.

- Drive to **Alajuela** (p104) and spend the night before embarking on a trip to **La Paz Waterfall Gardens** (p112) in the morning, where you'll hike around in the mist and see some of the region's most glorious plant life. Finish up with a visit to **Parque Nacional Volcán Poás** (p109) for a quick and rewarding 10-minute climb to the top.

Four Days of Culture & History

- Start in **Alajuela** (p104), at the **Museo Histórico Cultural Juan Santamaría** (p104), for a historical crash course on the Filibuster War, and catch a La Liga **soccer game** (p106) in the evening.

- The next day, head to **Cartago** (p113) to see the miraculous **Basílica de Nuestra Señora de Los Ángeles** (p114), **Las Ruinas de la Parroquia** (p113) and **Costa Rica Victoriosa** (p113) on Plaza Mayor.

- Spend the night in Cartago and visit the **Sanatorio Durán** (p118) and the **Ruinas de Ujarrás** (p119) on the third day before heading towards **Turrialba** (p130) and the ancient **Monumento Nacional Guayabo** (p133). Learn about the history of the **Jungle Train** (p131), and spend the night in Turrialba. Visit **Volcán Irazú** the following day.

AUGUST

August is a holy month in the Central Valley, during which Catholic devotees participate in the **Romería** (p114), a religious journey on foot from San José to Cartago. Prepare for rain and cooler temperatures in the evenings.

SEPTEMBER

September 15 is Costa Rica's **Independence Day**, so there will be parties and parades all over the historic Central Valley. Spend time in Cartago to witness the torch ceremony (p116). It's one of the rainiest times of the year.

OCTOBER

Enjoy amazing greenery and gorgeous flowers in the Central Valley, but beware of surprise rainstorms that can disrupt your **hikes**. At this time, you can find cheap accommodations.

DECEMBER

December is drier, cooler and full of the **Christmas** spirit around Costa Rica. It's an excellent time to go on longer **hikes and bike rides** in the Central Valley.

Alajuela

FOOTBALL FEVER | NATIONAL HISTORY | CULTURE APLENTY

GETTING AROUND

Most of Alajuela's main attractions are located around the center of town, which is very walkable. If you'd prefer public transportation, you can find a big bus station on the road out to the City Mall and a second across from Parque Calián Vargas that runs buses out to Ojo de Aguas and San Ramón every half hour. The train station is near San Rafael Hospital. Uber works in Alajuela, too.

TOP TIP

Visit the City Mall, a 20-minute walk from downtown Alajuela, for any last-minute needs. It has everything from beach clothes to strollers, is easy to navigate, has signage in English and Spanish, and is close to both the airport and town.

If you arrive at Juan Santamaría International Airport, you'll be a 10-minute taxi ride from downtown Alajuela, the historic Central Valley city that most tourists have never heard of. Famous for the drummer boy who defeated US mercenary William Walker, as well as the impressive La Liga soccer team, Alajuela has a lot going for it.

It's an excellent place to decompress and spend a day or two before embarking on your greater Central Valley trip or jumping on a bus for the coast. It's highly accessible, safe, walkable and filled with green spaces. Check out the Centro Alajuelense de la Cultura for a taste of traditional Tico music and dance or an artist lecture, visit the Museo Histórico Cultural Juan Santamaría to learn about Costa Rica's near-mythical hero, or simply grab your camera and spend some time snapping pictures of the candy-colored pastel buildings in the town center.

Fighting the Filibusteros

Meet Tico heroes

The **Museo Histórico Cultural Juan Santamaría** *(museo juansantamaria.go.cr)* is named for the pride of Alajuela, a drummer boy turned defiant hero who set an enemy stronghold ablaze during the Filibuster War's Second Battle of Rivas in 1856, dealing a costly blow to the colonialist forces of William Walker. His efforts and those of a 2000-strong citizen army called up by President Juan Rafael Mora Porras to defend their land successfully thwarted expansionist American dreams and kept Costa Rica independent.

The museum tells the story of this courageous effort through a permanent exhibit called 'Paths of Freedom,' which details the Costa Rican National Campaign, and through the murals of Antonio Ugalde Álvarez, which celebrate the country's Civil Guard. Visitors will also find plenty of artifacts and relics to peruse.

The museum space has had several different identities, including being a jail and a recreation space for the Alajuela

HIGHLIGHTS
1 Museo Histórico Cultural Juan Santamaría

SIGHTS
2 Catedral de Nuestra Señora del Pilar
3 Centro Alajuelense de la Cultura
4 Parque Calián Vargas
5 Parque General Tomás Guardia
6 Parque Juan Santamaría

SLEEPING
7 Alajuela Backpackers Costa Rica
8 Alajuela City Hotel & Guest House
9 Hildas Bed & Breakfast
10 Hotel Alajuela Costa Rica Airport

EATING
11 ChaRo Heladería & Cafe
12 Heladería Mango Mambo
13 Mercado Gastromino
14 Panadería y Cafetería Spigas
15 Soda Silvia Alajuela

DRINKING & NIGHTLIFE
16 Alkafe Coffee & Shop
17 Caffe Lejano
18 Coffee Dreams Cafe
19 Crema DELA Crema Café

ENTERTAINMENT
20 Municipal Theater

SHOPPING
21 Mercado de Alajuela

DRINKING IN ALAJUELA: OUR PICKS FOR COFFEE

Crema DELA Crema Café: Generously sized pastries, *batidos* (fruit shakes) plus cold and hot coffee drinks. *noon-6pm Tue-Sat*

Caffe Lejano: Decadent savory or sweet crepes, local ingredients and sweet cold coffee drinks. *noon-7pm Wed-Mon*

Alkafe Coffee & Shop: Gourmet coffee served with gorgeous presentation in an artistic and sunny space. *9am-7pm*

Coffee Dreams Cafe: Comfort food and traditional and artisanal coffee in a bright, family-friendly setting. *11am-7pm*

JUAN SANTAMARÍA DAY

Visit Alajuela on April 11, and you're bound to be greeted with music, drumming and partying in the streets of Costa Rica's former capital. Along with Independence Day (September 15), **Día de Juan Santamaría** is one of the nation's most joyful and patriotic celebrations. Juan Santamaría was the humble hero of the Filibuster War, famously dealing the foe a mighty blow by igniting a hostel that housed William Walker's men. His actions changed the course of the war during the Battle of Rivas. Tragically, Santamaría perished in the fire, but his legacy as both a martyr for the cause and the poor drummer boy who stood up to aggression has made him a mythical figure of sorts for Ticos.

BUDA MENDES - FIFA/FIFA VIA GETTY IMAGES

Estadio Alejandro Morera Soto

Command. Today, it's a well-appointed combination of indoor and outdoor areas where you could easily spend a few hours learning about the failed efforts of the *filibusteros* (p444). Admission is free; the museum is closed on Monday.

The Cathedral of Soccer

See La Liga in action

Estadio Alejandro Morera Soto *(lda.cr/ams),* nicknamed 'La Catedral del Fútbol' (The Cathedral of Soccer), is the triumphant stomping ground of Liga Deportiva Alajuelense (La Liga) and the Tigresses. It's 900m from Parque General Tomás Guardia and just outside the downtown core. Along with a pulse-pounding game of soccer, there are half-time shows featuring traditional Costa Rican entertainment that celebrates the cultural heritage of Alajuela and the Central Valley.

These games are family-friendly, with a strict code of conduct prohibiting rowdy behavior, and La Liga's lion mascot has a habit of visiting children in the stands during game breaks for photo ops. La Liga (men's team) and the Tigresses (women's team) compete in several games per week. You can get tickets online *(boleterialaliga.com);* prices change depending on the game. Highly contested bouts with rivals like San José tend to sell out quickly, so booking your ticket well in advance is a good idea.

The stadium can accommodate up to 16,200 people and is powered entirely by solar energy. It's also wheelchair-accessible. There's a shop with red-and-black La Liga shirts, jerseys, hats and socks to show your Alajuela pride back home.

EATING IN ALAJUELA: BEST SODAS

Soda Silvia Alajuela: Good for early birds, offering a yummy buffet so you can grab a quick bite. *7am-4pm Mon-Fri* $

Soda Pinticos: Big counter-lunch portions served with fries, salad and drinks. *7am-3pm Sat, Mon & Tue, to 5pm Wed-Fri* $

Soda Doña Olga: Western and Tico comfort food like *casados* (set meals), hamburgers and nachos. *6am-8pm Mon-Fri* $

Soda Los Ángeles: Fab place to get your late-night *salchipapas* (sausage and fries) and nachos fix. *2-10pm Sun-Wed, to 11pm Fri & Sat* $

Alajuela's Cultural Heart

Immerse yourself in art

A pastel pink building with deeply tinted mauve trim, **Centro Alajuelense de la Cultura** *(dircultura.go.cr)*, two blocks from the Mercado de Alajuela, is tough to miss. While you'll want to grab several snaps of the whimsical exterior, it's worth popping inside, too.

In 1979, it was named a Relic of Historical and Architectural Interest and acts as the beating cultural heart of Alajuela, with a calendar of workshops like sculpting, theater and painting. The National System of Musical Education also has an on-site presence and hosts regular classes that celebrate traditional Tico musical heritage.

Visitors can find frequent exhibitions, Q&As with local artists and ongoing festivals featuring folk dance, music and song. Admission prices vary; some performances and exhibitions are free to the public.

This Alajuela landmark is a fantastic place to visit as part of a larger city stroll or after enjoying a *cafí frio* in Parque General Tomás Guardia (p108). It's super-central, close to some excellent dining options and offers an unfiltered snapshot of the artistic bounty of this city.

LIGA & SAPRISSA RIVALRY

Alajuela's La Liga and San José's Deportivo Saprissa have a bitter rivalry that dates back to 1949, when the purple-clad, undefeated San José team first went toe-to-toe with the Alajuelense La Liga. Expecting an easy victory, Saprissa was stunned by the skill of La Liga and defeated by a single goal. Since that embarrassing introductory game, La Liga and Saprissa have squared off 327 times and Saprissa has a razor-thin lead by 28 games (at the time of writing). Each team has won 29 domestic league titles. The rivals regularly face down each other on the soccer pitch to the tune of deafening cheers from their fans and against a sea of red-and-black on one side and purple on the other.

Market Time

Shop and eat at Alajuela's markets

Wandering into the unassuming Mundo Cosmético store in Alajuela's downtown is like stumbling into Narnia. Venture far enough past eye-shadow palettes, and you'll find yourself in an utterly unexpected place: the **Mercado de Alajuela**, where fruit and veg vendors rub shoulders with barbershops and there's an authentic *soda* (place that serves a counter lunch) around every corner where you can get smoothies and *casados* (set meals) for about US$4.

You don't have to stroll far through the labyrinthine walkways to realize that this *mercado* is the real deal; it dates back to 1782 and is packed with locals. It's a fantastic spot to score high-quality goods like jewelry, leather bags and shoes, and it's open from 6am to 6pm Monday to Saturday (arrive early to avoid the crowds).

Most vendors don't take cards – cash is king, especially smaller bills. If you're craving more local eats and a fun vibe without the shopping, check out **Mercado Gastromino**, a five-minute walk away, which has a kids' play area.

EATING IN ALAJUELA: BEST ICE CREAM

Heladería Mango Mambo: Pet-friendly local shop offering fantastic sundaes and giant brownies. *10am-8pm* $

ChaRo Heladería & Cafe: Small space with plenty of seating and delicious milkshakes. *10am-7pm Mon-Sat, to 8pm Sun* $

Helaticos: Artisanal scoops and ice-cream bars in a friendly, comfortable location. *9am-8pm* $

Gusticos: Ice cream, parfaits and shakes with beautiful presentation. *8am-8pm Mon-Sat, from 11:30am Sun* $

A CHILLED-OUT CITY WANDER

Lace up your walking shoes, grab a *café para llevar* (coffee to go) and walk in the footsteps of Costa Rica's most famous son, Juan Santamaría.

START	END	LENGTH
Parque Calián Vargas	Catedral de Nuestra Señora del Pilar	650m; 1 hr

As you stroll, you'll enjoy grand parks, historical homes and monuments that paint a glorious picture of this one-time capital city. Start at ❶ **Parque Calián Vargas**, named after a union organizer. Here, you'll find a massive red 'Alajuela' sign, a great playground for kids and plenty of benches to unwind and enjoy that first cup of coffee. Then walk directly to your right across Calle 2 to ❷ **Parque Juan Santamaría**. A bronze statue of the hero and his torch dominates the park, surrounded by cannons. This area has several *sodas* (cheap eateries) and bakeries.

❸ **Parque General Tomás Guardia** is two blocks north, towards Avenida Central. You'll pass beautiful buildings rendered in shades of green, blue and pink. The park, also known as Central Park or Mango Park, is named after the former Costa Rican president from the late 1800s. This is a great place to play a game of checkers, grab a bit of respite from the heat under the big, leafy trees or enjoy music on Sunday mornings. It's right across from the ❹ **Catedral de Nuestra Señora del Pilar**, also known as Alajuela Cathedral, a stately marble building with jewel-toned stained-glass windows and an intricate mosaic on the left-hand side. It's generally only open on Sundays; on other days, you can still snap photos from the park.

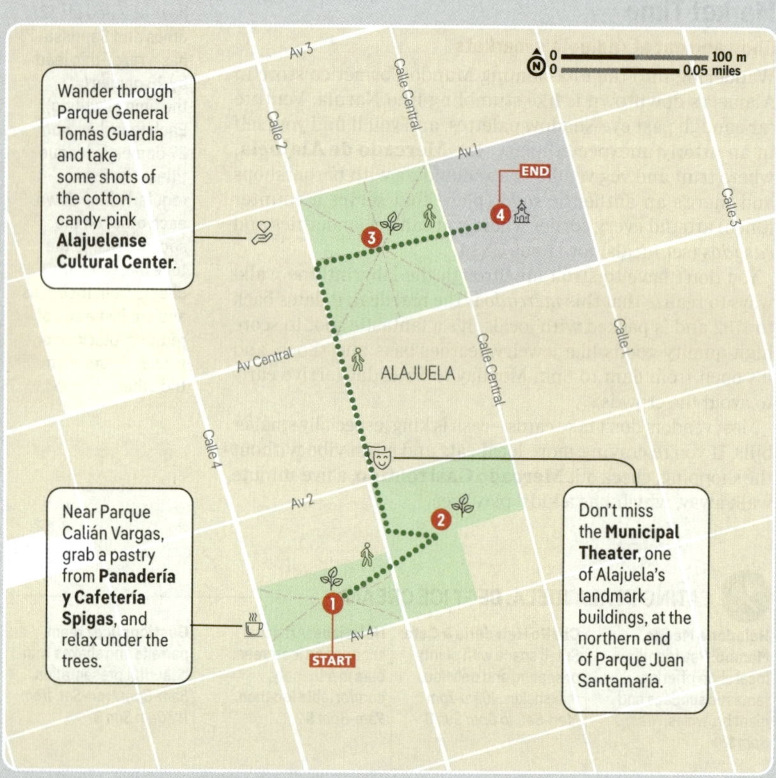

Beyond Alajuela

Alajuela province is a vast landscape of gentle hills, forests and fantastic local towns, each with something to share.

Alajuela itself is a buzzing city with a world-class sports team, but once you step out into the province, it will start to dawn on you just how bucolic and charming the Central Valley is. There's so much to see if you go north and west, from volcanoes and thundering waterfalls to artistic villages and tiny towns wreathed in clouds. There's also a wildlife rescue center where vulnerable macaws are bred to be repopulated in places like the Península de Nicoya, a whole town with whimsical hedges that looks like it's been ripped right out of a fairytale, and beautiful rural church after church surrounded by a small town square that really brings the sense of community home.

Places

Parque Nacional Volcán Poás

TIME FROM ALAJUELA: **55 MINS**

Hike to a majestic volcano

The highlight of **Parque Nacional Volcán Poás** *(sinac.go.cr; adult/child US$17/6)*, north of Alajuela, is a 2708m-tall stratovolcano. It's surrounded by a verdant cloud forest and anchored by the brilliant turquoise Laguna Caliente, whose vibrant acidic waters clash splendidly with grey volcanic rock. The national park's parking lot *(US$5.45 for light vehicles)* will put you within a 10-minute hike of the summit, where you can peep into the crater; along the way, try to spy some of the area's fascinating birdlife, including fire-throated hummingbirds and quetzals.

If you're feeling extra adventurous, check out the **Laguna Botos Circuit**, a 3.4km trek that takes you to Botos Lagoon and the volcano summit. It's a moderately challenging adventure with a 152m elevation gain, but you'll be rewarded with fabulous views of both the lagoon and crater.

As Volcán Poás is an active volcano closings are not uncommon, and you'll need to don a hard hat (provided for you at the ticket office) before heading towards the crater. The park is open between 8am and 4pm every day, but the last visitor entry is at 2pm.

GETTING AROUND

You'll need a car or someone to drive you around if you want to fully experience Alajuela province. There's really no other way to do it and see everything in any reasonable amount of time. You can rent a car at the Juan Santamaría International Airport and use it for this leg of the trip. Depending on the rest of your travel itinerary, you can rent for a single day or longer. Make sure to get insurance on the vehicle.

ROAD TRIP

Alajuela Rural Road Trip

Hop in the car and head west through greater Alajuela province. You'll find storybook towns full of fabulous topiaries, tiny cloud forests and glorious gardens with neon-colored blooms. Leave early and you can hit up every stop on this itinerary and return to Alajuela in time for dinner – all these destinations are close, so you'll have time for a wander and a bite to eat too.

1 Zarcero

This whimsical town, an hour's drive northwest of Alajuela, is sprinkled with delightful hedges sculpted into Seuss-style arches and life-size dinosaurs. The famous hedges in **Parque Francisco Alvarado** are a labor of love by artist Evangelista Blanco. Just past the topiary is **Parroquia San Rafael Arcángel**, Zarcero's iconic red-roofed church, where you can see handsome marble pillars and stunning artwork including a painting of San Rafael.

The Drive: Go south down Ruta 141 passing the hedges of Arbolitos El Grinch to reach your destination in just over 30 minutes.

2 Jardín Botánico Else Kientzler

A celebration of flora, from succulents and bamboo to orange, pink and purple blooms and wild hibiscus, the **Jardín Botánico Else Kientzler** is a restorative place where visitors follow winding paths to a serene lake or hike up to a well-appointed fruit garden and down through a copse of trees. There are 2000 species of plants from around the globe, organized into sections. Grab a coffee and have a wander.

The Drive: Sarchi is just six minutes to the south; you'll know when you reach it by the bright-orange bridge.

ALL A SHUTTER/SHUTTERSTOCK

Jardín Botánico Else Kientzler

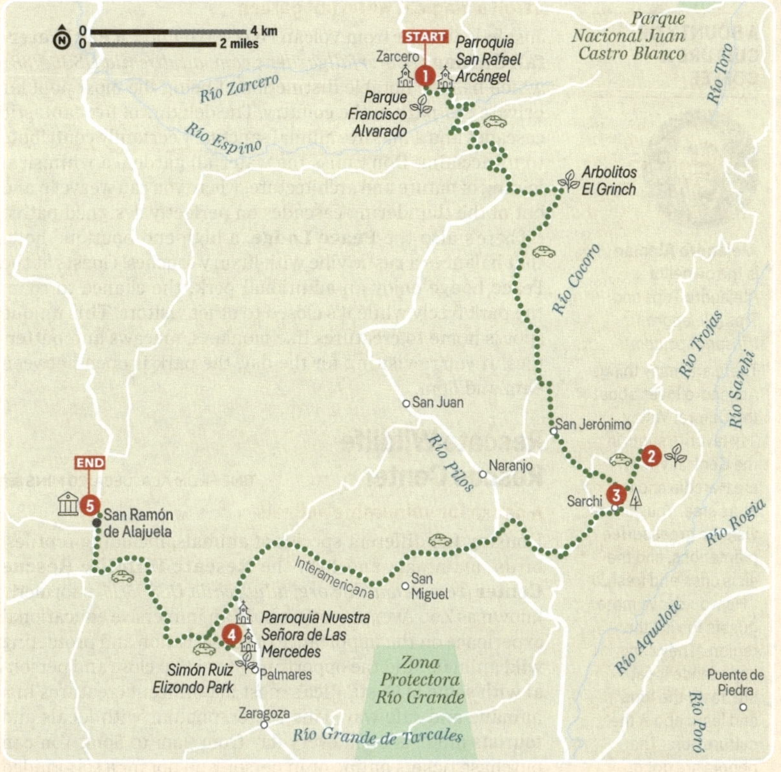

③ Sarchi

Sarchi's cheery bridge greets you as you ride into this artistic hub of the Central Valley. It's packed to the gills with clever curiosity shops selling handmade wares, but you can also experience **Bajos del Toro**, the wee cloud-forest town with the Río Agrio waterfall, and **Dino Land**, where kids can interact with their prehistoric favorites against a tropical backdrop (last entry is at 3pm).

The Drive: Continue for 20 minutes west on Ruta 1 past San Miguel and you'll arrive in Palmares.

④ Palmares

Except for two weeks in January, when the **Fiestas de Palmares** transform the town into a fun-filled carnival, Palmares is bucolic bliss, with stupendous mountain views and lovely **Simón Ruiz Elizondo Park** overlooked by the **Parroquia Nuestra Señora de Las Mercedes**, a cathedral made of stone and wood and surrounded by religious statues. Stop by **Panadería Campos del Parque** by the park for some pastries.

The Drive: It's just 10 minutes on Ruta 1 past Reserva Natural Madre Verde to San Ramón de Alajuela.

⑤ San Ramón de Alajuela

San Ramón de Alajuela is anchored by the **Parroquia San Ramón Nonato**, a dove-gray Catholic church full of color-saturated stained glass and intricate woodwork. It's a place of reflecting and learning, with the **Museo de San Ramón** and makeshift libraries made out of painted boxes around the town square. Don't miss the octagonal wood-and-bamboo 'bee hotels' that provide a haven for solitary bees and encourage pollination.

A BOUNTY OF CULTURE & COFFEE

Alejandro Alemán is the owner of Alejandro Trips and Tips *(alejandro tripsandtips.com)*.

There are many things Alejandro loves about the Central Valley. 'My favorite spots in the Central Valley are Heredia and the Poás area. You can visit the great coffee plantations, and the air is crisp and fresh.'

He would love more guests to visit the region. 'They can experience local life, taste the food and learn about the culture here. The people are good, friendly and open.'

Alejandro lives near Alajuela and is proud of his city's famous residents. 'Juan Santamaría saved Costa Rica from the filibusters. This is important history; it's how we got our freedom. Everyone should come to Alajuela and learn about it.'

Stroll a magical waterfall garden

Just half an hour from Volcán Poás you'll find **La Paz Waterfall Gardens** *(waterfallgardens.com; adult/child US$54/38)*, which has the notable distinction of being the most popular private eco-park in the country. The delights of five fantastic cascades and a massive animal sanctuary certainly contribute to its acclaim. Don't miss the waterfall garden, a whimsical joining of nature and architecture, where you can weave in and out of the thundering cascades on perfectly designed paths.

There's also the **Peace Lodge**, a high-end boutique hotel that balances a rustic vibe with luxury touches. Guests at the Peace Lodge enjoy an additional perk: the chance to roam the park freely while it's closed to other visitors. This unique spot is home to creatures like monkeys, macaws and butterflies. If you're visiting for the day, the park is open between 8am and 5pm.

Rescate Wildlife Rescue Center

TIME FROM ALAJUELA: **20 MINS**

A haven for vulnerable animals

Housing 125 different species of animals, including reptiles, birds, mammals and fish, the **Rescate Wildlife Rescue Center** *(rescatewildlife.org; adult/child US$35/15)* – formerly known as Zoo Avenue – offers both an immersive educational experience on the importance of conservation and protecting wild animals, and the opportunity to get up close and personal with some of Costa Rica's most magnificent creatures in a humane and safe way. This center, popular with locals and tourists alike, is open every day from 9am to 5pm. You can purchase tickets online or in person and opt for a self-guided tour or a guided one for an additional cost.

The center is a lifetime animal sanctuary, meaning that they provide enriching and secure habitats for animals that can't be released into the wild. There's an on-site animal hospital (not open to the public), where injured or rescued animals are rehabilitated, and the full amount of your ticket cost goes to fund these initiatives, as well as to keep the permanent residents of the center housed, fed and cared for. Well-marked, wheelchair-accessible paths connect each habitat, and you could easily spend half the day exploring.

You'll find reasonably priced food and drinks on sale (roughly US$7 for snacks and light meals and US$2 for beverages). You can also bring food into the park as long as you eat in the picnic zones. Alcohol is strictly prohibited.

Those who desire to help further can volunteer at the center as veterinary or wildlife interns. Volunteers interact more with the animals and are tasked with meaningful work, such as ensuring that the animals have enough enriching activities. Internship slots fill up quickly, so get your application in early if you're keen on exploring this opportunity.

Cartago

CATHOLIC MIRACLES | CURIOUS RUINS | MARVELOUS ART

When it comes to religious and cultural significance, it's hard to beat Cartago. This former capital is the final destination for the torch of independence, which travels from Guatemala every year on September 15 and symbolizes Costa Rica shaking off Spanish dominance. It's also home to the Basílica de Nuestra Señora de Los Ángeles, where the legendary *La Negrita* (Black Virgin) resides. This miraculous statue is the subject of a yearly pilgrimage by the faithful, a journey on foot from San José known as the Romería. Cartago can get creative, too, with an excellent art museum that's entirely free to the public and is surrounded by some of the prettiest and best-kept gardens you'll find in town. Indeed, it's a cosmopolitan and exciting city that's also the gateway to greater Cartago province and some of the most interesting sights in the Central Valley.

GETTING AROUND

You can cycle or walk around Cartago easily, and several local buses zip around the downtown area. The main sights are within a few blocks of each other. There are hop-on/hop-off bus tours that give you a good overview of the city and let you see some of the sights simultaneously. Uber works in Cartago, or you can pick up regular taxis if you need them.

Urban Ruins & Victorious Angels

Learn the history of Cartago

The 12m-high **Costa Rica Victoriosa** celebrates 200 years of national independence and looks down upon one of Cartago's most fascinating destinations: **Las Ruinas de la Parroquia**. The site of a failed parish originally started in the 16th century, it has been plagued repeatedly by earthquakes ever since. The ruins are the remains of an incomplete church supposedly haunted by a headless cleric who stalks the stone walls, looking for his missing head. While the lore is rife with restless ghosts and natural disasters, Las Ruinas de la Parroquia is a peaceful place, with little stone enclaves and shady spots, perfect for picnicking and grabbing a taste of nature in Cartago's otherwise hectic downtown. Visit on any given day and you're bound to see plenty of families enjoying this unique space. If you want to have the ruins a bit more to yourself, plan to arrive

TOP TIP

You're likely to find someone who can speak English at most of the hotels and tourist destinations in Cartago. Still, it's wise to have a few basic Spanish phrases down, especially if you're shopping in local markets and want to get off the beaten path. A few words will go a long way.

CARTAGO BY PEDAL POWER

Downtown Cartago has plenty of well-maintained bike paths connecting major destinations and attractions. These paths are part of a city initiative to introduce 6km of dedicated trails, which came on the heels of a similar initiative in San José that had great success. There are bike rental shops around town where you can pick up a speedy cruiser for a few hours or even a day, as well as places to park your bike near major attractions, so why not get a workout in and see the city from two wheels?

earlier or avoid weekends when it tends to be much busier in Cartago's central square.

Just outside the ruins, you'll find **Plaza Mayor**, a thoroughly modern place full of vendors and with plenty of seating. This square dates back to Spanish colonization and has been the hub of Cartago for 400 years. Today, it's a visual reminder of the city's righteous place in Costa Rica's story of independence and an excellent spot to snap photos of the ruins or of the giant statue, whose burnished silver frame gleams gorgeously in the sunlight. Costa Rica Victoriosa stands exactly where the city of Cartago signed the Act of Independence on October 29, 1821, freeing it from Spain, and was created by artist Ángel Lara Vargas under the patronage of the Municipality of Cartago.

The Virgin's Gift to Cartago

Legendary La Negrita

As the legend goes, the mysterious black-stone Virgin Mary, or *La Negrita*, was originally discovered in 1635. This icon refused to be moved, returning to a humble black rock if transported from the site that's now **Basílica de Nuestra Señora de Los Ángeles**, the most impressive cathedral in

Cartago. Stranger still, previous attempts to build a church in that location failed until the precious icon arrived, adding another layer to the story.

Calling Basílica de Nuestra Señora de Los Ángeles visually epic is an understatement; this cathedral is nothing short of awe-inspiring, with ornate, beautifully decorated pillars stretching to a ceiling patterned with gold arches and handsome woodwork. It's a holy place, and at the beginning of August every year, a million devotees participate in the **Romería**, a spiritual journey on foot from San José to Cartago to pay proper homage to *La Negrita*.

The street directly in front of the cathedral sells miniature replicas of the statue, religious materials, souvenirs and candles you can bring into the church for dedication and prayers. There's also a food market selling fruit, *empanadas* (stuffed turnovers) and beverages, with a small seating area. The Basílica de Nuestra Señora de Los Ángeles is centrally located, and you could easily couple a visit with a trip to Plaza Mayor. Most visitors spend about half an hour in the cathedral.

CARTAGO HOLY WATER

The magnificent Basílica de Nuestra Señora de Los Ángeles, with its detailed exterior design, sits atop a tucked-away spring that visitors often overlook. Follow the curving path down, and you'll find a small cistern of holy water, with the devout filling up cups and sampling it. A line of mostly local people generally waits to take their turn at the cistern.

As holy water isn't just reserved for people of the Catholic faith, visitors can take some too, but be respectful and don't touch the relics around the cistern. Photos are permitted. This hidden place stands in stark contrast with the church above, and you can't help but feel an air of reverence as you descend towards it.

Cartago's Art Scene

Immersive exhibits and engaging lectures

The **Museo Municipal de Cartago** *(muni-carta.go.cr)* sits surrounded by a vibrant flower garden behind a wrought-iron fence near the city's bus station. Its reserved presence is a bit out of place in the hustle and bustle of this area, where train tracks run parallel to bike paths and the busy market is in full swing across the street. If you didn't know it was there, you might walk on past.

Do stop on in. This museum is one of the best places to see well-preserved regional art and relics and hosts regular meet-and-greets with local and national artists. Offering permanent and guest exhibitions, lectures, films and special events, it's a cultural hub and free to visit (closed on Monday).

A former military command center, the museum is vast and surrounded by lovely, manicured gardens dotted with small statues. Multiple rooms feature the art of luminaries like Rafa Fernández, and a big mural depicts the Costa Rican triumphant struggle for independence.

As you leave the museum, you'll see a cafe to your right jammed with patrons. **La Flor del Café** *(laflordelcafe.com)* sells fresh cups of coffee as well as snacks. You can get a bag of ground-before-your-eyes gourmet coffee for US$5.

EATING IN CARTAGO: OUR PICKS

Q' Tortilla: Cheese-filled tortillas, *empanadas* and big traditional breakfasts. *8am-7pm Mon-Sat, 7am-6:30pm Sun* $

El Balcón Criollo: Karaoke and a party vibe meet comfort food: burgers, steaks and shakes. *11am-11pm Mon-Wed, to midnight Thu & Sun, to 1am Fri & Sat* $

Sonrisas Restaurante & Cafe: Fantastic pancakes, coffee and *batidos* (fruit shakes), in a bright, welcoming atmosphere. *10:30am-7pm Mon-Fri, from 8am Sat & Sun* $$

El Mosaica Coffee & Garden: Excellent salads and vegetarian options, plus delicious fruit smoothies. *8:30am-8:30pm Tue-Sun, from 11:30am Mon* $$

THE TORCH OF INDEPENDENCE

Visit Cartago on September 15 and you'll witness a patriotic celebration in Plaza Mayor as the torch of independence returns to the city. The torch is a pivotal part of the nation's history, carried all the way from Guatemala and entering Costa Rica from Nicaragua before finally arriving in Cartago. It symbolizes the news of Costa Rica shaking free of Spanish colonial power and gaining independence traveling through the province.

Visitors will be treated to parades, festivals, national dances, music, fireworks and massive festivities in the city. Simultaneous celebrations take place in nearby cities and towns, like Alajuela and San José. It's a family-friendly event and a fun way to participate in Costa Rican history and pride.

If you're having trouble finding the cafe, just follow your nose or look for the line out the door. Across the street and to the right is **Mercado Central** *(facebook.com/mercadocentraldecartago)*, where you can grab some fresh produce and cheap eats or simply take a stroll and do a bit of people-watching.

XMILOSK50/SHUTTERSTOCK

Basílica de Nuestra Señora de Los Ángeles (p114)

Beyond Cartago

A haunted sanatorium, mysterious ruins and a tour of Costa Rica's most famous coffee farm are all easy day trips from Cartago.

Places

Rough and scenic roads carry you out of Cartago city and far into the province itself, along mountainous roads and through charming villages where you'll be tempted to tarry and snap some pictures.

Family-friendly animal-rescue experiences rub elbows with abandoned sanatoriums full of lurid tales, and you can make a sweet stop to experience the history of Costa Rican chocolate-making and sample the good stuff for yourself. Explore the gardens and ruins of Paraíso, one of the prettiest towns in this part of the world, and spend some time in Heredia, where visitors sharpen up their Spanish and the college vibe is as strong as the local coffee.

San Isidro

TIME FROM CARTAGO: **40 MINS** 

Educate, rehabilitate, populate

Toucan Rescue Ranch *(toucanrescueranch.org; tours adult/child US$37/19),* near San Isidro, northwest of Cartago via Ruta 2, is a wonderful family find where you can see toucans, ocelots and sloths (but not touch them). This rehabilitation, education and breeding facility is the brainchild of American naturalist Leslie Howe and has been going strong for just over two decades. It's well organized and logically laid out, with a network of gravel paths connecting the different displays. The ground is level and wheelchair-accessible, but much of it is exposed to the elements, so bring sunscreen and water.

Visitors can take a virtual tour on the website and see these cute critters before booking an on-site daytime or nighttime visit. There are public and private tours and one- or two-day 'Ranch Experiences' where you'll meet Leslie Howe, visit the animal release site and learn about the vulnerable creatures housed and protected at the facility from the vet staff themselves. Toucan Rescue Ranch isn't open to the public, and you must book every tour online. There's a set number of available slots per day, so it's a good idea to reserve your spot early. Make sure you check the cancellation policy at the time of booking.

GETTING AROUND

Like in Alajuela province, it pays to have your own wheels or a dedicated driver in Cartago. Those relying on local buses would do well to choose a few destinations, like Paraíso and Heredia, to spend the majority of their time rather than try to hopscotch through the province by public transportation. While doable, it will cost you time and could add some unwanted stress to your otherwise tranquil Central Valley trip.

WHISPERS OF THE PARANORMAL

Although the official story is that Sanatorio Durán is absolutely not haunted, ghostly lore persists. There are rumors of a girl ghost lost in the children's wards, strange footsteps and phantom noises echoing throughout the men's and women's wards, and even apparitions in the morgue area. Common paranormal claims include cold spots, general unease and the feeling of being watched. Some people even say they've spied the ghost of Dr Durán himself walking the grounds. The facility strongly discourages these stories, and there's barbed wire around the exterior of the sanatorium, presumably to keep amateur ghost hunters away after closing hours. With or without the ghosts, this place has a tragic history, from the deaths of countless patients to its time as an orphanage and jail.

On your way out or back, stop in San Isidro and marvel at its ornate snow-white church, **Parroquia San Isidro Labrador**. It's generally only open for Sunday services, but you can still admire its exterior, grab a *batido* (fruit shake) or cone at **Oro Verde San Isidro**, and spend a bit of time in the park.

A sweet stop

Sibö Chocolate *(sibochocolate.com; tours US$36)* prides itself on top-quality, sustainable products, and its tastings show a reverence for the craft of cacao and the history of chocolate in Costa Rica. Guests are seated around a table and presented with pieces of premium chocolate, each of which tells the story of 3000 years of chocolate-making in the country. With inventive flavors like sea salt and spiced rum, you'll satisfy your sweet tooth while getting a crash course in Costa Rican cacao. It's a delicious deep dive that lasts an hour to an hour and a half and ends with a Q&A session.

Tours run Tuesday through Sunday at 10:30am. You need to make a reservation in advance. There's an online and on-site shop where you can pick up goodies and souvenirs, including bar chocolate and hot-chocolate blends.

Sanatorio Durán

TIME FROM CARTAGO: **24 MINS**

The shuttered tuberculosis hospital

Sanatorio Durán *(US$3.50)* was initially known as 'Carit Sanatorium' and opened in 1918 at the behest of the Costa Rica government; its current name is in honor of Dr Carlos Durán, who worked at the facility in 1931. It primarily housed tuberculosis patients, and the crisp, fine air of Central Valley was thought to do wonders for their lungs. Dr Durán had a personal connection to tuberculosis – his daughter suffered and tragically perished from it. At its peak, the sanatorium housed 300 patients, but when the epidemic faded, it was repurposed as a jail and orphanage. The facility closed for good in 1973, and the walls are significantly damaged.

Today, parts of the sanatorium are open to the public, and you can wander the halls of the men's, women's and children's wards. The latter are decorated with hundreds of semi-faded, colorful handprints, and each small room has a miniature bathtub about half the size of those in the men's and women's quarters.

One of the most somber (and clearly marked) areas is the morgue, a semi-open-air zone that overlooks a garden full of calla lilies. The gardens are well maintained and peaceful, contrasting with the melancholy and grim interior. There are footpaths through a small copse of trees, providing great views of the sanatorium. Although the public area of the building is structurally sound, you're not allowed in certain sections for safety reasons; many of the uneven paths inside are marred with giant cracks.

E ROJAS/SHUTTERSTOCK

Ruinas de Ujarrás

Paraíso

TIME FROM CARTAGO: **20 MINS**

Discover mysterious ruins

Like many ruins and religious sites in the Central Valley, **Ruinas de Ujarrás** have a mystical past that centers around decades of natural disasters and a mysterious painting of the Virgin Mary, discovered in a box that could not be moved. This painting became the focal point of the ruins. When the site was abandoned in the 1830s after waves of diseases and years of earthquakes and floods, it was rapidly reclaimed by the natural environment until it was restored in 2010 and opened to the public. Parts of the ruins are still largely intact, with phenomenal stonework dating back to the 1800s.

Today, the site is peaceful, surrounded by a well-maintained park full of gorgeous tropical flowers. It's perfect for picnicking, but no dogs, bicycles or alcohol are allowed. Entry is free, although small donations are accepted, and it's open from 8am to 4pm. It's only about 15 minutes away from Paraíso, a town famous for its potatoes. **Parque de Paris**, in the center of town, has a playground for kids and is a good place to grab lunch or a coffee after your adventures at the ruins.

A celebration of orchids

With 3000 different types of plants, including 600 orchid species, the 11-hectare **Jardín Botánico Lankester** *(jbl.ucr.ac.cr; adult/child US$10/7.50)* delivers a dose of heavenly fragranced natural therapy and helps you get your steps in, too. With myriad different ecosystems, plenty of winding paths to explore, a Japanese garden with a pond, towering bamboo forest and a tea house, it will appeal to those looking to take a breather and ecologists alike. There's a picnic spot and several food trucks if you're craving a snack.

A MAJESTIC NATIONAL FLOWER

The tropical climate of Costa Rica provides fertile ground for beautiful orchids of all kinds, with over 1500 varieties thriving throughout the country. Still, none is as majestic or impressive as the *guaria morada*. These towering, deep-lavender blooms are the national flower and flourish between January and April.

In 1939, Costa Rica crowned the vibrant and fragrant *guaria morada* as its national symbol, and since then, it's come to represent more than just a beautiful bloom. It's deeply tied to Costa Rican heritage and its commitment to nature and conservation. You'll mostly find these flowers on the Península de Nicoya, but you can also see them in Naranjo and Palmares in the Central Valley.

HEREDIA'S LONESOME WATCHTOWER

Next to Parque Nicolás Ulloa Soto you'll find **El Fortín**, a 13m-tall tower with dozens of windows cut deep into a thick layer of brick. The structure, the symbol of Heredia, is the vision of Fadrique Gutiérrez, the province's former governor who thought that no town was complete without a fortress. Originally, Gutiérrez' vision was to have four towers around the city, but only one was ever constructed. Its lone form looms above the park, overlooking children playing and families picnicking. Eventually, the city authorities plan to open up the structure so that visitors can climb to the top to enjoy panoramic views of Heredia and see what Gutiérrez' odd little tower looks like from the inside.

The garden is named after Charles Lankester, who came to the Cartago region to cultivate coffee but ended up selling the farm and focusing his green thumb on orchids instead. His legacy is now an important conservation area for the latter and other indigenous plant life. The Jardín Botánico Lankester is open from 8:30am to 4:30pm.

Heredia

TIME FROM CARTAGO: **1¼ HRS**

Explore the 'City of Flowers'

A launchpad for exploring the fertile coffee region beyond, Heredia is a college town with lots of history and a good spot to brush up on your Spanish skills. The so-called 'City of Flowers' is walkable and easy to navigate (though parking can be a pain), with almost everything clustered around the central **Parque Nicolás Ulloa Soto**. There are plenty of cafes, restaurants, shops and bars, so it's worth spending a few hours here.

Check out **Centro Cultural** *(facebook.com/culturalheredia)* for art exhibitions, performances and music, singing, dance and theater classes for all ages, or the **Casa de la Cultura** for rotating lecture series and art shows. You can also tap into the college-town energy of Heredia on Calle 9, where university students frequent spots like **Bar Stadium** *(facebook.com/stadiumheredia)* for cheap pints, pizza and music. You can even become a student yourself at one of Heredia's language schools like **Tico Lingo** *(ticolingo.com)*, which offers a summer camp and local homestays.

Some of Heredia's dining options include **Por Media Calle Mercado Gastronómico** *(facebook.com/PorMediaCalleMercadoGastronomico)*, an eclectic food hall with regular live music in the evening; **Estadero** *(estaderocr.com)*, which offers vegetarian food in a chill atmosphere; and **Vintage Cafeteria & Cupcakes**, which serves good coffee, baked treats and stuffed-full sandwiches and fries.

EATING IN PARAÍSO: OUR PICKS

Oasis Smoothies & Coffee: Open early and serving healthy smoothies and premium cups of coffee. *7:30am-5:30pm Mon-Sat, to 5pm Sun* $

Restaurante Orquideas: Excellent shrimp and rice, *ceviche* (marinated seafood) and a decent beer selection. *11:30am-11pm Tue-Thu, to midnight Fri & Sat, to 10pm Sun* $

Chicharronera Piso E' Tierra: Dine-in or takeaway traditional Costa Rican restaurant with a nice ambience. *1-9:30pm Fri, from 11:30am Sat, 11am-5pm Sun* $

Nono Café & Jardín: Fantastic baked goods, artisanal coffee and a welcoming atmosphere. *12:30-7:30pm Tue & Sat, from noon Wed-Fri, 1pm-5:30pm Sun* $

TOP EXPERIENCE

Britt Coffee Tours

While you can get Britt coffee virtually anywhere in Costa Rica, you must go to Heredia to find the source. The Britt Coffee Tours take you from the freshly picked burgundy bean to the intensely flavored cup of joe, with plenty of national history included and a multimedia tasting experience at the end. Learn about harvesting, roasting and enjoying this Costa Rican icon.

Classic Britt Coffee Tour

These thrice-a-day tours last 90 minutes. You'll be fully steeped in Costa Rican coffee culture, learn about picking and roasting, and sample premium blends in an immersive space. Guests also have Q&A time with the roasters.

Britt Coffee & Adventure Tour

Available daily at 8am, these tours are a six-hour fusion of a caffeine high and adrenaline. They start with an overview of coffee cultivation and roasting, proceed to zipline through the cloud forest, explore winding paths and see secluded waterfalls. Tours cost US$145 including transportation and lunch.

Britt Coffee & Waterfalls Tour

Combines the classic tour with a visit to La Paz Waterfall Gardens (p112), five incredible waterfalls and a wildlife sanctuary in the Central Valley. This eight-hour tour (US$149) includes gourmet chocolate, lunch and transportation.

Britt Coffee & Wildlife Tour

A joint venture between Britt Coffee Tour and Toucan Rescue Ranch (p117), this six-hour trip offers the full coffee harvesting tour and a chance to see some of Costa Rica's amazing creatures like macaws and sloths. The cost is US$125 including lunch and transportation.

TOP TIPS

- Taking photos is okay, but no video recording is permitted.
- Bring light layers as it can get chilly on the coffee plantation.
- If you need to cancel, do so at least 24 hours prior to the tour or you'll be fully charged.
- Tours from US$31 starting 8am and running several times a day

PRACTICALITIES

Scan this QR code for more information.

Orosí Valley

THERMAL BATHS | EXCITING HIKING | IMPRESSIVE DAM

GETTING AROUND

Buses run regularly between Orosí and Cartago – just look for the blue-and-white bus on the main drag near Super La Canasta supermaket. There's also a stop a bit outside of town, but the one in Orosí proper is easier. You can get around Orosí itself on foot, which will likely be the most enjoyable way. If you want to see the greater valley, you'll need a driver or your own car to get around.

TOP TIP

Arrive in Orosí before dark, even if your accommodations are secured, because everything closes early. Plus, you'll be able to enjoy twilight in a hammock, soaking in the clean air of the valley.

Orosí Valley is equal parts exciting and enchanting, with all of the promise of an unforgettable outdoor adventure coupled with breathtaking panoramic views of the mountains and big rivers that glide like glass. Get ready to lace up your hiking boots and hit the trail, sink down into a hammock for a well-deserved break and soothe your muscles in the thermal hot springs.

The town of Orosí is small but has all the essentials, including a bank, grocery store and a few pharmacies. There are plenty of accommodations here, a local mineral bath featuring an impressive Olympic-sized pool and lots of good eats on the main drag. Orosí Valley tends to close up shop early, with many of the establishments only staying open a few hours after sunset. Arrive early to make the most of your day and secure your lodgings and final meal of the day before nightfall.

Orosí's Religious Treasures

Tour a colonial-era cathedral

The longest continuously operated church in Orosí, the **Iglesia Colonial de Orosí** has stood in the center of town since 1766. Notable for its snowy-white exterior, cheerful tiled roof and bell tower, it's a masterpiece of minimalism with simple wooden pews and a flower garden surrounding the exterior. If you're looking for respite after a long hike or a place for a quiet prayer, this is it.

Don't miss the church **museum** *(US$1)*, located just to the right of the main building. Here, you can learn about the history of the Orosí Valley and its religious traditions. In the first two rooms, you'll find religious frescoes, including a magnificent depiction of Archangel Michael and the *Death of St Joseph*, an 18th-century confessional chamber and antique furniture that paints a picture of what life was like for clergy of days past. Everything is lovingly preserved, including the leatherwork, vestal garments and church relics. When

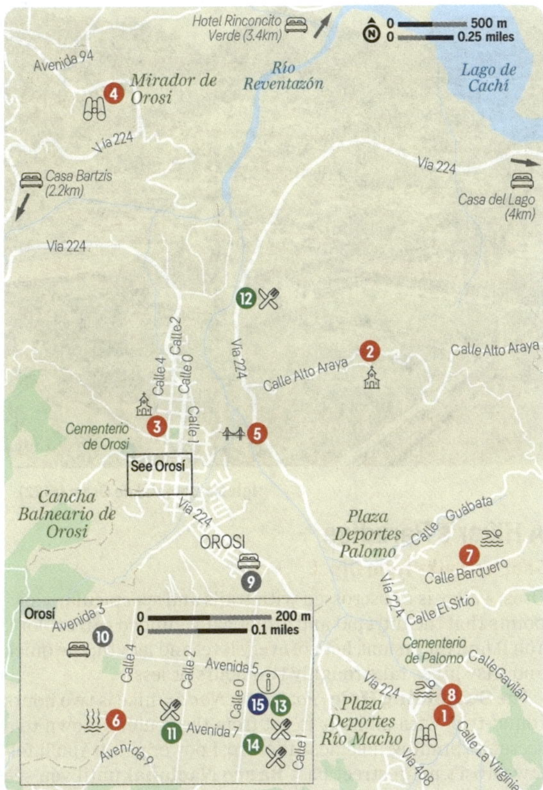

SIGHTS
1 Cruz de Alta Montaña
2 Iglesia Altos de Araya
3 Iglesia Colonial de Orosí
4 Mirador de Orosí
5 Puente Hamaca de La Alegría

ACTIVITIES
6 Balneario de Águas Termales Orosí
7 Catarata de Nano
8 Swimming Hole

SLEEPING
9 Hotel Tapanti Media de Orosi
10 Montaña Linda Hostel

EATING
11 Chenkos Gastronomía
12 Orosi al Natural Restaurante
13 Soda El Guayabo
14 Tony's Pizza Orosi

INFORMATION
15 Banco Nacional

you're done exploring, check out the *panaderías* (bakeries) and *sodas* (cheap eateries) along the streets flanking either side of the square.

The Valley at a Glance

Enjoy the views from Orosí Mirador

The **Mirador de Orosí**, a 10-minute drive north of town, is the spot to gaze down on the Orosí Valley and the mountains beyond or grab a few photos of the forested lands you'll be exploring over the next few days. It's open between 8am and 4:30pm, free to visit, and has picnic tables, secure parking and a kids' playground. A few trails nearby lead to other viewpoints, allowing you to stretch your legs. The hikes are relatively straightforward, short and scenic. It's a good preview of what to expect as you enter the valley: a natural, community-oriented place where you can truly let your hair down.

CONNECTING WITH NATURE

Following Calle 0 past Monster Shack Ice Cream, the road leaving town looks like a dead end. But if you keep going, and veer left at the fork where the pavement seems to end and the rougher road begins, you'll find yourself on the **Puente Hamaca de La Alegría**, also known as the 'Happy Hammock Bridge.' It's a pedestrian bridge, but you can easily take a bike across as long as you walk it. From the bridge, you can breathe in that pure Central Valley air, and take some photos of the landscape including sprawling views of the Río San Carlos.

WHY I LOVE THE CENTRAL VALLEY

Elizabeth Lavis, Lonely Planet writer

The emerald-green valleys and sparkling streams of the Central Valley captured my heart the first time I laid eyes on them, but what really made me keep coming back to this often-overlooked corner of Costa Rica was the slower, laid-back vibe. I felt enthusiastically invited to settle down into a hammock with a locally brewed cup of coffee, breathe in the fresh air and enjoy the stillness. Activities in the Central Valley are mostly nature-based, and after I'd gotten my fill of winding hiking trails and impossibly beautiful outlooks, I could slip into a soothing natural hot spring and ease my muscles. I also cherish the little things, from fresh Turrialba cheese and mango with bread to small town squares.

GIANFRANCO VIVI/SHUTTERSTOCK

Iglesia Colonial de Orosí (p122)

A Hiker's Paradise

Shorter walks from Orosí

Orosí Valley is crisscrossed with trails and spectacular viewpoints that the intrepid and athletically minded can explore. You'll find excursions here of every level and length; the quick and easy hikes take roughly two hours or less.

The **Swimming Hole** *(Pozo Para Nadar)* hike is two hours round-trip, with an hour to get from the center of town to a secret swimming hole near the Orosí power plant. You'll follow Orosí's main street past **Banco Nacional** until you see a split in the road near La Bomba gas station. Go right, and continue down the path until you spot two churches, then take the right path. At this point, you might be able to faintly hear the sounds of the river, which is where your final destination is. Pass through a small hamlet, then take the first trail left. Hop into the cool water and enjoy your relaxing reward.

The **Catarata de Nano** (Nano's Waterfall) is another simple hike from the center of Orosí that takes just 30 minutes, with a nice payoff at the end. Since it sits on private property, you'll need to pay US$7 to visit the waterfall (cash only in smaller bills) when you arrive. Expect tons of bright butterflies and birds as you make your way to the falls. To get there, walk down the main road to Banco Nacional, turn right, pass La Bomba gas station, make another right and continue walking

EATING IN OROSÍ VALLEY: OUR PICKS

Tony's Pizza Orosi: Cheap and cheerful pizza joint with good thin-crust pepperoni slices. *4-9pm Tue-Thu, from 3pm Fri, 11:30am-9pm Sat & Sun* $

Soda El Guayabo: Excellent *casados* (set meals), fresh hot coffee and comfortable seating. *11am-8:30pm Tue-Sat, to 7:30pm Sun & Mon* $

Chenkos Gastronomía: Great seafood and comfort pub grub, and a cute outdoor dining area. *4-8pm Tue-Thu, 11:30am-9pm Fri & Sat, to 7pm Sun* $$

Orosi al Natural Restaurante: Rustic family-style restaurant serving locally sourced food. *10am-5pm Tue-Thu, from 9am Fri, from 8am Sat & Sun* $$

for 20 minutes. The path can get steep in parts and slippery during the rainy season. You'll know when you're on Nano's property because you'll see a barbed-wire fence. Simply call out and pass along the fee. The owner might even show you around the property if he has time.

Big Gains & Fantastic Views

Intense hikes in the Orosí Valley

If you have the time and inclination to get your blood pumping in the fresh air of the Orosí Valley, two popular loop hikes take you far afield from Orosí and bring you right back. They last an average of four to five hours, depending on your speed and the weather conditions. Leave by 10am at the latest to ensure you're back before sunset (from 5:15pm to 6pm). By departing mid-morning, you can relax at some viewpoints or take your time on the harder bits.

The 'Pink Church' (referring to **Iglesia Altos de Araya**) hike has an elevation gain of 454m, with a steep slog in the middle that can get slippery in rainy conditions, and it will undoubtedly take a bit of grit to get up. To start, cross the Puente de Hamaca de La Alegría (Happy Hammock Bridge; p123) over the Río San Carlos, take the second trail on your right, and look for the 'Alto' road sign on your left. Take this path, the steep left path, and the right at the fork in the road. Here, the path starts to incline seriously, and you'll pass the hike's namesake salmon-colored church. After a few meters, it levels out at a coffee bean field and finally takes you into Cachí. Hikers will enjoy glorious views of the Cachí Reservoir and vast coffee bean fields, which make it all worth the effort. After Cachí, follow the main trail as it heads back down to Orosí.

The **Cruz de Alta Montaña** (High Mountain Cross) trail starts on Orosí's main street, where the Banco Nacional is. Follow the road, go right at La Bomba gas station, and find the Swimming Hole about an hour into the hike. If you arrive early enough, you can dip in the pool to steel yourself for the next part. You're in for some serious hiking up through the forest. The view from High Mountain Cross is epic and spans across the valley. You'll follow a series of prominent 'Aya' signs to get back to the main road to Orosí and wind up right near the town's church.

Keep safety in mind

While hiking in the Orosí Valley is generally safe and easy, it's essential to keep a few key things in mind. Many pathways are unpaved and can get relatively slick in bad weather, so good shoes with ankle support are a must. Additionally, there are a lot of stray dogs in Costa Rica. While most of them are friendly, and might follow you along the trail, reading their body language is key. Don't ignore growls, raised hackles or bared teeth. It's always better to err on the side of caution and reroute your path. With the exception of Nano's Waterfall, where the owner accepts visitors for a small fee, avoid trespassing on private property, and always let someone know where you're headed and for how long.

A RESTORATIVE SOAK

Give your muscles a well-deserved, post-hike soak in the healing waters of **Balneario de Aguas Termales Orosí** *(US$9.90)*, which at first blush looks like a series of public pools but is actually full of restorative minerals. These baths aren't steaming hot, so you can soak for longer than 20 minutes at a time, which is the recommended maximum time for most mineral springs. You'll find clean locker rooms, a small cafeteria and a special kids' area on-site. There are smaller pools for bathing, and an Olympic-size pool for doing laps in the fortified water beneath the shade of a mountain. These pools are cheaper than most hot springs you'll find in the Central Valley and are located right off the main street.

Beyond Orosí Valley

Rappel down cliffs, soak in thermal-bath infinity pools and visit the most whimsical house in all of Costa Rica.

Orosí Valley's natural splendor meets human-made excellence at Cachí Dam, a wonder of modern engineering that halted the regular flooding and preserved much of the Orosí Valley. Lago de Cachí is impressive from any angle, but especially so when you marvel at it from atop the dam.

You'll find hidden adventures and wonders in greater Orosí Valley, including Casa del Soñador, or 'the house of dreamers' adorned with fanciful woodwork, which is a relic of one of Central Valley's greatest artists. Visitors can relax in hot-spring infinity pools looking out over the mountains, coffee plantations and farms in every part of this phenomenal slice of the Central Valley. Slow down and take it all in as you cruise through paradise in search of adventure.

Lago de Cachí

TIME FROM OROSÍ VALLEY: **25 MINS**

A human-made wonder

While Costa Rica certainly isn't short on natural wonders, one of the most impressive sights in the Orosí Valley is distinctly human-made: the **Lago de Cachí**, spanned by the **Cachí Dam**. Prior to the 1970s, rivers ran through the valley, and devastating floods were common. Then the government built the Cachí Dam, which created a formidable reservoir and hydroelectric power plant. It's an impressive 80m-high structure that you can walk, drive and cycle across, and you can't beat the views of the gorge from the top. You'll find a queue of vendors lined up along the road, selling fresh fruit, kebabs and other food.

Lago de Cachí is a choose-your-own-adventure type of place where you can simply linger around taking in the views, set out on a leisurely loop around the lake or challenge yourself to a tough journey that will net you plenty of bragging rights. One of the most popular methods of taking in the Lago de Cachí is by bicycle. Pedaling around the lake is smooth, level sailing, and you'll likely run into plenty of other two-wheeled travelers. Local hotels often rent bikes to guests, and cycle tours can usually be arranged in Orosí.

Those who want a more challenging experience can opt for the **Lago de Cachí–Paraíso loop**, a 26km-long cruise with a 410m altitude change throughout the ride. You'll need a solid mountain bike and a bit of grit to handle the steep parts, but

GETTING AROUND

Like with much of the Central Valley, if you want to see all the hidden spots in this region, you'll need a car. Alternatively, you can cycle from Paraíso to Cachí Dam and beyond, even to Orosí. It's a strenuous slog, as you'll gain a lot of altitude, but if you want to use pedal power instead of four wheels, it's doable, especially during the dry and cooler season.

the payoff is tremendous. From the lush, rolling scenery of the Central Valley to the massive reservoir itself, this route is a true feast for the eyes. You'll likely encounter plenty of birdlife to keep you company as you pedal along. This trail is partially paved and can get a bit dicey in wet weather conditions, so check the forecast carefully if you're planning on heading out during the rainy season. Also, set out early from either Paraíso or Lago de Cachí to ensure that you're back well before the sun sets.

Thrilling ziplining and rock walls

Escalada Cachí, five minutes down the road from Cachí Dam past the Iglesia de Urasca, looks like a varsity-level natural rock-climbing wall, but it's suitable for confident beginners and intermediate climbers and interesting enough for those seasoned at the sport. This 100m-high cliff looks sheer and scary, but it's actually covered in handholds that will help you rappel down or shimmy up with ease. You'll also find amenities like clean bathrooms and on-site parking, indicating that this is, in fact, a tourist destination and not a madcap scramble up an unsupervised cliff. Instead, you'll be in the comfortable care of **Aventuras Cachí** *(facebook.com/aventurascachi; US$12-30, by reservation only)*, whose first order of business is to escort you to the 'Mega Rappel,' a lightning-quick zipline that sends you zooming over the frothing rapids of the Río Reventazón before depositing you on a lower platform positioned directly over the wall.

Once safely landed, visitors are clipped to a secure line and instructed on how to rappel down the wall to the riverbank. Though the drop is certainly sheer, you'll find lots of grips and rest comfortably, and the belay line will hold you in the event of a slip. It's an utterly thrilling experience, from the views to the adrenaline-spiking drop to the riverbank. While Aventuras Cachí operates every day except Sunday, reservations are requested. During busier periods, it's best to message them a few days or a week ahead to ensure you get your spot, especially if you're traveling with a larger group. Wear comfortable, breathable and close-fitting clothes that won't catch on the wall or the belay, and shoes with a lot of traction on them so that you can scale down like a champion. Aventures Cachí runs tours throughout the year, but it can get a bit wet and wild during the rainy season, so prepare for the mud and water if the forecast is looking stormy.

The whimsical house of dreams

Keep your eyes peeled on the road from Orosí Valley to Lago de Cachí, and you might spy a strange wooden house that looks ripped straight out of the pages of a fairytale. **Casa del Soñador** is the legacy of Macedonio Quesada, who left behind hundreds of intricate woodcarvings and a bewitching wooden house.

Casa del Soñador translates as 'house of the dreamer' and the property certainly embodies its name. Currently, Quesada's son tends the home, using it both as an exhibition area and a workshop. He will gladly give you a tour, let you take some photographs and offer you the chance to purchase a unique souvenir from Orosí Valley. Original sculptures start around US$25. You'll need some basic Spanish to communicate, as he doesn't speak English. The studio is on the main road, 1.5km south of the dam.

POWER & POTABLE WATER

The 1970s were a game-changing decade for the Central Valley, when the Cachí Dam, one of the first hydroelectric projects in the country was completed. Originally commissioned in 1966, the 80m-high arch-type dam covers 324 hectares, and spans Río Reventazón, providing astounding views of the verdant valley and generating ample electric power and potable water. This dam also created Lago de Cachí, a tremendous place for water sports, leisurely cycling and white-water rafting near the river head. The dam undergoes regular maintenance, most recently in 2015 when its hydropower capacity was increased to 160MW, and older infrastructure was updated to combat erosion and keep up with modern engineering standards.

FROM LEFT: PAUL ARAGÓN LEYTON/HACIENDA OROSÍ, PAUL ARAGÓN LEYTON/HACIENDA OROSÍ

Thermal spring, Hacienda Orosí

TOP EXPERIENCE

Hacienda Orosí

A five-minute drive from Orosí along Ruta 408, Hacienda Orosí is a huge family-friendly attraction with alfresco thermal hot springs, an animal farm, a restaurant and cafe, hiking and birdwatching opportunities and a coffee-farm tour. Visit and soak for the day, or spend the night at its premium hotel.

DON'T MISS

- Thermal hot springs
- Animal farm
- Coffee tour
- Coffee pickers' village
- Hiking and birdwatching

Thermal Hot Springs

Set up for peak indulgence, the seven thermal baths of Hacienda Orosí overlook the valley and beyond, seemingly floating over the landscape. Each pool is 37.7°C (100°F), and you can luxuriate and bathe in the steaming water or take advantage of a comfy deck chair nearby.

Overnight guests can use the thermal baths, or you can purchase a day or night pass, which includes a locker and towel as well as the animal and coffee farm experiences. You can also opt for spa treatments, such as exfoliation and mud masks, at an extra cost.

PRACTICALITIES

Scan this QR code for more information on opening times and entrance passes.

Coffee Tour & Animal Farm

The hacienda sits on ultra-fertile coffee-growing land and has an animal farm (La Granja de la Hacienda) that's perfect for children. You will walk a lot on the coffee tour, and some of the area is a bit steep, so wear comfortable shoes and bring ample sunscreen and water. Tours run between 8am and 4:30pm daily, with the last tour leaving at 3pm.

Stop by the charming red-painted barn to see cows, horses, peacocks, pigs and ducks. The cows at Hacienda Orosí are a unique, long-horned variety. The barn is near the starting point for the coffee tour, so it's a convenient place to stop before or afterward.

The tour itself goes up the side of a small nearby mountainside and includes 5km of hiking, where you'll have the opportunity to enjoy the fresh air and spot some of the 225 species of birds that call this valley home. Along the way, you'll learn about where the coffee beans come from, the harvesting practices and how the beans are roasted. If you're not up for the climb, you can always check out the area around the coffee tour, which has plenty of signage, bean-sorting machines and friendly folk who can answer your questions in English and Spanish.

Coffee Pickers' Village

Wake up to the intoxicating aroma of fresh coffee before you even brew your first cup at the coffee pickers' village. These individual villas balance rustic-inspired designs with modern amenities and can host up to six people per lodging.

You'll have your own fully stocked kitchen and enjoy free breakfast at Hacienda Orosí's restaurant. Costs vary depending on the time of year – the high season is generally more expensive – and which villa you choose. It's a good option for families who want to spend extra time in the valley, enjoy the hot springs, have animal encounters and do some hiking.

Hacienda Orosí viewed from adjacent hill

HACIENDA OROSÍ RESTAURANTS

There are two restaurants inside Hacienda Orosí: the main house restaurant and **Antojos Canuto**. You'll find fast food like hot dogs and *empanadas* at the latter and sit-down-style meals at the former. The house restaurant serves Costa Rican food like *gallo pinto* and *casados* as well as international dishes.

TOP TIPS

- Arrive early at the thermal baths to get the best spots overlooking the mountain, as they tend to fill up quickly.
- Look out for the friendly resident golden retriever hanging out by the barn, and give it a pet or two.
- A lovely greenhouse full of orchids is just to your left before you enter the restaurant. Pop in and take a sniff.
- You don't need to pay for a hot-springs day pass to eat at the restaurant or go on the coffee tour.
- Antojos Canuto's chicken tamales are ready in minutes, and have plenty of Linzano sauce for dipping.

Turrialba

ANCIENT MYSTERIES | SKY-HIGH VOLCANOES | STEAM-ENGINE HISTORY

GETTING AROUND

Turrialba doesn't have much in the way of public transportation, except for buses that go to Cartago, so your options are to get around on foot or drive. You can find some taxis in town, depending mainly on whether or not it's high season, and there are tour companies that can arrange airport shuttles and rides to other destinations, but just like in much of the Central Valley, nothing beats having your own wheels.

TOP TIP

Be kind to yourself and listen to your body when hiking around Volcán Irazú and Turrialba. The volcano sits at a full 3432m above sea level, which can give you mild altitude sickness and negatively impact how fast you can climb. Take it slow and easy when you're up there.

Even if the name Turrialba doesn't ring a bell, you might have sampled some of the cheese that shares its name with this region. Turrialba cheese (also known as *queso fresco*) is semi-hard, with a pale buttery color and mild taste. It's delicious on everything from fresh mango to sandwiches.

The town of Turrialba is on the edge of the Central Valley and makes a great base for adventure sports like white-water rafting and hiking. Also here is the Monumento Nacional Guayabo, an ancient site that's baffled archaeologists ever since it was first uncovered, and Volcán Irazú, whose dizzying height could cause altitude sickness.

In more recent Costa Rican history, Turrialba was an important stop on the Jungle Train, which connected San José and the Caribbean Coast and gave Central Valley farmers the chance to sell their wares across the country.

Turrialba's Historic Vibes

A stroll around the main square

Turrialba is a brilliant balance of off-the-grid and historic vibes. The town's main square is centered around where the old Jungle Train used to pass. **Paseo Las Palmeras**, a lengthy park by the railroad tracks, has a charming market where you can get fruit, veg or *ceviche* as well as souvenirs. A few blocks away is the **Templo Católico San Buenaventura de Turrialba** (San Buenaventura Catholic Temple of Turrialba), a pale, towering structure with vertical geometric lines built in 1974. Dedicated to a Franciscan mystic, it has been reconstructed several times and is an interesting counterpoint to the more traditional churches you'll find in the Orosí Valley. Walk towards the Río Turrialba, and you'll find **Casa de la Cultura Jorge Debravo de Turrialba**, a local focus for live performances and art exhibitions. Like most spots in the region, Turrialba goes to bed early, so you'll want to pack in your fun before about 9pm.

SIGHTS
1 Antigua Estación de Tren
2 Casa de la Cultura Jorge Debravo de Turrialba
3 Paseo Las Palmeras
4 Templo Católico San Buenaventura de Turrialba

SLEEPING
5 Boutique Hotel Casa de Lis
6 Turrialba Bed & Breakfast

Aboard the Jungle Train

Dine in a restored train car

The history of Turrialba is the history of steam-powered travel, starting in the 1880s when the Jungle Train connecting the Caribbean Coast with San José passed through the town. This new track opened up the city and the coast to local farmers looking to sell their produce and established Turrialba as an agricultural hub until an earthquake halted the transportation flow and the line closed in the 1990s.

Today, you can visit the historic tracks and grab a bite to eat at the **Antigua Estación de Tren** *(facebook.com/bysantopan)*, now home to Estación Atlantico Santo Pan restaurant. Menu items include traditional breakfasts for US$9, soups, lunch specials and desserts. You can really get into the spirit of the place and sit down in a restored train car located just outside the restaurant. It fills up quickly, so avoid the lunch or dinner rush if you want to score a seat. If you're not feeling hungry, you can pop in for a peek at what the long-gone Jungle Train used to look like.

WHITE-WATER RAFTING

Turrialba is the base for rafting on Río Reventazón and Río Pacuare (with Class II and Class III rapids), and there are family-friendly tours that are good for children seven years or older running almost daily. They generally last half a day, leave in the morning and include transportation from Turrialba to the rapids. The operators provide all of the equipment, snacks or lunch, depending on your package, and instructions on how to stay safe in the raft. Since it's bound to get wet and wild, bring an extra change of clothes and towels, and leave any valuables in your hotel. After you've mastered the rapids, your guide will take you back to Turrialba, where you can plan your next outdoor adventure.

Beyond Turrialba

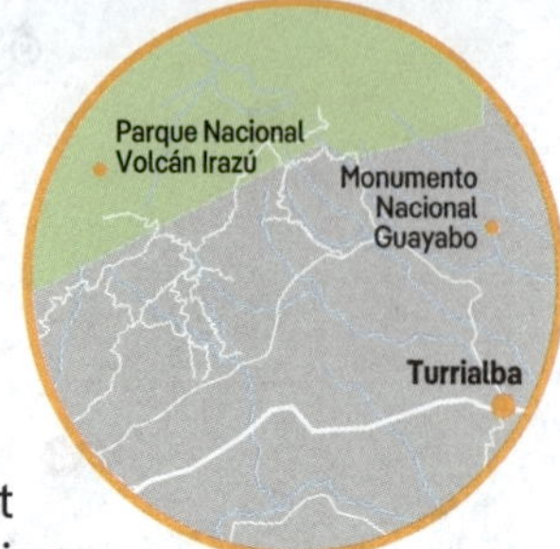

Explore the ruins of an ancient civilization that left only mysterious clues behind and a towering volcano with views of a sea and an ocean.

Places

Beyond Turrialba, you'll find nature in its most raw and powerful form, with volcanoes that scrape the sky and conceal deep blue-green lakes at their crater bases. The bragging rights you get from climbing Volcán Irazú – the largest and highest active volcano in Costa Rica and one of the few you can currently walk around – don't compare to actually seeing it in person.

You'll also discover the remnants of a long-lost civilization that left no clues as to why they made their home in this remote part of the Central Valley. The pre-Columbian city of Monumento Nacional Guayabo is one of Costa Rica's most enduring mysteries, and there's something both compellingly tragic and beautiful about walking through its ruins.

GETTING AROUND

Rent a car with a 4WD to explore the area beyond Turrialba properly. There are wide bits of open land between the attractions out here, so it's not feasible to walk. You can sometimes find taxis in Turrialba, but the cost stacks up quickly and the rides aren't guaranteed. You're better off using your own wheels or finding a driver for the day. Alternatively, you can opt for a tour to Volcán Irazú or Monumento Nacional Guayabo in Turrialba.

Parque Nacional Volcán Irazú

TIME FROM TURRIALBA: 1¼ **HRS**

Summit a volcano

Volcán Irazú is the highest volcano in Costa Rica, with a breathtaking 3432m summit, raccoons and *pizotes* (coatis), rocky craters with emerald-colored lakes, and, if you're lucky, a view of both the Caribbean Sea and Pacific Ocean on a clear day. The volcano's sky-high altitude means that conditions at the top can be fairly chilly, dipping below 10°C (50°F), so layers and waterproof clothing are absolute musts. Additionally, weather at high altitude is notoriously unpredictable, amplifying the effects of storms and making the trail difficult or even unpassable depending on the day. Check before you leave.

Volcán Irazú National Park *(sinac.go.cr; adult/child US$15/5)* is a protected area, designated a national park in 1955. As such, you'll see wide swathes of uninterrupted cloudy forests and impressive and untouched craters. Volcán Irazú hasn't erupted since the 1960s but remains an active volcano, so there is an underlying – and, frankly, exciting – bit of risk that comes with visiting. The park is open daily from 8am to 3:30pm, and there's a US$4 fee to park your vehicle. Visitors can't enter after 2pm, so it's a good idea to make Irazú a morning activity.

continued on p134

TOP EXPERIENCE

Monumento Nacional Guayabo

Monumento Nacional Guayabo is a mystery for the ages – the remnants of a vanished agricultural civilization that may have wielded political control over the Orosí Valley between 1000 BCE and 1400 CE but left only stone mounds as a record of their existence. This pre-Columbian city has fascinated historians and archaeologists ever since its excavation in 1891.

SAMOLI/SHUTTERSTOCK

What's Left Behind

The primary reason to visit Guayabo is to see the traces of a long-gone civilization. Aqueducts, drawer tombs, roads, stone-hewn storage tanks and the famous mounds paint a fascinating though incomplete story of a thriving place far removed in the forest.

Archaeologists suspect that the mounds were initially used as primitive home foundations, and the sophisticated aqueduct and storing systems supplied fresh potable water. The drawer tombs were carved directly into rough flagstone, and buried roads connected the whole system.

You can explore the ruins by yourself, and read plaques speculating on what the structures were used for, still coming away with a sense of wonder about Guayabo's significance.

Flora & Fauna

The path from the entrance to the ruins is well-marked and brief, but you'll have a chance to check out some impressive flora and perhaps even spot some fauna. The area is a riot of blooms like camarillo, orchids and fragrant magnolias, all enveloped in deep-green leaves that make the colors pop even more.

Toucans and woodpeckers nest nearby, while rabbits, *pizotes* (coatis) and tropical lizards are often scuttling around on the ground. These creatures remind us that, while humans come to Guayabo to connect with their past, it has been largely reclaimed by nature.

TOP TIPS

- You can camp near the park for an extra US$2 fee per night.
- Plan to arrive at 3pm at the latest so you have ample time to explore.
- The site offers guided tours for an additional fee.

PRACTICALITIES

Scan this QR code for admission times and ticket prices.

MANAGING THE HIGH ALTITUDE

Irazú's altitude is no joke. While you won't have to break out the crampons or belays to scramble to the summit, you might have to contend with bodily changes due to the lack of atmosphere. Altitude sickness can occur at 1500m above sea level, and this colossal stratovolcano is more than twice that.

Take things at a more leisurely pace if you start feeling winded or light-headed on the trail. Stay hydrated, carry some light anti-pain medication with you for sudden headaches, and treat yourself to a bit of chocolate over the course of the hike (it can help with the symptoms). Most of all, listen to your body. If you feel unwell, get back down from the volcano.

MILOSK50/SHUTTERSTOCK

Volcán Irazú crater

continued from p132

There's a cafeteria and an information booth with trail details outside the entrance. In and around the park, there are several trails, viewpoints and spots to grab a quick bite to eat. No serious mountaineering is required since the visitors center sits fairly close to the top of Volcán Irazú.

If you're looking for a leisurely but rewarding adventure, the **Craters Sector Loop** is a moderately easy 2km trail that yields views of the five craters, although occasionally you'll have to contend with a bit of fog depending on the weather conditions. The **Micaela Trail** is somewhat less spectacular but more introspective and private, with a chance to connect with Irazú's flora and fauna over the course of a 1.6km loop. This hike has a 132m elevation gain, so it's a tougher option.

Places We Love to Stay

$ Budget $$ Midrange $$$ Top end

Alajuela

MAP p105

Alajuela Backpackers Costa Rica $ Choose between dorms, private rooms and junior suites at this welcoming hostel. Airport shuttles available.

Alajuela City Hotel & Guest House $ Centrally located guesthouse with bright colorful rooms and a charming boho vibe.

Hildas Bed & Breakfast $ Slightly off the main square, this place is pet-friendly, serves good breakfast and has very nice staff.

Villa Garita Inn $ Family-friendly spot with stunning views, a fantastic swimming pool and clean rooms at a reasonable price.

Hotel Alajuela Costa Rica Airport $$ In the city center but 10 minutes from the airport, with traditional breakfasts included and good wi-fi.

Lagunillas del Poas $$ Spartan but sophisticated rooms with excellent views of the mountains; it's very close to Volcán Poás.

Rancho Amalia Lodge $$ Family-friendly, rustic-chic lodge with an excellent restaurant and a network of trails to explore.

La Finca Azul $$ Ecofriendly lodge tucked away in nature, with solar-heated water and a peaceful vibe.

Xandari Resorts $$$ Posh villas set in beautiful grounds with trails and waterfalls to explore nearby.

El Silencio Lodge & Spa $$$ Elegant jungle spa with lovely villas, outdoor hot tubs and incredible sunrises over the forest canopy.

Cartago

MAP p114

Casa Mora B&B $ Located near the central market and bus station, offering comfortable beds and good breakfasts.

La Casa de Mama Coyita $ Charming rooms and beautiful common spaces with plenty of places to sit among the plants.

El Guarco Hotel & Restaurante $ Modern, clean rooms, an on-site restaurant and a concierge who can help you find local tours.

Grandpas Hotel & Restaurant $ Individual cabins with reasonable prices in well-maintained and lovely grounds, plus a restaurant.

Glamping Campo Alegre $ Cozy triangular wooden cabins with big skylights; a good choice for couples.

Escapadita al Bosque $ Fun, communal glamping and more rustic camping options south of Cartago, with alfresco dining and trails nearby.

Navarro Mountain Dream Renewed $ Eclectic rooms with a family-friendly atmosphere and a gorgeous garden perfect for a morning coffee.

Secret Garden Cabañas Turísticas $$ Adorable individual cabins with an amazing view of the mountains. There's parking on-site.

Casa Lia $$ Nice B&B with excellent sunset views and a firepit outside for some evening stargazing.

Orosí Valley

MAP p123

Montaña Linda Hostel $ Funky hostel with single rooms, comfortable beds and some cute cats and dogs running around.

Casa Bartzis $$ Family-friendly two-bedroom house close to Orosi, with good wi-fi. Wheelchair-accessible.

Hotel Tapanti Media de Orosí $$ Centrally located hotel with balconies perfect for your morning coffee, clean rooms and a peaceful ambiance.

Hotel Rinconcito Verde $$ Ecofriendly hotel with bright, colorful rooms and great views. Enjoy an outdoor pool and good breakfasts. Good for families.

Casa del Lago $$ Spacious rooms, plenty of privacy and phenomenal views of Lago de Cachí, with good dining opportunities nearby.

Turrialba

MAP p131

Boutique Hotel Casa de Lis $ Cheap and cheerful hostel with a lovely garden, bright rooms and a nice common area.

Casitas Eco Bambú $ Quirky eco-hotel set on the edge of town, and a good base for hiking adventures.

Turrialba Bed & Breakfast $$ Beautifully decorated unique rooms in a classic B&B with free breakfast, fast wi-fi and a hot tub.

For places to stay on the Caribbean Coast, see p174

SIMON DANNHAUER/SHUTTERSTOCK

Above: Beach, Puerto Viejo de Talamanca (p163); Right: Turtle, Parque Nacional Tortuguero (p145)

Researched by
Anna Kaminski

Caribbean Coast

JUNGLE BEACHES, SPICY FOODS, DIVERSE CULTURES

From beach-hopping bike rides and rainforest hikes, to chocolate-making and white-water rafting, the Caribbean coast is the ultimate antidepressant.

For much of its history, the Caribbean was the coast less traveled, and home to some of Costa Rica's most distinctive cultures. Indigenous groups that held strong against the Spanish in the 1500s still follow the old ways in the Cordillera de Talamanca, and when Afro-Caribbean immigrant laborers were confined to this coast through the mid-1900s, they put down roots. Few leisure travelers set foot in the Caribbean before the turn of the 21st century, despite it featuring some of the country's prettiest beaches, wildest jungles and most alluring river.

KENCANNING/GETTY IMAGES

Now the secret is out, and the reasons to visit this rapidly changing coastline are multiplying. There's a 280km through-hike that connects the Caribbean to the Pacific, cultural centers in Puerto Limón and Puerto Viejo, and ongoing conservation efforts to keep turtle populations stable in Tortuguero, where nesting turtles and hatchlings crawling toward the sea draw nature-loving visitors.

To accommodate an increase in visitation, Hwy 32 from the capital to the Caribbean has been undergoing a years-long widening project – at the time of research it was slated to be completed before the end of 2025. All but the most isolated settlements are expanding – economically and physically – as the region's rich traditions and flavorful cuisine, adrenaline-spiking outdoor adventures and abundant wildlife take the spotlight. Whether the Caribbean can withstand higher visitor numbers and manage to protect its fragile ecosystems remains to be seen.

THE MAIN AREAS

TORTUGUERO
Wetland canals and turtle-dotted beaches. p142

PUERTO LIMÓN
History-laden port city. p149

CAHUITA
A Caribbean village frozen in time. p157

PUERTO VIEJO DE TALAMANCA
Burgeoning surf and party town. p163

Tortuguero, p142
An unspoiled canal system and marine park that protects sea turtles beside an eponymous village with lots of Afro-Caribbean charm.

CAR

The easiest way to get around the Caribbean is to have your own car: a high-clearance 4WD is necessary to explore inland or visit some of the indigenous communities. Parts of Hwy 32 within Parque Nacional Braulio Carrillo wash out during heavy rains.

BUS

Hop on any of the regular buses from San José to just about anywhere in the Caribbean (you'll need a bus/boat combo to reach Tortuguero and Parismina). Buses also connect most towns along the coast, from Sixaola, on the Panamanian border, to Puerto Limón.

BOAT & PLANE

Flights connect Puerto Limón to San José and Tortuguero daily. Tortuguero is reachable by bus from San José, then scheduled boat from La Pavona, or by private boat from Moín. For Parismina: bus to Siquirres from San José, then boat from Caño Blanco (or Moín).

Find Your Way

The Caribbean coast stretches for 200km. Puerto Limón is in the center, with Parque Nacional Tortuguero to the north. To the south, mesmerizing beaches, inland jungles and indigenous mountain territories are ripe for exploration.

Caribbean Sea

Puerto Limón, p149

A hardworking port, this provincial capital connects visitors with the history of Costa Rica and spicy Caribbean cuisine.

Cahuita, p157

With dirt roads, colorful homes on stilts and neighbors chatting in Mekatelyu, this seaside Caribbean village appears frozen in time.

Puerto Viejo de Talamanca, p163

This surfing and party town features stylish restaurants and vibrant nightlife, and is the gateway to the region's loveliest beaches.

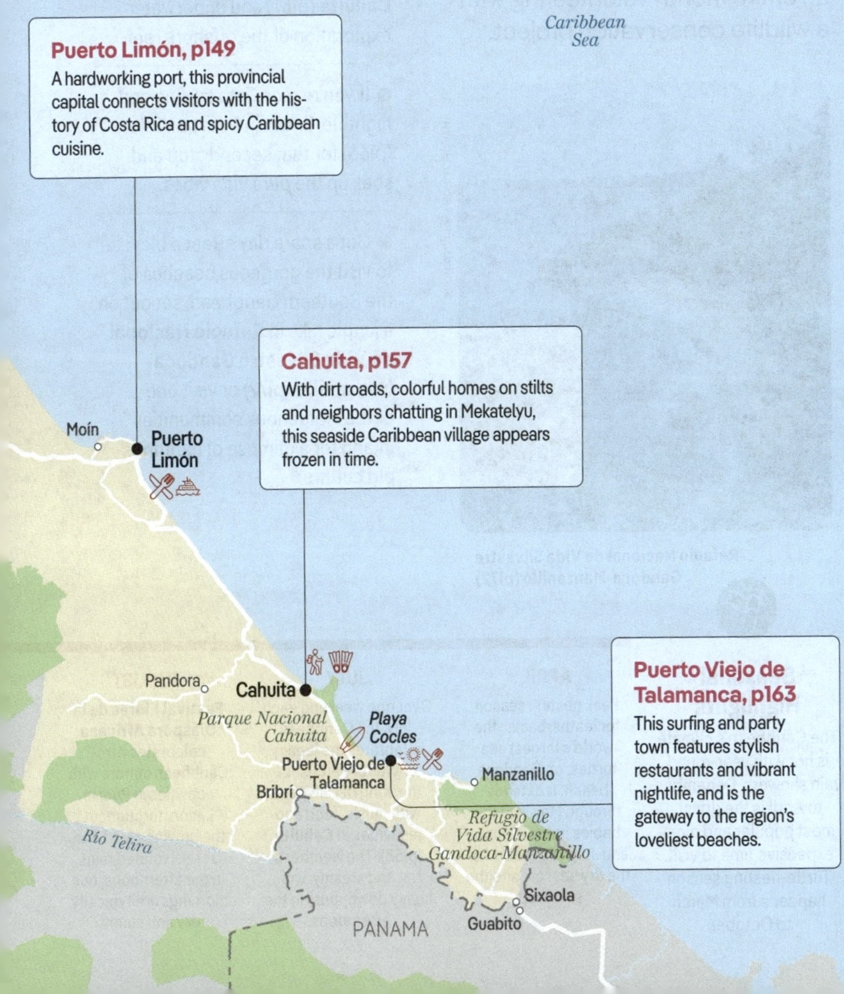

Moín
Puerto Limón
Pandora
Cahuita
Parque Nacional Cahuita
Playa Cocles
Puerto Viejo de Talamanca
Manzanillo
Bribrí
Río Telira
Refugio de Vida Silvestre Gandoca-Manzanillo
Sixaola
Guabito
PANAMA

Plan Your Time

The Caribbean is a choose-your-own-adventure kind of place. Spend days white-water rafting and jungle trekking, a week relaxing on assorted beaches, or an entire month volunteering with a wildlife conservation project.

MAREIKE WIELENS/SHUTTERSTOCK

Refugio Nacional de Vida Silvestre Gandoca-Manzanillo (p172)

Pressed for Time

- Shame on you for rushing through the super-chill Caribbean, but here's a quickie that hits the highlights. For an adrenaline-fueled introduction to the region's natural environs, raft **Río Pacuare** (p154) on your way east, then continue down to **Cahuita** (p158) for some jungle hiking in the adjacent **Parque Nacional Cahuita** (p157) and underwater exploration of the offshore reef.

- If you're more into surfing and nightlife, linger in **Puerto Viejo** (p163) for that second stop and soak up the *pura vida* vibes.

- Got a spare day? Rent a bicycle to visit the gorgeous beaches of the Southern Caribbean, set out on a jungle hike in **Refugio Nacional de Vida Silvestre Gandoca-Manzanillo** (p172) or visit one of the indigenous communities inland for a glimpse of centuries-old culture.

Seasonal Highlights

The Caribbean's climate is hot with year-round rain showers. December to April is the driest, most popular and most expensive time to visit. Turtle-nesting season happens from March to October.

APRIL

Peak nesting season for leatherbacks, the world's largest sea turtles, on Gandoca beach. It extends through May, and the babies hatch in June and July. It's the end of the dry season, and the surf is up.

JULY

Over one weekend each July, the Caribbean celebrates the legacy of Walter Ferguson, the 'King of Calypso,' with music, food and festivities in **Cahuita** (p158). The weather's hot and steamy, with heavy downpours in the afternoons.

AUGUST

Festival Flores de la Diáspora Africana celebrates Afro-Caribbean culture with activities in Puerto Limón, throughout the province (and San José). Isolated rains in the afternoons, but mornings are typically dry and sunny.

A Weeklong Stay

● Spend even more beach time in the southern Caribbean. Take a surf lesson, visit a wildlife conservation project or two, take a boat trip to the remote settlement of **Gandoca** (p173) and sign up for a walking and eating tour in **Puerto Viejo** (p163).

● If you really want to get adventurous, ascend a 25m-tall tree at **Nature Observatorio** (p169). On your way north, pop into **Puerto Limón** (p149) for a walk around its historical Old Town or the Quiribrí island adventure, and feast on delicious Caribbean cuisine.

● Then zip through the canals up to **Tortuguero** (p142), where you can spot wildlife from boats by day and go out in the evening with a guide to observe the timeless spectacle of nesting sea turtles.

If You Have More Time

● On top of the previous itineraries, be sure to add a trip to the further-flung **Laguna 4** (p148) to cruise coffee-colored canals and learn about local agriculture while staying in **Tortuguero** (p142).

● Then visit some little-explored villages along **El Camino de Costa Rica** (p147), a 280km through-hike that traverses national parkland, indigenous reserves, mountain ranges and fruit farms, ending at the Pacific Ocean.

● If you start in **Parismina** (p146), check out its wonderful turtle conservation project, and after you hike the trail in the incredibly biodiverse **Parque Nacional Barbilla** (p155), do a farmstay and learn about local indigenous culture. En route to San José, hike in the **Parque Nacional Braulio Carrillo** (p153), or stay deep in the jungle at **La Danta Salvaje** (p154).

SEPTEMBER

Barra del Colorado (p148) gears up for the tarpon- and snook-fishing season, which lasts three months. A mini dry season means calm waters are ideal for snorkeling and accommodations are cheaper than in summer.

OCTOBER

Carnival-style party for **Día de la Raza** (p151) in Puerto Limón. Tortuguero's **wild boat parade** (p142) signals the end of turtle-nesting season. One of the driest, cheapest and quietest months along the Caribbean coast.

NOVEMBER

Millions of vultures, hawks and other raptors flood the sky during the annual migration between North and South America (beginning in October). The rainy season begins and the surfing season kicks off.

DECEMBER

Surfers descend when the biggest swells start to hit the Caribbean coast. They last through March! There's some rain most days, with occasional all-day thunderstorms, so snorkeling and scuba diving are less good.

Tortuguero

WILDLIFE | NATURE | CULTURE

GETTING AROUND

From San José, you can reach Tortuguero by air or all-inclusive bus-boat shuttles. Budget travelers can save money by taking a bus from San José to Cariari (two hours), then another to La Pavona (one hour), followed by a scheduled boat at 1pm or 4:30pm. From the southern Caribbean, your best bets are with private boat operators from Moín or shuttle deals from Cahuita and Puerto Viejo. Once in Tortuguero, private and public water taxis are the only way to get around, and are easy to come by.

TOP TIP

Not all tour guides in Parque Nacional Tortuguero are certified or knowledgeable about the wildlife. Hire guides certified by the Asociación de Guías de Tortuguero who offer tours in English, Spanish and French.

Referring both to a popular national park created in 1970 and the eponymous village in the north-eastern corner of Costa Rica, Tortuguero translates to 'Land of the Turtles.' This is one of the world's most important nesting beaches for green turtles, along with leatherback and hawksbill turtles, and the birthplace of the turtle conservation movement.

In the early 20th century, Afro-Caribbeans settled the remote coastal region, and its waterways became arteries for boat traffic. International logging projects and hunting commenced, threatening the region's rainforests and nearly wiping out (mainly) green turtles. In the 1950s, a US turtle researcher created a landmark project to study and protect turtles, and villagers began to see how ecotourism could sustain them.

Drowning in bougainvillea, wisteria and oleander, the cluster of zinc-roofed wooden houses that sits on a thin sliver of land between the Tortuguero Canal and the ocean is welcoming visitors again, post-pandemic.

A Miracle of Nature

Turtle-spotting in the wild

Few experiences in nature rival the astonishing show that is turtle reproduction, and Tortuguero is one of the best places in the world to witness the spectacle. Four of the world's seven species of sea turtle frequent Tortuguero's beaches to lay their eggs, and visitors can observe both turtle nesting and – if extremely lucky – boils (explosions of recently hatched baby turtles from under the sand). The season stretches from June to October, when guided tours take place every night and cost US$35 to US$40 per person. In October, the end of turtle-nesting season is marked by Tortuguero's **wild boat parade**.

Guides collect their clients from Tortuguero's main dock in the evening before taking a jungle path that runs parallel to the beach. Upon arrival at a predetermined shelter site, they dispense turtle-related factoids while a few designated spotters comb the beach.

SIGHTS
1 Parque Nacional Tortuguero

ACTIVITIES
2 Casa Cecropia
3 Castor Hunter Thomas
4 Tortuguero Nature Native Guides

SLEEPING
5 Aracari Garden Hostel
6 Casa Marbella
7 El Icaco
8 Miss Junie's Lodge

EATING
9 Budda Cafe
10 Cocoman
11 Dorling Bakery
12 El Patio
13 Kame Sushi
14 Mi Niño
15 Soda D'Leite
16 Taylor's Place

INFORMATION
17 Cuatro Esquinas

This precautionary measure protects turtles coming ashore from becoming alarmed by hordes of waiting tourists (which will cause them to return to the ocean and dump their eggs). It can take upwards of an hour for the spotters to find a turtle and relay the location via radio. While sightings are not guaranteed, most visitors (particularly in the summer months) are rewarded for their patience.

Once a turtle has finished building her nest and started laying eggs, guides escort visitors to the beach assisted by the glow of infrared light, which turtles are unable to see (and therefore cannot be spooked by). Flashlights and cameras (including cell-phone cameras) are not allowed on the beach, and everyone must wear dark clothing. The waiting culminates with an opportunity to watch a turtle lay somewhere between 80 and 120 eggs, cover the nest and return to the ocean.

Incubation ranges from 45 to 70 days, after which palm-sized hatchlings break out of their shell and crawl to the ocean, moving as quickly as possible to avoid dehydration and predators. Once they reach the surf, they swim for at least 24 hours to get to deeper water. A turtle hatchling has a one in 1000 chance of surviving to adulthood and the females among them will return to nest on the very same beach.

TORTUGUERO'S BEST TOURS

Tinamon Tours: Zoologist and longtime Tortuguero resident Barbara Hartung and her team offer hiking, canoeing, culture and turtle tours.

Riverboat Francesca: These wildlife-viewing boat tours through the national park come highly recommended.

Tortuguero Nature Native Guides: Engaging family tours from knowledgeable guide Jungle Jon, who has an excellent eye for spotting wildlife.

Castor Hunter Thomas: Excellent local naturalist guide, who's been leading hikes, turtle tours and canoe tours for over 30 years.

Casa Cecropia: Biologist and naturalist Rafael specializes in cacao-farm tours. Also offers turtle-watching, ascents of Cerro de Tortuguero and more.

SALVADOR AZNAR/SHUTTERSTOCK

Boat tour, Canales de Tortuguero

Cruising Tortuguero's Canals

Wildlife-spotting along waterways

Waterborne excursions along the jungle-shrouded **Canales de Tortuguero** are the highlight of this incredible national park. These canals were built in 1974 to connect a series of lagoons and meandering rivers, and this engineering marvel allowed inland navigation between Limón and coastal villages in boats sturdier than a dugout canoe. Today, the variety and quantity of wildlife spotted as you glide quietly through the lowland tropical rainforest in a canoe, kayak or silent electric-motor boat is truly remarkable: this region is inhabited by 405 bird, 125 mammal, and 124 reptile and amphibian species.

Book a reputable guide in advance. It costs US$30 to US$40 for a three-hour tour, plus an admission fee to enter the park (US$15). Book online *(serviciosenlinea.sinac.go.cr),* which entitles you to a code that you'll share with your guide. On the morning of your tour, meet your guide at the main dock and travel by watercraft to the **Cuatro Esquinas** park office, where the guide will check you in.

From the ranger station, you'll paddle or motor down Río Tortuguero, a wide, brackish river that acts as an entrance to a network of aquatic trails. It's likely to be covered in water lilies, where waders such as herons, kingfishers and jacanas stalk insects and small fish. Look up: three species of monkeys –

EATING IN TORTUGUERO: OUR PICKS

Taylor's Place: Tortuguero's smartest restaurant in a garden setting; try beef in tamarind sauce or grilled shrimp in garlic sauce. *6-9pm* $$

El Patio: Buzzy 2nd-story restaurant overlooking the canal and serving up Caribbean and international favorites. *11am-9pm* $$

Budda Café: Trendy cafe with Tibetan prayer flags, ambient house music and river view. Delicious international food. *12:30-9pm* $$

Mi Niño: Coastal specialties such as garlic shrimp meet chicken fajitas and vegetarian pastas at this family-run spot. *8am-9pm* $$

howler, white-faced capuchin and spider – may be dangling in the trees alongside two- and three-toed sloths, while oversized iguanas and lanky basilisk lizards sunbathe on tree branches.

Soon you'll reach the entrances for Caño Chiquero and Canõ Mora, two narrower waterways where only kayaks, canoes and silent electric boats are allowed. **Caño Chiquero** is thick with vegetation, especially red *guacimo* trees and epiphytes. **Caño Mora** is about 3km long but only 10m wide and shaded by overhead trees. Meanwhile, **Caño Harold**, an artificially constructed canal that allows motorboats, is nonetheless inhabited by caimans and neotropical otters. Harder to spot are the timid West Indian manatees, which sometimes swim into the canals looking for food, and big cats, such as the mostly nocturnal jaguars and ocelots.

TURTLES ON THE PACIFIC COAST

Across Costa Rica, there are numerous turtle-watching and volunteering options up and down the Pacific coast. Check out recommended programs in **Playa Ostional** (p293), **Playa Grande** (p283) and the **Osa Peninsula** (p364).

Hiking Tortuguero's Jungle Paths

Trails in Parque Nacional Tortuguero

There are two sanctioned hikes within the vicinity of **Parque Nacional Tortuguero** *(sinac.go.cr/en-us/pages/default.aspx)*, both of which can be explored with a guide (from US$40) or without. While it may be tempting to wander the jungle on your own, it can be very rewarding to be accompanied by someone who knows how to spot local wildlife.

Behind Cuatro Esquinas ranger station, the well-trodden **Jaguar Trail** is a 2.5km linear hike that traverses the tropical humid forest and parallels a stretch of beach. Green parrots, monkeys and sloths are commonly sighted in the treetops, while leafcutter ants, poison dart frogs and butterflies march, hop and flit around the forest floor. The short trail is well marked, and when it's raining, you can rent rubber boots from a hotel near the park entrance.

A second hiking option, **Cerro Tortuguero Trail**, offers a moderately challenging hike along a plank-covered walkway, followed by 480 steps up to the summit (119m) of an inactive volcano – the highest point on the Caribbean coast – with panoramic views of the lagoon, village and coastline. Pay the entrance fee online *(serviciosenlinea.sinac.go.cr; US$2.26)*, and arrange for transport to the trailhead via a 15-minute boat to the town of **San Francisco**, north of Tortuguero, where you'll disembark at a ranger station.

PROTECTING THE TURTLES

In 1955, US sea-turtle expert Archie Carr started tagging sea turtles in Tortuguero. Sea-turtle populations were in decline worldwide, partly because of habitat destruction. In 1959, Carr founded the Sea Turtle Conservancy to help save sea turtles from extinction via scientific research, and the first-of-its-kind program has been monitoring turtle populations in Tortuguero ever since.

Today, green-turtle numbers seem stable along this coast, but leatherback, hawksbill and loggerhead are declining, largely due to poaching (locals may legally consume two turtles per week during nesting season).

EATING IN TORTUGUERO: OUR PICKS

Soda D'Leite: Pancakes, rice and beans with plantain, and fried chicken are all well-presented. *7am-9pm Wed-Mon* $

Kame Sushi: The chef serves handmade sushi rolls and *gyoza* dumplings to a soundtrack of chilled music. *5-10pm Sun-Fri* $$

Cocoman: Grab a beef patty alongside a coconut-based One Love cocktail at this colorful stand. *9am-9pm Mon-Fri, noon-5pm Sat & Sun* $

Dorling Bakery: A go-to for early-morning coffee and baked goods before a canal tour. Hardworking, friendly owners. *5am-6pm* $

Beyond Tortuguero

For a sense of what Costa Rica's Caribbean coast was like prior to mass tourism, head to these far-flung, seldom-visited destinations.

Places

The canal system surrounding Tortuguero is a liquid highway (complete with road signs!), connecting Costa Rica's wettest, most secluded coastal areas. You'll find diminutive villages and slick sportfishing camps, all-inclusive resorts and wildlife volunteer programs. An hour south of Tortuguero by boat, the sleepy fishing hamlet of Parismina and its long-standing turtle-conservation project monitors sea-turtle populations, while a bit further south Reserva Pacuare protects 8 sq km of tropical forest and a crucial nesting beach for endangered leatherbacks. These two lesser-visited destinations are now starting points for El Camino de Costa Rica, a 280km hike from the Caribbean to the Pacific that opened in 2018 but remains relatively lightly trodden.

GETTING AROUND

Running north–south, a canal system connects Reserva Pacuare, Parismina (both south of Tortuguero) and Barra del Colorado (north of Tortuguero) to each other and all of the common jumping-off points, including Moín, Caño Blanco and La Pavona. From Moín, there are private boats, while Caño Blanco (reachable by bus from San José or Limón; change in Siquirres) has scheduled boats to Parismina. Water taxis from Tortuguero abound.

Parismina

TIME FROM TORTUGUERO: 1 HR

Volunteering with turtles

There are many opportunities to help protect nesting sea turtles on the Caribbean coast, and grassroots **Asociación Salvemos Las Tortugas de Parismina** *(ASTOP; sustainablevision.org/astop.html)* is a particularly rewarding option.

ASTOP is based in **Parismina**, a coastal fishing village wedged between the Canales de Tortuguero and the Caribbean Sea and reachable only by boat. There isn't much gainful employment in the area, so ASTOP hires former poachers as turtle guides.

The group also maintains a turtle hatchery on a 6km section of beach. Volunteers help guard the hatchery and patrol the shoreline alongside the turtle guides. Depending on the time of year, they may also help with nest excavation, collecting data and hatchery building, or pitch in with community projects, such as home improvements, gardening and workshops with children.

Volunteers pay a one-time US$65 registration fee, and have to make their own way to Parismina, either by taking a private Tortuguero-bound boat from Moín and asking to be dropped off in Parismina en route, or by taking one of the scheduled daily boats from Caño Blanco (reachable by bus from Siquirres). Accommodations may be arranged ahead of time with the help of the useful Parismina website *(parismina.com)*,

Asociación Salvemos Las Tortugas de Parismina

whether it's a homestay (US$45 per night) with meals included or a village fishing lodge or basic hotel.

A handful of *sodas* (places that serve counter lunches) sprinkled around town serve *ceviche* (marinated seafood), tacos and other favorites, while a 3km hike south (or a short boat ride down the canal) brings visitors to the generator-powered **Green Gold Ecolodge** (p174), whose bilingual owners offer tours of their vanilla plantation. ASTOP volunteers may also participate in horseback riding and wildlife-viewing boat trips.

Hiking the Camino de Costa Rica

One of Costa Rica's most exciting outdoor adventures is **El Camino de Costa Rica** *(caminodecostarica.org),* a 280km coast-to-coast hike. Years of development work by nonprofit Mar a Mar went into creating this trail, which is divided into 16 stages. It begins on the turtle-dotted beaches of the Caribbean – either in Parismina or Reserva Pacuare (both of which are about an hour's boat trip from Tortuguero). At the shoreline, hikers visit a concrete marker indicating the start of the journey, then board a small boat and zip through the canals to **Muelle de Goschen**, where a challenging day lies ahead.

Over the first 25km, hikers experience the defining landscapes of the Caribbean: banana plantations and factories, pineapple farms, rural countryside, train tracks and trestles and clapboard homes on stilts. There's a cozy homestay option in the 200-person lowland village of **Cimarrones**, and from there hikers continue west through valleys and tropical forests, over mountain ranges and alongside volcanoes, and into indigenous territories and coffee plantations, making stops in a total of 16 rural communities (with lodgings available in each) before a triumphant finish in **Quepos** (p337) on the Pacific coast. The idea is to showcase regions of Costa Rica that have never received tourists before, and stimulate their economies. In experiencing the heartlands of Costa Rica, though, visitors are certain to benefit just as much, if not more.

BEST TURTLE CONSERVATION PROJECTS

Turtle Love: A team of biologists working south of the Pacuare river mouth to monitor 5km of nesting beach for green, leatherback and hawksbill turtles.

Ecology Project International: Offers volunteer opportunities on a turtle-protection project in Reserva Pacuare, along with gap-year wildlife programs.

Canadian Organization for Tropical Education & Rainforest Conservation: Nonprofit operating the Estación Biológica Caño Palma, 8km north of Tortuguero village.

Sea Turtle Conservancy: At Tortuguero's north end, the original turtle-conservation organization has a research station, visitors center and museum.

FISHING IN THE NORTHERN CARIBBEAN

Some 27km north of Tortuguero, the hard-to-access 912-sq-km **Barra del Colorado** is Costa Rica's biggest national wildlife refuge; its marshes, mangroves and lagoons, bisected by the San Juan, Colorado and Chirripó rivers, have long been a favorite of sportfishers. You can catch bass from September to December, while January to June is the best time to fish for tarpon and snook in the Río Colorado.

Visitors tend to opt for all-inclusive fishing packages in lodges around Barra, a logging village and the area's only settlement. Lodges here arrange 'catch and release' excursions for fish, including bluegill and rainbow bass in the rivers, or marlin, sailfish and tuna out at sea.

URRITREK/WIKIMEDIA/CC BY-SA 4.0

El Camino de Costa Rica (p147)

The trail can be hiked with or without a guide. Recommended companies include **UrriTrek** *(urritrekcostarica.com)*, **Walk CR** *(walkcr.com)* and **Ticos A Pata** *(ticosapata.com)*. If you're looking to tackle the trail without a guide, contact **Mar a Mar** *(WhatsApp on 6036-6199)* before setting off. For a short stretch of the trail, a local indigenous guide is required, and can be hired on-site.

Laguna 4

TIME FROM TORTUGUERO: 1 HOUR

Cruising to a remote farm

Living around Parque Nacional Tortuguero, locals support themselves with agriculture, and a half-day trip from Tortuguero connects visitors with one of these rural operations: **Laguna 4**. About an hour's boat ride away, the secluded cattle ranch and produce farm creates dairy products and harvests coconuts, lemongrass, cassava, taro, breadfruit and more. Several of the lodges north of the village offer this excursion.

You're picked up by boat at the main dock and then cruise up **Penitencia Canal** to **Caño Palma**. Surrounded by dense jungle, this canal draws its coffee-like color from tannins in the water. After spotting birds, lizards and monkeys, the tour continues along a narrow private canal to the **farm** run by Don Coco and Doña Katherine.

For more than a decade, they've been living off the land in this rural, isolated region, though both have previous experience working in Tortuguero's hotels and a keen interest in sharing their way of life with visitors. After a presentation on how they create products such as coconut oil, milk and cheese, the couple prepare a traditional meal over a wood stove. Together, guests drink fresh coconut milk and feast on fresh fruit, rice, beans, fish and whatever else might be available. There's also some time for lazing around in hammocks on the expansive farm and strolling the beach.

Puerto Limón

CULTURE | FOOD | ARCHITECTURE

The capital of Limón Province, Puerto Limón is the largest settlement on Costa Rica's Caribbean coast, with the country's largest Afro-Caribbean population. Cruise-ship passengers aside, this busy port attracts few visitors (besides transient ones, catching either a boat to Turtuguero or a bus further south), but Limón's historic significance and distinctive cultural heritage are worth your time.

In the late 1800s, thousands of Jamaicans, Trinidadians and Bajans arrived in Limón to work on the railroad between the Caribbean and San José, turbocharging the nation's fledgling economy, yet denied voting rights and forbidden from traveling freely until 1949. An independent culture emerged, with its own musical and gastronomic traditions. Today, you'll find a town slightly down-at-heel, with Jamaican dancehall, reggaetón and salsa blaring from bars, and locals of Jamaican descent conversing in a creole called Mekatelyu. Party-loving travelers shouldn't miss October's Día de la Raza carnival or the Festival Flores de la Diáspora Africana in August.

GETTING AROUND

Cruise ships dock in Limón between October and May, but smaller passenger boats bound for Parismina and Tortuguero use the port at Moín, about 7km west of town. Buses from all points west arrive at **Terminal Caribeño**, just west of the baseball stadium. Buses to all points south depart from the Autotransportes Mepe Terminal, on the eastern side of the stadium. A small airport south of the city has direct flights to San José and Tortuguero; there is talk of expanding the airport for international arrivals.

Spice It Up

Sample Caribbean cuisine

Distinctive from that of the rest of Costa Rica, Caribbean cuisine is steeped in indigenous, Creole and Afro-Caribbean flavors, and Limón is a hotbed of restaurants specializing in this regional cuisine.

In Limón's **Old Town**, follow your nose to **Soda El Patty**, a beloved and long-standing restaurant, for savory or sweet *patí* (essentially a Caribbean *empanada*); spicy beef with potatoes is a classic. If the line is too long, locals recommend heading a couple of blocks east to **Taylor's**, where the *patí* is almost equally satisfying and there's also a full menu of delicious Caribbean fare. Alternatively, head up to the cafeteria-style counter at **Restaurante Kalisi** and request a plate of coconut rice, red beans and whatever meat and veggies are cooking. Miss Roena Brown's umami-rich, slow-cooked oxtail stew is immensely satisfying, and should

TOP TIP

Inspiring accommodations are not the city's strong suit. Set expectations low if staying in the city proper, base yourself on Playa Bonita (en route to Moín), or visit on a day trip.

SIGHTS
1 Escuela General Tomás Guardia
2 G&E Chocolate Adventure Company
3 Parque Vargas
4 Post Office
5 Sacred Heart Cathedral

EATING
6 Bay Park Limón
7 Lizzie 1879
8 Maestros Wine & Grill
9 Mercado Municipal
10 Red Snapper
11 Restaurante Kalisi
12 Soda El Patty
13 Soda Sazón Colombiano
14 Taylor's

DRINKING & NIGHTLIFE
15 Bar Don Juan
16 Sol Mar Cocktails
17 Tsunami Sushi

TRANSPORT
18 Terminal Caribeño

be washed down with a glass of sorrel (a Jamaican hibiscus-ginger drink), followed by a slab of chewy cassava pudding.

True to its name, **Red Snapper** restaurant serves delicious whole fried snapper and fried plantains from its mountainside perch just west of Jamaica town on Calle Los Miranda; the views are as good as the food. Out on Playa Piuta, a string of hip restaurants includes a favorite with a staunch local following, **Lizzie 1879**. The name is a nod to the first ship to bring Jamaicans to Costa Rica. The foliage-bedecked place is decorated with old photographs and local art. The best dishes here include fiery jerk chicken, oxtail stew and *sopa de mondongo* (diced tripe and vegetable soup); *rondón*, a seafood gumbo, is served on Sundays.

MEKATELYU: LIMÓN CREOLE

When in Limón, you'll be exposed to a unique creole that combines Spanish with English patois expressions that arrived with Jamaican, Trinidadian and Bajan workers. While Spanish is taught in school and young Limonenses are more likely to speak it among themselves than the older generations, English is still widely spoken at home.

Carnaval!

Costa Rica's biggest party

If you happen to be in Puerto Limón's **Parque Vargas** on the Saturday preceding October 12, you'll find yourself reverberating with the bass from giant sound systems set up nearby, while extravagantly costumed locals – all sequins, feathers and bright colors – parade through downtown's streets to the sounds of calypso, ear-piercing whistles and tambourines. This

DRINKING IN PUERTO LIMÓN: OUR PICKS

Tsunami Sushi: This downtown spot gets busy on Friday and Saturday nights, when ragga and reggaetón artists and DJs take the stage. *10am-1am*

Reina's: On the beach at Playa Bonita; loud reggaetón and salsa, good vibes, *mariscos* (seafood) and fruity cocktails. *9am-9pm*

Bar Don Juan: Nondescript from the outside, this downtown spot is great for mingling with locals while catching a live reggae or reggaetón set. *11am-2:30am*

Sol Mar Cocktails: Skip the food and go straight for the strong cocktails, paired with sea views. *11am-10pm*

is the Grand Desfile – the highlight of the **Día de la Raza** – Costa Rica's biggest party. Unlike its glitzier brethren in Rio de Janeiro and Trinidad's Port of Spain that are tied to Lent, this Carnaval celebrates the arrival of Cristóbal Colón (Christopher Columbus) in the New World (and specifically in Puerto Limón).

Columbus' controversial legacy notwithstanding, it's an excuse for a massive celebration, with Ticos arriving from elsewhere in the country for revelry fueled by loud, bilingual ragga sounds and street stalls serving heaped servings of Caribbean and Tico classics. Revelers of all ages are made to feel included, with fairgrounds and candy floss for the youngest.

A Wild Island Adventure

Sail to Quiribrí

In 1502, on his final voyage to the Americas, Columbus allegedly anchored near a small, craggy island off the coast of present day Limón and named it La Huerta (the orchard). Indigenous inhabitants were already calling it **Quiribrí**, and today that's the official name, but locals also refer to it as **Isla Uvita**. Whatever you call it, a tour of this 11-hectare island about 3km from Limón is not to be missed.

On your way to the island, you'll cruise past fishing huts, a coast guard station and several large docks, before crossing the bay and disembarking onto a concrete walkway at the south end of Isla Uvita, then wading through shallow water to reach the island. A hike through thick tropical vegetation brings you to the remains of an 1886 **hospital**, where people with incurable illnesses (leprosy, smallpox, tuberculosis etc) were sent and placed under the care of nuns. There's also a concrete **lookout** built by the US Army during WWII. Continuing around the island, you'll scale hills for views of coral colonies and tide pools below; look out for brown boobies (large seabirds related to gannets) nesting on a neighboring islet. There are also opportunities for diving, snorkeling, fishing and swimming around the island, while Isla Uvita's reef break is popular with Limonese surfers.

Since the island is part of the Limón municipality, anyone can visit. The boat trip from Limón takes about 15 minutes and can be arranged by tour guides **Adriana Casco** *(8511-3736)* or **Hilario Wolf** *(2758-7795)*. Private excursions start at US$50, and you can spend as much time on the island as you like. There's also a public boat from **Transporte Acuático Island Uvita Eco Tour** on Río Limoncito, which costs US$20 per person and runs several times daily, depending on demand.

BRIEF HISTORY OF SEGREGATION

In the late 19th century when Limón became a trade hub and key export point for bananas, Afro-Caribbean workers were forbidden from leaving the province. Jamaican-born Marcus Garvey worked for the United Fruit Company from 1910 to 1912; the racism and deplorable working conditions he experienced later fueled his work in New York as a political activist and spokesperson for African American rights. Laborers staged bloody strikes against United Fruit and provided key support to revolutionary José Figueres during the 1948 civil war. When Figueres became president, he granted Afro-Caribbeans citizenship and the right to work and travel throughout Costa Rica.

EATING IN PUERTO LIMÓN: OUR PICKS

Bay Park Limón: Seaside gastropark with a pool and zipline, and many mini-restaurants operating out of shipping containers. *noon-10pm* $

Taylor's (p149): Popular old-school diner specializing in Limonese classics such as red snapper with shrimp sauce and oxtail *casado*. *7:30am-8pm* $$

Soda Sazón Colombiano: *Arepas* (cornmeal cakes), rice and beans combos and *empanadas* are all on the menu at this friendly downtown cheapie. *6am-5pm* $

Maestros Wine & Grill: At downtown's most sophisticated restaurant, pair *burrata caprese* and excellent risotto with decent wines and house sangria. *11am-10pm* $$

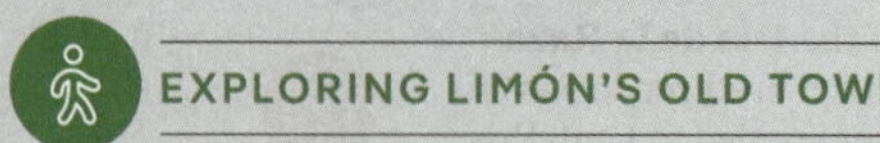

EXPLORING LIMÓN'S OLD TOWN

Take a stroll around Puerto Limón, and the historical significance of this port – along with new developments – will be revealed.

START	END	LENGTH
Parque Vargas	Taylor's	1.7km; 2 hrs

Begin at 1 **Parque Vargas**, a central green space commissioned by the United Fruit Company and opened in 1905. Royal palms shade an octagonal neoclassical gazebo surrounded by statues dedicated to those who built Limón's railroad, and to Columbus, who allegedly docked nearby. On the park's southwest side, and in front of the cruise terminal, is the 2 **G&E Chocolate Adventure Company**, a multifaceted business that sells inventive cacao products and offers cooking classes. The building once housed the United Fruit Company, where some of the most influential people in Central America worked in the early 1900s. A block north and another two west is Limón's 3 **Mercado Municipal**, constructed in 1893 and remodeled in 1941 – a chaotic, bustling market lined with mounds of locally grown fruit and vegetables, and numerous *sodas* in the interior serving inexpensive lunches. Catercorner from the market is the beautifully restored, 1911-built 4 **Post Office** – a fine example of 'Victorian Caribbean' architecture. A block west, admire the mint-green 5 **Escuela General Tomás Guardia**, an architecturally significant boys' school rebuilt in the 1940s, before heading north past 6 **Sacred Heart Cathedral**; its bell tower dates back to the 1890s and its stained-glass windows are striking. Finally, hit 7 **Taylor's** (p149) for *patí* (turnovers).

Opposite **Taylor's** is the charred facade of the Black Star Line building that once housed Marcus Garvey's Universal Negro Improvement Association (UNIA).

The new cruise-ship port south of **Parque Vargas** has improved the security situation in central Limón.

The **G&E Chocolate Adventure Company** includes a cultural center, art gallery and demonstration garden.

Beyond Puerto Limón

Little-explored jungles, an unusual wildlife sanctuary and the country's most extreme white-water rafting are awaiting your attention.

The road from San José to Limón is one wild ride: just east of the capital, Hwy 32 cuts directly through Parque Nacional Braulio Carrillo, an under-visited national park with towering trees, steep hills and yawning river canyons. The highway then snakes into the foothills of the Cordillera Central and through plantations to lowland Siquirres.

South of Siquirres lies one of the world's great rafting rivers, Río Pacuare, which winds its way for some 108km through primordial rainforest from the Cordillera de Talamanca to the Caribbean Sea, flowing through indigenous territories, some of which can be visited with a guide. Closer to Limón, the biologically diverse Parque Nacional Barbilla entices with its guided jungle trek.

Places

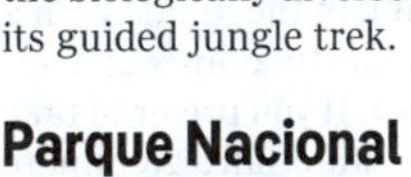

Parque Nacional Braulio Carrillo

TIME FROM PUERTO LIMÓN: 1¾ HRS

Hiking in a biodiverse wonderland

Encompassing jungle-clad hills, bisected by canyons with cascading rivers, cloud forest and lush, humid lowlands, plus the Barva and Cacho Negro volcanoes, the 500-sq-km **Parque Nacional Braulio Carrillo** *(sinac.go.cr/en-us/pages/default.aspx; adult/under-12 US$13.56/5.65)* is one of Costa Rica's largest and most biodiverse protected areas. Though mammals such as jaguars and ocelots are rarely sighted, you're quite likely to spot several species of monkeys, *tepezcuintle* (pacas, the park's mascot) and deer. Twitchers may want to bring their binoculars: toucans, hummingbirds and parrots are frequently seen here, while quetzals are found at higher elevations around **Volcán Barva**, Costa Rica's third-highest volcano.

The easiest way to access the park is via the **Quebrada González ranger station** *(8am-3pm)*, off Hwy 32, 45km north of San José and 114km west of Puerto Limón.

Of the three trails, the mostly flat, 1km-long **Sendero El Ceibo** passes a giant *ceibo* (cockspur coral) tree, a scenic overlook and other marked points of interest before looping back to the ranger station. The 2.5km-long **Sendero Botarrama** is a slightly more rugged spur trail (expect mud and exposed roots) that branches off Sendero El Ceibo and continues

GETTING AROUND

Frequent buses connect San José and Puerto Limón via Siquirres – the access point for Río Pacuare – but you can just as easily do rafting with a shuttle pick-up from your lodgings. To access Parque Nacional Barbilla and part of Parque Nacional Braulio Carrillo you need a 4WD, preferably a high clearance one. Landslides occur frequently when it's rainy in Braulio Carrillo, which can result in Hwy 32 closing for hours/days.

CHITO Y POCHO

On the outskirts of Siquirres, **Centro Turístico Las Tilapias** was once famous for an unusual attraction: the owner, Gilberto 'Chito' Shedden, performed stunts with Pocho, a 5m-long crocodile. Their unusual friendship was covered in the 2013 documentary, *Touching the Dragon.*

After Pocho died in 2011, Chito organized a funeral and preserved the reptile's body in a shrine. The Costa Rican government then outlawed crocodile training. The wildlife-teeming canals remain a great reason to stop by, particularly for anyone unable to visit Tortuguero. Chito and his daughter run boat tours and rent kayaks for fishing. There's also a lively restaurant-bar and some rustic cabinas perched above the canals.

another 1.5km to the junction of the crystal-clear Río Honduras with Río Sucio. Finally, the 1.6km, gravel-paved **Sendero Las Palmas** loop climbs gently into dense rainforest – prime territory for birdwatching.

A more strenuous outing involves summiting the 2906m Volcán Barva. To reach the trailhead at the **Barva Sector ranger station**, take the good paved road north from Heredia to Sacramento, and then an additional 4WD-only 3km stretch. From the ranger station, a 3km-long, signposted trail runs to the summit, with views of the crater lake. Shorter trails include the 1km-long **Mirador Vara Blanca** jaunt to a scenic lookout point and the birdlife-rich, 2km-long **Cacho de Venado** (Deer Cuckoo Trail).

A rustic jungle stay

If you've ever wanted to spend several days frolicking in the Costa Rican jungle, **La Danta Salvaje** *(ladantasalvaje.com)* is just the ticket. You'll drive a little over an hour east from Limón to reach **Guápiles** and meet up with your guide, who will bring you the rest of the way to a secret mountain location, a 410-hectare private rainforest reserve (altitude 800m) reached via a 45-minute 4WD trip and a three- to 3½-hour hike through the primary forest of Parque Nacional Braulio Carrillo. Rubber boots are provided and there are three river crossings en route, including one involving a cable ride.

You'll then sleep three nights in atmospheric cabins with no electricity (yes, it's a real ecolodge!) and share meals by candlelight. In the daytime, you'll go hiking in the jungle with a nature guide, splashing in waterfalls, spotting birds and animals and learning about the ecosystem. If you prefer to take it easier, there's a swimming hole with a waterfall a 25-minute walk away that you can do by yourself. Rates (US$400 per person) include transport from Guápiles, activities and meals. The owner's beef jerky is famous for a reason. Reserve ahead.

Río Pacuare

TIME FROM PUERTO LIMÓN: 1 HR

White-water thrills on Río Pacuare

Accessed from the town of **Siquirres**, 59km northwest of Puerto Limón, the mighty **Río Pacuare** is one of the world's top 10 rivers for white-water rafting. After ex-President Luis Guillermo Solís rafted the Pacuare, he signed a decree banning river dams until 2040. Yes, it's just that good. The 108km beast of a river plunges over Class III and IV rapids (and V in advanced areas) and is for many a traveler their highlight of the trip.

Imagine: you're floating on clear blue-gray waters through the lush jungle that lines the river canyon, waiting for the signal from your guide. White-water rapids churn ahead. 'Forward!' comes the shout, and you dig in with your oar and row with all your might, drenched in spray, as the raft pitches and rolls among the boulders and you come close to falling overboard. Then you're through, your heart beating wildly, laughing with relief...until the next patch of rapids, for three or four sweet hours.

There are two ways to tackle nature's rollercoaster: either via a day outing from San José or destinations along the

SAINTDAGS/SHUTTERSTOCK

Rafting, Río Pacuare

Caribbean coast with **Ríos Tropicales** *(tropicalrivers.com; US$110)* or **Exploradores Outdoors** *(exploradoresoutdoors.com; US$99)*, both of which have rafting bases near Siquirres, or as a multiday adventure, complete with a stay in one of the river lodges in the jungle. No prior experience is necessary, but the minimum age is 12.

More jungle adventures

If you want to combine adrenaline-packed rafting with jungle hikes, canyoning, ziplining, nocturnal wildlife-spotting hikes, spa treatments and immersion in the local Cabécar culture, opt for a stay at **Pacuare Lodge** *(pacuarelodge.com)*, one of Costa Rica's best accommodations, with its stylish, individually decorated suites and villas and an award-winning restaurant. **Ríos Lodge** *(rioslodge.com)* is a less expensive alternative, aimed at active travelers: river tubing, jungle hiking and horseback riding complement the river rafting, with excellent birdwatching opportunities to boot.

Further down the river, the **Ave Sol River Sanctuary** *(avesol.org)* is a remote, rustic retreat, built from sustainably harvested wood. It's actively involved in conservation and scientific study of this wildlife corridor that's essential to the survival of Costa Rica's jaguar. Rafting aside, you can go on nature walks with an experienced guide or interact with the lodge's Cabécar neighbors.

Parque Nacional Barbilla

TIME FROM PUERTO LIMÓN: 1½ **HRS**

Trekking a biodiverse trail

One of the most ancient and biologically diverse lowland rainforests in Costa Rica, the 119-sq-km **Parque Nacional Barbilla** *(sinac.go.cr/en-us/pages/default.aspx; US$5.65)* became a protected area in 1998 to support rare and endangered

BEST CARIBBEAN ADVENTURE PARKS

Veragua Rainforest Research & Adventure Park: Complex of elevated forest walkways, an aerial tram, reptile vivarium, insectarium, hummingbird and butterfly gardens.

Rainforest Adventures Braulio Carrillo: Take an aerial tram to the heights of the forest canopy, fly through the air on a zipline, go birdwatching, visit the orchid garden or take a frog night tour.

Pacuare Lodge: Deep in the jungle, this lodge arranges ziplining, canyoning, rafting, guided hikes, cultural experiences and more. Guests only.

Brisas de la Jungla: Smallish adventure park on the banks of the Río Blanco; its 10 ziplines include a particularly fast and exhilarating one.

THE TROUBLE WITH BANANAS

In the 19th-century, railroad baron Minor Keith hired immigrant laborers to build a railroad between San José and Limón. Keith grew bananas along the route to feed workers who managed to survive the arduous work. He carpeted much of the region in bananas and his company – United Fruit – became an economic giant and political puppet master. Today, Costa Rica is the third-largest exporter in the world of the problematic fruit. Because bananas are vulnerable to fungus, growers use an arsenal of chemicals harmful to the environment. Plantation workers face heightened risks of illnesses, including cancer, kidney disease and infertility. Some bananas are grown organically, for example, at Earth University in the Caribbean lowlands.

SAINTDAGS/SHUTTERSTOCK

Parque Nacional Barbilla (p155)

wildlife, including jaguars, ocelots and tapirs, along with the Cabécar people who inhabit the region, and the Dantas Watershed, a crucial source of drinking water.

A steep, 5.5km-long trail is open to the public for guided visits only; there's also a short, 330m-long trail for independent hikers. Visitors must make hiking reservations at least one day in advance; for an English-speaking guide, call a few days prior *(2200-5224)*. After a 17km ride south from Pacuarito (4WD only; a taxi from Siquirres costs US$30 to US$40), visitors arrive at the **ranger station** *(8am-4pm daily)* before noon to hike the longer trail, which takes around four hours to complete. Highlights include frequent wildlife sightings, three Río Danta crossings, two magnificent waterfalls and enlightening conversations with the Cabécar guides.

A Barbilla immersion

Barbilla Rainforest Lodge *(barbillarainforestlodge.com)* is an all-inclusive farmstay run by Swedish anthropologist Marine Hedström Rojas and her delightful family. Guests stay in the main house, an exquisite hardwood affair with five bedrooms and a wide terrace overlooking the rainforest, or a nearby three-bedroom cottage. You can opt for yoga and wildlife spotting, or else go horseback riding or hike a section of the long-distance **Camino de Costa Rica** that runs nearby.

The 60-hectare cattle farm has hosted scientists for decades, as Marine's father helped create Parque Nacional Barbilla. Over the years, she's befriended her neighbors, including the Cabécar people, learning their language, working to open better schools and writing children's textbooks. The inroads she's made allow her to build unique itineraries for guests: yucca harvesting and frying activities, guided waterfall hikes and other custom experiences with Cabécar families. Contact the lodge for accommodations and other rates.

Cahuita

WILDLIFE | BEACHES | SNORKELING

Tourism has exploded on Costa Rica's eastern coast, but compact Cahuita, some 45km south of Puerto Limón, has managed to retain the timeless, relaxed atmosphere of a bygone era. Bookended by two attractive beaches, Playa Blanca and Playa Negra, Cahuita is a quiet pocket of unpaved, palm-shaded streets lined with older homes on stilts, with locals (mostly descendants of Jamaican workers and settlers from Bocas del Toro in Panama) relaxing on their porches in the evenings and conversing with their neighbors in Mekatelyu.

Cahuita's most famous son, singer-songwriter Walter Ferguson (p158), moved here with his family in 1921 when his Jamaican father found work as a farmer with the United Fruit Company. Like many in the village, Ferguson's family now survives on tourism, owning a rental-cabin business.

With its handful of low-key restaurants, Cahuita remains an idyllic base for exploring Parque Nacional Cahuita and nearby beaches.

GETTING AROUND

If you stick around Cahuita, you can easily get by without a car, as there are frequent departures from the bus terminal on the main road to Puerto Limón (one hour), Puerto Viejo (30 minutes), San José (4½ hours) and Sixaola (1½ hours). But for travelers aiming to explore the area more deeply, a car is much more convenient. The best and most enjoyable way to get around Cahuita – especially if you're staying in Playa Negra – is on a beach cruiser; rent a bike (US$8 to US$12 per day) from **Mister Big J's** in Cahuita or **Brigitte's Ranch** in Playa Negra.

Small Park, Big Rewards

Hiking in Parque Nacional Cahuita

Easily walkable from town, 10-sq-km **Parque Nacional Cahuita** *(sinac.go.cr/en-us/pages/default.aspx; US$5.65)* comprises diverse habitats, including white-sand beach, coral reefs, coastal rainforest (primary and secondary) and mangrove swamp. The park (open 8am to 4pm) is bisected by a hiking trail that connects its two entrances, Playa Blanca and Puerto Vargas, off Hwy 36.

It's best to begin the hike at the **Playa Blanca** entrance, south of downtown Cahuita, next to the **Kelly Creek Hotel**. Once you sign a guest book and pay the entry fee, it's a good idea to hire an experienced guide at the ranger station to maximize your wildlife-sighting potential. Walk slowly along the first 1.5km between the entrance and Río Suarez. This stretch skirts the beach but also winds through the jungle,

TOP TIP

Tour operators can provide transport to further-flung experiences if you don't have your own wheels.

KING OF CALYPSO

One weekend each July Cahuita honors Walter Ferguson (1919–2023), aka the King of Calypso, with the eponymous **Walter Ferguson International Calypso Festival**. A musician of Jamaican-Costa Rican heritage, Ferguson invented the Costa Rican style of the calypso, which has been declared part of the national cultural heritage – you will often hear his music in local bars. During the festival, Cahuita comes alive with live bands and dancing, while the aroma of Caribbean cuisine wafts through the village.

HIGHLIGHTS
1 Playa Negra

SIGHTS
2 Parque Nacional Cahuita

ACTIVITIES
3 Cahuita Tours
4 Green Cahuita
5 Mister Big J's
6 Willie's Tours

SLEEPING
7 Alby Lodge
8 Casa Marcellino
9 El Encanto
10 Hakuna Matata Hostel
11 Kelly Creek Hotel

EATING
12 Aroma Coffee Bar
13 El Encanto
14 El Rincón del Amor
15 La Peruanita
16 Restaurante Pizzeria
17 Sobre Las Olas
18 Soda Kawe

DRINKING & NIGHTLIFE
19 Reggae Bar

and sloths, monkeys, eyelash pit vipers, coatis, raccoons and wetland birds are regularly spotted.

If you're up for a longer hike and are willing to get wet, cross Río Suarez and continue to Punta Cahuita. Inquire about conditions before you set out: this river is generally easy to wade across (particularly at low tide), but after heavy rains it can become impassable. Respect the red flag: it means that crossing is unsafe.

After the crossing, it's a further 2km to reach **Punta Cahuita**, where there are picnic tables and a coral reef just offshore. From here, you can turn back or continue 4.8km

EATING IN CAHUITA: OUR PICKS

La Peruanita: Authentic Peruvian dishes such as *ceviche, arroz chaufa* (fried rice) and *chicharrón de pescado* (fish crackling). *7am-9:30pm* $$

Sobre Las Olas: Delicious garlic shrimp and seafood pasta, accompanied by crashing waves and sparkling-blue Caribbean vistas. *1-9pm Thu-Tue* $$

Soda Kawe: With reasonably priced *gallo pinto* (rice and beans) and *casados* cooked over a fire, this humble place is always packed. *9am-7pm* $

Restaurante Pizzeria: Thin-crust pizzas fly out of the wood-fired oven at this Italian-run spot; the gnocchi is superb. *noon-9:30pm* $$

along a secluded beach to the **Puerto Vargas ranger station**. There isn't much shade, so make sure to hydrate. En route look out for roosting seabirds, sunning iguanas and shy hermit crabs.

Two trains lead to the park exit at the ranger station: a 2.3km beach trail, or the highly recommended **Cavitos Trail**, which is a 2.1km boardwalk path through lowland primary forest and mangrove habitat. Nature lovers often start at Puerto Vargas in the early morning and hike in the opposite direction to avoid crowds. The walk between Puerto Vargas and Cahuita is 3.5km along the coastal highway, but you can also catch one of the half-hourly buses in either direction; bring change in colones.

Under the Sea

Snorkeling in Parque Nacional Cahuita

Parque Nacional Cahuita (p157) includes a 224-sq-km marine protected area that contains one of the largest stretches of coral reef in Costa Rica – when the weather cooperates, **snorkel trips** in these waters are incredibly rewarding. Guides are mandatory for snorkeling the reef and half-day tours are offered by various operators (from US$40 per person). You might glimpse eels, sharks, stingrays or octopuses as well as large shoals of tropical fish. When you finish snorkeling, swim up on shore at Punta Cahuita. From here, hike back through the park, or return by boat.

BEST CAHUITA GUIDES

Cahuita Tours: Runs snorkeling trips, horseback riding, visits to indigenous reserves, rafting, birdwatching and hiking tours.

Brigitte's Ranch: Offers snorkeling, hiking, horseback riding on the beach, chocolate making and a *rondón* (seafood gumbo) cooking class, among other things.

Willie's Tours: Long-standing tour agency that provides guides for hiking and snorkeling the national park, and organizes visits to Bribrí villages.

Richard Robinson: Excellent wildlife guide who takes hikers/photographers on nature walks in Parque Nacional Cahuita and beyond.

Green Cahuita: Ludrick McLoud's team offer nature walks in Parque Nacional Cahuita, snorkeling trips, night hikes, birdwatching tours and waterfall jaunts.

EATING & DRINKING IN CAHUITA: OUR PICKS

El Rincón del Amor: Come for the herb-encrusted grilled snapper or grilled lobster with rice and beans, and stay for the friendly vibe. *11am-9:30pm Thu-Tue* $$

Aroma Coffee Bar: Excellent coffee, towering veggie burgers and all-day breakfasts await the hungry. *8am-6pm Fri-Wed* $$

El Encanto: Romance your sweetie at this elegant garden restaurant that serves international-Caribbean fusion and cocktails. *2:30-9:30pm* $$$

Reggae Bar: The place to be on Friday nights, with live reggae, calypso and DJ performances fueled by copious Red Stripes. *noon-11pm*

Beyond Cahuita

Hike to secluded waterfalls, learn the ways of indigenous tribes and birdwatch in the foothills of the Cordillera de Talamanca.

Places

There are only a handful of reasons to venture inland from Cahuita, but they're all good ones. The drive west on curvy Hwy 36 to Bribrí territory has turnoffs to waterfalls, which make for refreshing stops on day trips out to indigenous villages and cacao farms. You'll also likely pass through the town of Bribrí, a bustling agricultural center.

Heading northwest of Cahuita, drive through the small settlements of Penshurt, San Clemente and Bananito Sur and cross two rivers (4WD only) before reaching Selva Bananito. At the foot of Cerro Muchito, this 12-sq-km family-run farm has spent three decades developing sustainable ecotourism and protecting a large swath of tropical forest within a biological reserve.

GETTING AROUND

Driving in parts of the Caribbean coast can be stressful, particularly when you need to cross rivers or find indigenous villages that aren't accurately pinpointed on Google Maps. Be sure to rent a 4WD with high clearance, and watch where locals cross the rivers. Going with accredited local guides from ATEC to indigenous communities takes the stress out of the venture and allows you to participate fully in community life.

Selva Bananito

TIME FROM CAHUITA: **1 HR**

Visit an award-winning ecolodge

Some 42km northwest of Cahuita, **Selva Bananito** *(selvabananito.com)* was created in 1994. The Stein family turned 12 sq km of Caribbean lowlands into a private, biological reserve and built the award-winning **Selva Bananito Ecolodge** from recycled logging wood, employed solar energy and biodegradable products and committed themselves to preserving the Limón watershed.

Camera traps around their property record the movements of jaguars and other fauna, and the reserve is part of a vital wildlife corridor. Although the location is remote, there are plenty of adventures on offer, both for lodge guests and day-trippers (call ahead), such as gyrocoptering above virgin rainforest, tree climbing, birdwatching, waterfall hikes, abseiling and horseback riding; packages are available.

The lodge requires a three-night minimum stay. You need a 4WD to take the gravel road off Hwy 36, followed by a rough track that crosses several rivers.

Reserva Biológica Hitoy-Cerere

TIME FROM CAHUITA: **2 HRS**

Hiking Costa Rica's remotest trail

One of Costa Rica's most rugged and least-visited reserves, 99-sq-km **Reserva Biológica Hitoy-Cerere** lies some 27km west of

MARTIN PELANEK/SHUTTERSTOCK

Selva Bananito

Cahuita. Sitting on the edge of the Cordillera de Talamanca, and squeezed between Talamanca, Telier and Tanyí indigenous territories, it's characterized by varying altitudes, evergreen vegetation and epic amounts of rain: 4000mm to 6000mm annually.

Beneath its canopy – with some trees looming as high as 50m – and amid its orchids, bromeliads and tangle of lianas, wildlife thrives. Commonly spotted mammals include gray four-eyed opossums, tayras (a type of weasel), brocket deer, and howler and capuchin monkeys. It's not hyperbole to call it a paradise for birdwatchers: the area is home to more than 300 avian species, including keel-billed toucans, spectacled owls and green kingfishers, and the Montezuma oropendola, whose massive nests dangle from the trees. The ever-humid air and wet ground, in the meantime, keeps the place hopping with various species of poison-dart frog.

Besides a **ranger station** *(8am-4pm)* at the entrance, the reserve has no facilities. The tough 9km-long **Sendero Espavel** leads south to Río Moín, beginning at a muddy hill, and passing through primary and secondary forest before ascending another steep hill, littered with fallen trees and rocks; it's recommended for experienced jungle trekkers only, equipped with rubber boots, plenty of water and a compass.

A 4WD is essential for driving here. From Hwy 36, turn west onto Rte 234 at Penshurst and follow the signs to the reserve past a banana plantation and along a challenging dirt road.

Yorkín

TIME FROM CAHUITA: **2 HRS**

Deep-dive into Bribrí culture

Situated on the Río Yorkín in the Reserva Indígena Yorkín, the Bribrí village of **Yorkín** is only reachable by boat. **ATEC** (p162) in Puerto Viejo run day trips (US$125), with immersive one-night tours (from US$150 per person, including meals, transfers and experiences) also available. Getting there entails

INDIGENOUS RESIDENTS

The **Reserva Indígena KèköLdi** is home to some 200 Bribrí and Cabécar – two of the indigenous groups that have lived here since pre-Columbian times. The Bribrí tended to inhabit lowland areas, while the Cabécar made their home high in the mountainsThe reserve was established in 1976, with the recognition that indigenous culture was under threat. Threats still remain from banana plantations, logging, squatters and illegal hotel development, all stemming from lax government oversight. The Bribrí and Cabécar have distinct languages, though they share architecture, weapon and canoe styles, and the spiritual belief that the planet is a gift from *Sibö* (God).

VISITING INDIGENOUS COMMUNITIES

While it's possible to visit the Reserva Indígena KèköLdi and other Bribrí territories independently from Cahuita or Puerto Viejo, communities need to be contacted in advance. During your visit, bear in mind that these are people's private homes and work spaces, not tourist attractions. The most culturally sensitive and rewarding way to visit KèköLdi, Yorkín and Amubri is to book a tour organized by the Puerto Viejo–based **ATEC** *(ateccr.org)*. This grassroots organization has trained guides within these indigenous communities who can share their knowledge of their home territory while earning around 90% of the individual tour price. Book tours at least a day in advance, particularly if overnight stays are involved.

travel by dugout canoe followed by local demonstrations of roof thatching, bow-and-arrow making, the uses of medicinal plants and basket-weaving. You can tuck into a Bribrí-style lunch and learn the chocolate-making process. An optional hike in the highlands is also possible.

There's also a two-night trip that starts at the Amubri indigenous community, with overnighting in a traditional ranch, a morning hike along a nature trail, followed by a boat crossing of the Uren river, and visits to organic farms and local artisans, before finishing up with a second night in Yorkín.

Reserva Indígena KèköLdi

TIME FROM CAHUITA: **20 MINS**

Hiking and birding in Bribrí territory

Several tour companies run half-day and day trips (US$60) to the **Reserva Indígena KèköLdi**. **ATEC** offers an excursion that involves a 2½-hour hike through primary and secondary forest, with ample birdwatching opportunities, before traditional lunch cooked over a log fire at a traditional Bribrí community. **Gandoca Tours** *(gandocatours.com)* focuses specifically on birdwatching within the reserve. It's also possible to arrive in the reserve on foot and just pay the US$5 fee to visit the community. Check out their green iguana farm, created to boost numbers of the endangered green iguana – which was traditionally part of the Bribrí diet – by breeding them in captivity.

Watsi

TIME FROM CAHUITA: **1¼ HRS**

Shaman encounters and chocolate-making

The **Watsi** community, also within the Bribrí territory beyond Cahuita, offers interesting day-long cultural immersions, including learning about medicinal plants from a Bribrí shaman and experiencing a spiritual ceremony, plus a sweat lodge cleanse. Another Bribrí family in Watsi shows you how to weave traditional blankets and how to make artisanal chocolate using fresh cacao from their farm. Puerto Viejo-based Gandoca Tours offers day trips, as does the Playa Cocles-based **Ará Indómita** *(araindomita.com)*.

Meleruk

TIME FROM CAHUITA: **45 MINS**

A Bribrí chocolate immersion

In the Bribrí village of Meleruk, some 30km southwest of Cahuita, visitors can partake in an intimate cacao experience in conjunction with Gandoca Tours. Yoel and his family take their guests through every step of the chocolate-making process, including a hike through his family's permaculture farm, where bananas, coffee and cacao are staple crops. After the hands-on chocolate-making demonstration, you'll taste the results in various forms. Yoel's family provides a traditional lunch of chicken, rice and salad, all sourced on the farm. En route to Meleruk, your guide points out medicinal plants and natural materials used in construction of traditional Bribrí homes.

Puerto Viejo de Talamanca

BEACHES | SURFING | DINING

When locals contemplate Puerto Viejo de Talamanca, they barely recognize this formerly languid Caribbean beach town that has morphed into a surfer party spot. Sure, Bob Marley is still on blast and there's always a whiff of chicken Caribeño in the air. But as tourism has exploded in the southern Caribbean, these once-leisurely streets are now lined with international fusion restaurants, street vendors and luxury storefronts, and main thoroughfares are jammed with pedestrians, cyclists, dogs, motorists and even tuk-tuks.

During the pandemic, Puerto Viejo became a favorite for *josefinos* looking for new beach escapes, and many of them bought condos. Property prices subsequently are on the rise while tranquility is out the window, and more than a few of the town's long-standing business owners are cashing in and moving out. Travelers in search of a surf scene and late-night parties, on the other hand, will continue feeling right at home.

GETTING AROUND

This compact town is easy to walk or cycle around – pedaling out to beaches east of Puerto Viejo is a highlight. Frequent Autotransportes MEPE buses to Cahuita (30 minutes), Manzanillo (30 minutes), Puerto Limón (two hours), San José (4½ hours) and Sixaola (one hour) depart from La Parada on the waterfront Av 73. Shuttles, such as Interbus, offer door-to-door services to other tourist hot spots around Costa Rica and down the coast to Bocas del Toro (Panama). To reach Bocas del Toro, take a bus to Sixaola and cross the border.

Surf's Up

Hanging 10 on the Caribbean coast

Whether you're bold enough to surf **Salsa Brava** or prefer to watch from the eponymous bar as other people attempt the famous wave, this is definitely one of the most entertaining experiences in Puerto Viejo and one of the best (and gnarliest) breaks in Costa Rica.

Salsa Brava is named for the heaping helping of 'spicy sauce' it serves up on the sharp, shallow reef, continually collecting its debt of fun in broken skin, boards and bones. Just getting to the wave is difficult, as there are a series of canals that you must negotiate to reach it; it's for intermediate and advanced surfers only. Definitely ask a local to help you navigate this, and check that the conditions are appropriate first. The wave makes its regular, dramatic appearance when the swells pull in from the east, pushing a wall of water against the reef and

TOP TIP

Around midday at the beach, watch fishers haul in lobster and snapper, and in the early evenings people playing dominoes in the streets.

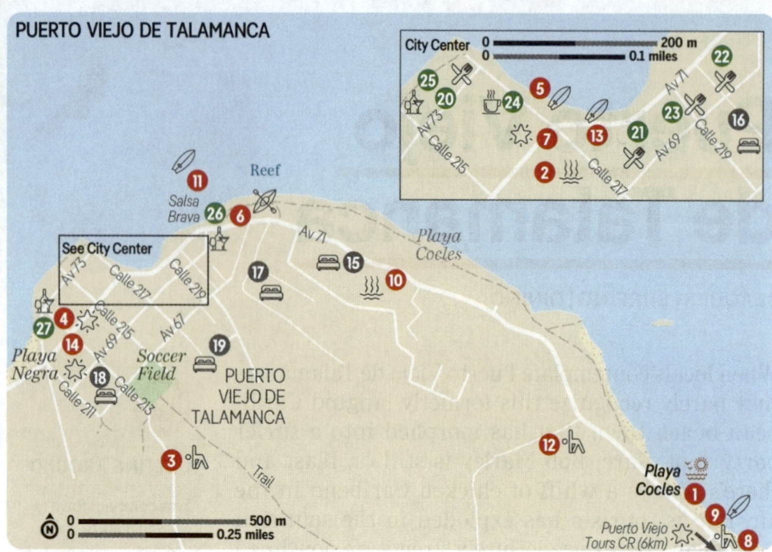

HIGHLIGHTS
1 Playa Cocles

ACTIVITIES
2 Aloha Spa
3 AmaSer
4 ATEC
5 Caribbean Surf School & Shop
6 Exploradores Outdoors
7 Gandoca Tours
8 KONA Wellness Shala
9 Pirate Surf School
10 Pure Jungle Spa
11 Salsa Brava
12 School of Love
13 Surf the Jungle
14 Terraventuras

SLEEPING
15 La Ruka Hostel
16 La Tribu
17 Olinka Boutique Hotel
18 Pagalú Hostel
19 Umami Hotel

EATING
20 Grow Puerto Viejo
21 KOKi Beach
22 Mopri
23 SOCA

DRINKING & NIGHTLIFE
24 Iriria
25 Johnny's Place
26 Salsa Brava
27 The Kat House

BEST TOURS

ATEC: Culturally sensitive tours to Bribrí communities.

Gandoca Tours: Visits to Bribrí communities, Manzanillo night walks, guided hikes in Refugio Nacional de Vida Silvestre Gandoca-Manzanillo and Cahuita hikes.

Exploradores Outdoors: White-water rafting specialist.

Terraventuras: Overnight stays in Tortuguero and Bribrí cultural tours.

Puerto Viejo Tours CR: Kayak excursions.

in the process generating a thick and powerful curl. There's no gradual buildup here: the water is transformed from swell to wave in a matter of seconds. Ride it out and you're golden. Wipe out and you may rocket into the reef. Some witty locals have dubbed it 'the cheese grater.'

If you prefer to look on from the bar with a mojito in hand, here's some fodder for conversation: this storied wave helped turn Puerto Viejo into a destination. More than 30 years ago the town was barely accessible. But bumpy bus rides and rickety canoes didn't dissuade dogged surfers from making

EATING & DRINKING IN PUERTO VIEJO: OUR PICKS

Iriria: Proper espresso and specialty coffees brewed from Terrazú region beans plus grilled cheese sandwiches and other light bites. *8:30am-7pm* $

Kat House: This breezy, elegant spot pairs natural wines and cocktails with tuna *tiradito*, shrimp tacos and sushi. *4-10pm Wed-Sun* $$

Salsa Brava: Take in the sunset over the eponymous surf break with two-for-one mojitos during happy hour, or grab a fish taco. *8am-midnight Wed-Mon* $$

Johnny's Place: Beloved bar serving innovative cocktails. Also DJs and occasional revelry; Wednesdays are liveliest. *11am-12:30am*

the week-long trip from San José. They camped on the beach and shacked up with locals, carb-loading at cheap *sodas*. Other intrepid explorers – biologists, Peace Corps volunteers, disaffected US veterans looking to escape the fallout of the Vietnam War – also materialized during this time, helping spread the word about the area's luminous sunsets, lush rainforests and monster waves.

Salsa Brava isn't the only wave in town, of course. For a softer landing, try the beach break at **Playa Cocles**, 2km east of Puerto Viejo, where the swell is consistent, the white water is abundant for beginners, and the wipeouts are more forgiving. Conditions are usually best early in the day, before the wind picks up. Meanwhile, **Punta Uva**, 9km east of Puerto Viejo, has a fun, semi-fickle right-hand point break for intermediates, and you can't beat the setting.

Waves in the area generally peak from December to March, but you might get lucky during the surfing mini-season between June and July. From late March to May, and in September and October, the sea is calm. Several surf schools around town charge US$50 to US$55 per person for two-hour group lessons and US$60 and up for private sessions. Locals on Playa Cocles rent boards from about US$15 per day. Recommended instructors work for **Surf the Jungle** *(surfthejunglecostarica.com)* and **Caribbean Surf School & Shop** *(puertoviejosurfandtours.com)* in Puerto Viejo, and **One Love Massage & Surf School** *(one-love-costa-rica.com)* and **Pirate Surf School** *(@pirate_surf_school)* in Playa Cocles.

BEST SPAS & YOGA IN PUERTO VIEJO

KONA Wellness Shala: Studio specializing in Vinyasa, Ashtanga, Kundalini, Hatha and Yin yoga styles; also offers sound baths.

Pure Jungle Spa: A full range of tropics-inspired massages, facials, manicures and pedicures, plus body treatments; jungle sounds come free.

School of Love: Satya and Navkiran offer Kundalini yoga to beginners and advanced practitioners alike; friendly vibe, go at own pace.

Aloha Spa: Seriously good deep-tissue massages, infra-red treatments, facials and more. Daniela is a wizard.

AmaSer: Daily Vinyasa yoga, plus twice-weekly Kundalini yoga and weekly Power yoga sessions in a lovely outdoor studio.

Sample Caribbean Flavors

A foodie walking tour

One of the best ways to get under Puerto Viejo's skin is to walk around town with a local, sample some of the traditional foods and learn about what the place was like before it became a popular tourist destination. Brothers Junior and Victor Palmer have lived here all their lives, and their tour companies – **Jungle Man Tours** *(facebook.com/junglemantours)* and **Wolaba Walking Tours** *(wolabawalkingtours.com)* – both offer a delicious and informative walking tour.

Without giving away the locations, we can disclose that they may indulge you with *pipa* (coconut water), cacao in all its decadent forms, classic chicken Caribeño, *patí* and a shot or two of *guaro* (local firewater). Come hungry and wear comfy footwear.

EATING IN PUERTO VIEJO: OUR PICKS

Mopri: Pick a side and sauce and dine on the freshest whole snapper, calamari, lobster and prawns around at this unprepossessing spot. *11:30am-9:30pm* $$

KOKi Beach: Expertly mixed drinks and mostly organic Latin American dishes served amid fairy lights, colorful local furnishings and art. *5-11pm Tue-Sun* $$

SOCA: Upmarket beach club with stellar service, exquisite cocktails and food-as-art dishes, such as flambéed red snapper and octopus with cassava foam. *5-11pm Tue-Sun* $$$

Grow Puerto Viejo: Adorable, innovative vegetarian restaurant right on the beach, dishing up delicious crepes, bowls, burritos and mocktails. *noon-9pm* $

Beyond Puerto Viejo de Talamanca

White-sand beaches, a mix of Caribbean and international cultures, and top-notch wildlife projects and jungle refuges await beyond Puerto Viejo.

Places

GETTING AROUND

Buses heading from Puerto Viejo to Manzanillo (six daily, 30 minutes) will stop at Playa Cocles, Playa Chiquita or Punta Uva on request. Alternatively, it's an easy and pleasant hour-long bicycle ride from Puerto Viejo to Manzanillo. Most motorists are respectful, but you should ride close to the shoulder so they can pass if necessary. Don't cycle without bike lights after dark, as this road is not lit. All beach communities are walkable.

Despite the rapid development of the southern Caribbean, you can still stumble upon a deserted beach east of Puerto Viejo, where a 13km road winds through coconut palm groves and lowland rainforest before dead-ending at the town of Manzanillo. Puerto Viejo also makes an excellent base for visiting Bribrí and other indigenous communities (p161).

Since the 1980s this coastline has seen the arrival of surfers, backpackers and holidaymakers – many of whom have stayed, adding European, Middle Eastern and North American flavors to the cultural stew. As the pace of the arrivals accelerates and new businesses and condos fly up, displaced creatures can seem ubiquitous, and wildlife conservation projects have become more important than ever.

Bribrí

TIME FROM PUERTO VIEJO DE TALAMANCA: **20 MINS**

Do go chasing waterfalls

North of Puerto Viejo, en route to Cahuita, it's well worth detouring along Hwy 36 in the direction of **Bribrí**. Without reaching the town, you'll pass turnoffs toward several impressive waterfalls; visiting them is an ideal way to cool down on a sweltering day.

First, follow the signposted road uphill (4WD only) to **Finca Las Brisas** *(8am-5pm)*, a private farm whose owner lets you splash in the smallish **Catarata Dos Aguas** with a refreshing dipping pool for a small parking fee (US$4). It's a popular picnic spot.

A little further west, another signposted road leads to **Catarata Ma-Cu**, also known as Bribrí Sparkling Waterfalls. When you go up the driveway, pay the entry fee (US$10) at the *palapa* (open-sided shelter) the falls are a steep 10-minute walk down, so wear water shoes with good grip. Choose between swimming in the deep pool beneath the falls or climbing the adjacent rocks and leaping in. There's a smaller, quieter waterfall with a swimming hole further up.

Catarata Volio

Finally, in the rainforest on the Bribrí reservation, is the gorgeous 15m **Catarata Volio** with a deep natural swimming pool. Getting there requires two shallow river crossings and a short jungle walk; it's best done with a guide, since occasional petty theft has been reported in the area.

Playa Cocles

TIME FROM PUERTO VIEJO DE TALAMANCA: **10 MINS**

Tour the Jaguar Rescue Center

Down at the east end of **Playa Cocles**, the well-run **Jaguar Centro de Rescate** *(jaguarrescue.foundation)* takes care of ill, injured and orphaned wildlife – sadly, their numbers are rising in step with development in the region. In 2022, 967 animals received care at the center, while in 2023 the number was 1001. On average, around 41% are successfully released back into the wild, 44% don't make it, and 15% survive but are unfit to be released. These become ambassadors whom you can meet on a tour of the facility.

Public tours *(US$27 per person)* take place at 9:30am or 11:30am daily. Book online in advance, and arrive a little early to find parking. A knowledgeable guide will then escort you through the verdant grounds to meet creatures such as Bobo, a booby bird who lost his fear of humans; Kivu, an ocelot with feline leukemia; and Sansa, an abandoned spider monkey who needed eye surgery.

The tours last 90 minutes and keep the operation – which receives no government funding – afloat. After the tour, grab a beverage and a snack at the on-site cafe and browse the gift shop. To support the center further, you can also volunteer for a minimum of four weeks, or opt to stay at at three properties around Puerto Viejo: **La Ceiba House** *(US$150 per night)*, **Ilan Ilan House** *(US$90 per night)* or **Jaguar Inn Bungalows** *(from US$180 per night)*, with proceeds going to the rescue center.

ACCESSIBLE BEACH ACCESS

In January 2024, Manzanillo became Costa Rica's third accessible beach, following similar initiatives in Manuel Antonio and Puntarenas on the Pacific coast. Nine tonnes of plastic bottle tops, collected at supermarkets around Costa Rica, have been recycled into retractable beach access walkways. They are durable and can traverse any terrain; Manzanillo's 33m-long stretch allows visitors with mobility issues to reach the beach using the amphibious wheelchair provided. Las Buenas Acciones Verdes, the environmental organization that's been key to the project, is planning further beach access projects that will open up more of the Caribbean coast to everyone.

WHERE THE BIRDS ARE

Haniel Rodriguez Rojas is a tour guide who specializes in wildlife and bird photography, and he's lived in Gandoca all his life. These are his favorite spots in the Caribbean to birdwatch. @haniel_tourguiderodriguez

Tucán Road: On this one road just behind Playa Cocles, I can regularly spot anywhere between 40 and 60 species of birds.

Gandoca: There are around 40 to 50 species in Gandoca, and right outside my door I can usually find hawks, toucans, tanagers, woodpeckers and hummingbirds.

Moín: The canals in Moín are a great place to see and photograph wading birds like herons and kingfishers. There are just so many.

Punta Uva

TIME FROM PUERTO VIEJO DE TALAMANCA: **20 MINS**

Spying on great green macaws

A 20-minute drive south of Puerto Viejo and set back in the jungle from Hwy 36 between **Punta Uva** and Manzanillo, **Ara Manzanillo** *(aramanzanillo.org; adult/under-12 US$20/free)* is an NGO devoted to saving the endangered great green macaw. It has successfully reintroduced dozens of endangered great green macaws to the lowland tropical forests of the southern Caribbean; to learn about their efforts and watch the macaws fly and feed in the forest, travelers can visit the field station at 3pm daily. This is the best chance you'll get to behold these wondrous creatures in their natural habitat.

Reserve the tour on the website and drive to the farm, where a guide will give a brief talk about the Caribbean arm of the project, which started in 2010. In addition to establishing a new population in an area where great green macaws were virtually extinct, the project is also assisting in their reproduction with artificial nests, running an education program with local schools and designing a strategy for forest management that increases the production of native foods for the birds.

EATING IN PLAYA COCLES: OUR PICKS

Soda Las Olas: Excellent *gallo pinto*, cheeseburgers, ample breakfasts and burritos, served on picnic tables next to the waves. *8am-6pm Wed-Mon* $

SAGE @ Playa 506: Plantain gnocchi, tuna burgers, mahi-mahi ceviche and *casados* are paired with craft beers at this hostel-adjacent restaurant. *7am-10pm* $

La Nena: Served beneath a *palapa*, ample portions of grilled chicken, jumbo shrimp and sea bass will get you through a siege. *noon-8:30pm Thu-Mon* $

La Pecora Nera: Splurge on a candlelit dinner of Italian seafood pasta and shrimp-topped starfruit, plus globe-spanning wines. *4:30-10pm Tue-Sun* $$$

ALBERT SCHWEITZER/GETTY IMAGES

Great green macaws, Ara Manzanillo

Macaws released by the project mostly find ways of feeding themselves, but every day at 3pm 30 to 40 of the multicolored birds swoop in to receive some supplemental nuts and seeds in the forest near a visitor lookout platform. Around the world there are only about 1200 of these birds, and about 350 of those reside in Costa Rica, making it an extra-special.

Manzanillo

TIME FROM PUERTO VIEJO DE TALAMANCA: **25 MINS**

Up in the canopy

Just 1.7km south of **Manzanillo**, and signposted off Hwy 256, **Nature Observatorio** *(natureobservatorio.com)* is a mind-blowing tree house located 25m up a Nispero tree; every seven years, it's moved to a different tree. While getting there is a challenge, the reward is enormous.

Reaching it requires a hike through dense rainforest; once you're there, you can opt to be strapped into a harness to ascend a rope like an arborist to the observation deck for a bird's-eye view of primary rainforest and the sea beyond, or go on a nature hike with an experienced guide to spot the critters living in the canopy and the undergrowth (or both!).

continued on p172

BEST FARM TOURS

Finca La Isla: Farm and botanical garden producing organic pepper, cacao and over 150 fruits and plants; chocolate workshops available.

Cacao Trails: Follow the chocolate-making process, from bean to bar, at this lush cacao plantation and chocolate museum.

Chocorart: Swiss-run cacao farm combines fun plantation and chocolate-making and sampling tours with wildlife-spotting.

Finca Tierra: Fantastic solar-powered permaculture farm that walks you through 'food forests' and teaches you how to grow medicinal and edible plants.

Jungle Man: Book via Le Cameleon Hotel for this private organic farm tour; pick herbs and fruit for a meal and spot wildlife.

EATING AROUND PLAYA CHIQUITA: OUR PICKS

Papaya Restaurant: Beautifully presented takes on *gallo pinto* and fish *tiradito* with passion fruit. Also creative cocktails. *7am-9:30pm* $$$

GypSea Cafe: Delicious organic coffee, eggs Benedict brunches, Buddha bowls and sandwiches, served with a side of sea views. *8am-2:30pm Tue-Sun* $

La Leyenda de L'Antico Forno: Authentic Italian food and some of the Caribbean's best wood-fired pizza, in a jungle setting. *3-9pm Tue-Sun* $$

Pura Gula: Dishes such as pad Thai, mahi-mahi *ceviche* and hummus draw on the chef-owners' global travels at this open-air spot. *3-10pm Thu-Tue* $$

CYCLE TOUR

Beach-Hopping in the Southern Caribbean

To really soak up the Caribbean vibe around Puerto Viejo, rent a beach cruiser from **Manú Bikes** or **Puerto Viejo Bike Rentals** and head east along the coast. Stop at each of the unique beaches, staying as long as you like and swimming at will (keep an eye out for riptides). Also recommended are stops for chocolate, coconut water, *patí* and anything else that calls to you along the way.

1 Caribeans Chocolate & Coffee

Bike down to this delightful **chocolate shop** and cafe opposite Playa Cocles to fuel up on cacao and coffee. The long-standing business also leads tours of its sustainable cacao forest and chocolate-creation lab, accompanied by gourmet chocolate tastings, and there's a refrigerated chocolate room where visitors can try several flavors of chocolate.

The Ride: Your first beach stop is right across the street, although it stretches down the coast for a good 2km.

2 Playa Cocles

Playa Cocles (p165) is the only Caribbean beach where lifeguards are on duty, and the waves here are ideal for beginner and intermediate surfers; rent a board from **Totem Surf** for around US$15 for the day. This is also a hot spot for beach volleyball, horseback riding and massages, and it can get pretty crowded on weekends.

The Ride: Cruise south along the coast for 3km, and consider popping into one of several chic beach clubs, such as **Da Lime**, for a coconut water or cocktail.

SIMON DANNHAUER/SHUTTERSTOCK

Punta Uva

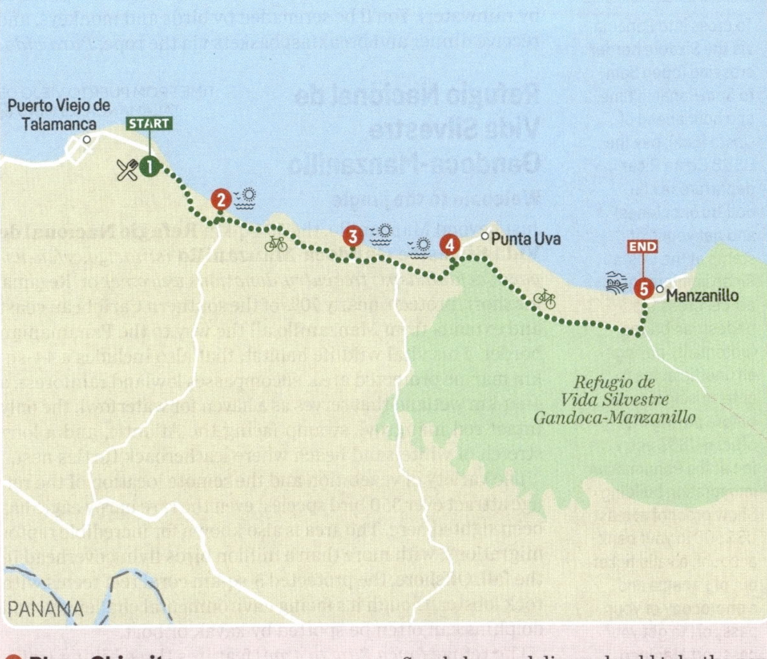

3 Playa Chiquita

When you reach the Playa Chiquita Trail, lock up the bicycle and hike through the jungle to hidden **Playa Chiquita**, a coco-palm-lined stretch of sand where you can escape the crowds in one of several isolated coves and take a dip in the Caribbean waters. This beach has been awarded the *bandera azul* (blue flag), meaning it is one of the cleanest beaches in the country.

The Ride: You'll pedal about 2km past entrances to some of the region's most upscale lodgings before arriving at Punta Uva.

4 Punta Uva

There are several entrances to **Punta Uva**, and all of them lead to blissful beaches. If you're interested in kayaking or surfing, take Calle Edén to **Panchos Place**. Snorkelers and divers should take the next left and continue to the **Punta Uva Dive Center** to rent gear or join tours to the extensive reef offshore. When the swell is kickin', this spot features a right-hand beach break suitable for intermediates.

The Ride: Another 4km of cycling along the road between the sea and the jungle takes you into the village of Manzanillo.

5 Manzanillo

Once a quiet outpost of Afro-Caribbean culture, Manzanillo is now abundant with lodgings and restaurants. At Cool & Calm Café (p172), enjoy fine Caribbean meals, cooking classes and 'reef-to-plate' tours (dive for your own lobster). Along **Playa Manzanillo** you can also rent snorkel equipment and kayaks or set off on a dolphin tour.

SIXAOLA-GUABITO BORDER CROSSING

To cross into Panama via the Sixaola border crossing (open 8am to 5pm Panama time, one hour ahead of Costa Rica), pay the US$8 Costa Rican departure tax (in dollars or colones) and get your exit stamp at the Costa Rican immigration office. Cross the pedestrian bridge (potentially paying an unofficial fee to enterprising locals) before paying the official US$3 entry fee at the Panamanian immigration building. Show proof of at least US$500 in your bank account, a valid ticket out of Panama and a photocopy of your passport to get your passport stamped. From Guabito, there are *colectivo* taxis to Almirante (one hour), where there are hourly water taxis (6:30am to 6pm) to Boca del Toro.

contined from p169

You may also opt for an overnight stay above the viewing deck, surrounded by the rustles and chirps of the nocturnal jungle. Suspended by nylon straps and built without the use of a single nail, the tree house features queen-sized beds, a hammock, a couch, a shower and a toilet (the last two powered by rainwater). You'll be serenaded by birds and monkeys, and receive dinner and breakfast baskets via the rope. *Pura vida!*

Refugio Nacional de Vida Silvestre Gandoca-Manzanillo

TIME FROM PUERTO VIEJO DE TALAMANCA: **25 MINS**

Welcome to the jungle

Just beyond Manzanillo, the 50-sq-km **Refugio Nacional de Vida Silvestre Gandoca-Manzanillo** *(sinac.go.cr/en-us/pages/default.aspx; free entry, donations welcome)*, or 'Regama' for short, protects nearly 70% of the southern Caribbean coast and extends from Manzanillo all the way to the Panamanian border. This vital wildlife habitat, that also includes a 44-sq-km marine protected area, encompasses lowland rainforest, a 4-sq-km wetland that serves as a haven for waterfowl, the only intact red mangrove swamp facing the Atlantic, and a long stretch of white-sand beach where leatherback turtles nest.

The variety of vegetation and the remote location of the refuge attract over 350 bird species; even the rare harpy eagle has been sighted here. The area is also known for incredible raptor migrations, with more than a million birds flying overhead in the fall. Offshore, the protected 5-sq-km coral reef teems with rock lobster, though it's facing environmental challenges, and dolphins can often be spotted by kayak or boat.

The refuge *(open 8am to 4pm)* features three hiking trails. A **coastal trail** extends 5.5km east from Manzanillo, and the first part of this path, which leads from Manzanillo to **Tom Bay** (about a 90-minute walk), is clearly marked, with excellent snorkeling at the end (bring own mask). Once you pass Tom Bay, however, the trail isn't very well-maintained, so ask about conditions before you set out, or hire a local guide.

A more demanding **12km-long trail** departs just west of Manzanillo and skirts the southern edges of the swamp, continuing to the small community of Gandoca. This trail is little-used, as most people access Gandoca by boat or from the park entrance at the northern edge of the refuge, on the road to Sixaola.

The 4km-long **'La Trocha' trail** takes visitors through thick forest along a mix of dirt track and boardwalk made of wood

EATING IN MANZANILLO: OUR PICKS

Cool & Calm Cafe: Sticky ribs, giant shrimp and chicken, smoky from the grill, await you at this popular Rasta-colored restaurant. *11am-9pm* $$

Maxi's Restaurant: Gaze at the sea as you wait for your grilled seafood, *pargo rojo* (whole red snapper) or *ceviche*. *noon-10pm Wed-Mon* $$

Mista Cook: Family-run place serving up ample portions of grilled fish with rice and beans, grilled chicken and excellent cocktails. *noon-8pm Tue-Sun* $

Colores Restaurant: Dig your toes in the sand and chow down on garlic shrimp with *patacones* or the fish *ceviche*. *noon-8pm* $$

DAMSEA/SHUTTERSTOCK

Refugio Nacional de Vida Silvestre Gandoca-Manzanillo

and plastic. Again, going with a guide maximizes your chances of spotting an incredible diversity of medicinal plants, exotic birds and animals. Recommended guides include **Abel Bustamante** *(8895-7394)* and **Florentino Grenald** *(8841-2732)*, who used to serve as the reserve's administrator, and charge around US$45 per person for the outing.

Gandoca

TIME FROM PUERTO VIEJO DE TALAMANCA: 1 HR

Exploring Costa Rica's southernmost settlement

Remote **Gandoca** (population 480) is Costa Rica's southernmost Caribbean settlement, and as it receives few visitors, it gives you an excellent taste of what the area was like before the advent of mass tourism. The best place to base yourself is the family-run **Colibrí Lodge** *(@colibrilodgegandoca)*, with simple, fan-cooled rooms, and access to the pool and to nature trails on the property. Owners Gladys and Aquiles maintain a garden, restaurant and trail leading to the boat launch, while daughters Elba and Eunice manage the place and cook meals.

Nearby, **Laguna Gandoca** is a crucial mangrove ecosystem for manatees, which are seen regularly, and the beach is a nesting site for green, hawksbill and leatherback turtles; Gladys and Aquiles' son Haniel gives top-notch wildlife tours.

EATING AROUND PUNTA UVA: OUR PICKS

Selvin: Top restaurant since 1982, specializing in shrimp, sautéed lobster, *rondón* and chicken Caribeño. Dress nicely. *12:30-8pm Thu-Sun* $$

El Refugio: Argentine restaurant featuring steak with *chimichurri* (savory Argentinian sauce), mussels in white wine and *dulce de leche* crepes. *noon-9pm Thu-Tue* $$$

Soda Alanita: A cornucopia of *gallo pinto*, *empanadas*, burritos and tacos; red snapper with rice and beans is more substantial. *8am-6pm* $

Restaurant Eden Beach: An idyllic beachside location paired with red snapper in Caribbean sauce, BBQ shrimp and daiquiris as big as your head. *11am-5pm* $$

Places We Love to Stay

$ Budget $$ Midrange $$$ Top End

Tortuguero

MAP p142

Aracari Garden Hostel $ Welcoming tangerine-colored hostel by the soccer field, with open-air kitchen, restaurant hammocks and on-site tour company.

Miss Junie's Lodge $ Upstairs rooms at Tortuguero's plantation-style original hotel overlook the sea. Hammock-hung garden and good restaurant are perks.

El Icaco $ Brightly painted rooms, beachside hammocks and friendly service define this simple beachfront hotel. Off-site swimming pool 200m away.

Casa Marbella $$ Super-central, naturalist-owned B&B features a devil's dozen of fan-cooled rooms. Excellent breakfasts served on the canal-side deck.

Parque Nacional Tortuguero

All Rankin's Lodge $$ Colorful garden cabins on stilts, run by one of Tortuguero's first family settlers. Boat transport/meals included.

Rana Roja $$ Frequent nature encounters and immaculate rooms, connected by raised walkways, are the best features of this jungle hideaway.

Tortuga Lodge $$$ Decorated with handmade textiles, this upscale lodge comes with private walking trails, saltwater pool and floating spa.

Laguna Lodge $$$ Superbly located lodge, decorated with gorgeous mosaic art, features three bars, buffet restaurant, and rooms with soaring ceilings.

Parismina

Green Gold Ecolodge $$ Rainforest beach hideaway 3km south of Parismina, with vanilla plantation, eight rustic rooms and kitchen (delicious meals available).

Río Parismina Lodge $$$ Swimming pool, English-speaking guides, fishing equipment, Jacuzzi and excellent meals are all boons at this jungle-fringed lodge.

Reserva Pacuare

Aventuras del Caribe $ Basic but comfortable collection of wooden cabins and a decent restaurant run by sweet Tico couple.

Lirio Lodge $$ Boutique canal-front lodge in the rainforest, with stylish hardwood cabins, kayaks for guest use and tours/meals included.

Barra del Colorado

Río Colorado Lodge $$$ Rambling tropical-style building with breezy rooms connected by covered walkways. Air-conditioning and river views a bonus.

Silver King Lodge $$$ Twelve large rooms, copious amenities: pool, Jacuzzi, sauna, fishing equipment, buffet-style meals and one cigar per day.

Kawe Lodge $$$ Intimate six-room (with air-con) sportfishing lodge 1km north of Barra, with hiking, kayaking, and birdwatching for non-fishing guests.

Parque Nacional Barbilla & Around

Barbilla Rainforest Lodge $$ Secluded farmstay with rainforest and mountain views from hammock-hung terrace. Wildlife-watching, horseback riding and indigenous cultural exchanges arranged.

Parque Nacional Braulio Carrillo

La Danta Salvaje (p154) $$ Atmospheric lodge without electricity in private rainforest reserve, reachable by 4WD and jungle trek; meals, transport and wildlife included.

Puerto Limón

MAP p150

Doña Koko $ Cheerful spot with friendly owner, guest kitchen, fan-cooled rooms and restaurant next door. A 15-minute walk from downtown Limón.

Hotel Playa Bonita $$ Whitewashed rooms and a breezy ocean-view restaurant, 5km from downtown Limón, make this seaside hotel a good choice.

Cahuita

MAP p158

Alby Lodge $ Palm-thatched bungalows on edge of the park with tropical gardens that attract howler monkeys and birds. Cash only.

Hakuna Matata Hostel $ Colorful decor, homey vibes and friendly owner make this place feel like a home away from home.

El Encanto $$ High-ceilinged bungalows (some with air-con) within landscaped grounds dotted with hammocks, pools and spa. Great pizza restaurant.

Casa Marcellino $$ Four spotless wood cabins (some with air-con) with kitchens and hammocks nestle in a garden inland from Playa Negra.

Puerto Viejo de Talamanca

MAP p164

Pagalú Hostel $ Welcoming hostel with airy doubles and dorms (with lockers and bunk-side lamps), open-air kitchen and quiet lounge with hammocks.

La Ruka Hostel $ Rent surfboards and snorkels from the friendly owners and hang out with fellow travelers in the lounge or kitchen.

La Tribu $ Delightful women-only hostel, with spa outings, cooking classes, movie nights and nature hikes organized for guests.

Olinka Boutique Hotel $$ Spacious, bright rooms, suites and villas with fans and air-con surround the garden and pool; numerous tours arranged.

Umami Hotel $$$ Adults-only hotel comprises design-forward rooms with hardwood features, chic pool area and restaurant serving a range of innovative international fare.

Playa Negra

Banana Azul $$ Splurge on the Howler Suite at this jungle-chic hotel with ocean vistas. Perks include restaurant-bar and bike/bodyboard rental.

Villas Piña $$ Four-person, one-bedroom villas amid jungle share a dazzling *rancho* with pool, restaurant and deck for sunbathing and stargazing.

La Prometida $$$ Immaculate seaside hotel offers individually styled villas, suites and cottages amid tropical gardens with an enticing pool. Tours arranged.

Playa Cocles

Playa 506 $ Beautifully decorated doubles, plus bunks and capsules with lots of thoughtful features, a beach bar and stellar waterfront location.

Physis $$ Comforts abound at this friendly four-bedroom, air-conditioned B&B, including free Netflix movies, mini-fridges and garden with water features.

Playa Chiquita

La Kukula $$ The boldly decorated doubles, family room and deluxe apartment at this jungle lodge come with mosquito nets.

Tree House Lodge $$$ Whimsical self-catering *casitas* (cottages), including a tree house, and converted school bus; Jacuzzis; jungle walkways to the sea.

Punta Uva

aWà Beach Hotel $$ Design-forward adults-only boutique hotel in the jungle, close by the beach. Individually conceived rooms, kind staff and delicious food.

Casa Viva $$ Handcrafted hardwood houses with kitchens and wraparound verandas benefit from direct beach access and wildlife-spotting from hammocks.

Cabinas Punta Uva $$ Right near the waves, these *cabinas* with polished-wood verandas and hammocks share an open-air kitchen and verdant garden setting.

Playa Manzanillo

Cabinas Manzanillo $ Cheery rooms inside the eight super-clean *cabinas* feature carved masks, industrial-strength ceiling fans (or air-con) and large beds.

Congo Bongo $$ Pop-art paradise of repurposed and recycled materials: eight *cabinas* with terraces and hammocks within a former cacao plantation.

Almonds & Corals Lodge $$$ Surrounded by jungle, this beachfront spot consists of palm-roofed bungalows with netted walls and hammock-hung patios.

IAN BOTTLE/ALAMY

Pool, Banana Azul

Researched by
Sarah Gilbert

Northwestern Costa Rica

ECOTOURISM AND ADVENTURE

Relish the bountiful biodiversity, from the beaches and dry forest of the lowlands to the volcanic peaks and misty cloud forest in the mountains.

Defined by the ocean in the west and the mountains in the east, Northwestern Costa Rica is a region of startling and delightful diversity. The far northwest is a wide, flat expanse of grasslands and tropical dry forest, where sweeping savanna vistas are broken only by windblown trees. To the east, the Cordillera de Guanacaste rises majestically out of the plains in a line of simmering, steaming volcanic peaks. Further south, the higher altitudes of the Cordillera de Tilarán create misty cloud forests that are teeming with life. There's an unrivaled array of ecosystems and adventures.

The region features a couple of top-tier destinations. The cloud forests of Monteverde and Santa Elena are not easy to get to, but worth the effort for the mystical, magical environment and the myriad adventure opportunities. The national parks of Rincón de la Vieja and Palo Verde are also popular (and worthwhile) destinations, especially for day-trippers coming up from the coast.

But many of the region's highlights are unexpected, unsung attractions. Swathes of rainforest, dense and undisturbed; ancient volcanoes, hissing and steaming with geothermal power; deserted beaches and historic battle sites – they're all here, in one compact corner of the country. What's most surprising is how accessible these destinations are, thanks to the international airport in Liberia and the Interamericana (Ruta 1) that snakes through the region.

CHARLES WOLLERTZ/GETTY IMAGES

THE MAIN AREAS

For places to stay in Northwestern Costa Rica, see p218

JAKUB MACULEWICZ/SHUTTERSTOCK

Left: Cerro Pelado (p202); Above: Río Celeste (p194), Parque Nacional Volcán Tenorio

Find Your Way

This region stretches from the Pacific Coast in the west to the Guanacaste mountain range in the east. From the Nicaraguan border, it extends down to the Golfo de Nicoya. Ruta 1 runs its length, from north to south.

Parque Nacional Santa Rosa, p212

Protecting the country's largest tract of tropical dry forest, this national park also features superb surf breaks and a significant historic site.

Rincón de la Vieja, p207

The national park is a volcanic hot spot, but there's a host of other river adventures here too, such as waterfall hiking.

Cañas, p201

More of a Tico town than a tourist destination, Cañas gives easy access to hiking, river rafting, waterfall swimming and world-class wetlands.

CAR
The most efficient way to travel around Northwestern Costa Rica is by car, especially with Ruta 1 connecting several of the main destinations. In some places, poor roads will slow you down, especially during the rainy season.

SHUTTLE BUS & TOUR
Private shuttle services offer relatively quick and comfortable service to popular destinations, including Santa Elena and Liberia. Once you reach these hubs, you'll need tours and taxis to get around. In Santa Elena, in particular, local transportation is included with many activities.

PUBLIC BUS
Public buses ply Ruta 1 on a regular basis, offering easy access to main hubs such as Cañas, Bagaces and Liberia, which are useful jumping-off points. Santa Elena is also accessible by public bus. Buses run less frequently (or not at all) to smaller towns and villages.

Río Celeste, p194
The turquoise-blue river lends its name to the entire region, which is dense with rainforest, waterfalls, abundant wildlife and inviting ecolodges.

Monteverde & Santa Elena, p182
With countless cloud-forest and rain-forest reserves, there's endless opportunity for adventures, birdwatching and wildlife encounters.

Plan Your Time

Destinations in Northwestern Costa Rica are so varied that it's important to choose carefully what you want to do – perhaps wildlife-watching, adventure activities or water sports – and design your itinerary accordingly.

VICKY GOSSELIN/SHUTTERSTOCK

Reserva Biológica Bosque Nuboso Monteverde (p182)

On a Quick Trip

- If you only have a day or two in the region, you should choose a destination that is easy to access, like **Rincón de la Vieja** (p207). Spend the night in a rustic lodge in **Curubandé** (p210) and spend the day at the national park, marveling at the volcanic activity along the **Sendero Las Pailas** (p207), swimming under waterfalls and soaking in the mineral-rich water of the **Río Negro Hot Springs** (p208).

- On your second day, go on a watery adventure, hiking, swimming and climbing the scenic river canyon to **La Leona waterfall** (p210). Don't miss dinner at **El Mirador** (p211) for spectacular sunset panoramas. If you're short on time, you can do all this in one very full day.

Seasonal Highlights

Guanacaste is the driest region of the country. It still rains in the rainy season – practically every day – but you're also likely to get a daily reprieve with a few hours of sunshine.

FEBRUARY

The dry weather is perfect for exploring the **national parks**. Resplendent quetzal breeding season starts mid-month, making February to June the best time to spot these beauties in Monteverde's cloud forests.

MARCH

Fiestas Cívicas – weeklong celebrations of *sabanero* (cowboy) culture – take place in Liberia in February and in Cañas in March, with plenty of live music, traditional food, horse parades and rodeos.

MAY

The green season begins, bringing more rain and lower prices for accommodations, quieter national parks and better deals on car rental across the region. **Surfers** will enjoy the increasing swells.

Five Days to Travel Around

- After a few days in the dry forest, it's time to ascend into the cloud forest around Monteverde and Santa Elena. Explore the trails of the **Reserva Biológica Bosque Nuboso Monteverde** (p182), walk through the clouds in **Reserva Bosque Nuboso Santa Elena** (p188), or whizz over the forest canopy on a **zipline** (p186). Between February and June, keep an eye out for the region's celebrity bird, the resplendent **quetzal** (p186).

- Make time for one of the more unusual tours on offer, such as **tree-climbing** (p190) or a sustainable **coffee tour** (p187). Learn to rustle up Tico treats at a **cooking class** (p190) or try some of the one-of-a-kind **restaurants** (p191) around town. And be sure to swim under at least one **waterfall** (p192).

If You Have More Time

- If you want to see more wildlife, be sure to fit **Río Celeste** (p194) into your itinerary. Stay at one of the many **ecolodges** (p196) near the national park or closer to Bijagua, marvel at the river's sky-blue waters, and you're bound to see monkeys, sloths and lots of birds, too.

- Avid birders will want to spend a day or two exploring the wetlands of the **Parque Nacional Palo Verde** (p204), cruising down the Río Tempisque.

- If you're ready to relax on a beautiful beach, head up to the **Golfo de Santa Elena** (p217) to find your favorite sweep of sand. Stop at **Santa Rosa** (p212) on the way to learn about a game-changing event in Costa Rican history.

JULY

On July 25, **Día de Guanacaste** commemorates the country's 1824 annexation of Guanacaste with parades and parties, especially in Liberia. There's still sunshine to be found at the beaches.

SEPTEMBER

September and October are the rainiest months across the region. Prolonged heavy rainfall means roads can become muddy and sometimes impassable and national parks can sometimes close briefly.

NOVEMBER

The rains become less heavy while the wind picks up at Bahía Salinas, kicking off **kitesurfing** season, which lasts through April (the best kite months are December to the end of March).

DECEMBER

Prices for accommodations soar, tours are at their busiest and beaches are more crowded during the last two weeks of December, unofficially starting peak tourist season which lasts until April.

Monteverde & Santa Elena

CLOUD FOREST | ADRENALINE-FUELED ADVENTURE | BEAUTIFUL BIRDS

GETTING AROUND

Driving around Santa Elena and Monteverde can be notoriously difficult, due to steep hills and some unpaved roads, especially in wet weather. Nonetheless, it's useful to have your own vehicle, as the attractions are sprawled out for kilometers in all directions. Many tours and reserves provide transportation from hotels and lodges in the area (free of charge or for an extra fee). Travelers without a vehicle can arrive in Santa Elena by bus from San José and La Fortuna (via Tilarán), or by tax-boat-taxi.

TOP TIP

The biggest population center is the bustling village of Santa Elena. This is where buses arrive and depart, and where most restaurants and budget lodgings are located. Santa Elena stretches seamlessly into its southern neighbor, the smaller village of Cerro Plano, and then tiny Monteverde.

In the 1950s, Quakers fleeing US conscription settled on this lush hillside, high on Costa Rica's mountainous spine, swirling in clouds and enveloped in vegetation. They dubbed it Monteverde, or 'Green Mountain.' They developed the land for agriculture but agreed to preserve a third of their property.

The Quakers later joined environmental organizations to purchase more land, establishing the pioneering Reserva Biológica Bosque Nuboso Monteverde (Monteverde Cloud Forest Biological Reserve) in 1972. Soon, naturalists and nature lovers arrived to explore this unique hotbed of biodiversity, and the conservation movement blossomed.

Today, the Monteverde Reserve is the most famous one, but the whole area is a green patchwork of public and private land dedicated to protecting this precious landscape. All trails lead to scenic overlooks, waterfalls, wild encounters and adventures waiting to happen. There may be increasingly luxe lodges to sleep in and refined restaurants to dine in, but Monteverde's still wild at heart.

Meet the Green Giant

The original cloud-forest reserve

Wandering the trails through the dense forest, dripping in vegetation and drizzling with mist, it's easy to understand why the Quakers named this place Monteverde, or 'Green Mountain.' Due to the near-constant cloud cover, layer upon layer of plant life sprouts from every surface, including the trees.

The moisture is inescapable in the cloud forest: you'll see it gather on the outsized leaves, hear the trickle of streams, sink into the spongey ground underfoot and feel the dampness in the air all around you. Welcome to the **Reserva Biológica Bosque Nuboso Monteverde** *(cloudforestmonteverde.com; day pass adult/child US$26/13).*

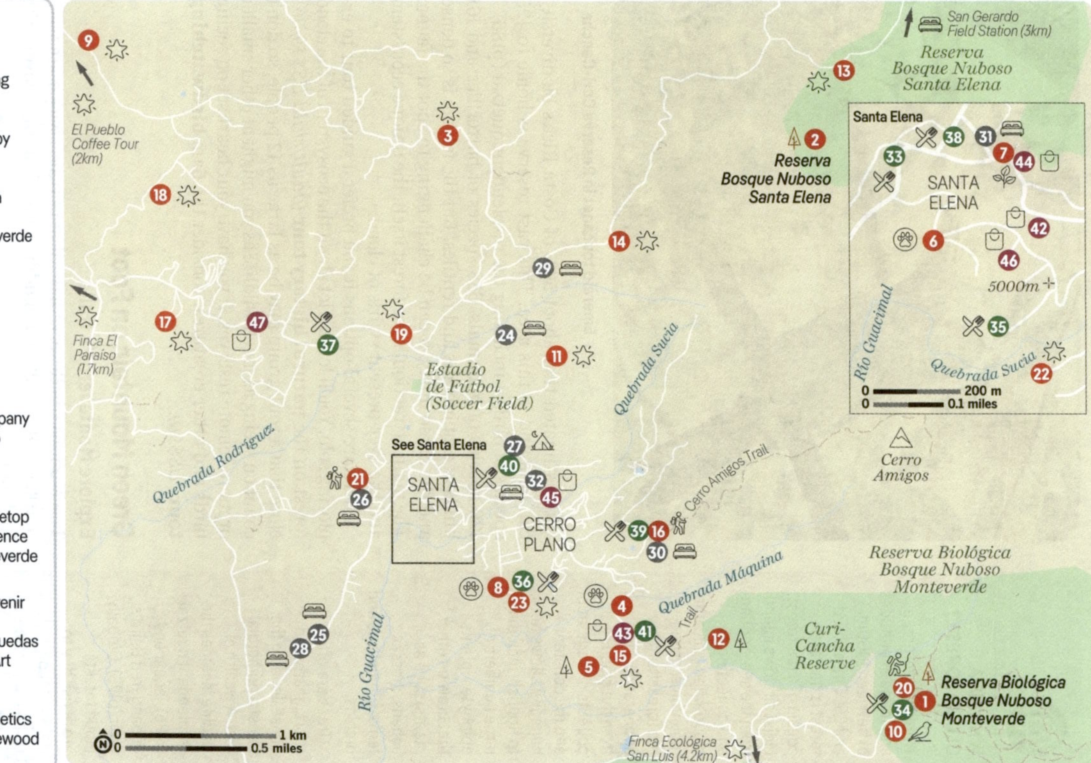

HIGHLIGHTS
1 Reserva Biológica Bosque Nuboso Monteverde
2 Reserva Bosque Nuboso Santa Elena

SIGHTS
3 100% Aventura
4 Bat Jungle
5 Bosque Eterno de los Niños
6 Frog Pond Ranario
7 Jardín de Orquídeas
8 Monteverde Butterfly Gardens
9 Monteverde Extremo Park
10 Monteverde Hummingbird Gallery
11 Original Canopy Tour
12 Reserva Curi-Cancha
13 Selvatura Park
14 Treetopia Park

ACTIVITIES
15 Café Monteverde
16 Cerro Amigos
17 Don Juan Tours
18 Finca Modelo
19 Horse Trek Monteverde
20 MonteTours
21 Pasión Costa Rica
22 Santuario Ecológico
23 Valle Escondido

SLEEPING
24 Cabinas Capulín
25 Casa Batsu
26 Casa Jungle Monteverde
27 Chira Glamping Monteverde
28 El Nido Lodge
29 Hidden Canopy Treehouses
30 Hotel Belmar
31 Pensión Santa Elena
32 Senda Monteverde Hotel

EATING
33 Boca2 Café
34 Cafe Colibrí
35 El Jardín
36 Farm to Table Escondida
37 Monteverde Brewing Company
38 Raulito's Pollo Asado
39 Restaurante Celajes
40 San Lucas Treetop Dining Experience
41 Stella's Monteverde

SHOPPING
42 Brillante Souvenir
43 CASEM
44 Ferlander Arguedas
45 Monteverde Art House
46 Monteverde Natural Cosmetics
47 Souvenir Rosewood

WHAT IS A CLOUD FOREST?

Tropical, evergreen and found at altitudes of between 1000m and 2500m, a cloud forest is the rarer cousin of a rainforest. Moist air flows inland from the sea, cooling and collecting as cloud when it hits the mountains, giving the forest its misty appearance. Moisture from the clouds collects on vegetation and the constant humidity allows flora to flourish, including large numbers of epiphytes (plants that grow on other plants) such as lichens, mosses, ferns, bromeliads and orchids.

Trees are often short, gnarly and dense, lending the forest a primordial feel. A wealth of wildlife includes the resplendent quetzal (p186), jaguar and endangered Baird's tapir (p198). Globally, cloud forests are at risk due to deforestation and rising temperatures, so protecting Monteverde is all the more important.

DANIEL HUMBERTO UMANA/SHUTTERSTOCK

Emerald toucanet in Reserva Curi-Cancha

It's estimated that about 50% of Costa Rica's biodiversity can be found in this area. This vast reserve is home to 425 species of birds – including the resplendent quetzal (p186) – 120 species of mammals, 658 species of butterflies and 161 kinds of amphibians and reptiles. But the foliage is so dense and the air so misty, it can be challenging to spot the fauna. The main attraction is the forest itself: the unique ecosystem and the ever-present swirls of cloud.

There are several options if you prefer a guided tour to exploring solo. You'll learn a lot about the ecosystem of the cloud forest on the **natural history tour** *(adult/child US$49/36)*. Note that a tour group may be as large as 12 people, so don't count on seeing as much wildlife as you might at other smaller or more remote reserves. If you have your heart set on seeing birds and other creatures, consider the 6am **birdwatching tour** *(US$90)*.

Green Mountain on Foot

Explore Monteverde's trails

The Monteverde Reserve has 13km of trails, which are well-marked but sometimes muddy. This 5km loop covers the highlights.

From the ranger station, follow the **Sendero Bosque Nuboso** through the mist. This is a popular trail, so if you want to (try to) avoid other hikers, you might opt for the parallel **Sendero Camino**. The latter is wide and flat – less interesting visually, but better for birding.

Both trails end at a short trail that climbs to the **Mirador La Ventana**. At 1550m, this is a scenic 'window' over the Continental Divide – the convergence of the Pacific and Caribbean slopes, where dry air meets moist air. If the cloud cover is not too dense, the vista stretches east across the plains and valleys and west all the way to the Golfo de Nicoya.

From La Ventana, double back toward **Sendero Wilford Guindon**. Here you'll come across a 100m-long suspension bridge, swaying with your step, but offering an incredible perspective on the cloud-forest canopy. The final leg of the hike follows **Sendero Tosi** to a small but sweet waterfall. From here, you can take **Sendero Cuencha** back to the ranger station.

QUETZAL-SPOTTING

Monteverde is one of the best places in Costa Rica to spot a resplendent quetzal. The other is **San Gerardo de Dota** (p373).

Find Some Feathered Friends

Tick off your birdwatching hit list

Whether you are a budding birder, an avian expert or don't know your trogon from your tanager, the birdwatching in Monteverde is epic. Upward of 400 bird species pass through here at one time or another.

On the edge of the Monteverde Reserve, **Reserva Curi-Cancha** *(reservacuricancha.com; entry adult/child US$25/15; birding tours from US$125/115)* is a cattle ranch turned private reserve, with trails winding through primary, secondary and open forest. It's at a slightly lower elevation and hosts many of the same bird visitors but fewer human ones.

This is a top spot for Monteverde's most in-demand species, including the resplendent quetzal and the three-wattled bellbird, but there are a couple of hundred other gems here as well, such as the orange-bellied trogon and blue-crowned motmot. Rowdy toucans and evocatively named hummingbirds – violet sabrewings, green-crowned brilliants, coppery headed emeralds – are practically guaranteed.

The reserve opens at 6:30am for birdwatching: bring a guide, book a 4½-hour tour with one of its expert naturalist guides, or come on your own from 7am.

Make Like Tarzan

Fly over the cloud forest

For some adrenaline-fueled adventure, whizz over the cloud-forest canopy on the state-of-the-art zipline in **Selvatura Park** *(selvatura.com; adult from US$80)*. One of the longest and highest zipline courses in town, Selvatura has 13 thrilling cables and 15 platforms, all zigzagging over an incredible stretch of primary cloud forest. There's a Tarzan swing for extra fun and you can strike a Superman pose on your last cable.

Neighboring two vast private reserves and with its own large area of protected land, the zipline comes with unbroken

MY FAVORITE HIKE

Marcos Méndez Sibaja, naturalist guide and founder of Pasión Costa Rica, reveals his favorite hike in Monteverde. *@pasioncr*

My favorite place for a 'hardcore' hike is **Cerro Amigos**, the highest peak in the area (1842m). It's not an official trail but rather a dirt road up to the radio towers, or 'Las Torres.' It's often windy and misty at the top. But on a clear day (which is rare), you can see all the way to Volcán Arenal. To get there, take the dirt road behind Hotel Belmar in Cerro Plano. It's a steep uphill walk that takes 45 to 60 minutes each way.

EATING IN SANTA ELENA & MONTEVERDE: OUR PICKS

Monteverde Brewing Company: Sample some creative craft beer, perfectly paired with a top-notch burger (there's a vegan option, too). *noon-10pm* $$

Raulito's Pollo Asado: A local favorite, Raulito will fix your roast-chicken cravings at this friendly chicken joint. *8am-9:30pm Mon-Sat, to 3pm Sun* $

Boca2 Café: Tasty, wallet-friendly dishes with plenty of vegetarian and vegan options; don't miss the Donkey Kick coffee smoothie. *7am-5pm Mon-Sat* $

Stella's Monteverde: Santa Elena landmark serving healthy breakfast bowls, delicious sandwiches, sensational salads, just-baked quiches and more. *8am-4pm* $$

forest views. This high-speed canopy tour is a favorite with adrenaline junkies (age four and up), but Selvatura has a range of other attractions that will appeal to wildlife lovers, including a butterfly garden, a snake house, a sloth sanctuary and a fantastic 3km trail of suspension bridges.

While a researcher near Sarapiquí created the first zipline to explore the forest canopy, the first canopy tour for thrill-seeking travelers was launched in Monteverde in the 1990s. The **Original Canopy Tour** *(canopyoriginal.com; adult/child US$79.10/56.50)* is still operating, with 10 ziplines plus the chance to rappel down a towering tree. **100% Aventura** *(aventuracanopytour.com; adult/child US$67.80/56.50)* offers a similar set up with a super-long zipline; **Treetopia Park** *(treetopiapark.com; tours adult/child from US$100.60/80.20)* is home to the 3km SkyTrek zipline and the region's only SkyTram; and at **Monteverde Extremo Park** *(monteverdeextremo.com; tours from US$67.80)* you can bungee-jump into a 143m-high canyon.

CAFFEINE CRAZE

Coffee production is still biggest in the **Central Valley** (p121), but nowadays it's being cultivated all over the country.

QUANTITIES OF QUETZALS

Monteverde's most famous feathered resident, the aptly named resplendent quetzal, is on every birder's bucket list. This stunning – and hard-to-spot bird – has vibrant, shimmering green and blue plumage, with a striking scarlet belly and a pseudo mohawk. During mating season, adult males grow twin tail feathers that form a flowing train up to 1m long to impress a would-be mate. The best places to find quetzals are the Monteverde and Curi-Cancha Reserves from February through July, in the early morning. They nest in the hollows of decaying tree trunks, and feed on insects, lizards and fruit – they love wild avocados, especially *aguacatillo* (little avocado). Go with a local naturalist guide for the best chance of a sighting.

A Monkey's-Eye View

Hike along hanging bridges

Monteverde's hanging bridges are a slower and more serene way to explore the cloud-forest canopy, and you'll certainly see more wildlife. So, transport yourself to the treetops, look down on a seemingly endless patchwork of shifting greens and see the forest as monkeys, sloths and birds do.

Immerse yourself in the forest along **Selvatura Park**'s *(adult/child US$49/44.10)* 3km Treetop Walkway, combining forest trails and eight suspension bridges ranging in length from 50m to 170m. **100% Aventura** *(adult/child US$40/34)* offers two-hour guided walks along its 3km of trails and eight hanging bridges; you'll be able to borrow your guide's binoculars and peer through the scope as you learn about the flora and fauna. And **Treetopia Park** *(adult/child from US$47.50/32.80)* is home to the original SkyWalk hanging bridges soaring to a vertigo-inducing 50m; you can go it alone or with a guide.

Things That Go Bump in the Night

Embark on an after-dark adventure

To experience a very different side to the cloud forest, sign up for a night walk. The sun usually sets around 5:30pm, and by 6pm, the forest will be enveloped in darkness. You'll engage all your senses as you pick your way along the trails, serenaded by the frog chorus, the night air thick with the smell of damp vegetation.

You never know what you might see – your guide's torch might pick out the golden eyes of a kinkajou (a cross between a monkey and a small bear), or a somnolent three-toed sloth supine on its twig bed, a slumbering keel-billed toucan with its long bill resting along its back, or – far more deadly – a

FLO-SMITH/SHUTTERSTOCK

Hummingbird, Selvatura Park

venomous side-striped palm-pit viper coiled by the side of the trail. There'll be lots of interesting insects about, too.

Reserva Curi-Cancha *(US$30)* offers a two-hour guided night tour from 5:30pm with a maximum of nine people. **Pasión Costa Rica** *(pasioncostarica.com)* organises private night walks, choosing the best location on the day; some night tours can get crowded.

Wake Up & Smell the Coffee

An organic coffee tour

A farm tour at **Café Monteverde** *(cafedemonteverde.com; adult/child US$40/12)* is like a lesson in sustainability and a coffee date all in one. This impressive project is an association of 20 families that are committed to conservation, education and – most importantly – coffee. You'll see the whole process here, from seeds to trees to 'ripe cherries' to sun-dried beans to a delicious cup of joe.

Depending on the season, you might even get a chance to help out with the picking. Most fascinating, you'll learn about the sustainable practices the farm has implemented. Finish it off with a coffee cupping, sampling the various roasts and blends to find your favorite. They serve a farm-to-table lunch, too.

Down on the Farm

Get hands-on at Finca El Paraíso

For a perfect kid-friendly tour, head to **Finca El Paraíso** *(fincaparaisocr.com; adult/child US$30/15)* in Las Tornas. The farm has been around since the 1950s and is now split between three generations of family members. Around half the land is used for dairy farming, while the rest has been preserved as primary forest. The farm went organic several

Q&A ON HUMMINGBIRDS

Marcos Méndez Sibaja is a naturalist guide and founder of Pasión Costa Rica. *@pasioncr*

How many species of hummingbirds are there in Costa Rica? Costa Rica has 53 species, two of which are considered endemic: the coppery-headed emerald and the mangrove hummingbird. There are more than 20 species around Monteverde.

What's a fun fact about hummingbirds? Cuba's bee hummingbird is the smallest bird in the world, just 6cm long.

What's your favorite thing about hummingbirds? Their ability to fly forward, backward and upside down.

Where's the best place in Monteverde to see them? Cafe Colibrí outside the trailhead at the park, and there are often hummingbird nests near some of the trails. To avoid the crowds, especially in high season, go after 3pm.

SHOP LOCAL IN SANTA ELENA & MONTEVERDE

Brillante Souvenir: This boutique supports local artisans with an artfully curated collection of handcrafted goods.

Ferlander Arguedas: This abstract artist puts his colorful work on T-shirts, tote bags, umbrellas and more.

Monteverde Art House: Boutique selling locally made products, and a coffee shop, surrounded by lush gardens.

Monteverde Natural Cosmetics: All-natural, eco-conscious products that smell delicious – think cinnamon and organic-coffee soap.

CASEM: This nonprofit artisan cooperative is dedicated to improving the lives of local women artists.

Souvenir Rosewood: Jose Luis makes beautiful bowls, plates and more using sustainable rosewood; ask to see his workshop.

San Gerardo Field Station

years ago and adopted regenerative farming practices; the cows move daily, munching their way through one field at a time.

If you've ever wanted to milk a cow, they'll teach you the hands-on technique. And you can help to feed their super-cute calves, piglets and chickens. After, it's time to try artisanal cheese-making, separating the curds and whey before straining it through a cheesecloth. In no time, the soft, mild cheese is ready to enjoy with just-baked tortillas. You can learn how to bake bread and *empanadas* (stuffed turnovers), too.

The Trails Less Traveled

Getting off the tourist trail

Swirling with mist, echoing with birdsong and literally dripping with life, the cloud forest is an environment unlike any other. Although Monteverde is more famous, there are two other vast protected patches of cloud forest that receive fewer visitors.

If you've ever wondered what it's like to walk through the clouds, the wilds of the **Reserva Bosque Nuboso Santa Elena** *(reservasantaelena.org; adult/child from US$18/9)* are actually at higher altitude, making them just a little more nebulous – in a good way. The Santa Elena Cloud Forest Reserve is dense with life, and the slower you go, the more you notice. Keep an eye out for high-profile highland bird species, including the resplendent quetzal, the three-wattled bellbird, the long-tailed manakin and the emerald toucanet.

A guide also helps, but there's plenty to see and hear if you prefer to go it alone along the 12km of well-marked trails. Finish up with a stop at the observation tower which, on a clear day, offers a view over four volcanoes. If you can't see much, wait around. Clouds come and go, as do the views.

The long-standing **Bosque Eterno de los Niños** *(acmcr.org; adult/child from US$18/10.80)*, or the Children's Eternal

Rainforest, is Costa Rica's largest private reserve, and 100% of its proceeds go back into conservation, reforestation, research and education. Spanning 227 sq km, it's one of the most biodiverse places on the planet for its size. It has several zones: set out on foot for **San Gerardo Field Station**, high on the Caribbean slopes; while **Bajo El Tigre** has 4.5km of trails that wind through dryer forest, with two lookouts offering views over the Golfo de Nicoya.

Birding Bliss

For serious birders

If you're serious about your birds – and willing to go the extra mile (quite literally) – consider a visit to **San Gerardo Field Station** *(acmcr.org/en/san-gerardo; entry US$18)*, a remote outpost in the Children's Eternal Rainforest.

It's a 3.5km hike to reach the station, which takes a couple of hours, departing from the Santa Elena Cloud Forest Reserve, and you can go for the day or stay over at the rustic lodge (book in advance for food, lodging and tours), which includes three home-cooked meals a day.

The trail is famously muddy – bring proper boots – and your destination is set high on a Caribbean slope among lush premontane forest, draped in epiphytes and bursting with life. Beyond the forest looms the majestic Volcán Arenal and its namesake lake.

You could probably check off a few species from the lodge's balcony, but there are 9km of trails to explore and more than 300 species of birds to spot. The birding prize here is the endangered bare-necked umbrellabird, so named for its Elvis-style quiff. The males have a bright-red throat with no feathers, which puffs up during mating season (March through June). There's a host of mammals, reptiles and amphibians, too.

Two Wheels or Four Legs

Explore by bike or on horseback

Monteverde is prime mountain-biking territory, and **MonteTours** *(elbosquemonteverde.com; tours from US$99)* offers guided rides for all levels on top-notch electric mountain bikes. Remember, you're at high altitude here but you can make it as easy or hard as you like.

Everyone can enjoy the 4:30am sunrise tour (May through November), as you watch the sun peer over Volcán Arenal. On the sunset tour (December through April), watch as the setting sun streaks the Golfo de Nicoya pink and gold. For intermediate riders, the year-round Cloud Forest tour takes in some of Monteverde's most beautiful backroads. Advanced mountain bikers can take on the challenge of riding all the way to Laguna de Arenal and back, with some jaw-dropping views en route.

If you'd prefer to explore on four legs, **Horse Trek Monteverde** *(horsetrekmonteverde.com; tours from US$59)* has horseback-riding tours for all abilities. Marvin will take beginners on a gentle 2½-hour walk around this far-reaching family farm, with sweeping views over the rolling countryside. More experienced riders

WHY I LOVE MONTEVERDE

Sarah Gilbert, Lonely Planet writer

Monteverde showcases so many things I love about Costa Rica. The multisensory magic of a morning walk through the cloud forest. Picking over root-laced trails flanked with giant vegetation, dripping in moisture and wrapped in swirling mist, while listening to the soundtrack of wake-up whistles, whoops, chirrups, caws and trills. Marveling at towering trees trapped in a strangler fig's embrace, lofty branches festooned with bromeliads, feather-like ferns and dainty orchids. Spotting a primary-colored toucan perched on a branch like a flamboyant flower or listening to the wings of jewel-hued hummingbirds flitting between blossoms. The profusion of flora and fauna is awe-inspiring. So is the communal commitment to protecting it, rooted in the very history of Monteverde.

UP-CLOSE ANIMAL ENCOUNTERS IN MONTEVERDE & SANTA ELENA

Monteverde Butterfly Gardens: Take a tour of four unique butterfly habitats with more than 30 species of *mariposas,* plus lots of insects.

Bat Jungle: Fascinating exhibit about your favorite flying mammal, with around 90 bats flying freely about the enclosure.

Monteverde Hummingbird Gallery: Spy on jewel-colored hummingbirds as they hover around the feeders in the gorgeous gardens.

Herpetarium, Selvatura Park: A guide will introduce you to snakes, lizards and other cold-blooded critters in the custom-built terrariums.

Frog Pond Ranario: Up to 28 species of colorful frogs hop around their transparent enclosures. They are more active at night.

Restaurante Celajes

can spend a day in the saddle discovering *sabanero* (cowboy) culture, as they explore the mountains and lunch by a waterfall.

What Goes Up Must Come Down

Climbing and canyoning

At **Finca Modelo** *(familiabrenestours.com; tours adult from US$35),* the Brenes family has found some engaging ways to pass the time using ropes and rappels, such as climbing a vertigo-inducing 40m-high ficus tree.

There are three different ways to tackle the towering tree during this two-hour tour – all with a harness and safety lines, of course. You can climb up inside its hollowed-out trunk, or clamber up the outside with the aid of metal rods, similar to a *via ferrata.* The most challenging option is to climb a rope to the top. Whichever way you do it, you'll emerge onto a platform with 360-degree views over the *finca* (farm) and forest before rappelling down again.

For some more high-octane adventure, combine tree-climbing with canyoning in the cloud forest. After being strapped into your equipment, a short hike through the forest and a safety briefing, you'll rappel down six scenic waterfalls, the tallest of which is 40m. Be prepared to get wet.

Rustle Up Rice & Beans

A Costa Rican cooking class

Combat the craving for *gallo pinto* once you get home, and learn how to recreate your Costa Rican meal in your own kitchen at the **Santuario Ecológico** *(santuarioecologico.com; classes US$48),* where Doña Mireya Salazar leads the hands-on cooking classes.

Gallo pinto is one of the most traditional ways to start the day – a mix of rice, beans, peppers, onions and spices, it appears at lunch and dinner, too, perfectly paired with handmade corn tortillas and washed down with a cup of homegrown coffee.

You can learn to cook up *arroz con pollo* (rice with chicken), and perennial Costa Rican favorite, *casado* (set meal). Or learn how to rustle up a traditional snack, such as *chorreada,* a filling corn pancake; sweet, deep-fried *prestiños,* perfect for an afternoon coffee break; or *empanadas de chiverre. Chiverre* is a member of the squash family, used to make a sweet preserve, popular around Holy Week.

This family farm is committed to permaculture, conservation and ecofriendly practices. You can walk the trails through the recovering forest or book a creative coffee ritual.

Foodie Rica

Unique eating experiences

When you grow weary of *gallo pinto,* get a taste of the surprisingly sophisticated dining scene in Monteverde and Santa Elena. Splurge at one of the following restaurants, where the focus is on local ingredients, creative cookery and one-of-a-kind settings.

At **El Jardín**, the acclaimed restaurant at **Monteverde Lodge & Gardens** *(monteverdelodge.com),* you'll dine on creative gourmet fare crafted from top-notch local produce, surrounded by hanging greenery and brilliant blooms. The greenhouse setting is a delight – especially when the orchids are in bloom (January to April). There are plenty of options for vegetarians and vegans.

You can't get more local than **Farm to Table Escondida** at **Valle Escondido Nature Reserve Hotel & Farm** *(valleescondidocr.com).* It grows most of its ingredients onsite and the result is irresistible fresh salads and brick-oven pizzas. Explore the lovely grounds and gardens to see where your meal came from, then drink in the stunning views over the 'hidden valley' as you dine – it's wonderful at sunset.

At venerable **Hotel Belmar** *(hotelbelmar.net),* **Restaurante Celajes** is a wonderful place to end the day. From the balcony, you'll enjoy sweeping views of the cloud forest – all the way to the Golfo de Nicoya on a clear day. The menu epitomizes farm-to-table cuisine, using ingredients cultivated in the hotel's organic garden or at the family's nearby farm, Tierra Madre. Even the lounge serves beers that are brewed on-site and craft cocktails made from fresh seasonal ingredients. Come for 'Tico time' (aka happy hour), from 4:30pm to 5:30pm, to take in the sunset vistas and drink a toast to *pura vida.*

The **San Lucas Treetop Dining Experience** *(sanlucas.cr)* promises (and delivers) a captivating 'gastronomic adventure' and makes a regular appearance on 'the world's most romantic restaurant' lists. High on a hillside overlooking Santa Elena, private glass pods are suspended in the sky, looking down through the clouds. The menu is a closely guarded secret – a nine-course extravaganza that celebrates the region, the country and its native produce. Every course tells a story about the geography, culture and cuisine of Costa Rica to a forest soundtrack. There are two sittings per night: go for the early one.

MORE FARM & GARDEN TOURS IN MONTEVERDE & SANTA ELENA

Valle Escondido: At this nature reserve, hotel and farm, take the sustainability tour to learn about the principles of permaculture.

Finca Ecológica San Luis: This farming family has opened its primary forest for hiking, river swimming and birdwatching. There's no-frills camping, too.

El Pueblo Coffee Tour: Go bean-to-cup at this small, family-run farm, ending with a tasting and homebaked cakes in its hilltop cafe.

Jardín de Orquídeas: Shady trails wind past more than 450 orchid species in this gorgeous garden, including blooms a few millimeters across.

Don Juan Tours: Discover the process behind Costa Rica's most important products, in this hands-on coffee, chocolate and sugarcane tour.

Beyond Monteverde & Santa Elena

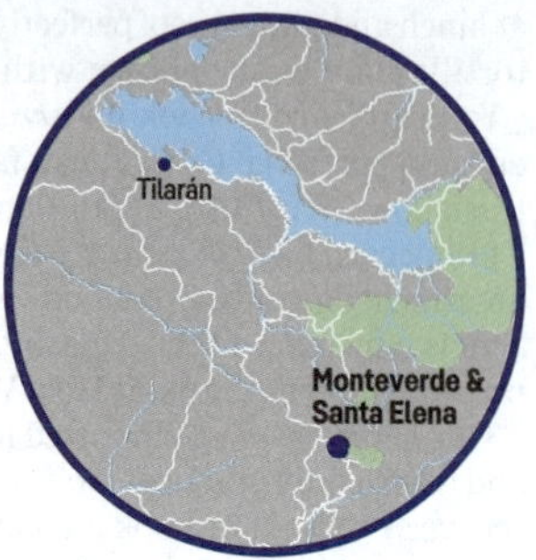

Hike to hidden waterfalls and cool off in sweet swimming holes between Santa Elena and Laguna de Arenal.

Places

Tilarán p192

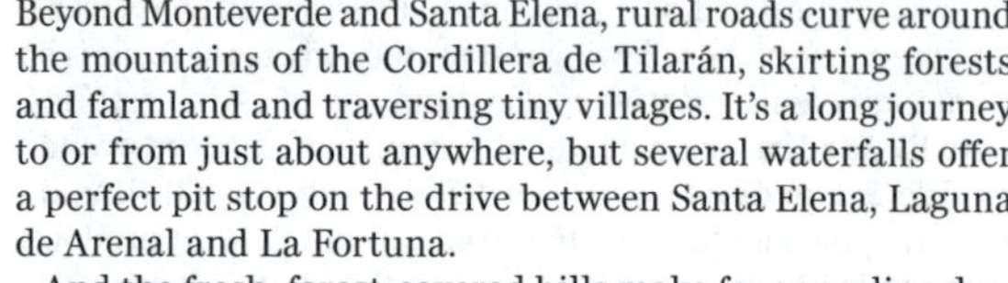

Beyond Monteverde and Santa Elena, rural roads curve around the mountains of the Cordillera de Tilarán, skirting forests and farmland and traversing tiny villages. It's a long journey to or from just about anywhere, but several waterfalls offer a perfect pit stop on the drive between Santa Elena, Laguna de Arenal and La Fortuna.

And the fresh, forest-covered hills make for appealing destinations in their own right, especially when they hide wondrous waterfalls – from gentle streams to powerful ragers, rushing over rocks or dropping down cliffs to create enticing swimming holes. If you don't swim under at least one waterfall while you are in the vicinity of Monteverde, you are doing it wrong.

GETTING AROUND

Ruta 145 between Monteverde and Tilarán is winding, mountainous but very scenic. It's a mix of paved and dirt road and takes around 1½ to two hours. It can get potholed and muddy, especially during the rainy season, so a high-clearance vehicle is recommended. Avoid driving it after dark as there are no guardrails. There are regular buses between Santa Elena and Tilarán (around 2½ hours); from there you can get an onward bus to La Fortuna.

Tilarán

TIME FROM MONTEVERDE & SANTA ELENA: **1 HR 20 MINS**

Wondrous waterfalls

El Tigre Waterfalls *(eltigrewaterfalls.com; adult/child from US$33/22)* is an adventurous and sometimes challenging 8km hike that includes four gushing falls, 10 hanging bridges and countless swimming holes along the way. The trail is well marked but often muddy, so wear boots. If you want to avoid the uphill slog on the way back, spring for the 'full package,' which includes returning on horseback or by 4WD. This is a half-day outing, around 10km north of Santa Elena.

Close to Tilarán, 25km northwest of Santa Elena, community-run **Cataratas Viento Fresco** *(facebook.com/senderosvientofresco; US$12, cash only)* is the perfect place to break up the drive between Monteverde and La Fortuna. The hiking trail is steep and sometimes precarious, with lots of earthen steps, but it leads past three picturesque waterfalls of varying sizes, with one more on view in the distance. The highlight is the 75m **Arco Iris**, which casts a rainbow in the lower right corner of the pool. You can climb up behind the falls and jump off the cliff on the right-hand side. It's scary, but not as scary as it looks from below.

JOSE COSTA RICA/RUTAS ANCESTRALES MONTEVERDE LTDA

El Tigre Waterfalls

If you prefer your hikes guided and your trails well manicured, you'll appreciate **La Piedra del Indio** *(lapiedradelindiowaterfalls.com; self-guided tour adult/child US$17/$10, guided tour adult/child US$30/$20)*. It's family-run, and Alejandro and his guides lead visitors on hikes along a magnificent multilevel cascade, regaling them with their extensive knowledge of the flora and fauna along the way. Take a dip in the refreshing swimming hole at the bottom – lunch is included in the guided hike – then hike or ride horses back.

You'll need your own vehicle to access these destinations, with the exception of El Tigre, which offers a shuttle service from Santa Elena for an additional fee.

WATERFALL-SWIMMING SAFETY TIPS

1. Conditions can change dramatically, especially following heavy rains. It's important to assess the risk each time you swim.
2. Always comply with posted restrictions and warnings indicating unsafe swimming areas.
3. Look out for hard-to-spot underwater hazards, such as boulders and logs, before getting in.
4. Test the depth of waterfall pools by wading in rather than jumping in headfirst.
5. Avoid swimming directly under the waterfall, where the pressure of the water could force you under.
6. Be careful of strong currents that could pull you into rocks or boulders, especially at times of high water flow.
7. Wear shoes that grip and watch out for slippery rocks around the waterfall.

EATING AROUND TILARÁN: OUR PICKS

Restaurante y Pizzeria Donde Jossy: Popular spot that serves a mean Neapolitan pizza; wash it down with a glass of sangria. *11am-8pm Thu-Tue* $

Sunset Coffee: Wallet-friendly, all-day dining cafe offering stunning views, particularly at sunset – perfect with a delicious burger. *8am-8pm* $

Restaurante Brisas del Lago: Local and international flavors; think Thai shrimp and a perfectly cooked steak. *noon-2:30pm & 5:30-9pm Mon-Fri, noon-9pm Sat* $$

Restaurante Florida: Look out for the popular vegetarian *casado* (set meal) and don't miss a glass of sugarcane juice from their own press. *7am-7pm* $

Río Celeste

TECHNICOLOR LANDSCAPES | WILD NATURE | COMMUNITY TOURISM

GETTING AROUND

Driving to the park is straightforward; it's around two hours from Santa Elena and 1½ hours from La Fortuna. There's no public transport to the national park or the surrounding area, so if you don't have a car, consider staying in Bijagua and booking a tour (or taking a taxi or private shuttle) to the park. There are regular buses to Bijagua from Cañas (one hour), but it's a long journey from Santa Elena with a change at La Irma.

TOP TIP

The paving of the road to Parque Nacional Volcán Tenorio resulted in a massive increase in traffic to the national park. The park service limits the number of people admitted, so book your tickets well in advance on the Sinac (Sistema Nacional de Areas de Conservación) website; you can choose your time slot.

From the icy-blue waters of its namesake river to the deep greens of the surrounding forests, the Río Celeste region shimmers with vibrant life. You can spend your days hiking and swimming amid the technicolor landscape.

The Parque Nacional Volcán Tenorio is a cool, misty and magical place with four volcanic peaks soaring up to a skyscraping 1916m. Its 189 sq km are dense with primary forest – cloud forest at higher altitudes and rainforest lower down – all teeming with wildlife, including more than 500 species of birds.

Bijagua de Upala is the gateway to the region. This small farming center, set in an idyllic valley between Volcán Tenorio and Volcán Miravalles, about 9km west of the national park, has become a trailblazer in rural community tourism. Bed down in one of the ecofriendly lodges to immerse yourself in this incredible natural environment.

River Blue & Forest Green

Hiking the Río Celeste

The **Parque Nacional Volcán Tenorio** *(sinac.go.cr; entry adult/child US$13.60/5.70)* is an entracing place, covered by cloud forests and teeming with life. Soaring 1916m above the forest is the park's namesake volcano; below is the remarkable **Río Celeste**, which winds its way through the park in a series of waterfalls and lagoons.

A 6km out-and-back trail leads from the park entrance at **Puesto Pilón**. Some parts of the trail are steep – and most parts are muddy, so you'll need boots – but it showcases the park's highlights; allow yourself three or four hours to see it all.

You'll pass the **Catarata de Río Celeste**, a milky-blue waterfall that cascades 30m down the rocks into a fantastically aquamarine pool. There are around 250 steps down to the waterfall (and 250 steps back up), but it's worth it.

Afterward, stop at the *mirador* (lookout point) to enjoy grand views over the four volcanic cones of the Tenorio volcanic massif. Further on is the spectacular **Laguna Azul** (Blue

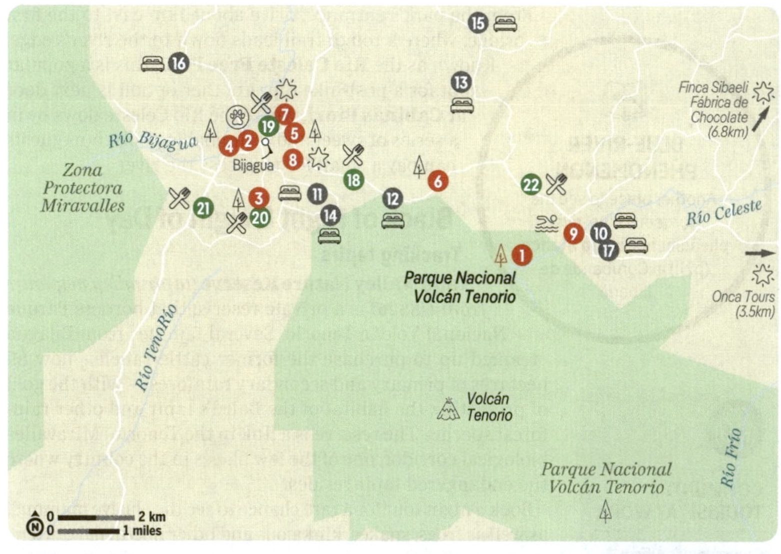

HIGHLIGHTS
1 Parque Nacional Volcán Tenorio

SIGHTS
2 Bijagua Ranas
3 Finca Verde Lodge
4 Frog's Paradise
5 Spring Paradise Bijagua
6 Tapir Valley Nature Reserve

ACTIVITIES
7 Bijagua Rainforest Tours
8 Jungle Life Costa Rica
9 Río Celeste Free Pool

SLEEPING
10 Cabinas Piuri
11 Casitas Tenorio B&B & Farm
12 Celeste Mountain Lodge
13 Finca La Amistad Cacao Lodge
14 Heliconias Rainforest Lodge
15 La Carolina Lodge
16 Mei Tai Cacao Lodge
17 Río Celeste Hideaway

EATING
18 Blue River Brewery
19 Café Semilla
20 Hummingbird Café
21 La Choza del Maíz
22 Restaurante Metamorphosis

Lagoon) and the sulfur-smelling **Borbollones**, fissures and cracks through which hot volcanic gases escape. The trail loops around the lagoon until you arrive at the confluence of rivers known as **El Teñidero** (The Dyer), where two small rivers mix to create the Río Celeste's famed blue hue.

Note that heavy rains can stir up dirt and sediment, which makes the water appear more brown than blue. If you're at the Río Celeste after heavy rains, it's worth asking your accommodations to check the color of the water before you set off; there are also color updates on the park's Facebook page.

Cool Blue Pools

Swimming in the Río Celeste

You'll have to fight an irresistible urge to jump into this refreshing and beguilingly blue water – swimming is strictly forbidden everywhere in the national park. Luckily, if you want to submerge yourself in these enticing waters, there are a few options.

WHY SO BLUE?

According to Costa Rican legend, when God finished painting the sky, he dipped his paintbrush in the Río Celeste. But there's also science behind this river's jewel-colored water. El Teñidero sits at the junction of two rivers; one is the Río Buenavista, and the other is Quebrada Agria (Sour Creek), both with a high concentration of minuscule mineral particles (including aluminum and silicon) suspended in the water that can reflect the blue component of sunlight. Scientists believe that when they mix, it's the chemical reaction between the acidic water of the Quebrada Agria and that of the more PH-neutral Río Buenavista that gives the water an amazing azure appearance.

From the park's entrance, drive about 1km east to the first bridge, where a rough trail leads down to the river's edge. Known as the **Río Celeste Free Pool**, this is a popular spot for a post-hike dip. Another option is next door at **Cabinas Piuri**, where the Río Celeste flows by in a series of sweet and swimmable pools; non-guests can pay a small fee to access the river.

BLUE-RIVER PHENOMENON

Another place to see the gorgeous blue-river phenomenon is **Río Blanco** (p211) in Curubandé de Liberia.

Black of Night & Light of Day

Tracking tapirs

Tapir Valley Nature Reserve *(tapirvalley.net; tours from US$26)* is a private reserve that borders Parque Nacional Volcán Tenorio. Several families from Bijagua teamed up to purchase the former cattle ranch – now 89 hectares of primary and secondary rainforest – with the goal of protecting the habitat of the Baird's tapir and other rainforest species. The reserve is a link in the Tenorio–Miravalles biological corridor, one of the few places in the country where the endangered tapir resides.

Book a night tour for a rare chance to see the elusive mammal, as well as frogs, snakes, kinkajous and other nocturnal critters. Or, if you're more of a morning person, opt for the three-hour **birdwatching tour** at 6am. It's an incredible birding destination, thanks to its diverse habitats and the minimal human presence along its 6km of hiking trails that wind through the forest at various altitudes as well as through wetlands.

Three different **viewing platforms** provide an ideal perspective over the forest, the wetlands and a hummingbird garden. Among the rare avian species here are the ornate hawk eagle, the colorful cotinga and the bare-necked umbrellabird. The super-knowledgeable naturalist guides will help you find them.

COMMUNITY TOURISM AT WORK

Community tourism in Bijagua de Upala (p199) started in 1991, when a group of 23 local families rallied together to protect 73 hectares of primary rainforest on the edge of the national park. The land had been designated for distribution to local farmers, but the families formed a community association that agreed to conserve the forest instead of clearing the land for farming. They founded **Heliconias Rainforest Lodge**, the first ecolodge and private reserve in the area, which became a model for conservation efforts. The association has since helped many of its members to invest in their own property, creating their own projects and turning Bijagua into the community-driven ecotourism center that it is today.

Totally Tubular

Floating on the Río Celeste

Spend an adventurous half-day in an inner tube, floating across the turquoise pools and riding the white water of the Río Celeste. This is a perfect combo of thrill and chill, although the balance varies, depending on recent rains and the resulting water levels. Either way, your river guide will be on hand to keep you safe and help you navigate the obstacles.

Remember that you are riding an inner tube, so you're completely soaked the whole time (dry bags are provided). When you want to take a break from the tube, you can jump in for a swim. **Onca Tours** *(riocelestehiking.com; adult/child from US$55/40)* offers a half-day, 4km-long tubing trip (the country's longest), ending with a Tarzan Swing over the river.

Take a Bird's-Eye View

Hanging bridges and hummingbirds

Get a bird's-eye view of the rainforest when you hike the Heliconias Hanging Bridges Trail, on the grounds of the **Heliconias**

Heliconias Rainforest Lodge

Rainforest Lodge *(heliconiascr.com; adult/child US$14/7)*. It's a 2.2km trail through primary forest, with sweeping views across the old-growth forest from three suspension bridges. The unique perspective from the bridges gives a real sense of their size and strength. Gazing down from the leafy canopy to the forest floor – a distance of around 35m – is awe-inspiring.

Before or after your hike, take a tour of the family-run **Finca Verde Lodge** *(fincaverdelodge.com; tours from US$15)*, stopping off to admire the fabulous tropical flora and spot a sloth or two. Stay to eat at the **Hummingbird Café**, where the menu makes the most of the homegrown organic produce. The garden setting is a delight, with hummingbirds flitting about.

View a Volcanic Crater

Hike around Lago Danta

Volcán Tenorio is made up of four volcanic peaks and two craters. These summits are mostly off-limits, except for the small but picturesque crater lake known as **Lago Danta**, or Tapir Lake. Now extinct, the crater fills with rainwater and becomes a popular watering hole for resident creatures, particularly (as the name suggests) tapirs.

The trailhead is at **Heliconias Rainforest Lodge** *(with guide US$40)*. Along the Heliconias Hanging Bridges Trail, there's a turnoff to the **Sendero Laguna Danta**, a 3km spur that leads

BEST NATURE TOURS IN BIJAGUA

Bijagua Rainforest Tours: Naturalist guide Marlon Brenes and his team lead hikes around the region, plus mountain-biking and horseback-riding tours.

Bijagua Ranas: Named after the frogs (best seen at night), this small reserve is famous for its resident sloths, perhaps due to all the cecropia trees.

Frog's Paradise: Formerly used for cattle-grazing, this wetlands is a habitat for frogs including the blue-jean poison-dart frog. Popular spot for a night tour.

Jungle Life Costa Rica: A family-run outfit has preserved a tract of forest and leads day and night tours to spot sloths, birds, frogs, monkeys and more.

Spring Paradise Bijagua: Guides take you through primary and secondary forest, where you can spot sloths, snakes and other wildlife.

EATING AROUND RÍO CELESTE: OUR PICKS

Restaurante Metamorphosis: Delightful spot near the national park entrance with traditional food in a lovely garden setting. *8am-10pm* $

Café Semilla: This cute cafe caters to all dietary requirements, with filling breakfasts, big salads and fresh-fruit smoothies. *6:30am-9pm* $

Blue River Brewery: Stop for a cold, home-brewed Blue Morpho, and nachos with *patacones* (fried green plantains). *noon-10pm Wed-Sat, to 9pm Sun* $$

La Choza del Maíz: A Bijagua favorite, this simple *soda* features the region's staple ingredient: corn. Try *chorreadas* (corn pancakes). *7am-8pm* $

up to the crater lake. The trail is steep and challenging and takes around five hours; national park regulations require you to hike with a professional guide, and you'd get hopelessly lost without one.

The trail ascends to 1350m, transitioning from rainforest at lower altitudes into the cloud forest at the summit. This offers a remarkable opportunity to observe the contrasts between the two forests – not only the habitats but also the native birds and beasts. Monkeys, sloths and coatis are often spotted, along with many varieties of birds and frogs. It's not common to see larger mammals, but they're out there – keep your eyes peeled for tapir and puma tracks in the mud.

TAPIR TERRITORY

The country's largest population of tapirs resides around the La Sirena Ranger Station in **Parque Nacional Corcovado** (p396). They prefer to forage at night when it's cool, so only overnight visitors might catch a glimpse.

Sweet Like Chocolate

Go from bean to bar

Chocoholics will love the sweet experience at **Finca Sibaeli Fábrica de Chocolate** *(chocolatesibaeli.com; adult/child US$35/15),* set in a lush forest around 45 minutes east of Bijagua. This organic farm is a family affair; Juan Carlos and his wife Maria are passionate about all things chocolate, and will take you from bean to bar on a 90-minute tour.

As you stroll through the organic cacao plantation – yes, chocolate is technically a fruit; the farm also grows coconuts, bananas and papayas – you'll hear about the history of cacao, in addition to smelling and tasting it. Then you'll be immersed in the chocolate-making process, from the fermentation and drying of the cacao, to the roasting and grinding. You'll get to sample chocolate in its purest form and with different percentages of cacao, before enjoying a traditional chocolate drink. Then snap up some bars to take home.

Finca Sibaeli Fábrica de Chocolate

JORGE EZEQUIEL BERBENA MURILLO/ CHOCOLATE SIBAELI

DEETS ABOUT DANTAS

Officially called Baird's tapir, or the Central American tapir, it's known locally as a *danta*. Often confused for an anteater (in fact, it's distantly related to rhinos and horses), this gentle giant is one of four species of tapir and Costa Rica's – and Central America's – largest land mammal. This herbivore can weigh up to 300kg; for the record, it requires around 40kg of vegetation per day to maintain that weight. Baird's tapir is chiefly nocturnal and solitary and its tough skin, distinctive light patches and long, bendy nose – perfect for swimming and sniffing the air – make it stand out in the wild. Today, tapirs have few natural predators but are listed as endangered due to habitat loss.

Beyond Río Celeste

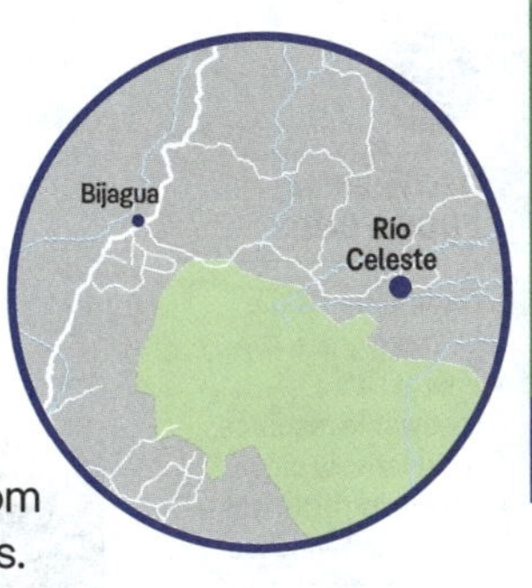

Explore the environs of Volcán Miravalles, from picturesque waterfalls to volcanic hot springs.

At 2028m, Volcán Miravalles is the tallest in the Cordillera de Guanacaste and has been protected by the Parque Nacional Miravalles–Jorge Manuel Dengo since 2019. Although the main crater is dormant, the fires are still roiling and raging deep beneath the earth's surface and it's become an under-the-radar hot-springs destination, where you can soak up the energy.

Miravalles is home to the country's first geothermal power plant, constructed in 1994 to harness the energy of the earth. You'll see the pipes and tubes snaking and steaming around the flanks of the volcano. This area is much less developed than some other volcano sites, but it's an attractive destination scattered with hot springs, and the volcano views will blow you away.

Places

Bijagua p199

Bijagua

TIME FROM RÍO CELESTE: **30 MIN**

Hiking and hot springs

It may be technically dormant – the only volcanic eruption on record was a small steam explosion in 1946 – but **Volcán Miravalles** generates enough energy to supply five power plants, which provide electricity for much of the country. The plants and pipes are belching and steaming along the roads all around this area, and you can spot the volcano through the clouds from **Bijagua**, but it's a 30km drive to the volcano slopes.

The best place to see volcanic action up-close is at family-run **Las Hornillas Volcanic Activity Center** *(hornillas.com; adult/child from US$40/30)*, which has its own active crater. A short trail around the barren landscape winds around bubbling pools, multihued gurgling mud pots and steaming fumaroles. It's a truly surreal scene in the midst of the forest greenery.

Also pay a visit the rustic geothermal 'spa.' The circuit starts in the geothermal sauna to open the pores, followed by a full-body mud 'mask' to take advantage of the therapeutic properties, and then a soak in the warm thermal pools. The final step is a dive into the cold pool to close the pores – not for the fainthearted.

If you want to make a day of it, there's also a wonderful guided **waterfall hike** *(adult/child US$65/55)* on the property, starting with a hokey but fun tractor ride to the trailhead.

GETTING AROUND

Volcán Miravalles is 27km northeast of Bagaces, near the villages of Fortuna de Bagaces and Guayabo. It's a 30km drive from Bijagua, if you take the rural road via Cuipilapa. This route has an extremely steep incline, known to locals as La Gigante: it is paved but it takes some courage. The alternative is the 88km route via Ruta 1, which takes about 30 minutes longer. Buses from Bijagua to Bagaces change at Cañas (around two hours).

GEOTHERMAL PROS & CONS

Geothermal is the ultimate green energy: it's a renewable resource, it's relatively clean, producing little waste and no greenhouse gas emissions, and it's not dependent on weather conditions, unlike solar, wind and hydropower energy. Currently, Costa Rica produces around 11% of its electricity from geothermal sources, including power plants at Miravalles and Rincón de la Vieja. Considering the benefits, it seems a no-brainer for the country to expand its geothermal power capacity. However, there is an obstacle: geothermal energy is location-specific and the plants must be in areas where that energy is accessible. In Costa Rica's case, most of these areas are within national parks, which are legally protected from exploitation for any commercial purposes.

TONOCB/SHUTTERSTOCK

Volcán Miravalles (p199)

The 2km hike takes in two waterfalls, including one stunner that's spanned by a 40m hanging bridge, as well as lunch.

Luxury lodge with ample adventure

The area around Volcán Miravalles is sprinkled with small, family-run facilities offering simple lodgings and volcano-heated hot springs. But – broadly speaking – it lacks the fancy facilities you might find near Volcán Arenal (p231) or Rincón de la Vieja (p207). The exception is the gorgeous high-end resort, **Río Perdido Hotel & Thermal River** *(rioperdido.com; day pass from US$109).*

From Bijagua, it's a 35km drive south to Río Perdido, which is set on a vast private reserve at the junction of two volcanic river canyons, surrounded by dry tropical forest and scrubby dwarf forest higher up. This rare ecosystem is breathtakingly beautiful and ripe for adventure, from hiking and mountain biking to river tubing and ziplining. At the center of the property is a volcano-heated river, with dozens of natural thermal pools of varying temperatures; there's a serene nature-inspired spa, too.

The bungalows are sustainably designed and architecturally stunning, with private terraces and panoramic forest views. All this fabulousness doesn't come cheap, but non-guests can get a taste of the action with a good-value day pass.

EATING AROUND MIRAVALLES: OUR PICKS

Borrego Negro: Unassuming roadside bar and grill with tasty (and huge) burgers and other grilled meats. *5-10pm Tue-Fri, from noon Sat & Sun* $$

Volcano: Burgers, steaks and chicken grilled to perfection at this Guayabo favorite with a hospitable owner. *noon-10pm Tue-Sun* $$

Los Juanchos Pizzeria: Open-air Yökö Termales joint serving wood-fired pizzas, and Nutella and strawberry dessert pizzas. *5-9:30pm Tue-Sun* $$

Restaurante Sotavento: Popular *soda* with an extensive meaty menu and daily chalkboard specials, plus a bar area. *11am-10pm Mon-Sat, to 9pm Sun* $$

Cañas

COWBOY CULTURE | RIVER RAFTING | WILDLIFE-FILLED WETLANDS

Come out of the mountains and down to the hot, dusty plains of Guanacaste. This is cowboy country, where cattle ranches spread out across the landscape and life moves at a leisurely pace – except during the Fiestas Cívicas in March.

In Cañas, *sabanero* (cowboy) culture is on full display, from herds of Brahman cattle being driven through its sweltering streets, to the barbecue restaurants and rough-and-ready saloons. It's a small town with a distinctive Catholic church and a big bullring, a stage for rodeos, *topes* (horse parades) and Toros a la Tica, or Costa Rican–style 'bullfighting' – the bull isn't killed, but it's still a controversial tradition in this animal-loving country.

Sleepy Cañas is more authentic Tico town than tourist destination, but its location on Ruta 1 makes it an easy jumping-off point for adventures around the region, including rafting, hiking and exploring the watery wonderland of Palo Verde's wetlands.

GETTING AROUND

It's easy to get to Cañas, as it's right on Ruta 1. Buses ply this highway frequently, heading north to Bagaces or Liberia, south toward San José, and east to Bijagua. You'll need your own transport (ideally a 4WD) to reach Cerro Pelado, but the other experiences are close at hand.

A Tale of Two Rivers

Rafting adventures in Cañas

Arid and flat, Guanacaste isn't known for its rivers and rapids. But here on the outskirts of **Cañas** there are a few waterways that will get your adrenaline pumping.

RCR Rafting *(raftingguanacaste.com)* offers full-day rafting tours on the Río Tenorio *(US$130),* which provide some powerful white-water action with Class III/IV rapids, as well as an intense 3m drop – your stomach will catch up later. Alternatively, opt for a more tranquil half-day floating trip along the Río Corobicí *(adult/child US$80/68),* a wide river with fewer rapids but lots of monkeys, birds and other wildlife to spot, including caimans and crocodiles.

Both tours end up at the **Restaurante Rincón Corobicí** for excellent international fare and wonderful views over the

TOP TIP

There's a dearth of places to stay in Cañas, so if you want to explore this region, base yourself in the small but appealing village of Bijagua de Upala (40km along Ruta 6) or livelier Liberia (50km north along Ruta 1).

THE SIX CATS OF COSTA RICA

Jaguar: Central America's biggest cat – a male can weigh up to 120kg – has a stunning spotted coat.

Puma: Athletic cat with a powerful, muscular body and plain coat; it's able to adapt to different habitats.

Ocelot: Medium-sized spotted cat famous for its *manos gordos* (fat hands) that allow it to climb trees with ease.

Jaguarundi: Strange-shaped cat, with a long body, small head, short legs and no spots. It's diurnal and can survive in a range of habitats.

Margay: Looks like a small ocelot but with a longer tail and enormous eyes. It's a skilled climber and loves to leap through the treetops.

Oncilla: The smallest of the cats weighs 2kg on average and resides in the higher altitudes of the cloud forest.

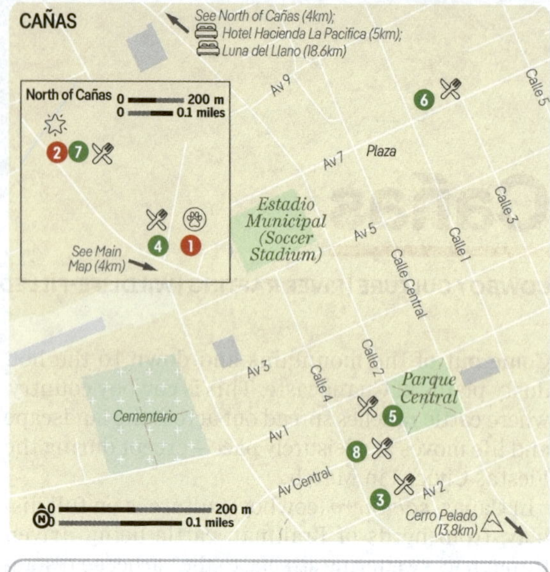

SIGHTS
1 Centro de Rescate y Santuario Las Pumas

ACTIVITIES
2 RCR Rafting

EATING
3 Bastos Restaurante
4 Cocobolo
5 Restaurante El Parque
6 Restaurante Mimi
7 Restaurante Rincón Corobicí
8 Soda Don Rogelio

Río Corobicí and – on a clear day – Volcán Tenorio. There's also a sweet river-swimming spot, in case you haven't got wet enough.

Bare-Hill Hike

Watch the sunrise from Cerro Pelado

The word is out about this majestic mountain around 12km southeast of Cañas. At 680m, **Cerro Pelado** *(8838-3645; entry US$12, parking US$6)* is an extinct volcano that's barren at the summit – hence the name, which translates as 'bare hill.' What this means for hikers is incredible, uninterrupted vistas on all sides, and it's a wonderful place to catch the sunrise or the sunset.

EATING AROUND CAÑAS: OUR PICKS

Bastos Restaurante: Contemporary restaurant serving international and vegetarian dishes and delicious desserts. *11am-10pm Mon-Sat, to 8pm Sun* **$$**

Restaurante Mimi: Right by Ruta 1, this *soda* offers big breakfasts and a buffet of typical dishes like *empanadas*. *6am-9pm* **$**

Cocobolo: Dine alfresco on home-style dishes at this family-owned roadside restaurant close to Las Pumas. Don't miss the coconut flan. *6am-8pm* **$$**

Soda Don Rogelio: Try the famous *leche dormida* drink, perhaps flavored with vanilla and cinnamon. Pair it with their *enyucadas* (cheesy pastries). *8am-6pm Mon-Sat* **$**

Early-morning party people sometimes sleep in their car (or camp) at the trailhead before setting out around 4am, while afternoon hikers should set out around 3pm. Either way, on this 5.5km out-and-back trail, you'll be rewarded with fantastic views of endless rolling hills and an ever-changing sky. Either way, you'll be doing half the hike in the dark, so bring a flashlight.

The trail is well maintained but it can be a slog at times, particularly the short, steep section at the beginning, with loose stones and gravel, so a walking stick is helpful (they're available at the trailhead). The lack of vegetation means that the sun and wind can be extremely harsh, especially November through January, so slap on the sunscreen and carry plenty of water; it's worth calling ahead to check conditions, particularly in the rainy season, and navigate to 'Entrada Cerro Pelado.'

Save the Felines

An innovative animal rescue center

Cat-lovers will want to make a stop at **Centro de Rescate y Santuario Las Pumas** *(laspumascr.org; adult/child US$15/10)*, one of Costa Rica's largest and longest-standing animal rescue centers. You'll find five of the country's six feline species here – jaguar, puma, jaguarundi, ocelot and margay – along with other wild residents, such as spider monkeys and scarlet macaws.

This nonprofit's aim is to rehabilitate rescued animals and return them to the wild. The animals on show – perhaps because they are injured or too tame – reside in the sanctuary, an area of spacious, natural enclosures, where you can read their backstories and learn a lot about wildlife conservation.

You can reserve a free guided tour a day or two in advance online. It's 4.5km north of Cañas, right off Ruta 1, and an easy stop on the way to or from the coast.

LECHE DORMIDA

When passing through Cañas, don't miss the opportunity to sample the local Guanacaste drink, *leche dormida* (literally 'sleeping milk'). It was created by Cañas native Don Rogelio Gutierrez in 1946, and the recipe for this one-of-a-kind milkshake has been passed down through the generations – a mix of milk, sugar, cinnamon and vanilla, plus a top-secret ingredient. It's thought that the name was inspired by the preparation: after mixing the ingredients, the drink must sit for at least an hour to settle and allow the milk to curdle. Then the drink is chilled, ice is added and a final whirl in a blender results in a creamy, refreshing treat. Sample it at Soda Don Rogelio (p202) or **Restaurante El Parque**.

Beyond Cañas

Guanacaste may be Costa Rica's driest province, but it's home to one of its most extensive and important wetlands.

Places

Guanacaste's aridity is palpable – especially during dry season. The towns are dusty, the sun is scorching and the landscape takes on a golden-brown hue. People flock to the region's cooling waters for respite from the heat, and so does the wildlife.

In the midst of the dry forest and farmland, about 40km west of Cañas, is one of the country's largest wetlands, protected by Parque Nacional Palo Verde. Even during dry season, when the river basin shrinks dramatically, a number of shallow permanent lagoons remain. These become a focal point for wildlife, especially birds and crocodiles. The large concentrations of animals, in turn, become a focal point for wildlife-watchers.

GETTING AROUND

A gravel road leads around 20km from Ruta 1 to the entrance of Parque Nacional Palo Verde, and another 10km to the OTS research station. If you don't have your own vehicle, local boat-tour operators can arrange transport for an extra fee and there are plenty of guided tours from the beach towns. If you're staying at the OTS lodge, ask about transportation from Bagaces. There are frequent buses to Bagaces from Cañas, Bijagua, Liberia and San José.

Parque Nacional Palo Verde

TIME FROM CAÑAS: **50 MINS**

Dry forest and wetlands

At the head of the Golfo de Nicoya, amid the lowlands of Guanacaste, the region's major rivers all drain into this ancient basin, creating a mosaic of 11 distinct habitats. Here, the **Parque Nacional Palo Verde** *(entry US$12, cash only)* protects one of the largest and most important wetlands in Central America, as well as a rare intact tract of tropical dry forest. The **Organization of Tropical Studies** *(OTS; tropicalstudies.org)* operates a **research station** here, with a simple lodge and tours catering to scientists and nature-loving tourists.

The wetlands of the lower Río Tempisque watershed are home to an incredible diversity of birds, especially aquatic birds, including the endangered jabiru stork and the stunning black-crowned night heron. During dry season – when the rest of Guanacaste dries up – birds and other animals crowd around the park's permanent lagoons, making them easy spotting for eager wildlife-watchers.

The life aquatic

The best way to see the wetlands and its resident waterbirds is a boat tour on the Río Tempisque, where you're likely to spot a host of aquatic avians, especially grebes, cormorants, herons, ibises, spoonbills and jacanas, as well as birds of prey, such as falcons and caracaras. There's also a huge population

KRYSSIA CAMPOS/GETTY IMAGES

Black-bellied whistling ducks, Parque Nacional Palo Verde

of iguanas and large crocodiles, not to mention white-faced capuchins and howler monkeys, bats and other mammals.

The OTS runs three **boat tours** *(adult/child US$51/40)* daily, starting at 7:30am. The national park doesn't open until 8am, so the early-morning tour and afternoon tour are only available to OTS lodge guests. Outside the park, **Palo Verde Boat Tours** *(paloverdeboattours.com; from US$67.80)* in Ortega offers 90-minute boat tours along the Río Tempisque in the **Refugio de Vida Silvestre Cipancí**. And **Jabiru Tours** *(jabirutours.com; from US$55)* runs two-hour boat tours, with the option to be picked up from the coast.

The **Rancho Humo Estancia** *(ranchohumo.com; tours from US$44)* is part working cattle ranch, part protected reserve and part eco-conscious boutique hotel sitting to the west of the national park. It offers tours of the wetlands, river, ranch and more. **Hacienda El Viejo** *(elviejowetlands.com; tours from US$70)* is a private wetlands reserve bordering the national park, where you can combine boat tours with a sugarcane experience and rum tastings.

On terra firma

On dry land, you can hike four different trails within the park. The OTS also offers guided nature walks for non-guests *(adult/child from US$34/23)*, as well as night walks and early-morning birding walks for lodge guests. The mosquitoes are fierce, so cover up and bring repellent.

Climb the short, steep **Sendero Roco** up to a scenic lookout over the lagoon, or follow **Sendero Mapache** to traverse three distinct habitats (deciduous lowland, limestone, evergreen forest).

Sendero El Guayacán cuts through the heart of the park, with views of the lagoon and Tempisque plains. At the far end of the park, you can hike 1400m along the **Sendero La Cantera** to a splendid lookout that takes in the whole area.

BIRDWATCHING IN PALO VERDE

Jabiru stork: This sizeable stork is easy to spot, standing around 1.5m tall with a 2.5m wingspan and a long black beak.

Roseate spoonbill: This flamboyant pink-hued wading bird is named after its spoon-like bill.

Great curassow: Males are shiny black with white bellies, yellow beaks and a head of distinctive curly feathers.

Yellow-naped Amazon: This critically endangered parrot species is vivid green with, as its name suggests, a patch of yellow on its neck.

King vulture: The largest of the Americas vultures, it can grow to almost 1m tall and weigh around 4kg.

Glossy ibis: These waders have iridescent black plumage and sickle-shaped bills.

CRUCE DE FAUNA

Ruta 1 has seen many upgrades in recent years, including widening the road in many places – good for drivers, but not so good for the animals that might want to cross to the other side. Anecdotal evidence and academic studies show the impact of increased traffic and speeding cars on the welfare of animals, and it's not pretty. The good news is that the Ministry of Public Works and Transportation (MOPT) now requires all road projects to include roadkill mitigation measures, including yellow 'Cruce de Fauna' (Wildlife Crossing) signs with an image of a tapir and other wild creatures, as well as underground and arboreal crossings. Drivers can also play their part by slowing down and looking out for animals on the road.

REBECA BOLANOS/SHUTTERSTOCK

Llanos del Cortés

Bagaces

TIME FROM CAÑAS: **20 MINS**

A day at the cascade

The picture-perfect **Llanos del Cortés** *(8777-3014; adult/child US$7/4)* is a captivating cascade just 30km north of Cañas and 6km west of **Bagaces**. Follow the stairs down from the parking lot to the wide and welcoming falls – 28m high and 12m wide – that drop into a tranquil pool (there's a line for safe swimming). There's even a small sandy beach for your picnicking pleasure; bring your own, as there's no food for sale here, but there are restrooms and changing rooms.

Stop for a quick dip or stay all day; it makes a great break from driving Ruta 1. It's open from 8am to 4pm – get there early or later in the afternoon to dodge the tour groups and avoid weekends when it gets crowded with locals. In the rainy season, the pool might be closed for safety reasons, or the access road may get flooded, so it's worth checking in advance.

If you don't have wheels, any bus traveling this part of Ruta 1 can drop you at the turnoff to Llanos del Cortés, 5km from Bagaces, from where it's about a 1.5km walk to the waterfall. Near the highway, you'll pass **Luna de Llano**, a welcoming family-owned hotel and restaurant.

Rincón de la Vieja

VOLCANIC POWER | WONDERFUL WATERFALLS | THERMAL SPRINGS

Rincón de la Vieja is one of Costa Rica's most active volcanoes, with powerful eruptions as recently as 2023 and frequent minor ones. While hiking to the crater isn't permitted, you can still witness volcanic activity on its slopes – gurgling mud pools, steaming fumaroles and bubbling hot springs – in the surrounding national park.

All this activity at the surface is evidence of the enormous reserves of geothermal energy below, and in the last 14 years the Costa Rican Institute of Electricity has opened two state-of-the-art geothermal power plants in this area, which you'll see belching and steaming as you drive to the park.

There are two entrances to the Parque Nacional Rincón de la Vieja: the main entrance at Sector Las Pailas, near Curubandé de Liberia about 10km south of the park, which makes a great base; and a second, lesser-used entrance at Sector Santa María, about 10km to the east.

GETTING AROUND

The 20km road to Sector Las Pailas is paved from the highway to Curubandé. After that, the road traverses Hotel Hacienda Guachipelín's private property, so all non-guests must stop to pay a charge of US$800 per person for driving the rest of the way to the park. To get to Sector Santa María, take the gravel road past Río Negro Hot Springs and continue for about 7km. Buses run from Liberia to Curubandé three times a day; your accommodations may be able to arrange transportation.

TOP TIP

All visitors to the park must buy entry tickets through the Sinac website, as cash or card payments can't be made on-site. The Oropendola waterfall and Río Negro Hot Springs aren't included in admission; to visit, contact Hotel Hacienda Guachipelín.

Volcanoes & Waterfalls

Hike volcanic slopes

At **Parque Nacional Rincón de La Vieja** *(sinac.go.cr; adult/child US$17/6, book online),* you can take a walk around **Sector Las Pailas** to get a glimpse of the furious energy roiling just beneath the earth's surface. The **Sendero Las Pailas** is only a 3.5km trail, but it bubbles with multihued fumaroles, tepid springs and steaming, flatulent mud pots, as well as a young and feisty *volcancito* (little volcano). Although you can't go to the crater, this trail will give you a good idea of what's going on up there. Arrive early to beat the tour buses; it's closed on Mondays.

There's a short waterfall hike at **Hotel Hacienda Guachipelín** *(guachipelin.com; adult/child US$20/15).* It's better to get your tickets online in advance, but you'll still need to check in at the hotel reception. It's a 20-minute walk through the forest and over a hanging bridge to reach the **Catarata**

VOLCANIC POWER

Standing at 1916m tall and 15km wide, Rincón de la Vieja is Guanacaste's largest and most active volcano. Bridging the Continental Divide, this colossus is thought to be around 600,000 years old. It's an andesitic volcanic complex formed by felsic lava, which is high in silicates, and the active crater holds a 500m-wide acid lake. The last significant eruption in 2023 produced a plume of volcanic material and water vapor that rose 3km above the crater and generated lahars (a mix of mud and hot water) on the cone's northern side that landed in several of the surrounding rivers. But don't panic – the park is safe and volcanic activity is closely monitored; stay informed about current conditions and follow the guidance.

HIGHLIGHTS
1 Parque Nacional Rincón de la Vieja

ACTIVITIES
2 Río Negro Hot Springs

SLEEPING
3 Casa Rural Aroma de Campo
4 Hotel Hacienda Guachipelín
5 Rinconcito Lodge

INFORMATION
6 Sector Las Pailas Ranger Station
7 Sector Santa María Ranger Station

Oropendola – a spectacular 25m cascade that drops into a sparkling sky-blue pool. You can take a dip here, and even jump off the cliffs when the conditions are safe. The Hacienda offers a variety of tours; the One-Day Adventure Pass includes ziplines, tubing and the Río Negro Hot Springs.

For a more strenuous hike, you might want to spend the better part of a day in the national park, as there are two additional trails – **Sendero Escondida** (8.6km) and **Sendero La Cangrega** (10km). Both trails lead to scenic, but technically unswimmable, waterfalls.

Soothing Soak

Take the thermal waters

Recover from a volcano or waterfall hike with a hot-spring soak, allowing the thermal power to soothe your muscles and restore your energy.

The most popular option is the privately run **Río Negro Hot Springs** *(guachipelin.com; adult/child US$36/30)* on the way out of the park, in a scenic setting on the river 6km from the Hotel Hacienda Guachipelín. The thermally heated water is pumped into 10 small, stone-built pools and ranges from warm to super-hot. You can cool off in the river and slather yourself in healing mud, too. There are changing rooms, showers, lockers and towels available, but you'll want to bring water shoes for the river. You can also access the four **Cataratas Río Negro**, with picturesque swimming pools.

For a more rustic and all-natural experience, drive 30 minutes east to the less-visited **Sector Santa María** (closed Tuesday). Less volcanic and more verdant, this sector is home to white-faced monkeys, tapirs, deer and even jaguars. The **Sendero Aguas Termales** trail leads 3km through the **Bosque Encantado** (Enchanted Forest), past a lovely waterfall to sulfurous hot springs, or *aguas termales,* surrounded by tropical forest. You're not supposed to bathe in the springs but a short side trail, the **Sendero Morpho**, leads to a captivating cascade where you can take a dip.

Go off the Volcanic Road

MTB on an active volcano

If you've ever wanted to cycle around an active volcano, now is your chance. **Hotel Hacienda Guachipelín** *(tours from US$107.10)* has created 30km of shaded, single-track trails with stunning views over Volcán Rincón de la Vieja. If you want to go it alone, rent a bike and explore the 12.5km beginner's trail, traversing dirt tracks and crossing pastures, while spotting the resident wildlife. The trail is well marked.

If you want to whizz around at high speed and take on some dizzying descents and difficult climbs, tackle the intermediate (16km) and advanced (30km) trails with a guide. You can have a wallow in a waterfall pool to cool off. And if you're up for an Ironman-style challenge, the **Iron Horse Mountain Bike Tour** is a multi-sport adventure. It's a test of stamina as you spend the day horseback riding, mountain biking, river tubing and ziplining, finishing off with a dip in a hot spring. There's also a half-day option that only involves two wheels and four legs.

WHAT'S IN A NAME?

According to indigenous legend, there once was a powerful tribal chieftain whose daughter, Princess Curubandá, fell in love with Prince Mixcoac from a rival clan. Their forbidden love affair so angered the chieftain that he threw Mixcoac to his death down into the volcano crater. But Curubandá would not abandon her lover; she spent her life as a recluse high on the volcano's slope – she even sacrificed her infant son to the volcano so he could be with his father. Over time, she learned the power of medicinal plants and became a renowned healer and, in her old age, the volcano itself became known as 'the old woman's corner,' or Rincón de la Vieja.

Beyond Rincón de la Vieja

Adventure awaits in the charming village of Curubandé de Liberia, where waterfalls and white water will get your adrenaline pumping.

Places

Curubandé is a farming community on the fringes of the national park. It's just 15km from Liberia but feels far from the urban jungle. Many visitors motor through on their way to the park, but it's worth stopping to experience authentic Tico culture, explore the hiking and biking trails, the wonderful waterfalls and – best of all – the ravishing rivers that flow through here.

Curubandé is tucked between the Río Blanco to the north and Río Colorado to the south. The two rivers share unusual geological features – their deep limestone gorges and intense blue color – making them spectacular settings for some wet and wild adventures. Save money (and have a more rewarding experience) by booking tours with a local guide.

GETTING AROUND

The turnoff to Curubandé is on Ruta 1, 5km north of Liberia, and it's a further 10km to the center of the village. If you don't have your own wheels, buses ply this route three times a day. Once in Curubandé, book a tour to get to the activities on offer and they can arrange transport for an additional charge.

Curubandé

TIME FROM RINCÓN DE LA VIEJA: **25MIN**

River canyon adventure

Book in advance for a guided hike to **La Leona Waterfall** with **Don Rafa Adventure Tours** *(guanacastewaterfall.com; from US$30, transport to/from Curubandé US$20)*. It's one in a series of waterfalls along the Río Blanco near **Curubandé**; the name means 'White River' but it's actually a heavenly blue, due to the mineral deposits on the riverbed.

Expect to get wet (they supply life jackets and dry bags, but take a waterproof pouch for your phone) on this adventurous hike through the canyon involving river crossings, scrambling over rocks and tree roots, crawling through caves and cliff jumping (if you dare). You'll pass three waterfalls on the way, including one dazzling cascade hidden inside a cavern. The two-hour tour also includes access to Finca Don Rafa's pools and facilities.

Ride the river rapids

Get soaked in the aqua-blue waters of the Río Colorado, about 15km from Parque Nacional Rincón de la Vieja. Sign up for a tubing tour with **Colorado Adventure Tours** *(coloradoadventurecr.com; adult/child from US$35/30)* or **Un Tico y Una Gringa Tours** *(facebook.com/unTicounaGringaTours;*

TANGUY DE SAINT-CYR/SHUTTERSTOCK

Río Colorado

from US$40) – they also combine tubing with La Leona Waterfall – for a heady dose of chilling and thrilling.

One moment you'll be drifting down the river, feeling the sun on your face and taking in the gorgeous scenery of the river canyon. The next, you'll be hanging on for dear life as you careen over rapids, bounce off rocks and fly through a refreshing spray of river water. And during the quieter moments of the tour, there's time for river dips and cliff jumps.

Swim the Coyotes

While away an afternoon or longer in the true-blue waters of the Río Blanco. About 17km from the national park, near Curubandé, you'll find a series of picture-perfect, sapphire-colored swimming holes, known as **Poza Los Coyotes** *(instagram.com/pozaloscoyotes; adult/child US$7/4)*.

Take your time and explore. Follow the well-marked trails to swim in *las pocitas* (literally 'little puddles'), jump off the rocks and float through the namesake cave, and don't miss the mini waterfall. Different-sized tubes are available for rent at the office – life jackets, too – so you can explore the cave and float lazily along the river at your leisure to a soundtrack of howler monkeys.

You'll need your own wheels but there's a fast-food restaurant on-site; it's popular with locals at weekends, so try to go during the week or early in the morning (it opens at 8am).

A SECLUDED SPOT

Pablo Camacho Calvo and **Sara Garrett** of Un Tico y Una Gringa Tours reveal their favorite weekend destination near the Río Blanco bridge. *@untico_unagringatours*

We usually head down the river to a more hidden spot, for swimming and rock jumping. If you're a little crazy (like Pablo), you can jump in from the tree.

A bit further, there's another secret swimming area, with a rock that forms a natural (cold-water) Jacuzzi. We spend many Sundays swimming and soaking there. We always spot blue morpho butterflies, birds, iguanas and even monkeys.

From the Mini Super in Curubandé, head west for 1.6km, until you reach the bridge. The secluded spot is down the river to the left (west).

EATING AROUND CURUBANDÉ: OUR PICKS

El Mirador: Large portions and spectacular views over the Guanacaste lowlands, especially at sunset. In Cañas Dulces. *noon-10pm* $$

La Ventanita: Charming pastry shop for picking up a pre- or post-hike snack. Try the savory *empanadas* or the sweet *dulce de leche* cookies. *hours vary* $

Rancho Los Gavilanes: Family-friendly restaurant by the Río Blanco, surrounded by greenery. Pair the crispy chicken wings with an ice-cold beer. *11am-9pm Thu-Mon* $

Soda Curubanda: This traditional *soda* serves typical dishes, including *casados* and tacos, plus fresh juices and *batidos* (fruit shakes). *8am-7pm* $

Parque Nacional Santa Rosa

HIKING | HISTORY LESSONS | WAVE RIDING

GETTING AROUND

La Casona and the ranger station are 7km off Ruta 1. Buses from Liberia or La Cruz can drop you at the turnoff, but you'll have to walk or catch a ride the rest of the way. The roads through the park are very rough and require a 4WD year-round (they're often closed to vehicles, so check in advance), and beyond the ranger station you need to be entirely self-sufficient. It's easier to get to the beaches on a surfing tour from Playas del Coco or Tamarindo.

TOP TIP

There aren't many places to stay near the park. Consider staying in the lively city of Liberia, 40km to the south. Another option is La Cruz, 30km north, or one of the villages on the Península de Santa Elena. And you won't get far in the park without a 4WD.

In Costa Rica's northwestern corner, Parque Nacional Santa Rosa (or Sector Santa Rosa) is part of the Área de Conservación Guanacaste (ACG). It protects a vast swathe of savanna, marshlands and rare tropical dry forest, one of the largest remaining pockets of tropical dry forest in Central America. Its protected marine areas include Playa Nancite, one of the world's largest nesting sites for olive ridley turtles.

Apart from its great ecological importance, Parque Nacional Santa Rosa was the site of not one, not two, but three game-changing historic events, where invading enemies were defeated. The most important was the 1856 Battle of Santa Rosa, which turned the tide in the Filibuster War and set the stage for lasting Costa Rican independence and peace. There are not a lot of historical sites in the country, and even though there's not much to see at Santa Rosa, this is an important one.

Where History Happened

Costa Rica's battleground

Parque Nacional Santa Rosa *(acguanacaste.ac.cr; adult/child US$17/7)* was founded in 1966 to protect the large tract of tropical dry forest, but also the hacienda's historic building, known as **La Casona**. Sadly, the building was destroyed in a fire in 2001, so the one you see today is a replica, but still a symbol of freedom.

It is home to a small museum displaying farming utensils and other relics from the hacienda's time as a large cattle ranch. The main exhibit details the actors and events of the Filibuster War and the 14-minute Battle of Santa Rosa – one of Costa Rica's defining moments (p214). Another exhibit covers the flora and fauna of the tropical dry forest. There is also an art gallery with beautiful nature photographs of the park.

After learning all about the battle, you can climb up the steep staircase behind La Casona to reach the **Monumento a los Héroes**, dedicated to patriots who died defending their

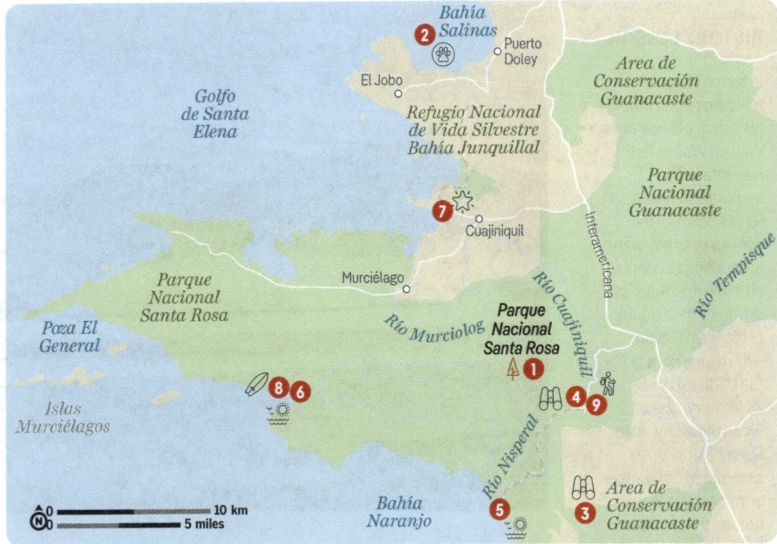

country in 1856 and 1955. From here, enjoy a sweeping panorama of three volcanoes to the east, including Rincón de la Vieja.

Take to the Trails

Explore the tropical dry forest

Parque Nacional Santa Rosa's vast landscape is made up of tropical dry forest, oak forest, mangroves, estuaries and wild coastline, and even on a short visit you can encounter birds, monkeys, deer and coatis. There are jaguars, too, but they're usually shy. In the dry season, when the trees lose their leaves, wildlife gathers around water sources, making it easier to spot.

The park is crisscrossed by self-guided trails, although many are challenging and – depending on the weather – inaccessible, so always check in with a park ranger before you set off. And remember to take plenty of water if you plan to hike, as there's very little shade.

The **Sendero Indio Desnudo** (Naked Indian Trail) is a lovely circular trail that's accessible to all, including wheelchair users, and it has audio information (in Spanish) for the visually impaired. Named after a native tree famous for its striking peeling bark, it wends for 800m through tropical dry forest to spot flora and fauna and ancient petroglyphs.

Another short but atmospheric trail is the linear **Mirador Valle Naranjo**. Only 1.2km long, it passes through tropical dry forest and is perfect for birders. It ends with stunning views over Playa Naranjo (p214) and Witch's Rock. There's another spectacular view from the more challenging **Mirador Tierras Emergidas** trail, this time over the Golfo de Santa Elena.

HIGHLIGHTS
1 Parque Nacional Santa Rosa

SIGHTS
2 Isla Bolaños National Wildlife Refuge
3 Mirador Valle Naranjo
4 Monumento a los Héroes
5 Playa Naranjo
6 Playa Potrero Grande

ACTIVITIES
7 Cuajiniquil Tours
8 Ollie's Point
9 Sendero Indio Desnudo

HISTORY LESSON

In March 1856, US mercenary and (briefly) president of Nicaragua, William Walker led his ragtag army of marauders into Costa Rica. Known as the *filibusteros*, they were attempting to conquer all of Central America, driven by their doctrine of Manifest Destiny – the divine right of the US to expand its territory. Costa Rican president Juan Rafael Mora Porras assembled a volunteer army of civilians to defend the northern border, and on March 20, the patriots took the Filibuster army by surprise while they were resting at La Casona in Hacienda Santa Rosa, winning the battle in a record-breaking 14 minutes. The hacienda was also the site of battles between Costa Rican troops and invading forces from Nicaragua on two separate occasions during the 20th century.

Surfing Safari

Remote beaches with legendary waves

The beaches of Parque Nacional Santa Rosa are famous for their incredible surf breaks and stunning setting, as well as their notorious inaccessibility – making them all the more desirable to die-hard surfers.

Experienced wave riders seek out **Playa Potrero Grande** for the famous break known as **Ollie's Point** after Oliver North, who notoriously aided the Nicaraguan Contras using a secret jungle airstrip around these parts. Some say this wave is the best right in all of Costa Rica – the surf break certainly serves a sweet, long ride, especially with a southwestern swell. It's only accessible by boat (shared or private charter) from Playas del Coco (p270).

Combine it with another favorite of surfers-in-the-know, the wild and wonderful **Playa Naranjo**. Called Roca Bruja or **Witch's Rock** after the ancient offshore rock formation, the break is famous for its fast, hollow 3m rights. The rough-and-rocky road through the park to Playa Naranjo is currently closed to vehicles, so it's a challenging (and sweltering) 12km walk from La Casona. There's an off-the-grid campground (closed Tuesday) around 2km along the beach from the rock; you need to book your spot in advance and be entirely self-sufficient.

TURTLE NESTINGS

Playa Ostional (p293) – part of the Refugio Nacional de Vida Silvestre Ostional and open to the public – is another of the world's largest nesting sites for olive ridley turtles.

GIANFRANCO VIVI/SHUTTERSTOCK

Witch's Rock

Magnetic Marine Life

Under-the-radar wildlife havens

Among Parque Nacional Santa Rosa's protected marine areas are the **Islas Murciélagos** (Bat Islands), a spectacular snorkeling and diving destination only accessible by boat, usually from Playas del Coco (around 70 minutes across the Golfo de Papagayo) or Tamarindo (p278).

The islands are no longer open to visitors – they're a nesting site for green and black sea turtles – but snorkelers can swim with turtles, Pacific giant mantas and large schools of smaller devil rays. The big draw for experienced divers is a deep dive site dubbed **Big Scare**, a popular haunt of fearsome bull sharks. Tours run from May through November, when sea conditions are at their best – it's also a great time to spot migrating humpback whales.

From July to November, the park's pristine **Playa Nancite** (currently only open to researchers) is the site of *arribadas,* the mass synchronised nesting of olive ridley turtles. The busiest months are September and October; the turtles gather offshore for several days, coming to the beach in their thousands to lay their eggs around the time of the new moon.

Offshore in Bahía Salinas, the national wildlife refuge of **Isla Bolaños** is an important nesting site for brown pelicans in January and February and magnificent frigate birds from November to June. Access is limited but you can circle the rugged island by boat.

If you want to get out on the water, contact **Cuajiniquil Tours** *(cuajiniquilcr.com)* for boating, kayaking, snorkeling and scuba-diving excursions.

WILDLIFE-SPOTTING

Olive ridley turtle: One of the smallest sea turtles, it's named after its olive-green shell. It nests in very few places, hence its vulnerable status.

Jaguar: The population of this near-threatened big cat is growing within the park, thanks to the plentiful prey.

Silky anteater: The world's smallest anteater weighs just 280g and consumes up to 5000 ants a day. Tree-dwelling and nocturnal, it's hard to spot.

White-tailed deer: They're prey for larger predators, including jaguars and pumas, and venomous snakes such as the fer-de-lance.

Variegated squirrel: This multihued species primarily feeds on nuts, seeds and fruits, but in this hot climate it doesn't need to hide its nuts for winter.

FOR HISTORY BUFFS

Read our essay on p444 for more on the Filibuster War and the Battle of Santa Rosa.

Beyond Parque Nacional Santa Rosa

In this unheralded corner of Costa Rica, you can lounge on a near-deserted beach or catch the wild wind and fly.

There was a time not so long ago when this corner of Costa Rica was the sole domain of dedicated kiteboarders, who traveled over the roughest roads in search of the strongest winds. That all changed with the opening of a sprawling all-inclusive resort just meters from Playa El Jobo, and the subsequent paving of roadways.

The glorious sandy beaches and sparkling waters have been officially 'discovered.' The good news is that beaches are open to all and are now much easier to reach. The other good news is that the wind is just as wild. Best of all, the Península de Santa Elena is lined with glorious, pristine beaches, many of which are still under the radar.

GETTING AROUND

It's a 20-minute drive to the village of El Jobo from La Cruz and 75 minutes from Liberia. Public buses run several times daily from La Cruz via Playa Papaturro and Playa Copal. Most of the lodgings are within walking distance of at least one beach, but it's useful to have a vehicle to explore this area.

Bahía Salinas

TIME FROM PARQUE NACIONAL SANTA ROSA: **50 MINS**

Harnessing wind power

If you want to ride the wind, you're in the right place. This remote northwestern region of Costa Rica is the country's kitesurfing capital. The beaches facing **Bahía Salinas** are too windy for casual lounging and swimming (head to the west-facing beaches for warm waters and gentle breezes); from the end of November to the end of April, the wind howls all day every day and the surrounding hills reliably funnel it into the bay. Wet suit not required.

Playa Copal is as wide and wild as they come and the perfect place to catch the wind and go for a ride; it's also perfect for novice kitesurfers. A few kilometers to the northwest, **Playa Coyotera** purportedly receives the best wind swell in the bay, so hang on tight.

Kitesurfers should be experienced (and ideally certified) to rent equipment and surf independently. Instruction is available at the local kiteboarding schools. Check out **Blue Dream Kiteboarding School** *(bluedreamhotel.com; 3hr private lessons US$180)* and **Kiteboarding Costa Rica** *(kiteboardingcostarica.com; 3hr private lessons US$180);* both offer private and group lessons, equipment rental and basic beachfront lodging, and they can also arrange transportation from Guanacaste airport in Liberia.

Golfo de Santa Elena

TIME FROM PARQUE NACIONAL SANTA ROSA: **40 MINS**

Find your own deserted beach

Southwest of La Cruz, there's a little piece of coastal Costa Rica that's largely untouched by international tourism. Around the edge of the **Golfo de Santa Elena** is a string of tiny fishing villages and idyllic beaches, all surrounded by forest and farmland and with spectacular views across the gulf. The beaches are only accessible by private vehicle or taxi. The following are heading from south to north.

The road is rough to reach the pristine forest-backed beach of **Playa Cuajiniquil**, but you'll find few people here. Humpback whales are often spotted in the bay in September and October.

Playa Escondida is a sweet little beach with no sign. Just offshore, a tiny island decorates the seascape and invites exploration. If you're hoping to find a deserted beach, this could be the one.

Part of the eponymous **wildlife refuge** *(junquillallacruz.com; adult/child US$14/6),* **Playa Junquillal** is a gorgeous crescent of sand in a calm, quiet bay that's perfect for swimming and kayaking. It's a popular spot for iguanas, and Tico familes at weekends; you can camp there, too. For your money, you'll get plenty of picnic tables, as well as bathrooms and showers. Two short trails hug the coast, traversing tropical dry forest and leading to a marine-bird lookout in one direction and to the mangroves in the other. There's a turtle project there, too.

South of **El Jobo**, tiny **Punta Manzanillo** is not for swimming, but it's worth a stop to see colorful fishing boats bobbing at their lines and local fisherfolk hauling and cleaning their catch.

Off the road to **Playa Rajada**, a rough road leads 500m south to a secret spot – and it's a stunner. At **Playa Las Pilas**, striated cliffs flank the rocky beach, which is otherwise surrounded by forest.

Lined with shady picnic tables, **Playa Rajada** curves around a bay, creating a placid swimming area. At the southern end, the outgoing tide leaves a lagoon of jumping fish and scurrying crabs. You can also sneak over to the tiny, hidden **Playa Rajadita**, stopping to admire the ocean views.

NAVIGATE TO NICARAGUA

The border post of **Peñas Blancas** (6am to midnight daily) is the only official crossing between Costa Rica and Nicaragua. There are frequent public buses from Liberia (one to 1½ hours), La Cruz (30 minutes), Cañas (two hours) and Upala (three hours), as well as shuttles and taxis from Guanacaste airport. Exit tax (US$8) can be paid in advance through Banco de Costa Rica (BCR), either online *(bancobcr.com)* or in a branch (keep the receipt). Or pay at the border by machine or in person. After passing through Costa Rican immigration, keep your passport, small bills and a pen to hand. It's a short walk to Nicaraguan immigration where, after your exit stamp is checked, you'll pay a US$1 municipal charge and arrival tax of US$13. Hold on to your paperwork, especially if you plan to re-enter Costa Rica.

EATING AROUND BAHÍA SALINAS: OUR PICKS

Restaurante La Copaleña: With sweeping views over Playa Copal, the menu focuses on fresh seafood – don't miss the *ceviche*. *11am-8:30pm* $$

Naked Indian: Tasty surf and turf (Tomahawk steak and lobster Thermidor), strong drinks and live music Friday nights. Near El Jobo. *noon-9pm* $$

El Fogón de Juana: Roadside gem near Playa Copal, with quirky decor and a menu of fresh fish, *ceviche* pasta and good pizza. *8am-8:30pm Mon-Fri, to 9pm Sat & Sun* $

Seafood Restaurante Las Mareas: Enjoy fabulous fish and seafood at this family-run restaurant, from seafood soup to *ceviche* and fried red snapper. *6:30am-10pm* $$

Places We Love to Stay

$** Budget **$$** Midrange **$$$ Top End

Monteverde & Santa Elena

MAP p182

Casa Jungle Monterverde **$** Comfortable, good-value rooms, a helpful host and a delicious breakfast, all within walking distance of downtown Santa Elena.

Pensión Santa Elena **$** Central and accommodating budget-friendly option. A variety of room types, friendly service and good vibes.

El Nido Lodge **$** Simple, wallet-friendly rooms. Feast at the restaurant or make use of the shared kitchen before hanging out around the firepit.

Casa Batsu **$$** Delightful B&B in a family farmhouse with design innovations and artistic touches, plus indulgent breakfasts.

Cabinas Capulín **$$** Simple, spacious log cabins lined up on a hillside, with a working farm and hiking trails on-site.

Hidden Canopy Treehouses **$$$** Just six gorgeous tree-house chalets, with private decks and floor-to-ceiling windows giving serene views over the cloud forest.

Chira Glamping Monteverde **$$$** A treetop glamping experience; the geodesic dome tents come with air-con, wi-fi and minibars. There are outdoor showers and hot tubs, too.

Hotel Belmar **$$$** Classy place with understated luxury and true eco-credentials, plus breathtaking views over cloud forest and gulf.

Senda Monteverde Hotel **$$$** Embrace sustainable luxury at this contemporary hotel set among beautiful grounds, right next to the Aguti Reserve.

Río Celeste

MAP p195

Casitas Tenorio B&B & Farm **$$** Attractive Bijagua *casitas* (cottages) set amid farm and forest, where you can expect visits from sloths, howler monkeys and birds.

Finca La Amistad Cacao Lodge **$$** Wooden *casitas* surrounded by a sustainable cacao plantation. The family will share their love of all things chocolate.

La Carolina Lodge **$$** Rustic retreat on a working cattle ranch, with river swimming, a hot tub and a rustic spa and yoga shala.

Mei Tai Cacao Lodge **$$** Six sunny chalets scattered about a lovely landscaped farm, complete with a pond, hiking trails, birds and wildlife.

Celeste Mountain Lodge **$$** Floor-to-ceiling windows yield stunning views from the stylish rooms at this innovative ecolodge.

Río Celeste Hideaway **$$$** Luxurious lodge next to the national park with capacious *casitas* scattered among gorgeous jungly grounds.

Heliconias Rainforest Lodge (p196) **$$$** Immerse yourself in nature at this rustic lodge, complete with hiking trails and hanging bridges.

Volcán Miravalles

Paraiso Volcano Lodge **$** Between two volcanoes and close to all the action, a handful of cabins are set in gorgeous grounds with attentive hosts.

Colinas del Miravalles Hotel & Hot Springs **$$** Spacious cabins sit in lovely gardens at this family-run favorite, with hot-spring pools and volcano views.

Río Perdido Hotel & Thermal River **$$$** A contemporary, high-end lodge set in an expanse of wild nature, with adventurous activities and a spa on offer.

Cañas

MAP p202

Luna del Llano **$$** Close to the entrance to Llanos de Cortés, surrounded by forest and farmland, this eco-conscious, super-friendly bolthole serves wonderful home-cooked meals.

Hotel Hacienda La Pacífica **$$** Former hacienda on an expanse of tropical dry forest, frequented by deer, agoutis, howler monkeys and birds.

Parque Nacional Palo Verde

Rancho Humo Estancia $$ This stylish – and remote – boutique lodge is perfect for exploring the park and its own private reserve, by boat, on foot or on horseback.

OTS Palo Verde Research Station $$ This rustic lodge in the national park offers boat and walking tours with top-notch naturalist guides.

Rincón de la Vieja

MAP p208

Casa Rural Aroma de Campo $$ Close to Las Pailas, the top spot for a personable and peaceful stay is this wonderful guesthouse complete with hammock-strung patio.

La Anita Rainforest Ranch $$ Remote, peaceful and luxurious accommodations on a cacao plantation with hiking trails and a fantastic restaurant.

Hotel Hacienda Guachipelín $$ This sprawling place is good value, with rainforest hikes, hot springs, waterfalls and adventurous tours aplenty, close to Las Pailas.

Rinconcito Lodge $$ Near to Sector Santa María, simple tiled rooms look over glorious greenery, plus there's a large swimming pool and excellent breakfasts.

Bahía Salinas

Blue Dream Hotel $ Laid-back lodgings on Playa Papaturro, including dorms and suites, plenty of hammocks and a highly rated kiteboarding school on the doorstep.

Treehouse Camping Zone $ Super-clean and safe camping ground, with a mini-kitchen for each camping zone. There are small *cabañas* (cabins) if you don't have a tent.

Golfo de Santa Elena

Camping Los Malinches $ This peaceful campsite on Playa Junquillal is wrapped in nature; just basic facilities, drinking water and a spectacular stretch of sand.

Rinconcito Lodge

For places to stay in Arenal & the Northern Lowlands, see p262

PARKO/SHUTTERSTOCK

Above: Volcán Arenal (p231); Right: Horse riding, Río Fortuna (p227)

Researched by Christa Jiménez

Arenal & the Northern Lowlands

FROM FARMS TO FORESTS

The flatlands of the northern Caribbean slope, this rich region includes the country's most vibrant tourist center and some of its most remote wilderness.

Arenal and the Northern Lowlands stretch from the volcanic peaks of the Cordillera de Tilarán to the Nicaraguan border and eastward across the lush Caribbean slope. This diverse region, where the continental divide begins, blends majestic mountains with sprawling lowlands rich in both biodiversity and adventure.

Volcán Arenal stands as the crown jewel, its iconic cone dominating the skyline around La Fortuna and across the Laguna de Arenal. While often shrouded in clouds, when the volcano emerges from the mist the view is nothing short of spectacular. That's why the image of Volcán Arenal graces postcards across the country.

At the volcano's base lies La Fortuna, the region's thriving epicenter and one of Costa Rica's most popular tourist destinations. Bursting with energy, this lively town offers an array of adventure activities, from ziplining to canyoning, alongside ample opportunities to encounter the area's rich wildlife.

Venture beyond bustling La Fortuna, and the pace slows in the remote lowlands. Past banana and pineapple plantations, winding roads lead to hidden swimming holes, exhilarating white-water rapids, secluded fishing spots and prime birdwatching locales. In this quieter corner of Sarapiquí, life revolves around nature. Stay in an ecolodge surrounded by dense jungle and discover a sense of peace amid the region's unspoiled beauty.

DAVOR LOVINCIC/GETTY IMAGES

THE MAIN AREAS

VOLCÁN ARENAL & LA FORTUNA
Lush rainforest and majestic volcano. p226

SARAPIQUÍ VALLEY
Wild forests flanking the mighty river. p248

CAÑO NEGRO
Remote wetlands with abundant birdlife. p258

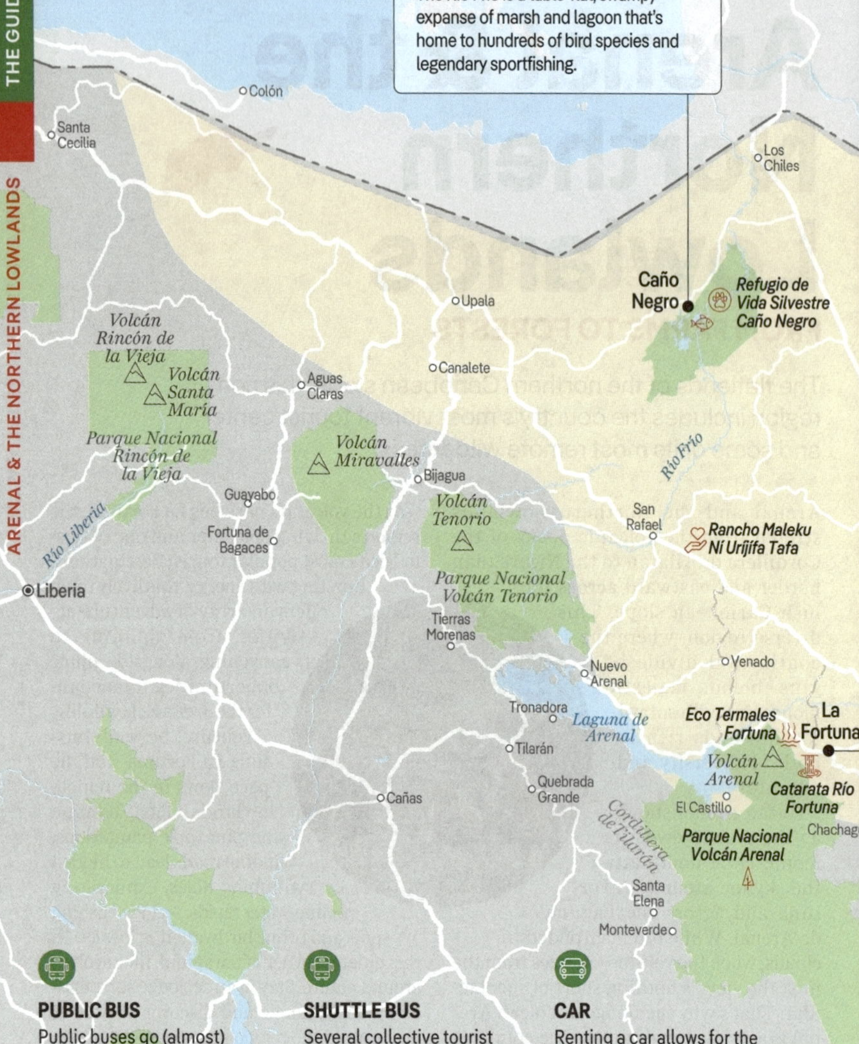

PUBLIC BUS

Public buses go (almost) everywhere. They can be slow (and sporadic), especially in rural areas, but you'll eventually reach your destination. Taxis and organized tours from the hubs can help you reach the good stuff.

SHUTTLE BUS

Several collective tourist shuttle services offer relatively quick and comfortable transportation between popular destinations, including La Fortuna and Puerto Viejo de Sarapiquí. You can also find private shuttles, but you'll need taxis and tours to see the sights.

CAR

Renting a car allows for the greatest flexibility – not only for reaching your destinations but also for doing all the activities on your hit list. Accessing the remote areas is much easier with a car.

Find Your Way

This expansive region includes La Fortuna and the Arenal volcano and lake. It covers much of the northern border with Nicaragua and the Caribbean slope. In this region, the lesser-known, less-traveled destinations are the region's gems.

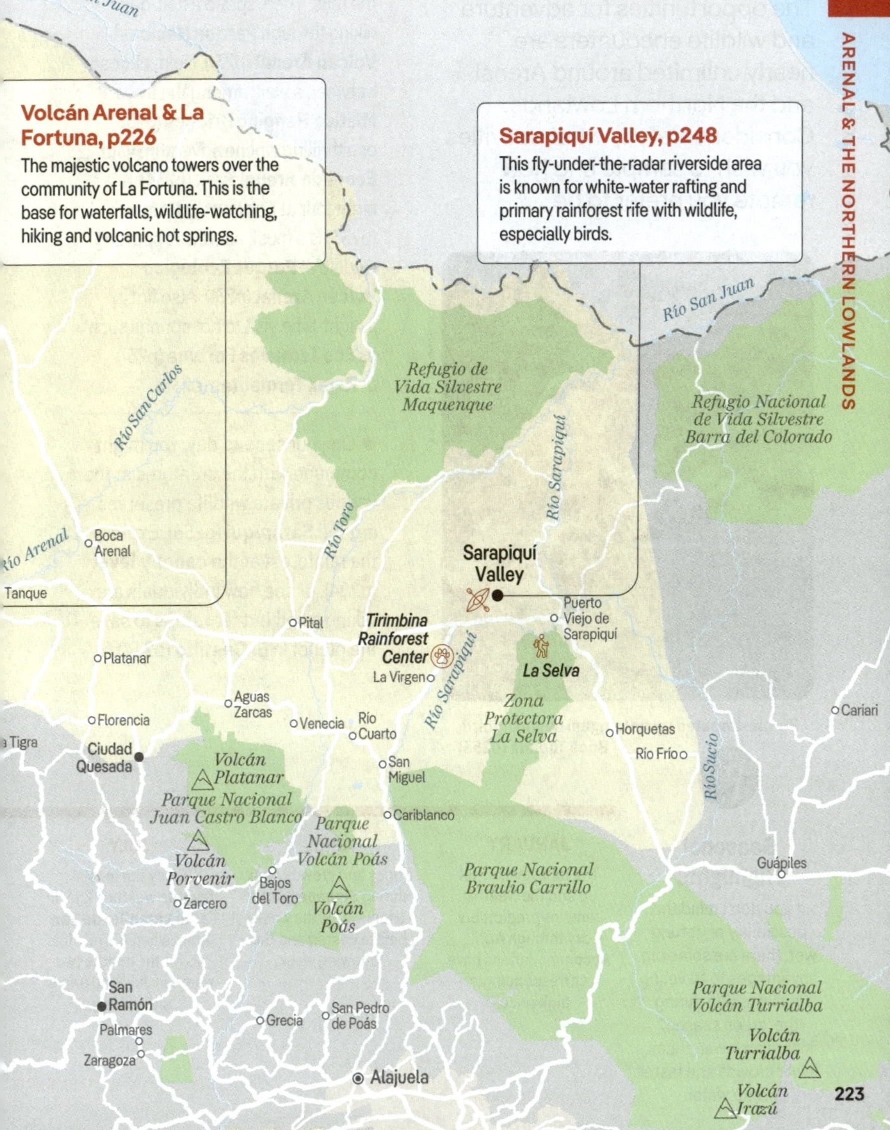

Volcán Arenal & La Fortuna, p226

The majestic volcano towers over the community of La Fortuna. This is the base for waterfalls, wildlife-watching, hiking and volcanic hot springs.

Sarapiquí Valley, p248

This fly-under-the-radar riverside area is known for white-water rafting and primary rainforest rife with wildlife, especially birds.

Plan Your Time

The opportunities for adventure and wildlife encounters are nearly unlimited around Arenal and the Northern Lowlands. Consider carefully what activities you wish to sample and how remote you prefer to be.

JIM CUMMING/SHUTTERSTOCK

Purple-throated mountaingem hummingbird, Boca Tapada (p256)

If You Only Have a Few Days

- Head straight to **La Fortuna** (p226) and the majestic **waterfall** (p226) for a thrilling descent to the falls. Then, spend a half-day hiking through **Parque Nacional Volcán Arenal** (p231). Next, choose between a walk among the trees at **Mistico Hanging Bridges** (p233) or a thrilling zipline adventure with **Ecoglide Arenal Park** (p234). A night tour at **Ecocentro Danaus** (p233) is a must, as well as spotting wildlife at **Parque Ecológico Volcán Arenal** (p231). Also fint in a night-time visit to hot springs such as **Eco Termales Fortuna** (p231) or **Relax Termalitas** (p238).

- On your second day, you might commune with the creatures at the various private wildlife preserves around **Sarapiquí** (p256). Explore the rainforest at the **canopy level** (p254), or see how individuals are taking small but real steps to save the planet in **El Castillo** (p244).

Seasonal Highlights

If you don't mind the possibility of getting wet, there are some big advantages to traveling in this region during the 'green season,' including lower prices, fewer crowds and faster white water.

JANUARY

The rain starts to let up and the weather remains predictably dry through April. Accommodations have correspondingly high prices.

APRIL

Prices and crowds peak during **Semana Santa** (Holy Week, the week before Easter) and the following week.

JULY

Enjoy the locals' favorite weather, known as **el veranillo de San Juan**, when the rain lets up for the middle two weeks in July and prices are still low.

Five Days to Travel Around

- After hanging out in **La Fortuna** (p226) for a day or two following the previous itinerary, you'll want to escape the crowds at one of the region's lesser-known destinations.

- The **Sarapiquí Valley** (p256) has some fantastic ecolodges that are surrounded by their own private forest reserves, so the lush rainforest is at your doorstep, rife with flora and fauna. Don't bypass the outdoor adventures, such as riding the rapids on the **Río Sarapiquí** (p248).

- But you might just want to spend most of your time at your lodge, exploring rainforest trails, going for river swims and spying on birds, kinkajous and howler monkeys from your balcony. The private reserves in this area are still virtually untouched, allowing you to enjoy endless hiking and wildlife-viewing.

If You Have More Time

- Dedicated bird nerds should spend at least one day in **Boca Tapada** (p256) and another at **Caño Negro** (p258). They offer different experiences – with many species of birds – and it's worth carving out time for both places. Boca Tapada attracts birds in dense primary forest, while Caño Negro's wetlands offer species not found elsewhere.

- If your bird list is not the main priority, spend your extra time at **Maquenque Eco Lodge** (p253). Cruise the Río San Carlos, explore the lush grounds, look for spider monkeys swinging through the trees, enjoy a riverside dinner and – at the end of the day – lay yourself down to sleep in a treehouse. It's an experience you will remember.

SEPTEMBER

The start of the rainiest part of the **rainy season**. Expect rain every day (not necessarily all day) in September, October and peaking in November.

OCTOBER

Heavy rains characterize October in this region – torrential rains can last all day, obscuring the volcano and making birdwatching difficult.

NOVEMBER

After months of rain, the biggest **white-water rapids** on the Río Sarapiquí usually occur in November and December.

DECEMBER

Lodging prices shoot up during the last two weeks of December, with peak rates continuing through the beginning of January.

Volcán Arenal & La Fortuna

ICONIC VOLCANO | MINERAL HOT SPRINGS | ENDLESS ADVENTURE

TOP TIP

Restaurant prices in La Fortuna and its surroundings are higher than in other areas. To keep costs down, rely on small, local restaurants called *sodas*. Also look for accommodations where breakfast is included. Don't forget the supermarket – **Súper Christian** is a local favorite with several locations in the area.

Volcán Arenal, the region's iconic centerpiece, towers over lush forests and farmlands like a slumbering giant. Once famous for its nightly eruptions, the volcano's fiery displays drew crowds for years, transforming nearby La Fortuna from a quiet farming village into a bustling tourist hub. Although Arenal went dormant in 2010, La Fortuna's charm and reputation were already firmly established.

Even without glowing lava, Arenal's grandeur captivates visitors. Exploring its trails and unwinding in its thermal pools make for a memorable day. Yet, the area offers far more. La Fortuna is a hot spot for wildlife-watching, and private reserves teem with biodiversity. Waterfalls, canopy tours, rainforest hikes and sustainable farms promise days of adventure. The town also boasts exceptional restaurants and accommodations for every budget. Tourist-centric? Absolutely – but there's no better place to embrace being a tourist than in La Fortuna.

A Natural Wonder

Take a dip in La Fortuna waterfall

Almost every visitor dreams of bathing in cold river water at the base of a raging Costa Rican waterfall, and **Catarata Río Fortuna** *(cataratalafortuna.com; US$20)* delivers in spades.

GETTING AROUND

Renting a car or hiring a private driver in this area is your best bet, but it can also be more expensive. The area is widely spread out and activities are not generally near each other. Many of the midrange hotels offer tours with transportation included, and tours that originate downtown are close to the budget accommodations. Many tours offer drop-off and pickup at your hotel, but keep in mind they usually spend an hour dropping off and picking up people at their accommodations. Local buses do not run through the area, but it's easy to get a direct public bus from other parts of the country. Local taxis are reliable, but prices are high. It's a good idea to find out which points of interest include transportation to and from the experience, which can help you save some cash.

VALERIJA POLAKOVSKA/SHUTTERSTOCK

Catarata Río Fortuna

Upon arrival, you'll find changing rooms and bathrooms to help you prepare for your descent. Buy your ticket online in advance or on-site, and keep in mind that your fee directly funds important community projects in La Fortuna. An early start guarantees you'll be done before the bigger tour buses start to arrive around 10am.

Snap an iconic photo from the **viewing platform** before beginning your 530-step descent to the base of the falls. The stairs are metal and cement, and accessible for most visitors. You'll begin to feel and hear the power of the crashing falls, and rest stops give you ample opportunities for taking photos and videos.

Prepare to be awed at the base of the falls as rushing water crashes into the pools below. For the best photo, plan to walk over some slippery rocks. Next, opt for a leisurely dip in the swimming holes further downstream. Lifeguards on-site keep visitors safe. Then you'll head back up all those stairs; factor in a 15-minute descent and a 30-minute ascent.

Alternatively, choose to go to the falls on horseback. **Alberto's Horses** *(facebook.com/albertoshorses; US$100)* offers a tour leaving from the family farm and finishing with a traditional home-cooked meal. This option will take three

continued on p230

HISTORY OF A VOLCANO

For most of modern history, local farmers called this landmark Cerro Arenal, or 'Arenal Peak,' with no thought that it was actually a volcano. That changed in July 1968, when the volcano unexpectedly erupted, spewing lava, ash and rock, far and wide. Eruptions continued for several days; farmland and villages were destroyed, and 87 people were killed.

For 42 years, Volcán Arenal remained extremely active, producing menacing ash columns, massive explosions and streams of glowing molten rock, almost daily. The activity ceased – rather suddenly – in 2010. Volcán Arenal is still considered active, however, and you can sometimes see smoke escaping from the crater. But volcanologists predict that the explosive activity will not resume any time soon.

DRINKING IN LA FORTUNA: OUR PICKS

Lava Lounge: Reliably good food, colorful drinks, friendly service and good-vibes live music make this place a long-standing favorite. *11:30am-10pm*

La Fortuna Pub: This is the place to sample Tico craft beers, including their own *cervezas* brewed on-site. *noon-11:30pm Mon-Sat, to 10pm Sun*

Voodoo Bar: The mixologist serves some fancy drinks at the cocktail bar in Mercadito Arenal in downtown La Fortuna. *noon-10pm Wed-Mon*

Jungle Love: Craft cocktails with expansive views of the Arenal volcano and lake. A cozy sunset from a tropical bar; reservations recommended. *11am-8pm Tue-Sun*

VOLCÁN ARENAL & LA FORTUNA

HIGHLIGHTS
1 Catarata Río Fortuna
2 Eco Termales Fortuna
3 Parque Nacional Volcán Arenal

SIGHTS
4 Ecocentro Danaus
5 Mirador El Silencio
6 Parque Ecológico Volcán Arenal

ACTIVITIES
7 Alberto's Horses
8 Arenal 1968
9 Arenal Oasis Wildlife Refuge
10 Arenal Vida Campesina
11 Arenal Wilberth Stables
12 Baldí Hot Springs
13 Bike Arenal
14 Ecoglide Arenal Park
15 El Fogón de Chela
16 Finca Paraíso Orgánico
17 Kalambú Hot Springs
18 Maquique Adventures
19 Mistico Hanging Bridges
20 Outback Adventures
21 Red Lava Tours
22 Relax Termalitas
23 Río Chollín
24 Sky Adventures
25 Springs Resort & Spa
26 Tabacón Hot Springs
27 Termales Los Laureles

SLEEPING
28 Arenal 360
29 Arenal Backpackers Resort
30 Arenal Manoa
31 Arenal Oasis
32 Hotel Campo Verde
33 Hotel El Silencio del Campo
34 Hotel Monte Real
35 Hotel San Bosco
36 La Choza Inn

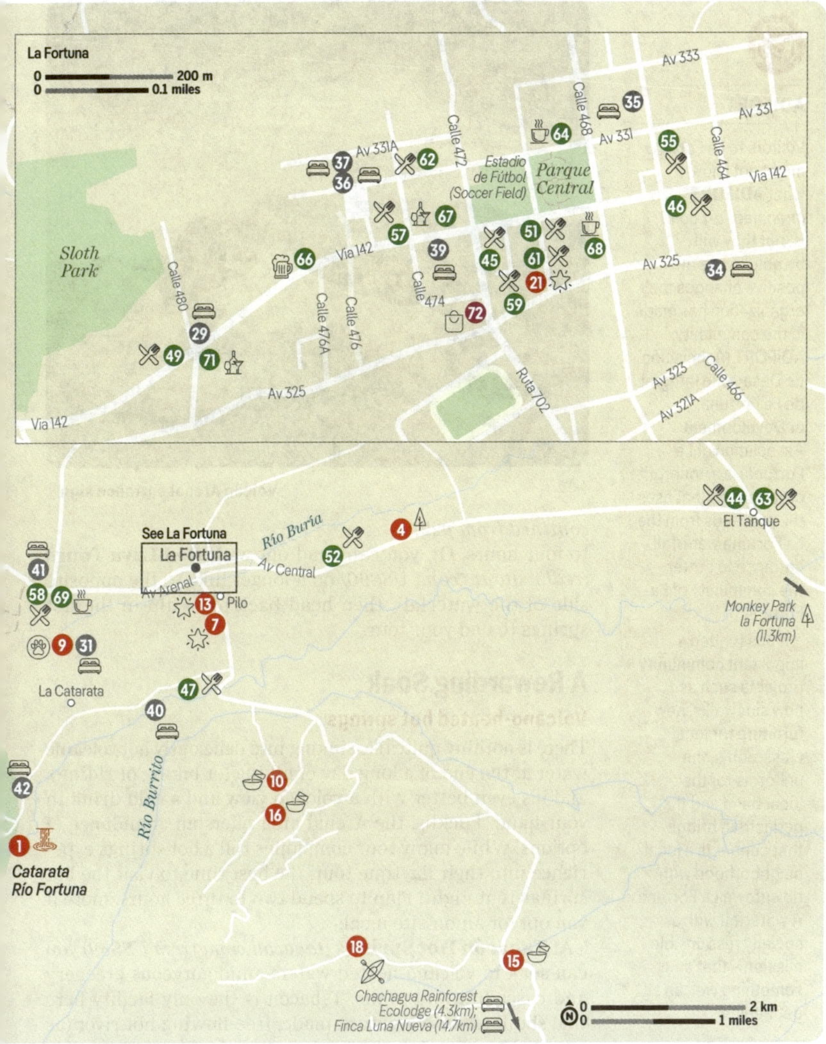

37 La Fortuna Suites
38 Los Lagos Hotel & Resort
39 Poshpacker Arenal
40 Rancho Cerro Azul
41 Roca Negra del Arenal
42 Ti-Fakara
43 Volcano Lodge & Springs

EATING

44 Antojitos Isa
45 Chifa La Familia Feliz
46 Don Rufino
47 El Chante Verde
48 El Novillo del Arenal
49 Kenko
50 La Mesa de Mamá
51 La Parilla de María Bonita
52 Las Tablas
53 Mirador Arenal
54 Mirador Doña Luisa
55 Pollos La Familia
56 Qué Rico
57 Restaurante Fortueño
58 Soda El Turnito
59 Soda la Hormiga
60 Soda La Palma
61 Soda Leo
62 Soda Melania
63 Victorino's

DRINKING & NIGHTLIFE

64 Chocolate Fusión
65 Jungle Love
66 La Fortuna Pub
67 Lava Lounge
68 Rainforest Café
69 Red Frog Coffee Roasters
70 Sloffee
71 Voodoo Bar

SHOPPING

72 Súper Christian

ADIFORT

Visitors to La Fortuna might not know what **ADIFORT** *(arenaladifort.com)* is, but they will be able to see the positive changes the organization has made in the community. ADIFORT (Asociación de Desarrollo Integral de La Fortuna, or Development Association of La Fortuna) is a nonprofit organization that uses the proceeds from the La Fortuna waterfall entrance to better the community of La Fortuna.

It has funded important community projects such as new sidewalks, new furniture for local classrooms, the uniforms for the local band and the pedestrian bridge that connects a local neighborhood with downtown La Fortuna. A waterfall with a socially responsible mission – that's something we can all get behind.

ANASTASIIA MOSINA/ALAMY

Volcán Arenal entrance sign

contined from p227

to four hours. Or, you can head out with **Red Lava Tours** *(redlavatours.com; US$90)* on a longer hike to the opposite side of the waterfall, then head back for a dip in the hot springs to end your tour.

A Rewarding Soak

Volcano-heated hot springs

There is nothing quite like sinking into deliciously hot volcanic water at the end of a long day of hiking (or biking or riding), and it's even better with a volcano view and a cold drink in your hand. Luckily, the Arenal area offers an abundance of options. While many tour companies roll a hot springs experience into their daytime tour, the best time to visit the hot springs is at night. Plan to spend two to three hours, more if you opt for an on-site meal.

At **Tabacón Hot Springs** *(tabacon.com; from US$89)* you can soak in volcano-heated waters amid gorgeous greenery and cascading waterfalls. Tabacón is the only facility here that'sbuilt around a nature-made, free-flowing hot river (as opposed to pumping the heated water in from below). Numerous natural and human-made pools surround the river, ranging in temperature from 22°C to 40°C, with water flowing freely between them.

EATING IN LA FORTUNA: OUR PICKS

Kenko: Bustling sushi restaurant with pizza, nachos and traditional Costa Rican food. Top service and superb volcano view. *11am-11pm Sun-Thu, to 1am Fri & Sat* **$**

El Novillo del Arenal: Casual pizzeria with floor-to-ceiling glass walls, guaranteeing a phenomenal volcano view from every table. *noon-9pm* **$$**

Restaurante Fortueño: This long-standing local restaurant does wood-fired chicken, grilled steak and delicious salads. Fabulous views and friendly service. *7am-10pm* **$$**

Chifa La Familia Feliz: Chef Martin is a true believer and effective evangelist of this surprising Peruvian-Chinese fusion. *10am-10pm* **$$**

A more affordable option is **Eco Termales Fortuna** *(ecotermalesfortuna.cr; from US$49)*, set in a verdant secondary forest. Although this isn't the fanciest 'hot springs' experience in La Fortuna, it does benefit from a gorgeous natural setting, with lush greenery all around. The large human-made thermal pools range in temperature from 32°C to 40°C. Eco Termales is open for daytime (9am to 4pm) or evening (4pm to 9pm) admission.

In either place, you can soak in the mineral-rich pools, stand under waterfalls for a hydro massage, and bring your body temperature down in cool water pools. This is nature at its most luxurious. Order a cocktail from the bar and sink into the warm, healing waters.

Opposite the entrance to Tabacón Hot Springs (7km east of the national park), a gravel path leads down to **Río Chollín**, a bubbling, volcano-heated river, crafted by nature itself. It's free – and less safe – because of strong currents and slippery rocks. But if you're up for a mini adventure, this is a fun and authentic experience for travelers in the know. You'll park along Ruta 142 and walk along the main road to the entrance to the river. Sunday is the busiest day to visit as locals who are off work visit come with picnics and music for a full-day experience.

In the Shadow of the Volcano

Hikes around Volcán Arenal

The mighty Volcán Arenal is surrounded by protected land and many chances to explore the volcano and witness its effects. At **Parque Nacional Volcán Arenal** *(sinac.go.cr; adult/child US$16.95/5.65)* you should arrive early to beat the heat and the crowds.

There are basically two interconnected circular trails. The **Sendero Las Coladas** branches around the volcano for 2km, passing the lava field that remains from the 1992 eruption. You can hike up the old lava flow, culminating with a spectacular vista of Arenal. The 3km **Sendero El Ceibo** is a semicircular loop that branches off from Las Coladas deeper iwnto the rainforest – don't miss the massive 400-year-old ceiba tree. End your hike at the **Mirador Principal** for a photo op.

Arenal 1968 *(arenal1968.com; US$26)* is a private reserve right next to the national park that offers a very similar hiking experience on and around the lava flows from the 1968 eruption.

Another excellent option is **Mirador El Silencio** *(mirador elsilencio.com; US$10)*, where some of the trails are more challenging, but the view of the volcano is spectacular, and there are generally fewer visitors.

Parque Ecológico Volcán Arenal *(parqueecologicocr.com; US$17)* is the hike that brings you to the closest point to the volcano. You'll climb over boulders to a spectacular 360-degree view of the entire valley.

KNOW YOUR MONKEYS

Four species of monkeys live in Costa Rica.

Howler monkeys: Most commonly sighted (and heard!), this is the world's loudest land mammal. It 'howls' to mark its territory or attract a mate.

Geoffrey's spider monkey: The largest species is also the most acrobatic, thanks to the strong prehensile tail, which acts as a fifth limb.

White-faced capuchin: Looks like a monk, acts like a monkey. They are omnivores and can be aggressive, especially when it comes to food.

Squirrel monkey: The smallest species is less than 30cm long, nose to tail, weighing in at 1kg. They are also the least common, found only in the South Pacific and the Península de Osa.

WHAT'S SO LUCKY ABOUT LA FORTUNA?

For most of its history, La Fortuna was a sleepy agricultural village, 6km from the base of Cerro Arenal (Arenal Hill). It's true that the village had the 'good fortune' to escape destruction, after the massive explosion of Volcán Arenal in 1968 – following nearly 400 years of inactivity – buried the small villages of Pueblo Nuevo, San Luís and Tabacón. But, contrary to legend, this was not the inspiration for its name. In fact, the village has been called La Fortuna since its official incorporation in 1952, when it was named for its fertile lands – its original source of wealth and good fortune.

ROAMING PANDA PHOTOS/SHUTTERSTOCK

Mistico Hanging Bridges

Wlidlife Galore

Spot wild creatures in the forest

Two things are sure to be on your bucket list in Costa Rica: seeing sloths and seeing monkeys. In La Fortuna, you can check off both achievements in one day!

The best place to spot sloths and other rainforest creatures is with a guide at **Arenal Oasis Wildlife Refuge** *(arenaloasis.com; tours from US$68)*. Opt for a morning or late-afternoon tour, as rainforest creatures usually spend midday hiding. A guided tour is highly recommended, as the charismatic yet elusive sloths can be extremely well camouflaged. Fortunately, guides know where to look and can focus their scopes so you'll get a good look too. Often, they will also let you take photos through the scope. Reservations are required.

At **Monkey Park** *(monkeyparkcr.com; US$20)*, 25km east of La Fortuna, the primates are the main attraction. Both howlers and capuchins pass through these parts. Of course, there are no guarantees – these are wild animals, after all –

EATING IN LA FORTUNA: HEARTY, CHEAP EATS

Soda La Hormiga: Locals swear this is the best and cheapest plate of food in town. *6am-3:45pm Mon-Sat, from 7am Sun* $

Soda La Palma: The *soda* (cheap eatery) with the best view of the volcano, and a handy supermarket next door. *6:30am-5pm* $

Soda Leo: This tiny buffet is adjacent to the bus terminal in La Fortuna. Cheap, fast and easy. *4:30am-8pm* $

Pollos La Familia: Adorable family-run restaurant right by the park. Mom cooks and son is the waiter – a family affair! *11am-8:30pm* $

Antojitos Isa: A great option on the outskirts of La Fortuna. Delicious *casados* (set meals) and homemade juices. *6am-9pm Tue-Sat, to 4pm Mon* $

Soda Melania: Unfussy *soda* overlooking La Fortuna park. Next door to the laundromat, so you can eat while you wait. *8am-8pm* $

La Mesa de Mamá: Located in El Castillo and worth every kilometer. Don't miss the homemade plantains. *8am-8:30pm* $

Soda El Turnito: Tiny, cheap *soda* with a simple, consistent menu. *7:30am-9pm* $

but there's a pretty good chance you'll see some of them. The friendly resident raccoon will likely accompany you on your 2.5km stroll through the primary forest, though you can also hire a guide. Fresh juice and a snack await on your return. Even though it's a 'monkey park,' you might see sloths, anteaters, armadillos, frogs and other creatures here too. There are lots of mosquitoes, so long pants are highly recommended and insect repellent is essential.

Next, drive about 20km east to the town of **Muelle**. Just 2km north of the main intersection, Ruta 35 takes a sharp turn to cross a narrow bridge. Here, on either side of the river, green iguanas hang out in the trees above the river. These prehistoric-looking creature can be massive! Walk across the pedestrian bridge to see how many you can count, or get a good look from the viewing platform at the **Centro Turístico Las Iguanas** *(facebook.com/lasIguanassancarlos)* on the west side. This is also a good place to grab lunch or ice cream.

Around 80% of rainforest animals are nocturnal. That's why almost every nature preserve offers a night tour: so you can see the frogs, bugs and spiders – and even some mammals – that only come out at night. **Ecocentro Danaus** *(ecocentrodanaus.com; adult/child US$35/17.50)* seems to specialize in frogs, including the red-eyed tree frog. Flashlights are provided. Reserve in advance for all tours.

MORE VOLCANOES

You can only see Volcán Arenal from a distance. To get up close and personal with live volcanic activity, visit **Parque Nacional Volcán Poás** (p231), **Parque Nacional Rincón de la Vieja** (p207) or Las Hornillas on the slopes of **Volcán Miravalles** (p199).

Rainforest Canopy Craze

See the rainforest from above

Much rainforest activity takes place in the treetops, from birds to bugs to monkeys. There are a couple of ways you too can experience life at the canopy level, whether you want to slowly observe the ecosystem or fly past it at high speed.

If you get more excited by a bird sighting than a thrill ride, head to **Mistico Hanging Bridges** *(misticopark.com; tours from US$32)*, 20km west of La Fortuna, near the Arenal dam. Here, 3km of paved trails wind through 250 hectares of tropical rainforest, crossing 16 bridges along the way. Tucked between the lowlands and the highlands, the park contains a vast number of species of flora and fauna. You'll see more of it if you opt for the guided walk, but it's an enchanting experience even if you don't.

EMBRACING THE RAIN

Some people might try to avoid visiting Costa Rica when it's raining, but the true lovers of the country know that the rain makes (almost) everything better. This is especially true for adrenaline adventures. Rain makes the rivers run faster for more exciting rapids. Rain makes the cables on ziplines and rappels literally sing with speed. There's nothing more satisfying than running an ATV through a huge, muddy puddle. And sipping a cocktail under a warm rain while immersed in volcanic hot springs? Well, there's nothing like it. So act like a local and enjoy the rain!

EATING IN LA FORTUNA: OUR PICKS FOR A SPLURGE

La Parilla de María Bonita: Lebanese and Costa Rican dishes served in downtown La Fortuna. Gyros and baklava, anyone? *noon-9:30pm Sun-Wed, to 11pm Thu-Sat* $$$

Don Rufino: Book ahead for this popular spot serving excellent grilled meats and tantalizing fusion fare with expert wine pairings. *noon-9pm* $$$

Victorino's: Stellar soups, *ceviche* (marinated seafood), chicken and beef dishes, as well as excellent cocktails. *6am-midnight* $$

Las Tablas: Offers a variety of fine cuts of grass-fed beef paired with traditional Costa Rican sides in a welcoming atmosphere. *11am-10pm* $$

ETHICAL ANIMAL-SPOTTING

The La Fortuna area has always been an excellent place to see many rainforest animals in their natural habitats, especially sloths. The nature of wildlife-spotting means that the animals are not always in the same place, and can be hard to see – if you see them at all! To avoid uncertainty for tourists, the latest eco-park craze has caused many businesses to guarantee that visitors will see certain animals at certain times of the day or year. Many of these parks operate under the title of 'sanctuary.' If you are concerned about animal treatment, your best bet is to do your own research before you visit. Check for a current MINAE (Ministry of Environment and Energy) certification.

For nature with a healthy dose of adrenaline, your destination is **Ecoglide Arenal Park** *(arenalecoglide.com; from US$56.50)*. The guides will suit you up with helmets and climbing gear, and put you on a test line so you know how everything works. After a 15-minute bumpy ride up to the first platform, you'll hook into your first cable. Take a fantastic flight through the trees on a thrilling 11-cable zipline course. Only the most daring will opt for the Tarzan Swing, where riders drop almost 40m into the rainforest before enjoying a lazy swing back and forth among the trees.

You can combine the hanging-bridges walk and a zipline course with **Sky Adventures** *(skyadventures.travel; from US$40)*, on the road to El Castillo. Opt for a three-in-one package that includes an informative guided hanging-bridges walk (Sky Walk) and a shorter seven-cable zipline (Sky Trek), as well as a 20-minute gondola ride (Sky Tram) for volcano and lake views. Each adventure can also be done separately, making this a great option for groups where every rider wants a different experience. Reservations required.

Wet & Wild

Rappel through the rush

Waterfalls are lovely to look at and delightful for a dip. But if you want to take your adventure to the next level, it's time for waterfall rappelling. That's right, scaling down the face of a cliff while you feel the rush of a mighty waterfall all around you. (Yes, you'll get completely soaked.)

Offered by **Maquique Adventures** *(maquique adventure.com; US$101)*, this exhilarating half-day tour takes you through a gorgeous forest-covered river canyon and rappelling down three waterfalls along the way. The scenery is spectacular, further enhanced by the adrenaline rush that accompanies it. You'll finish the day with a short hike leading to the area's only tandem zipline, where you and a friend will zip through the trees side by side, or engage in a friendly race to the bottom.

No special skills are required – just moderate physical condition to complete the hike on well-maintained trails. The rappelling does require some strength, but the guides are skilled at working with anyone who may require extra assistance. Water shoes and quick-drying clothing are recommended. A photo package is also available for purchase

EATING IN LA FORTUNA: DINING WITH A VIEW

Qué Rico: A casual pizzeria with floor-to-ceiling glass walls, guaranteeing a phenomenal volcano view from every table. *11am-10pm* **$$**

El Chante Verde: Airy space with a veg-friendly menu of sandwiches, salads and *batidos* (fruit shakes). Booking recommended. *11:30am-9pm* **$$**

Mirador Arenal: Excellent choice for perfectly cooked and reasonably priced steaks, with lovely volcano views. *noon-10pm Thu-Tue* **$$**

Mirador Doña Luisa: Grilled meats and seafood alongside Costa Rican classics such as *chifrijo* (rice and pinto beans). *noon-9pm Thu-Mon* **$$**

BOB HILSCHE/SHUTTERSTOCK

Sky Tram at Sky Adventures

after every tour, so you don't have to bring a camera. Did we mention that you'll get wet?

Just Like Grandma Made

Exercise your chef skills

It won't take long for you to fall in love with La Fortuna's food – it's as fresh as it gets. If you want to take home the flavors of Costa Rica, Chela Jiménez Romanini of **El Fogón de Chela** *(6049-5192; from US$55)* helps you achieve just that.

At her cooking school, you'll learn the business's origin story. Choose the dish you want to make from her grandmother's recipe book and prepare to work. As the food is cooking, you'll enjoy natural drinks while you make your own tortillas. Once all the food is ready, gather around Chela's large wooden tables to enjoy your meal with new friends.

To discover where your food comes from and how it's prepared, **Finca Paraíso Orgánico** *(facebook.com/fincaparaiso organicofortuna; from US$55)* offers a highly entertaining tour that might include making (and sampling) a drink from sugarcane or a chocolate candy from dried cacao seeds. Finish with a homemade lunch, prepared with ingredients grown right here on the *finca* (farm).

THE PERFECT CUP OF COSTA RICAN COFFEE

Chef Isela 'Chela' Jiménez Romanini is the owner of El Fogón de Chela cooking school.

To make a hot cup of Costa Rican coffee (we call it *café chorreado*), you need a *chorreador*. It's a wooden stand with a fabric filter that looks like a sock. First, boil one to two cups of hot water (preferably over the fire). Place two teaspoons of ground Costa Rican coffee at the bottom of the 'sock,' and then place a coffee cup in the middle of the stand. Slowly pour the hot water over the coffee, letting it drain through the filter until your coffee cup is full. Add sugar or milk if you want, and enjoy the coffee with friends.

DRINKING IN LA FORTUNA: OUR PICKS FOR A CAFFEINE FIX

Red Frog Coffee Roasters: This place will make you freshly roasted coffee and serves pretty fabulous food too. *7am-8pm*

Sloffee: Locally owned, bustling to-go coffee stand located on the road between La Fortuna and Arenal. *7am- 4pm*

Chocolate Fusión: Serious baristas prepare every coffee drink under the sun. Find it in downtown La Fortuna. *9am-8pm*

Rainforest Café: A perfect downtown stop for a lingering coffee break. Don't miss the traditional *café chorreado. 7am-10pm*

MAD FOR MACAWS

If you have your hopes set on spotting the great green macaw, be sure to spend a few days in Boca Tapada, on the edge of the **Refugio Nacional de Vida Silvestre Mixto Maquenque** (p256), one of the last nesting areas of this magnificent bird.

A farm-to-table experience at **Arenal Vida Campesina** *(arenalvida.com; from US$50)* includes a tour through the extensive vegetable gardens, where you'll pick ingredients and learn about medical plants before making your own meal alongside local women.

Choose Your Ride

Epic views and adventure

There's nothing quite like plowing through the rainforest on an ATV. You'll see plenty of terrain in a short amount of time, and have a blast while doing it. Start with a short drive and quick hike over lava boulders for a stunning view of Volcán Arenal. Then spend an hour or two plowing through rivers and down dirt roads, and splashing through the occasional mud puddle – all while enjoying different vantage points of the volcano. **Outback Adventures** *(outbackquads.com; from US$85),* located about halfway between La Fortuna and Lake Arenal, will set you up with expert local guides who facilitate the perfect balance between safety and adrenaline.

If you'd rather power your own wheels, you can go cycling with **Bike Arenal** *(bikearenal.com; from US$90),* which offers both single-track mountain biking and road-bike trips in the area. These tours aren't for beginners, but if you love cycling, splendid volcano views and spotting animals from your bike, this is for you. A full-day road-bike tour to Pital and back is for advanced riders. Or choose between varying difficulties of a single- or double-track mountain-biking adventure.

DO I NEED RESERVATIONS?

The tension between a laid-back, *pura vida* vacation and not wanting to miss any of the adventures is something Costa Rican travelers often experience. If you are wondering whether to make a reservation for your tour, here are some quick tips:

Do you need transportation?
If you need someone else to transport you to your destination, you'll want a reservation.

How important is the tour?
Some tours are can't-miss, while others you might feel indifferent about. Book the ones you really love.

Do you need a guide?
If you'd like an expert Costa Rican guide, you should arrange tours in advance.

Volcán Arenal

TANGUY DE SAINT-CYR/SHUTTERSTOCK

WHY I LOVE LA FORTUNA

Christa Jiménez, Lonely Planet writer

I have lost count of the number of times I've seen the Volcán Arenal, and it never ceases to amaze me. There's nothing like watching the clouds slowly move to reveal the majestic cone at the top. If you're lucky, you'll be at one of my favorite viewpoints – right downtown in the middle of the park, enjoying a delicious *copa* from the local vendor. A *copa* is a snow cone with powdered milk in the middle and sweetened condensed milk on top. It's a purely Costa Rican confection, and one you can't miss while in La Fortuna.

Arenal Volcanic Hot Springs

There's something awe-inspiring about being in the shadow of an active volcano – seeing its conical top, hiking volcanic rock, soaking in naturally heated waters. Volcán Arenal may not be spitting fire any longer, but its power is still on full display. The healing powers of volcanic hot springs are for many the whole reason to visit Arenal.

Where to soak if you love...

Intimate Settings

Eco Termales Fortuna (p231) These reservation-only hot springs limit the number of people allowed per entry, allowing for a personalized experience. Purchase your tickets online in advance, and plan for a four-hour window.

Springs Resort & Spa This large upscale resort attracts thousands of honeymooners each year. But you can book a day pass and enjoy a bit of romantic luxury without the high price of accommodations.

TANYA KEISHA/SHUTTERSTOCK

Springs Resort & Spa

Tabacón Hot Springs (p230) At the most photographed hot springs in Costa Rica, wander the perfectly groomed paths between natural and artificial pools. Sit under the waterfall for a massage, or head to the adults-only section for a quiet soak. Book in advance.

A Party Vibe

Baldí Hot Springs This ostentatious resort is the largest in Costa Rica, billed as the 'largest hot springs in the world.' Enjoy its 25 pools, multistory waterfalls and water slides. Kids love the dedicated area, and the bartenders mix excellent cocktails.

Los Lagos Hotel & Resort (p262) Practically at the base of the volcano you'll find Los Lagos, a resort popular with locals and big tour groups alike. A bustling bar serves draft beer and cheap eats while pumping top Latin hits. Gorgeously groomed gardens surround hot and cold pools.

Soaking with the Locals

Termales Los Laureles Hot springs, soccer fields, grills, cabanas and a great on-site restaurant. Costa Ricans spend the entire day here, and you'll get a good soak in some of the seven pools as well as a taste of local life.

Relax Termalitas Don't be fooled by the super-cheap entry fee to this little property. You can choose from 10 pools and enjoy a few waterslides here.

A Family Affair

Volcano Lodge & Springs (p262) Soaring volcano views accompany the main cold pool, where you'll find lots of families. As you go deeper into the property, there's a hot pool with a wet bar and several other smaller, more intimate pools.

Kalambú Hot Springs This family property has a kids' pool with a huge water feature. Teens will love the waterslides, while adults can relax in lounge chairs or in the infinity pools at the back of the property.

WIRESTOCK CREATORS/SHUTTERSTOCK

Tabacón Hot Springs (p230)

HOW TO

Before you go You'll want to have your bathing suit, of course, and check if towels are available on-site, as not all hot springs offer them.

When to go The best time to visit the hot springs is at night when the temperatures dip and both the hot and cold pools feel heavenly.

Book ahead Once you've determined which hot springs you want to visit, check online to see how much space they generally have. Some need to be booked well in advance (Eco Termales Fortuna) and others are walk-in (Baldí).

Budget Many hot springs offer optional meal packages within their day passes, which can be an economical way to enjoy the springs.

A Seamless Hot Springs Experience

Each of these hot springs provides the relaxing benefits of hot and cold water, but some are artificially heated. If you prefer actual volcanic waters, research before you visit. Also consider location, as few hot springs resorts provide transport to/from the property, so it's best to arrive by rental car or taxi. Luckily, taxis in this area are abundant and reliable. You won't need a guide or tour to visit these properties, so showing up on your own can save money.

Almost all of the hot springs resorts have changing rooms and showers on-site. If you decide to use them, find out if lockers are available and how much they cost. Decide what to do with your phone while you're in the pools – consider a waterproof pouch that also holds money and keys. If you plan to consume food or drink at the wet bars, take cash or a credit card with you to the pools.

A visit to the hot springs is best in the evening, as the water can be blistering-hot under the sun. Don't be afraid of the rain – there's nothing more luxurious than being submerged in a hot-water pool while cool rain comes down from above.

Beyond Volcán Arenal & La Fortuna

Beyond La Fortuna, you'll find luscious lakes, charming villages, challenging hikes and wildlife encounters, all with a stunning volcano backdrop.

Places

GETTING AROUND

This area is very spread out and best explored in a rental car. You can also arrange organized tours to all of these places, but you'll pay a hefty premium for transportation. There are three daily buses to Tilarán, with stops at Nuevo Arenal and other lakeside destinations. There are also two daily buses between El Castillo and La Fortuna. Schedules are subject to change, so be sure to check in advance at the bus terminal.

In most places, a lake as scenic as Laguna de Arenal would be the focal point. In this case, the 88-sq-km lake takes a back seat to the steaming volcano, but it's still a source of fabulous vistas and myriad recreation opportunities.

Perfectly poised at the lake's edge, the tiny village of El Castillo is a beautiful, bucolic alternative to La Fortuna, offering rejuvenating retreats, sustainable farm tours and wildlife experiences (all with amazing, up-close views of the looming mountain). For extreme-adventure lovers, this is also the base for a challenging two-day trek to Monteverde.

East of town there are a number of private wildlife reserves, offering the region's best opportunities to spot monkeys, sloths, iguanas and more.

Laguna de Arenal

TIME FROM VOLCÁN ARENAL & LA FORTUNA: **45 MINS**

Life is better at the lake

With its true-blue waters and volcanic backdrop, the **Laguna de Arenal** – about 25km west of La Fortuna – is as captivating as they come. Most visitors will make the scenic drive around the lake at least once, en route to or from La Fortuna. If you believe the best lakeside experiences require getting at least a little bit wet, here is your chance. You'll need your own vehicle to do these activities independently, but if you book a tour, **Jacamar Naturalist Tours** *(jacamartours.com; from US$70)* will provide transportation from La Fortuna.

Book a tour with **Arenal Kayaks** *(arenalkayaks.com; from US$40)* in Nuevo Arenal or **Canoa Aventura** *(canoa-aventura.com; from US$78)* in La Fortuna, and spend a morning paddling among the flora and fauna of Laguna de Arenal. There's plenty of wildlife to see, including waterbirds, otters and the occasional iguana. The pace is relaxing and the views are rewarding.

The west end of the lake is a windy wonderland as the tradewinds blow across the Caribbean and get funneled through the mountains. This creates strong and stable conditions to catch the breeze on Laguna de Arenal. From December

CARMELA SOTO/SHUTTERSTOCK

Laguna de Arenal

through April only, make advance arrangements to rent windsurfing gear or take lessons from **Tico Wind** *(ticowind.com; rental from US$100 per hr)*.

Glide across the lake with the volcano in view. **Desafío Adventure Co** *(desafiocostarica.com; from US$80)* will equip you, brief you for safety, and then deposit you in the middle of the lake. You'll paddle to the other side, with a break on a scenic island. Calm waters and wonderful scenery make for a peaceful morning. Alternatively, rent a SUP from the **Arenal Boat Rental Association** *(8876-1849; 2hr US$50)* and strike out on your own. Look for the turnoff about 3km past the dam.

You can also motor across the lake with a tour guide. **Blue Pass Arenal** *(bluepasshub.com; adult/child US$19/10)* offers boat tours every hour at the *embarcadero* (wharf) also located 3km past the dam. Hop aboard a covered boat and enjoy views of the volcano while looking for the caimans. Halfway through the trip, stop for a short hike on paved paths in Parque Nacional Volcán Arenal before heading back across the lake.

A lakeside stop in transit

Another way to enjoy the lake and an easy way to travel between La Fortuna and Monteverde is via a taxi-boat-taxi combo. Travel from La Fortuna to Laguna de Arenal, where you'll meet a boat and cross the lake. On the other side, a 4WD picks up passengers and continues to Santa Elena. It's an efficient – and scenic! – transportation option. Book with **Aventuras El Lago** *(aventurasellago.com; US$30)*.

Alternatively, turn the journey into an adventure by doing it under the power of your own two feet. A guided hike to Monteverde offered by **Red Lava Tours** *(redlavatours.com; US$155)* requires two days of trekking over rough terrain a 1000m

continued on p244

HISTORY OF A LAKE

The Laguna de Arenal was not always the grand beauty it is today. The 1979 construction of the Represa Arenal, or Arenal Dam, expanded the lake's size by about three times, making it the largest lake in the country (and the second largest in Central America).

The project also destroyed two villages in the process. The villages were subsequently rebuilt on higher ground, giving us Nuevo Arenal on the north coast and Tronadora on the south. The upside is that the resulting hydroelectric dam generates about 12% of the country's energy needs.

To learn more, the **Arenal Observatory Museum** in the national park shows an interesting documentary film about the history of the Arenal dam project.

ROAD TRIP

A Lakeside Road Trip

The small town of Tronadora is a gorgeous destination many visitors pass by on their way to Monteverde. But the vistas – shimmering lake, rolling hills, smoking volcano – are spectacular. You also get a fascinating close-up view of the wind farm, which might just blow you away. There are no gas stations along this route, so make sure you fill up when you can. You'll stay on Hwy 142 for almost the entire route.

1 Mirador El Silencio

You'll want to get an early start (before breakfast) from La Fortuna to avoid rain in the winter and heat in the summer. Start your morning with a hike up to the breathtaking viewpoint at **Mirador El Silencio** (p231).

The Drive: Continue toward Laguna de Arenal, and then to Nuevo Arenal; the drive takes about 45 minutes.

2 Tom's Pan

A German breakfast? Yep! Stop by **Tom's Pan** in Nuevo Arenal for some of the most delicious German breads in the world. Enjoy a traditional German breakfast – sausage and all – you earned it.

The Drive: After Nuevo Arenal, continue on Ruta 142 for about 24km to reach Mirador Tilarán.

INTREEGUE PHOTOGRAPHY/SHUTTERSTOCK

Laguira de Arenal, viewed fom Mirador Tilarán

3 Mirador Tilarán

Some of the most gorgeous views of both the Arenal lake and volcano are just off the road at **Mirador Tilarán**. Stop here to snap photos and talk to locals selling souvenirs. This can be a windy spot, so a jacket is a good idea.

The Drive: Head back onto Ruta 142 for about 5km before you turn left onto Ruta 926. This will take you through the town of Tronadora, where you'll take a left at the park, and another left at Monte Terras Hotel. You'll see the Cove straight ahead.

4 The Cove

You have to get off the beaten path to sail the lake on a catamaran, and the **Cove** is the place to do it. This popular birding spot/hotel also offers guided sailing experiences on the Laguna de Arenal. If you aren't up for a sail, the stand-up paddle boards are a blast on a calm day.

The Drive: Head back through town on Ruta 926 (the same way you came) until you get to Ruta 142. Stay on it until you get to the Wind Farm.

5 Wind Farm

You'll see firsthand Costa Rica's deep commitment to being carbon-neutral by 2050 as you gaze over the massive government-run **wind farm**. The gigantic turbines look otherworldly at the base of the volcano. If you have an automobile, skip this stop, as the road is rocky.

The Drive: Head back around the lake towards Nuevo Arenal. Drive for 7km and look for Café & Macadamia on your right just after Cabinas Vista Lago Arenal.

6 Café & Macadamia

You won't want to miss the sunset at this iconic **restaurant** with breathtaking views of the lake. Take your time here – this is your last stop before you head back to La Fortuna for a delicious dip in the volcanic hot springs.

contined from p241

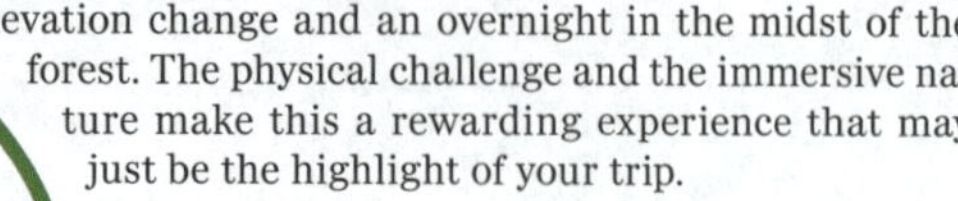

elevation change and an overnight in the midst of the forest. The physical challenge and the immersive nature make this a rewarding experience that may just be the highlight of your trip.

YOGA RETREATS

Costa Rica has become something of a yoga destination, but most yoga retreats take place at the beach. Check out the options in **Nosara** (p289) and **Santa Teresa** (p313).

El Castillo

TIME FROM VOLCÁN ARENAL & LA FORTUNA: **20 MINS**

Conservation and sustainability

Across Costa Rica, individuals are taking steps to preserve their little piece of the planet. Head to the tiny village of **El Castillo** to see how two people have taken different paths to transform deforested land into eco havens. If you don't have a car, a taxi is the easiest option for these experiences.

Your first stop is **Rancho Margot** *(ranchomargot.com; tours US$60)*, an off-the-grid, self-sustainable working farm. Reserve in advance for a two-hour regenerative farm tour around the spectacular property to learn how the ranch produces almost all the food and energy that it needs – not only to support the on-site resort, but also to make generous contributions to the surrounding community. The tour ends with a fabulous lunch, so you can taste the results of the ranch's efforts.

After lunch, head up to the **Butterfly Conservatory** *(butterflyconservatory.org; US$20)* into 'Upper Castillo.' Once a cattle ranch, these 5 hectares now house a nature education center that claims the country's largest butterfly exhibition. The 30-some species of butterflies are indeed spectacular, but that's just the beginning. There's also a frog house, flower gardens and hiking trails through the regenerated rainforest. You can easily spend all afternoon exploring the grounds and planning how you might preserve your little piece of the planet too.

Boost for the body, mind and soul

Come to **Essence Arenal** *(essencearenal.com)* in El Castillo, 25km southwest of La Fortuna, to refresh, renew and absorb the positive energy. Perched on a 22-hectare hilltop with fabulous volcano and lake views all around, the setting is absolutely spectacular – an inspiring spot for some DIY you-time. Guests choose when to come, how long to stay and what to do – a custom-designed retreat, as it were.

You'll start your days with 75 minutes of sun salutations in the open-air yoga shala. Nourish yourself with fabulous vegetarian meals and fresh fruit juices, both using ingredients from the on-site permaculture farm to which guests have unlimited access. Explore the grounds on 5km of hiking trails, replete with animals and birdlife. Pamper yourself at the on-site spa as your stay includes daily access to the sauna, steam bath and Jacuzzi (with a fabulous volcano view). Sweat Lodge, Reiki and nutrition consults with experts are available.

It's worth noting that this is not a luxury retreat experience. Accommodations are clean and comfortable, but decidedly not fancy. You'll choose rooms with either shared or private bathrooms. Choose between a standard room, a glamping

TIPS FOR A LOW-IMPACT TRIP

Juan Sostheim, founder of Rancho Margot, shares tips for a sustainable tourism experience in Costa Rica, to help make your trip as low-impact as possible. *@ranchomargot*

Reuse: Bring your own reusable water bottles and reusable bags. Costa Rica is one of the few places in Latin America where you can drink the tap water.

Research: Look for accommodations with a carbon-neutral certification or sustainable tourism certification.

Carbon offset: The longer your flight, the longer you should consider staying in Costa Rica.

Eating: Choose restaurants that use local ingredients and local labor.

DANVANPELT/SHUTTERSTOCK

Butterfly, Butterfly Conservatory

tent or a treehouse. Digital nomads will find work and wellness seamlessly merge.

The property is expansive and rugged, requiring a fair amount of walking to get around. But for immersive nature, glorious views and healing *pura vida* vibes at an affordable price, it's a winner.

Essence Arenal offers transportation to and from San José airport. When you care to explore the greater area, there are two or three daily shuttle buses between El Castillo and La Fortuna (passing the national park and other attractions along the way). Otherwise, Rancho Margot , offering horseback tours, and the Butterfly Conservatory as well as several good, local restaurants are within walking distance in the town of El Castillo if you need a change of pace.

Nuevo Arenal

TIME FROM VOLCÁN ARENAL & LA FORTUNA: **30 MINS**

A meal at the gingerbread house

Located 44km west of La Fortuna, the **Gingerbread Hotel & Restaurant** *(gingerbreadarenal.com)* is a Nuevo Arenal gem serving innovative fusion fare. The menu changes daily, offering delights like escargots, tuna poke or chicken schnitzel. Meals are served family-style, which is fortunate because you will want to try everything.

AN AGED CAVERN

The Cavernas del Venado date back to the Miocene epoch, which means they are between five million and 23 million years old (this is relatively young by cave standards; the caverns at Parque Nacional Barra Honda on the Península de Nicoya are estimated to be some 60 million years old). Indigenous Maleku people long knew about the Cavernas del Venado, naming them Gabinarraca, which means 'where God sits' (according to one guide). They were officially 'discovered' in 1945, and extensive exploring started in 1969.

The cave network extends about 2700m, and 10 separate caverns have been mapped. About half the cave network is open to tourists. Inhabitants include four types of bats, as well as spiders, crickets and fish.

EATING IN EL CASTILLO: OUR PICKS

El Patio Al Carbón: Stunning volcano views, excellent food and a killer passionfruit margarita. Don't miss the gigantic burger. *10am-9pm* $$

La Ventanita: Cool vibe, cooler drinks and unbeatable tacos, burritos and *chifrijo* (a dish with rice, beans and fried pork). *11am-9pm Wed-Mon* $

Fusión Arenal: This place takes things up a notch with its elegant dining area, sophisticated presentations and scenic environs. *7am-9pm* $$

Howler's Bar & Grill: Congenial lakeside spot with excellent pub food, a pool table and a menu of craft brews. *11:30am-8:30pm Tue-Sun* $$

ALL ABOUT SODAS

The Costa Rican *soda* is a small, inexpensive and locally owned restaurant that serves traditional Costa Rican food. *Sodas* are where locals gather to eat, and they are generally open for breakfast and lunch. The specialty is the *casado* dish. The word's literal meaning in Spanish is 'married'; this hearty lunch plate is a set meal that consists of rice, beans, a choice of protein, fried ripe plantains and salad. The *casado* usually costs between US$5 and US$10 and comes with an ice-cold glass of homemade juice. Looking for a delicious *soda?* Ask a local for the *soda del pueblo* and they'll know exactly where to send you.

The real star, however, is Chef Eyal, a charismatic, larger-than-life host who entertains guests with bold recommendations and outrageous stories. His passion for food is infectious: 'I love food, and I want to do it better than anyone else.'

If you care to have a few drinks with dinner (or you just need a place to spend the night), the Gingerbread also has six fun and funky guest rooms. Reservations are required.

Cavernas del Venado

TIME FROM VOLCÁN ARENAL & LA FORTUNA: **1 HR**

Explore the Earth's darkest depths

Your journey to the center of the Earth begins in the **Cavernas del Venado** *(cavernasdelvenado.com; adult/child US$35/28)*, located 40km from La Fortuna. The guide will lead you on an adventurous excursion into an eight-chamber limestone labyrinth that extends for almost 3km. You'll squeeze through narrow passages and crawl (or swim) through tunnels, only to emerge into impressive halls, bedecked with stalactites and stalagmites and other intriguing formations. Keep a lookout for the insects and bats who call these caves home.

Water shoes are ideal for this venture; otherwise, you'll be given rubber boots (along with a headlamp and helmet). You'll get dirty and wet, but there are showers and a pool available afterward. If only part of your group wants to spelunk, those who stay behind can use the swimming pool for US$4 per person. If you don't have your own wheels, **EcoTerra** *(ecoterracostarica.com; adult/child US$86/52)* runs a tour that leaves from La Fortuna.

Dining with a 360-degree panorama

On your way home from Cavernas del Venado, you'll be hungry. Set aside an evening for dinner at **Jalapas Restaurant** *(facebook.com/jalapasrest)*, for one of the best views in the area. The reasonably priced restaurant is perched atop a ridge that separates La Fortuna from the Northern Lowlands, offering unobstructed volcano views, as well as a grand panorama stretching north all the way to Nicaragua. The sunset turns

EATING IN NUEVO ARENAL: OUR PICKS

Casa Italia: Chef Christian will take you to Palermo with brick-oven pizzas, homemade pastas and cannoli. *noon-8:30pm Thu-Tue* **$$$**

Moya's Place: This is a local favorite, serving unusual sandwiches, well-stuffed wraps and thin-crust pizza. *11:30am-9pm* **$$**

Los Platillos Voladores: Sit on the patio and enjoy fabulous homemade pasta and other Italian delights. *noon-8:30pm Tue-Sun* **$$**

Soda La Parada: This *soda* in Nuevo Arenal is beloved for good-value local fare, especially the *casados*. *5am-4pm Mon-Fri, to 2pm Sat* **$**

Café & Macadamia (p243): Bakery and pizzeria also serving traditional Costa Rican food. A local favorite for decades. *8am-7pm* **$$**

Equus Bar-Restaurant: Rustic for sure, serving cold beer and irresistible barbecued meats. Occasional live music. *10:30am-8:30pm* **$$**

Tinajas Arenal: Jaw-dropping lake views and fabulous food. The sunset and cocktails are out of this world. *8:30am-8:45pm* **$$**

Lake Arenal Hotel & Brewery: Solar-powered beer brewing. Farm-to-table meals. Volcano views. What more do you need? *7am-10pm* **$$**

AA WORLD TRAVEL LIBRARY/ALAMY

Cavernas del Venado

the sky a million shades of orange, pink and purple before it eventually fades to black. Arrive by 5pm to see the show.

The extensive menu includes a balance of seafood and steaks. You'll feast on tropical *ceviche,* Caribbean chicken and other Costa Rican classics with a modern twist. Cocktails, smoothies and local beers accompany your meal.

Husband-and-wife team Luis and Yorllinela treat their guests like old friends, guaranteeing a delightful evening. Jalapas is about five minutes' drive past the Springs Resort & Spa (p238). Reservations are recommended during the high season; it's open from noon to 9pm.

CHOOSING THE RIGHT ACCOMMODATIONS

Josué Arroyo, the manager of Ti-Fakara and Noah's Forest hotels, shares his tips on booking accommodations.

There are myriad lodging choices in La Fortuna. My best advice is to choose your location carefully. Consider whether you want to be close to certain activities, or close to a variety of restaurants downtown. It's also a good idea to decide if you want to have hot springs on-site, or if you prefer to visit different pools in the area. Find out if your hotel offers an included breakfast, as most hotels in the area offer a hearty breakfast. And, finally, make sure your chosen accommodations fit within your budget.

Sarapiquí Valley

WHITE-WATER RAFTING | BIRDWATCHING | PRIMARY RAINFORESTS

GETTING AROUND

Ruta 4/126 runs parallel to the river and connects the towns and villages in this region (La Virgen, Chilamate, Puerto Viejo, Horquetas). You can make any of these small towns your base. If you don't have a car, buses ply this route frequently. Taxis are few and far between. For farms, night tours and rainforest hikes, a car is the way to go. Lodges in Boca Tapada will provide transportation to/from Puerto Viejo, La Fortuna or San José. You won't need a car once you're in the Boca Tapada area.

TOP TIP

Sarapiquí has riverside hostels and dorm-style eco-retreats that provide an immersive rainforest experience and won't bust your budget. Book one day longer than you think is enough because once you're here you won't want to leave.

The Sarapiquí Valley is already something of an 'off-the-beaten-track' destination, even if you stick to the main drag. In recent years, the Río Sarapiquí has gained acclaim as a white-water destination. The wild river also provides a dramatic backdrop for some excellent ecolodges, most of which are surrounded by their own private forest reserves. Crisscrossed by hiking trails and teeming with life, the landscape merges seamlessly into the unexplored northern reaches of Parque Nacional Braulio Carrillo, making this one of the country's premier destinations for wildlife-watching and biological research.

Sarapiquí offers a glimpse of rural Costa Rica, authentic and unaffected, without the impact of contemporary commercialism or tourism. Immerse yourself in picturesque villages and dense tropical rainforests to gain firsthand insight into why Costa Ricans are immensely proud of their country. On the farm or in the forest, nature-made and ecofriendly, sustainable living is what Costa Ricans do best.

Run the Río

Ride the rapids, float the boat

The rivers are the lifelines of the Northern Lowlands, watering the fertile farmlands, transporting the produce, and providing endless entertainment for adventure seekers and wildlife-watchers. Whether you float among the flora and fauna on the Río Puerto Viejo, ride the rapids on the Sarapiquí or just go for a dip, a day on the river is a day to relish and remember.

If you feel the call of the river, you have your choice of vehicle. Inflatable, durable river rafts are the most popular option as they serve both for the adventure of white-water rafting and birdwatching on a river float. Rafts are easy to navigate and great for families or large groups. If you'd rather go in your own transport, tubing the river is a memorable experience. The

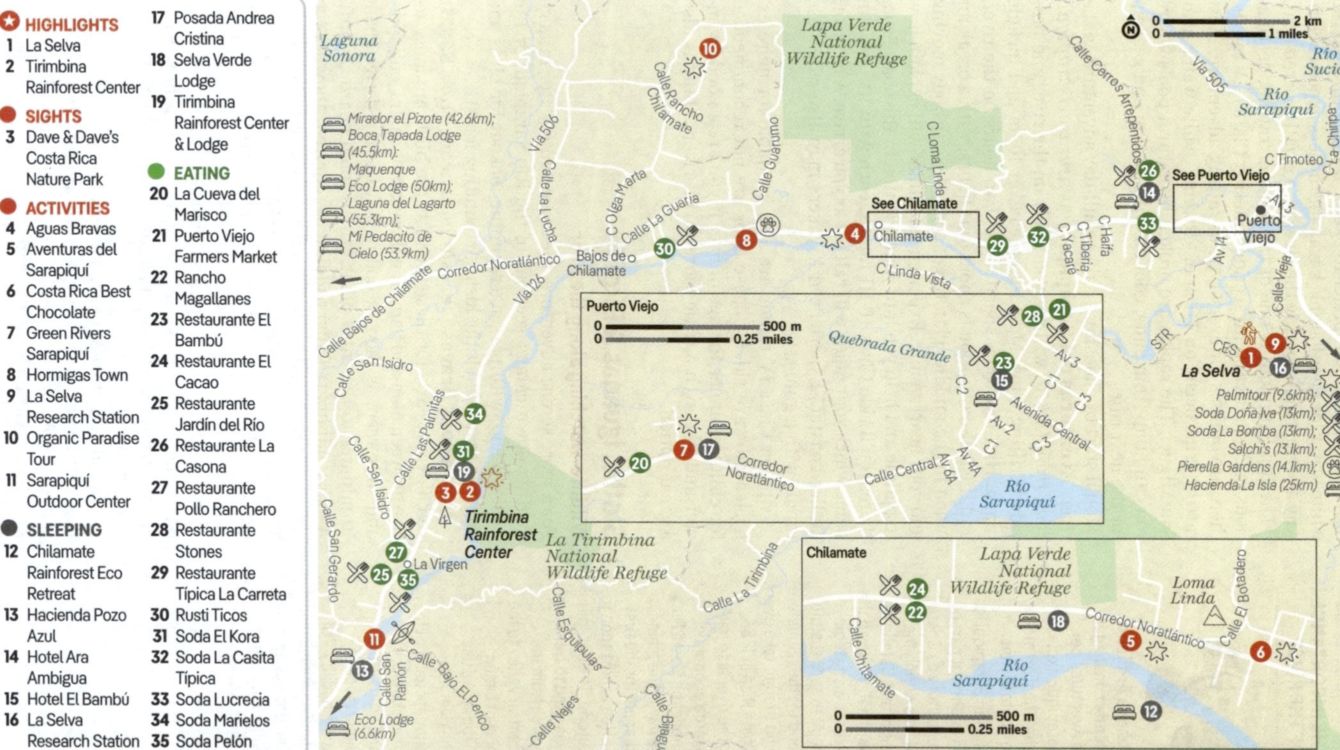

HIGHLIGHTS
1 La Selva
2 Tirimbina Rainforest Center

SIGHTS
3 Dave & Dave's Costa Rica Nature Park

ACTIVITIES
4 Aguas Bravas
5 Aventuras del Sarapiquí
6 Costa Rica Best Chocolate
7 Green Rivers Sarapiquí
8 Hormigas Town
9 La Selva Research Station
10 Organic Paradise Tour
11 Sarapiquí Outdoor Center

SLEEPING
12 Chilamate Rainforest Eco Retreat
13 Hacienda Pozo Azul
14 Hotel Ara Ambigua
15 Hotel El Bambú
16 La Selva Research Station
17 Posada Andrea Cristina
18 Selva Verde Lodge
19 Tirimbina Rainforest Center & Lodge

EATING
20 La Cueva del Marisco
21 Puerto Viejo Farmers Market
22 Rancho Magallanes
23 Restaurante El Bambú
24 Restaurante El Cacao
25 Restaurante Jardín del Río
26 Restaurante La Casona
27 Restaurante Pollo Ranchero
28 Restaurante Stones
29 Restaurante Típica La Carreta
30 Rusti Ticos
31 Soda El Kora
32 Soda La Casita Típica
33 Soda Lucrecia
34 Soda Marielos
35 Soda Pelón

THE IMPORTANCE OF THE RIVER

Johana Argüello Méndez, manager of Aventuras del Sarapiquí, explains what the river means to Costa Ricans.

The Río Sarapiquí is an important part of our history as Costa Ricans during the important Batalla de Sardinal. We used the river as a strategic point to successfully fend off the filibusters who tried to take over Costa Rica in 1856.

The river also had a large economic impact on Costa Rica as it was the main channel for the first coffee exportation to Europe. The Sarapiquí was used to transport coffee from the Central Valley to the port of Limón.

Today, we use the river as an educational tool to teach both locals and tourists the importance of sustainability – of keeping rivers clean and protecting local wildlife for future generations.

brave and crazy might prefer to paddle a kayak through the white water (or an inflatable kayak for the less experienced). Any age can enjoy floating the river on a small covered boat.

The Río Sarapiquí is one of the premier rafting destinations in Costa Rica. With sections offering Class I–IV rapids, there are options for every type of rafting adventure. Most rafting trips occur on 14km of 'extreme' white water near San Miguel. The rapids are broken by natural pools where you can jump from cliffs, cool off with a swim and gear up for the next run.

You'll start by choosing a half- or full-day adventure on the river. **Aventuras del Sarapiquí** *(aventurasdelsarapiqui.com; from US$73)* will get you safely on the river and provide thrilling trips. Most tours leave at 10am and include lunch. Half-day tours spend about two hours on the river, and the full-day option is about four hours, with a break for lunch in the middle. Plan to get soaked, your body moving and your heart racing. Experienced guides will explain how to paddle and help you into your position in the boat. From there, you'll ride Class II–III rapids, each with its own fun name which your guide will call out as you arrive. A favorite? 'Roller coaster.' Experienced kayakers may also run these rapids with a guide.

Trips on Class IV rapids are also available for more experienced wave riders. These trips are not recommended for children under the age of five. If you are a good swimmer and like even a little more thrill, river tubing is also a great option.

Sloths, Iguanas & Birdlife

Wildlife-watching along the river

For a more serene adventure, the same white-water rafts go floating down calmer sections of the Río Sarapiquí or Río Puerto Viejo, with passengers on the lookout for birds and animals that inhabit the lush surrounding forest.

With **Aguas Bravas** *(aguasbravascr.com; from US$75)*, you'll depart early for these tours, as the birds are most active between 6am and 9am. You'll want binoculars, bug spray and sunscreen, as the raft doesn't have a roof. Drive about 10 minutes to the entry point, where you'll board the raft. Aboard, minimal (if any) paddling is required, allowing you time to sit back and enjoy the quiet river as you float along. The variety of waterbirds is incredible – ibis, herons and egrets are just a few of the many waterbirds you can see. If you're lucky, you'll spot playful otters and sleepy sloths, and monkeys, caimans and countless iguanas sunning themselves on the muddy riverbanks. At the conclusion of the float, you'll enjoy a hearty Costa Rican *casado* lunch and debrief your trip with your guide.

Alternatively, if you'd like to power your own boat, a kayak float with a guide is a lovely option. **Sarapiquí Outdoor Center** *(costaricaraft.com; from US$75)* is the area's leader for kayak tours. **Green Rivers Sarapiquí** *(sarapiquigreenrivers.com; from US$95)* offers a peaceful yoga float.

Rafting, Río Sarapiquí (p248)

Mysterious Noises in the Night

Night tours at Tirimbina

While daytime wildlife-spotting is magical, there is something even more enchanting about finding nocturnal animals in nature. The Sarapiquí region has some of the best night tours in Costa Rica due to the high concentration of primary and secondary rainforest. Insects and animals are hidden in the night, cleverly disguised in the trees, under leaves and along the rainforest floor.

Head toward the village of La Virgen and then to **Tirimbina Rainforest Center** *(tirimbina.org; US$36)*, where you'll spend 1½ to two hours tromping through the rainforest with a knowledgeable bilingual guide. These tours should be booked in advance. You'll need a flashlight, lots of bug repellent, closed-toe shoes and an open mind. Embrace a rainy tour, as the nocturnal creatures love to come out and play in the rain.

Red-eyed tree frogs come alive at night, and spiders calmly weave their webs undisturbed. Bats sleep upside down in the trees, and caimans slide onto the banks of the river to hunt. That bump in the night? Probably not a snake, though you'll see several of those. More likely, you are coming across a kinkajou, porcupine or sloth. The highlight of the Tirimbina tour is the walk across the suspension bridge at night. You might be tentative at first as you imagine what could be beyond the swaying bridge. Once you get used to the movement of the bridge, you'll enjoy an unforgettable, one-of-a-kind Costa Rican nature experience.

Travel Your Tastebuds

Palmito, pineapple and chocolate

The Northern Lowlands is one of Costa Rica's most important agricultural regions, with vast banana, palm and pineapple plantations, as well as smaller family *fincas* of all sorts. With

THE FROGS OF SARAPIQUÍ VALLEY

Green and black poison-dart frog: Known for its striking colors, this tiny frog is elusive and fast.

Blue Jeans frog: Also named the strawberry poison-arrow frog, this tiny creature emits a chirp you can hear from far away.

Glass frog: This transparent frog makes it hard to spot. Look at the underside to see the organs functioning!

Masked tree frog: The 'Batman' of frogs, this one is a bit larger than the others. The black mask around its eyes helps camouflage it.

Golden poison frog: This frog is more elusive than you'd think. It's named for its deep yellow color.

BANANA HISTORY

In the 19th century, the flat steaming lowlands of northern Costa Rica were part of the vast banana plantations owned by the United Fruit Company. Boats laden with fruit plied the Río Sarapiquí as far as the Nicaraguan border, then turned east on the Río San Juan to the sea. Lying at the confluence of the Ríos Puerto Viejo and Sarapiquí, Puerto Viejo de Sarapiquí was Costa Rica's most important port during this time. In 1880 a railway connected rural Costa Rica with the port of Puerto Limón, and Puerto Viejo became a backwater. Although it's no longer a transportation hub, Sarapiquí Valley is still an agricultural region, blanketed in banana, pineapple and *palmito* (heart of palm) plantations, as well as smaller family *fincas* (farms).

TINA CHIU/COSTA RICA BEST CHOCOLATE

Costa Rica Best Chocolate

the growing interest in environmental health, many farmers are eschewing chemicals and implementing sustainable methods, with delicious and healthy results. Book ahead for tours (all of which include degustations).

Start at **Palmitour** *(facebook.com/Palmitour; US$45)* in **Horquetas**, where María Luz Jiménez has been growing peach palms for 20 years. She discovered that the *palmito* – the soft edible heart of the palm – is more delicious and versatile than anyone ever imagined. Now you can tour the plantation, learn how the palms are grown and harvested, and sample the products at the on-site restaurant.

Your next stop is the **Organic Paradise Tour** *(organicparadise tour.com; US$28),* located in **Chilamate**. Take a bumpy ride on a tractor-drawn trailer and learn everything you ever wanted to know about pineapples, including how to choose your pineapple at the supermarket. The tour focuses on sustainable practices, such as compost fertilization and natural herbicides. But the highlight is the taste test (of course), when your guide will pick a pineapple from the plant and slice it open with a machete (as you do).

If you did it right, you saved the best for last – dessert! After you have had your fill of pineapple, head up the road to learn about another fruit: cacao. At **Costa Rica Best Chocolate** *(crbestchocolate.com; adult/child US$37/25),* they share the secrets of how to turn cacao seeds into the world's favorite delicacy. Be prepared to help with every step of production, especially the taste tests.

If you want to try your hand at cooking traditional Costa Rican food, the Costa Rican Campesina Cooking Class offered through **Chilamate Rainforest Eco Retreat** *(chilamate rainforest.com; US$40)* is a true delight. You'll walk to a local's home near the village of **Linda Vista** and learn to prepare a snack or a meal, and then eat it alongside the family.

A Garden Paradise

Birds, frogs and bats

When you arrive at **Pierella Ecological Garden** *(pierella.com; US$40)*, you'll be astounded by the lush forest surrounding the property. You'd never guess that it used to be a pasture for dairy cows until William Camacho and Cristal Barrantes transformed it into a beautiful secondary-forest wildlife sanctuary. They started with a butterfly project, and over the years, the butterflies started to attract other wildlife. Today, there are many species of birds, frogs and bats as well as a butterfly garden. After your tour, enjoy a traditional Costa Rican lunch. Chocolate tours are offered on-site, too.

An Ant's Life

Learn all about leaf-cutters

At the very least, this place gets an A+ for originality. Located at Aguas Bravas, it's called **Hormigas Town** *(aguasbravascr.com; US$20)* and it's run by a guy known as 'the ant man.' Leo Herra spent years studying ants and setting up this little city – three colonies – so he could share his knowledge with the world. Suffice to say, he earned his title.

You might think ants aren't that interesting, but you will be surprised at how fascinating and complex these insects are. Specifically, you'll learn more than you ever wanted to know about leaf-cutter ants, including their complex social structure and division of labor, their diets and their methods of reproduction. (Spoiler alert: it ends badly for the males.)

A Treetop Sanctuary

Sleep in a treehouse

You don't have to stay in a treehouse when you come to **Maquenque Eco Lodge** *(maquenqueecolodge.com)*. After all, the regular bungalows are tasteful and lovely and, you know, on the ground. You'll have a pleasant visit – delightful, even – if you stay in a bungalow.

But if you want to gaze out over the rainforest canopy as if it's your backyard, to fall asleep to the humming and thrumming

EXPERT BIRDWATCHING TIPS

Adolfo González, manager of Laguna del Lagarto Eco Lodge, shares his top tips for birders.

Dress: We are in a rainy area, so unless you want to get wet, it's never a good idea to go birding without a rain jacket or poncho. You'll also want waterproof hiking shoes or rubber boots.

Watch: You'll want your own binoculars to see the details of each bird up close.

Local experts: Bring a guide from the area with you. They are an unending source of knowledge about not only the area but each of the species.

EATING IN PUERTO VIEJO: OUR PICKS

Restaurante El Bambú: Downtown location with lots of choices for both traditional and international cuisine. *6am-10pm* **$$**

Restaurante La Casona: This friendly restaurant serves great pizzas alongside Costa Rican dishes. *7am-9pm* **$$**

Soda La Casita Típica: Traditional Costa Rican fare. Stop for a meal or a snack – the *empanadas* are gigantic. *6:30am-7pm Mon-Sat, 7am-4pm Sun* **$**

Restaurante Típica La Carreta: This local favorite serves huge portions alongside a quick and cheap lunch buffet. *7am-8pm* **$**

La Cueva del Marisco: Sample pasta, paella or *ceviche* with fresh seafood, less than 100km from the Caribbean Sea. *11am-8pm Tue-Sun* **$$**

Soda Lucrecia: Traditional Costa Rican fare in an unassuming lunch-counter atmosphere. *5am-9pm* **$**

Restaurante Stones: International and Costa Rican bar food run by locals who love the Rolling Stones. *11am-11pm* **$**

Puerto Viejo Farmers Market: If you visit on a Saturday, try fresh fruit and vegetables directly from local farms. *6am-noon Sat* **$**

THE BEST PALMITO RECIPES

María Luz Jiménez, owner of Palmitour plantation, reveals some local recipes.

Each of these dishes showcases the versatility of one of Costa Rica's most beloved ingredients:

Heart-of-palm salad: A classic green salad elevated with fresh *palmito* rounds.

Chorreada: This traditional Costa Rican corn pancake gets a twist with *palmito* fruit, perfect with coffee.

Heart-of-palm lasagna: Layers of homemade pasta sauce, lasagna noodles, white cheese and *palmito* create a savory delight

Ceviche de palmito: A vegan spin on traditional *ceviche* (seafood marinated in lemon or lime juice), replacing raw fish with *palmito* marinated in lime juice.

of frogs and bugs and wake up to the grunt of howler monkeys and the chatter of birds – in short, to immerse yourself in the sights and sounds of the rainforest – then you do have to stay in a treehouse. And your 12-year-old self will thank you for it.

There are eight **treehouses** scattered about the 80 hectares at Maquenque Eco Lodge. To get there, you'll walk about 10 minutes from the main lodge on well-groomed trails through dense forest. And you'll climb a staircase that takes you about 12m off the ground to your treehouse at canopy level. Once you arrive, the view from your balcony is endless, lush primary rainforest – and little else. (The reception provides walkie-talkies in case of emergency.)

The treehouse itself is wonderful. There is a wide, welcoming balcony for birdwatching and stargazing. The interior is properly equipped with comfy beds and stylish decor, and there's also a wall of windows (or screens, to be exact) for unfiltered sensory input from the outside. Best of all, the bathroom opens up to an outdoor shower, taking the concept of a 'rainforest shower' to a whole new level.

Back at the main lodge, guests enjoy an excellent **restaurant**, with a surprisingly diverse menu. There's also a sweet **swimming pool**, birds rallying around the feeder and spider monkeys swinging through the trees. Various tours are on offer, including farm tours, boat tours, a night walk and kayaking.

But it's OK if you prefer to just hang out in your treehouse. You might even find yourself entertaining some coatimundi visitors up there.

Welcome to the Jungle

A walk in the wild

In the Sarapiquí region, there's no shortage of nature parks and private reserves to get lost in the rainforest (figuratively speaking, we hope). They all have something to offer, but the biggest and most famous is **La Selva**, a nature preserve and 'biological research station' that hosts scientists and students from all over the world.

La Selva is 16 sq km of premontane wet tropical rainforest, bordering the massive Parque Nacional Braulio Carrillo. The whole area contains a great diversity of life. More than 886 bird species have been recorded here, as well as 120 mammal species (including 70 species of bat and five species of cats), 1850 species of vascular plants (especially from the orchid, philodendron, coffee and legume families), and thousands of insect species, with 500 types of ants alone.

EATING IN LA VIRGEN: OUR PICKS

Soda Marielos: A perennial local favorite. Try the *casado* with *pollo a la plancha* (grilled chicken). *6am-9pm* $

Restaurante Pollo Ranchero: Lots more than just chicken, but the *arroz con pollo* (rice with chicken) is delicious. *6am-10pm* $$

Restaurante Jardín del Río: Great appetizers including spicy chicken wings, and fun bar vibe, often with live entertainment. *11:30am-11pm Tue-Sun* $$

Soda Pelón: Fun taco, burger and *empanada* combos alongside Costa Rican fare. Great delivery service. *6am-8pm Mon-Sat, 7am-6pm Sun* $

SALPARADIS/SHUTTERSTOCK

Strawberry poison-dart frog, La Selva

The best way to experience La Selva is to stay at the research station **lodge** *(tropicalstudies.org; from US$65 per night),* which is managed by the Organization for Tropical Studies. The price of accommodations includes a nature walk with a naturalist guide, but you'll also have access to explore the 57km of trails on your own throughout the duration of your stay.

Otherwise, day visitors can take advantage of various guided walks (reservations required). Every day, there is an early-morning birdwatching outing. (You know they are serious about birding when the bird walk starts at 5:45am.) Non-bird nerds might prefer the less specialized nature walk, which has the additional advantages of being later, longer and cheaper. Either way, you'll see some cool creatures and learn a lot.

Wildlife Photographer's Day Out

Line up the perfect shot

You're bound to capture some fabulous photos of Costa Rica's animal residents. But some places make it easier by creating the perfect setting to lure your subject closer to your camera. These venues in the Sarapiquí area are guaranteed to enable top-notch photos of the creatures of the river and rainforest.

You can visit **Dave & Dave's Costa Rica Nature Park** *(daveanddaves.com; US$45, cash only)* in La Virgen, where

THE LOWDOWN ON LEAF-CUTTERS

Long processions of busy leaf-cutter ants traverse the forest floors and trails of Costa Rica, appearing like slow-moving rivulets of green leaf fragments. Don't confuse them with the predatory army ants.

Leaf-cutter ants are incredibly strong. They can carry up to 50 times their own body weight. A colony might house up to 10 million ants, each with a specific job to do. Leaf-cutter ants don't actually eat leaves. What? They literally take the leaves to compost them, facilitating decomposition and creating fertilizer to grow their favorite food, which is a type of fungus. The ants 'cut' the leaves (and other stuff) with their razor-sharp jaws, which vibrate at a super-fast rate to saw through the greenery.

EATING IN HORQUETAS: OUR PICKS

Salchis: Huge menu with everything from traditional Costa Rican dishes to bar food. A local favorite. *11am-midnight* $

Soda La Bomba: Conveniently located at the bus stop in Horquetas, you can go for à la carte or the buffet option. *24hr* $

Palmitour (p252): If you don't have time for the tour, the restaurant is still worth a stop. The lasagna *de palmito* is second to none. *7am-5pm* $

Soda Doña Iva: Serves traditional breakfast and lunch. The homemade juices and smoothies can't be missed. *5am-7pm Mon-Sat* $

A UNIQUE WILDLIFE REFUGE

The **Refugio Nacional de Vida Silvestre Mixto Maquenque** *(refugio maquenque.com)* was established in 2005; the impetus for the refuge was to protect the unique habitat of the great green macaw. It's a wild and luscious bit of rainforest, tucked away in a remote corner of the Northern Lowlands, close to the Nicaraguan border. Straddling both sides of the Río San Juan, the refuge protects some 520 sq km of mostly virgin forest and wetlands. Maquenque is a 'mixed-use' wildlife refuge – the first of its kind in Costa Rica. It allows human residents to continue living and working within its boundaries. However, activity is drastically restricted – especially activities such as logging and farming, which contribute to deforestation.

IMAGEBROKER/CHRISTIAN HANDL/GETTY IMAGES

Brown-hooded parrots, Laguna del Lagarto Eco Lodge

father and son Daves welcome you for a guided walk around this delightful bird habitat. A viewing platform overlooks the forest, while trails wind down to the river, where you'll see toucans and tanagers flitting about. On the back balcony, some seven species of hummingbirds buzz at the feeders ingeniously crafted from heliconia flowers. The *colibríes* are accustomed to the setting, so you can get up close and personal. The two-hour walks take place at 8am, 10am, 1pm and 3pm; reservations are required.

If you're feeling adventurous, an overnight in **Boca Tapada** will guarantee not only the best wildlife shots but also a relaxing escape away from technology. Boca Tapada is a sort of birding mecca, thanks to the diversity of habitats, ranging from wetlands to rainforest to open pastures, which in turn attract many bird species. Professional ornithologists and amateur birders alike flock to this remote outpost, and especially to **Laguna del Lagarto Eco Lodge** *(lagunalagartoecolodge.com; from US$150)*. This whole place is set up to cater to birders, from the hummingbird garden to the photography

EATING IN CHILAMATE: OUR PICKS

Restaurante El Cacao: Tasty traditional dishes and intriguing pizzas, including the house special Theobrome ('food of the gods'). *11am-8pm Tue-Sun* $$

Rusti Ticos: Roadside stop featuring huge homemade tortillas and an ice-cream shop. *6am-9pm* $$

Rancho Magallanes: The specialty of the house is succulent chicken, roasted in the brick oven and served with tortillas and banana salsa. *8am-8pm* $$

Soda El Kora: Serves Mexican specialties, including *empapelados* (fish cooked in foil) and *casados*. *8am-8pm Mon-Sat* $

platforms to the vulture 'blind' (which allows lucky birders to observe the elusive king vulture). Boat tours and canoes *(from $65)* go in search of aquatic birds, and 10km of trails crisscross the forest. And, indeed, the birding never stops here, as there are feeders hanging off the balcony for your viewing pleasure while eating lunch or lounging in a hammock. More than 350 species have been spotted at this birding hot spot, which bodes well for your bird list.

A Relaxing Float

Cruise the Río San Carlos

For a superb riverboat tour on the Río San Carlos, head to Maquenque Eco Lodge (p253) in Boca Tapada. Half-day excursions generally leave from the dock at 9am, so if you wanted to book this from Sarapiquí and drive up, you would have time. Covered boats cruise downstream on the Río San Carlos. Flora and fauna are bountiful in this remote corner of Costa Rica, and your naturalist guide will point out crocodiles, tortoises, bats, herons, kingfishers, king vultures and countless aquatic birds. Make sure to bring your own binoculars if you want to spot the elusive species before they go away; otherwise, your guide will have some lenses to share. These boats do a fair amount of floating, which reduces the breeze and means mosquitoes, so make sure to have your repellent in tow.

Halfway through the morning, you'll stop in the tiny village of **Boca San Carlos**, on the Nicaraguan border. The vast Indio Maíz reserve is just across the border. Food, drinks and souvenirs are for sale, and you'll have the opportunity to speak to locals and wander the village.

You'll then float back to Maquenque, where you can head to the restaurant for a delicious lunch or go back to Sarapiquí. If you don't dine at the lodge, stop at **Centro Familiar Cuyito** *(facebook.com/centrofamiliarcuyito)*, about 2km south of Boca Tapada, for tasty seafood dishes, refreshing *batidos* (fruit shakes) and a wonderfully scenic riverfront setting that's a great place to view macaws. From December to June (their breeding season in Costa Rica), a pair of great green macaws nest in the almond tree on the property. Macaws are monogamous and they always nest in the same place, so this pair is a reliable fixture at Cuyito. They're particularly loud and squawky just after sunrise and for a while before sunset. Enjoy a cold Imperial and a traditional *casado* lunch before you head back to your accommodations.

RAINFOREST BATHS

Meghan Casey, co-owner of Chilamate Rainforest Eco Retreat and certified Forest Therapy Guide, shares tips on rainforest baths.

Follow these steps for a successful Forest Therapy Session:

Get comfortable: Activate all of your senses in the rainforest and begin to notice new things around you.

Stay in the moment: We will move slowly – maybe too slowly! – until you are hyper-aware of your presence in the rainforest.

Drink the forest: After you've entered the contemplative space, you'll enjoy a tea ceremony, literally drinking in the forest with a natural team from the area.

Enjoy the benefits: You'll take with you lower blood pressure, lower stress and a general sense of well-being.

Caño Negro

BIRDWATCHING | FISHING | RIVER FLOATING

GETTING AROUND

Tour operators can offer relatively inexpensive trips to Caño Negro, mainly from La Fortuna. However, it's much more rewarding (and cheaper) to rent some wheels (or hop on a bus), navigate the rutted road into the rural flatlands and hire a local guide from Caño Negro village or through your lodge.

Buses travel to Caño Negro village several times a day from Los Chiles and Upala.

North of the village of Caño Negro, the slender Río Frío divides a looming forest. During the wet season, the river expands and breaks its banks to form one immense 800-hectare lake, becoming a table-flat, swampy expanse of marsh and lagoon. But when the rains stop, the water recedes. And by April it has almost completely disappeared – until the May rains begin. This cycle has proceeded without fail for millennia. The small fishing communities around the river's edges adapt to each seasonal nuance, as do the waterfowl, the fish and the other animals that inhabit these waters.

But they are all at risk. In spite of Caño Negro's protected status as a national wildlife refuge, deforestation continues to be a concern in this area, as is the shrinking lake. The pineapple plantations surrounding Caño Negro require extensive irrigation and intensive agrochemical use, which may be part of the problem.

Kingfishers & Caimans

Cruise a bird-filled lagoon

Nature lovers come to **Refugio Nacional de Vida Silvestre Caño Negro** *(sinac.go.cr; US$5.65)* for the birds – more than 300 species of aquatic birds, rainforest birds and migratory birds that pass through these parts. They can't help but also get a kick out of the caimans, with their toothy grins. Not to mention the green iguanas (which are sometimes orange) and the striped basilisks (aka Jesus Christ lizards, because they walk on water), as well as the three kinds of monkeys and the two-toed sloths. Indeed, Caño Negro is a wildlife wonderland that is still (relatively) undiscovered by tourists.

Considering the very wet environment at Caño Negro, almost all the wildlife-watching occurs from a boat, which is a very civilized way to commune with the creatures. You'll leave early, around 6am or 7am, with an expert guide (who often doubles as the boat driver). Local experts have a knack for spotting

TOP TIP

You'll hear a lot about the 'density' of birds and wildlife during the dry season, when animals congregate around limited water supplies. But there's plenty to see during 'green' season, too. You might have to move around a bit more to find them, but you're in a boat, so sit back and enjoy!

SIGHTS
1 Caño Negro Experience

ACTIVITIES
2 Paraíso Tropical Caño Negro

SLEEPING
3 Caño Negro Natural Lodge
4 Hotel de Campo Caño Negro
5 Poponjoche Lodge
6 Tocu Tent Camp

EATING
see 3 Caño Negro Natural Lodge
7 Rancho Pitín
8 Restaurante Fogón Caño Negro

birds and animals that other people just wouldn't notice. Spending time on a boat with **Caño Negro Experience** *(canonegro experience.com; US$97)*, owned by Tatiana Guerrero, is an absolute delight. If they are booked, **Chambita's Tours** *(facebook.com/chambita.romero; from US$65)* is also a fun morning on the river.

But back to the birds. During the dry season, as water levels drop, the bird populations are concentrated around the remaining wetlands. From January to March, the sheer density of birdlife is astounding. The variety of species is also impressive. Look out for loads of aquatic birds such as herons, egrets, sandpipers, jacanas, kingfishers and shorebirds. And in the winter months, there are huge congregations of migratory ducks. You will also have a decent chance of spotting some species that are near impossible to see in other regions, such as the jabiru stork, glossy ibis, Nicaraguan grackle and lesser yellow-headed vulture.

Gotta Get a Garfish

Cruise a fish-filled lagoon

Before there was birding, there was fishing. The communities around Caño Negro have been living off the lake for centuries. Still today, small boats bob on the Río Frío, pulling in freshwater fish of all shapes and sizes, to feed their families and sell at the markets. From August through November, river tarpon is a big attraction (literally big – these guys might be 50kg to 150kg). In the drier season, anglers go for snook and garfish.

There are several ways to enjoy fishing in this area. For a cultural experience, book an **artisanal fishing tour**. It's great for families, and you'll use your sardine as bait and fish for tilapia as the locals have done for centuries. At the end of the tour, you may even get to cook your fish and eat it.

PURA VIDA, INDIGENOUS STYLE

Hiqui Morera, owner of Rancho Maleku Ní Uríjífa Tafa, invites travelers to engage with the indigenous Maleku culture.

Many visitors to Costa Rica focus on spending time at the bigger tourist sights, such as popular beaches and the volcanoes. But to miss an authentic indigenous experience is to miss a huge part of Costa Rica's cultural identity. I encourage visitors to schedule at least one authentic cultural experience during their trip, whether it be taking a Maléku Jaíka language class, experiencing a traditional indigenous cooking class, or a walk through nature with an experienced indigenous guide, because those experiences are the 'real' Costa Rica.

ARTISANAL FISHING

Rosi Arguedas Sequeira, co-owner of Paraíso Tropical tour agency, shares insight on artisanal fishing in Caño Negro.

For hundreds of years, fishing has been the lifeblood of the Caño Negro community. Locals head out to the river from their homes, look for sardines, hook them on improvised fishing poles and set out in search of the *guapote* fish. Community members of every age can participate, from the very youngest to the very oldest. And everyone knows the best fishing spots. It's a tradition that for many generations was a way to survive; today most people fish only to feed their own families and as a way to build community. At the end of a successful day of fishing, families share the fish for a meal, thus continuing a generations-old Caño Negro tradition.

There are also plenty of opportunities for sportfishing. Keep in mind that for sustainability reasons, sportfishing in this area is catch and release. You'll experience the adrenaline of the fight, but none of the secondary effects of overfishing. These tours are for those with previous sportfishing experience. Experienced fishers can also enjoy fly fishing in this area.

For all fishing tours, book directly with **Paraíso Tropical Caño Negro** *(canonegrotours.com; from US$100)*. It's run by local guide Joel Sandoval, who just happens to hold a world record for catching a 14.5kg tropical garfish. Paraíso Tropical also offers spectacular birdwatching tours led by Joel's extremely knowledgeable wife Rosi.

Meet the Maleku

Costa Rica's indigenous gem

On your way to Caño Negro, an excellent stop is at the **Rancho Maleku Ní Uríjífa Tafa** *(8559-1767; from US$42)*, located in the **Guatuso Indigenous Reserve**. The Maleku are the indigenous people who have long inhabited northern Costa Rica. Their reservation was originally over 295 sq km. But similar to the story of many indigenous peoples around the world, today less than 15% of the original land is in the hands

EATING IN CAÑO NEGRO: OUR PICKS

Rancho Pitín: Great-value local dishes paired with some birdwatching? Yes, please. *hours vary* $

Restaurante Fogón Caño Negro: 'Downtown' restaurant featuring traditional meals cooked over a wood fire. *7am-9pm* $

Rancho Tabacón: Feast on homemade bread and baked fish native to the Caño Negro area. *hours vary* $$

Caño Negro Natural Lodge: Farm-to-table Costa Rican cuisine served in the lodge. *7am-9pm* $$

Río Frío, Refugio Nacional de Vida Silvestre Caño Negro (p258)

of the tribe. The rest of the land has slowly been taken over by cattle farmers who have deforested the land.

The deforestation makes it very difficult for the Maleku people to maintain their culture, which focuses on nature, community and spirituality. But the Maleku are fighting to keep their traditions alive. Today, schools on the reservation have hired bilingual (Spanish and Maleku) teachers who teach the Maléku Jaíka language alongside native traditions and customs. These classes play a vital part in maintaining indigenous culture in the area.

You can learn firsthand about Maleku culture at the Rancho Maleku Ní Uríjífa Tafa, where Hiqui Morera invites visitors to participate in ancient Maleku traditions alongside her community. Spend a half-day at the ranch, where you'll paint your face with traditional markings before trying your hand at using a bow and arrow.

Then, it's time to try your hand at art. Some of the coolest Maleku handicrafts are created from the shell of the jicara, the fruit of the calabash tree. The Maleku have long used these shells for functional vessels like bowls and canteens. Now you might also find decorative objects like vases, and musical instruments, especially wooden drums carved from balsa wood, painted and topped with iguana skin for the drum head. The shell is dried and painted, often with stylistic depictions of rainforest flora and fauna, which you have the opportunity to create. Or, you can support the tribe by purchasing one of their (expert) works.

Finally, participate in a traditional Maleku ceremony alongside your new friends before you head home. This is one stop you won't regret making.

BE AN EARLY BIRD

The best time for birdwatching is almost always at sunrise, or at least early in the morning. Many travelers book a tour in La Fortuna and come to Caño Negro for a day. These tours generally start in Los Chiles and float down the Río Frío in the vicinity of the wildlife refuge.

But it is our strong recommendation – for both ethical and ornithological reasons – to skip the tour and spend at least one night in the village of Caño Negro. Your lodging can organize an early-morning tour with a local guide. You'll see more and your tourist dollars will go directly into the hands of locals, thus encouraging communities in the area to protect wildlife.

Places We Love to Stay

$** Budget **$$** Midrange **$$$ Top End

Volcán Arenal & La Fortuna

MAP p228

Arenal Backpackers Resort $ The original 'hostel-resort' in La Fortuna, offering a variety of rooms and tents. Epic outdoor pool and volcano views.

Poshpacker Arenal $ A smaller version of the hostel resort, this newish place has a nice pool and a very inviting hammock garden.

La Choza Inn $ An old-fashioned hostel in a rambling old house on the edge of town. Everything is a bit worn around the edges but the place is friendly.

Hotel San Bosco $$ Small hotel in town offering volcano views; breakfast included. Free access to the hot springs at sister property Volcano Lodge.

Finca Luna Nueva $$ Regular classes are offered at the open-air yoga pavilion, in addition to the roster of retreats at this lodge south of La Fortuna.

Rancho Cerro Azul $$ Cute, shingled cabins that back up to the forest, with private porches overlooking trees.

La Fortuna Suites $$ An in-town option with many amenities, excellent service and fabulous volcano views.

Hotel Monte Real $$ Smart, modern property on the Río Burio. Location combines the convenience of town with forest rusticity.

Hotel Campo Verde $$ Stay in comfy *casitas* (cottages) with private porches in the shadow of the volcano.

Roca Negra del Arenal $$ Spacious rooms and a luscious pool amid a bird- and bee-filled tropical garden, bursting with blooms.

Arenal Oasis $$ Dark but cozy bungalows surrounded by rainforest – and its residents. Located 3.5km southwest of town.

Volcano Lodge & Springs $$ Family-friendly resort with hiking trails, a playground and suites with your very own hot spring.

Los Lagos Hotel & Resort $$ Sparse but comfortable accommodations. Private volcano viewpoint overlooking – you guessed it – a lake.

Arenal Manoa $$ Lush gardens, hot springs and a great restaurant. Quietly secluded yet in the heart of the Arenal area.

Ti-Fakara $$$ This boutique hotel, as well as its sister property Noah's Forest, offers modern, spacious rooms and on-site frog- and sloth-viewing tours.

Hotel El Silencio del Campo $$$ About 5km west of La Fortuna, this is a luxurious lodge and working farm. A hot spring heats a series of thermal pools on the hotel grounds.

Arenal 360 $$ Adorable, comfy wood cabins facing a majestic volcano view. Kitchenettes give these a homey feel.

Chachagua Rainforest Ecolodge $$$ Located on a private reserve 15km south of La Fortuna. Guests enjoy gorgeous lodgings, hiking trails, hot springs and swimming holes.

Laguna de Arenal

Living Forest $ A wide, covered yoga deck faces the forest and the rushing Río Sabalito. A free-standing sauna is perfectly placed for cooling dips in the river.

Mystica Lodge $$ Overlooking the west end of Lake Arenal, this gorgeous property has a yoga 'sanctuary' surrounded by forest and a wellness studio in the treetops.

Lucky Bug B&B $$ Former horse stables are now an art-bedecked B&B immersed in rainforest. Excellent on-site restaurant.

Agua Inn $$ Intimate B&B on the Río Cote's banks with a jungle-shaded pool and private lake trail.

Toucan Lane $$ Expect super hospitality at this delightful guesthouse, which has sweet suites overlooking bird-filled grounds.

La Mansión $$$ Colorful villas with mural-painted walls, private balcony and wonderful lake views. Highly lauded European restaurant.

Hotel Laguna Arenal $$$ Mid-century modern meets eco-chic at this lakeside retreat with stylish bungalows and attentive service.

Lost Iguana $$$ Swanky rainforest resort near the Arenal dam, with luxurious rooms, a bi-level pool and well-equipped spa.

El Castillo

Rancho Margot $$ Off-the-grid-farm with yoga classes, swimming in natural, spring-fed pools, fishing in the tilapia pond and hiking amid rainforested mountains. Meals included.

Chateau Arenal $$ Simple, comfortable rooms with phenomenal sunset volcano views.

Nepenthe $$ Simple, colorful rooms in a delightful setting, with a spring-fed infinity pool overlooking the lake.

Linda Vista $$ Light-filled panoramic-windowed rooms, spectacular infinity pool, recommended restaurant and nearby hiking trails.

Sarapiquí Valley

MAP p249

Boca Tapada Lodge $ Clean, comfortable rooms overlooking the river. Perks include well-placed hammocks, outdoor showers and warm welcome.

Hotel Ara Ambigua $$ Well-equipped rooms, gorgeous grounds, blooming gardens and three swimming pools; about 1km west of Puerto Viejo.

Tirimbina Rainforest Center & Lodge $$ Vast reserve with 9km of trails and two suspension bridges. Accommodations are nothing special.

Chilamate Rainforest Eco Retreat $$ Riverside accommodations housed on a private reserve. Simple lodgings and home-cooked meals.

Laguna del Lagarto Eco Lodge $$ A birdwatcher's paradise, with a photography platform. Rooms are basic but comfortable and the meals are excellent.

Hacienda Pozo Azul $$ 'Glamping' resort near La Virgen's southern end with comfy tents and en suite bathrooms at the forest edge, and plenty of activities.

Hotel El Bambú $$ 'Downtown' Puerto Viejo hotel with comfortable rooms, a good restaurant and giant swimming pool.

Posada Andrea Cristina $$ Quaint, colorful cabins at the edge of Puerto Viejo with forest-facing terraces, perfect for birdwatching.

Pierella Garden (p253) $$ Attractive wooden bungalows in a gorgeous eco-sanctuary in Horquetas. The genuine, warm hospitality is the selling point.

Hacienda La Isla $$ A colonial-style *hacienda* (estate) that offers simple rooms, super service and rainforest trails.

Mi Pedacito de Cielo $$ Comfortable cabins have private porches overlooking the river. Fantastic home-cooked meals are a highlight.

Mirador el Pizote $$ Small riverside lodge that caters to birders, especially bird photographers, with carefully placed perches and blinds.

Maquenque Eco Lodge (p253) $$$ Bungalows and treehouses set on a working farm. You'll cross a river to get to the lodge – it's unforgettable.

Selva Verde Lodge $$$ Chilamate *finca* turned lodge and 200-hectare rainforest reserve. Shiny rooms above the river or in the trees.

Caño Negro

MAP p259

Poponjoche Lodge $ A family-run place that provides good-value, top-notch service and endless nature.

Caño Negro Natural Lodge $$ Attractive lodge on an island in the lagoon with well-appointed rooms and a leafy garden.

Hotel de Campo Caño Negro $$ Tiled *casitas* scattered about an orchard overlooking the lagoon. The Italian owners run a tasty kitchen.

Tocu Tent Camp $$$ Glamping tents surround a freshwater pool filtered by UV rays. The on-site restaurant does Maleku-inspired cuisine.

Hotel Laguna Arenal

Researched by
Elizabeth Lavis

Península de Nicoya

WIDE GOLDEN BEACHES AND FABULOUS SURF

Pristine beaches meet party towns and chill artistic communities in this incredible natural paradise.

Península de Nicoya's epic coastline was made for beach-hopping and impromptu exploration, from the family-friendly gateway to the Pacific, Playa del Cocos in the north, down to rowdy Tamarindo and luxe Nosara. Santa Teresa is a surfing haven, with swells ranging from beginner-friendly to experts only, while Montezuma's raw nature and splendid waterfalls are guaranteed to spark your sense of wonder.

The Península de Nicoya is situated perfectly between the Golfo di Nicoya in the east and the tumultuous expanse of the Pacific Ocean in the west. Beyond the sandy shore, you'll find an emerald-green jungle teeming with fabulous tropical flora and elusive fauna, and its designation as a Blue Zone – one of only five worldwide – means that the water is potable and delicious. Whether your mission is to surf the big waves of Suck Rock or Playa Langosta, find a slice of zen in Nosara, or cruise by ATV through Nicoya's southern beaches and charming towns, you'll find all manner of outdoor splendor here.

Nicoya is also home to Playa Ostional, where you can witness the annual turtle *arribada* – the spectacle of hundreds of olive ridley turtles making their way to the shore to lay their precious eggs. The Daniel Oduber Quirós International Airport (LIR), west of Liberia, is only 37 minutes from the nearest beach, and buses and shuttles run the length and width of the peninsula. You can explore even more if you have a car, hitting secret beaches and small local towns.

GROGL/SHUTTERSTOCK

THE MAIN AREAS

PLAYAS DEL COCO
Family-friendly beach, swimming and sportfishing. p270

TAMARINDO
Party central and fabulous natural park. p278

NOSARA
Surf resorts and sea turtles. p287

SANTA TERESA
Huge variety of surfing beaches. p296

MONTEZUMA
Artistic vibe, hiking and waterfalls. p304

For places to stay in Península de Nicoya, see p312

JOSHUA TEN BRINK/SHUTTERSTOCK

Left: Playa Santa Teresa (p299); Above: Playa Tambor (p309)

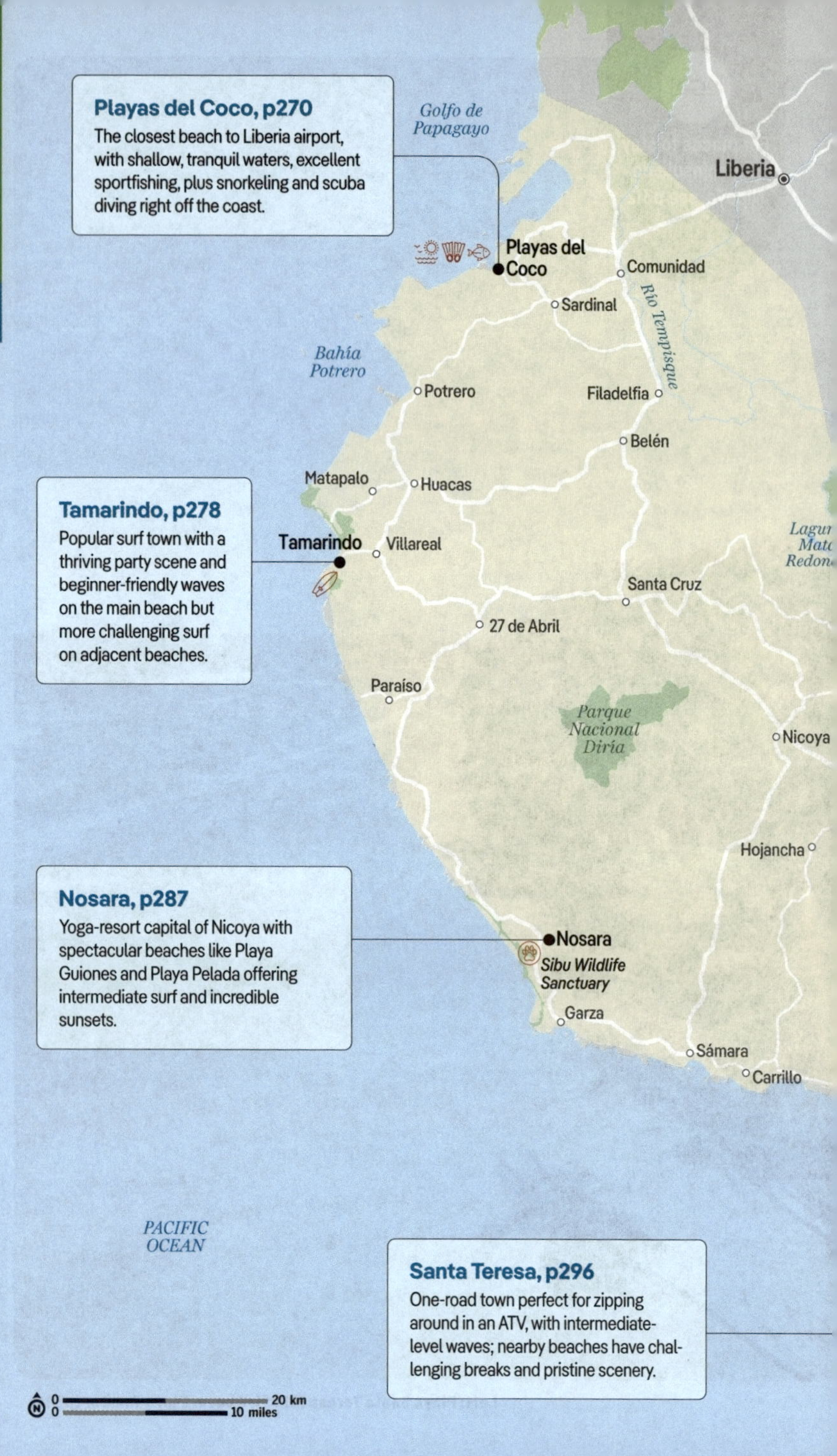

Playas del Coco, p270

The closest beach to Liberia airport, with shallow, tranquil waters, excellent sportfishing, plus snorkeling and scuba diving right off the coast.

Tamarindo, p278

Popular surf town with a thriving party scene and beginner-friendly waves on the main beach but more challenging surf on adjacent beaches.

Nosara, p287

Yoga-resort capital of Nicoya with spectacular beaches like Playa Guiones and Playa Pelada offering intermediate surf and incredible sunsets.

Santa Teresa, p296

One-road town perfect for zipping around in an ATV, with intermediate-level waves; nearby beaches have challenging breaks and pristine scenery.

Golfo de Papagayo
Liberia
Playas del Coco
Comunidad
Sardinal
Río Tempisque
Bahía Potrero
Potrero
Filadelfia
Belén
Matapalo
Huacas
Tamarindo
Villareal
Santa Cruz
27 de Abril
Paraíso
Parque Nacional Diriá
Nicoya
Hojancha
Nosara
Sibu Wildlife Sanctuary
Garza
Sámara
Carrillo
PACIFIC OCEAN

0 20 km
0 10 miles

Find Your Way

The roads in the Península de Nicoya can be unpredictable, poorly maintained or even impassible during the rainy season, so 4WD vehicles are a good bet. ATVs are the best way to get around at the bottom of the peninsula.

BUS

Buses run every hour from 4:30am to 8pm from the Liberia airport to Playas del Coco and Tamarindo and inland to Nicoya. To get to Santa Teresa, you'll have to take the bus to Nicoya, switch buses toward Sámara, and get a taxi down the coast.

ATV

ATV is the best way to get around the southern part of the peninsula. You can cruise between Santa Teresa and Montezuma on a well-marked ATV route through the jungle, although this path can get dicey in the rainy season when the mud and water piles up.

CAR

You have freedom in this region if you have a car. Make sure you get one with a 4WD as many roads, particularly near the beach, are not very good. You can rent a car at the airport or fly into towns like Tamarindo or Sámara.

Montezuma, p304

Artistic and mellow town with plenty of hiking trails, waterfalls, and a secret pink-hued beach dominated by a river-to-ocean waterfall.

Plan Your Time

If you have a car, you can squeeze a lot more into your Nicoya trip than by relying on public transportation. Consider what you want to see and the logistics of getting around, especially if pressed for time.

KRYSSIA CAMPOS/GETTY IMAGES

Playa Hermosa (p298)

Three Days of Mind & Body Restoration

- Start by renting a car at Liberia airport or heading to **Nosara** (p287) by bus. If you're doing the latter, you'll want to take the Liberia airport bus to Nicoya, then transfer to the Nosara bus.

- In Nosara, check in to **Bodhi Tree Yoga Resort** (p289), **White Palms Nosara** (p312) or **Gilded Iguana** (p312) for a day of meditation, yoga and spa treatments. Watch the sunset at **Playa Guiones** (p287) through the almond trees.

- On day two, take a taxi, car or bus to **Sámara** (p291) for easy surfing or kayaking to **Isla Chora** (p292) for some solitude and snorkeling. On the last day, rent a golf cart or ATV, explore **Playa Barrigona** (p295) for relaxation in the tidal pools, and then **Playa Carrillo** (p294) for a fantastic sunset.

Seasonal Highlights

Peninsula de Nicoya is dotted with beautiful beaches, with fantastic surfing year-round and balmy seas ideal for swimming. See the sparkling bioluminescence from December to May.

JANUARY

Surfers will want to ride the big waves in Nicoya, especially in places like Santa Teresa. The weather is sunny, dry and excellent for all kinds of outdoor adventures like ATVs and **hiking**.

FEBRUARY

The average temperature is about 27°C (80°F) – the perfect **beach-weather** sweet spot where the ocean is refreshing and you can lie on the sand all day long. There's also very little rain this time of year.

MARCH

The weather is balmy and glorious, but you could encounter more crowds because of two holidays, **Día de los Boyeros** and **Día de San José**. Easter **Semana Santa** (Holy Week) sometimes falls in March, too.

Four Days of Seeking Surf

- You'll want to rent a car for this adventure since it involves plenty of *playa*-hopping. If you do one thing, make sure you get to **Suck Rock** (p299) near Santa Teresa for some of the gnarliest surf in the country.

- Drive to **Tamarindo** (p278) for an afternoon of surfing and partying. Spend the night, then rise early for a trip to **Nosara** (p287), where you'll hit the gentle giants on **Playa Guiones** (p287), before going to **Sámara** (p291) for some more relaxed evening surf and a night of live music at **Blue Iguana** (p312).

- Next up is **Santa Teresa** (p296), where you'll have a full dance card of beaches ranging from the comparably easy **Playa Hermosa** (p298) to the wickedly fun Suck Rock and, finally, the swells of **Playa Santa Teresa** (p299) itself.

Five Days of Party Vibes & Sweet Rides

- Rent a car, take the Liberia airport bus or grab a shuttle to **Tamarindo** (p278), check into your hostel and hit the beach. Start the party at **Volcano Brewing Company** (p280) for the sunset, then head to **Sharky's** (p278), **Kinky Tamarindo** (p278) or **HandleBar** (p278) for evening shenanigans. Take some surf classes, explore **Playa Grande** (p283), then enjoy your evening the next day at the Tamarindo **night market** (p281).

- Take a combination of bus and taxi or drive to **Santa Teresa** (p296), where you'll rent an ATV for two days. Explore **Malpaís** (p301) and **Playa Hermosa** (p298), and enjoy Santa Teresa's chill beach bars at night.

- Finish the trip in **Montezuma** (p304) with an ATV ride up to the waterfalls and beach beers on the *playa* or karaoke on the main strip.

MAY

May is the very start of the wetter season in Costa Rica, so you'll get a bit more precipitation, but not so much that it will spoil your outdoor fun. It's an excellent month for **swimming**, as the ocean averages 28°C (83°F).

JULY

Visit Nicoya in June for **Día de Guanacaste**. On June 25, most towns hold a parade or celebration. It's a great time to connect with local people and participate in a meaningful tradition.

NOVEMBER

This is the tail end of the rainy season, and you'll start to enjoy an average of five hours of sunshine per day. Average temperatures are 30°C (87°F), so it's an excellent time to cool off with **water sports**.

DECEMBER

You'll have the chance to check out Playa Ostional's annual olive ridley turtles' **arribada** (p293). This is also an excellent time to view **bioluminescence** (p310) in Ballena Bay and other areas of Paquera.

Playas del Coco

BIG FISH | SUPERB SNORKELING | HORSEBACK RIDING

GETTING AROUND

Everything you need in Playas del Coco is within a 15-minute walk from the beach, including the **Mega Super El Coco** and the **Parada Pulmitan** bus terminal, where you'll get dropped off if you're coming from San José and Liberia. You don't need a car; the roads are well-marked, maintained and suited for walking. Crossing the street near the Maxi Pali on the far end of town can be challenging, as the vehicles don't seem to slow and there's no traffic light.

TOP TIP

The best time to visit Playas del Coco to fish and relax on the beach is March. March tends to be warm and dry, with long sunny days ideal for beach basking. It's also a great time to go sportfishing, as it's neither windy nor rainy on average.

Playas del Coco is the closest beach town to the Liberia airport, with a wide, pale-golden beach and tranquil waters perfect for swimming. There's a fun mix of high-end and budget-friendly, starting from the mega supermarkets lining the far end of the main drag, which stock everything from European wine to local ice-cream tubs. Walk down the drag, and you'll find *soda* (cheap lunch counter) after *soda,* stalls selling bikinis and T-shirts, and even a fish spa where you can stare out at the ocean as your feet are gently nibbled.

Sportfishing is huge here, and you can reel in marlin, roosterfish and mahi-mahi. Dive or snorkel near the Islas Pelonas, the islands visible from the shore. Although a statue of a shark stands in the middle of town, Playas del Coco has no such fearsome creatures near its waters. Instead, you'll float with a flurry of tropical fish as you explore the crystal-clear sea.

The Perfect Sunday

A morning at Pamela's Coco Sunday Market

If you find yourself in Playas del Coco on a Sunday morning, between 9am and 2pm, head to Hotel La Puerta del Sol and browse the rows of just-picked produce, homemade edible goodies, original art, clothing and jewelry, and fantastic souvenirs at **Pamela's Coco Sunday Market** *(facebook.com/pamelascocosundaymarket).* You can also get fresh fish straight from Golfo de Papagayo. Arrive early for the best selection and support the local fishers while taking home a choice filet.

Named for its late founder, this market is a staple of the local community and an excellent way to meet people and get a read on the beach's vibe. It's a great place to grab breakfast on the go, with fresh coffee and baked goods on offer in every aisle. The market hosts live music, including traditional Costa Rican bands, so be sure to check its Facebook page to see if you're in for a treat. It's two blocks from the beach, so visitors can pair their morning market wanders with a stroll down the *playa* and be finished by lunchtime.

ACTIVITIES
1 Kuna Vela Sailing Tours
2 Life & Dive
3 Sea Bird Sailing Excursions
4 Sport Fishing Blue Marlin

SLEEPING
5 Claudio & Gloria Beach Front Coco
6 Hospedaje Combi Dream Bird
7 Hotel M&M Beach House
8 Laura's House B&B

EATING
9 Buzzed Monkey BBQ & Grill
10 Café Corazón
11 Johann Bistro
12 Soda Teresita

SHOPPING
13 Pamela's Coco Sunday Market

Snag Your Supper

Reel big fish

The waters off Playas del Coco teem with big game fish like marlin, which can clock in at over 200kg and need a talented hand and a tonne of patience to get into your boat. There's also medium-sized fry, like roosterfish, mackerel, tuna and mahi-mahi. You'll find plenty of operators and vessels of all shapes and sizes that will whisk you off the sunny shores of Coco and into the rich waters to catch your dinner, including **Sport Fishing Blue Marlin** *(sportfishingbluemarlin.com; half-/full-day tours from US$520/750)*.

Plan to be on a boat anywhere from four to nine hours, depending on the type of fish you're hunting, but these vessels have everything you need for a long day on the waves, including water, beer, soda and fruit. You just need to bring sunscreen and a towel in most cases. Check with your tour operator before embarking on a multi-hour outing just to be sure.

Although beginners can try for the big fish, being honest with yourself and your tour operator about your skills is important. That way, they can get you the help you need to reel in a heavyweight successfully. Also, many operators will descale and debone your fish for you, leaving you with just the filets.

EATING IN PLAYAS DEL COCO: OUR PICKS

Café Corazón: Excellent cold-brew coffee, takeaway baked goods, and comfy chairs if you want to dine in. *8am-5pm Thu-Tue* $$

Soda Teresita: Open for early birds, this *soda* offers seaside views and big portions of *gallo pinto* (rice and beans) and lunch *casados* (set meals). *6:30am-10pm* $

Buzzed Monkey BBQ & Grill: Enjoy big plates of barbecue and a good beer selection in a lively spot a few blocks from the beach. *noon-10pm Sat, Mon, Wed & Thu, to 11pm Fri* $$

Johann Bistro: Sandwich platters with gluten-free options on request, sashimi and sushi bowls, and an upscale but relaxed vibe. *9am-5:45pm Tue-Thu, to 8:45pm Fri-Sun* $$

BIG FISH & GREAT SUNSETS

Juan Carlos Delgado is the founder of Sport Fishing Blue Marlin in Playas del Coco. *@sportfishingblue marlin*

For Juan, the town's primary draw is its sense of community. 'It's like coming home. In most places, people speak English, and everyone is friendly.' Delgado and his crew help foreign guests to catch the big prizes off the coast.

Juan recommends exploring the local waters for big fish and going under the waves, too. 'Snorkeling is really popular here. You'll find incredible sea life and get panoramic views of the shore from your catamaran.' Delgado suggests visiting the *playa* in summer for technicolor sunsets. 'Between December 15 and April, you have the most amazing sunsets. It's strange not to have a great sunset between those months.'

JOSHUA TEN BRINK/SHUTTERSTOCK

Islas Murciélagos

Sportfishing happens all year round in Playas del Coco, but it can get pretty windy out there during January and February, and October tends to be rainy, which makes visibility more difficult.

Bald Islands & Underwater Worlds

Majestic marine life awaits

Gaze into the tranquil gulf at Playas del Coco, and you'll spot the **Islas Pelonas**, or 'Bald Islands,' just off the coast. These twin islands get their name from annual vegetation loss, which happens during the dry season and renders them completely craggy. On a windless day, you can reach the islands in 10 minutes by sea kayak, or you can set out by boat from the shore for snorkeling. Flocks of bright fish, occasionally smaller rays, and seahorses are all there for delightful discovery.

Boats run at all times during the day, but sunset cruises and snorkeling outings are especially popular. If you're only in Playas del Coco for a short while and want to maximize your time with a two-for-one sunset and snorkeling adventure, try to get on one of these. Space is limited and generally fills up quickly during the busy season. Check out **Sea Bird Sailing Excursions** *(seabirdsailingexcursions.com; from US$95)* or **Kuna Vela Sailing Tours** *(kunavela.com; from US$99)*. Alternatively, you can ask on the beach and get loads of options.

If you're inclined to delve deeper, you can also scuba-dive near the Islas Pelonas, but you'll need to be PADI-certified. Operators like **Life & Dive** *(lifeandive.com; from US$135)* can help you get your certification, and there are plenty of shops where you can pick up gear. If you plan on staying in Península de Nicoya for longer or traveling down to Las Catalinas, your newly minted PADI certificate will let you see the large rays and bull sharks that roam these waters.

Monkey Around for Good

Support a cause at Monkey Farm

A haven for people down on their luck and animals in need of help, where each works to restore and heal the other – this is the core ethos of **Monkey Farm** *(themonkeyfarm.org; farm tour US$16)*, a family-friendly destination just 12 minutes' drive outside the center of Playas del Coco or roughly 47 minutes on foot. Although the roads are unpaved, dusty and rural, you'll find clearly marked directions to Ocotal and signs advertising Father Rooster and Monkey Farm. Follow them, and you can't miss the place.

Since Monkey Farm is a rehabilitation facility for both animals and community members, you need a reservation to visit and tour *(8853-0165 or info@themonkeyfarm.org)*. The cost of other experiences varies, and proceeds go directly back to caring for vulnerable animals and people. It's a free faith-based residential recovery program, using equine therapy to help local people manage and conquer their addictions. As such, your admission fee may be tax-deductible.

The interactive farm tour is among the most popular experiences and a great way to spend the day with your animal-loving kiddos. It includes bottle-feeding and milking animals, learning about the medicinal flora that flourishes all around Monkey Farm, and learning about 'monkey bridges.' These pathways span busy roads and circumvent power lines to help monkeys safely get from point A to point B. You can also help cook meals for the human residents of Monkey Farm, contributing directly to the rehabilitation process.

Monkey Farm also offers ethical horseback-riding adventures that range from one to three hours, and sharp-eyed bilingual guides who can point out monkeys and birds in the trees. Choose between jungle or beach rides, or both. Monkey Farm offers regular moonlight rides on the beach, but these fill up quickly, so make sure you check the website and reserve your place in advance.

Although Monkey Farm is technically in Playas del Coco, it hasn't entirely caught on as a tourist destination, so there's a good chance that you'll enjoy plenty of hands-on time with the animals while supporting an excellent cause.

GETTING TO THE 'BAT ISLANDS'

Islas Murciélagos (p215), or 'Bat Islands' – across the Golfo de Papagayo from Playas del Coco – are a superb bet for snorkeling and scuba diving with marine life like sea turtles, octopuses and gentle nurse sharks. Part of the Parque Nacional Santa Rosa, their clear waters are perfect for spotting all sorts of elusive creatures. The park admission fee may be included if you're traveling from Playas del Coco, so check with your tour operator. You can only go to the Bat Islands for snorkeling during the rainy season because it's too windy during the rest of the year. If you book in advance, check with your tour operator before the day and reschedule if it's too windy to set sail.

Beyond Playas del Coco

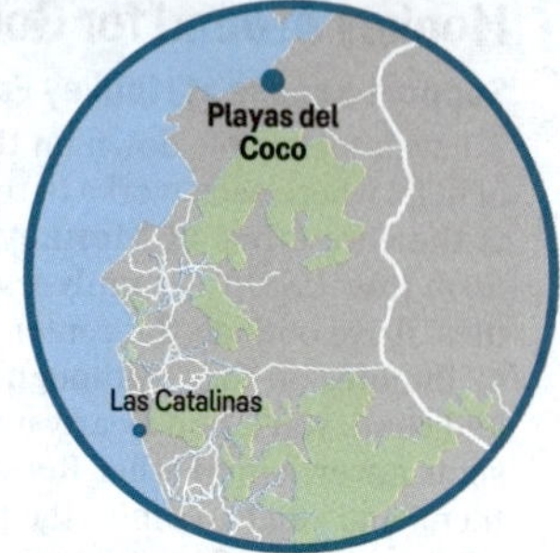

Playas del Coco is the northern gateway to the Península de Nicoya's Pacific Coast beaches, ranging from the posh to the private and pristine.

Places

Las Catalinas p274

The Pacific side of the Península de Nicoya is a beautiful area, balancing raw nature with surf party towns and sophisticated, sprawling resorts with humble hideaways where you can buy a rum-spiked coconut from a cart and sprawl out on a beach of white shells. You can drive this dynamic and naturally diverse coastline in under two hours between Playas del Coco and Tamarindo. Still, you'll want to spend some time in the intentional resort community of Las Catalinas, on the secret shores of Playa Pan de Azúcar, and near the calm waters of the Bahía Culebra, where the ocean temperature is balmy and the water is tranquil and ideal for a midday swim.

GETTING AROUND

You'll need a car, preferably a 4WD, to get around this part of the country. In a pinch, you can take buses, which pass through Nuevo Colón in the upper part of Guanacaste, but you'll be on the road for much longer and see less. Your wheels, or a dedicated driver, are the way to go. These roads also get tricky in the rainy season, and there can be detours. Pack your patience.

Las Catalinas

TIME FROM PLAYAS DEL COCO: **53 MINS**

A bit of Europe in Guanacaste

Smack-dab in the middle of Guanacaste's beach-dotted western coast, you'll stumble on a pristine, pastel-colored community that looks like it was transported directly from Europe, with a Disney-esque, squeaky-clean flair that seems out of sync with the surrounding jungle. Welcome to **Las Catalinas** *(lascatalinascr.com)*, arguably Guanacaste's most interesting and unusual intentional beach community. where you can live, rent property or just visit.

There's plenty of free parking outside the town, and if you keep your eyes peeled and skyward, you could even see some congo monkeys scrambling around in the trees. The vibe is very different within the town, with pretty, well-maintained, light-colored structures, lots of shopping, and a big fountain right in the plaza's center. Aside from the adjacent parking, Las Catalinas is car-free, a refreshing and family-friendly perk that keeps the manicured streets hazard- and pollution-free. One of Las Catalinas' biggest draws for residents and visitors alike is **The Beach Club** *(visitor day pass US$70)*, with swimming and lounging pools, a play area for the kids, and a bar and fitness room.

17 LIVING ART/SHUTTERSTOCK

Las Catalinas

If you don't want to pay to lounge by the pool and get your laps in, you can frequent some of the restaurants and bars that line Las Catalinas' central square. **Papagayo Brew House** *(papagayo-brewing.com)* is a good choice, with a lineup of local drafts and spectacular views over the sea, and **La Pampa Grill** *(pampagrillrestaurant.com)* is a smart place to score locally sourced seafood prepared simply and elegantly.

There are also 42km of hikeable and bikeable trails snaking all around Las Catalinas, with maintained paths and fabulous views of the jungle and sea. You'll likely encounter coatis and monkeys on your travels – a gentle reminder that while Las Catalinas looks like something out of a storybook or a provincial European town, it's actually deeply rooted in wild Guanacaste. Staying at Las Catalinas certainly isn't for everyone, but it's worth stopping by, if only for a few snaps of the square and a more-than-decent cup of artisan coffee.

DIVING WITH GIANT MANTA RAYS

Graceful giant manta rays, reef sharks, turtles and the occasional dolphin await just off the coast of Las Catalinas. Oceanic manta rays are the biggest draw, and the best time to see them is between November and April, but there's a bevy of sea life any time of year. **El Clásico** (nicknamed 'Shark Alley') is one of the most popular dive sites, with a flurry of reef sharks and abundance of coral reefs; mantas can also be found here. Divers make the journey from Playas del Coco or Playa Flamingo. Participants must be PADI-certified, but anyone can engage in some exploration on nearby **Playa Dantita**, where the tide pools and tranquil, shallower waters offer a glimpse into the underwater world.

DRIVING TOUR

Hopping Down the Gold Coast

The Península de Nicoya's western coast, dubbed 'Gold Coast' for its glittering, wide beaches, is an inspiring place to road-trip. It's a great and cheap way to see the country and swim in balmy, clear waters. You'll need a decent vehicle to traverse these roads; some are muddy, unpaved, bumpy and even impassable during the rainy season, requiring you to seek smoother pavement inside the peninsula and drive back to the coast.

1 Playa Panama

Tucked into the calm waters of Bahía Culebra, **Playa Panama** is a gently sloping swimming beach with phenomenal sunset views. You'll find plenty of sand for sunbathing and a boardwalk that runs the length of the beach, ideal for wheelchairs and strollers. It's about a three-minute walk from **Eco Camping Papagayo**, a nature-oriented campground with shops and villas. This beach is less popular than Playas del Coco, so you're more likely to have a quiet space to enjoy nature.

The Drive: Depending on the road conditions, drive roughly one hour either through Playa Hermosa or inland toward Guardia and Comunidad. Follow the Las Catalinas signs and continue north until you see a sign for Sugar Beach.

2 Playa Pan de Azúcar

Playa Pan de Azúcar, or 'Sugar Beach,' is a well-hidden little spot just north of Las Catalinas. Scan the roadside to see a small sign directing you to a thin trail through the jungle and down to the beach. Park,

PANDORA PICTURES/SHUTTERSTOCK

Playa Flamingo

then descend about 100m down a bumpy but well-marked path. This tiny beach is only accessible during low tide; the semi-clandestine location and gorgeous scenery make it a private slice of *pura vida* without the crowds, fishing boats or beach bars.

The Drive: Drive 13 minutes down Camina Las Catalinas, which turns into Ruta 911. You'll pass the town of Potrero, Playa Penca and Playa de la Paz on your way.

3 Playa Potrero

Playa Potrero has a livelier vibe than Playa Pan de Azúcar and makes an excellent stop if you want to vary your beach experience. You'll find plenty of bars and restaurants all along the main drag, such as **Hemmingways**, which has live music and superb views. Activities include catamaran tours and sportfishing, depending on what time of day you arrive. This beach is also great for swimming, as it's shielded from the big waves by Bahía Potrero.

The Drive: Drive a scenic seven minutes down the Bahía Potrero coastline. You'll spot Marina Flamingo as you enter the beach. Drive a bit further and take in the views from Mirador Flamingo.

4 Playa Flamingo

Playa Flamingo is full of high-end resorts, a massive marina, and kilometers of white-sand beaches ideal for taking in a Gold Coast sunset; you can even spot Isla Plata, just off the coast. You'll find a plethora of fish in these waters, including bright-green parrotfish and mahi-mahi, and tours eager to take you out on the sea to catch your supper. You can also head to **Mirador Flamingo**, a less hectic, family-friendly spot further up the coast.

Tamarindo

PARTY VIBES | APPROACHABLE WAVES | SEA TURTLES

GETTING AROUND

Tamarindo itself is pretty walkable, with bars, restaurants, accommodations and the beach all within about 20 minutes of each other, but if you want to explore some of the other beaches, like Playa Conchal or Playa Brasilito, you'll want to have a car or hire a taxi. You can get to Playa Grande by boat from the far end of Playa Tamarindo and walk to Playa Langosta in less than half an hour. Shuttles and buses regularly run between Liberia airport and Tamarindo.

TOP TIP

Tamarindo is safe, but like in other beach party towns, there's petty theft and crimes of opportunity. Separate your cash and cards, and only take what you plan to spend for the night. Avoid very dark stretches of beach after sundown to be extra secure.

Tamarindo is the Península de Nicoya's raucous and wonderful party hub, with sports bars and clubs on every corner, a lively Thursday night market, and plenty of cheap and cheerful hostels where you can get a bed for US$13 a night on average, depending on the season, and make friends with fellow travelers. The surf is beginner-friendly, and you'll find lots of spots on the beach to score some lessons. If you want more of a challenge, head to Playa Grande or Playa Langosta.

Playa Tamarindo's broad, golden beach is flanked by a pale blue ocean on one side and bars, shops and restaurants on the other. The party vibe is infectious, from the cheerful patrons making their way from Tamarindo's busy streets to the bustling beach and the frenzy of activity that seems to be happening around the clock in this town.

Surf by Day, Party by Night

Tamarindo nightlife

If you like your beach with a side of booze, Tamarindo is a fab place to party it up and enjoy some beginner surfing waves at the same time. Hang out in the central hub, and you'll bump into other travelers with the same vibe. You can also check out **Tasty VIP & Local Experiences** *(@tasty_cr)* for a list of nearby parties and events. Plenty of hostels also have their lineups, including pub crawls and pool parties, listed. Plus, true to party form, Tamarindo stays open late, with many places closing at or after 2am.

Tamarindo is also a gay-friendly beach town, with spots like **Kinky Tamarindo** *(kinkytamarindo.club)* serving drink specials, DJs and drag. **Sharky's** *(facebook.com/CostaRicaTamarindo)* is an excellent place to watch the game and catch some earlier fun, and **HandleBar** *(handlebartamarindo.com)*, a newer edition to the scene, is part craft beer, part bicycle repair shop.

Ocho Beach Club *(ochoartisanbungalows.com)* is an excellent place to catch the sunset and get some beach drinks. **El Be**

SIGHTS
1 Playa Tamarindo

ACTIVITIES
2 Carlos' Surf School
3 Costa Rica Surf Institute
4 Iguana Surf
5 Native's Way
6 Tamarindo Diving
7 Tidal Wave Surf & Travel
8 Wonder Away

SLEEPING
9 Tamarindo Diria Beach Resort
10 Wet Hotel

EATING
11 El Mercadito de Tamarindo
12 Jardín Food Truck Park
13 La Palapa Seafood & Grill
14 Lobster & Co
15 Nogui's Restaurant
16 Sushi & Poke
17 Tama Market

DRINKING & NIGHTLIFE
18 CATA Agave Bar
19 Chili Guaros
20 El Be
21 HandleBar
22 Kinky Tamarindo
23 Langosta Beach Club
24 Ocho Beach Club
25 Pacífico Bar Tamarindo
26 Papagayo Brewing
27 Sharky's
28 Volcano Brewing Company

(facebook.com/elbeclubtamarindo) offers snacks, meals and frosty beverages under a canopy of blinking outdoor lights; it's great for sunset and early evenings. **Selinas** hostel also hosts regular events, including body-painting contests and pool parties, although it was changing ownership at the time of writing so the schedule may vary.

A Friendly Sea

Chill swells and good snorkeling

The big, gentle waves of **Playa Tamarindo** are suitable even for most surfing newbies, but you can find more challenging watery terrain if you head south on the beach of Playa

CRAFT BREW CENTRAL

Looking to satisfy your thirst for hearty craft beer made with local ingredients? The breweries around Tamarindo deliver the goods.

Potrero Brewing Company: A welcoming vibe, trivia nights, live music, beer, cocktails and nonalcoholic drinks. Try the citrus-forward Hazy IPA.

Volcano Brewing Company: Look for the big black-and-white sign on Tamarindo's main drag. Gato Malo stout is a fan fave here.

Brothers of Ale Brewing: Beer flights, huge burgers and live music. It's worth the drive, especially for a pink Dry Irish Stout flavored with local cacao.

Papagayo Brewing: A name you're probably familiar with if you've spent any time in Costa Rica. The Beach Lager is a drinkable, refreshing sip.

NICOLA PULHAM/SHUTTERSTOCK

Horse riding, Playa Tamarindo

Langosta (p283), making this area a win for people of every aptitude level. With few rocks, consistent waves and your pick of top surf schools and rentals on and near the beach, Tamarindo is the place to go if you've ever craved a surfing adventure but don't want to chance a ferocious ocean. The Pacific is chill here. Peak surfing time varies by time of year and day but it's generally in the early morning and evening. Check the Tides Chart *(tideschart.com)* for up-to-date information and to chart your following day. Alternatively, you can always ask on the beach. Beginners will want to look for gentle, long waves that break easy.

You can also get some self-care time between surfing sessions in the form of massages and pedicures, with a great view of Bahía Tamarindo, or treat yourself to a snack or beverage at one of the many **beach bars**. With plastic chairs right out in the sand and an unfettered view of the sea, it's tough to beat.

While the waves are this area's biggest draw, there's quite a bit going on beneath the surface, too. Snorkeling tours are popular, and you can customize the length of your trip to pack more in before or after your adventure. Winds and rainy conditions can affect the sea's clarity, so always check the day before to make sure that your tour is still on. Expect to see a flurry of deeply hued tropical fish, smaller rays and the occasional reef shark, depending on how far you venture out.

DRINKING IN TAMARINDO: BEST BARS

Chili Guaros: Fun cocktails, regular beer specials and homemade chili *guaro* (local firewater made with sugarcane). *11am-2am*

Langosta Beach Club: Day passes available, and excellent bay views. Try the craft margaritas and house-made red or white sangria. *8am-8pm*

Pacífico Bar Tamarindo: Artisan cocktails, local craft beers and live music – a good place to meet people. *11am-11pm*

CATA Agave Bar: Sophisticated vibes and excellent selection of mezcal and agave; easy beach access. *4-11pm Thu-Tue, 4pm-midnight Wed*

Some tours go to Las Catalinas and combine a day at sea with diving, where you'll be treated to giant manta rays and sea turtles. PADI certification is required to dive. **Tamarindo Diving** *(tamarindodiving.net; diving/snorkeling tours from US$130/80)* is an excellent place to get your snorkeling and diving fix.

Equine Adventuring

Horseback riding on Playa Tamarindo

Playa Tamarindo's wide, level beach is ideal for horseback riding, where you can soak in the dense, deep-green jungle on one side and the endless Pacific on the other. Walk down the popular sections of the beach, and you'll spot horses relaxing and waiting with their guides, ready to take you down the expanse of the *playa*. Some tours take you riding the length of Playa Tamarindo, as far as Playa Grande. Others start on neighboring beaches, like Playa Brasilito, and traverse the snow-white shell beach of Playa Conchal. **Native's Way** *(nativeswaycostarica.com; US$65)*, a Tamarindo-based agency, will pick you up from your accommodations and take you to Playa Conchal, Playa Potrero, Playa Langosta or Playa Flamingo for a two-hour ride.

Wonder Away *(wonderaway.com; US$50)* runs morning and sunset tours that last an hour and a half, and **Riding Escapes** *(ridingescapes.com; lessons/tours from US$40/60)* offers regular tours, lessons and riding holidays. While these tour companies might be preferable if you're a well-in-advance planner and want to schedule your days before you arrive, nothing beats walking down the beach and getting to know the horses for yourself. You might click with that particular mare, support a local not on social media, and have a fantastic equine companion in Tamarindo.

Fresh & Fabulous Eats

Tamarindo's markets

Small markets, courtyards and charming alfresco community spaces are found all over Tamarindo. The **Thursday night market** runs officially from 6pm to 9pm, but, unofficially, the party keeps going until 9:30pm, and it's a tremendous spot for cheap and scrumptious eats like vegan *empanadas* (stuffed turnovers) and popsicles. You'll find art, souvenirs and clothing, including a selection of one-of-a-kind bikinis, plus live music and plenty of local beer. It's right off the main drag near **Sharky's** (p278). Make sure you check out the second level when you visit, as it's easy to miss.

Jardín Food Truck Park *(facebook.com/jardintamarindofoodtruckpark)* is another chilled-out, family-friendly space to sample some of Tamarindo's finest: artisanal cocktails, smoothies, cold-brew coffee and local beer on tap, plus a huge collection of food trucks offering ice cream, churros, hot dogs, burgers and seafood. There's a separate area where you can get Oracle card readings or massage therapy. This is a good place to bring kids, with a nice park and picnic area,

BEST SURFING SCHOOLS

You'll find a slew of instructors at Playa Tamarindo. For a more formal surf-camp experience, these four are great picks.

Iguana Surf: Tamarindo go-to for rentals, lessons and tours around Guanacaste, and has a beachfront hostel environment.

Costa Rica Surf Institute: Lessons in Spanish and English tailored to all levels, with maximum six people. Stay in a dorm-style setting or with a local family.

Carlos' Surf School: With one-on-one attention, it's great for beginners and intermediate surfers. Also covers Playa Grande for more intense waves.

Tidal Wave Surf & Travel: Daily private, semi-private or group surf lessons tailored to your level. Couple them with other activities like yoga.

STRANDED IN THE SHALLOWS

Marring – or perhaps adding to – the beach scenery, depending on your personal sense of aesthetics, is the confounding wreck lying in the Playa Tamarindo shallows. You can't help but spy it the moment you visit the beach, and it makes a cool photo op and an interesting juxtaposition to the warped, rusting hull against the cerulean sky. According to locals, the wreck washed up in a big storm and has been sitting here ever since. The doomed seacraft is on the beach near Selina's mega beach hostel. The best time to visit the wreck is at sunset when the different colors play on the water and glint on the non-rusted bits of metal from the hull.

STEFAN NEUMANN/SHUTTERSTOCK

Playa Grande

and a serene air about it that's a shade different than anything else you'd find in Tamarindo; and since it's partially roped-off, you run less risk of lost partygoers stumbling into the park.

El Mercadito de Tamarindo *(facebook.com/mercaditodetamarindo)* is tucked back on the main road, but you'll know when you reach it because there are two rearing white horse statues on either side of the entrance. It's a cocktail and food market with excellent alcoholic drinks, *batidos* (fruit shakes), a bakery and many dining options such as tacos and gourmet pizza. Say hello to the friendly resident cats and pick up a pear pastry to snack on later. This market is close to the beach, so it's a handy place to stop for a quick bite on the way back to your accommodations.

Guanacaste is a Blue Zone, meaning that people in this part of the country generally live longer and suffer fewer diseases than in many other parts of the world. The water in Guanacaste is completely potable, so you can refill your reusable water bottle straight from the tap. Pick up fresh fruits and veg from **Tama Market**, the farmers market open from 8am to 2pm on Saturdays and Sundays. The market is also a solid place to find clothing, souvenirs, jewelry and semi-prepared local goods to take on your travels. Shopping here supports local farmers and likely gets you better deals on in-season produce than at big stores. Embrace the Blue Zone and the local diet!

EATING IN TAMARINDO: BEST SEAFOOD

Lobster & Co: Fantastic lobster rolls and French fries, with alfresco seating in a nice courtyard. *11:30am-9:30pm Mon-Sat, 11am-9pm Sun* $$

La Palapa Seafood & Grill: Best views in town, big portions of fresh seafood and sides, and happy-hour specials. *11am-9pm Mon-Sun* $$

Sushi & Poke: Ultra-fresh and healthy seafood and vegetable bowls just a few meters from the beach. Try the tuna sashimi. *noon-10pm Mon-Sun* $

Nogui's Restaurant: Tasty fish tacos, *patacones* (fried green plantains) and chocolate cream pie, as well as a good beer selection. *7am-9pm* $$

Beyond Tamarindo

White-shell beaches, ancient mangroves and the swells at Playa Grande and Playa Langosta are a quick trip from the heart of Tamarindo.

Tamarindo sits smack in the center of Parque Nacional Marino Las Baulas, so you don't have to go too far to explore the fabulous ecosystems that make up this part of Nicoya. Flanking Tamarindo to either side are Playa Langosta and Playa Grande, where you can surf some considerably big waves and possibly even glimpse a sea turtle as you paddle out.

Playa Conchal, Nicoya's white-shell beach, is just down the road before the Gold Coast opens up to the northern beaches on the way to Playas del Coco. It's hard to imagine that howler monkeys and sea turtles exist right on the fringes of Tamarindo, but you just need to step outside the developed downtown to enter a whole new world.

Places

Playa Grande

TIME FROM TAMARINDO: **40 MINS**

A wide, secluded beach

You can spot **Playa Grande** from the far end of Playa Tamarindo. However, getting there by car takes a deceptively long time because you must go far inland to avoid Parque Nacional Marino Las Baulas. It's better to talk to the local fishers near the end of Playa Tamarindo and see if they'll take you by boat across the **Tamarindo Estuary**. Taking this route will get you to the secluded, vast, lovely shores of Playa Grande far quicker than a two-wheeled land ride.

This beach is a far cry from its more boisterous cousin. There are a few properties, such as the **Café Mar Azul**, which serves incredible fish tacos, and a few set-back Airbnb rentals. This is an excellent place to forage for sea shells and sea glass, or seek the larger swells that you won't find in Tamarindo. You won't have to wait in the line or deal with throngs of fellow surfers – you'll have some one-on-one time with the sea. The nearest town from this end of the beach is around 1.5km away. You'll find a cute village with *sodas* and shopping if you fancy a walk.

GETTING AROUND

You can get to Playa Grande by walking down to the far end of the beach and taking the water taxi, and to Playa Langosta by either crossing over Punto San Francisco on the beach or walking down the main road in town. Book any tour for Parque Nacional Marino Las Baulas in Tamarindo, and your transportation will be covered. To see Playa Conchal, you'll either need a car or to hire a taxi.

Playa Langosta

TIME FROM TAMARINDO: **15 MINS**

Serious surf and sea turtles

Playa Langosta's varsity-level waves and double break are an easy, quick trip from Playa Tamarindo. You can drive, hike

TIPS FOR TAKING THE FERRY

The Playa Tamarindo–Playa Grande ferry *(transbordador)* is a locally known shortcut to get between the two beaches. Head to the far end of Playa Tamarindo, where several small boats are waiting. Each boat can fit up to five or six people; every person must pay US$4 (bring small money).

The trip takes about 10 minutes, and they'll drop you at the far end of the beach, so you need to walk a bit to get to a prime surfing spot. These boats have no set schedule except for their cut-off time, but they're usually out in the morning. If you arrive too early, find a *soda* on the beach and enjoy your breakfast. The last boat runs to Playa Tamarindo at 5pm, and if you miss it, you'll have to take the long land trip back to Tamarindo.

down the road, or go along the more difficult but much more scenic beach route at low tide. Walk left down Playa Tamarindo toward **Punto San Francisco** and scramble over the rocks. During high tide, this route is impassible, and it can be slick and tough to navigate even when the seas are lower. Morning is the best time to try to pass between the beaches, but your mileage may vary. Don't underestimate the mighty Pacific.

Playa Langosta is a good compromise between barren, beautiful Playa Grande and busy Playa Tamarindo. There's a small village nearby, so you don't need to bring provisions from Tamarindo. It's also much more peaceful, and the waves are enormous and broad, but you'll have to contend with a tricky coral reef out near the break, with left and right breaks. While you're likely to have some of the beach to yourself depending on the time, you might spot some leatherback turtles, who hang out near the reef. Its proximity to Parque Nacional Marino Las Baulas makes Playa Langosta a prime spot for swimming leatherbacks, although they rarely come to the beach. You need to get wet, wild and full in the surf to see them.

Playa Conchal

TIME FROM TAMARINDO: **30 MINS**

A snow-white shell beach

The impossibly beautiful white-shell shores of **Playa Conchal** are just a half-hour drive from Tamarindo. The **Westin Reserva Conchal** *(marriott.com)* sits directly in front of the beach but you can't access it through the hotel unless you're a guest. There's a cut-around through Playa Brasilito that takes just 10 to 15 minutes, winds through the jungle and deposits you on the shores of Playa Conchal. You'll find a free parking lot near the entrance to Playa Brasilito, and the trail to Playa Conchal is just a few steps away to the left. Lock your vehicle and stow or take any valuables – Playa Brasilito is less frequented than other beaches, there's no on-site security, and cars get broken into in this area.

As you walk down the path, keep a lookout for vendors selling coconuts or iced drinks along the way. At Playa Conchal, you can swim in shallow, balmy waters with a glassy-smooth surface thanks to the protection of Bahía Brasilito. It's an excellent spot for snorkeling; you'll see jewel-bright parrotfish and pufferfish circling right below the surface. You can also try spearfishing on the rocky outcrops right offshore. If you venture further out, you'll find the big fish, like tuna, marlin and mahi-mahi.

Most people come to Playa Conchal for relaxation with a capital 'R,' and since it's not as well known as some of the other

EATING IN PLAYA GRANDE: BEST RESTAURANTS

Taco Star: Enjoy fantastic fish tacos and traditional Costa Rican food, accompanied by cold beers. *10am-5pm* $

Pots & Bowls: Good acai bowls and breakfasts, excellent coffee and a family-friendly vibe. *7:30am-8pm Mon-Thu, to 9pm Fri-Sun* $

Santo Bandido: Choose from beautifully prepared tapas made from local ingredients and an excellent wine list. *5:30-10pm Mon-Sat* $$$

Las Olas Brewing: Towering burgers and local craft pints in a laid-back atmosphere with regular live music. *11am-10pm Wed-Mon* $$

PAVEL TOCHINSKY/GETTY IMAGES

Playa Conchal

beaches on the Pacific coast, you'll likely have a slice of sand to yourself. Just arrive early and stake out your territory. Ticos know about the beach, so you'll see bigger crowds during Semana Santa and other big Costa Rican holidays when families and kids frequent the *playa* for picnics, sunbathing and swimming.

If you don't have a car, catch a taxi from Tamarindo, although getting one back to town can be difficult.

Playa Brasilito

TIME FROM TAMARINDO: **25 MINS**

Sunset strolls and gentle waves

Make some time to stop by **Playa Brasilito** while in Playa Conchal. This wide, dark-sand beach is a great place to picnic and take a stroll, especially at sunset. The waves here are rolling and gentle, suitable for body surfing and bathing, and the water is clear, balmy and free of rip tides. Brasilito itself is charming, with plenty of small *sodas* and shops to check out. Enjoy locally sourced seafood and a great view at **Patagonia del Mar** *(facebook.com/patagoniadelmar),* which overlooks the surf and wide expanse of the *playa*. **Soda Brasilito** is a good pick for traditional local fare at reasonable prices; it opens at 7am. Playa Brasilito's proximity to Playa Conchal means you can easily experience both beaches on a single morning or afternoon and make it back to Tamarindo for some dinner, an evening surf session and a bit of partying downtown.

SURF INTENSITY: A MATTER OF GEOGRAPHY

At first blush, it may seem counterintuitive that Playa Langosta and Playa Tamarindo would have such dramatically different swells, given that they're right next to each other. It all comes down to a matter of geography. Playa Tamarindo sits squarely in a massive bay, formed by Punto San Francisco on one side.

Playa Langosta is on the other side of this rocky point and is subject to the tempestuous whims of the Pacific Ocean. Therefore, you'll find bigger waves and more unpredictable ocean patterns than at its sister beach. Swimming at Playa Tamarindo is also better than at Playa Langosta because the water is far calmer. Watch out for rip tides when in the water at Playa Langosta.

EATING IN PLAYA LANGOSTA: BEST RESTAURANTS

Bistro Langosta: Western and Tico-style breakfasts, acai bowls and big salads – great for vegetarians. *8am-10pm Mon-Wed, to midnight Thu-Sat* $$

Tandoor Indian Restaurant: Tonnes of vegetarian options including pakoras and mushroom tandoori, but also seafood and meat. *10:30am-11pm* $$

Pizzeria El Sapo: Artisanal pizzas and excellent burrata salads; they can accommodate gluten intolerances. *5-10pm Thu-Tue* $

Fish & Cheeses: Premium seafood and Italian comfort food, not far from the beach. *11am-9pm Mon-Sat* $$

TOP EXPERIENCE

Parque Nacional Marino Las Baulas

Land and sea creatures, ancient mangroves and breathtaking flora await at Parque Nacional Marino Las Baulas, which encompasses the Tamarindo Estuary, Playa Langosta, Playa Grande and Playa Ventanas. Spot leatherback turtles, tiny howler monkeys and fabulous tropical birds and reptiles on a guided tour or by taking the boat from Playa Tamarindo.

KRYSSIA CAMPOS/GETTY IMAGES

Playa Langosta

Mangroves & Ancient Forest

The Tamarindo Estuary is an incredible place to see the park's colossal black and red mangroves with serpentine root systems dipping deep into the waters. These trees are an essential piece of the ecosystem, and you can gently take a boat between them. You'll also find deciduous and semi-deciduous dry forest flora, including black olive, *carao* and laurel trees, for a total of 117 tree species in the park.

Impressive Wildlife

The park teems with animals, including crocodiles, boa constrictors, reptiles and howler monkeys. If you want to check out the entire pantheon of amazing critters, take a joint land and water tour and keep your eyes peeled for fish and reptiles among the mangroves and tiny, loud howler monkeys lurking in the trees. Howler monkeys are tricky to spot, but a good guide can tell you exactly where to look.

Leatherback Turtles

The *baula* for which the park is named is the mighty and magnificent leatherback turtle that nests on the beaches near these waters, specifically on Playa Langosta, Playa Grande and Playa Ventanas. Sea turtles' numbers are dwindling rapidly, putting the creatures at risk of extinction, so it's even more critical to ensure that they have safe beaches to lay their eggs on.

TOP TIPS

- Visit during sea-turtle nesting season (October to February) to join an official tour. **Chelonia Tours** *(tamarindomangrove.com; US$70)* is a good option.
- Bring good, waterproof shoes if you're exploring the Tamarindo Estuary.
- Most people spend quite a bit of time in the park, so bring water and a snack.

PRACTICALITIES

Scan this QR code for opening times and entrance prices.

Nosara

YOGA RETREATS | INTERMEDIATE SURF | WILDLIFE SANCTUARIES

Sprawling, posh Nosara is two hours down the coast from Tamarindo, and depending on the road conditions, you may have to go inland to access it. This stretch of the Península de Nicoya is rough, and a 4WD will be your best friend as you navigate the potholes and dirt roads that lead to the heart of town.

Filled with expensive yoga retreats that offer surfing lessons and spa packages alongside asanas, barren and beautiful beaches and deep jungle to every side, Nosara is an intensely natural and wild place. The waves here are big and glorious, thundering down Playa Guiones and Playa Pelada. It's also one of the priciest spots on the peninsula, with organic grocery stores and accommodations charging double what they do in other areas. High-end dining rubs shoulders with tiny bars that sell beach beers in this multifaced, marvelous town.

GETTING AROUND

Nosara is huge, so you'll need a sturdy 4WD vehicle to get around the town and up the nearby mountains. Walking is doable but takes a long time. Alternatively, you can rent tuk-tuks at your hotel or by flagging them down in town; they cost US$10 per ride. It's smart to get the WhatsApp number of your preferred tuk-tuk driver so you can text them if you're in a more remote area.

Almond Trees & Crashing Surf

A day at Playa Guiones

You have to work to get to the beach in Nosara. If you stay outside **Playa Guiones**, your tuk-tuk will drop you somewhere in downtown Guiones. Follow the main drag for about 15 minutes until it intersects with Calle de Olas, continue on Calle de Olas and follow the path through the dark-green-leaved almond trees to Playa Guiones. It's a huge stretch of golden-colored natural beach, with a glittering, swelled ocean crashing to the shores, and some jaw-dropping sunsets, when the entire sky is lit up in flaming orange and pink.

The waves here are intermediate to advanced, and the beach is mainly untouched because it belongs to the Refugio Nacional de Vida Silvestre Ostional. Playa Guiones is, by far, the most popular beach for surfing in Nosara, but less congested than Tamarindo or Sámara. There are a few surf instructors on the beach, ready to give an impromptu lesson or tips on where to catch the break, and you'll find surf schools set back from the beach. Try **Lotus Surf School** *(lotussurfschool.com; from*

TOP TIP

On average, Nosara is more expensive than other parts of the peninsula. If you're on a budget, consider outdoor activities like hiking and surfing. Eat at *sodas* and spend more time in Playa Pelada, which is cheaper and has more of a local flair than Playa Guiones.

HIGHLIGHTS
1 Sibu Wildlife Sanctuary

SIGHTS
2 Playa Guiones
3 Playa Rosada

ACTIVITIES
4 Lotus Surf School
5 Mindful Waves
6 Nosara Independent Surf
7 Outpost Nosara

SLEEPING
8 Bodhi Tree Yoga Resort
9 Gilded Iguana
10 Jungle's Edge
11 Socialtel Nosara
12 Villa Mango B&B
13 White Palms Nosara

EATING
14 Destiny Cafe
15 El Local Nosara
16 Naked Foods
17 Sendero Nosara

US$80), **Nosara Independent Surf** *(nosaraindependentsurf.com; US$90)* or **Mindful Waves** *(mindfulwaves.com; from US$99)*. Intermediate and advanced surfers will jump at the chance to tackle Nosara's big waves, but novices should approach cautiously – the rips here are no joke.

Breathtaking Clandestine Beach

Hike to Playa Rosada

Playa Rosada is south of Playa Guiones, and you can walk there when the tide is low. It takes 45 minutes to an hour, and you'll be rewarded with a perfect, pink-tinged beach and very little company. Time your departure well: Playa Rosada becomes inaccessible from the mainland once the tide rolls in. High tide changes depending on the season and day, but you can expect it to start moving in around 8pm.

If you're feeling extra athletic, try out the Playa Rosada loop, a moderately challenging jaunt through the forest and beach that spans 4km and takes about an hour. You'll see plenty of wildlife, like iguanas and shorebirds. Good shoes are essential, as there are a few steep, scrambly bits, and it can get tricky to navigate during the rainy season.

Find Your Peace

Posh yoga resorts in paradise

Nosara is full of bougie yoga resorts set against the backdrop of the jungle and sea. Those who don't want to shell out for a yoga retreat can book individual classes or spa services and get a small taste of the experience for a fraction of the price.

The **White Palms Nosara** *(whitepalmsnosara.com; classes from US$40)* is a surf and yoga retreat with nine rooms, infinity pools, waterfalls, palm trees and an on-site restaurant offering ultra-fresh local fare and cooking classes. Private suites have pool access steps away from your patio. Yoga classes and spa services like facials with volcanic clay are available.

Bodhi Tree Yoga Resort *(bodhitreeyogaresort.com; classes from US$40)* is part retreat center and part luxury yoga hotel with a robust schedule of daily classes. Non-residents can book individual classes, ranging from spin to meditation and yin yoga to Bodhi vinyasa. Both Bodhi Tree and White Palms are set back from the beach, and you have to trek up a dirt road to find them, lending to their exclusive nature.

The **Gilded Iguana** *(thegildediguana.com)* is on Playa Guiones' main drag, and you can't miss it if you're heading down to the beach. A surf hotel and spa with a prominent burnt-orange-and-gold logo, this is a more family-friendly venue, but you'll still get the high-end perks, including an organic restaurant, yoga classes, surf instruction and spa treatments such as the Iguana Surf Signature Massage *(US$161 per 90min).*

LOCAL WELLNESS COMMUNITY

If you want to experience meditation, zen and the benefits of yoga and dance without going to the pricey retreat centers, connect with the local community. Nosara regularly hosts ecstatic dance on the beach, meditation, yoga practices in the open air, cacao ceremonies and women's dance workshops, where you'll pay a fraction of what you'd spend at the resorts and get to connect with the locals.

Check out the **Yoga Community of Nosara** *(facebook.com/groups/nosarayogacommunity)* or **Outpost Nosara** *(outpostnosara.com),* a coworking and wellness space. These events tend to fill up quickly, so reserve your spot early, especially during the high season. Unless advertised as such, events will not necessarily be in English, so be prepared to exercise your Spanish-speaking skills.

EATING IN PLAYA GUIONES: BEST RESTAURANTS

Destiny Cafe: Healthy choices include vegetable and rice bowls, smoothies and plenty of vegan and vegetarian options. *6am-3pm Tue-Sun* $$

Naked Foods: The menu features all-vegetarian and vegan dishes like the breakfast superfood parfait and the bliss-bean burger. *8am-3pm* $

El Local Nosara: Serves farm-to-table dishes and big portions; pair them with craft beers or artisanal cockails. *noon-midnight* $$

Sendero Nosara: Alfresco dining steps from the beach. Order big hamburgers and truffle French fries; good dessert. *7am-9pm* $$

TOP EXPERIENCE

Sibu Wildlife Sanctuary

Sibu Wildlife Sanctuary, a 10-minute drive from Nosara, offers a safe haven for injured or psychologically damaged animals with a special focus on primates. The sanctuary isn't a zoo, and you won't have contact with any of the creatures. Instead, it's an ecologically and conservation-centered experience where visitors can learn how to better coexist with our animal friends.

SIBU WILDLIFE SANCTUARY

Howler monkey

Build-a-Bridge Initiative

As more development encroaches on the jungle in spots like Nosara, vulnerable howler monkeys have their routes bisected by power lines and roads. 'Monkey bridges' can help solve the problem by providing safe passage for these creatures and shielding them from electrocution, dog attacks and traffic. The staff from Sibu Wildlife Sanctuary's Build-a-Bridge initiative regularly erect such bridges. You can talk to the staff about how monkey bridges help animals in need or donate to their construction on the sanctuary's website.

Volunteer Opportunities

Sibu Wildlife Sanctuary accepts full- and part-time volunteers with a three-month commitment (US$300 per person monthly). Volunteers are responsible for the day-to-day maintenance including cleaning habitat and sleeping areas, helping with tours and preparing food for the animals. They do not have direct interaction with the animals. You can sign up to be a part-time volunteer for either the morning shift (6:45am to 10am) or the afternoon shift (2:30pm to 5:30pm). The sanctuary accepts volunteers from all backgrounds but is particularly interested in those with wildlife rehabilitation, conservation, fundrasing or marketing experience. Apply on the website.

TOP TIPS

- The tour is short (2½hr), but the terrain is rugged and includes some stairs.
- The Sanctuary asks visitors not to come if anyone in your group is sick.
- Pay 50% upfront online for your tour, and the rest later.

PRACTICALITIES

Scan this QR code for more information and booking (which is required).

Beyond Nosara

Visit one of the most famous turtle-nesting beaches in the country, and explore quirky and welcoming artistic towns around Nosara.

Nosara's beaches are part of the Refugio Nacional de Vida Silvestre Ostional – an 85-sq-km coastal refuge that extends from Punta India in the north to Playa Guiones in the south – so they're gloriously unencumbered by massive development and make excellent places for surfing and beachcombing. Just beyond Nosara is Playa Ostional, the site of one of the biggest *arribadas* (mass nestings of the olive ridley sea turtles) in the country. If you visit between July and December, you'll have the chance to experience this incredible natural phenomenon for yourself. Sámara is Nosara's sister town right down the coast, with beginner surf waves, a family-friendly atmosphere and a thriving international and local community.

Places

Sámara

TIME FROM NOSARA: **50 MINS**

A perfect beach town

Sámara walks the line between a family-friendly beach town and an artistic community full of wonderfully wacky souls. Its infectious charm is evident in popular spots like **LoCoworking** *(locoworkingcostarica.com; day pass US$16-25)*, a hive for digital nomads and those looking to connect with the local community. If you're lucky, you might even spot the resident coati curled up near the entrance. **Roots Bakery** *(facebook.com/rootsbakerysamara)* has excellent pastries, coffee and fresh fruit, best enjoyed sitting outdoors.

Rise early, and you'll catch the **Saturday Feria** *(facebook.com/feriasamara)*, open from 7am to 2pm. This market is one of the best spots in town for iced coffee, and you'll find all manner of wares, from fresh fruit and veg to whimsical clothing and jewelry. It's also a fun place to people-watch and drink in the vibe. Or stay up late for live music and libations at **Blue Iguana** *(blueiguanasamara.com)*, a modest hostel with an expansive pool and bar area that regularly features local artists and jam sessions. Pop by after sunset. Surfers will enjoy the gentle beginner waves and relatively few rip tides at Playa Sámara, and there are surf schools and instructors aplenty on the shore for those who want to get their feet wet. Don't miss the epic sunsets on the beach – the best place to catch them is right near Gusto beach, across from the Natural Center (p292).

GETTING AROUND

You'll need a car or a reliable driver to get between Nosara and Playa Ostional. The road is rough; you need to ford part of a shallow river, and it can be impassible, especially during the rainy season. Pad in some extra time to make it there. Sámara is less than an hour away by car, or you can take the bus to Nicoya and then another bus back out to Sámara.

NATURAL CENTER: A ONE-STOP-SHOP

The **Natural Center** *(visitplayasamara.com/natural-center)* is about 100m from the big 'Sámara' sign and across from the Gusto beach cut-through. It's the only place in Sámara to work out, sample some fine local microbrews and dine under a thatched roof in a breezy, semi-open-air environment that pays perfect homage to the beach.

You can book excursions at Natural Center Tours, and work off your dessert at Natural Center GYM, which has month or day passes available depending on how long you're in town for. The Natural Center is family-friendly, has regular local entertainment, and is an excellent spot to meet up before or after hitting the beach.

ALEXANDER LIESS/GETTY IMAGES

Isla Chora

Journey to Isla Chora

The pale, salmon-tinged sands of **Isla Chora**, just off the coast of Sámara, are a spectacular place to spend a lazy afternoon, and the island bliss is only made more enjoyable if you work a bit for it. You can sea-kayak there in about 30 to 45 minutes, depending on the wind and wave conditions, across a thin stretch of open ocean to the island's quiet shores. This kayaking adventure is a workout, even if the sea is tranquil, and you'll be paddling in intense heat, so have a bottle of water tucked into your boat and some strong SPF.

As you glide through the waves, spare a few moments to turn back and spot the entirety of Playa Sámara in panoramic glory behind you. Once ashore, you can snorkel in the shallows or take a leisurely hike around the island, spotting sizable iguanas and raccoons along the way. Be sure to save up a bit of energy for the paddle back, although the natural motion of the waves will help ferry you back to mainland Sámara easily. Tours are tide-dependent, and timing varies if the sea is temperamental. Always check with the tour operator on the day to make sure that nothing has changed. Rainy season and excess wind can also affect the tour schedule. Visit **Natural Center Tours** *(naturalcentertours-samara.com; kayaking/snorkeling tours US$57, boat tours from US$62)* to book.

EATING AND DRINKING IN SÁMARA: BEST CAFES

Roots Bakery (p291): Big breakfasts and excellent iced coffee, plus nice indoor/outdoor seating. *7am-6pm Mon-Sat, to 2pm Sun* $

Sweeties by Celia: Great coffee and homemade desserts and meals daily. Next to the Pali supermarket. *11:30am-9pm Mon-Sat, noon-8:30pm Sun* $

Malehu Coffee: Excellent macchiato, croissants and pastries, and fruit smoothies. It's off the mean drag in Sámara. *7am-5pm Mon-Sat, to 1pm Sun* $

Marea Surf Shop Cafe: Cute clothes and good breakfasts and coffee, including avocado toast and fruit smoothies. *7:30am-5pm Mon-Sat* $

Playa Pelada & Playa Marabella

TIME FROM NOSARA: **52 MINS**

Titanic waves and varsity-level surf

If you crave more adventure, head to **Playa Marabella** for the impressive, giant waves that dwarf even the colossal ones at Playa Guiones. You can rent an ATV or take a 4WD; it's about 52 minutes up the coast toward Tamarindo and can be challenging to get to during the rainy season. Plan accordingly, and check the weather.

Playa Pelada, a more local-oriented beach next to Playa Guiones, also has some challenging surf with big, choppy waves. You can take a detour and cut between the two beaches by walking to the far north end of Playa Guiones, turning right at the rocks, and taking the path. The route is steep and passes through the jungle, so wear decent shoes and prepare for a workout. Otherwise, grab a tuk-tuk in town (US$10) for the 10-minute trip by the main road. You'll find cheaper eats in Playa Pelada, and plenty of space to paddle out and try your hand at the more formidable waves.

Playa Ostional

TIME FROM NOSARA: **23 MINS**

See nesting olive ridley turtles

Between July and December, olive ridley turtles make the arduous journey from the deep sea to **Playa Ostional** for the *arribada,* or mass nesting event, where you can see hundreds of turtles depositing their eggs in the sand, then trekking back into the sea. The journey between Nosara and Playa Ostional can be challenging, especially during the rainy season, and you'll need a suitable 4WD vehicle to get there or hire a driver in Nosara (US$40). Part of this journey involves fording a shallow river. While there's a general idea of when the *arribada* will happen, it's tough to predict it day by day.

The most likely scenario is that you'll find out one or two days in advance and, if you're lucky enough to be in Nosara, be able to attend. Visitors can see the *arribada* very early in the morning or at night. During the morning, you can see the sun rising over Playa Ostional and have a full view of the turtle-packed beach; in the evenings, you'll have to use red lights to watch the animals lay their eggs. White lights and camera flashes can spook the turtles and are forbidden. The streetlights in Playa Ostional also use red bulbs instead of traditional ones.

BABY-TURTLE BLUES

Sea turtles are not overly maternal creatures; tamping down the sand to protect their nests is virtually their only parental gesture. While olive ridley turtles lay dozens of eggs at a time, few of them ever survive to adulthood. Dogs and raccoons prowl turtle-laying beaches, dig up the fresh nests and feast on the newly laid eggs. If the eggs hatch, they face a host of other problems – the blazing sun, sea birds and crabs. The journey to the beach is easily the most perilous time in their little lives. Those who get to the sea will encounter new aquatic predators until they're old enough to fend for themselves. One in a thousand turtle eggs reaches maturity, making the *arribada* a genuine numbers game for species survival.

EATING IN PLAYA CARRILLO: OUR PICKS

El Colibri Hotel & Steakhouse: The place to go for big portions of excellent steak and seafood. *7am-10pm Tue-Sun, from 9am Mon* $$

Restaurante Los Delfines: Delicious whole fish dishes, breaded shrimp appetizers, and comfort food in a relaxed environment. *noon-9:30pm* $

Soda La Plaza: Popular *soda* with fast service and traditional Tico foods like *gallo pinto* and *casados*. *7am-9:30pm* $

La Puesta del Sol: Fantastic views, great seafood and excellent food presentation. Try the tuna and asparagus. *2-10pm Wed-Mon* $$

WHY I LOVE SÁMARA

Elizabeth Lavis, Lonely Planet writer

The second I landed in Sámara, I fell in love with it. The small-town, artistic vibe and wide beach with the spectacular sunsets were precisely what I was looking for. Sámara isn't too big or too small; it's just right with a mixture of big stores, *sodas* and boutiques. I loved the sea kayaking, tried and fumbled at surfing, and hiked and biked through the outskirts of town.

One of my favorite activities was renting a golf cart and checking out the nearby playas, Barrigona and Carrillo. What sold me on Sámara was the community. As soon as I arrived, I felt like I was part of a family; or as we called it, 'our Samily.'

LUIS GOMEZ/GETTY IMAGES

The **Asociación de Guias Locales de Ostional** *(facebook.com/guiasaglo; US$20)* runs these tours in English and Spanish. You pay in cash, receive a wristband, and wait in a sheltered area with plenty of seating. You'll watch a short movie about turtle conservation until your guide is ready, then hit the beach.

Your group needs to stick together, avoid blocking the turtles' passage from the sea to the beach, or vice versa, and avoid touching the animals. With literally hundreds of turtles emerging from the water to deposit eggs, navigating around them can be a dance. Each turtle digs a hole with her fins, drops her eggs into it, and then tamps down the sand over her precious nest before turning and journeying back into the sea.

Playa Carrillo

TIME FROM NOSARA: 1 HR

Chill out in a hammock

Wide, palm-tree-fringed **Playa Carrillo** is a prime spot to hang up a hammock, read a book and soak in the calm vibes. While nearby Sámara and Nosara are known for surfing, Playa Carrillo has a different vibe; its waters are warm, peaceful and swimmable, and it's flanked by two coral reefs where you can see plenty of tropical fish in the clear water. This beach is popular with Ticos and full of cheap treats like ice-cold *pipa* (coconut water). Gaze out at the horizon, and you'll spot a few fishing boats trawling for roosterfish and mahi-mahi in the bright-blue waters.

Since it's so close to Sámara, you can easily couple your Playa Carrillo and Sámara adventure into one day. It's wise to visit

Playa Barrigona

Sámara early in the day and save your sunset time for Playa Carrillo, as the pink- and orange-tinged sky looks epic from this vast, flat *playa*. If you opt for a two-for-one Sámara and Playa Carrillo, rent a golf cart in Sámara and ride it the 15 minutes or so between the beaches. You can also take a taxi or even walk the distance in an hour. A golf cart is your best bet if you want to check out Playa Barrigona, too.

Playa Barrigona

TIME FROM NOSARA: **34 MINS**

A solitary beach scene

Playa Barrigona is barren and breathtaking, with multiple tide pools and wide, smooth indentations in the rocks where you can lay and let the surf wash over you. It's populated by thousands of tiny hermit crabs that will scuttle your way as you bask in the sun. It looks, in a word, prehistoric, with massive pockmarked rocks spreading across the beach and far into the ocean and rich jungle foliage on the edge. If you want solitude and to admire a stunning natural scene, this is it. Bring everything you need, as there are no shops or vendors in Playa Barrigona. It's just you and the sea.

The road to Barrigona, 37 minutes from Playa Carrillo and half an hour from Sámara, is challenging even in the dry season and can become impassable when it's raining. ATVs or golf carts are the way to go. You'll likely have to pass through a few flooded zones, but nothing too deep as long as it hasn't been storming.

Santa Teresa

INTERMEDIATE SURF | BOUTIQUE SHOPPING | ATV TRAILS

GETTING AROUND

Most of Santa Teresa sits on one long road. It's uneven, potholed and dirt in most places so walking isn't advisable, especially with ATVs zooming by. Instead, do as the locals do and rent an ATV to cruise around the town. There are plenty of spaces to park, and you'll have access to some of Santa Teresa's further-away beaches, making the most of your days in this part of the peninsula.

Super-cool Santa Teresa is the best place to surf in the southern part of the Península de Nicoya. It's a trendy town with opulent beach bars and excellent shopping, with one big road that runs down the center. You can walk the length of Santa Teresa, but many prefer to cruise by ATV from the south to the north end and the beaches beyond.

Santa Teresa's waves are intermediate-level and get more challenging at high tide, but you can find mellower surf north in Playa Hermosa. If you want to go in the opposite direction, Suck Rock is a great place to flex your chops and challenge yourself. Santa Teresa has a similarly exciting and adventurous vibe on land. Ride your ATV to Malpaís or beyond on a well-marked trail that can get muddy and flooded during the rainy season, but which is always a fantastic journey.

Rent Some Wheels

Hit the trails for adventure

Santa Teresa is built on one long, bumpy road. Rent a rough-and-ready ATV and hit the beaches, explore the whole town or even cruise to Malpaís or Montezuma if the trail conditions permit. Some spots might be mud-clogged and impassible during the rainy season.

To rent an ATV, you'll need a deposit of a few hundred dollars in most places. Shop around; Santa Teresa is spoiled for choice when it comes to rental spots – try **ATValerios** *(atvalerioscostarica.com)*, **Savannah X-treme Tours** *(savannahatvtours.com)* or **True Nature Adventure Tours** *(santa-teresa-atv-rentals.com)*. Prices vary depending on the season and demand but start from US$70 per day.

You might be asked to leave your passport, but it's best to avoid doing this if you can. It's a good idea to take a few photos of the ATV, especially if it looks a bit dinged up, so you're not charged later. Always return it on time and with a full tank of gas. Alternatively, you can always

TOP TIP

Surf conditions change depending on what time of year you come. During the dry season, expect smaller waves; during the rainy season, the swells are much larger. For glassy, consistent waves any time of the year, surf Playa Santa Teresa and nearby Playa Hermosa in the mornings.

SIGHTS
1 Playa Hermosa
2 Playa Santa Teresa

ACTIVITIES
3 ATValerios
4 Savannah X-treme Tours
5 True Nature Adventure Tours
6 Zuma Tours

SLEEPING
7 Akih Pods Hostel
8 Don Jons Surf & Yoga Lodge
9 Funky Monkey Lodge
10 House of Somos
11 Lost Boyz
12 Zeneida's Surf Garden

EATING
13 Banana Beach Restaurant
14 El Carmen
15 Manzú a Beachfront Restaurant
16 Shambala Beachfront Restaurant

SHOPPING
17 Pacific Wolf Factory
18 Studio Colectiva
19 Tica Surf
20 Wave Boutique Mall Santa Teresa

join an ATV tour. **Zuma Tours** *(zumatours.net/atv-tours; US$120)* offers four-hour packages that cover Santa Teresa, Montezuma and Malpaís.

A Shopping Spree

Santa Teresa boutiques

On-trend Santa Teresa is a goldmine of boutique shopping, with plenty of options on the main road. At **Wave Boutique Mall Santa Teresa** you can stock up on bathing-suit cover-ups,

continued on p300

WOMEN-LED SURF INSTRUCTION

Tica Surf, founded by Veronica Quiros, one of Costa Rica's most celebrated surfers, sells comfortable, functional, brightly colored surf gear for women. Quiros and a team of female surf instructors offer regular lessons to women who are just getting started, want to improve their game or need some expert advice *(book on 6139-7950 or @ticasurfbikinis)*.

DRIVING TOUR

Surf Seeking & Beach Tripping

Talk to any serious surfer about where to catch waves in Nicoya, and they'll likely mention Santa Teresa. This hub of all things salty and gnarly is blessed with beach after beach, offering waves suitable for ambitious beginners, intermediate surfers and experts alike. Rent yourself an ATV, Santa Teresa's top choice of transportation, and head out for a day of adventure.

1 Playa Hermosa

Your journey starts just north of Santa Teresa, in **Playa Hermosa**, where the waves are a bit more beginner-friendly, the beach is less crowded and there are fewer dangerous rip tides in the surf. Have an easy, breezy session to start your day of surfing and enjoy the splendid views from Playa Hermosa's golden shores. The only issue you might have is parking, so get there bright and early for some good, glassy waves and a decent spot.

The Drive: Drive your ATV for about seven minutes down the road toward Santa Teresa until you see the signs for Roca Mar restaurant.

MAREMAGNUM/GETTY IMAGES

Playa Carmen

❷ Suck Rock

After a refreshing, gentle start in Playa Hermosa, it's time for **Suck Rock**, a notorious break with enormous swells next to Roca Mar. Suck Rock is advanced-grade surfing only, so if you're looking for something a bit milder, skip this stop and head to Playa La Lora instead – it's just down the road in the direction of Playa Santa Teresa.

The Drive: Drive your ATV for about eight minutes to Playa Santa Teresa. If you're heading to Playa La Lora, it's about five minutes away, depending on your speed.

❸ Playa Santa Teresa

The waves at **Playa Santa Teresa** are an advanced-beginner to intermediate level and get tricky or more fun when the tide is high, depending on your ability. The beach also varies; the waves near Selina's North, closer to Playa Hermosa, tend to be a touch bigger than those to the south. This beach is a fantastic place to spend a few hours and grab a surf lesson.

The Drive: Drive your ATV for 15 minutes toward Playa Malpaís and you'll find Playa Carmen just before the tide pools.

❹ Playa Carmen

Sugary-white beaches and a grab-bag of reef and beach breaks make **Playa Carmen** an appealing destination for surfers who like a challenge. If you're a beginner, choose your waves wisely, especially around the reef breaks. Advanced surfers will love the opportunity to show off their skills and relax on Playa Carmen's snowy shores for sunset.

TRAVELING BEYOND SANTA TERESA

It's possible to take an ATV from Santa Teresa through Malpaís and across to Montezuma; the 21km trail is a bumpy, scenic ride. Depending on your pace, you can also hike the trail in four to five hours. There's plenty of signage, and the route is relatively safe and well-traversed. Otherwise, shuttle services like **Santa Teresa Travels** *(santateresatravels.cr)* run regularly between the three spots.

If you take the bus, you must transfer in Cóbano. Buses run several times a day from Santa Teresa and Montezuma and drop you off at Cóbano Pollolandia, which doubles as a bus terminal for people going to Malpaís. A Scotiabank in Cóbano lets you withdraw the equivalent of US$400 with the same fees as Banco LAFISE, which only allows you to withdraw US$200.

contined from p297

jewelry, flowy dresses and custom T-shirts. There's a cute shaded area in the back that sometimes hosts events. **Pacific Wolf Factory** *(facebook.com/pacificwolffactory)* is an eco-conscious brand selling flattering, minimalist pieces made from good-quality fabrics; you can get a bikini that will last you for the long run. **Studio Colectiva** *(studiocolectiva.com)* has souvenirs, candles, homeware and clothing in a bright showroom. All of its pieces are made by local designers, so you're getting a one-of-a-kind item. You'll also find pop-up shops and storefronts around Selina's North mega-hostel near the beach.

Santa Teresa

ROB FRANCIS/ALAMY

EATING IN SANTA TERESA: BEST BEACH RESTAURANTS

Shambala Beachfront Restaurant: Artisan pizza, *ceviche* (marinated seafood) and pasta with a gorgeous beach view. *8am-10pm Wed-Mon, from 8:30am Tue* $$

Banana Beach Restaurant: A great place to watch the sunset over the cocktail of the day, appetizers to share and great burgers. *7am-11pm* $$

Manzú a Beachfront Restaurant: Dine by the surf on an inspired menu of local dishes, including seafood and fresh fruit bowls. *7am-10pm* $$$

El Carmen: Tasty hamburgers and tuna tartare, good breakfasts and morning coffee. There's live music too. *hours vary* $$

Beyond Santa Teresa

The otherworldly rocky shores of Malpaís and the snorkeling and diving paradise of Isla Tortuga are less than an hour away.

Places

If the frantic pace of Santa Teresa's roads is getting you down, simply hop on your own ATV and take a trip to Malpaís, about 20 minutes away down a well-marked path with plenty of signage. You'll find an astoundingly barren and gorgeous beach full of rock formations that look like they're straight out of another galaxy.

You can even cruise further to Montezuma and see the other side of the peninsula. Isla Tortuga is a popular day trip that you can book anywhere in Santa Teresa. It will afford you a full day of sand and sea.

GETTING AROUND

If you're interested in land adventures, an ATV is the best way to get around Santa Teresa. You'll have access to the surfing spots in the north, and you can get to Malpaís and Montezuma in about half a day.

You can also get to Malpaís by bus, but you'll have to change buses in Cóbano.

You can also make this journey by car in under 30 minutes.

Malpaís

TIME FROM SANTA TERESA: **20 MINS**

Pristine beach and tide pools

If you have a car or ATV, getting to **Malpaís** is fairly simple. Just shoot 20 minutes down the road is a whole new zen zone dominated by rocky beach, unruly surf and some of the most pristine, raw stretches of sand in Nicoya.

If you're traveling by bus, it's a bit more complicated. You need to head inland toward **Cóbano**, then back out to Malpaís. The bus (US$1) will drop you off on Calle Carmen near Nicoya Villas Rd, and you'll need to walk several blocks down to the beach. There's a cut-through on your right directly before the cemetery, and if you hit the park, you've gone too far.

Playa Malpaís is stunning. As you leave the main drag, you'll walk through a pathway full of emerald-green foliage and bright tropical flowers, opening wide onto a barren stretch of beach with several rough-hewn rock formations scattered about the surface and tide pools swirling gently in their concave indents. The water on this *playa* is impossibly deep teal, like something out of an ultra-saturated photo.

Since you'll navigate your way over rock and sand, good-soled flip-flops will serve you well. Keep your eyes peeled for iguanas and shorebirds. There are comparably few people in Playa Malpaís, but the wildlife is abundant. Turn right and wander down the *playa* to see more otherworldly rock formations and spy tiny sea creatures in the tide pools. If you're keen for more, you can go to the official Malpaís tide pools – wide, shallow pools full of life six minutes north of Playa Malpaís by car. While you're there, visit **Playa Ventanitas**, a superb sunset spot.

JOAN VENDRELL/SHUTTERSTOCK

Snorkeling, Isla Tortuga

TOP EXPERIENCE

Isla Tortuga

An island teeming with sea and land life, covered in gorgeous flowers and foliage, and ringed with snowy white beaches perfect for melting into a beach chair and watching the ocean waves slowly roll by – this is Isla Tortuga, just 45 minutes by boat from Santa Teresa and easily one of the most memorable day trips you'll take in Costa Rica.

DON'T MISS

- Wreck scuba diving
- Spotting monkeys and peccaries
- Snorkeling near the shore
- Island hike
- Lunch on the beach

Snorkel in the Shallows

The fine, clear waters of Isla Tortuga make it a prime spot for snorkeling. Spot graceful orange- and sapphire-colored angel fish, lime-green parrotfish and even small rays. If you're lucky, you might be able to see turtles or smaller, benign reef sharks.

Some tour companies take you a bit offshore for snorkeling, but you could also do it right off the white-sand beaches of Isla Tortuga. Snorkeling is good all year round, but the visibility is better during the dry season. Plus, a bright, sunny day makes the entire island experience all the better. Your tour company should provide the proper gear, but you can also rent it on the beach.

PRACTICALITIES

Scan this QR code for more information on opening times and entrance fees.

Scuba-Dive among the Sharks

Isla Tortuga is a fantastic dive site with a volcanic reef and a wreck, frequented by white-tip reef sharks. You'll also see a glorious array of marine life, such as spotted eagle rays, octopuses and green turtles. Lucky divers might also encounter dolphins or whale sharks. Between the wreck and the reef, there's plenty to explore. While PADI-certified divers will have the opportunity to explore deeper and more remote areas, non-certified visitors can participate in a 'discovery dive' where you can dive up to 7m deep under strict supervision.

Keep your eyes on the wreck's smaller crevices and dark corners to spot moray eels and different kinds of tropical fish that have made their homes in these clandestine spaces. If you want diving included in your Isla Tortuga tour, prepare to pay extra when booking. Prices vary depending on the operator and season, but if you're keen on seeing marine life and don't mind the technical aspects of navigating a wreck, this activity could be for you.

Explore the Island's Flora & Fauna

While the sea will undoubtedly have your attention for at least part of your time on Isla Tortuga, the land is worth checking out, too. All manner of fantastic beasts populate this region of Costa Rica, including peccaries (small boars), monkeys, peacocks, macaws and armadillos. You can see some of these animals right on the beach, take an **Ecological Tour** *(US$5)*, or explore the terrain yourself.

Schedule your Ecological Tour at the small shop in the middle of the beach, next to the bathrooms. As Isla Tortuga measures about 500m across and about 1.5km long, you can cover quite a bit of distance. While the walk is short, the elevation is substantial, 88m near the beginning of the trek.

Catch Some Rays

Isla Tortuga was made for maximum relaxation, so slot in some time to chill out on the beach and enjoy the views. You can rent beach chairs for about US$8 and use them for the entire day. There's a bar a bit back from the shore, and your tour will likely provide lunch and snacks, including cold, freshly cut fruits and water. If you feel like moving, you can jump into a game of beach volleyball, rent a kayak or paddleboard, or take a stroll in the surf. The vibe and pace are *pura vida* at its most distilled and finest.

THE TURTLE ISLAND

There's a wealth of wildlife on and around Isla Tortuga, but the name *tortuga* (literally 'turtle') doesn't come from the green turtles that swim near its wreck and reef. Instead, it's named as such because of its shape. From the air, Isla Tortuga looks like a giant turtle, with its head extended and all four legs splayed out. If you squint and use your imagination, you can totally see it!

TOP TIPS

- If possible, visit during the dry season. You'll have better beach weather, and the snorkeling will be superior.
- Don't approach the peccaries. They are used to people, but can become aggressive if threatened.
- Cash is king. Bring small bills to pay for drinks or souvenirs, as many places can't accept change.
- If you're a vegetarian, vegan or have dietary restrictions, let your tour company know. They can likely accommodate you.
- Look for dolphins on the way to and from Isla Tortuga. They often like to play and jump next to tour boats.
- **Zuma Tours** *(zumatours.net; US$140)* is a convenient choice in Santa Teresa.

Montezuma

BOHO VIBES | EXCELLENT TRAILS | JUNGLE WATERFALLS

Montezuma is located on the Golfo de Nicoya and has a much more relaxed and boho feeling than Santa Teresa. You won't find too many ATVs zooming around here, but you'll discover little boutiques along the winding streets, artist markets, tranquil parks and a hiking path taking you down to a waterfall that empties directly into the sea. Montezuma's trio of waterfalls is one of the town's biggest draws, located right off the main drag.

You can swim in the deep waterfall pools, zipline through the canopy and visit a butterfly farm nearby, all while having time to get back to Montezuma for the sunset.

The town is also a transportation hub, with water shuttles running back and forth to Jacó. Travelers who want to tack mainland Puntarenas to their Costa Rica itinerary would be well served to stop in Montezuma for a few days before heading there.

GETTING AROUND

You won't need a car to get around as everything in Montezuma is in the same downtown area, but you can rent an ATV to explore the waterfalls or head across the peninsula toward Santa Teresa. El Chorro Waterfall, the main attraction outside central Montezuma, is accessible by horseback or hiking. You'll find many horseback-riding tours by the beach, or you can hike for 1½ hours down the coast to get there.

TOP TIP

Montezuma has only one ATM and it doesn't always work, so have cash on hand when you visit. Many vendors don't take cards or may charge more for a credit-card transaction. If you need to take out extra money, you'll have to go to Cóbano where there are several banks, and you can withdraw up to US$400.

Zooming Through the Canopy

Zipline over Montezuma's mountains

If speeding through the jungle canopy on a sky-high wire is your idea of thoroughly getting to know a place, you'll love Montezuma. The **Montezuma Waterfalls**, a trifecta of cascades perfect for hiking, are the backdrop of the best ziplines in town. **Sun Trail Tours** *(suntrails.com; US$55)* takes you on a circuit of nine ziplines across 13 platforms for comprehensive bird's-eye views of the mighty falls. While you're speeding along, you might encounter some wildlife, including white-faced capuchin monkeys. **Raccoon Travels** *(raccoontravels.com; US$55)* offers a similar two-hour tour suitable for children over five with multiple platforms and different ziplines.

Paquera Costa Rica *(paqueracostarica.com; US$62)* lets you spend 30 minutes at the waterfalls, where you can take a cool dip before resuming the high-flying adventures, and uses

HIGHLIGHTS
1 Montezuma Waterfalls

ACTIVITIES
2 Montezuma Tours
3 Sun Trail Tours

SLEEPING
4 Chorotega Hotel Arte y Sol
5 Downtown Montezuma Hostel
6 Hotel Cabinas Mar y Cielo
7 Pura Vida Hostel
8 Sano Banano Hotel

EATING
9 Bakery Cafe Montezuma
10 Chicos Bar Montezuma Beach
11 Soda El Artesano
12 Soda La Naranja

SHOPPING
13 Mercado de Artesanos de Montezuma

multiple ziplines to see the canopy properly. You can book online. Ziplining is possible all year round, but the tour operator may cancel if there's a chance of thunderstorms, as being up on the line during severe weather can be dangerous. Check the weather on the day of your adventure, and confirm with the guide if it looks windy and stormy. Sprinkles or even a light downpour are fine – a little rain doesn't hurt the ziplining experience, and you'll probably want to get wet in the waterfalls anyway.

A Splendid Trio of Cascades

Explore Montezuma's three waterfalls

Montezuma's collection of cascades is just a 15-minute walk from the beach and a perfect way to experience the nearby jungle and return to town for an incredible sunset. Follow the well-marked signs to the **Riverbed Trailhead**, toward Río Montezuma. You'll see a soccer field on your left and a colorful map of the grounds where the official trail to the **Montezuma Waterfalls** begins. This area is free to access; a series of maintained trails will lead you to the falls. Each one has a deep, glassy pool at the bottom, perfect for bathing, and these impromptu dips make for fun respites on your journey to the top.

EATING IN MONTEZUMA: OUR PICKS

Soda El Artesano: Excellent *gallo pinto* and iced coffee, in a welcoming atmosphere close to the beach. *6am-10pm* $

Soda La Naranja: Really good seafood at reasonable prices, excellent *casados*, and a friendly resident cat. *noon-9pm Mon-Sat* $

Chicos Bar Montezuma Beach: Comfort food like burgers and fries, plus a solid craft-beer selection. Excellent sea views. *11am-10pm Mon-Fri, to 9pm Sat & Sun* $

Bakery Cafe Montezuma: Good coffee, fresh fruit smoothies and freshly baked treats served in a bright and cheerful interior. *6am-6pm* $

RENTING AN ATV

ATVs aren't as prevalent in Montezuma as they are in Santa Teresa, but you'll still see plenty of them on the roads. By renting an ATV from operators like **Tiko Tours** *(tikotours.com; from US$70 per day)*, and you can venture to Malpaís, Santa Teresa or off-the-grid beaches. You can also take your ATV to the Montezuma Waterfalls. Parking costs between US$2 and US$4 depending on the season, and it's a secure place to stow your ATV while exploring. If you don't want to rent and go on your own, you can take an ATV tour that includes Montezuma highlights like the waterfalls and the beach. **Ollie's Adventures** *(olliesadventures.net; US$120)* and **Montezuma Tours** *(montezumatour.com; from US$150)* offer packages ranging from a few hours to a full day.

The journey itself is steep, studded with rocks and tree vines, narrow at points, and definitely will require more than a bit of effort to scramble up, but the views are stunning and photo-worthy, and there's plenty to admire as you make your long slog up Montezuma's trifecta of falls. Proper shoes with grip are important, as the trail can get slippery if it's been raining. The entire climb takes between 30 and 45 minutes at a leisurely pace.

You'll find lots of people at the lowest falls, an excellent swimming place. While swimming is permitted, jumping from the top of the falls into the pools below is a no-no. Also, avoid swimming in the pools right under the cascades themselves, as the washing-machine pressure of the mighty rapids can suck you under.

Ascend to the upper two, and you'll have to pay US$4 to access Sun Trail Tours (p304) private property. It's worth the few dollars for the views, and you might even see some zipliners gliding above you as you wind your way up. This is the steepest part of the ascent, with some stairs.

You can also start at the top of the falls and work your way down via the **Canopy Tour Trail**, a popular route for those accessing this area by ATV. It's also a good option for those with small children and limited mobility, as it affords spectacular scenery without the grueling climb.

Journey to the Pastel-Pink Beach

Ride to Playa Cocolito

Pristine, pale-pink **Playa Cocolito** is notoriously challenging to get to, gorgeous and remote. Its highlight is the sky-high **El Chorro Waterfall**, which crashes dramatically down a cliff and into the sea. There are a few ways to get to Playa Cocolito, but the easiest and most enjoyable is using horse power.

DAVE STAMBOULIS/ALAMY

El Chorro Waterfall

Find your gallant steed and expert guide anywhere near Playa Montezuma. Tours last about three to four hours, depending on the operator. You'll start on Playa Montezuma, make your way through Playa Grande and arrive at Playa Cocolito, where you'll have time to relax in the sun, enjoy some refreshments and take a cool dip in the ocean before heading back to Montezuma.

While you'll get water and fruit along the way, it's a good idea to bring a little extra hydration with you for the ride, especially if the sun is blazing. Additionally, you'll want to wear long, loose, breathable pants to stay comfortable atop your horse. Toss your swimsuit in a carry-along bag, or wear it under your clothes so you don't miss out on bathing in the pristine waters near El Chorro. These excursions are suitable for families since the horses are well trained and trot slowly. If you want your steed to go a bit faster, simply let the guide know and get ready for an inspired ride across the wide beaches.

A Haven for Sea Turtles

Volunteering at the Romelia wildlife refuge

The **Refugio Nacional de Vida Silvestre Romelia** *(refugioromelia.com),* 10 minutes from Montezuma, is a sea-turtle conservation and rescue center where you can volunteer to directly affect the well-being and safety of vulnerable baby turtles, including tagging nesting sea turtles for future tracking and studying and collecting eggs. The refuge runs a hatchery, where the eggs are shielded from both human and animal predators that raid the nests. Volunteers also assist with beach clean-ups, general maintenance and gardening. If your idea of a perfect vacation is a quiet beach, simple and healthy local meals and the company of some of the sea's most majestic animals, it's worth checking out. You can visit even if you're not volunteering and recharge on Montezuma's quietest stretch of pristine beach.

SENDERO EL SUENO VERDE

Horse riding is one way to get to Playa Cocolito, but you can also use your own power. The **Mercado de Artesanos de Montezuma** leads to the Montezuma Playground, with shady spots to sit and a kids' play area. Follow it all the way through, head right, and you'll see signs for the **Sendero Sueno Verde** (Green Dream Trail). It will lead you straight to the beach. **Cascada Piedra Colorada** is 10 minutes down the trail, **Playa Grande** is 30 minutes at a moderately fast clip, and **Cascada Cocolito** is 1½ hours away. While the trail is marked and maintained, you'll have to cross a few freshwater streams, which can be difficult depending on the tides. Go in the early to mid-morning so that you have plenty of time to enjoy yourself on the secluded Playa Cocolito.

Beyond Montezuma

Discover Costa Rica's very first nature reserve, camp on a bioluminescent beach or check out luxury accommodations just beyond Montezuma.

Places

Sitting right at the bottom of the Península de Nicoya, Montezuma is both an access point to mainland Puntarenas (by boat) and a tourist destination all on its own. However, before you board that ferry on the way to Jacó, it's worth checking out the area immediately surrounding Montezuma. The Reserva Natural Absoluta Cabo Blanco, the first nature reserve in Costa Rica and a model for all other parks that followed, is a mere taxi or bus ride away. Plus, there's Tambor, a study in contrasts between the posh all-inclusive resorts and humble Tico-style camping. A few minutes away from Tambor itself, you'll find Playa Pochote, where you can fish by day and see bioluminescence by night.

El Chorro Waterfall

TIME FROM MONTEZUMA: **30 MINS**

See the waterfall from above

Seeing **El Chorro Waterfall** from Playa Cocolito (p306) is a fantastic experience, but if you really want to have the whole adventure and don't mind getting a little sweaty and muddy, why not see it from above? Drive out of Montezuma on Ruta Nacional 160 until you see Escuela La Abuela. Make a right immediately before the school and drive down until you see a parking lot on your left near Jardín Date Daniela, a large, fenced-in property with an adjacent lot and the trailhead to the right. The road is not well maintained and is full of potholes, so a 4WD vehicle would be best for this part of the journey, especially during the rainy season. Take it slow, and you'll get there.

This is where you leave your vehicle and make your way down the trail. It's slippery, steep and full of tree branches, so wear closed-toe shoes and keep an eye out for slick spots. The trail is also very thin and overgrown in parts, but there are small signs that say 'Cascada' (meaning 'waterfall') and it's hard to get lost if you stick to the main path. You'll walk for about 15 minutes and arrive at the top of El Chorro. The rocks are extremely slick, and there's no barrier, so be very careful if moving toward the edge. Get close enough, and you can see the falls crashing into the rocks and ocean below and a slice of Playa Cocolito in the distance. Very adventurous hikers can even cross the river on large rocks about 3m from

GETTING AROUND

The best way to get around the Montezuma area is either by car or traveling by sea. You can pick up tour boats heading toward Playa Pochote in Montezuma. If you have wheels, you have options, specifically for seeing areas like the top of El Chorro Waterfall, which is down a dirt road that is difficult or impossible to walk along. Consider renting a car in Montezuma if you want to explore.

JOSHUA TEN BRINK/GETTY IMAGES

Playa Tambor

the edge and follow a trail on the other side. You won't find many people out on this trail, and the rest area near where the water plummets down is only big enough for three or four people to fit comfortably, but it's a fabulous way to admire the beauty of El Chorro in a completely different way. The hike back up is mildly easier, as you're less likely to slip, but caution is still needed.

BEWARE OF THE POCHOTE TREE

The thin-trunked, spiky *pochote* tree is native to Costa Rica, and you'll find it throughout the country. Watch out for it about halfway down the hike to El Chorro, as there's a cluster of them right before the trail opens up at the top of the falls. You'll be tempted to reach out and grab a trunk to maintain your balance, but if you grasp a *pochote,* you'll bear the full brunt of its natural spikes. Costa Ricans use these trees as a way to naturally protect their homes, because the spikes are an effective deterrent to would-be intruders. The *pochote* tree is also considered sacred, and its red-brown wood is ideal for furniture and carved items because it naturally repels insects.

Playa Tambor & Playa Pochote

TIME FROM MONTEZUMA: **30 MINS**

The beaches of Ballena Bay

The beaches of Tambor and Pochote sit right on tranquil Bahía Ballena, offering calm seas for swimming, beach camping and a relaxed atmosphere ideal for families. The bay is also an excellent place to see bioluminescence, a phenomenon where organisms emit light, lending the sea a glittering, neon-blue sheen. You can drive to **Playa Tambor** or take the bus operated by **Transportes Cóbano** *(laterminalcostarica.com)*. It will drop you off near the beach; as Tambor is small, you can get around pretty quickly and easily.

Playa Pochote is on the opposite side of the bay and 30 minutes' walk or a seven-minute drive. You can cover the entire distance on the beach. You'll find a selection of higher-end digs, more modest lodging and camping facilities.

This area is also a less popular conservation spot for olive ridley turtles, facilitated by **Tambor Bay Turtles** *(tamborturtlerescue.wixsite.com/tamborbayturtles)*. The organization accepts volunteer applications to care for the

THOSE PRETTY PLANKTON

You can thank the plankton for the luminescent waters in Bahía Ballena, Paquera, Oso, Puerto Jiménez and Manuel Antonio. This phenomenon is the product of a chemical reaction and is a heatless glow created for myriad purposes, including communication.

Disturb plankton-filled waters, and you'll see a blossom of blue swirling from the depths. It doesn't harm the plankton when you swim with them, but take precautions to ensure that your spangled swimming experience is both enchanting and plankton-friendly.

Don't put on sunscreen, perfume, lotion or makeup before you go under. Some of these products can negatively impact the ecosystem. And don't be surprised if you return with a souvenir or two. People have reported seeing flashes of light from sea-water-soaked swimsuits.

nests and vulnerable turtle populations. You can also make donations through the website or adopt a turtle.

You'll find plenty of places to rent out paddleboards and sea kayaks – a joy to cruise around on the benign bay waters, with a fantastic view of the mainland. Playa Tambor is also excellent for picnicking, with its lovely, wide, family-friendly sands that reward beachgoers with incredible sunsets. If you take a bioluminescence tour from Santa Teresa or Montezuma, there's a good chance you'll be hanging out near Playa Pochote and maybe even make a pit stop on the beach for sunset.

Night swimming

Floating in a sea of sparkling neon-blue is an experience you can only have in a few places on the planet, and the **Bahía Ballena** off Playa Pochote is one of the best in Costa Rica. Booking a tour at a spot like Don Trino Camping (p313) or at one of Montezuma's or Santa Teresa's tour agencies is the way to go. The guides know precisely where the magic happens, and you can hop into the sea for a transcendental night swim that will make you feel like a Disney princess.

Tours leave around 4pm and generally make a stop in either Playa Tambor or Playa Pochote before heading out into the bay. The cost varies depending on the season and demand, but it starts at around US$65 per person. This price includes transportation to Bahía Ballena and some light snacks. Bring your swimsuit, a change of clothes and a lightweight layer to wear after your nighttime dip, as it can get a bit chilly in the evenings. Tours last anywhere from four to five hours, and a lot of that is contingent upon how long you and your group want to spend in the water.

Once your guide finds a good patch of bioluminescence, they will stop the boat and briefly demonstrate how it works by dumping a pail of glittering water aboard and pointing out the tiny fleck of teal inside. Then, you have the opportunity to jump in and ignite the bioluminescence yourself by paddling, diving or simply treading water in a flurry of the sparkling ocean. These wonders of nature do come with a small cost: the bioluminescence can be home to tiny sea insects that inflict a not-severe, but still jarring, sting upon impact. The stings are not dangerous, only hurt for an instant and are more shocking than actually painful, but it's something to be aware of if you're swimming in a neon sea in Bahía Ballena or anywhere else.

Playa Pochote (p309)

IMAGEBROKER/MORITZ WOLF/GETTY IMAGES

Places We Love to Stay

$** Budget **$$** Midrange **$$$ Top end

Playas del Coco

MAP p271

Hospedaje Combi Dream Bird $ Stay overnight in a converted bus and enjoy a big outdoor area in this relaxed accommodations in Playas del Coco. Payment in cash only.

Hotel M&M Beach House $$ Clean, spacious rooms just steps from the beach with a nice outdoor area with hammocks for relaxation; friendly staff. Book early during the high season.

Claudio & Gloria Beach Front Coco $$ Cheerful rooms and exterior, and staff that will help you find cool things to do in town. Make sure you try the traditional Costa Rican breakfasts on offer, and enjoy them on the beach.

Laura's House B&B $$ Nice outdoor pool and speedy wi-fi at this pet-friendly B&B with plenty of parking nearby. Enjoy complimentary breakfast with your reservation. Cash only.

Hotel RIU Guanacaste $$ Huge resort with multiple pools, Jacuzzis and an on-site spa located right on Playa Matapalo. Amenities include exercise classes, regular activities and tours.

Santarena Hotel at Las Catalinas $$$ High-end hotel with several suites near Las Catalinas, with ocean access, an excellent rooftop restaurant and concierge service.

Tamarindo

MAP p279

Wet Hotel $$ Adults-only hotel with a good restaurant and pool, and plenty of outdoor and indoor communal space. The rooms have big balconies and there's speedy wi-fi throughout the property.

Grateful Hotel $$ Fun accommodations on Playa Grande near the Tamarindo Estuary, offering a great vibe with regular live music, a nice restaurant and plenty of outdoor trails and areas to meet other guests.

Zen Garden Tamarindo $$ These beautiful, bright apartments near Playa Langosta provide a reprieve from the party vibe of Tamarindo. You can relax by the pool and catch a glimpse of some of Tamarindo's wildlife.

Tamarindo Diria Beach Resort $$$ Massive beach resort with several pools, spa services, on-site restaurants and spacious rooms with balconies overlooking the sea. Centrally located.

Nosara

MAP p287

Blue Iguana $ Humble private rooms, a fun outdoor pool area and regular live music. It's very close to Sámara beach, and you'll meet many other travelers here.

Socialtel Nosara $ Formerly Selina's, near Playa Guiones but set back a bit in the mountains. There are dorms and private rooms, an on-site restaurant and pool, yoga classes and regular activities so that you can meet fellow travelers.

Villa Mango B&B $$ Tucked into the mountains with spectacular views over Nosara, this B&B offers an outdoor pool and nice rooms with comfortable beds, plus an excellent traditional breakfast with fresh fruits and *gallo pinto*.

Jungle's Edge $$ With options for staying in rooms or glamping, this spot provides martial arts classes in a dedicated dojo, surfing lessons and a pool. It often hosts retreats but you can book a private room as well.

Gilded Iguana $$$ A surf resort with spa services, on-site yoga and wellness classes and a spacious outdoor area. It's a family-friendly option right near Playa Guiones and close to several restaurants.

White Palms Nosara $$$ A quiet and restful yoga resort and wellness retreat with sprawling outdoor space and several pools. You can book yoga and meditation classes and dine at a world-class restaurant.

Santa Teresa

MAP p297

Lost Boyz $ Cheap housing where you can choose between a tent and a room, with a great community and young vibe, plenty of hammocks to hang out in and surf lessons available.

Zeneida's Surf Garden $ Wellness, surf and yoga hostel with private rooms and dorms, outdoor area with ice baths and showers, and a restaurant serving excellent smoothies in the morning. Reasonable pricing and a community atmosphere.

Akih Pods Hostel $ Clean, bright dorms with privacy curtains or individual 'pods' with private bathrooms, offering surf and yoga packages including multiday surf camps. The vibe is young and there are a lot of community areas.

Don Jons Surf & Yoga Lodge $$ Beautiful and rustic lodging, including dorms and private rooms, in a big space right on the beach. Surfing lessons and yoga classes available.

Funky Monkey Lodge $$ Vacation rentals great for families or couples, with an outdoor pool, surf and yoga lessons, and plenty of local wildlife and jungle scenery around.

House of Somos $$$ High-end yoga and surf lodge experience with two on-site restaurants, deluxe suites and rooms as well as dorms and camping. Price varies drastically on whether you go for private rooms or camping.

Montezuma

MAP p305

Pura Vida Hostel $ Cute hostel with lots of outdoor space, hammocks and laundry service, a common kitchen and a community vibe. Close to the Montezuma bus station.

Downtown Montezuma Hostel $ Humble and tidy private rooms in a family-owned hostel with a good restaurant downstairs. About three blocks away from the beach and close to the Montezuma Waterfalls.

Don Trino Camping $ Friendly and modestly priced rustic campground popular with Ticos, with spectacular views of Bahía Pochote. Basic amenities and electric hookups are available.

Hotel Cabinas Mar y Cielo $$ Lovely wooden cabins with a rustic feel but modern amenities just a few steps away from Montezuma beach. The balconies provide great views.

Sano Banano Hotel $$ About two blocks from the beach, next to a small market, with hot showers and breakfast included. You'll dine either outside on a patio or inside on comfortable couches. They can also organize tours.

Chorotega Hotel Arte y Sol $$ Beautifully decorated rooms and phenomenal views of the jungle and sea in a tranquil environment. Plenty of communal experiences, including morning yoga classes.

Hotel Bahia $$ Beachfront hotel in a quiet location, with 48 rooms and big balconies overlooking the sea, plus an outdoor pool with lots of space to rest in the sun. It offers off-season promotions but gets busy during the high season.

Tambor Beach Resort $$ Adults-only beach resort set back from Playa Tambor, offering secluded rooms, spa services and an on-site restaurant.

Barceló Tambor $$$ All-inclusive resort right on Playa Tambor with ocean-facing rooms, athletic facilities and international dining at El Rancho restaurant.

JENARI/SHUTTERSTOCK

The Gilded Iguana

For places to stay on the Central Pacific Coast, see p362

MARTINA CLERC/SHUTTERSTOCK

Above: Humpback whale breaching; Right: Punta Uvita (the Whale's Tail, p355)

Researched by
Marisa Megan Paska

Central Pacific Coast

SURF, WATERFALLS AND WILDLIFE GALORE

From awe-inspiring waterfalls to breaching humpback whales and incredible foodie finds, endless adventures await on the Central Pacific Coast.

Costa Rica's Central Pacific Coast may be small in area (it's only a 3½-hour drive from top to bottom), but don't be fooled – this little ocean-side zone is jam-packed with amazing activities for all types of travelers.

Start up north at the Pacific Coast's port town, Puntarenas, where seafood restaurants and mangrove estuaries set the scene. Then, head over one particularly crocodile-infested river to find some of the country's best birdwatching, just down the road from Jacó, a surf and party town so close to San José you could visit on a day trip.

Make your way down south past sleepy beach towns where tiny turtles scurry to the sea before heading into the hills to hike incredible jungle trails to crystal-clear blue swimming holes. Then make a beeline back to the coast to check out Costa Rica's most visited national park, Manuel Antonio, and its many animal residents.

Next on your list is Dominical, a laid-back surf town with jungle-backed beaches, set in front of hills that hide some of the most spectacular waterfalls you've ever set eyes on. If you've not been wowed yet, stop by Uvita, where humpback whales breach in the distance, extraordinary sea caves await your discovery and exceptional food abound. There's so much to explore in this tiny slice of paradise.

U. EISENLOHR/SHUTTERSTOCK

THE MAIN AREAS

JACÓ
Surf and nightlife near the city. p320

MANUEL ANTONIO
Pristine beaches, haute cuisine, wildlife-spotting. p331

DOMINICAL
Surfers' paradise and breathtaking waterfalls. p342

UVITA
Humpback whales, coral reefs, hippy festivals. p351

Jacó, p320
This grown-up surf town is also the Central Pacific Coast's nightlife hot spot where adrenaline sports, jungle hikes and crocodiles reign.

Manuel Antonio, p331
Home to Costa Rica's most visited national park, this little hillside town has a plethora of international eats, hidden coves and animals in the wild.

BUS & SHUTTLE

Buses and shuttles are one of the easiest ways to get around in the area, especially if you're sticking to the main towns. Schedules vary and can change without notice, so book at least a day in advance to confirm the departure time.

AIR

If you're short on time or long drives aren't your style, you can fly to the coast from Juan Santamaría International Airport in San José. There's a tiny airport in Quepos serviced by Sansa Airlines; the 30-minute trip runs nine times daily in high season.

CAR

Having a car will give you a lot more freedom to explore some of the area's most exciting offerings like the waterfalls, beaches and wildlife reserves. Roads are typically paved, so outside the rainy season a 4WD isn't essential in most cases.

Find Your Way

While you can get to and from all of the Central Pacific Coast's main spots by bus, having your own wheels will give you the freedom to explore the jungles, waterfalls and beaches further afield.

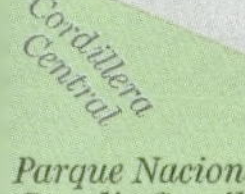

Dominical, p342

The southern Pacific's main surf town is an authentic Tico affair, where locals gather to watch sunset daily and attend the weekly farmers market.

Uvita, p351

Breaching humpback whales line the horizon, while pristine, empty beaches stretch out for miles and impressive culinary options lie just out of town.

Plan Your Time

The Central Pacific Coast is fairly compact, so you won't need weeks on end to see the main sites, but the longer the stay, the more treasures you'll find in this tropical paradise.

IMAGEBROKER.COM/SHUTTERSTOCK

Crocodiles, Río Grande de Tárcoles (p326)

A Week of Waves & Waterfalls

- Base yourself in **Jacó** (p320) for beginner waves, advanced partying and a swim at **Catarata Manantial de Agua Viva** (p320). If the swell is on, head north to **Boca Barranca's** (p327) epic point break or just south to **Playa Hermosa** (p325) where peaky A-frames await.

- When cravings for freshwater kick back in, detour inland to **Rainmaker** (p339) to cool off in some amazing natural swimming pools, then make your way down to **Dominical** (p342), where the surfing faithful will find waves for all abilities.

- From there, a trip to the **Nauyaca Waterfalls** (p346) is an absolute must, or stop at the lesser-known **Eco-Chontales** (p349) waterfall before packing up your board and swimsuit and heading back to San José.

Seasonal Highlights

Like most of Costa Rica, the Central Pacific has a wet season and a dry season. From December to April, expect hot days and tourist crowds; May to November brings rains, lower prices and quiet to the coastline.

JANUARY

With sunny skies, the coast is in full swing, so you can surf, hike and swim to your heart's content – or join the electronic-music faithful in Jacó for the **Ocaso Festival** (p323).

MARCH

Slightly cooler temperatures and clear skies are ideal for hiking and horse riding. The **Envision Festival** (p356) kicks off just outside Uvita, so expect regional crowds and a party atmosphere.

MAY

May is the perfect month for wildlife-spotting, and although the rainy season has just begun, it's still an excellent time to visit the national parks without the crowds.

A Weekend Trip to National Parks & Foodie Havens

- On your way to the coast from San José, stop at the **Río Grande de Tárcoles** (p326) to see the world's most croc-infested river – it forms the northern border of the **Parque Nacional Carara** (p326), one of the country's best spots to see scarlet macaws.

- Detour to Jacó's **Café Bohío** (p322) for the best coffee on the coast on your way down to **Parque Nacional Manuel Antonio** (p334), where a plethora of tropical wildlife awaits. Dig in at one of the town's many **international restaurants** (p333).

- Next, make your way to Uvita's **Parque Nacional Marino Ballena** (p354) for a gander at sea turtles, dolphins and humpback whales, then end your trip in **Ojochal** (p360) for a five-star meal at one of this town's culinary hotspots.

Five Days of Outdoor & Wildlife Adventures

- Start off in **Manuel Antonio** (p334)with a **white-water rafting** (p333) adventure. Opt for a **Zip Coaster** (p336) ride, then head south to Dominical's **Hacienda Barú** (p345) for some animal adventures. Overnight in the Hacienda's jungle reserve to see the creepy crawlies that come out after dark, then take to the hills for a high-flying trapeze lesson at **Airborne Arts** (p349).

- Back down at the coast, make a beeline to **Playa Ventanas** (p360) for kayaking to sea caves, then stop at **Costa Rica Coral Restoration** (p359) or **Alturas Wildlife Sanctuary** (p350) to see amazing conservationists in action. If you're in town during humpback season, hop on a **whale-watching tour** (p352) from Uvita to end your trip right.

JUNE

If you're on a budget, June is a fantastic time to visit the northern part of the coast. Towns like Jacó offer plenty of indoor activities to fill even the rainy season's grayest days.

SEPTEMBER

On September 15, Ticos celebrate Independence Day, so keep an eye out for local lantern parades. September is also peak whale-watching season, marked by the **Whales and Dolphins Festival** (p353) in Uvita.

NOVEMBER

November may be one of the best months to travel, as the rains have ended and the crowds are yet to arrive, although waterfalls and rivers can still be raging.

DECEMBER

December starts the Pacific Coast's peak season, marked by high temperatures, tourist crowds, excellent waves and bright-blue sunny skies.

Jacó

NIGHTLIFE | WATERFALLS TREKS | WILDLIFE-SPOTTING

GETTING AROUND

Jacó is a hub for the Pacific Coast. It's just two hours from San José by bus, shuttle or car. A shuttle boat (Zuma Tours Boat Taxi) services Montezuma on the Península de Nicoya. There are multiple buses and shuttles daily to Manuel Antonio, which is just an hour away by car.

Jacó is walkable, though a bicycle or scooter can be handy to get around. For nearby beaches like Playa Hermosa, having a car is ideal. Note that parking is a bit chaotic, especially around dinner time – park a bit further out and walk to avoid the mayhem.

TOP TIP

If you're keen on convenience but not on the crowds, book a place just outside Jacó to get some peace and quiet. Just down the road at Playa Hermosa you'll find both, with quick and easy car access to the main town.

The closest beach to San José, Jacó has long been a go-to spot for surfing and sunshine, and has a well-earned reputation as a nightlife hot spot. Yet sand, waves and beers isn't nearly all that Jacó has to offer.

This highly accessible mini-city has all the conveniences of home – banks, supermarkets, breweries and salons – while still being surrounded by stunning natural settings where pristine waterfalls, world-class birdwatching and a crocodile infested-river all set the scene. The adventurous can climb, trek, skate or deep-sea fish their days away, while the laid-back crowd will find plenty of memorable sunsets, yoga classes and outdoor markets to enjoy.

Whatever your vibe, this well-developed coastal town has more than enough exciting adventures around to fill an entire trip, so if you're looking for a fun fusion of partying, surfing and exploring (and you don't want to travel far to get it), head to Jacó.

Cascading Beauties

Hike to Jacó's waterfalls

The hills surrounding Jacó are home to some of the region's most impressive waterfalls – the trickiest part is choosing which one to visit. One of the most popular is the **Catarata Manantial de Agua Viva** *(US$20)*, just a 40-minute drive from town. It's one of the country's tallest waterfalls, and the steep, 3km hike to its base requires sure-footing, solid shoes and a bit of stamina. However, it's very much worth the trip.

For a more wallet-friendly experience, head to the **Catarata El Salto Gamalotillo** *(US$7)*, a smaller waterfall with a great swimming hole, whose low-crowd factor makes it an attractive option if you have your own wheels. Alternatively, try **Catarata El Encanto** *(US$4)*, a lesser-known spot most commonly visited by adventure tour groups for canyoning and rappelling. If you arrive on your own, you can enjoy some wonderful fresh-water swimming.

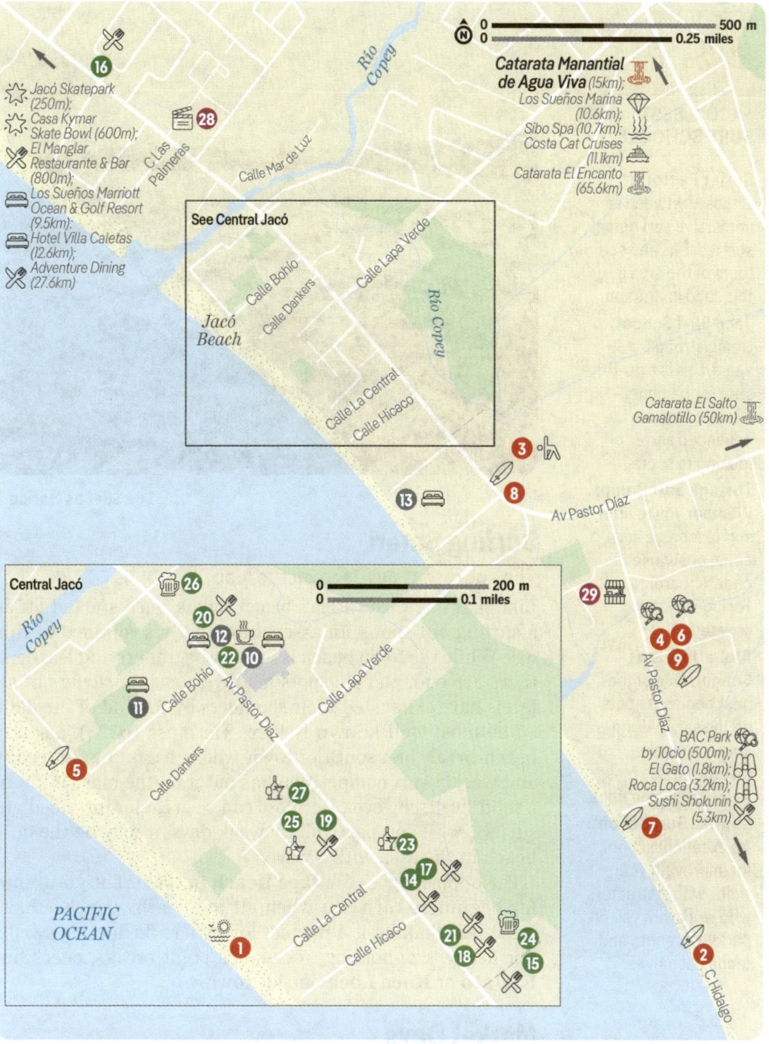

SIGHTS
1 Jacó Beach

ACTIVITIES
2 Aloha JoSi Surf School
3 Aurora Yoga
4 Beach Body Gym
5 Jacó Surf School
6 Pura Vida Jiu Jitsu
7 Sunrise Surf School
8 Surfer Factory
9 Tortuga Surf Camp

SLEEPING
10 Buddha House
11 Hotel de Haan
12 Jacó Inn
13 Selina Jacó

EATING
14 Amancio's Pizza
15 Graffiti Restro Cafe + Wine Bar
16 La Artesanal
17 Lemon Zest
18 Los Mahi Tacos de Cholo
19 Pachis Pan and Bakery
20 Restaurante Mundaka
21 Ridiculous Burgers

DRINKING & NIGHTLIFE
22 Café Bohío
23 Jacó Bar
24 PuddleFish Brewery
25 Republik Lounge
26 The Beer House
27 The Green Room

ENTERTAINMENT
28 Sunset Cinema

SHOPPING
29 Jacó Farmers' Market

JACÓ'S BEST SURF SCHOOLS

Surfer Factory: Choose between an immersive surf camp, surf lessons and surf tours of the area at this Jacó institution.

Jacó Surf School: Going strong for 35 years, this is a go-to spot for beginner, intermediate and advanced surfers looking to score.

Tortuga Surf Camp: Whether you're after surf lessons, a surf camp or sunrise paddleboarding, Tortuga's got you covered.

Aloha JoSi Surf School: One of the best beginner spots on the sand, Aloha JoSi is a family favorite whose class times follow the tides.

Sunrise Surf School: An excellent school for improving your skills, with instructors who work with you on paddle strength and technical moves.

GIANFRANCO VIVI/GETTY IMAGES

Los Sueños Marina

Surfing Safari

The sport that put Jacó on the map

Like many of Costa Rica's beach towns, Jacó started off as a surfing hot spot – an association that it's retained to this day. While the town beach is best for beginners and learners, there are enough epic spots nearby to ensure surfers of all levels have exhausted their shoulders by the end of the day.

The most well known is Playa Hermosa (p325), a sandy beach break just south of town whose barreling 2m peaks and weekly surf competition has put it on the map. Without a solid swell, however, Hermosa can be great for intermediate surfers, while on particularly weak days, it may be the only beach in the area with a wave.

The opposite goes for **Jacó Beach** in town. The go-to spot for beginners turns on when all the nearby beaches have sized out, making it a magnet for surfers during big swells. For heavy, size-holding, rock-laden point breaks, check out **El Gato** or **Roca Loca** outside town.

Market Days

Jacó's outdoor farmers market

Every Thursday evening and Friday morning next to the Garabito Clinic you'll find Jacó's weekly *feria,* or outdoor **farmers**

EATING & DRINKING IN JACÓ: BREAKFAST CAFES

La Artesanal: Small bakery known for French-style fresh bread and great coffee; the top spot for all-day breakfasts. *6:30am-6pm Thu-Tue* $$

Café Bohío: This family-owned roastery on the main strip may just have the best coffee on the Central Pacific Coast. *7am-6:30pm* $$

Pachis Pan & Bakery: An artisanal bakery that opens its doors for early birds, and serves some of the best croissants in the area. *6am-8pm* $

Restaurante Mundaka: Smoothie bowls, pancakes, eggs galore plus plenty of gluten-free options make this a breakfast haven. *7am-2:30pm* $$

market. Open from 5pm to 10pm on Thursday and then 7am to 2pm on Friday, the *feria* is the best place to get locally grown, fresh produce, as well as artisanal cheese, yogurt, chocolate and other foods. There are even some stalls selling handmade jewelry, cosmetics and clothing, making it the perfect place to take care of both your weekly shopping and to get some cool souvenirs.

On the Water

Catamaran cruises and sportfishing

A great way to enjoy local nature is to get out on the water, and whether you opt for a sunset tour or some sportfishing, you're bound to have a great time.

The Central Pacific Coast is one of the best regions for year-round sportfishing in Costa Rica. Billfish, mahi-mahi, sailfish, blue marlin and yellowfin tuna are all on the list of possible catches, and thanks to an abundance of fish in the water, visiting anglers are seldom disappointed.

Head just north of Jacó to Playa Herradura's **Los Sueños Marina** to meet your boat. Both **Pelagic Pursuits** *(catchfish costarica.com; from US$750)* and **Allin Sport Fishing** *(fishingcostaricaexperts.com; from US$675)* are excellent options, offering deep-sea, in-shore and near-shore trips on both a half- and full-day basis.

If simply cruising is more your speed, sign up instead for a day trip to Isla Tortuga or a sunset catamaran cruise with **Costa Cat Cruises** *(costacatcruises.com; from US$96)*.

Rock Out at Ocaso

A festival of electronic music

At the end of January, crowds converge on Jacó in anticipation of one of Costa Rica's premier electronic music festivals – the **Ocaso Festival** *(ocasofestival.com)*.

What started in 2017 as a gathering of a few hundred people on the beaches of Tamarindo (p283) quickly grew into a much-awaited yearly event, and in 2024 Ocaso moved to Jacó to accommodate its ever-expanding crowds. Although attendance is still capped to maintain a family-like atmosphere, Ocaso's new home at the Jacó Amphitheater just inland of town has allowed space for its growth to continue organically. For a festival that's had names like Bob Moses, Dixon and Damian Lazarus all grace the stage, it's no wonder all the hype.

Ocaso is also an important supporter of Central American talent – 50% of the artists are from the region.

RAINY SEASON IN JACÓ

Jacó's rainy season stretches from May to November, and although it may not seem so at first, this can be a great time to visit. Besides being less busy, prices are cheaper, the landscape is lush and waterfalls are overflowing. Plus, unlike other areas of the coast, Jacó is developed enough to offer alternative indoor activities if the rainfall gets heavy, such as the **Sunset Cinema**, Herradura's **Sibo Spa** at the Los Sueños Marriott Ocean & Golf Resort, and a number of fitness options like **Aurora Yoga** *(aurorayogajaco.com; from US$1.60)*, **Beach Body Gym** or **Pura Vida Jiu Jitsu** *(sydneymachadobjj.com; from US$20)* to keep you entertained.

EATING IN JACÓ: HIGH-END DINING

Graffiti Restro Cafe & Wine Bar: Bistro-style restaurant known for internationally inspired, locally sourced meals and creative cocktails. *5-10pm Tue-Sun* $$$

Lemon Zest: Jacó's first fine-dining restaurant is still a favorite spot for chic eats, with a seafood-heavy menu. *5-10pm Mon-Sat* $$$

Shokunin Sushi: This surprisingly affordable Japanese joint serves fresh sushi and creative fusion plates. *3-10pm Mon-Wed, from 12:30pm Thu-Sun* $$

Adventure Dining: Unique, mountaintop restaurant with its own tropical gardens and waterfall views. Reservation only. *from 4.30pm* $$$

JACÓ'S BEST NIGHTLIFE SPOTS

The Green Room: This cafe-restaurant-bar puts on live music every night, with salsa dancing on Tuesdays from 7pm (lessons included).

Jacó Bar: A Jacó institution with live music and DJs, cold craft pints and decent cocktails. It gets rowdier as the night goes on.

The Beer House: An in-town bar with great pub fare, a chilled-out atmosphere and rock'n'roll on the stereo – a great place to start the night.

PuddleFish Brewery: At the back end of town, this sizable microbrewery has outdoor seating and a semi-enclosed area where local bands play.

Republik Lounge: Lounge, pool party and a nightclub all in one – Republik may seem a bit kitsch but it throws a pretty good party.

ROBERTO ARREDONDO/SHUTTERSTOCK

BAC Park by 10cio

Adrenaline Rush

Skate, BMX-bike and climb away

Surfing isn't the only adrenaline-pumping sport in town – Jacó also has some cool spots for skateboarding, BMX riding and even climbing, right in town. Start off at Jacó's free in-town **skatepark**, a small but well-organized outdoor affair with both street and transition zones, before heading over to Casa Kymar's covered **skate bowl** *(from US$5 per hour)* for lessons or a blissful free skate (by reservation only).

If you're looking for a bigger playground, **BAC Park by 10cio** *(10ciobikeshop.com; from US$5 per hour)*, just off of the Pacific Coastal Rd, has got you covered. This indoor, warehouse-style skatepark is actually most popular with BMX riders, but skaters are also welcome. Both BMX and skate lessons are available, while the on-site shop offers gear both for purchase and rental. Still have some energy after your session? Check out its outdoor bouldering wall on the street side of the shop.

EATING IN JACÓ: LAID-BACK RESTAURANTS

El Manglar Restaurante & Bar: Relaxed riverfront restaurant with surf-and-turf cafe fare, colorful cocktails and live music. *noon-10pm* **$$**

Los Mahi Tacos de Cholo: Arguably the area's best fish tacos; opt for the burrito-size flour wrap or the traditional-size maize coverings. *11am-9pm Tue-Sun* **$**

Amancio's Pizza: No surf town is complete without its Italian fare and pizza spot, and for Jacó, Amancio's is the place. *3-10:30pm Thu-Tue* **$$**

Ridiculous Burgers: This burger joint does fully loaded sandwiches with every topping imaginable. *11:30am-11pm Mon-Thu, to 2am Fri & Sat, to midnight Sun* **$$**

Beyond Jacó

The area around Jacó is a goldmine for incredible waves, feathered fliers and seafood goodies – if you know where to look.

Just beyond Jacó you'll find more than a few amazing, and sometimes overlooked, attractions that are almost more exciting than the big town itself. To the north lies a Tico port where seafood reigns and mangrove estuaries hide both wildlife and wildlife refuges, followed closely by a beach boasting the second-longest left-hand point break in Costa Rica.

Birdwatchers will want to make straight for a lesser-known national park just north of town, with more unique feathered species than anywhere in the country. Meanwhile, surfers can park up just south of town at the region's most breathtaking beach, where fantastic waves, cold beers and surf competitions make for a perfect weekend getaway.

Places

Playa Hermosa

TIME FROM JACÓ: **10 MINS**

The most beautiful beach

Just a short drive south of Jacó sits the most beautiful (and aptly named) beach in the area – **Playa Hermosa**. This 7km-long stretch of black sand is also the surfing epicenter of the region, known for its standout peaky, sometimes barreling, beach breaks when the swell is on. The northern end of Hermosa has a small collection of restaurants and guesthouses, while further south the beachfront constructions dwindle out, making this handsome stretch of sand the perfect place to escape the crowds (although beware: there's little shade to escape the sun).

Confident surfers can paddle out at North Hermosa for bigger sets, or increasingly smaller waves as you head further south. Currents tend to be strong, so unless the swell is tiny, this isn't considered a beginners' beach. If you're more keen to watch the action, head to Hermosa on a Saturday afternoon to check out the weekly local surf competition, hosted by one of the oldest beachfront restaurants on the sand.

GETTING AROUND

All of the attractions in this region sit on or just off the Pacific Coast Hwy (Costanera Sur National Route), making getting to and from anywhere a breeze. While you can easily catch a bus from Jacó to Puntarenas, Playa Hermosa or Parque Nacional Carara, you'll be less limited by timetables – and able to make stops along the way – if you have your own wheels. For shorter distances like Playa Hermosa to Jacó, taxis are another solid option.

Esterillos & Playa Bejuco

TIME FROM JACÓ: **30 MINS**

A few good beaches

Continuing south down the main road, you'll come to another quiet surf town called Esterillos, a huge swath of real estate that stretches along three hamlets – Esterillos Oeste,

SURF COMPETITIONS

Playa Hermosa, a year-round, A-frame beach break, was the first place in the country to host surfing competitions. It's since been the site of both national circuit and international surf events, thanks to community support and the waves' own incredible consistency.

The local surf scene centers around **Vida Hermosa** restaurant, which has been hosting a weekly surf competition on Saturday afternoons (around 4pm) to provide a stage for local groms and pros looking for sponsors.

While the competition is worth watching year-round (although cancellations are frequent during the rainy season), you'll want to head to Hermosa in the spring, during south swell season, if you're looking for a real show.

Esterillos Este and Playa Bejuco. Although it's just south of the bustling streets of Jacó, Esterillos is such a sleepy little beach town it's easy to forget that civilization exists anywhere nearby.

Pristine, tropical-forest-lined beaches stretch out to the horizon, with virtually no oceanfront construction to obstruct your views. Favorite local activities include horse riding on the beach with **CR Beach Barn** *(crbeachbarn.com; from US$75)*, watching the turtle hatchlings being released into the sea with **Vida Tortuga** *(facebook.com/vidatortugacr; free)*, or surf lessons with **Aloha Surf** *(facebook.com/surf.lessons.rentals; from US$50)*. The waves are smaller and much less crowded than in the Jacó region.

Just south at **Playa Bejuco**, longboarders will find a long, mellow, left-hand point break that stretches from the breakwater to the beach on a good day, and isn't known for having huge crowds.

Parque Nacional Carara

TIME FROM JACÓ: **30 MINS**

Birdwatching at the 'River of Lizards'

Just north of Jacó on the road to Puntarenas sits the **Parque Nacional Carara** *(serviciosenlinea.sinac.go.cr; US$10, payable online only)*, a lesser-known national park that's easily one of the best birdwatching destinations in the country.

Carara, which in indigenous Huetar language means 'River of Lizards' (referring to the crocodiles of the **Río Grande de Tárcoles**), has the only transition forest in the Central Pacific, along with a number of unique ecosystems, such as the swamps that were made by the seasonal flooding of the Tárcoles river basin, as well as dense, tall, gallery forests located on the banks.

The park is home to more than 360 different species of birds – including favorites like the scarlet macaw – plus more than 1400 types of plants (the water lilies that cover the lagoon are particularly attractive).

Carara is also known for its accessibility. There are numerous trails with universal access, making it a great national-park destination for movement-limited birdwatchers. History buffs should keep their eyes out for the vestiges of pre-Columbian indigenous groups found around the park, although unfortunately they're not well signed and in some cases, not open to public visits.

EATING IN PLAYA HERMOSA: OUR PICKS

Vida Hermosa: Tacos, poke bowls and juicy burgers are the stars; the *gallo pinto* (rice and beans) isn't bad either. *7am-10pm Mon-Thu, to 11pm Fri-Sun* $$

Elixir Bar: Hermosa's go-to stop for vegetarians and vegans, with unique offerings like ceremony-grade cacao, CBD kombucha or kava. *10am-5pm Wed-Mon* $$

Empanadas Argentinas: Three cheers for *empanadas* (turnovers)! These Argentine pocket snacks are made with Tico ingredients. *9am-8pm* $

Animal: Chic wine bar and restaurant serving delicious seafood (and land-based) dishes, just across the road from the beach. *11am-10pm* $$

SEKARB/GETTY IMAGES

Scarlet macaws, Parque Nacional Carara

HUETAR INDIANS

The indigenous Huetar were once the most organized, powerful people in the territory of present-day Costa Rica. At the time of the Spanish conquistadors' arrival in the mid-16th century, the Western Huetar Kingdom (aka the Lordship of Garabito) was the main indigenous society along the Central Pacific Coast. The Western Kingdom spanned the Central Valley and Pacific Coast, stretching from the Río Virilla to the ocean along the basin of the Río Grande de Tárcoles (which these days is most famous for its crocodile population). The kingdom was led by King Garabito, who is considered by many to have been the most important indigenous leader in the region during the Spanish invasion.

Puntarenas

TIME FROM JACÓ: 1¼ HR

Catch a wave at Boca Barranca

Just south of Puntarenas is a river-mouth beach whose long, high-quality left-hand point break has made it a magnet for surfers in the area. **Boca Barranca** is known to be one of the better point breaks in Costa Rica – arguably second only to Pavones – that offers over 700m-long rides when the swell is on.

Thanks to the beach's easy access from San José, it can get quite crowded, yet due to the mostly mellow nature of the waves, localism isn't typically too intense. Drive to the end of the bridge and pay for parking to avoid break-ins; keep an eye out for crocodiles near the river mouth.

Wander around Puntarenas town

Puntarenas is the local port town of the region, and although most travelers only know it as the place to catch a ferry to the Península de Nicoya (p264) or the legendary dive site Isla del Coco (p328), there's more to this town than meets the eye.

Built along an 8km-long peninsula that's only 600m across at its widest point (and 100m at its narrowest), Puntarenas was once an important tourist hub, and still receives cruise ships at its port. Take a walk along the **Paseo de los Turistas**, visit the **lighthouse** at the far end of the peninsula,

continued on p330

EATING IN ESTERILLOS: OUR PICKS

Los Almendros: A mix of Latin American, Asian and American cuisine is served at this friendly restaurant in Esterillos Oeste. *noon-9pm Wed-Mon* $$

Soda Margarita: Just off the beach, this laid-back *soda* (cheap eatery) offers fresh local dishes. Breakfast and lunch only. *7am-3pm* $

El Patio: Tex-Mex, seafood and wood-fire pizza are fan favorites at this expat gathering spot with live music and game nights. *noon-10pm Thu-Tue* $$

La Rioja: Spanish-style tapas, pasta and juicy burgers at a colorful restaurant just off the main drag. *11am-10pm Mon-Sat, from noon Sun* $$

Hammerhead sharks

TOP EXPERIENCE

Isla del Coco

Isla del Coco is a small, volcanic island that sits about 550km off Costa Rica's Pacific Coast. A national park since 1978 (and UNESCO site since 1997), it has no permanent inhabitants besides the park rangers, making it the world's largest uninhabited tropical island. It can only be reached by sea and is a bucket-list stop for divers looking to see large marine animals in the wild.

DON'T MISS

- Wafer Bay sunset
- Chatham Bay
- Wafer Bay's waterfall
- 'The Moai' cliffs
- Alcyone dive site
- Dirty Rock dive site

History

Isla del Coco was discovered in the first half of the 15th century by navigator Johan Cabezas (the actual date is debated). Over the next two centuries, it became a place of rest and refuge for whalers, corsairs and pirates, thanks to its abundance of freshwater, wood and fishing. From the late 1700s to the early 1900s, expeditions to Coco turned more scientific in nature, although the island did spend a few short years as a criminal colony and then as an agricultural outpost at the end of the 1880s.

PRACTICALITIES

Scan this QR code for more information on opening times and entrance passes.

Visiting the Island

These days, Coco is uninhabited, meaning there are no accommodations on land, so visitors stay on live-aboard vessels in one of the island's two main bays – **Wafer** or **Chatham**. While it's possible to visit by your own boat or hydroplane, most travelers have to take part in a guided tour. The latter typically last 10 to 11 days, giving you a full seven days on and around the island, and can range from US$3500 to US$7500 depending on the preferences of your accommodations. **Undersea Hunter** *(underseahunter.com)* is a popular operator for enthusiastic divers.

On Land

The island itself is nearly 24 sq km in size, and roughly rectangular in shape. It's lined by sea cliffs that reach up to 180m in height (nicknamed **'The Moai'**), covered with tropical forest and punctured by three peaks – the tallest being **Cerro Iglesias** at 634m. There are freshwater rivers that cascade into waterfalls, along with a number of bugs, birds and reptiles that call Isla del Coco home (there are no native land mammals). The island has a large percentage of endemism, including three endemic bird species, two endemic freshwater fish, two endemic reptile species and 70 endemic species of vascular plants.

To actually step foot on the island, you'll need a permit from the **Costa Rican National System of Conservation Areas** *(SINAC; US$50 per day)*, arranged in advance – your tour operator should sort this out before departure.

Any island excursions, such as a hike to Wafer Bay's waterfall, are accompanied by the park rangers, who are knowledgeable about the island's unique geology, flora and fauna.

Diving

Most people who visit the island are there to spend time underwater. Thanks to the deep waters and counter-currents that surround it, Isla del Coco is the ideal natural habitat for large marine species, and is considered to be a world-class dive spot. Divers are likely to encounter hammerhead, silky and Galapagos sharks (among others), giant manta ray and dolphin pods, whale sharks, blue marlins, swordfish and more.

Some of the main dive sites include **Submerged Rock**, a swim-through playground; **Islas Dos Amigos**, a current-heavy site where you can hold on to the rocks and watch the marine show; and **Dirty Rock**, a popular option for mating manta rays and schooling scalloped hammerheads.

Alcyone, which is one of the main places divers go to get full-frame images of swimming hammerheads, is widely considered to have the best diving on the island, and visitors who've been to Isla del Coco argue that it's one of the best dive sites on the planet.

PIRATES

According to lore, Isla del Coco hides buried treasure. Thanks to its many years as a favorite pirate stopover, the island gained the reputation as the site where famous pirate captains hid their stash. Hundreds of expeditions have set out in search of the horde of famed Portuguese pirate Benito Bonito, English captain Bennett Graham and the famous Treasure of Lima. While small hordes have been found, no one has ever hit the mother load.

TOP TIPS

- Many of Isla del Coco's dive sites have strong currents, so stick to sites that are within your comfort zone and skill level. This isn't the best destination for novices.
- There are no health and safety facilities on the island, and a trip to the mainland can take up to 48 hours by boat, so make sure you have health insurance that covers emergency airlifts.
- Permits to the island are issued for less than 1500 people per year, so if Isla del Coco is on your must-see list, start planning your trip as early as possible.

ESTUARY RESERVES

Near Puntarenas are two important estuary reserves that protect the flora and fauna of the area's mangrove habitats. The first, the estuary of Puntarenas (also called **Manglar El Establo**), is an 8km wildlife refuge on the inner part of the Golfo de Nicoya, visited mostly by fishing boats, sailboats and tourist yachts. On the land side of the mangroves, the **Natuwa Wildlife Sanctuary** *(natuwa.com)* is a wild-animal rescue center with animal education programs, frequently visited by families and school groups from San José (tours in English are available). The second is the **Mata de Limón** estuary near Caldera (a town known for its artisanal fishing practices) that's exceptional for birdwatching (including seabirds).

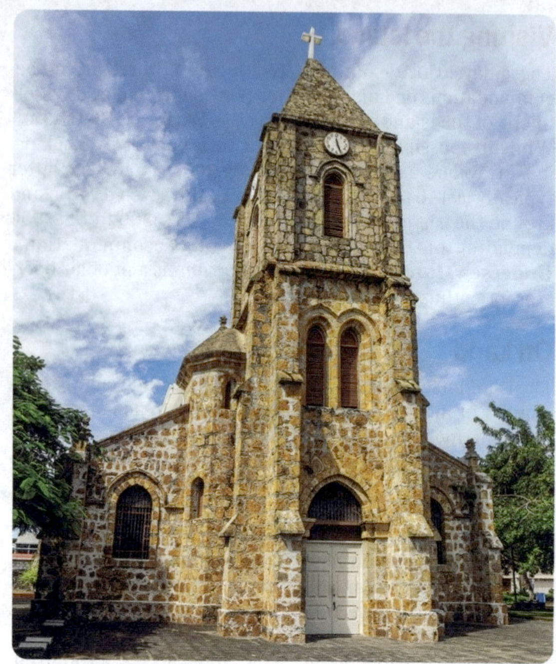

ARTUSH/SHUTTERSTOCK

Catedral de Puntarenas

contined from p327
or check out the **Catedral de Puntarenas**, the town's stone cathedral from the early 1900s, before heading off for a swim at the beach to cool off.

This hardworking Tico town also has a pleasant marina that's packed with enough incredible alfresco seafood restaurants to make a day trip here very much worth your while.

After dinner, head to the marina's green space, **Parque Muellero**, to relax in a hammock, or indulge in a perfectly decadent local shaved-ice and ice-cream treat called a *Churchill*, which comes topped with sweetened condensed milk, syrup and fresh fruit.

EATING IN PUNTARENAS: BEST SEAFOOD

Marisquería de Mis Suegris: Family-run seafood stand on the bay side of the peninsula where fresh fish is cooked in front of you. *10am-3:30pm Mon-Sat* $$

Isla Coco's Bar & Grill: Amazing fish tacos and strong drinks, right next to Puntarenas' ferry dock – perfect for a pre-boat meal. *noon-10pm Wed-Mon* $$

El Código Beach: Beachfront restaurant with delicious local-style seafood dishes; don't miss out on the deep-fried fish. *11am-midnight Thu-Tue* $$

Lunarossa: Cool seafood joint serving fresh *ceviche* (marinated seafood) and pasta in a date-night ambiance. *4-11pm Wed-Fri, 2-11pm Sat, noon-10pm Sun* $$$

Manuel Antonio

WILDLIFE-SPOTTING | HIDDEN BEACHES | INTERNATIONAL EATS

An upscale, hillside town that stretches up and down along winding roads, Manuel Antonio is one of Costa Rica's most popular destinations.

This area was originally home to the Quepoa, an indigenous group thought to have arrived from the Amazon in 900 CE. The Quepoa were difficult to defeat – they defended their land from Spanish conquistador Juan Ponce de León in 1519, then again from Juan Vázquez de Coronado in 1563. It wasn't until the following century, when pirates began to arrive in the area, that the Quepoa territory succumbed to foreign occupation.

These days, the area's treasure lies in breathtaking secluded beaches, expansive ocean views, delectable international cuisine and prolific wildlife – not to mention the crown jewel of this Central Pacific Coast hamlet, the town's namesake national park. Whether you're into beautiful sands, tropical hikes or wildlife-spotting, Manuel Antonio is a must on any Costa Rica itinerary.

Crash-Landing

An abandoned airplane turned restaurant

Across from Selina's mega-hostel, an airplane sits on the hillside, enveloped in a wooden structure where tourists calmly enjoy their ocean-view meals. Yet **El Avión** *(elavion.net)* isn't just a casual dining joint – it's a relic from a Cold War arms sale gone terribly wrong.

Its history dates back to the 1980s, when the United States' Reagan administration was embroiled in international arms sales aimed at negotiating hostage release and funding counter-revolutionaries in Nicaragua and Cuba. The 'Iran–Contra Affair' was aggressively denied by the CIA until a US-funded Fairchild C-123 aircraft was shot down over Nicaragua in 1986. When the crew told of CIA-funded arms sales to Iran, the C-123s were abandoned – including El Avión's C-123, which was left in Manuel Antonio.

GETTING AROUND

Manuel Antonio is well connected by public transportation. There are regular shuttles and buses to/from San José, Jacó and other main towns; a local bus runs from Quepos through Manuel Antonio. You can catch a short flight to the Quepos La Managua Airport from San José if you're not up for the three-hour drive from the capital.

The town itself is spread out along hillside roads, so walking around can be tiring. If you don't have a car, pack good walking shoes or take taxis to the beach or the park. If you're driving, you'll have to pay for parking nearly everywhere.

TOP TIP

This hillside hamlet offers spectacular sunsets. Catch it at one of the town's up-high cafes, on a sunset cruise, or simply head to the town's main beach.

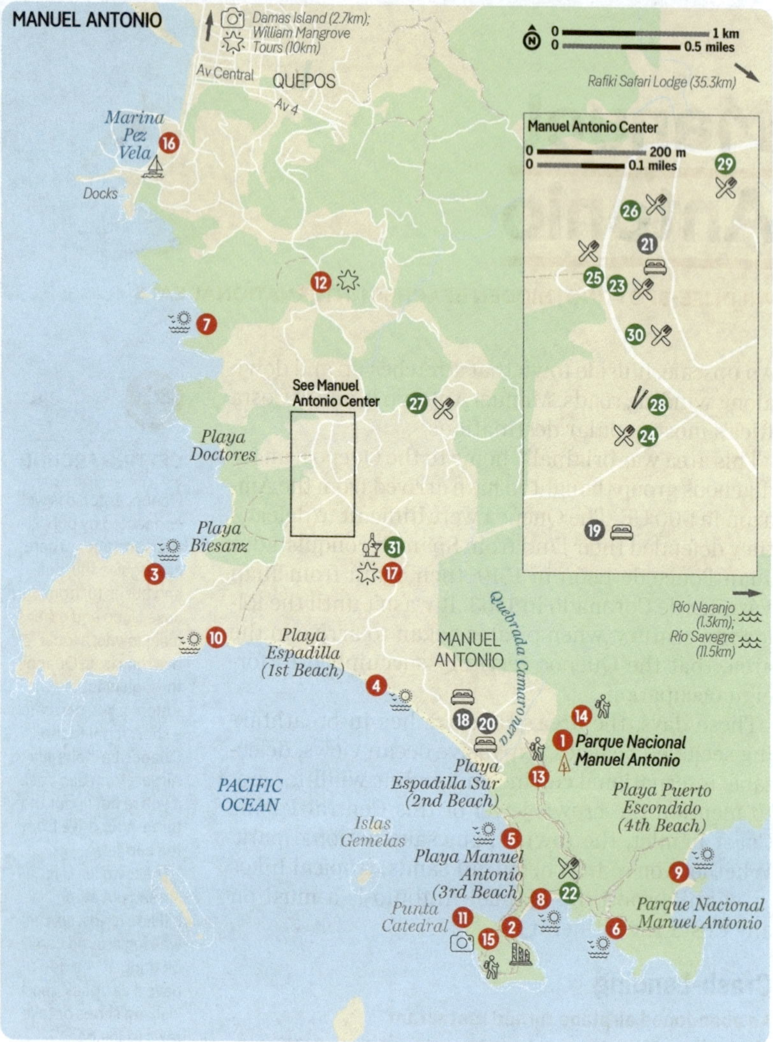

MANUEL ANTONIO

Damas Island (2.7km); William Mangrove Tours (10km)
Rafiki Safari Lodge (35.3km)
Río Naranjo (1.3km); Río Savegre (11.5km)

QUEPOS
Av Central
Av 4
Marina Pez Vela
Docks
See Manuel Antonio Center
Playa Doctores
Playa Biesanz
Playa Espadilla (1st Beach)
MANUEL ANTONIO
Quebrada Camaronera
Parque Nacional Manuel Antonio
Playa Espadilla Sur (2nd Beach)
Playa Puerto Escondido (4th Beach)
PACIFIC OCEAN
Islas Gemelas
Playa Manuel Antonio (3rd Beach)
Punta Catedral
Parque Nacional Manuel Antonio

Manuel Antonio Center

HIGHLIGHTS
1 Parque Nacional Manuel Antonio

SIGHTS
2 La Trampa
3 Playa Biesanz
4 Playa Espadilla
5 Playa Espadilla Sur
6 Playa Gemelas
7 Playa La Macha
8 Playa Manuel Antonio
9 Playa Puerto Escondido
10 Playitas
11 Punta Catedral

ACTIVITIES
12 Amigos del Rio
13 Sendero El Perezoso
14 Sendero La Catarata
15 Sendero Punta Catedral
16 Sunset Sails
17 Zip Coaster

SLEEPING
18 Art Hostel Costa Linda
19 La Mariposa Hotel
20 La Vela Boutique Hotel
21 Peace of Paradise

EATING
22 Cafeteria
23 El Patio de Café Milagro
24 Emilio's Cafe
25 Falafel Bar
26 Namaste Indian Restaurant
27 Restaurante Cerdo Feliz
28 Samui Thai
29 Soda El Angel
30 Varuna

DRINKING & NIGHTLIFE
31 El Avión

These days, the airplane plays a new role as a cocktail bar (yes, you can sit in the cockpit), while the scene itself has become a popular restaurant with impressive views.

Ride the Rapids

White-water rafting for all

Just 20km south of Manuel Antonio, the **Río Savegre** is perfect for a white-water rafting adventure. The river is raftable almost year-round and its Class II and III rapids are suitable for first-timers and families – plus the scenery is spectacular. Tours leaving from town run about six hours end-to-end, though you'll only spend about four on the water. More advanced rafters should head to the **Río Naranjo** on the border of the Parque Nacional Manuel Antonio, whose Class III and IV rapids challenge experienced white-water paddlers from June to November. The advanced crowd can sign up for a four-hour trip with **Amigos del Río** *(amigosdelrio.net; from US$95)* through the 'Chorro' section of the river, where rapids are Class IV and V (best in March and April).

All Aboard

A chic sunset sail

Manuel Antonio is the land of spectacular sunsets, and whether you're watching them from the beach, one of the town's hillside cafes or your hotel room, you're sure to be wowed. For a particularly special sundowner, however, try a catamaran tour. The four-hour trip with **Sunset Sails** *(sunsetsailstours.com; from US$20)* takes you around Manuel Antonio's beaches and offshore islets, past historical sites like the Quepoa Indian Burial Grounds, and through the crystal blue waters where dolphins and migrating whales often play.

Glide Through the Mangroves

Kayak the waters of Damas Island

Damas Island is a small mangrove-laden peninsula just outside Quepos, with abundant wildlife. Join a kayak tour through the area to see some of the monkeys, sloths, herons and mangrove hawks that call the estuary home – the best are run by **William Mangrove Tours** *(williammangrovetours.com; from US$80)*, a family-owned local operator. William is

continued on p336

SLOTHS OF COSTA RICA

Of the six sloth species in the world, two of them are native to Costa Rica – the Hoffmann's two-toed sloth and the brown-throated three-toed sloth. Of the pair, the three-toed is slightly more active, while the two-toed is primarily nocturnal, so if you see one during the day, it's likely to be hanging upside down having a nap (sloths can spend up to 90% of their lives hanging upside down).

A few other fun facts? Sloths can live up to 12 years in the wild; they're actually quite good swimmers; and once a week they risk their lives to head to the ground and poop, although biologists still don't know why they won't poop from the trees.

EATING IN MANUEL ANTONIO: INTERNATIONAL FARE

Varuna: Lovely little vegan cafe serving creative savory dishes, delicious desserts and smoothie bowls to the health-food crowd. *8am-9pm* $$

Samui Thai: With views that reminded the owner of her home in Koh Samui, this Thai joint is as authentic as it gets, albeit a bit expensive. *12:30-9pm* $$$

Falafel Bar: Laid-back falafel bar with counter service and a buffet of toppings for your Middle Eastern wrap. *10am-9pm* $$

Namaste Indian Restaurant: Mouthwatering Indian dishes served with sunset views in a charming dining room. Date- and family-friendly. *noon-10pm* $$

AUTUMN SKY PHOTOGRAPHY/SHUTTERSTOCK

Playa Espadilla Sur

TOP EXPERIENCE

Parque Nacional Manuel Antonio

The Parque Nacional Manuel Antonio is the most popular protected area in Costa Rica, receiving more visitors than any of the other national parks, even though it's one of the country's smallest. Wander through tropical forests, mangroves and along postcard-perfect white-sand beaches, all the while keeping your eyes peeled for the hordes of animals that call this park home.

DON'T MISS

- Playa Manuel Antonio
- La Trampa
- Playa Espadilla Sur
- Playa Puerto Escondido
- Sendero Punta Catedral
- Sendero El Perezoso

History

Manuel Antonio National Park was born from community efforts. In the late 1960s, as plans for development appeared, local residents realized the need for conservation and began advocating for preservation of the zone. Their voices were heard, and in 1972 the government named 682 hectares of land the Parque Recreativo Nacional Playas de Manuel Antonio (National Recreation Park Beaches of Manuel Antonio), with another 61 hectares added in 1984.

PRACTICALITIES

Scan this QR code for more information on opening times and entrance passes. Entry is timed and ID is required.

Wildlife

Manuel Antonio is home to nearly 350 unique plant species, 184 types of birds and 109 of mammals, with two- and three-toed sloths, white-faced capuchin monkeys and scarlet macaws being some of the park's most popular. Also look out for for howler monkeys, titi monkeys, coati, agouti, toucans and white-tailed deer, along with plenty of marine life and corals if you remembered to bring your snorkel.

Guides & Tours

You don't need a guide to visit the park, but a knowledgeable guide (carrying a high-powered telescope) will enhance your experience, and even if you aren't part of a tour, you can easily hire a guide at the park's gate. While they're not officially the park's staff, guides stationed outside the entrance are specially licensed to work within its confines, and are extremely informative about the local flora and fauna.

Hiking Trails

The park has 11 trails of varying lengths and difficulty levels; at times, some may be closed for maintenance, especially in the rainy season. Others, like the **Sendero La Catarata**, which leads you to the park's only waterfall, are only worth taking during or just after the rainy season, as the waterfall dries up during the rest of the year.

One of the first habitats you'll see when entering the park are the mangroves, a salt and fresh-water habitat that covers about 18 hectares of the park. Try to spy for the tiny red crabs scurrying as you walk along **Sendero El Perezoso**, a raised-walkway trail.

Beaches

There are four beaches within the park limits: **Playa Espadilla Sur**, **Manuel Antonio**, **Gemelas** and **Puerto Escondido**.

Espadilla Sur and Manuel Antonio beaches are the closest to the park's entrance, and are separated from each other by the *tómbolo,* or natural land bridge. Both have tide pools and are considered good for snorkeling, although Espadilla Sur does have strong currents at times.

On Manuel Antonio beach, you'll find the remains of a semi-circle fish trap in the rocks, called **La Trampa**, formerly used by indigenous people for catching marine life. Further along, Gemelas beach is made of two gray rocky coves, while Puerto Escondido is a long, idyllic stretch of sand that's the furthest from the park's entrance.

Punta Catedral

Formerly an island, the *tómbolo* turned **Punta Catedral** into a peninsula, and it's great for views and monkey-spotting. There are three lookout points on the ocean side of **Sendero Punta Catedral**, the trail offering wide sea views and, in season, the possibility of seeing a migrating humpback whale or two.

ACCESSIBILITY

Manuel Antonio is considered to be one of the more accessible national parks in Costa Rica. Some of its main trails are wheelchair-friendly, like **El Manglar,** a 726m path that begins at the park's entrance and is built on wide, flat, raised platforms with interpretive and Braille signage as well as 10 resting points along the way. With prior reservation the park also provides amphibious chairs to enter the ocean (2777-5185).

TOP TIPS

- While you're not allowed to bring food into the park, there's a **cafeteria** in the park's center that serves pizzas, burritos, sandwiches and salads, plus coffees, juices and ice cream. There are also plenty of full-fledged restaurants just outside the entrance.

- Swimming is allowed at the beaches within the park's limits, so remember to throw a bathing suit and towel in your bag. There are even showers and dressing rooms so you can change and keep hiking, though note that using soap or shampoo isn't allowed.

MANUEL ANTONIO'S BEST BEACHES

Playa Biesanz: This river-meets-white-sand beach with breathtaking backdrops and exceptional snorkeling (on clear days) is a fan favorite.

Playa La Macha: Secluded beach kept free of crowds thanks to its lack of direct car access (it's about a 40-minute hike from the main road).

Playa Espadilla: Manuel Antonio's town beach is where you'll find all the action. Easily accessible, breathtakingly beautiful and full of fun.

Playitas: The far north end of Playa Espadilla is accessible by a 4WD-friendly road. Parking is limited; expect surfers on swell days.

Playa Manuel Antonio: Located inside the national park, this beach gives you a look at what life was like before humans came to town.

PHOTO_TRAVELLER/SHUTTERSTOCK

Damas Island mangroves (p333)

contined from p333

a former marine biologist whose passion for wildlife clearly shines through. Those less intent on paddling can opt for an equally educational boat tour – either way, the trip ends with a delicious home-cooked meal.

Zipping Away

Take a ride on the Zip Coaster

Manuel Antonio's **Zip Coaster** *(manuelantonioadventurepark.com; from US$12)* is quite a fun ride, located along the main road just below El Avión. Somewhere between a zipline and a roller coaster, it takes you along a winding, up-and-down path through the treetops that's not for the faint of stomach. If you're nervous about canopy tours, opt for the motorized-bike tour, which allows you to sit down as you calmly glide through the air, without worrying about hanging on or how you'll stop. It's perfect for smaller children, too.

EATING IN MANUEL ANTONIO: EASY EATS

Soda El Angel: The best local eats on the hillside – the perfect mix of good value and great taste. Getting a table can be tricky. *6:30am-9pm Fri-Wed* $

El Patio de Café Milagro: Exceptional coffees and tasty meals, served up with a wonderful view. Its sibling, Café Milagro, is in nearby Quepos. *6:30am-9:30pm* $$

Emilio's Cafe: Long-standing favorite known for its breakfasts, hearty meals and exceptional views. Don't miss the cake. *7am-9pm Wed-Mon* $$

Restaurante Cerdo Feliz: Easy eats – burgers, burritos, *ceviche* and pork ribs – with friendly service at great prices. *8am-10pm Tue-Sat, from 10am Mon* $$

Beyond Manuel Antonio

Rainforest romps, wildlife refuges, coastal treks and Tico-town fun all await in the areas outside Manuel Antonio.

While it's been overshadowed by its shiny new neighbor, the dusty *pueblo* of Quepos, just northwest of Manuel Antonio, is still the best place to escape the expat crowd and get back to some local-style living. Named after its original indigenous inhabitants, the little town is also the top site in the area for sportfishing or for heading off on a rather extreme coastal hike to all of the nearby cove beaches. For a different kind of activity, push inland, where both a wildlife reserve and a community ecotourism project sit hidden in the jungle, offering you more sustainable options for enjoying the beauty of this Central Pacific paradise.

Places

Quepos

TIME FROM MANUEL ANTONIO: **8 MINS**

Main Quepos haunts

Quepos is best known as the gateway town to Manuel Antonio, but this square-shaped local hamlet has quite a lot going on in its own right. Start off at **El Malecón**, Quepos' seafront boardwalk, where you can stroll along the sand and take in the ocean views. If you're in town on a Friday (noon to 8:30pm) or Saturday (6am to noon), you'll find the Feria del Agricultor, or Quepos' **Farmers Market** *(facebook.com/feriadelagricultorquepos)*, just below El Malecón, where you can purchase locally grown produce, handmade crafts and Costa Rican delicacies.

At the far left end of the Malecón (looking at the ocean) is the **Marina Pez Vela** *(marinapezvela.com)*, the defacto social gathering location for tourists and expats alike, while just below the breakwater by the beach is the surfers' gathering point – a mellow left-hand wave that's perfect for longboarders. On the southern side of the marina you'll find one of the town's best-kept secrets, **Parque Nahomi**. This peaceful oceanfront park is a local favorite for swimming, sunsets and kayaking.

GETTING AROUND

Buses run between Manuel Antonio and Quepos, and the hikes are easily accessible from either town. If you're looking to head up to any of the rainforest destinations, however, you'll need to have your own set of wheels or organize with a tour group, taxi or shuttle in order to get to and from sites that are further out of town.

SPORTFISHING SEASON

Quepos has been one of the country's sportfishing meccas ever since 1991, when a world-record 26kg black snook was landed near Mogot, one of the area's coastal islands. Visitors flock to the Marina Pez Vela (p337) hoping for their own big-game trophy – although note that what you'll catch depends on the time of year you plan to visit. Sailfish, for example, are most abundant from November to April, while marlins are found across the zone from September to November. Yellowfin-tuna season covers both those windows, while snook season runs from March through May (and sometimes September to November as well). Dorado can be found from late May to October, while wahoo, snapper and roosterfish are possible catches all year round.

KAREN BURGESS/SHUTTERSTOCK

Finca Anita

TIME FROM MANUEL ANTONIO: **25 MINS**

Saving the rainforest's wild residents

Located on 33 hectares just inland of Quepos, **Kids Saving the Rainforest** *(kidssavingtherainforest.org; adult/child US$60/45)* is a wildlife rescue, rehabilitation and conservation center that started as its name suggests– two little kids who wanted to save the rainforest. Janine Licare and Aislin Livingstone created the nonprofit in 1999, when they were only nine years old, pooling their pocket money to facilitate reforestation and conservation work. Years later, the center is an educational campus where visitors can learn about the challenges facing the Costa Rican rainforest, and about the projects that help to save endangered animals. Book a 1½-hour guided walking tour through the on-site sanctuary to learn about the history and mission of the nonprofit and the group's recent schemes. You'll get to meet the center's animal residents – sloths, spider monkeys, kinkajous – unfit to be released into the wild, and hear their stories. There's also an option for jungle night tours.

Quebrada Arroyo

TIME FROM MANUEL ANTONIO: **1 HR**

Eco-adventures at Los Campesinos

Up in the hills, in the small village of Quebrada Arroyo, a group of local families gathered together and decided they wanted to share their piece of paradise with the world. **Los Campesinos Ecolodge** *(loscampesinosecolodge.com; day visits from US$11)* is the result, and this lovely community-tourism project is more than worth a visit. On-site you'll find jungle trails, waterfalls and hanging bridges – including a 127m suspension bridge – as well as natural pools, viewpoints and a great local restaurant. There are 15 small cabins available for those who want to spend the night immersed in nature. Roads are rough, so having a 4WD is recommended (although if you're arriving in dry season, you might be able to slide by with a 2WD SUV),

Rainmaker Conservation Park

otherwise opt for the shuttle service from Quepos or Manuel Antonio. Trails are mostly easy and animal-spotting is abundant, making this a great spot for families. Longer, guided treks and horse rides are also available depending on the season.

Parrita

TIME FROM MANUEL ANTONIO: **40 MINS**

Trekking the Rainmaker

Rainmaker Conservation Park *(rainmakercostarica.com; from US$23)* is a tropical-rainforest conservation project with tourist-friendly hiking trails, suspension bridges and waterfalls that's one of the best jungle attractions in the region. The trail itself is well marked and maintained, making it easy to navigate without a guide. There are two routes: the upper, where you'll find the suspension bridges and lookout points; and the lower, with the waterfalls and crystal-clear swimming holes. Opt for a circular route to see it all (we recommend hiking up then down, so you sweat first then cool off after), or choose just one of the trails – the lower route is easier, and better for those with a fear of heights.

WILDLIFE BRIDGES

One of the most difficult things for societies living hand-in-hand with the tropical rainforest is learning how to keep the wildlife safe in the face of human development. Costa Rica has a particularly tricky time with these questions, and vulnerable species are too often found electrocuted or run over on freeways. To combat this, nonprofits work with the government to install wildlife corridors, which connect natural habitats once cut up by roads, as well as wildlife bridges to keep animals from transiting along the power lines. Kids Saving the Rainforest has spearheaded a particularly successful Wildlife Bridge Program that, since its inception in 2000, has built over 170 bridges.

EATING IN QUEPOS: OUR PICKS

Marisquería Sabromar: An all-local seafood joint serving incredibly fresh and delicious dishes at wallet-friendly prices. *11am-10pm* $

La Cuchara de la Rana: Big portions of local food served here; there are some picky-eater menu options as well. *7am-9pm Tue, Wed & Fri-Sun* $

Soda Sánchez: Head to this lovely little eatery with friendly service for *gallo pinto* and *casados* (set meals). *6am-11pm* $

De La Finca: Unassuming spot with a cozy dining room serving dishes made from high-quality organic ingredients. *noon-10pm Mon-Fri, from 5pm Sat* $$

Gabriella's Steakhouse: This intimate, romantic restaurant delivers exactly what its name suggests – in style. *noon-10pm* $$$

Cuba Libre: Terrace grill with excellent views over the marina. *11am-10pm Mon-Fri, to 9pm Sat & Sun* $$

Tentación: Colorful cafe with a cool interior serving beautifully presented plates, salads and wraps made with fresh ingredients. *7am-10pm* $$

Gelatería Amorosi: Ice cream made with real ingredients in a variety of flavors. A perfect way to end your day. *10am-10pm* $

HIKING TOUR

El Reto MAE Hike

There aren't many free activities around Manuel Antonio, but one of the coolest hikes here is free to all – **El Reto MAE**. In Spanish, *reto* means 'challenge,' and MAE (which is also common Costa Rican slang for 'guy') stands for Manuel Antonio Extreme, as this 10km trail began its life as a hiking race. These days, the race is no longer held, but the challenging route is still tons of fun.

1 The Trailhead

The main trailhead starts on the hill behind the Marina Pez Vela, near the Quepos tourist police. There's a sign at the trailhead, and from here you'll start hiking through jungle.

The Hike: The route isn't entirely well marked, but it is beautiful. When the trail seems to split about 800m in, choose the path that goes down.

2 Playa La Macha

The first beach you'll hit is **Playa La Macha**, a secluded cove that's usually free of crowds. Take a quick swim, or continue along the coastal trail. If you'd like to shorten your hike by about 1km, you can start from this point as well.

The Hike: It's only 500m to your next stop, although just past Playa La Macha you'll want to stop and enjoy the fantastic views.

3 Playa La Vaca

This tiny, hidden beach is more than idyllic and only accessible by trail, so it's typically people-free and can be great for animal-watching. Try to plan your hike

SIMON DANNHAUER/SHUTTERSTOCK

Playa Espadilla

around low tide, as the beach virtually disappears at high tide.

The Hike: You'll pass a Reto MAE signpost and two lookout points before arriving at your next destination just over 1km later.

❹ Playa Tulemar

This wide, sandy beach with exuberant vegetation is very paradisiacal, so no surprise that there's a rather large resort hidden in the jungle just behind it. Expect beach chairs and umbrellas, and the chance to buy a cold coconut.

The Hike: It's another 1km up and down forest-covered hills to your next destination. The trail never goes more than 300m from the coastline.

❺ Playa Rocosa

Rocky Beach, as it's aptly called, is rather full of large rocks. If you hit this beach at high tide, you'll be scrambling over said rocks to continue your trek.

The Hike: It's only another 800m to your next destination, with more forest than lookout points.

❻ Playa Biesanz

This small beach cove is gorgeous, although not quite so secluded these days. Popularity has its benefits – you can get a cold beer or coconut, hire a kayak or grab a snorkel before continuing the hike.

The Hike: The last stretch of the walk takes you straight up the paved road until you see a gravel road entrance on your right. Hike down.

❼ Playa Espadilla

End your hike on the far north end of Manuel Antonio's town beach. Stay for sunset, then head up to the main road where you can catch a cab back to your hotel.

Dominical

SURFING | TICO VIBES | ECOFRIENDLY LIVING

TOP TIP

As in many small towns on the Pacific Coast, sunset is a village-wide event. Head to the beach about an hour before sundown with a cold beer or kombucha for social hour, and to watch the surfers put on their nightly show.

Tucked away on the south-central coastline, Dominical is one destination that hasn't yet lost its authentic Tico atmosphere. Like most surf towns, this charming little *pueblo* started its life as a fishing community, growing from nothing in the 1960s and '70s after the road was open from San Isidro to the coast. In the late '80s, expats began to arrive, drawn by the relaxed lifestyle and some great waves, and over time the fishing village grew into a small tourist center, where family-owned restaurants, surf shops and yoga studios share the strip with small guesthouses and ecofriendly supermarkets.

If even that seems like too much tourist action, head just a few minutes down the road to Dominicalito, a small hamlet that's still home to a traditional fishing community. Whether you're here to catch waves, chill out or swim in fresh-water cascades, Dominical is the perfect, jungle-backed escape on the Central Pacific Coast.

Join the Wave Addicts

Nonstop surf

Surfing is the main activity on **Playa Dominical**, and whether you're looking to learn, practicing your skills or simply keen

GETTING AROUND

Dominical can be reached via the coastal highway or the San Isidro road, and it's only a few hours from the Península de Osa, meaning you have plenty of options for heading to and from town. The fastest route from San José runs along the coast, or you can catch a local bus from Jacó or Quepos. If you're heading to Chirripó or Parque Nacional Los Quetzales, take a bus to San Isidro; or to Piedras Blancas if Península de Osa or Panama is your next destination. You can also catch a national flight to the Quepos La Managua Airport and grab a bus or transfer from there.

Once you're in town it's easy to walk around; however, if you're keen to hit up other surf spots or spend time in Dominicalito, having a car is more than helpful. If you visit in the rainy season, opt for a 4WD.

SIGHTS
1 Playa Dominical

ACTIVITIES
2 Costa Rica Surf Camp
3 Danyasa Yoga
4 Dominical Surf Adventures
5 Dominical Surf School
6 Casa Madreveda Holistic
7 Rockstar Yoga
8 Sol Circle
9 Sunset Surf School
10 Todo Sano Surf School

SLEEPING
11 Danyasa Yoga Retreat
12 Hotel Rio Lindo
13 Hotel Tropical Sands
14 Mavi Surf Hotel

EATING
15 El Pescado Loco
16 La Junta
17 Lori Restaurant
18 Moromo Forneria

SHOPPING
19 Eco Feira

to catch some waves, this surfing town has plenty to offer. The main beach is an extensive sand-bottomed beach break that stretches along both sides of the river mouth, with powerful, A-frame peaks that offer open face, long rides and the possibility of barrels if the swell is up. On small swells, the beach turns into a beginner-friendly and longboarding paradise, with consistent, glassy waves. While the best time to surf is just before and after high tide – lower tides tend to bring more hollow waves that often close out – crowds are still heaviest in the early morning and around sunset.

When Dominical is big, you can make your way south to **Playa Dominicalito** for friendlier waves, or if it's too small, head down to **Playa Hermosa** just outside Uvita, the area's swell magnet. At huge swells, the left-hand point break **La Punta** lights up; ask a local to show you the spot.

A Fisher's Life

See, surf and stay in Dominicalito

A traditional fishing town that straddles the Inter-American Hwy, Dominicalito lies just south of Dominical. On the ocean side you'll find a small conglomeration of fishing boats, beachfront businesses and a few resident families, while across the highway is the main community of artisanal fishing families and more than a few surfers.

Playa Dominicalito is known for its soft, beginner-friendly waves, best surfed around high tide (you can rent boards right on the beach), while the town side has a freshwater escape called **Pozo Azul**, a deep-blue swimming hole that's perfect for beating the afternoon heat.

The main expat offerings in Dominicalito are centered at the **Aracari Square** by Casa Kia Ora, where you'll find the

DOMINICAL'S BEST SURF SCHOOLS

Dominical Surf School: The area's only women-owned surf school offers lessons, surf training and female-only surf camps.

Costa Rica Surf Camp: This camp has excellent instructors for all levels of surfers and a location right along the beachfront road.

Sunset Surf School: A family-friendly surf school offering standard surf classes as well as tailored packages for rippers of all ages.

Todo Sano Surf School: Todo Sano's systematic approach to surfing is applicable to all-level surfers and includes photo analysis to help you ace your skill sets.

Dominical Surf Adventures: Family-owned ecotourism company specializing in water-based sports like surfing and white-water rafting.

Kunjani Cafe *(kunjanicafe.com)* that serves delicious lattes and smoothie bowls, plus lovely shops, a salon and massage rooms (Tica masseuse Isa González works miracles; *irag29@gmail.com*).

Stretch It Out

Yoga classes around town

Surf and yoga go hand in hand, so it's no surprise there are plenty of yoga options in Dominical. The nearest to the town's main entrance is **Rockstar Yoga** *(rockstaryoga.org; drop-ins from US$16),* where classes are held at a covered, raised yoga deck by the river and range from Vinyasa set to soul-grooving music, to AcroYoga or slow flows.

Closer to the beach is another hip yoga spot – **Danyasa Yoga** *(danyasa.com; US$16),* whose evening candlelit classes are a real treat. Located inside a hotel and retreat center, Danyasa offers 10 public classes a week.

Dominicalito has a lovely outdoor yoga studio, just behind the town's football field. **The (Yoga) Shala** *(theshalacr.com; drop-ins from US$14)* at Casa Kia Ora offers a daily class at 9am, plus a smattering of pilates, breathwork and meditation sessions during the week.

EATING IN DOMINICAL: IN-TOWN EATS

La Junta: This gourmet cafe and sandwich shop with a secret backyard patio makes everything from scratch using local ingredients. *noon-8pm* $$

El Pescado Loco: Fish tacos, fish and chips and fried-fish sandwiches are all reasons to stop at this laid-back tacos spot. *11am-8pm Mon-Sat* $$

Lori Restaurant: Vegan restaurant and deli serving creative, plant-based fare made with lots of love on a very green outdoor patio. *9am-8pm* $$

Moromo Fornería: Mouthwatering bakery with all kinds of breads, sweet treats and stone-baked pizza, plus cool seating and great coffee. *7am-9pm* $$

RICCARDO OGGIONI/ALAMY

White-faced capuchin monkey, Hacienda Barú

A Reserve to Remember

Explore the offerings at Hacienda Barú

A top choice for hiking and wildlife-spotting in the area is found just off the highway in Dominical. **Hacienda Barú** *(haciendabaru.com; self-guided trails US$17; night tour US$80)* is a 330-hectare private wildlife reserve where most of the area's native species – such as white-faced monkeys, sloths, scarlet macaws and toucans – can be seen. The hacienda was formerly a cattle farm, but in 1990 its owners sold their cattle to dedicate their lives to reforestation, conservation and ecotourism. The effort quickly paid off, and in 1995, with the return of many of the native species, Barú was declared a National Wildlife Refuge by the Costa Rican government.

Explore the 7km of well-maintained trails running through wetlands, grassland, primary and secondary forest and along the beach, or join a night tour or overnight jungle stay to discover what goes on in the forest after dark.

Friday Market Mornings

Shop at Dominical's Eco Feria

Every Friday morning from 8am to 1pm, Dominical hosts the **Eco Feria** *(ecoferiadominical.com),* an adorable outdoor market at the Plaza Deportes Dominical where vendors sell local produce, artisan food, handicrafts and artistic creations. While crafts do outnumber the food stands and the vibe is undeniably hippy, this charming community get-together is very much worth a visit. If you're aiming to get fresh fruit and veg, be sure to arrive early as the stands are few and sell out quickly. For souvenirs, plant medicines, live music or just to enjoy the atmosphere, arrive anytime before the *feria* ends.

The local agriculture producers also offer an online store with weekly deliveries during different times of the year.

RETREAT YOURSELF

Sol Circle: Lovely retreat center up in the hills where sound healing is so prevalent they even have their own on-site music studio.

Jungle Gayborhood: This place caters specifically to the LGBTIQ+ community, with sexuality, medicine and yoga retreats all on the calendar.

Airborne Arts: Looking to fly? Head to Airborne Arts to learn the trapeze and other circus arts.

Casa Madreveda Holistic: A rustic retreat center focusing heavily on holistic healing and the sacred feminine.

Dominical Surf School: Go surfing with really cool chicks at a women's-only surf retreat by a women-owned surf school.

SILVERMANI/SHUTTERSTOCK

TOP EXPERIENCE

Nauyaca Waterfalls

A stop at Nauyaca Waterfalls, considered to be one of the most beautiful waterfalls in Costa Rica, is a must on any Central Pacific Coast itinerary. The massive falls are divided into two sections: the upper, with a 54m straight drop, and the awe-inspiring lower, a 26m magical tiered waterfall that's sure to impress.

DON'T MISS

- Upper falls
- Lower falls
- Cliff jumping
- Swimming
- Horse riding

The Entrances

There are two different ways in to Nauyaca. The first is via the traditional Nauyaca Waterfalls entrance just 15 minutes from the center of Dominical town. From here you can hike, horse ride or hop in the back of a 4WD to the cascading beauty. Alternatively, 30 minutes down the road, on the other side of the falls, is the newly minted **Nauyaca Waterfall Nature Park** *(nauyacawaterfall.com),* which offers groomed trails, easier 4WD access and enhanced customer service for a more seamless adventure.

PRACTICALITIES

Scan this QR code for more information on opening times, tours and entrance passes.

Hiking In

Hiking to the falls is by far the most budget-friendly option; however, this fairly difficult 6km trek isn't for everyone. If you have your own car, you can cut the distance to 4km, but in either case, the main recommendation is to start early. While you can just show up and buy a ticket, reserving one in advance is preferable.

Horse Rides

Horse riding is one of the most popular ways to Nauyaca. Only available at the falls' original entrance, the 4½-hour ride is suitable for all levels. You'll follow the same 6km trail that hikers use to reach the falls, and upon arrival, you'll have plenty of time to swim and enjoy Nauyaca before getting back on your horse to head home. Advance booking is required and the fee includes a guide, your horse, admission to the falls and lunch.

Nauyaca Waterfall Nature Park

From the Nauyaca Waterfall Nature Park office to the park itself it's a 2.7km trip. You can opt to go on foot (it's mostly downhill) or hop on a 4WD to the park's *rancho* (small house), where you'll find hammocks, bathrooms, water and wi-fi. From there, there's no vehicle access, although it's only about a 10-minute walk (again, downhill) to the falls.

Swimming

While the falls themselves are strong, there are plenty of options for swimming. The lower cascades has a huge, 7m-deep swimming pool that's great for adults, while just a few meters further down the river is an easily accessible 'beach' with calm, shallow water that's ideal for kids and families. The upper falls also have a small swimming spot that can be nice, depending on the time of year and the rainfall.

Cliff Jumping

For the really adventurous, Nauyaca also offers an unofficial cliff-jumping option, although it's not for the faint of heart. You'll have to climb up the rocks against the falling water to get to a small, rocky platform about midway up the falls – the local location for jumping off. The height plus the energy of crashing water all around you is as adrenaline-pumping as it gets – and that's before you've even jumped. If you're game, however, ask some of the guides to show you the route to the jump spot (solo jumping isn't allowed).

WHAT'S IN A NAME

While there is also an indigenous legend about a forbidden love, most agree that the waterfall's name comes from one very venomous snake. Long before the falls were a tourist attraction, locals hiking through the area would come across impressive numbers of snakes – the most common being the feared fer-de-lance, a Central American viper species known among the locals as *nauyaca*.

TOP TIPS

- If you want to see the falls without the crowds, make sure you arrive just as the park opens and choose the 4WD option.
- Bring a waterproof bag and a change of clothes – getting wet is inevitable.
- If you're sensitive to mosquitoes, don't forget your repellent.
- Food is allowed, so pack some fruit, snacks and water.
- Unless you're on a horse ride, there's no set departure time, meaning you can stay at the falls until closing time.

Beyond Dominical

The area around Dominical is blessed with extensive, empty beaches, colossal waterfalls and wonderful wildlife sanctuaries.

Places

Dominical is rich with natural offerings, so it's no surprise that areas surrounding the humble surf town would be even richer. As you head inland, you'll find green hillsides where mind-blowingly tall waterfalls sit nestled amongst verdant jungle, and artistic crowds have unique immersive offerings for those looking for a new challenge. Also in the area, a wonderful group of humans committed to conservation run a wildlife sanctuary that's as educational as it is inspiring.

Closer to shore, empty beaches where sea turtles lay their nests provide a blissful escape from the crowds, along with one of the most special culinary experiences in the area. Get excited.

GETTING AROUND

Between Dominical and Matapalo, getting buses (or grabbing a cab) is easy enough, but as you head into the hills, having your own wheels will serve you well. If you're without a car (or without a 4WD), ask at your accommodations about shuttle services or grab a 4WD taxi to get you between sites.

Matapalo

TIME FROM DOMINICAL: **15 MINS**

Enjoy the beach

A little coastal hamlet north of Dominical, **Matapalo** is the perfect place to escape the crowds. There are only a few small hotels in this town of mostly locals, along with a virtually empty beach that stretches off into the distance where you can swim, sunbathe, surf or take a leisurely stroll without a soul in sight. It's also a great place for wildlife-spotting, as there's hardly any noise to scare the animals away. Keep your eyes peeled for monkeys, toucans and sloths; or from June to December, head out at night to catch a glimpse of the olive ridley, hawksbill and Pacific black turtles that come here to nest (peak arrival time is from August to October).

Matapalo Supper Club

Just off the beach in Matapalo, one restaurant is offering a unique culinary experience. The **Matapalo Supper Club** *(facebook.com/matapalosupperclub)*, owned and run by Costa Rican Darlenny and her German husband Daniel, is an open-air, no-fixed-menu restaurant serving exceptional, fresh cuisine based on the best ingredients of the day. Chef Daniel serves huge portions and excels in meat dishes cooked over an open fire; however, the seafood, fresh pasta and carpaccio mains all play starring roles. Dinner is by reservation only, and while service is a bit slow, the dishes offered at the Matapalo Supper Club are very much worth the wait.

MARIDAV/SHUTTERSTOCK

Playa Matapalo

Las Tumbas

TIME FROM DOMINICAL: **30 MINS**

Wonderful waterfalls

More than a few amazing waterfalls await in the hills behind Dominical. While you've probably heard of Nauyaca (p346), there are two other falls not far away that are equally impressive. The first, **Eco-Chontales** *(ecochontaleswaterfall.com; US$10),* sits on family-owned land; it's a relatively easy hike to the falls where you can swim, relax in the sun or even challenge yourself to a 7m-high cliff jump into the water. There's a good local restaurant on-site, as well as some cabins you can rent and a *rancho* for camping if you're looking to stay the night.

For a more challenging hike, head to **Diamante Waterfall** *(pacificjourneyscr.com; day hikes from US$89; overnights from US$135),* one of Costa Rica's tallest at 180m. It's a magical place where you can sleep in a cave behind the falls – an incredible experience for those who like sunsets, night hikes, bonfires, candlelight dinners and (optional) waterfall rappelling. Note that even if you opt for a day trip, guides are required for all hikers.

Learn to fly at Airborne Arts

If you've ever dreamed of running away and joining the circus, **Airborne Arts** *(airbornearts.com; classes US$75)* is the

SEA TURTLES

Although it doesn't have the hype of Ostional, Playa Matapalo is one of Costa Rica's key sites for nesting sea turtles. Olive ridley, hawksbill and Pacific black turtles all come to the beaches to lay their eggs, an event which typically takes place from late June to December. Nests remain in incubation for five to seven weeks before the baby hatchlings are born and make their way to sea, which usually happens from August to November (with September being the most likely time to see both nesting and hatching). During turtle season, volunteers around the country patrol the beaches at night to ensure the safety of the nests, protecting them both from wild animals and potential poachers.

EATING BEYOND DOMINICAL: OUT-OF-TOWN EATS

La Parcela: This ocean-view joint hidden off at the end of Dominicalito beach serves incredible, fresh *ceviche* (marinated seafood). *11am-9pm* $$

nFusion Bistro: Getting to Villas Alturas on-site restaurant requires a 4WD and intense uphilling, but the views and food make it worth while. *7am-9pm* $$$

Scala: This upscale restaurant takes luxe eating to a new level. Food, presentation, service and drinks are all incredible but expect prices to match. *noon-9:30pm* $$$

Beyan: New, unassuming roadside restaurant near Playa Hermosa that surprises and wows with exceptional food and service. *7am-9pm* $$

WILDLIFE SANCTUARIES

There are other amazing wildlife refuges on the Central Pacific Coast, like **Kids Saving the Rainforest** (p338) outside Quepos and **Natuwa Wildlife Sanctuary** (p330) near Puntarenas, to name only a couple.

place for you. Located in the hills above Dominical near the Diamante and Nauyaca waterfalls, this training and retreat center offers cool immersions into the circus arts of high-trapeze flying, aerial silks and partner acrobatics.

Classes are for all levels (from beginners to pro), and all are incredibly fun and confidence-building. You'll end up doing tricks you never imagined possible, like jumping, swimming, back flipping and even being caught mid-air by a professional trapeze artist. It's as fun to watch as it is to do. Trapeze classes run in two-hour sessions, while silks lessons and partner acrobatics are one-hour long. Note: you'll want to wear yoga clothes that cover your belly and legs to avoid skin abrasions, especially on the silks.

Wildlife up high

The Dominical region is home to an amazing wildlife sanctuary dedicated to rescuing, rehabilitating and (in the best cases) releasing sick, orphaned or injured native animals back into the wild. **Alturas Wildlife Sanctuary** *(alturaswildlife sanctuary.org; tours adult/child US$33/17)* has a 24/7 veterinary clinic for injured animals (in case you find a fallen sloth on the road), and is also home to furry or feathered friends who are unable to live a life in the wild. Visiting the sanctuary is a way to support the nonprofit's mission; 1½-hour guided tours are offered by reservation at 9am, 11am or 1pm Tuesday to Sunday. You'll get to see the resident animals while learning about ethical wildlife tourism, including the *#stopanimalselfies* movement that Alturas supports. You can also apply for a volunteer position at the center on a daily or overnight basis, or as a local resident of the Costa Ballena area.

WHY I LOVE THE COSTA BALLENA

Marisa Megan Paska, Lonely Planet writer

The Costa Ballena, which runs from Dominical down to Ojochal, is one of my favorite parts of the country – and it's not just because of the whales. Besides the fact that you can find great, uncrowded waves up and down the coast, or that on a clear day, the diving and freediving around the national park is exceptional, this region has some of the most beautiful beaches you've ever seen in your life, and even the tiny, local town ones are pristine. Mostly, however, I love this region because, unlike other, more popular coastal zones of the country, the Costa Ballena hasn't developed away from its local roots. It still feels like a small string of jungle-backed Tico towns – and just like coming home.

Raccoon, Alturas Wildlife Sanctuary

JEROEN MIKKERS/SHUTTERSTOCK

Uvita

WHALE-WATCHING | BEACH FESTIVALS | UNDERWATER WONDERS

Uvita de Osa, better known as Uvita, is a fast-growing town along Costa Rica's Costa Ballena (which translates as 'Whale Coast'). Its main claim to fame is the Parque Nacional Marino Ballena, the country's first marine national park, where migrating humpack whales come to breed and raise their young.

This beachfront park features a cool whale-tale-shaped beach. While it's best seen from the air, the beach is worth a ground-level visit – as are the rest of the park's beaches, which are beautifully preserved and empty of the typical tourist crowds.

Uvita isn't all oceans and beaches, however. On the land side of town, you'll find hill country, waterfalls and creative communities. And if you take one of the many dirt roads into the mountains, you can still discover some secret natural gems tucked away in the rainforests.

GETTING AROUND

Uvita's bus terminal is pretty large; it's where you can pick up direct buses to Jacó or San José, because the ones going through Dominical might not stop in those places. Buses generally stop running from Uvita to nearby cities after sunset, and taxis between towns can get expensive if you miss your window.

Uvita itself is not a walkable town. Buses will drop you off on the main road near the supermarket, about 3km from the beach. There are plenty of taxis near the bus terminal, or you can walk down the main road and follow the signs for Parque Nacional Marino Ballena.

Get Underwater

Diving and free-diving on the Costa Ballena

Uvita is one of the Central Pacific Coast's most popular areas for snorkeling and diving, largely thanks to its huge preserved marine zone, **Parque Nacional Marino Ballena**. Within the national park are a few great dive sites like Whale Rock, a rock formation just 2km off the coast with thriving coral reefs and an impressive amount of marine life. Another reason is the easy access to Isla del Caño just off the Península de Osa, which has incredible marine biodiversity and excellent dive sites for divers of most levels.

If you've never done a dive before, Uvita is also an excellent place to get certified. Operators like **Costa Rica Dive & Surf** *(costaricadiveandsurf.com; from US$659)* offer Open Water PADI courses for beginners, along with Advance Diver, Divemaster and Rescue Diver for those looking to further their skills.

SIGHTS
1 Catarata Uvita
2 Marino Ballena National Park
3 Playa Colonia
4 Playa Hermosa
5 Playa Uvita
6 The Whale's Tail

ACTIVITIES
7 Bahía Aventuras
8 Ballena Tour
9 Bodhi Surf + Yoga
10 Costa Rica Dive and Surf
11 Freediving Uvita
12 Pacific Expeditions
13 Uvita 360

SLEEPING
14 Bungalows Ballena
15 Cabinas Los Laureles
16 Flutterby House
17 Karandi Hostel

EATING
18 Indómitos Café & Bar
19 Las Esferas
20 Marino Ballena Restaurant
21 Mosaic Wine & Sushi Bar
22 Que Tuanis Café
23 Soda Ranchito Dona Maria
24 Tribu
25 Whale Tail Brewery CR

TOP TIP

The Whale Coast lives up to its name. Twice a year, from July to November and December to March, throngs of humpback whales visit the shores. You can see them from land, breaching in the distance, or join a whale-watching tour to get up close to these majestic creatures.

For an alternative underwater experience, consider exploring the ocean without an oxygen tank. **Freediving Uvita** *(freediving-uvita.com; from US$140)* offers free-diving tours, PADI free-diving certification and even spearfishing expeditions for qualified free-divers (spearfishing courses are also available).

Humpback-Spotting

Whale-watching galore

The Costa Ballena, aka the Whale Coast, isn't just a name. Every year, thousands of humpback whales migrate to this part of the Costa Rican coastline, stopping in the area's temperate, food-rich waters to breed and rear their young.

There are two different migrations during the year. From late December to early March, humpbacks arrive from the areas around California and Washington state, USA; mid-July to November brings the southern-hemisphere humpbacks, migrating up from Antarctica.

While there are often other species of whales around – including false orcas and pilot whales – the humpbacks are the main draw, and there are plenty of boat tours in the area that will get you up close to these gentle giants.

EATING IN UVITA: BEST LOCAL OPTIONS

Que Tuanis Café: One of the area's best *sodas* serves tasty *gallo pinto*. Friendly service and fair prices. *7am-8pm* $

Las Esferas: This restaurant close to the park's main entrance has some of the best Tico food in the area. Expect big portions. *7am-9pm* $$

Soda Ranchito Doña María: Breakfast and lunch joint offering the best-value around, serving flavorful, slow-cooked meals in a friendly setting. *7am-4pm Mon-Fri* $

Marino Ballena Restaurant: Ranch-style restaurant serving local and international fare, plus drinks and cocktails. *6:30am-10pm Mon-Thu, to 11pm Fri & Sat, to 9pm Sun* $$

If you're looking to join a tour, **Bahía Aventuras** *(bahiaaventuras.com)*, **Ballena Tour** *(ballenatourcostarica.com)* and **Pacific Expeditions** *(pacificexpeditionscr.com)* are all reputable operators who follow wildlife conservation protocol *(3-hour tours from US$75)*.

Uvita Waves

Learn to surf without the crowds

Uvita isn't a hot spot for surfing, but that fact alone makes it a pretty decent place to catch a wave. While the waves here aren't world-class, there's a much smaller number of surfers on this stretch of the Costa Ballena, meaning you might just have the ocean all to yourself.

For beginners, Uvita's Playa Colonia (also called Playa Chaman; p355) is a recommended place to start surfing. Beginners will be able to practice on small, consistent, uncrowded waves within the national park, without having to worry about heavy currents or collisions with other surfers. Book your two-hour beginner class with **Uvita 360** *(uvita360.com; from US$65)* or head to **Bodhi Surf & Yoga** *(bodhisurfyoga.com; from US$65)* for surf lessons, surf clinics or week-long surf and yoga camps.

Experienced surfers should head north of town to Playa Hermosa (p343), a beach-break swell magnet that typically offers slightly bigger waves than Dominical on any given day. There are lifeguards on-site, but strong currents are prevalent.

Live Your Cowboy Dreams

Horse-riding paradise

Rancho La Merced *(rancholamerced.com; hikes from US$40, horse riding from US$65)* wears many hats. Besides being the annual site of Envision Festival (p356), this is a wildlife reserve that encompasses 506 hectares of primary and secondary tropical forest, mangrove and beach zones adjacent to the Parque Nacional Marino Ballena. It's part of the Path of the Tapir Biological Corridor, is Blue Flag–certified, and on top of all that, it's a working cattle ranch where you can realize your dreams of becoming a Costa Rican cowboy.

While its main activity is cattle breeding, the ranch is open to tourists looking to hike the reserve's trails, horse ride along the beach or immerse themselves in life on the farm, learning cowboy skills such as how to rope, ride and herd cattle, check cows and calves and more.

WHALES & DOLPHINS FESTIVAL

Every September, at the height of the humpback-whale migration, the local community comes together to celebrate the gentle giants that grace the coastline during the **Festival de Ballenas y Delfines** (Whales and Dolphins Festival). Uvita hosts a community fair with traditional dances, art displays, live music, food, vendors and more, while tour operators provide educational information about whales and dolphins to promote conservation efforts in the region. Visitors of all ages can learn about the role humans play in supporting the large marine populations, highlighting the significance of sustainable and ecofriendly practices. There's also the opportunity for discounted whale-watching tours for the duration of the festival.

CL-MEDIEN/SHUTTERSTOCK

Punta Uvita (the Whale's Tail)

TOP EXPERIENCE

Parque Nacional Marino Ballena

Stretching along 15km of pristine coastline between Uvita and Piñuela beach, Parque Nacional Marino Ballena protects some of the most important coastal, transition and marine zones in the country. Created in 1992, the national park aims to preserve the delicate ecosystem of mangroves, beaches, coral reefs and especially whale-breeding grounds found around Uvita.

DON'T MISS

- The Whale's Tail
- Wildlife-spotting
- Islas Tres Hermanas
- Isla Ballena
- Playa Uvita
- Playa Colonia

Under Water

The national park protects 5160 hectares of marine area, principally located around the breeding and nursery grounds for the visiting humpback whales.

The massive marine mammals aren't the only ones that benefit from the conservation zone, however. False orcas and pilot whales are often also present, along with spotted, beluga and bottlenose dolphins, olive ridley turtles, Pacific sea turtles and more.

PRACTICALITIES

Scan this QR code for more information on opening times and entrance passes.

The park's area also encompasses a few islands, like **Isla Ballena** (Whale Rock), a rock formation 2km from shore that's home to a number of birds and iguanas as well as coral reefs and their inhabitants, as well as **Islas Tres Hermanas**, three offshore rock formations important for nesting sea birds.

Beaches

Although Parque Nacional Marino Ballena's coastal zones only amount to 171 hectares of land, the park protects some of the most beautiful beaches in the country. All of the park's beaches are blissfully uncrowded – although you'll sometimes find families with hammocks and grills set up between palm trees – but do require an entry fee to visit. **Playa Uvita** is the main beach, with the best access to the Whale's Tail, while Bahía, **Colonia**, Ballena, Arco and Piñuela beaches are all good alternatives if you're looking for solitude.

The Whale's Tail

One of Parque Nacional Marino Ballena's main draws is Punta Uvita, more commonly known as the **Whale's Tail**.

This *tómbolo,* or natural land bridge, when seen from above, is the spitting image of a whale's tail – all too fitting on a coastline that attracts more humpbacks than anywhere else in the country.

The *tómbolo* is the result of natural sedimentation caused by converging currents, and is only visible (and can only be visited) at low tide. While the best way to see the tail is from up high, if you don't have access to an airplane, you can drive up into the hills just behind Uvita for views from the road. Walking along the Whale's Tail is also worth the experience.

Check the tide charts, then head to the park's main entrance at Bahía Ballena, from where it's only a 15- to 20-minute walk to the tail. The rocky formation is covered with tide pools teeming with life, and also offers excellent views of the jungle-backed coastline. Note that there's no shade, and sturdy shoes may help for walking along the rocks.

Onshore Wildlife

Onshore, Parque Nacional Marino Ballena is teeming with diverse wildlife. Many of Costa Rica's famous monkeys – including howler, capuchin and squirrel monkeys – are present, along with two- and three-fingered sloths, raccoons and even the occasional puma or ocelot. If birdwatching is more your style, look out for toucans, sandpipers, pelicans and white-tailed hawks, amongst other feathered flyers.

Entrance Fee

Parque Nacional Marino Ballena has four official accesses, all located just off the South Inter-American Hwy: Uvita, Colonia, Ballena and Piñuela. It costs US$7 to enter (free for children under 11 and seniors), and your fee is good all day for multiple entries at any of the park's beaches.

MARINE ANIMALS

Humpback-whale-watching in season happens twice a year (mid-July to November and late December to early March), during which time you can see these majestic beasts even from shore. There are also plenty of marine animals during the rest of the year, like the resident dolphins that are ever-present in the area, numerous sea turtles that come here to nest, or manta rays, sharks and parrotfish that sometimes appear near the rocky outcroppings.

TOP TIPS

- If you arrive before or after the official opening hours, the gates may be closed.
- Pets are not allowed in the park, meaning you can't bring your dogs to the beach here.
- Alcohol and smoking are prohibited within the park.
- While campfires are not allowed, above-ground BBQ stoves are okay if you're planning a picnic lunch.
- Snorkeling is permitted from shore, but diving fins are not allowed.

BORUCA & THE PARK

The indigenous Boruca people have an important connection with the Parque Nacional Marino Ballena. Although the tribes live in the mountains and are best known for their colorful masks, they also have another art that has connected them to the beaches around Uvita throughout their history. During the waning moon, the Boruca would travel down to the beaches of the Costa Ballena to carry out an important tradition – the natural dyeing of threads and fabric using an endemic coastal snail, known as *múrice*. The unique purple color of Boruca clothes is testament to of this tradition, and although it's undertaken quite rarely in the modern era, the park concedes free entry to all Boruca, as its grounds are considered a part of their cultural heritage.

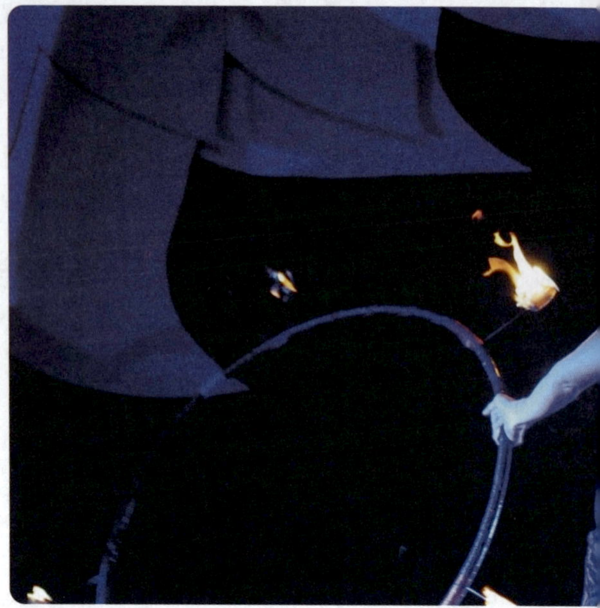

Festival Daze

Join the area's largest music festival

Every year in early March, a horde of spirituality-seeking electronic-music lovers gather near Uvita for a four-day music, art and movement festival. Held just outside Playa Hermosa, on the grounds of Rancho La Merced, **Envision Festival** *(envisionfestival.com)* attracts over 8500 attendees from around the world.

During the day, expect art, workshops, performance artists, an artisan market and full agendas of yoga, meditation and spirituality classes. Music performances take place mostly at night, and range from house, techno and world bass to reggae beats or the more psychedelic trance or 'medicine music.'

Local opinions about the festival are mixed – while it does bring economic benefits, some argue that the large influx of festival crowds disrupts the laid-back local lifestyle and can have a negative impact on the area's fragile, protected environment.

Whether you opt to attend or not, expect a much higher number of people at the beach, waterfalls and restaurants if you're in town during festival time.

LINDSAY FENDT/ALAMY

Envision Festival

A Waterfall with a Twist

Enjoy the Catarata waterslide

Just inland of Uvita's main road, a verdant, waterfall-filled jungle paradise awaits. While you won't find any skyscraper-size falls like around Dominical, there's one waterfall in Uvita that's quite popular (and inexpensive), **Catarata Uvita**, a small waterfall and swimming hole with a natural waterslide along one of its cascades. It's located only about 1.5km from the main drag – an easily accessible five-minute drive or 30-minute walk.

There are two entrances to the falls, and both are privately owned. They each have bathrooms, parking and a small restaurant. The lower entrance, called **Catarata Uvita y Jardín de Mariposas** (Uvita Waterfall and Butterfly Garden), is closer to town and has a small butterfly garden as well as a larger parking area (US$4). The upper entrance (US$3) has less parking. Both offer well-maintained trails to the falls, and both are quite popular, so come early to beat the crowds.

BUTTERFLY-SPOTTING

There are over 1200 species of butterflies in Costa Rica, and at the lower entrance of the Catarata Uvita, there's a small butterfly garden where you can see some of these beautiful flying insects. Keep an eye out for some of the most notable. The blue morpho is a favorite – it's one of the world's largest butterflies, with wingspans reaching up to 20cm, and an iridescent-blue color that's actually an optical illusion from the light-reflecting scales on the backs of its wings. You might also see a glasswing butterfly – there are 64 different types of glasswings, all with completely transparent wings – or an owl butterfly, a nocturnal species whose wing patterns resemble an owl's eyes.

EATING IN UVITA: INTERNATIONAL EATS

Indómitos Café & Bar: Veggie restaurant that knocks every dish out of the park, from smoothie bowls to farm-fresh salads, wraps and croquettes. *11am-8:30pm* $$

Whale Tail Brewery CR: Family-friendly microbrewery and gastropub with a rock-and-roll soundtrack and chilled atmosphere. *noon-9pm Tue-Sun* $$

Mosaic Wine & Sushi Bar: Chic, open-air wine and sushi bar, serving cocktails and tapas that are as delicious as each other. *noon-9pm Mon-Sat* $$

Tribu: Fresh, healthy eats served in style at this fairly priced establishment that favors using locally grown ingredients in its dishes. *1-8pm Tue-Sat* $$

Beyond Uvita

Amazing haute cuisine and isolated villas, stupendous sea caves you can kayak through and inspiring conservation projects lie just beyond Uvita.

Places

GETTING AROUND

Although there are a few public buses, the area around Uvita is best explored by car. Ojochal is accessible by public transportation, but getting in and around town is much easier with your own wheels – plus, to access many of the best B&Bs, it's 4WD or bust. You'll need to take a car, taxi or tour to get you to Playa Ventanas, and if you're heading to see the turtles further south, a 4WD vehicle is required.

While Uvita itself has some incredibly cool offerings, there is so much more past the town limits. In the areas surrounding this Tico town you'll find dark-sand beaches with seductive sea caves; just 20 minutes to the south, there's a fine-dining paradise and hidden luxury cabins that are the perfect spot for a jungle getaway.

Don't miss a stop by one of the area's impressive nature conservation projects. While one group is saving endangered sea-turtle populations and protecting vulnerable nesting sites, the other is working to restore the area's coral reefs, protect the marine park and educate the population on sustainable practices that can help save our oceans.

Ojochal

TIME FROM UVITA: **20 MINS**

A hidden, hillside town

Ojochal doesn't seem like much on arrival. This tiny enclave is spread along a few streets, culminating at a supermarket and *soda* with not much else in sight. Look a bit deeper, however, and you'll find that this expat favorite is a hot spot for a reason.

Most visitors are drawn by the area's high-end culinary offerings. Although restaurants skew on the more expensive side, this foodie paradise offers fusions of French, European and Costa Rican flavors in the jungle version of a fine-dining setting.

If you decide to stay, you'll also find that Ojochal offers incredible accommodations, with secluded cabins and B&Bs immersed in pristine swaths of jungle yet with magnificent ocean views. Grab your 4WD and enjoy a weekend escape.

Catch some live music

Ojochal is spread out, secluded and typically pretty quiet. Most tourists come here for peace and quiet, meaning that there's hardly any nightlife to be found. If you are really keen to mingle, however, there are two decent options for live music in town.

The first is the **Bamboo Room** (*almacr.com*; p360), a cool restaurant and bar at the Alma de Ojochal Hotel with sunset views and live music sets on Friday, Saturday and Monday evenings at 6pm. Option two is **Los Gatos Locos**, a mostly

El Pavón waterfall

Mexican-food joint with live music on Friday and Saturday, and open-mic night on Sunday (also from 6pm). Both close before 10pm.

Discover El Pavón waterfall

Like most towns on the Costa Ballena, Ojochal also has its own little waterfall. While **El Pavón** isn't the largest, it's very peaceful, beautiful and, unlike most falls in the region, still free to visit. Despite its location deep in the jungle, you can usually arrive in any vehicle, although in the rainy season you'll want a 4WD to get there.

You can park near the tilapia farm and follow a short 100m trail to the falls where crystal-clear waters await. Don't miss a stop at the **Tilapias El Pavón** restaurant on your way out for some of the best local food in the area.

Ballena

TIME FROM UVITA: **10 MINS**

Restoring the reefs

While most of the conservation nonprofits in the region work on land, there's one project just outside Uvita that's dedicated to protecting the sea. The **Costa Rica Coral Restoration** *(CRCR; costaricacoralrestoration.com)* project is exactly what it sounds like – a nonprofit organization that works to protect and restore the coral reefs in the Marino Ballena area. Besides having coral gardens where fragmentation reproduction is undertaken, the group also has its own coral laboratory, and is the only coral restoration project in the country working on sexual reproduction.

CORAL BLEACHING

Coral bleaching happens when ocean temperatures rise. The heat forces the corals to expel the algae that live in them (and create their colors), which causes the corals to turn white and become susceptible to disease. While the corals are still alive, they're in a very vulnerable state – a risk to the health of both the reef and all its residents. The most recent El Niño (a cyclical phenomenon during which sea temperatures rise and fall) caused widespread coral bleaching in the Parque Nacional Marino Ballena, which puts both ocean health and local fishing and tourism industries at risk. Reef restoration efforts work to grow and replant healthy coral to support and replace the bleached specimens – especially strains that have proven more resistant to bleaching.

CRCR is located within the park, and the founders work closely with the park's authorities to ensure their work supports both the natural environment and the national park itself. CRCR built park-ranger housing and recently got permission to add public wheelchair access to the beach near their site. The organization is devoted to education initiatives – in 2024, they brought 20% of the local population to their lab to learn about ocean conservation. The official visitors' program is still in the works, but send them a message and they'll happily show you around their site.

Playa Ventanas

TIME FROM UVITA: **13 MINS**

Sea caves adventures

Just over 10km south of Uvita, **Playa Ventanas** is a lovely little beach that's a favorite amongst Tico tourists. Head down the gravel road to the beach (you'll need a car to get here) where you can rent a sunbed, wander the sandy stretch or explore the beach's namesake caves – Ventanas, or tunnel-like 'windows,' can be found on the far side of the beach from the entrance, and are accessible only at low tide.

There are more caves to be explored just offshore, and you can join a sea-kayaking adventure with Uvita 360 (p353) for US$80 to check them out – but be realistic about your sea-kayaking skills, as waves and changing currents can make for a vigorous upper-body workout. If you're game, scan for local wildlife, of which there is plenty. Note that tours are dependent on the tides and waves, and generally don't run in the rainy season.

EATING IN OJOCHAL: OUR PICKS

Panadería del Francés: French-style cafe serving amazing bread, pastries, sandwiches and pizzas. *8am-4pm Mon, to 9pm Wed-Fri, 4-9pm Sat & Sun* $$

Exotica: This fine-dining spot has well-conceived mains, nouveau-French dishes and an impressive wine selection. *5-10pm Tue-Sun* $$$

Bamboo Room: Wonderful classic dishes and excellent seafood, with sunset views and live music. *noon-8:30pm Mon & Wed-Sat, from 4pm Sun* $$

Citrus: The restaurant that put Ojochal on the map offers Asian and French fusion cuisine. *noon-10pm Mon-Sat* $$$

L'Epicerie: Offers ready-made meals and sandwiches plus French-inspired ingredients. *8am-8pm Mon-Sat, to 6pm Sun* $$$

Heliconia: Refined food that caters to the healthier, slightly less fancy crowd. Make a reservation. *11am-9pm Tue-Sat, 2-8pm Sun* $$$

El Castillo: Ocean-view restaurant and bar located inside El Castillo Hotel. It's not family-friendly. *noon-9pm* $$$

Tagua Café: Family- and dog-friendly open-air coffee shop with baked goods, plus a cool community vibe. *7:30am-3pm Tue-Sat* $$

PLAYA TORTUGA RESERVE

Situated along Ojochal's coastline, Playa Tortuga is an important nesting ground for olive ridley turtles, and in 2009, a group of Costa Rican researchers and scientists from the region decided to dedicate themselves to research and conservation of this spectacular species. The group formed the **Reserva Playa Tortuga** *(reservaplayatortuga.org)*, a nonprofit organization focused on scientific research, education and conservation of both the turtles and their natural habitats.

This reserve doesn't have a fixed visiting schedule, and doesn't offer paid tours (although donation is encouraged); however, you can follow its Instagram account to see when baby turtle releases will happen, and join in to see the tiny creatures scurry to the sea for free.

Turtle, Reserva Playa Tortuga
FELIPE THOMAS/RESERVA PLAYA TORTUGA

Places We Love to Stay

$** Budget **$$** Midrange **$$$ Top End

Jacó

MAP p321

Hotel de Haan $ A friendly, laid-back surfer option seconds from Jacó beach, with a massive surfboard-themed swimming pool and a party atmosphere.

Buddha House $ Bold colors and modern art create an artistic atmosphere at this boutique hostel, where the best private rooms are spacious suites.

Jacó Inn $ This hip hostel even has a few private rooms built from a recycled airplane hangar. Plus there are free open-air yoga classes and a cool, community vibe.

Selina Jacó $$ This edition of the Selina hostel empire has a pool and bar overlooking Jacó's surf break, and nicely decorated private rooms and dorms.

Hotel Villa Caletas $$$ With amazing views over the Pacific and a unique architectural fusion, these ultra-exclusive accommodations perched high on a dramatic hillside are worth the splurge.

Los Sueños Marriott Ocean & Golf Resort $$$ With a golf course behind and marina in front, this sprawling resort at Playa Herradura embodies upscale comfort with a hacienda-style aesthetic.

Playa Hermosa

Cabinas Brisa del Mar $ A classic no-frills surfers' crash pad popular with Ticos, this place has basic rooms with air-con and a communal kitchen to boot.

Hermosa Bungalows $$ Two- and three-bed tropical-style bungalows (some with an ocean view) sit surrounding a central swimming pool. With individual owners, each is a bit different.

Tortuga del Mar $$ Sheltered amid shady grounds, this beachfront lodge has nine clean and stylish beach-themed rooms housed in a two-story building, plus an oceanside deck to watch the surfing action.

Backyard Hotel $$ Well-put-together rooms with individual terraces and a communal, beachfront pool that sit just in front of the main surf break.

Manuel Antonio

MAP p322

Art Hostel Costa Linda $ Jovial, tropical digs just a few minutes' walking from the beach or national park. The price point excuses all imperfections.

Peace of Paradise $$ Bungalows and private apartments slightly set back in the jungle, with plenty of wildlife-spotting from your window.

La Vela Boutique Hotel $$$ Secluded boutique hotel a short walk from Playa Espadilla, with a swimming pool and possibly more monkeys than guests.

La Mariposa Hotel $$$ Three-star hotel with exceptional views over the ocean and national park, some private balconies and an elegant on-site restaurant.

Rafiki Safari Lodge $$$ Luxury jungle-safari lodge where tents have beds, bathrooms, hot water and private porches. The pool and waterslide are fed by a natural spring and the jungle is your backyard.

Dominical

MAP p343

Hotel Río Lindo $$ Friendly hotel with comfortable, retro rooms centered around a tropical garden and large pool; near the north end of town.

Mavi Surf Hotel $$ Higher-end surf hotel that's unabashedly painted lime-green. A two-minute walk to the beach, with a clean pool, kitchenettes, surf racks and excellent breakfast.

Danyasa Yoga Retreat $$ Refurbished container rooms set amid tranquil greenery (some are quite snug). There are shared outdoor bamboo showers, a guest kitchen and on-site yoga classes.

Hotel Tropical Sands $$ A lovely little hotel at the southern end of town, with comfortable rooms, hammock-strung porches and verdant grounds almost on the beach.

Pacific Edge Eco Lodge $$ Cozy cabins or fully equipped bungalows perched on a high-up ridge with unbelievable views, plenty of local wildlife and friendly and helpful hosts.

Villas Alturas $$$ Gorgeous posh collection of hillside villas with balconies and awesome panoramic views of the Pacific. Units come with self-catering kitchens.

Matapalo

Jardín de los Monos $$ A quiet, relaxing stay, this adult-only B&B is just steps from the beach, with well-finished rooms, a tropical garden and a swim-up pool bar.

Dreamy Contentment $$ Spanish-colonial-style beachfront bungalows equipped with kitchenettes and terraces – opt for the villa if you're looking for a bit of luxury.

Rafiki Beach Camp $$$ Unique, luxury safari-style beachfront tents – with electricity, tiled bathrooms and hot shower – around a laid-back, ocean-view ranch with a communal kitchen. Sister property of Rafiki Safari Lodge (you can arrive by kayak).

Uvita

MAP p352

Flutterby House $ A collection of colorful Swiss Family Robinson–style tree houses and dorms with an open-air communal kitchen, on-site restaurant and bar.

Cabinas Los Laureles $ This 14-room choice slightly uphill from the main drag offers basic rooms and authentic Costa Rican hospitality, plus an on-site restaurant serving delicious meals.

Karandi Hostel $ Super-comfortable four-person dorms with a central garden filled with lawn chairs, hammocks and local wildlife. It has an open-air kitchen and is a great location for beach-lovers.

Bungalows Ballena $$ Rustic bungalows and apartments that are popular with Ticos and families – it's no wonder, with an on-site playground and a whale's-tail-shaped pool.

Finca Bavaria $$ This German-run inn with tidy, tile rooms, jungle-lined walkways and sweeping ocean views is a great getaway from the crowds.

Oxygen Jungle Villas $$$ Stylish mountaintop cabins constructed almost entirely of glass make you feel like you're part of the rainforest even from your plush, four-poster king bed.

Hotel Cristal Ballena $$$ Hillside boutique hotel set on 12 hectares of private nature reserve, with faraway Pacific views and unrivaled birdwatching.

Ojochal

El Castillo $$$ Perched 180m above the Pacific Ocean, this ultra-luxe hotel is decked out with four-poster beds and rain showers, and has tremendous views from the infinity pool.

La Cusinga Lodge $$$ A lovely ecolodge with breezy wood-and-stone rooms and sustainable practices. The perfect place to unplug and take yoga classes, hike, swim or birdwatch.

WHIT RICHARDSON/ALAMY

Flutterby House

Researched by
Marco Ferrarese

Southern Costa Rica & Península de Osa

UNMATCHED BIODIVERSITY AND ANCESTRAL ROOTS

Immersive jungle adventures, pristine natural wonders and engaging experiences with the country's indigenous past await you in Southern Costa Rica and the Península de Osa.

For travelers looking to experience rural and indigenous culture, the southern region of Costa Rica offers intimate opportunities to connect with the land and its people. You won't find fancy hotel chains, and high-speed internet is scarce, but you will be immersed in the country's biodiversity. Here, visitors will encounter various microclimates and terrains, with infinite types of excursions for every type of traveler. The highlands villages of Los Santos are a coffee lover's dream and a jungle gym for extreme sports enthusiasts. San Gerardo de Rivas is a charming cloud-forest village in the heart of the Cordillera de Talamanca, home to the highest peak in Costa Rica.

The Península de Osa is the most southern region along the country's Pacific coast and also the most sparsely populated. Its 180,000 hectares contain 2.5% of the world's biodiversity, even though it covers less than one-millionth of the planet's surface. *National Geographic* named it 'the most biologically intense place on Earth' because of its abundance of rare flora, fauna and land and marine species that thrive at Parque Nacional Corcovado. Because of the delicate and unique ecosystem, there's a deep focus on conservation amid ecotourism options.

Visitors can also learn more about the indigenous communities of the Brörán and Boruca people in Térraba via museums, workshops and homestays.

BOIVIN NICOLAS/SHUTTERSTOCK

THE MAIN AREAS

LOS SANTOS
Birdwatching in the highlands. p370

SAN GERARDO DE RIVAS
Summit Costa Rica's highest peak. p377

TÉRRABA
Connect with indigenous past and present. p386

BAHÍA DRAKE
Boundless biodiversity. p392

PUERTO JIMÉNEZ
Rural ecotourism, unique nature excursions. p404

For places to stay in Southern Costa Rica & Península de Osa, see p416

LOUIS-MICHEL DESERT/SHUTTERSTOCK

Left: Parque Nacional Corcovado – La Leona (p414); Above: Parque Nacional Corcovado – La Sirena (p396)

Los Santos, p370

Crisp air and the country's cleanest rivers flow in the Cordillera de Talamanca highlands. Watch hummingbirds, toucans and, if lucky, quetzals soar above the cloud forest.

San Gerardo de Rivas, p377

This quaint town attracts expert hikers excited to summit Cerro Chirripó. It also welcomes nature enthusiasts seeking cloud forests and birdwatching adventures.

Guácimo
Caribbean Sea
Moín
Puerto Limón
SAN JOSÉ
Tres Ríos
Cartago
Turrialba
Paraíso
Tucurrique
Lago de Cachí
Cachí
Orosí
Aserri
San Ignacio de Acosta
San Gabriel
Frailes
San Marcos
Santa Maria de Dota
Parque Nacional Tapantí-Macizo Cerro de la Muerte
Parque Nacional Los Quetzales
Los Santos
Providencia de Dota
Cerro de la Muerte
San Gerardo de Dota
División
San Gerardo de Rivas
Parque Nacional Barbilla
Moravia
Río Pacuare
Río Chirripó Duchi
Pandora
Cahuita
Bribrí
Bratsi
Amubri
Río Telira
Parque Nacional Chirripó
Cerro Chirripó
Cerro Ventisqueros
Cerro Terbi
Cordillera de Talamanca
Cloudbridge Nature Reserve
Quepos
Río Savegre
Reserva Forestal Los Santos
Rivas
Parque Nacional Manuel Antonio
San Isidro de El General
Río Chirripó
Cerro Durika
Parque Internacional La Amistad
Cerro Kamuk
Matapalo
Palmares
Cajón
San Pedro
Platanillo
Dominical
Río General
Buenos Aires
Uvita
Bahía de Coronado
PANAMA
Parque Internacional La Amistad

CAR

Driving allows for slow travel, small-town pit stops and epic mountain views. However, consider the dangerous curves of Cerro de la Muerte (Mountain of Death) en route to San Gerardo de Rivas along with bumpy, unpaved roads and spotty cell-phone service in Providencia.

PLANE

The best option when you're short on time and heading to the Península de Osa. It's a one-hour flight from San José into Bahía Drake or Puerto Jiménez in a cozy propeller plane with awesome aerial views.

BUS

A cheaper way to explore the southern region without the stress of driving unknown roads. There are also boats to Bahía Drake and Puerto Jiménez, an eight- to 10-hour journey from San José.

Find Your Way

This region of Costa Rica includes some of the country's most remote areas and unmatched biodiversity. Because of its geography, you can experience highlands, cloud forests, rainforests and one of four tropical fjords on the planet.

Plan Your Time

Take a meandering road trip through serpentine mountain highways and cloud forests. Drive along dirt roads and rainforest paths to fully appreciate this region's spectacular natural beauty and abundant wildlife.

CARMELA SOTO/SHUTTERSTOCK

Cerro Chirripó (p380)

Three Days in the Cordillera

- Hide out in the highlands of **Los Santos** (p370). This remote region is among the best places in Costa Rica to see the mythical quetzals, the multicolored birds sacred to the Maya, and half of Costa Rica's 52 species of hummingbirds. Brave and athletic adventurers can try extreme sports like rock climbing, climbing inside trees or ziplining at Providencia's **Extreme Forest Park** (p372).

- Hike to **Catarata El Pocerón** (p373), a stunning waterfall in the middle of a cloud forest featuring some of the country's cleanest water. You can swim there or at other local waterfalls.

- Coffee fans will be in heaven since some of the best coffee grows here – a tour at **Coopedota** (p375) will unveil the secrets.

Seasonal Highlights

Summer, or dry season, coincides with the high season from December through April. The dry weather is ideal to fully experience the various outdoor adventures, but attractions can be crowded.

JANUARY

Start of the dry season and **high tourist season** throughout southern Costa Rica. It's a great time for traveling, but accommodation prices are higher and it's necessary to book visits to Parque Nacional Corcovado ahead.

FEBRUARY

On the last Saturday of February, runners gather for **Carrera Chirripó** (p381), an annual 21km foot race up and down Cerro Chirripó, starting at 1350m in San Gerardo de Rivas and ending at 3400m at the Base Crestones.

MARCH

March brings the best conditions for **surfing** off the Península de Osa and Golfo Dulce in particular, with consistent waves and sunny weather.

A Week from High to Ancestral Lands

- Traverse **Cerro de la Muerte** (p375) to spend three to four days in **San Gerardo de Rivas** (p377) where **Cerro Chirripó** (p380) – Costa Rica's highest peak – stands tall. If you've been training and have a reservation, you can climb up to spend the night on the mountain before returning the next day.

- For a less strenuous but still magnificent hike, visit **Cloudbridge Nature Reserve** (p384). Savor more gorgeous mountain views as you arrive in **Térraba** (p386), where the indigenous Brörán and Boruca communities live.

- Spend the rest of your week with a local family, learning about how ancient traditions intersect with modern life.

Ten Days in the Peninsula

- Fly or bus it to **Puerto Jiménez** (p404) for 10 days of ecotourism adventures in the Osa. Hike the beachside **Sendero Madrigal** (p415) in Parque Nacional Corcovado's La Leona sector and stay overnight just outside the park on a wild beach.

- Stop at **Matapalo** (p411) the next day and swim with dolphins in a rare tropical fjord or surf in world-class waves. Then head inland to **Dos Brazos de Río Tigre** (p408) to learn about gold mining and spend a few days relaxing and hiking the trails and falls at **Bolita** (p410).

- Take a flight or the *colectivo* to **Bahía Drake** (p392) for epic snorkeling, scuba diving and maybe a day trip to Corcovado's **La Sirena** (p397) sector. Leave Bahía Drake by boat and head to **Río Sierpe** (p399) for a mangrove tour teeming with the Osa's diverse wildlife.

APRIL

Even if these mythical birds are present year-round in this area, April is one of the best times for **quetzal watching** in Los Santos because it's mating season.

AUGUST

Peak **humpback-whale-watching** season begins and lasts until October, though you may see migrating whales throughout April, especially coming from the northern hemisphere seeking warmer waters for breeding and calving.

OCTOBER

The rainiest month in the region, which means slick roads, landslides and flooding that closes parks and cancels excursions. It's best to avoid this season even though accommodation prices are at their lowest.

DECEMBER

Over a raucous three days from December 30 to January 2, the Boruca community celebrates the **Fiesta de los Diablitos** (p387), commemorating indigenous resistance against colonization.

Los Santos

RURAL ECOTOURISM | HUMMINGBIRDS | RIVER VALLEYS

GETTING AROUND

A car is necessary because Los Santos is a spread-out area in the mountains along winding and oftentimes unpaved roads, where there's minimal public transportation – buses to Pérez Zelédon can drop you on the highway turnoffs, but it's a long way on foot from here. A 4WD is recommended when the roads are especially wet and slippery in the rainy season.

A two-hour drive to the southeast of San José in the mountains off the Carretera Interamericana Sur, the highland zone of Los Santos straddles the country's center-south. The three regions of Dota, Terrazú and León Cortés Castro, where most towns have a saint's name, are made up of a series of intermontane valleys in the highlands of the Cordillera de Talamanca, one of Costa Rica's major coffee production areas. The towns of Santa Maria de Dota, San Providencia de Dota and San Gerardo de Dota have developed rural ecotourism and are all reachable by venturing south of Ruta 2 on stunning (it sometimes harrowing) drives on cliffs and alongside the pristine rivers for which the region is renowned. The Parque Nacional Los Quetzales is the guidepost to turn off the highway and begin the descent to Providencia, where four rivers run: Río Brujo, Río Garaffa, Río Roncador, and Río Savegre – considered the cleanest in Costa Rica and Central America.

Breathtaking Birdwatching

Spotting rare quetzals

While Costa Rica is known for its variety of tropical birds (such as toucans and macaws), quetzals are a rare and special sight. These vibrantly colored birds live in specific climates, so you can only see them in this region because of its crisper temperatures and higher altitudes. Quetzals have a cultural and mythical significance to Central America's Maya and Aztec peoples as a sacred and divine bird – connected to their fight against Spanish colonization. You can recognize the machos (males) by colorful plumage that spans their backs, creating the illusion of a long tail. They have vivid red bodies, aqua and verdant-green feathers and a yellow beak to impress their female counterparts while also distracting their enemies. The female quetzals are also colorful but are less bright, so they can camouflage themselves more easily from predators as they guard their nests.

TOP TIP

Arrive before the sun goes down because you'll be driving through a mountainous cloud forest on unfamiliar and narrow, bumpy roads. Give yourself ample time, especially if driving from San José, because traffic is unpredictable. It can be stressful in the dark and you'll miss the incredible mountain and river views.

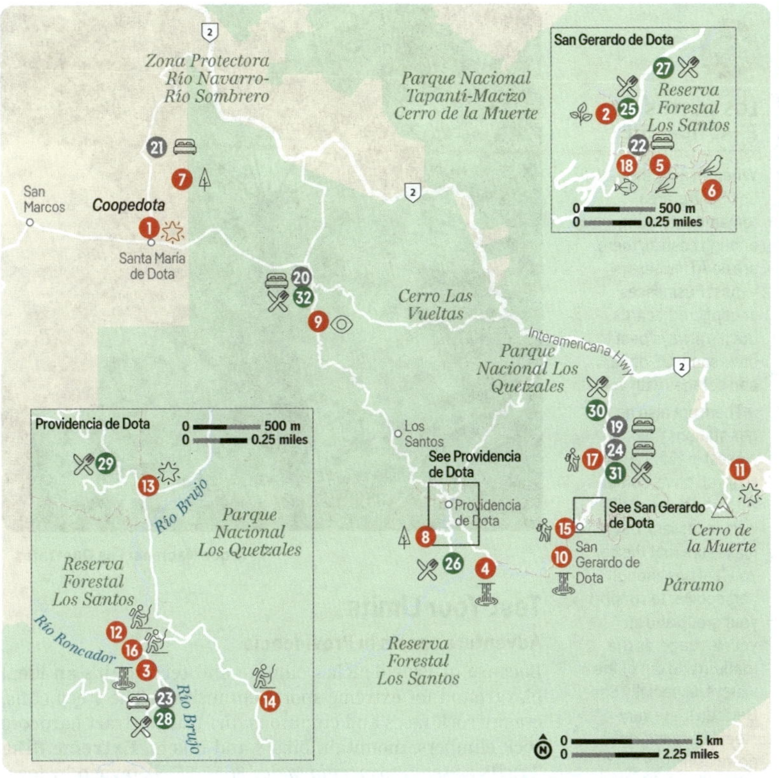

HIGHLIGHTS

1 Coopedota

SIGHTS

2 Batsù Gardens
3 Catarata El Pocerón
4 Catarata el Salitre
5 La Quebrada Trail
6 Los Robles Trail
7 Los Santos Forest Reserve
8 Parque Nacional Los Quetzales
9 Providencia Road
10 Rio Savegre Waterfall

ACTIVITIES

11 Cerro de la Muerte
12 El Oso Maravilloso
13 Extreme Bike Trails
14 Extreme Forest Park
15 La Catarata Trail
16 La Piedra
17 Rio Savegre Waterfall Trailhead
18 Savegre Hotel

SLEEPING

19 Dantica Cloud Forest Lodge
20 El Toucanet Lodge
21 Quinta Galeón Lodge
22 Savegre Hotel
23 Tamí Lodge
24 Trogon Lodge

EATING

25 Alma de Árbol
26 Armonia Ambiental Soda
27 Café Kahawa
28 Cascadas del Savegre
29 Mario's Soda
30 Miriam's Quetzals
31 Restaurante Doña Marlen
32 Toucanet Restaurante

One of the best places to spot the birds is a sprawling farm tucked into a mountain off the main road, accessible via a tour guide. After a 1km hike through lush forest trails, the path reveals majestic views of the Cordillera de Talamanca and acres of green farmland. The quetzals congregate in the *aguacatillo* trees (a cousin of the avocado) sprinkled throughout the farmland, feeding in the early mornings. Your best chance to see quetzals is to start your hike shortly after sunrise to give yourself a few hours of peak birdwatching time.

LOS SANTOS PRACTICALITIES

When visiting the Los Santos area, remember to bring enough cash as there are no ATMs here – most businesses accept credit cards, but it's always best to have some US dollars and colones with you.

There are also no gas stations (the closest is 25km away), so if you drive, come with a full tank. 4WD is unnecessary, but make sure that the car you rent has enough horsepower to support your group and all your luggage, as the roads in and out of the valleys, especially San Gerardo's, are very steep. Likewise, drive down using low gear to avoid exerting your brakes and potentially causing damage to your rental vehicle.

AGA PRZYBYLSKA/SHUTTERSTOCK

Parque Nacional Los Quetzales

Test Your Limits

Adventure sports in Providencia

Because of Providencia's climate and terrain, it's an ideal playground for extreme sports enthusiasts. The steep cliffs, craggy rock faces and circuitous dirt trails attract hardcore rock climbers, mountain bikers and hikers. **Extreme Bike Trails** *(@senderosprovidencia; 8669-2565)*, owned by local guide David Retana, organizes tours through hilly, twisting mountain-biking trails for experienced riders or beginners who want to challenge themselves.

The Cordillera de Talamanca provides natural routes for rock climbing and rappelling during the dry season. Bouldering, a form of ropeless climbing where climbers focus on executing difficult moves near the ground, is especially popular in the area. **La Piedra** (the Rock) is a part of Providencia known especially for boulders ripe for climbing. **El Oso Maravilloso** (the Wonderful Bear) is a highlight for many climbers and is easily accessed on the trail that leads to Catarata El Pocerón.

For travelers who want a less death-defying excursion, there's the **Extreme Forest Park** *(reservation necessary; 2541-2020, info@santostours.net)*. In this adventure park, visitors can

EATING IN PROVIDENCIA DE DOTA: OUR PICKS

Mario's Soda: Family-owned restaurant (part of a lodge) serving tasty typical Tico cuisine. Reservations are required. *11am-8pm* $

Armonia Ambiental Soda: Restaurant and lodgings in beautiful grounds. Dishes use locally grown ingredients from the family farm. *10am-8pm* $

Cascadas del Savegre: Part of the Tamí Lodge, dishes up *casados* (set meals) and fresh drinks amid beautiful mountain views. *noon-3:30pm & 5-8:30pm* $$

Toucanet Restaurante: In Copey de Dota, this lodge restaurant offers refined local dining with locally sourced ingredients, such as trout. *noon-8pm* $$

climb inside a strangler ficus tree, walk across a slackline, single-rope 'Monkey Bridge' 50m above the ground and fly through the air via the 'Tarzan Swing' canopy zipline. It's certainly a challenging workout but lighthearted and fun once you catch your breath.

Discover Los Santos' Cloud Forest

Explore Los Quetzales National Park

Set right off Ruta 2 by the turnoff to Providencia de Dota, **Parque Nacional Los Quetzales** *(sinac.go.cr; US$10)* may disappoint those who come looking for the beautiful bird – although quetzals live in this cloud forest, a tour with a knowledgeable guide is necessary to see them. However, it will reward those who want to experience a less crowded cloud forest or have never walked into one.

The reserve has two linear trails. The **Circular Trail** is a 400m-long concrete path with some metallic stairs passing through dense mossy undergrowth and is the easiest of the two. **Ojo de Agua** is 2km-long and goes through a secondary forest, taking about two hours to complete. It feels a bit wilder because it's unpaved, but if you stay at some of Dota's ecolodges, most of which have private jungles, you may find better trails elsewhere.

Hike to Majestic Waterfalls

Revel in Los Santos' nature

The Los Santos area has quite a number of waterfalls, including a couple of options for those short on time or energy. For a more relaxed experience, visit **Catarata el Salitre**, a small double waterfall that's not swimmable but is quite mesmerizing. It's easily accessible from the main road with clear signage, and only requires a short walk to witness its splendor. Do like the locals and bring food and drink for a picnic. Or take a brisk dip at **Catarata El Pocerón**, a popular swimming hole close to the main road. The waterfall isn't as high as many others in Costa Rica, but the pool is large and refreshing (ie cold).

Another beautiful waterfall is the **Rio Savegre Waterfall** in San Gerardo de Dota, but be warned that the 2km trail's conditions are pretty neglected. The track is fine past some wild swimming spots until the first cascade, but only expert hikers should attempt to reach the main waterfall, which lies 700m ahead on a track whose staircases and bridges are in poor condition – be careful. Start hiking from the **trailhead** near **Trogon Lodge** for about 200m until a trout farm. Don't follow the pink signs on the trees – instead, go past the farm and stay on the trail for another 200m until you see a waterfall sign. The two swimming holes are both within 300m from that junction, and the first waterfall (where you can swim) is further on after a metallic bridge. The second is 700m onwards along a sketchier trail.

QUETZAL HOT SPOT

The San Gerardo de Dota area is possibly the best place to see the resplendent quetzal in Costa Rica. The region is said to host the largest population of the vividly colored bird in the world because of the bountiful supply of the quetzal's favorite food – the fruit of the *aguacatillo* tree. These remarkable birds migrate by altitude, moving up and down in elevation, following the fruiting wild avocado trees. But because the changes in elevation in San Gerardo de Dota's area are so dramatic, there are always fruiting *aguacatillo* trees, which keeps the quetzals in the area year-round. The nesting season from late January to April sees the birds' most active.

BEST BIRDWATCHING LOCATIONS

Providencia Road: By day spot trogons, azure-hooded jays and flame-throated warblers; by night see owls.

La Catarata Trail: Runs along the Río Savegre and is a good place to see the torrent tyrannulet and, if you are very lucky, quetzals.

Los Robles Trail: Inside the Parque Nacional Los Quetzales, tall oak trees host the Costa Rican pygmy owl, spotted wood quails and silvery-throated jays.

La Quebrada Trail: Inside the private reserve of Savegre, this path is full of Talamanca's bird species.

Los Santos Forest Reserve: Bordering Los Quetzales, this reserve is home to many birds and big cats including ocelots and jaguars.

Learn About the Hummingbird

Get personal with the smallest birds in the Americas

Los Santos is one of the world's best endemic bird areas and has possibly the largest number of *colibrí* (hummingbirds) in Costa Rica. An easy place to see and learn about them is **Quinta Galeón Lodge**. Perched at 2050m above Santa Marta de Dota's valley, the lodge offers the **Colibrí Experience** *(hummingbirds-costarica.com; US$100 per person including lunch)*, a four-hour program that starts with a local Terrazú coffee degustation and a presentation about hummingbirds. The best part of the time is dedicated to observing and photographing the bounty of hummingbirds that flock here. The experience is focused on bird photography: in a day, it's possible to see 10 to 15 hummingbird species out of the 26 recorded at this spot – a remarkably high number, considering that Costa Rica has 52 species. The tour ends with a home-cooked lunch served on the lodge's beautiful terrace overlooking the valley.

For a less organized experience, try the bird-feeding terrace at the back of **Miriam's Quetzals** *(miriamquetzals.com)*, a restaurant in San Gerardo De Dota that exploits its position above a cloud forest with feeders that attract all sorts of local birds, including hummingbirds and toucans. You just have to order something from the menu to watch and take photos.

EATING & DRINKING IN SAN GERARDO DE DOTA: OUR PICKS

Restaurante Doña Marlen: Family-run and serving excellent trout, hearty *casados* and sweet treats at reasonable prices. *7am-8pm* $

Café Kahawa: Drinks and alfresco dining at this riverside spot with variations like trout in coconut sauce and trout *ceviche*. *7:30am-6pm* $

Miriam's Quetzals: Popular cafe serving coffee, cakes and Tico meals, but the birds who drop by their terrace feeder steal the show. *7am-7pm* $$

Alma de Árbol: The Batsù Gardens' restaurant has an eclectic local menu with vegan and gluten-free options, homemade bread and freshly caught trout. *11:30am-8pm* $$

ROSALIE KREULEN/SHUTTERSTOCK

Coppery-headed emerald hummingbird

Drink Santa Maria's Coffee

Town and farm tours at Finca Coopedota

Besides hummingbirds, Santa Maria de Dota is famous for its coffee. The local **Coopedota** *(coopedota.com; 8306-2619; US$30 per person; closed Mon)* produces delicious arabica and also organizes educational tours that start with a city tour of Santa Maria and move to the roasting plant, where machines and coffee-making processes are explained. This is followed by a visit to an organic farm and coffee degustations. Coffeeholics can sign up for the **Kaffeina Lover tour** (US$40), which also includes a coffee cupping experience.

Peak Mountain Hiking

Epic views

Driving or hiking up the **Cerro de la Muerte** (Mountain of Death) might sound ominous, but here you'll find some of Costa Rica's most impressive views. At 3451m, it's the country's second-highest peak after Cerro Chirripó (p380) and the hiking trail to the summit will take you through four types of vegetation and two different ecosystems: rainforests and cloud forests.

If you choose to drive, the summit is around 30 minutes from Providencia de Dota, along a winding stretch of the Interamericana Hwy (Ruta 2) known for its dangerous curves, blind spots and monumental views of the Cordillera de Talamanca.

The 15km hike to the peak and back takes approximately 7½ hours. Because of the altitude and terrain changes, this challenging trail is only recommended for people in good physical condition and with some hiking experience. Birdwatchers will be treated to a multitude of high-altitude species along the route. Bring a light jacket and/or poncho to be prepared for cold and potentially rainy weather.

COFFEE COUNTY

Costa Rica is the only country in the world where it is illegal to produce coffee that's not 100% arabica. A 1989 law prohibits planting low-quality beans, pushing local farmers to pursue true excellence. The Tarrazú coffee region in Los Santos, surrounded by the Talamanca Mountains, is one of the most famous among Costa Rica's eight distinct coffee regions, renowned for its red soils that produce excellent coffee with a slightly acidic taste that's heavy in aromas. It has a light, clean flavor and a subtle chocolate hint. Coope Tarrazú is a famous producer in San Marcos de Tarrazú and San Pablo de León Cortés.

PAN-AMERICAN HEIGHTS

Cerro de la Muerte is the highest point on the Pan-American Hwy from Prudhoe Bay, Alaska, to Ushuaia, Argentina - considered the world's longest drive. The name 'Mountain of Death' comes from the past, when crossing from Costa Rica's Valle Central was at least a three- to four-day journey on foot or horseback, causing many ill-prepared travelers to die because of the cold and rain.

The peak is now very accessible, with a drivable track leading from the highway's Km 89 to the peak - a sign marks the Pan-American Hwy's highest point at 3335m. At the beginning of the 20th century, three rest stations were created along the route - one of them, the Casa Refugio Ojo de Agua, has been restored into a small museum.

IMAGEBROKER/MORITZ WOLF/GETTY IMAGES

Cerro de la Muerte (p375)

The trail officially starts at **Savegre Hotel** in San Gerardo de Dota, and because it's private property, hikers are charged a US$10 fee for a wristband to enter. Tours from various hotels in the area can ease navigating this relatively untraveled trail. For something even more challenging, local guide **David Retana** *(8669-2565)* organizes four- to six-day hiking expeditions from Cerro de la Muerte and across the mountains to the coast at Quepos (p337).

An Avian Lover's Heaven

Photograph birds in the Batsù Gardens

Batsù Gardens *(batsucr.com; tours from US$30)* is a must-see for birdwatchers and photographers, especially those interested in hummingbirds. The gardens are designed specifically for photographers to experience the variety of local birds in their natural habitat while catching the best shots. Located in San Gerardo de Dota, 9km south of the Pan-American Hwy, it offers various morning or afternoon packages that include access to the facilities, transportation from area hotels, and coffee and snacks. Even if you're not a photographer, the park offers guided birdwatching tours and a specific tour to view quetzals.

San Gerardo de Rivas

CLOUD FOREST | STEEP MOUNTAINS | FINE BIRDWATCHING

San Gerardo de Rivas is a quaint cloud-forest village 20km northeast of the regional hub San Isidro de El General. It attracts daring hikers, avid birdwatchers and budding biologists and is the home of Parque Nacional Chirripó, which shelters Costa Rica's highest peak, Cerro Chirripó (3820m), the main attraction for most visitors to this less-developed and visited region. Chirripó translates to 'land of the eternal waters' and is a part of the Cordillera de Talamanca, a mountain range within La Amistad International Park split between Costa Rica and neighboring Panama. Even though the Cordillera de Talamanca is home to vast rainforests, San Gerardo de Rivas' altitude surpasses 1500m and spurred the formation of cloud forests with some of the country's coldest temperatures and stunning views. Don't expect a flawless tourist infrastructure, even though foreign developers and expats continue investing in this naturally lush small town, gentrifying it rapidly.

TOP TIP

If you're planning to hike Cerro Chirripó, give yourself time before and after the scheduled date of your hike to acclimate to the altitude and explore the village. Most of all, you'll want to have time to rest and recharge, perhaps in front of a cozy fireplace, after a strenuous but epic hike.

GETTING AROUND

San Gerardo de Rivas is tucked up a steep mountain road leading to Cerro Chirripó's trailhead and is certainly best reached by car. Once in town, the small, steep and windy road is best navigated on foot. If your reason for coming here is relaxing or hiking without the need to visit any nearby attractions, it's easy to get here by bus from San Isidro de El General, 20km away. Hernández Solis *(hernandezsolis.com)* runs four daily departures to San Gerardo de Rivas from the **bus station** behind San Isidro de El General/Pérez Zeledón's market. Buses from San Gerardo de Rivas return to Pérez Zeledón four times daily from 6:30am, from where **Tracopa** *(tracopacr.com)* and **Grupo Blanco** *(grupoblanco.cr)* buses continue north to San José or south to Puerto Jiménez, Golfito and the Panama border at Paso Canoas. Note that there are fewer departures on Sundays. Note also that there are no gas stations or ATMs at San Gerardo de Rivas, so ensure your vehicle has a full tank and you carry enough cash. Most businesses in town accept credit cards, but it's good to have cash for smaller vendors, when leaving tips for cleaning staff, or to avoid extra fees for using a card.

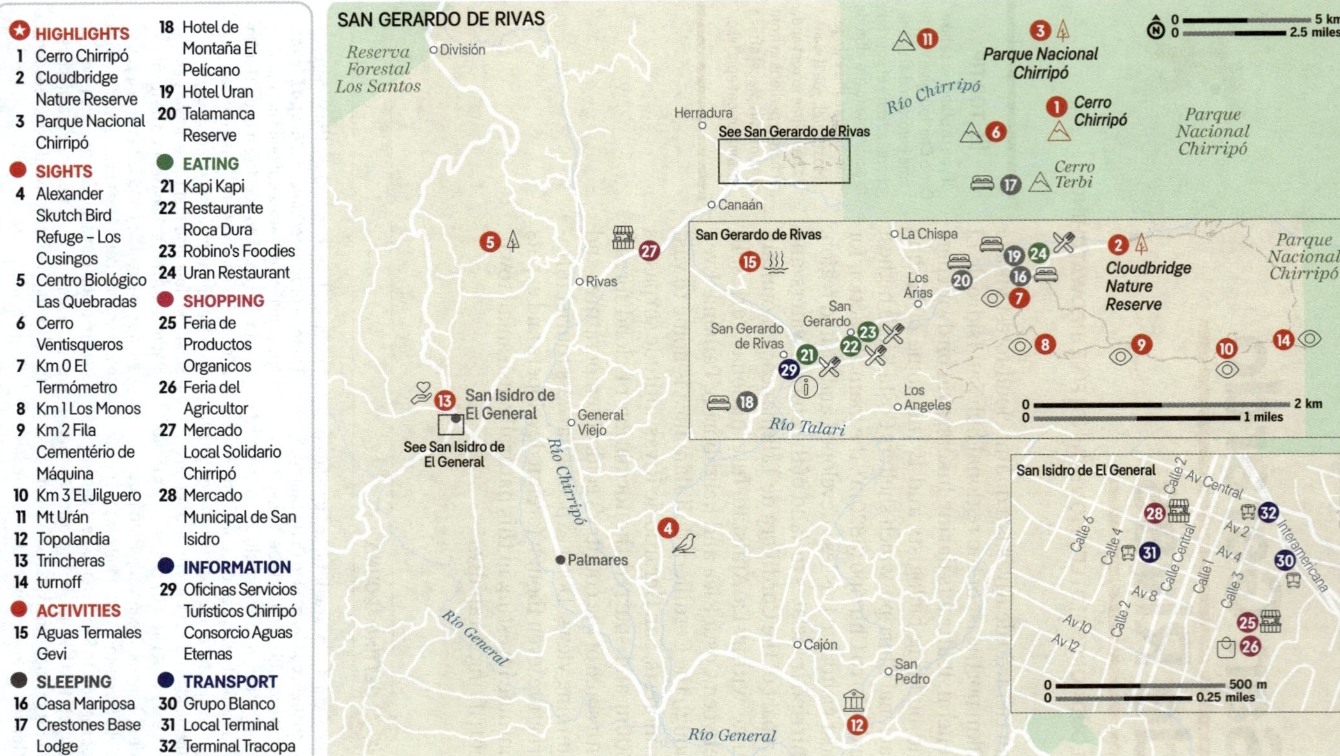

HIGHLIGHTS
1 Cerro Chirripó
2 Cloudbridge Nature Reserve
3 Parque Nacional Chirripó

SIGHTS
4 Alexander Skutch Bird Refuge – Los Cusingos
5 Centro Biológico Las Quebradas
6 Cerro Ventisqueros
7 Km 0 El Termómetro
8 Km 1 Los Monos
9 Km 2 Fila Cementério de Máquina
10 Km 3 El Jilguero
11 Mt Urán
12 Topolandia
13 Trincheras
14 turnoff

ACTIVITIES
15 Aguas Termales Gevi

SLEEPING
16 Casa Mariposa
17 Crestones Base Lodge
18 Hotel de Montaña El Pelícano
19 Hotel Uran
20 Talamanca Reserve

EATING
21 Kapi Kapi
22 Restaurante Roca Dura
23 Robino's Foodies
24 Uran Restaurant

SHOPPING
25 Feria de Productos Organicos
26 Feria del Agricultor
27 Mercado Local Solidario Chirripó
28 Mercado Municipal de San Isidro

INFORMATION
29 Oficinas Servicios Turísticos Chirripó Consorcio Aguas Eternas

TRANSPORT
30 Grupo Blanco
31 Local Terminal
32 Terminal Tracopa

Relax in Nature's Hot Tub

Hot springs and fanatastic panoramas

The **Aguas Termales Gevi** *(US$7)*, San Gerardo's natural thermal hot springs, seem tailor-made to soothe sore hikers' muscles. Two thermal pools overlook the area's vast mountains and valleys, while colorful local birds flutter in the garden's hibiscus bushes. The larger pool looks like a big tiled swimming pool you might see at a community park, while the smaller one sits on a platform above it connected by a small staircase. Don't expect a hot tub or sauna experience. The water temperature is warm rather than hot, which still feels rejuvenating and allows visitors to stay longer and safely without getting overheated or dehydrated. Both pools are also covered so you can enjoy them year-round whatever the weather.

Aguas Termales Gevi is a 10-minute drive from the entrance of Parque Nacional Chirripó. There are bathrooms and changing rooms available, as well as benches for picnicking or leaving your things, so feel free to bring lunch or snacks, or order typical local Tico dishes, like *casados*, at the on-site restaurant.

Spread Your Wings

Enter Costa Rica's birdwatching birthplace

Alexander Skutch Bird Refuge – Los Cusingos *(loscusingos.com; US$20/7 adult/child)* is a 40-minute drive from San Gerardo de Rivas and comprises 78 hectares of land. Some of the most prominent species among the 225 avian visitors that can be seen here are the turquoise cotinga, golden-naped woodpecker, Baird's trogon, black-hooded antshrike and orange-collared manakin, along with tanagers and antbirds.

This private reserve is where Dr Alexander Skutch (1904–2004) lived and conducted his world-renowned research. A well-respected naturalist and expert in neotropical birds, Skutch spent most of his life studying and writing about his findings in Costa Rica. He co-wrote *A Guide to the Birds of Costa Rica* (1989), still considered the preeminent text and the go-to source for birders exploring the country's avian wildlife.

The bird sanctuary is currently managed by the Tropical Science Center that bought it after his death and continues to maintain the property and his mission of conservation. As well as Skutch's home there are two trails. The **Naturalist Trail** is enclosed by tall trees, so it can be more difficult for novices to spot birds. The shorter **Aves Trail** goes closer to the Río Peñas Blancas, so beginners may see more birds. Even if you're an expert birdwatcher, it's recommended to go with a guide since they are local experts and know the land.

ALTERNATIVE ROUTE TO CHIRRIPÓ: EL CERRO URÁN

As if summiting Costa Rica's highest peak from San Gerardo de Rivas wasn't challenging enough, experienced hikers with official guides can also attempt the grueling 43km multiday trek that enters the Talamanca reserve from the west, taking in **Cerro Urán**. The trek heads from Herradura de Rivas toward the hostel at Paso de los Indios (approximately 14.5km), where hikers spend the first night after passing through Urán's peculiar flagstone-type stones. The second day is another 14km to Cerro Urán, which is very close to Cerro Nudo, and finally on to Chirripó. On the second night, hikers sleep in Los Crestones Base Camp and, on the next day, descend the better-known path to San Gerardo de Rivas.

EATING & DRINKING IN SAN GERARDO DE RIVAS: OUR PICKS

Kapi Kapi: Organic smoothies, superfoods and kombucha in a big dining room overlooking the forest. Popular for co-working and relaxing. *10am-8pm* $

Robino's Foodies: Hip pizza place in San Gerardo's square that spills tables on a balcony overlooking the forest. *noon-7pm Sat-Thu* $

Uran Restaurant: Refuge-style restaurant with mountain views close by the Chirripó trailhead, popular for sandwiches, burgers, rice and meat dishes. *8am-10pm* $

Restaurante Roca Dura: Stalwart standby, serving local food, drinks and comfort dishes like wood-fired pizzas. *8am-10pm* $

PAVEL TOCHINSKY/GETTY IMAGES

TOP EXPERIENCE

Cerro Chirripó

Costa Rica's highest mountain is a bucket-list experience for hiking aficionados. On a clear day, you will have breathtaking views of the Caribbean Sea and Pacific Ocean from the peak. But you will work for that view. It's a steep 36km hike round trip, and only 52 permits are given for overnight hikers, making it a rare experience worth bragging about.

DON'T MISS

- Los Crestones Base Camp
- Valle de Conejos
- Chirripó Summit
- Cerro Ventisqueros
- Los Crestones

Chirripó in a Nutshell

Tours start at the San Gerardo Sector entrance of **Parque Nacional Chirripó** for a steep 14.5km hike with a steady ascent to Los Crestones Base Camp, where hikers sleep for the night. Then it's another 5.5km to the top of 3820m-high Cerro Chirripó via Valle de Conejos (Rabbit Valley), the park's most important cirque glacier, which once had many rabbits before weather conditions and human impact dispersed them.

Most visitors do an overnight hike, ascending on the first day, summiting at sunrise the next day, and then heading back down

PRACTICALITIES

- Consorcio Rurál Comunitario Chirripó *(8549-8022)*
- Permits US$20 per per day.

to San Gerardo de Rivas. However, local experts recommend spending two nights at base camp: use the first day to hike up, summit the next day and explore the area and trails around the peak, and then descend on the last day. There are various trails and a lake at the top, including the trail to 3812m-high **Cerro Ventisqueros**, Costa Rica's second-highest peak, and the dramatic rock spires **Los Crestones**. Incredibly strong hikers can summit and descend in a day, but it's a hard slog.

Plan in Advance

Permits to visit the park can be reserved online *(serviciosenlinea.sinac.go.cr)* six months in advance for up to four people and a specific date, and can be paid for using a credit card. Make your reservation as soon as possible, as there's a daily limit for park permits. You'll receive a confirmation email with details about extra payment details for food and lodging at Los Crestones Base Camp. You have five days to confirm your reservation and discuss payment, as non-residents can only pay in person upon registration. Email *info@chirripo.org* or phone *8549-8022* with your entry permit number.

High season, January through April, is the best time to climb because there's minimal rain plus less cloud cover and fog. Weekends, especially during high season, and Semana Santa (Easter Week) are especially popular and sell out months in advance. Consider booking a slot during the week when there is less demand or in May and December when torrential downfalls are less likely.

The park closes the last two weeks of May for trail maintenance and the last weekend in February for **Carrera Chirripó** *(carrerachirripo.com)*, a grueling foot race from San Gerardo de Riva to Los Crestones Base Camp and back.

Spending the Night

No camping is allowed in the park making **Los Crestones Base Camp** *($US35 per person, per night)*, a no-frills dormitory-style lodge 14.5km from the trailhead, the only overnight option. The hotel accommodates 52 guests with beds, bathrooms, a communal dining area with hot meals for sale, and limited solar-powered electricity. Hikers can also bring their own cold food; cooking is not allowed. Don't expect a hot shower after a long day of hiking: there's no hot water and temperatures can drop below 0°C (32°F) at night. While the hotel provides soap, towels, sheets and light blankets, bringing a warmer sleeping bag and appropriate clothing is a good idea.

You need to check in by 4pm at the Parque Nacional Chirripó office to pay for your accommodations, get your permit and wristband for the next day's hike to the summit, as well as the **Consorcio Aguas Eternas** office just down the road from the park's office to pick up food and accommodation vouchers for the base camp.

DON'T TAKE THIS HIKE LIGHTLY

Because of the strenuous terrain and high altitude, visitors should be experienced hikers. This means physical and mental training because of the cold, the rain and the considerable altitude gain. While it's not mandatory, arriving at the base camp before dark is advisable, meaning you'll have to maintain a steady walking pace. Tours often leave before sunrise to ensure plenty of time to arrive in daylight.

TOP TIPS

- This hike is steep and demanding. If you're concerned about carrying your stuff to the base camp, hire someone to transport it up and down the mountain. The cost is generally US$5.40 per kg, but sometimes there's a flat rate.
- Stay in a hotel close to the trail entrance so you can easily start your hike before sunrise and, on your return, have a hot shower and comfy bed waiting.
- Reserve to stay in San Gerardo de Rivas for a few days after your hike. Take a day to relax and visit the thermal pools. Your muscles will thank you.

MUST-VISIT MARKETS IN PÉREZ ZELEDÓN REGION

Immerse yourself in local culture by exploring these markets.

Feria del Agricultor: Held every Thursday and Friday, this bustling farmers market offers fresh produce, artisanal cheeses and handmade crafts.

Mercado Municipal de San Isidro: A lively indoor market with food stalls, local goods and affordable meals.

Mercado Local Solidario Chirripó: A small, community-driven market in Rivas showcasing the best of local farmers and artisans.

Feria de Productos Orgánicos: Fresh produce market where you can find organic coffee, herbal remedies and homemade jams.

Visit a Hand-Dug Tunnel House

Go underground at Topolandia

Family-friendly and an Instagrammer's delight, **Topolandia** *(topolandiacostarica.com; US$20)* is Costa Rica's self-proclaimed first underground archaeological museum. Located in San Pedro de Pérez Zeledón, an hour's drive from San Gerardo de Rivas, the 'museum' was built by a family who created caves over 16 years using hand tools. There's kitschy art everywhere: bright yellow suns on the walls, flowers of various colors that line the entrance and even carved images of the Flintstones. Fun, strange and full of surprises, it's an off-the-beaten-path stop but something joyous for a rainy day. You can also sign up for tours that include an underground dining experience.

Green Trails & Waterfalls

Visit the Centro Biológico Las Quebradas

Only about 15-minute drive to the north of San Isidro de El General, looming viridian hills host the **Centro Biológico Las Quebradas** (*fudebiol.com; US$6*). This lesser-known nature reserve, situated between 1100 and 2400m above sea level in the river basin of Río San Isidro, is part of the Cordillera de Talamanca. Visitors can spend hours walking more than 4km of forest trails, horse riding, birdwatching or bathing in one of the reserve's many waterfalls. It's also possible to volunteer here.

Engage with San Isidro's Art Scene

Meet local creatives at bookstore Trincheras

Artist, musician and music producer Albán Corráles García has kept the regional art and music scene alive for over a decade at **Trincheras** *(trincherascr.com)*. Set on a hill on the outskirts of town, this former wooden mansion turned cool secondhand bookstore, artisanal and cultural center is the place to meet local creatives and enjoy a cuppa in the simple back-of-house coffee shop overlooking avocado trees and views of the barrage of hills behind San Isidro's church. It often hosts talks, film screenings and live music shows. Come browse a large collection of secondhand Spanish and English books and discover what's happening in and around town.

UNDER THE SHADOW OF CHIRRIPÓ

Walk on the mountain's flanks without the need to summit and enjoy San Gerardo de Rivas' beautiful nature.

START	END	LENGTH
Km 0 El Termómetro	Km 0 El Termómetro	7.3km; 5 hrs minimum

This hike allows you to have an alpine experience even if you can't book your Chirripó hiking slot (p381), taking you along the main path for about 4km and then on a loop back and down to San Gerardo de Rivas, from where you start and end the hike. Ensure you have acclimatized and leave early enough in the morning.

Start at ❶ **Km 0 El Termómetro**, the beginning of the Chirripó trail, adjusting to the steep incline until reaching ❷ **Km 1 Los Monos**, and then continue climbing up until ❸ **Km 2 Fila Cementério de Máquina**, from where it's another steep climb to ❹ **Km 3 El Jilguero** at 1990m.

Continue until the ❺ **turnoff**, leaving the main Chirripó trail to turn north and descending to ❻ **Cloudbridge Nature Reserve** (p384). You'll have to pay for an entry ticket to continue exploring the reserve. Otherwise, keep on the trail and proceed west until you bypass it.

From here, it's about a 2km walk west along a descending path, definitely the easiest part of the hike, that soon connects with the main road until you'll reconnect at Km 0 El Termómetro, completing an almost perfect circular loop on the Chirripó's western flanks.

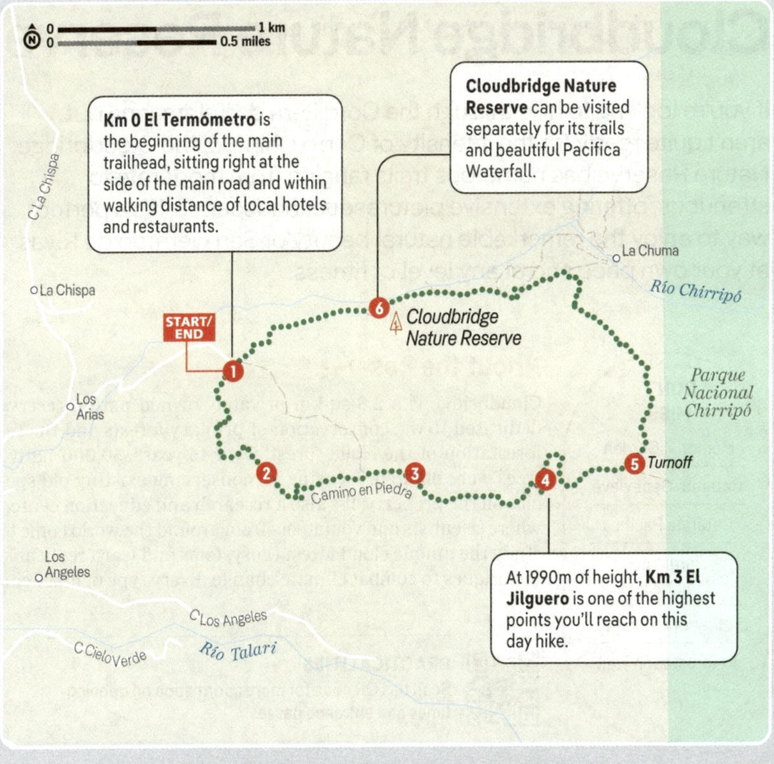

0 — 1 km
0 — 0.5 miles

Km 0 El Termómetro is the beginning of the main trailhead, sitting right at the side of the main road and within walking distance of local hotels and restaurants.

Cloudbridge Nature Reserve can be visited separately for its trails and beautiful Pacifica Waterfall.

At 1990m of height, **Km 3 El Jilguero** is one of the highest points you'll reach on this day hike.

C La Chispa
La Chispa
START/END
Los Arias
Los Angeles
C Los Angeles
C Cielo Verde
Río Talari
Camino en Piedra
Cloudbridge Nature Reserve
La Chuma
Río Chirripó
Parque Nacional Chirripó
Turnoff

TRAVELVIEW/SHUTTERSTOCK

TOP EXPERIENCE

Cloudbridge Nature Reserve

If you're looking to hike through the Cordillera de Talamanca but aren't quite ready for the intensity of Cerro Chirripó, the Cloudbridge Nature Reserve has numerous trails ranging from moderate to strenuous, offering extensive picturesque landscapes. It's a perfect way to enjoy the remarkable natural beauty of San Gerardo de Rivas at your own pace and at any level of fitness.

DON'T MISS

- Memorial Garden
- Catarata Genevieve
- Catarata Pacifica
- Jardín de Meditación
- Mirador del Valle
- Reforestation Trail

About the Reserve

Cloudbridge is a 2.8-sq-km privately owned nature reserve dedicated to the conservation of primary forests and the reforestation of the cloud forest. Over 15 years, 50,000 native trees were planted, focusing on conserving existing old species on the property. It's also a research and education center, where scientists and volunteers from around the world come to study the unique cloud forest ecosystems and learn replicable techniques to combat climate change. Every type of hiker can

PRACTICALITIES
Scan this QR code for more information on opening times and entrance passes.

enjoy the land: there are leisurely 600m trails with scenic waterfalls and rugged 8km treks through the cloud forest where Ticos and visitors train for summit Chirripó.

Best Trails for Trekking

One of the simplest and shortest trails is the Waterfall Trail, a 1km route leading to the **Memorial Garden** and to the three different waterfalls so you can experience the gorgeous terrain without a demanding hike. You'll also pass by the **Jardín de Meditación**, which has a fun labyrinth path made of stones. Take a moment to sit, relax, breathe and spin around in the labyrinth. This trail, in particular, can be quite slippery during the rainy season because of mossy rocks, but it is relatively doable for families with older people and small children, especially during the dry season.

For those who want something more challenging, there's a steep hike up Sendero Principal to **Mirador del Valle** (Valley Lookout) with panoramic mountain views. It's the starting point for longer trails that are less demanding and more rustic. The Sendero Montaña is a strenuous hike offering steep ascents up zigzagging grassy paths, but you're rewarded with awesome views of clouds rolling up the valley. The Cloudbridge North Trail winds through the Río Uran valley, past the only remaining pasture in the Cloudbridge valley. It clearly reflects how much reforestation has been done in the area, thanks to the reserve. Check with the Welcome Center before you head in that direction because parts of the trail are susceptible to landslides.

Hire a Tour Guide

Guided tours are available for individuals and small groups in English and Spanish, and sometimes French and German, but should be booked a minimum of 48 hours in advance. You can choose a 3-4 hour general tour or specialized versions focusing on primary forest, birdwatching or even nocturnal wildlife. If you're bringing a larger group, definitely inquire about their specialty topics, which include cloud-forest flora and fauna, the local history of reforestation and global climate.

Spend the Night

Three cabins (sleeping between one to four people) are available for rent for those who want to stay on the property for a minimum of two nights. The two cabins at the reserve's entrance have electricity and wi-fi, while the remote Galivan cabin, a one-hour hike from the reserve's entrance, does not.

PARTICIPATE IN CLOUDBRIDGE'S CONSERVATION

Casey McConnell, Executive Director, Cloudbridge Nature Reserve

The best way to experience Cloudbridge is to join our participant program. It's a very accessible option that allows you to spend time in and learn about the cloud forest in the company of motivated and knowledgeable researchers. Be prepared to be challenged by the steep terrain, and remember to breathe clean air and go at your own pace.

TOP TIPS

- The reserve is open daily from 7am to 5pm. Arrive as early as possible to see the most wildlife and to avoid peak high temperatures or midday and afternoon rain showers.
- Wear hiking shoes or boots with good traction and ankle support. They are necessary during the rainy season but a safe bet during the dry season too since it is a cloud forest.
- Spend some time in the Welcome Center at the entrance. There's a wealth of information about the wildlife in the park, including safety tips and a whiteboard where visitors track what animals they see.

Térraba

INDIGENOUS CULTURE | LOCAL CRAFTS | ARCHAEOLOGY

GETTING AROUND

A car is recommended to most easily explore Térraba – it is a beautiful scenic mountain drive along the Río Térraba. While there are buses from Pérez Zeledón to Buenos Aires and local buses into Térraba, the timetable can be unreliable.

Térraba's inhabitants are descendants of the pre-Columbian Chiriquí civilization, dating back 10,000 years, who thrived all over what is modern-day Costa Rica until the Spanish arrived in the 16th century. The Spanish missionaries and the military moved much of the Térraba population to the southwestern region of Costa Rica, near Boruca and the Río Grande de Térraba. Through violence and disease from the conquistadors, the Térraba community was largely destroyed, but those who remained maintained the culture and fought for recognition and rights from the government. By 1977, legislation guaranteed indigenous groups an inalienable land right. Since then, the Brörán and Boruca communities have had several showdowns with corporate and government interests that have cut down forests and tried to build on their sacred land. Tourism is a growing industry to promote and maintain Térraba culture. The area's main town is Buenos Aires, with restaurants and grocery stores.

TOP TIP

Spend a few days at a homestay with Brörán and Boruca families who have opened their homes for cultural exchange *(boruca.org; 2730-5178; laflordeboruca@gmail.com)*. It's the best way to support indigenous families and to learn about their culture respectfully. Inquiring about bringing donations (goods for local schools, for example) is appreciated before you arrive.

The Stories Behind the Art

Attend weaving and mask-making workshops

Traditional art and its ancestral techniques are foundational to the Boruca culture. Art is a means to tell stories about history and honor spiritual traditions, particularly within indigenous communities. When visiting Térraba, you'll find activities such as mask-making and weaving workshops led by local Boruca artisans.

Women are the keepers of the weaving tradition, using large pre-Columbian backstrap looms. Workshops demonstrate the impressive complexity of weaving the various threads in an imposing loom and how the Boruca use various plants and natural materials, for example, turmeric and *mata azul* to dye their thread. The artisans will show you how they extract these hues from various plants, and you can see how the thread transforms into colors in minutes.

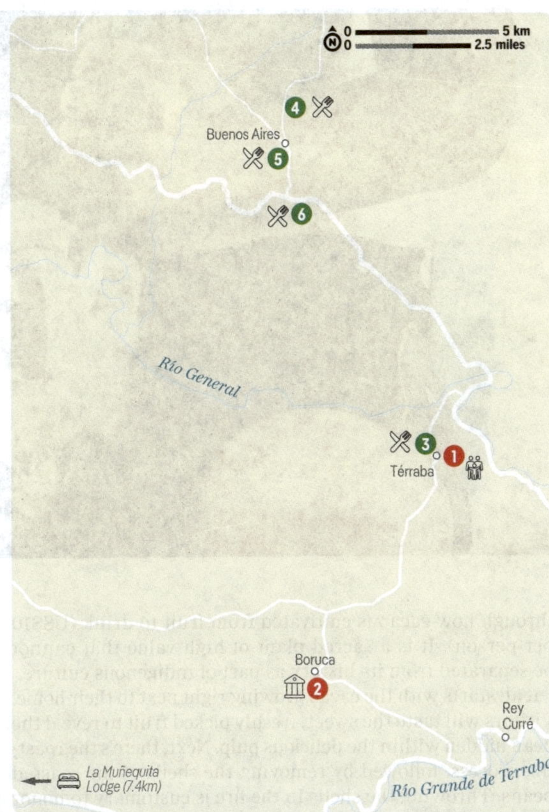

SIGHTS
1 El Descanso
2 Museo Comunitario Indígena de Boruca

EATING
3 Flacos Bar
4 Mau's Pizza
5 Pepe El Pollo Buenos Aires
6 Restaurante Los Pinos

Visitors can also attend mask-making workshops to watch skilled Boruca artists craft intricate masks out of cedar. The masks depict nature motifs and fierce warrior faces, and they honor their ancestors who fought the Spanish conquistadors. The masks are used in their **Fiesta de los Diablitos** in late December and early January to reenact the bravery of their forebears. There has been a revival in the last decade, as local men are taught this ancestral skill as a means to reconnect with the culture and as a way to support themselves independently as artists. It has traditionally been a men's art and the resurrection of this skill has renewed a pride in their history and culture.

From Bean to Beverage

Dive deep into cacao

Learning about cacao from the Brörán people is distinct from other similar activities geared toward tourists throughout Costa Rica. Cacao is deeply regarded by indigenous communities and their pre-Columbian ancestors. When visiting **El Descanso** *(eldescansoterraba.com)* in the morning or mid-afternoon, the owner, Jeffrey Villanueva, will walk you

CRAFTS IN BORUCA & BRÖRÁN CULTURE

Térraba's Boruca and Brörán communities make significant efforts to maintain their cultural traditions and land. Because of their geographic location, they remained relatively isolated during Spanish colonization, but were not immune to assimilation. The schools in these communities teach the children indigenous languages and spiritual, historic and ancestral stories. Craft making is central to this education but is also important to the livelihood of many adults through mask-making and weaving. There's a conscious effort by many Boruca and Brörán leaders to work with youth to instil a sense of pride and preservation of their powerful history and rich cultural heritage.

through how cacao is cultivated from fruit to drink (US$10 per person). It is a sacred plant of high value that cannot be separated from its history as part of indigenous culture.

It all starts with the cacao growing right next to their home. Visitors will taste the sweet, freshly picked fruit to reveal the bean hidden within the delicious pulp. Next, there's the roasting process, followed by removing the shells of the roasted beans. Throwing the shells in the fire is customary to honor the ancestors. Once the beans are sorted, you can use large stones to try the official ancestral grinding process. The women in the community, particularly the grandmothers, often did the grinding and would sing traditional Brörán songs while doing this work together.

Villanueva explains the cultural significance of each step, infusing stories from his family and upbringing. After grinding with stone and more modern hand machines, Villanueva's mother steps in to transform the beans into a drink. The final payoff is a delectable warm chocolate beverage and conversation with the family. Other activities include a mask-painting workshop (US$10 per person) and a guided walk to a petroglyph (US$8) set 400m away from the property.

Indigenous Roots

Visit a museum dedicated to pre-Columbian life

In the hills of Térraba amid the Boruca community, a small museum gives insight into pre-colonial life in this region of Central America. At the entrance is a Diquís sphere – a smooth stone sphere about 1m high and 1.5m wide that is one of the most well-known and remarkable indigenous artifacts from Costa Rica's pre-Columbian societies.

YANNICK MARTINEZ/SHUTTERSTOCK

Carving a traditional wooden mask

Museo Comunitario Indígena de Boruca *(facebook.com/laflordeboruca; free)* exhibits how Boruca communities lived before colonization, particularly through replicas of thatched-roof homes, their living quarters and cooking tools. It also emphasizes how they worked together as a community. A notable illustration shows the complete difference in their lifestyle before and after the Spanish conquistadors invaded, especially in their dress, homes and language.

A significant portion is dedicated to Boruca art. One section is full of powerful paintings and sculptures portraying many of their gods, goddesses and revered warriors. Another area explains and displays the various goods that indigenous artisans made, including drums, vases, plates and weapons. Take some time to look at the walls of photos of cherished local community leaders who helped build and support the museum, as well as the detailed photo book at the exit. The gift shop stocks gorgeous colorful bags, wallets, table runners and a vast assortment of wooden Boruca masks made by local artisans.

PRESERVING INDIGENOUS TRADITIONS

Jeffrey Villanueva, Brörán community leader and owner of El Descanso, explains the importance of his history.

A lot of the conversation about our tribes and families is as if we were completely annihilated or extinct. We are talked about in the past tense, and our presence is erased. But we are here, continuing an important relationship with Mother Earth, who provides us with medicine, raw materials for crafts, food, water and clean air. My family and I love to host travelers from all over the world to share our culture on the land of my great-grand-parents. We want visitors to Costa Rica to learn about our rich history and how we are continuing the legacy of our ancestors by building our community.

EATING IN & AROUND TÉRRABA: OUR PICKS

Pepe El Pollo Buenos Aires: Cure your crispy fried chicken and French fries cravings at this local fast-food joint. *10am-9pm* $

Restaurante Los Pinos: Fast-food local restaurant in Buenos Aires serving burgers, fried fish and a range of ice creams and desserts. *9am-9pm* $

Flacos Bar: In Térraba town, this is a popular place specializing in seafood and scrumptious burgers. *9am-5pm Mon-Sat* $

Mau's Pizza: Family-friendly restaurant and delivery service with a robust menu of pizza toppings and combinations. *10am-10pm* $

HELP ME PICK:

Parque Nacional Corcovado: Trails & Stations

Covering 424 sq km or a third of the Osa Peninsula, Parque Nacional Corcovado is the area's main draw, the largest national park in Costa Rica and one of Central America's largest lowland tropical forests. It's the only park in the country where you can see all four species of endemic monkeys and much other wildlife. However, this large area has many access points, and knowing where to go and what to expect is important.

Where to go if you love...

Wildlife Sightings

La Sirena (p397) is the most visited and developed sector, easily reached by boat from either Bahía Drake or Puerto Jiménez. On the one hand, this is the most popular part of Corcovado, with up to 240 day-trippers and 100 overnight visitors per day, but it is also the area that pretty much guarantees wildlife sightings – monkeys, anteaters and Baird's tapirs are commonly spotted near the beach and the riverbanks. The drawbacks? More people on the trails and overnights at the station's dorms are expensive and not necessarily better than the day trips – trails are off-limits from 5pm to 6am.

Multiday Hikes

To feel Corcovado's full majesty, sign up for a two- or three-day walking circuit from **La Leona** (southeast station near Carate; p414) or **Los Patos** (northern station south of La Palma) to La Sirena, where you must overnight, before exiting the park. It's a more immersive adventure, but it comes at higher costs (about US$350 for a two-day trip).

Coastal Jungles

La Leona (p414), west of the sleepy hamlet of Carate, is Corcovado's southeastern-most entrance and sees little foot traffic. It's either an entry or exit point for the multiday treks or a standalone day-trip destination offering five-hour walks along the thick coastal jungle and chances to see both land and marine mammals. Some large fig trees here have giant, spectacular buttress roots.

The **San Pedrillo** sector on the peninsula's western coast also extends beyond a beach and has a web of trails ending at a modest waterfall. There are many birds here but fewer wildlife sightings compared to La Sirena (p397).

Off the Beaten Track

El Tigre (p408), Corcovado's northeastern sector, is easy to access by *colectivo* from Puerto Jiménez and is managed by the local community of Dos Brazos de Río Tigre, but sees very little foot traffic. It's a less expensive day tour (US$170 for two people) along a 7km **trail** (p408) that's disconnected from all others and offers great birdwatching and the possibility of seeing monkeys. It's not impossible to spot tapir here, but as these are shy animals, unaccustomed to seeing hordes of tourists like at La Sirena, don't count on it.

TANGUY DE SAINT-CYR/SHUTTERSTOCK

Parque Nacional Corcovado – La Sirena

HOW TO

When to go The dry season between January and April is peak, but it's also the best time to go, exploiting the good weather to stay dry and see more wildlife.

Booking ahead You must reserve in advancefor La Sirena, especially in January and February. Other stations are less difficult, but as guides are necessary, booking ahead is best.

Getting there Once you are in Bahía Drake or Puerto Jiménez, local tour operators include return transportation to the station of your choice as part of any package.

Budget Corcovado is expensive wherever you decide to go, but El Tigre has the cheapest entry and tour fees.

Guides, overtourism & other considerations

It's mandatory to enter Corcovado National Park with a licensed tour guide. If you start from Bahía Drake, **La Picolina Tours** (p410) is recommended as they keep their groups small (about eight people), while in Puerto Jiménez, **Osa Wild** (p410) is a well-reputed company supporting local community tourism. Both can organize tours to all the park entrances except for El Tigre, which is managed by **Acodobrarti** (p408) in Dos Brazos.

Given the steep price tag of tours, many visitors expect to see animals, and La Sirena is best for that. Consider, however, that the animals there have grown habituated to the constant human presence found on those trails, and their behavior has adapted because of it. For a more authentic experience that feels less like an overcrowded open zoo, trek in other parts of the park where the wildlife remains elusive. That said, if your goal is spending a half day in the forest and seeing animals, especially if you are traveling with older people or children, La Sirena remains an easy and rewarding option. For something in the middle, day trips to La Leona are also recommended, while El Tigre will highlight Corcovado's over 400 species of birds.

Bahía Drake

UNSPOILED BEACHES | SEA EXPLORATION | WILDLIFE ENCOUNTERS

TOP TIP

Bahía Drake has no ATMs or banks, so get cash before arriving. While many businesses accept credit cards and PayPal, others only accept cash. You also avoid credit-card fees using cash.

The Península de Osa, part of the Puntarenas province on the southwest coast, is one of the most remote places in Costa Rica. Bahía Drake is on the peninsula's northern side, usually reached with a scenic boat ride through the mangroves of the Río Sierpe.

Bahía Drake (Drake Bay) is named after Sir Francis Drake, the British explorer, pirate and slave trader, who purportedly conducted his raids and hid treasure here in the late 1500s.

Today, this is one of the most popular destinations in the Osa Peninsula because it's a gateway to Parque Nacional Corcovado. Most visitors stay in the small coastal town of Agujitas for easy access to the park and snorkeling and diving tours to the stunning reefs surrounding Isla del Caño. But Bahía Drake also offers many other activities and opportunities to experience its incredible biodiversity.

Swim with Sharks

Diving and snorkeling in a biological reserve

Península de Osa's notable biodiversity can be explored through aquatic adventures at **Isla del Caño**, 24km west of Bahía Drake. The island and its surrounding crystal-blue waters are a biological reserve and attract scuba divers thanks to excellent visibility during diving season (December to April). Only

GETTING AROUND

Bahía Drake has a small **airstrip** with flights to and from San José and Puerto Jiménez (also in the Península de Osa). Two bridges over rivers have made the bay accessible to any car with decent front clearance. However, consider that once in the bay, there's little need to drive unless your accommodations are far inland from the main town, Agujitas de Drake. Tracopa *(tracopacr.com)* direct buses to Sierpe leave San José at 8:30am and 3pm. Take the morning departure to connect to the last one-hour 'ferry' speedboat ride from Sierpe to the bay's beaches. From Monday to Saturday, another *colectivo* leaves La Palma to Agujitas at 11pm and returns to La Palma at 4am.

HIGHLIGHTS
1 Parque Nacional Corcovado - La Sirena
2 Reserva Biológica Isla del Caño

SIGHTS
3 Playa Caletas
4 Playa Cocalito
5 Playa Colorada
6 Playa Danta
7 Playa el Rincón de San Josecito
8 Playa San Josecito

ACTIVITIES
9 Costa Rica Adventure Divers
10 Divine Dolphin
11 Drake Bay Diving

SLEEPING
12 Cabinas Murillo
13 Corcovado & Drake Inn
14 Drake Bay Backpackers
15 Martina's Place
16 Our Home Corcovado
17 Rancho Corcovado Lodge
18 Río Agujitas Eco Farm Hostel

EATING
19 Claudio's Grill
20 El Bucanero
21 Marisquería Roberto's
22 Soda Mar y Bosque

TRANSPORT
23 Drake Airstrip

a limited number of visitors are allowed to go scuba diving or snorkeling each day, so you will need a reservation and have to go with a certified tour guide. Reef-safe sunscreen and rash guards are highly recommended.

Snorkeling trips cost US$95 per person and usually begin around 7am, including two sessions of snorkeling, lunch and some beach time, ending in the early afternoon. Afternoon tours start around 1pm and end around sunset at 5:30pm. The 45-minute boat ride to the island offers great views of the Península de Osa's coast. It's possible to see schools of dolphins and even whales during migrating season.

The amount of marine life is astounding: it's normal to snorkel among various types of sharks – including whale and bull sharks – octopus, sea turtles and dozens of fish species. Beginners and expert divers will enjoy exploring the wondrous caves and sprawling coral reefs. Some diving shops, including **Drake Bay Diving** *(drakebaydiving.com)* and **Costa Rica Adventure Divers** *(costaricaadventuredivers.com)*, offer night options for certified divers.

The 300-hectare island also features pre-Columbian spheres like those on Finca 6 (p402) and was a burial ground for

WALK THE SENDERO DRAKE

Enjoy Bahía Drake's nature and stunning sea views by skirting the coast along this challenging hiking trail.

START	END	LENGTH
Playa Colorada	Playa El Rincón	10km; 3 hrs one way

The Sendero Drake (Drake Trail) is a jungle coastal route that's one of the bay's highlights. To complete the whole walk, start at daybreak from 1 **Playa Colorada** (p395), walking west past **El Bucanero** (p395). Go across a 2 **suspension bridge** and follow the coast to the northwest past **Claudio's Grill** (p395). The trail crosses another river on a 3 **second suspension bridge** and continues west via stone staircases and a paved path toward 4 **Playa Cocalito** (p395), a beautiful cove and the final destination for most people who come for a swim and rest. If you decide to continue, follow the well-marked trail along the coast, passing smaller beaches until arriving at the crescent of 5 **Playa Caletas** (p395). Swim and take a break before tackling the next 2.2km stretch to 6 **Playa Danta**, and then swerve to the southwest across the mouth of the 7 **Río Claro**, from where it's another 1.3km to 8 **Playa San Josecito** (p395). This is where several tour boats stop for lunch – arrange a ride back to Playa Colorada if you wish, or push on for another 1.8km to the long and windswept 9 **Playa el Rincón de San Josecito**. From here, hardcore hikers can follow a loop that almost reaches Corcovado National Park's 10 **Playa San Pedrillo** (p395), but consider time and the more than 10km return trip – it gets dark before 6pm.

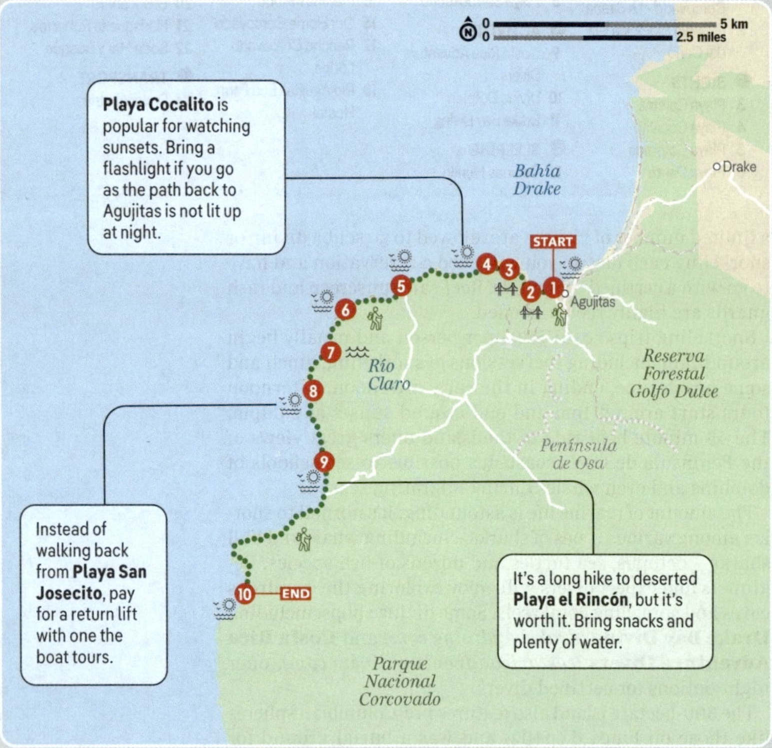

Playa Cocalito is popular for watching sunsets. Bring a flashlight if you go as the path back to Agujitas is not lit up at night.

Instead of walking back from **Playa San Josecito**, pay for a return lift with one the boat tours.

It's a long hike to deserted **Playa el Rincón**, but it's worth it. Bring snacks and plenty of water.

0 5 km
0 2.5 miles

Bahía Drake

Drake

START

Agujitas

Río Claro

Reserva Forestal Golfo Dulce

Península de Osa

END

Parque Nacional Corcovado

FIREBIRD007 SHUTTERSTOCK

Playa San Josecito

the Chiriquís people in the 700s and 1500s. Tourists, however, have not been permitted to visit the island since the onset of COVID-19, and it's unclear when it will reopen.

Encounter Creatures of the Night

Night Tours with 'The Bug Lady'

Tracie 'The Bug Lady' *(thenighttour.com; US$50 per person)* is a biologist and researcher who has been doing tours in Bahía Drake for over 25 years. Even if you're creeped out by critters, this 2½-hour experience will give you a new appreciation for nocturnal wildlife because of the seemingly infinite knowledge and passion of Tracie and her naturalist/photographer husband, Gianfranco. You might spot bats roosting under leaves and discover trapdoor spiders concealed in their intricately crafted burrows, leaving you with a newfound appreciation for after-dark animals and how these creatures profoundly impact our lives. If requested, guests receive a list of the animals they saw on their nocturnal exploration and links to additional reading materials – a perfect keepsake to

continued on p398

BEST BAHÍA DRAKE BEACHES

Playa Colorada: One of the bay's main beaches and very popular. Many restaurants and shops along the shore.

Playa Cocalito: A 30-minute walk from the bay, it's often deserted despite its proximity to the area's hotels and is a fine spot to watch the sunset.

Playa Las Caletas: Secluded beach with rock formations and plenty of fauna within walking distance from Playa Colorada. Stay close to the shore when swimming.

Playa San Josecito: Hike the Bahía Drake Trail to spend the day at this quiet, golden sand beach, perfect for relaxing. Beware of strong currents when bathing.

Playa San Pedrillo: It's a demanding six-hour hike to this secluded beach, as far-flung and paradisiacal as it gets.

EATING & DRINKING IN DRAKE BAY: OUR PICKS

Marisquería Roberto's: On a large covered terrace overlooking the bay, enjoy breakfast-type dishes, sandwiches and coffee. *5:30am-10pm* $

Claudio's Grill: At the Jinetes de Osa hotel, this coast-hugging spot offers a mix of Tico dishes, and vegan/vegetarian choices. *1pm-8:30pm* $$

El Bucanero: Beachside shack with a range of local dishes, pizzas, pastas, seafood and cocktails. Good location for a sundowner. *8am-10pm* $$

Soda Mar y Bosque: Centrally located. Serves hearty *casados* and a choice of guacamole, nachos and fresh fish. *6am-9pm* $$

DUARTE DELLAROLE/SHUTTERSTOCK

Isla del Caño

TOP EXPERIENCE

Parque Nacional Corcovado – La Sirena

The last great original tract of tropical rainforest in Pacific Central America contains 2.5% of the world's biodiversity and spans 33% of the Península de Osa. As soon as you enter this remote park, you'll see that unique flora and fauna are on full display. Traverse rainforests and rivers amid various species of remarkable birds, mammals and reptiles, including Baird's tapir and the giant anteater.

DON'T MISS

- Boat ride from Bahía Drake
- La Sirena Station
- Río Claro
- Baird's tapir
- Anteaters
- Howler monkeys

Osa's Natural Marvel

Parque Nacional Corcovado is one of the biggest attractions for visitors to Bahía Drake. The park occupies roughly a third of the peninsula and contains 42,570 terrestrial and 5375 marine hectares, including 500 marine meters from the coastline. Corcovado contains various ecosystems, including forests, beaches, coral reefs, mangroves and freshwater marshes.

PRACTICALITIES

Scan this QR code for more information on opening times, entrance prices, booking guides and boat transfers.

La Sirena

There are multiple ways to enter the park from different points around the peninsula (p390), but **La Sirena** is the closest to Bahía Drake and the most visited because of its proximity to Uvita and popular destinations along the Pacific coast. To visit Parque Nacional Corcovado and nearby Isla del Caño (p392) you need a reservation and a guide certified by the Costa Rican Tourism Board (ICT), which many tour operators can easily arrange for you. La Sirena remains a great spot to see wildlife, but don't expect to be alone: since 2023, the previous limit of 100 visitors a day has increased to 240 per day (split between visitors entering at either 7am or 10am) and the place can feel cramped.

Accessing the Park

Most visitors come with group tours (about US$115 per person) to do a five- to six-hour hike winding through a portion of the park's extensive rainforest trails. To do so in a day, the only way to enter at La Sirena is by a shared **speedboat 'shuttle'** with your fellow travelers. Tours leave in two trenches, the first around 5:45am and the second at 8am, timed to access the park at 7am or 10am.

The boat ride tends to be choppy, especially during the rainy season, so be prepared. But it's worth it since you may be treated to whale sightings, particularly new moms and their calves. Schools of dolphins swimming next to the boat are relatively common and gleeful. After an hour-long ride through Bahía Drake, the boat will approach Corcovado's shore for a 'wet landing' – be prepared to jump out of the boat into calf-deep water and walk up to the beach to enter the park. There's an area with showers to wash the sand off your feet and benches to put your shoes back on. A park ranger at the entrance checks your bags to ensure you don't bring food (and thus garbage) into the park. There are bathrooms at the entrance before you begin your guided hike.

A Bounty of Wildlife

Wildlife is truly at every turn – on the ground, in the trees, in the air, in the water. The nocturnal tapir is a coveted sight; these mammals have been on the planet for over 33 million years. Eagle-eyed guides point out sloths, owls, multiple species of monkeys and toucans in the trees. Wild turkeys and peccaries might cross your path. Snakes could slither down the trail, and caimans and crocodiles may float along the **Río Claro**. During the high/dry season, it may be harder to see the wildlife because of large groups of day-trippers on the trail simultaneously, so visiting during the off-season maximizes your chances of seeing the park's nonhuman inhabitants.

RAINFOREST FACTS

Around 60% of Parque Nacional Corcovado is primary forest – meaning it has never been cut down. And 40% is considered 'secondary', thriving again through reforestation or regeneration. Reforestation means planting seedlings or trees; regeneration lets new native plants grow from the forest land. Reforestation prevents the land from becoming barren, and regeneration lets nature create new life from the old earth.

TOP TIPS

- Stay overnight. Day tours can feel rushed because guides want visitors to experience as much of the park as possible within a few hours. Overnighting means you'll be in the park when the sun rises to take advantage of the early-morning animal activity and fewer people on the trails.
- Wear rubber boots (with good traction) for solid protection from snakes, and only pass through the river in shallow water where you can see the bottom and any approaching predators.
- Bring a refillable water bottle to stay hydrated. It's hot and humid all year and the hikes span hours.

HOW TO BEST EXPERIENCE BAHÍA DRAKE

Olman Brenes of La Picolina Tours shares his favorite ways to enjoy the bay. *picolinatours.com*

A night walk is very special because you can see a lot of noctural critters, amphibians and insects you can't see during the day.

For Parque Nacional Corcovado – La Sirena (p397), a day tour is possible. There are two times to go in the morning, but remember that seeing animals doesn't depend on timing; it depends on luck. Rest assured, it's practically guaranteed to see them – not a huge number, but you'll be pleased.

El Manglar, a mangrove area going out of the bay into the Sierpe Wetlands, is highly recommended to see birds and animals. Tours leave the main beach by boat and explore the mangroves for half a day.

PAUL ATKINSON/SHUTTERSTOCK

Dolphin, Bahía Drake

contined from p395

remember the night's discoveries. For logistical reasons, the Night Tour is only available to guests lodging in and near the village of Agujitas, and booking in advance is essential, especially in the high season.

Chase Whales & Mega-Pods

Marine biologist-led tours in the bay

Learn more about the wonderful marine life that inhabits Bahía Drake on tours run by the long-established **Divine Dolphin** *(divinedolphin.com; US$120 per person)*. Led by certified marine-biologist guides, tours start at 8am at the main beach and return between 1pm and 2:30pm. Each day is unique: during peak whale season in mid-July to October, boats stay close to shore, while at other times, they venture further out to look for mega-pods of dolphins that can sometimes number in the hundreds or even thousands. An on-board hydrophone helps hear the sound of the marine mammals. Tours include a vegan lunch served in reusable containers, and when the ocean conditions are right, boats stop to let guests snorkel using the gear provided.

Paddle in the Bay

Guided or self-powered kayaking adventures

Another great way to experience the bay is in a kayak, gliding into the web of mangrove-draped canals that go inland from the coast. **Ivan Mora** *(8529-1738)* runs guided marine or river kayak tours (US$50 for two hours) that exploit the tides to give different impressions of the bay's natural environments. Alternatively, rent a kayak (from US$20 for two hours) and strike out independently.

Beyond Bahía Drake

Explore former gold-mining villages and wildlife sanctuaries and take the river to an enigmatic archaeological site.

Many tourists visit Bahía Drake to stay a couple of days to check Parque Nacional Corcovado off their bucket list and then return to more popular and populated parts of the Pacific coast. And yet, endless adventures are available beyond Agujitas and the park's La Sirena sector.

Rural ecotourism is an excellent way to learn about Tico life outside tourist areas and build cultural connections with people who have been in Costa Rica for generations. An hour outside Bahía Drake by boat or car, you'll find immersive experiences in nature that are unique to the Península de Osa, where you can take a break from group tours and experience the region through a local's eyes.

Places

Sierpe

TIME FROM BAHÍA DRAKE: **1 HR**

Glide along Río Sierpe's mangroves

The small town of **Sierpe** is best known for having Diquís spheres on display in the city park and as the launching pad for travelers going to Bahía Drake. However, the town's geography and topography make the Río Sierpe the perfect location for wildlife-watching amid the astonishing mangroves.

The region's biodiverse mangroves play an important protective role for the land and thousands of species of flora and fauna. This vast network of trees prevents erosion when the rivers rise during the rainy season, contributes to the nutrient-rich soil along the river and filters carbon from the earth. The elements create a distinct ecosystem where mammals, reptiles, birds, insects and plants can thrive.

While the Río Sierpe is the major crossing for visitors headed to the Península de Osa, travelers staying in nearby coastal towns – such as Uvita (p351) – take a day trip to Sierpe specifically for the mangrove tours. Sierpe is an hour's drive from Uvita, so the tour is a popular ecotourism excursion. It's a 45-minute ferry (motorboat) ride from Bahía Drake, so if you do a morning tour, you'll still have plenty of time to catch the last boat before sunset. Book with an experienced and knowledgeable local guide who knows the land; for example, Enoc Espinoza Villalobos via **Sierpe Azul Tours** *(facebook.com/sierpeazul; US$95 per person for two people or US$65 joining a larger group).*

GETTING AROUND

It's common to drive to Sierpe, park in the paid parking lot, and take the shuttle boat to and from Bahía Drake – a good way to have a quick taste of the Térraba Sierpe National Wetlands. Alternatively, a *colectivo* leaves Bahía Drake Monday to Saturday at 4am and sometimes 1pm (check locally), reaching La Palma at about 6am, from where it's possible to catch onward connections to Puerto Jiménez and points north.

OSA PENINSULA'S MOST ICONIC WILDLIFE

Baird's tapir: The region's largest land mammal is a shy yet much-coveted sight at Corcovado – La Sirena.

Scarlet macaw: The distinctive squawk of these large, spectacularly colored parrots resonates across the Osa, where they are found in large numbers.

Anteater: Several species of this long-snouted mammal are found in the Osa, including its smallest and completely tree-dwelling version.

Coati: These highly social mammals live in groups and are often seen in the peninsula, even on the grounds of ecolodges.

Panamanian white-faced capuchin: A highly intelligent monkey with a pink face and white on much of the front of the body.

Rancho Quemado

TIME FROM BAHÍA DRAKE: **45 MINS**

Slow down in the country

Rancho Quemado *(visitranchoquemado.com)* is a quaint village where some Tico families have opened their homes to create sustainable ecotourism encounters that show tourists what daily life is like outside the beaches and national parks. There are many options: nature and native-plant tours, hikes to hidden waterfalls for swimming, fishing in a local laguna or taking a cooking class. Walk with Don Carlos and his jovial brother through the tropical fruit trees of their farm before a canoe trip along the river to spot the area's native birds: snow egrets, toucans and more. You'll eat a fresh and delicious meal sourced from the farm; say yes if they offer you sugarcane juice. There is also a homestay option.

Pan for gold

In the decades before Parque Nacional Corcovado was established in 1975, gold panning was a livelihood for many people in the Península de Osa. Dos Brazos (p409) is famous for its history as a gold-panning community, but the area around Rancho Quemado also shares this history. The gold present in the soil is unique to the Península de Osa and large companies came into these areas to capitalize on the natural resources. Because of the effect on the environment and delicate ecosystems, the government decided to protect the land by establishing national parks.

At **Finca Las Minas** *(US$35)* you can try mining for gold in a local creek. The owner, Don Juan Cubrillo, explains the story of gold mining, its significance to the region and information about his indigenous heritage. He also guides you to the nearby river, where you observe and experience panning for gold in the iron-rich ochre soil. Afterward, his wife Rosa provides a savory, traditional Tico home-cooked meal from their outdoor kitchen using local ingredients.

Los Planes

TIME FROM BAHÍA DRAKE: **25 MINS**

Rainforest cascades

While much of Bahía Drake's tourism focuses on Parque Nacional Corcovado or being out on the water, there are some stunning hiking trails and waterfalls only a few kilometers inland. Drive to **Los Planes** for a day of hiking and exploring the Naguala Falls along the Río Agujitas, one of the cleanest rivers in Costa Rica.

The **Naguala Jungle Lodge** offers accommodations and ecotourism experiences, such as day trips where visitors can

EATING & DRINKING IN SIERPE & PALMAR NORTE: OUR PICKS

Donde Jorge: Sierpe's unofficial embarkation point to Agujita de Drake has coffee, cocktails, finger food and some amazing river views. *6:30-9pm* $

Restaurante Wah Lok: Asian twists on Tico dishes, coffee and frozen *batidos* at this beloved Palmar Norte joint. *11am-9pm Mon-Sat* $

Las Vegas Marisquería: Another embarkation point in Sierpe that has *casados*, coffee and snacks, and can organize secure car parking. *7am-11pm* $$

Ristorante La Piccola Fragata: In Sierpe's northern suburbs serving tasty pizza, pasta, seafood and burgers in a nature-surrounded setting. *6-9pm Tue-Sat* $$

TIM FLEMING/ALAMY

Gold panning, Dos Brazos

trek through the rainforest and swim beside three spectacular waterfalls on the property. Some tours arrange lunch after the hike along with transportation, or visitors can stay overnight in the on-site cabins, relaxing in the open-air hammocks.

The roughly 15km hike to see all three falls meanders through creeks and riverbeds, leading visitors deeper into the rainforest and further away from cell-phone service. Move cautiously on the trails and pause to appreciate the pristine landscapes. It's extraordinary during the rainy season when the lush-green foliage drips with water that reflects rainbows from the sunshine. On the flip side, it's slippery during the rainy season and hikes may be canceled because of flooding.

La Palma

TIME FROM BAHÍA DRAKE: **2 HRS**

Find sloths up in the trees

When grandmother Nai Quirós Valverde was told to start walking to maintain her health, her grandchildren thought of creating a pathway in the remaining patch of rainforest on their 10-hectare farm. Little did they know that moving slowly around the property, Nai started noticing that her home hid something almost as slow as herself: sloths.

Today, **La Perica Sloth Garden** *(facebook.com/tierradeperezosos; US$75 per person)* in **La Palma** has become a prominent sloth sanctuary in the Osa Peninsula, going to great effort to reforest the area to help the sloths survive instead of using the land for cattle farming. Guides from the Valverde family will walk you around the forest, pointing at the many sloths hidden in the trees. They can also point out birds, insects, monkeys and various plants with great insight, and the yummy homemade lunch of empanadas and fruit included with the tour seals the deal.

COMMUNITY TOURISM IN THE PENINSULA

Ifigenia Garita Canet, naturalist and founder of Osa Wild, suggests some rural community tourism initiatives worth supporting. *@osawild. travel*

Ecoturístico La Tarde, a rustic lodge with cabins and dorms, is near Corcovado's entry point of Los Patos and perfect for forest walks, night tours and birdwatching.

I recommend our Heart of Palm tour, a combination of gastronomy and local knowledge, to learn about *palmito*, a nutritious food grown locally at the Jacana Rey palm plantation.

You can't miss a gold-panning tour, an experience that can only be experienced in Osa, where the soil is still rich in gold.

Rancho Raices de Osa is a local farm that runs tours that perfectly mix chocolate, nature and local culture.

FEDE90/SHUTTERSTOCK

Diquís spheres

TOP EXPERIENCE

Finca 6

Finca 6 is a UNESCO World Heritage Site and the second archaeological location in Costa Rica open to the public. The museum tells the story of the mysterious Diquís spheres of the Diquís delta, where they were created and unearthed. Visitors can walk throughout this ancient land to observe the spheres and other artifacts in their original size and site.

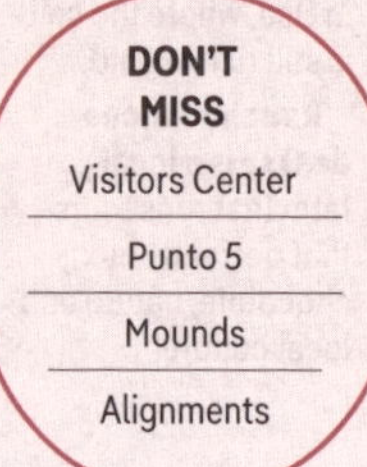

DON'T MISS

- Visitors Center
- Punto 5
- Mounds
- Alignments

Getting There

Drive 1½ hours south along Ruta 223 from Térraba through Palmar Norte and follow the signs. Turn carefully onto the dirt path leading to the visitors center. Cross a narrow, one-way bridge before arriving at the parking lot.

Visitors Center

Not only is this the place where you buy your tickets and can use the restroom, it also helps visitors get to grips with the site's unique history. As you enter, an animated movie tells

PRACTICALITIES

Scan this QR code for more information on opening times and ticket prices.

stories of indigenous legends, and there are cases full of artifacts and information about the relevance of the spheres (in English and Spanish). There are ancient vessels and small replicas of what indigenous homes looked like. Exhibits explain how the environment affected all aspects of their lives, helping visitors imagine pre-Columbian life and understand what they see on the grounds.

Punto 5/Point 5

It's worth spending the time to take the Settlements Trail (1150m) to see the full site. The first stop, **Punto 5**, was formerly a funeral and burial ground, but because of years of looting and farming, it's no longer recognizable as such. There are gatherings of relatively small stones halfway submerged in the earth, scattered fragments of artifacts and a sign explaining the effect of looting on the land and the culture.

Mounds

After walking past a cable railway connecting to an adjacent banana farm, the next section houses two spheres used as base structures for pre-Columbian homes. Although the houses no longer exist, a diagram on the site explains how cone-shaped structures were created as a way of showing community rank and power, and also to prevent flooding

Alignments

The largest part of the site are the 'in-situ' spheres, which means they are half-buried and were never moved. You only see a portion of the sphere sticking out of the ground – a piece known as the 'crown' – not the full spheres as on display in the Mounds section or in Museo Comunitario Indígena de Boruca (p389).

The spheres were aligned and arranged intentionally by the land's original inhabitants, particularly to mark where celebrations took place and also to show hierarchy. The signage notes how these massive stone spheres were made and mobilized and hints at the community's collective effort. From April through August, the group of three spheres aligns with the sun at its peak.

Collection of Spheres

This section contains over a dozen various-sized spheres that you can touch and inspect. The Museo Nacional de Costa Rica (p59) recovered them from various looters through numerous court proceedings, seizures and returns.

WHERE ARE THE OTHER SPHERES?

Besides San José's Museo Nacional de Costa Rica, the other 300 Diquís spheres recorded are scattered around the country. Many are in the southwestern region of Costa Rica. One is in the park across from the ferry dock where the mangrove tours and shuttles to Bahía Drake depart from in Sierpe. Finca Batambal, near Palmar Norte, takes reservations for tours. Isla del Caño (p392) has others but has been closed to tourists since the COVID-19 pandemic.

TOP TIPS

- As the museum does not offer English tours, if you don't speak Spanish, your best bet is to use the services of a guide via a tour company.
- Bring a hat or an umbrella to protect yourself from the sun, or visit in the morning.
- There's no public transportation to the site, so it's best to come with your own vehicle or organize a tour from Sierpe or Palmar Norte.

Puerto Jiménez

TROPICAL FJORDS | BEACHES | CORCOVADO'S BACKDOOR

TOP TIP
Aim to spend a week in the Puerto Jiménez area. Mix up days of planned excursions with days where you can lie on the beach or explore the peninsula on your own. **Osa Wild** (p410) is a great tour company for booking quality ecotourism adventures with local experts.

Puerto Jiménez is a tranquil coastal town on the southeastern part of the peninsula and a springboard for endless ecotourism excursions. It sits along Golfo Dulce, one of only four tropical fjords on the planet. It's attractive to snorkeling fans, tourists who want to visit Corcovado and sportfishers, many of whom own property along the coast.

Corporate investment has been a source of tension in this small agricultural village that has teemed with natural resources for over a century. The delicate environment has been threatened by the United Fruit Company in the 1930s, the US-based Osa Forest Products in the 1970s, and currently the Hilton Hotel conglomerate, all wanting to 'develop' the Península de Osa. In the 1960s, gold mining was booming for Ticos in Puerto Jiménez but halted after Parque Nacional Corcovado was established in 1975. By the 1990s, ecotourism had become one of the area's biggest economic drivers and remains so today.

GETTING AROUND

Puerto Jiménez has a tiny airport and an **airstrip** for domestic flights *(flysansa.com)* to and from San José, with a quick stop in Bahía Drake (p392) to pick up and drop off passengers. Transporte Blanco Lobo has a direct bus from San José to Puerto Jiménez at noon (which makes stops at Quepos, Uvita and Palmar Norte on the way) and one from San Isidro de El General at 6:30am. Alternatively, get a Golfito-bound bus to connect with the *lanchas* shuttling across the gulf to Puerto Jiménez (7am, 10am, 1pm and 4:30pm Monday to Friday, 8am, 11am and 3pm Saturday, 10am and 3pm Sunday) or get off at the Chacarita junction and connect with the 3pm departure to Puerto Jiménez. There's a rental-car office around the corner from the airport. If driving, take Ruta 2 to Ruta 245 along the coast.

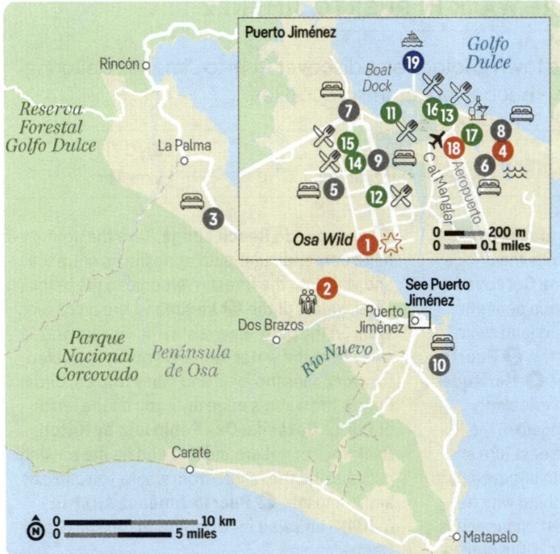

HIGHLIGHTS
1 Osa Wild

SIGHTS
2 Cacao Farm
3 Finca Köbö
4 Laguna

SLEEPING
5 Anluka House
6 Botanika Osa Peninsula by Hilton
7 Cabinas Jiménez
8 Corcovado Beach Lodge
9 Hotel Hoja de Oro Corcovado
10 Iguana Lodge

EATING
11 Brisa Marina Corcovado
12 Hellen's Chill House
13 Marisquería Corcovado
14 Panaderia Monar
15 Pizzamail.it
16 Soda Marbella

DRINKING & NIGHTLIFE
17 Sport Bar Marvitos

TRANSPORT
18 Airstrip
19 Ferries to Golfito

Enthralling Crystal Waters & Wildlife

Explore a rare tropical fjord

Golfo Dulce, one of only four tropical fjords worldwide, draws international researchers to study its depths. It's a sparkling snorkeling utopia teeming with schools of dolphins and groups of sea turtles.

It's is a sanctuary for various shark species and humpback whales who use it as a breeding ground to raise their offspring, thus whale sightings are a normal occurrence. Parque Nacional Corcovado and Parque National Piedras Blancas border this body of water, offering fantastic verdant views of the lush Península de Osa in every direction from your boat. Some surrounding beaches, like Playa Blanca, are designated Blue Flag or 'Bandera Azul', meaning they are nationally recognized by the government for their cleanliness.

Travelers can enjoy Golfo Dulce through various excursions. For those wary of the water, the numerous beaches around the gulf are excellent. Snorkeling tours are a family-friendly way to encounter the striking water and marine wildlife. Dolphins

EATING IN PUERTO JIMÉNEZ: OUR PICKS

Hellen's Chill House: Popular cafe owned by a local Tica: coffee and sandwiches for hiking. *10am-7pm Mon-Sat* $

Pizzamail.it: Long-established and surprisingly delicious way to assuage random pizza cravings. Get a heart-shaped pie. *4pm-midnight* $

Soda Marbella: The certified local go-to spot in Puerto Jiménez for seafood, especially *ceviche. 11am-10pm Wed-Mon* $$

Brisa Marina Corcovado: The burgers and fish fillets are yummy at this cafe and cocktail bar that's walking distance to the pier. *10am-10pm* $$

TOWN & NATURE WALK IN PUERTO JIMÉNEZ

Get out of the anonymous town gridlock and discover Puerto Jiménez's alluring beaches and natural side – but beware of the crocodiles.

START	END	LENGTH
Panadería Monar	Puerto Jiménez Airstrip	1.5km; 1 hr

Start at 1 **Panadería Monar** and walk past the sports field toward the coast, cross the bridge past cocktail bar 2 **Brisa Marina Corcovado** (p405) and watch fish in the lagoon beneath you. Keep walking along the coast (and swim with the locals, if you wish) past the 3 **Puerto Jiménez pier** and maybe stop at 4 **Marisquería Corcovado** for some seafood overlooking the bay. Keep walking and looking up in the trees for birds, and then take the east turn and proceed for about 200m along an unpaved path past 5 **Sport Bar Marvitos** (behind which flocks of white herons usually rest on branches in a lagoon) and walk for another 200m until 6 **Corcovado Beach Lodge**. Take the right-hand perpendicular path opposite its entrance and walk into the forest. Welcome to the brackish inner waters of the 7 **Laguna** where crocs lurk. Walk on the path, always staying vigilant and away from the water, keeping your eyes peeled for crocodiles (no joke) and many tropical birds. Follow the water's edge until you hit the fence of the 8 **Botanika Osa Peninsula by Hilton**. Backtrack or get around it to end on the walking paths inside the resort, from where you can exit and bump into 9 **Puerto Jiménez Airstrip** (p404) – and wait for a departing Cessna Grand Caravan plane.

will likely swim next to your boat while en route to Piedras Blancas, where the shallow reefs are ideal for snorkeling.

Adventurers can rent kayaks for river tours of the mangroves around Playa Platanares or the Río Rincón. Another awesome activity in the gulf is the bioluminescence sunset kayak tour around the coast of Puerto Jiménez, which is offered by several agencies, including Osa Wild (p410). Once night falls, the surrounding waves glow, thanks to this magical chemical phenomenon.

Sweet & Savory Farm Fun

Learn cacao cultivation and culture

Finca Köbö *(fincakobo.com)* is a family-owned and operated cacao farm plantation that's a 25-minute drive (17km) from the center of Puerto Jiménez. Visitors are first led to the traditional plantation, full of cacao fruit and flowers to learn more about the cultural significance of this sacred plant to the Maya. Tour guides share details of what happened to the land when the first Europeans arrived and the effects of colonialism on cacao plants, such as the emergence of the destructive plant disease Monilinia.

Next, you'll pass through a biological corridor between farms where animals can eat and safely hang out without much interference. It's a home for monkeys, coatis, sloths and tons of insects and birds that are endemic to the region – this portion of the visit emphasizes the importance of living in harmony with our surroundings. There's also a short walk through some secondary forests full of native plants and new occupants, which leads to the cacao cultivation area. Guides show off different species of cacao fruit that visitors can taste. Also, in the cultivation area, you'll see where the cacao is fermented and dried and the transformation process of going from the bean to a pure chocolate bar. Finish the tour with fresh fruit, a chocolate fondue and great conversation in the tropical garden.

PACKING LIST MUST-HAVES

If you're planning to spend some time traveling around the Península de Osa, here are a couple of things you must pack:

A wet bag: to keep your purse, wallet, keys and phone dry when traveling on boats or hiking in the rain. Many activities include a boat ride, so having a wet bag will give you peace of mind that your important things will stay dry.

Sunglasses and a hat: to provide protection from the glaring sun. While (reef-safe) sunblock and sunscreen are just as important, a hat can block and limit sun damage. Sunglasses block UV rays, prevent eye strain (especially when driving), and block the wind when on speedboats.

Beyond Puerto Jiménez

Gold-mining history, waterfalls and hidden trails await inland, while the Osa's southeastern coast beckons with surf and wildlife.

Places

The rugged road along the peninsula's southeastern coast leads to the former mining outpost of Carate, today a sleepy entry point to Corcovado National Park's La Leona station, from where experienced hikers can start or end multiday reserve crossings on foot. Midway is Matapalo, a surfers' beach backed by thick jungle and upmarket ecolodges, with surprisingly abundant wildlife in the trees, bushes and water. Twenty kilometers inland from Puerto Jiménez is the former gold-mining outpost and charming Dos Brazos de Río Tigre village. Named after its location along the 'two branches' of the Río Tigre, it boasts farms, hidden waterfalls, community tourism and Sendero El Tigre – yet another lesser-visited trail through Corcovado National Park.

GETTING AROUND

The area is served by *colectivos*. A Carate-bound van passes by Matapalo twice daily, departing Puerto Jiménez at 6am and 1:30pm and passing Playa Matapalo on its return trip at about 9:30am and 4:30pm. Dos Brazos and Puerto Jiménez are also connected by *colectivos* leaving Jiménez **BM Pali Supermarket** at 6am, 11am and 3pm Monday to Saturday. Contact driver *Luz (8771-9414)* for reservations.

Dos Brazos de Río Tigre

TIME FROM PUERTO JIMÉNEZ: **35 MINS**

Visit Corcovado's backdoor

Dos Brazos is the access point for the **El Tigre** sector of Parque Nacional Corcovado, an excellent day-trip option to experience the park's enveloping biodiversity without a long drive or busy trails. The 7.7km **Sendero El Tigre** has a steep ascent and then loops around a portion of the park but does not connect to other trails. Tours cost US$170 for two people with a Spanish guide and US$190 with an English guide, take about seven to eight hours and are suitable for anyone, including children. There's also a 3km, three-hour-long route option. While it may not have the same abundance of wildlife as La Sirena, tapir and anteaters have been spotted here, and it's a popular birdwatching trail with wondrous plant life.

You'll need a certified guide to access the El Tigre trail (just like at the other Corcovado entrances). Contact **Acodobrarti**, the Conservation Association of Dos Brazos del Tigre *(corcovadoeltigre.com)*, directly to make a reservation. It's helpful for coordination and is recommended, as it only works with local guides and women who cook and prepare food, so money is

TIM FLEMING/ALAMY

Río El Tigre

reinvested into the community and the maintenance of the Salón Eco Culturál, which helps support local children.

Pan for gold

Before Corcovado National Park was established in 1975 to protect one-third of the peninsula's landmass, the Osa was considered an 'unwanted place' due to its virgin landscape and lack of inhabitants. The discovery of gold in the region in the 1930s changed everything, convincing many to migrate here to exploit the gold rush.

Dos Brazos became one of the most important gold-mining centers thanks to the bounty of the Río Tigre's exceptionally high-grade natural gold, which uniquely accumulates on riverbanks in the form of sedimentary gold. Unlike larger nuggets, these sediments can be mined in a laborious artisanal process known as gold panning. Acodobrarti organizes interesting **gold-mining tours** *(US$40/50 with Spanish/English guide)* lasting three hours. You'll follow an expert guide down to the river to take part and understand the laborious extraction method using a gold pan to separate the precious metal from sand and gravel. Be warned, it's hard work, and come well protected from the scorching sun. Whatever gold you'll find – and you will – is given to you as a very special keepsake.

For a more immersive experience, consider taking the two-day hiking tour along gold miners' routes from Dos Brazos to Carate (from US$277 per person). You'll follow the Río Tigre and the boundaries of Corcovado National Park to overnight at Piedras Blancas, a former gold-mining community where you'll have a gold-panning demonstration the next morning before ending at Carate near Corcovado's La Leona Station (p414).

HOW TO ENJOY DOS BRAZOS

Esther Coronado Silva, President of Acodobrarti, the Conservation Association of Dos Brazos del Tigre, has tips on enjoying the region. *corcovadoeltigre.com*

Dos Brazos de Río Tigre has everything for a tailor-made experience to suit everyone – accommodations are plentiful, from rental houses with pools to cabins with shared bathrooms and ecolodges surrounded by lush mountains and the waters of the mythical Tigre River. Spend a couple of nights in town, either joining a gold-panning tour or exploring the river alone. Or you can employ one of our local guides to take you into Corcovado's lesser-known El Tigre trail. Use another day to hike Bolita Hostel's system of trails or just relax. Nature and fun are guaranteed!

BEST OSA PENINSULA TOUR COMPANIES

Osa Wild: Run by a Tica biologist and conservationist, it offers various outdoor adventures, expert guides, and a co-working space in Puerto Jiménez *(osawildtravel.com)*.

La Picolina Tours: Established Bahía Drake operator offering tours to Corcovado, snorkeling at Isla del Caño and more, including transportation around the peninsula.

Lokal Travel: Boutique ecotourism firm providing experiences that support Ticos and uplift local culture.

Sukia Travel: Osa-based operator focused on adventurous multiday trips and safaris around the peninsula.

Corazón de Osa: Specializes in community-based tourism and volunteering within Rancho Quemado.

ROSTASEDLACEK/SHUTTERSTOCK

Chase remote trails and waterfalls

Founded by Canadians Ronnie Engel and Val Rosiana 20 years ago, **Bolita** *(bolita.org)* is not just a beautiful solar-powered eco-hostel, but an excellent alternative Osa jungle experience at a fraction of Corcovado's prices. Set on a lush hill at the westernmost limits of Dos Brazos and rubbing borders with the national park's limits, Bolita's office is at the end of the village, from where it's a 10-minute walk to a river crossing, and another 20 minutes uphill slog through the forest to the accommodation proper.

Besides the abundance of birds and potential animal sightings, the beauty here is the remote quiet and 15km of trails snaking across 60 hectares of property, including four different waterfalls and two lookouts from where views stretch to the Barú volcano in Panama. It's important to know that Bolita is the only clothing-optional hostel in Costa Rica, so staying may not be suitable for everyone, but the trails are open to anyone for a lifetime access fee of $10. The perfect three-hour-long loop starts at the hostel along the Banana and the Big Banana trails to the Valle Frijol junction and proceeds upward, snaking around a creek for great views of the jungle stretching to the Pacific. Take the southwestern junction on the Bonanza trail and walk to the two namesake waterfalls, of which the 10m-high **Bonanza 2** is the grandest – remember you have to walk into the water and up the creek to the left as soon as you descend. Slog back up, take the Fila Quemada trail to the **Go-to-Go Viewpoint**, soak in the views, and descend to headquarters.

Playa Pan Dulce

Matapalo

TIME FROM PUERTO JIMÉNEZ: **40 MINS**

Down with the surf

Surfers flock to the Península de Osa's most remote corners to take advantage of the unique currents and strong breaks. Matapalo is nothing more than a gorgeous tract of coast backed by a slew of accommodations and wild nature about 18km south of Puerto Jiménez in the direction of Carate. This area has become an attractive spot for foreign investors and expats, and thanks to its varied waves, it's also the training ground for some of Costa Rica's best surfers. Tour companies offer lessons here for beginners on some gentler beaches, such as **Playa Pan Dulce** and **Backwash Beach**, which is also the most quiet and swimmable – we spotted dolphins when we visited last. Expert surfers go further south to the beaches of Cabo Matapalo (a 4WD is preferred), where swells from the west and southwest churn up strong but potentially dangerous waves. Near the beach, a 15-minute narrow and adventurous jungle trail leads to **King Louis Waterfall** – ask around, as it can dry up between February and April.

EATING & DRINKING AROUND PUERTO JIMÉNEZ: OUR PICKS

Pulperia El Cayman: Dig into burgers, *salchipapas* (sausages and fries) and *casados* on a beautiful, cool terrace overlooking the Río Tigre. *7am-7pm Tue-Sun* $

Minisúper Río Tigre: Friendly Dos Brazos supermarket serving *casados* and organizing local tours and even places to stay. *6am-7pm* $

La Cuchara Tica: The restaurant of Amazonita ecolodge serves typical Tico mains and international wines. Reservations are essential. *11am-9pm* $$

Martina's Bar: Popular Matapalo hangout, crowded with locals and expats on Friday nights. Its pork chop is recommended. *9am-9pm* $$

CROSSING INTO PANAMA

Catch the *lancha* from Puerto Jiménez to Golfito and an onward bus to the Paso Canoas border. This highly trafficked border can be chaotic. Pay Costa Rica's exit tax (US$8) either in advance at the Banco de Costa Rica website or the small Impuestos building across from the Costa Rica Migration office. Look for the 'Salida' window to get stamped out. It's a 10-minute walk to the Panama Migration office. Come prepared with a printed hotel reservation, proof of funds (a credit card should do) and, most importantly, proof of onward travel out of Panama. There are *colectivos* to David on the Panamanian side of the border. If you're on a visa run, note that at the time of research, the Costa Rica passport stamping offices had been moved 5km west of the border.

PHILIPPUS/SHUTTERSTOCK

Surfing, Pavones

Pavones

TIME FROM PUERTO JIMÉNEZ: **3 HRS**

Chase the easternmost surf breaks

Right across the gulf from Puerto Jiménez, Pavones is an even more secluded beach town on the interior coast of the Golfo Dulce, and a significant sojourn for dedicated surfers. It has recorded the second-longest waves in the world, as measured by length, height, speed and swell, so surfers flock here to experience the legendary breaks for themselves. The best come during the rainy season – April through October – but that's also when it's hardest to navigate wet roads and potentially flooded rivers along the mostly unpaved roads. It's a half-hour ferry ride from Puerto Jiménez to Golfito (6:15am, 7:45am, 11am and 3pm Monday to Friday, 7am, 9:30am and 2pm on Saturday, and 7:30am and 2pm on Sunday) and then a two-hour drive on unpaved roads from Golfito (a *colectivo* leaves at 10am and 3pm) until the end of the road deep in the coastal jungles. A 4WD is recommended to visit, and it's wise to have cash on you and a full tank of gas because there are no ATMs or gas stations nearby.

WILDLIFE & BEACH WALK

Take a walk along Matapalo's coast to discover that these beaches harbor plenty of wildlife and not just surf breaks.

START	END	LENGTH
Start Matapalo *colectivo* stop	King Louis Waterfall	1.5km; 1 hour

Start at the 1 **Matapalo colectivo stop** and walk down the forested road Calle Pan Dulce to 2 **Playa Pan Dulce** (p411). If you have a surfboard, this is a perfect, quiet spot for learning to surf or enjoying the long breaks sweeping in. Otherwise, make your way to the 3 **northern side of the beach**, paying attention to the forest and the water as it's common to see scarlet macaws flying overhead, pelicans fishing by the coast and spider monkeys swinging from the trees.

Then, walk back toward the beach's southern end and keep going south along a well-marked coastal trail through the forest and on to the southern end of Pan Dulce, where you'll find the 4 **Backwash Beach's Trailhead**. If you are lucky, as you walk through the forest you may bump into groups of capuchin monkeys. It's a short walk to the ample bay of 5 **Backwash Beach** (p411), the area's most suitable beach for swimming. Dolphins can sometimes be spotted jumping out of the water, so pay attention as you walk south.

You can either take the west turn onto a backroad that returns up toward the *colectivo* stop and maybe stop at 6 **Encanta la Vida** for a drink or continue walking for another kilometer to 7 **Cabo Matapalo** and, from there, to 8 **King Louis Waterfall** (p411).

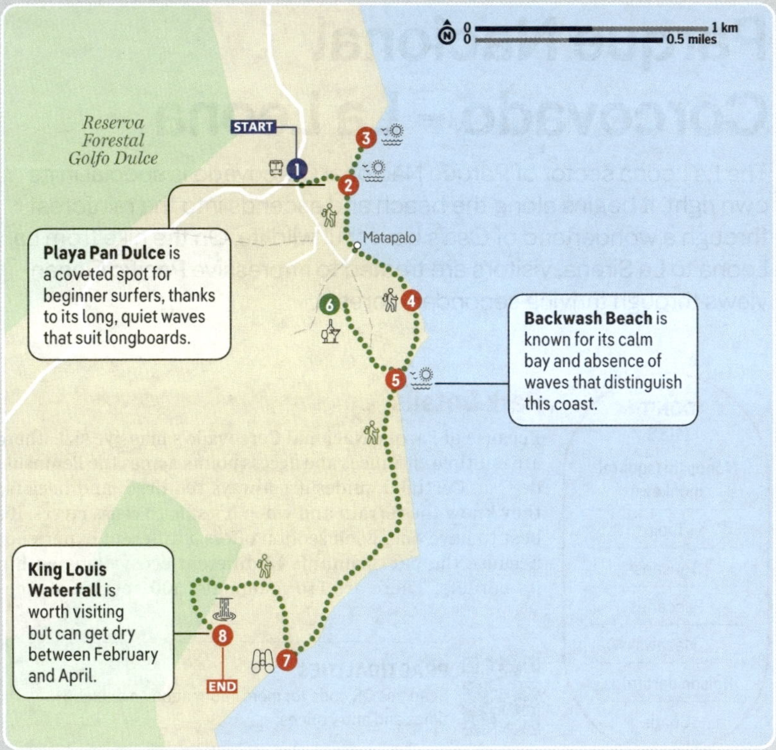

0 — 1 km
0 — 0.5 miles

Reserva Forestal Golfo Dulce

START

Matapalo

END

Playa Pan Dulce is a coveted spot for beginner surfers, thanks to its long, quiet waves that suit longboards.

Backwash Beach is known for its calm bay and absence of waves that distinguish this coast.

King Louis Waterfall is worth visiting but can get dry between February and April.

MR. JAMES KELLEY/SHUTTERSTOCK

TOP EXPERIENCE

Parque Nacional Corcovado – La Leona

The La Leona sector of Parque Nacional Corcovado is special in its own right. It begins along the beach and ascends into the rainforest through a wonderland of Osa's bountiful wildlife. On the hike from La Leona to La Sirena, visitors are treated to impressive Pacific Ocean views through thriving secondary forests.

DON'T MISS

- Monos titi (squirrel monkeys)
- Tapir
- Toucans
- Peccaries
- Macaws
- Poison dart frogs
- Coatis

Park Details

Because of Parque Nacional Corcovado's massive size, there are multiple entrances and access points across the Península de Osa. Certified guides are always required, and because they know the terrain and when it's safe to cross rivers, it's best to have one. Each section offers a different experience because the park contains 13 different ecosystems within its borders. There are 140 mammals, 500 species of trees

PRACTICALITIES

Scan this QR code for more information on opening times and entry prices.

and thousands of insect species in the park, which contains 2.5% of the world's biodiversity.

Hiking Trails

Visitors only spending a short time in the Osa usually take a quick day trip through the La Sirena sector (p397) near Bahía Drake. **La Leona** is for travelers wanting a more intimate experience with Parque Nacional Corcovado and the Península de Osa's all-encompassing ecosystems. Set on the southeastern side of the park, the La Leona trails are more demanding as you navigate varying terrain: beaches, rainforests and rivers.

Day-trippers can enjoy a five-hour hike on the **Sendero Madrigal**, with picturesque coastal cliffside views and well-maintained jungle paths. La Leona is also the entry point for the roughly nine-hour trek to La Sirena, a journey that will appeal to travelers who have endurance for long hikes and want to spend the night in Corcovado. Most visitors hike a portion of this trail and then return to Carate, but that can feel grueling and rushed.

Getting There

The La Leona entrance is a two-hour drive from Puerto Jiménez to Carate along unpaved rocky roads and across rivers. A 4WD is recommended in the rainy season, but cars with high clearance can also navigate it for the rest of the year. Some travelers hire drivers or group transportation with a tour, while others drive themselves and meet their guide in Carate. The drive makes the case for sleeping overnight in the park or at the beach before the station, where there are lodges. Day tours leave Puerto Jiménez at 5:30am for a potentially exhausting day of hiking in the park for five hours, and then another two-hour drive to get back.

Wildlife

The hike starts on the beach, walking a few kilometers to **La Leona Ranger Station**. It's possible to see four different species of sea turtles nesting along the route, depending on the time of year. As you enter the park, you'll be on the Sendero Madrigal that traverses the coast. Along the trail, you'll pass a cemetery used by the ancient inhabitants of the La Leona area centuries before it became a national park. Its rock formations and caverns can be seen at low tide. While La Sirena is one of the best spots to see wildlife running free, there's still plenty to see in the La Leona sector if you're not making that 17km trip.

LOCAL ADVICE

Ifigenia Garita Canet, President of Osa Wild

If you want to visit Corcovado, the best experience is an overnight tour. Other excellent options less saturated with tourists are day tours of the La Leona sector or the El Tigre sector, which the local community manages. The magic of Corcovado is lost when so many people are on the same trail.

TOP TIPS

- Be prepared for any type of weather. It can rain even during the dry season, so pack a poncho or light rain jacket.
- It will likely be hot and humid, so bring plenty of water, only in reusable bottles because single-use plastic is not allowed inside the park.
- A lot of the trail is uncovered, so wear a long-sleeve SPF shirt that protects you from sunburn and the heat. Always have a hat, especially one that covers your neck.
- Ensure you have sturdy hiking boots or shoes for walking on the beach, muddy trails and across rivers.

Places We Love to Stay

$ Budget $$ Midrange $$$ Top End

Los Santos

MAP p371

Trogon Lodge $$ Established lodge with beautiful gardens and wooden cabins set by the riverside, facing cloud forest views.

Tamí Lodge $$ Spacious African-style tents: a unique mountainside glamping experience. Connect with nature because there's no electricity.

El Toucanet Lodge $$ Birding-focused lodge with six homey rooms built with local woods, and balconies to enjoy the views and the birds, plus two suites featuring hot tubs.

Dantica Cloud Forest Lodge $$$ Luxuriate in gorgeous bungalows overlooking San Gerardo de Dota Valley. Private terraces, ecofriendly chimneys, hot tub.

Savegre Hotel $$$ The most upmarket hotel in town is set on a sprawling property next to the Savegre River and features a spa, private hiking trails, viewpoints and restaurants.

San Gerardo de Rivas

MAP p378

Casa Mariposa $ Cozy nature lodge with a shared kitchen, lounge area and five jungle-facing rooms, some en suite, set 50m from the entrance to Cerro Chirripó trailhead.

Hotel Uran $ Refuge-type hotel and restaurant set by the start of the climb to Chirripó, which also offers physiotherapy and massage sessions for tired hikers.

Hotel de Montaña El Pelicano $$ Mountain hotel with spectacular views and comfortable rooms; a 300m walk from Chirripó's ranger station.

Talamanca Reserve $$$ Room service and a private cloud-forest patio at this hotel with on-site trails and waterfalls.

Térraba

MAP p387

El Descanso $ Cabin homestay on Brörán land – family vibes and home-cooked meals.

La Muñequita Lodge $ Delightful working farm with cabins in Palmar Sur.

Bahía Drake

MAP p393

Drake Bay Backpackers $ Hostel run by the Corcovado Foundation that offers budget accommodations with all proceeds reinvested into environmental programs.

Martina's Place $ Stalwart budget option offering private rooms and dorms in the center of the village, yet shrouded by vegetation in a quiet garden.

Our Home Corcovado $ Rustic house, a 10-minute walk to the village, with only two en-suite doubles. Set in a private garden with excellent forest views. Also has a kitchen and is perfect for budget travelers.

Cabinas Murillo $ Good-value cabins right in the village's center. Choose one in the back row of their two-story buildings for stunning bay views.

Río Agujitas Eco Farm Hostel $ Rustic yet beautiful forest concept ecolodge set in the jungle about 1.5km from the bay, featuring doubles with mosquito nets and a campsite. Also offers a circuit of trails, night walks and tours.

Corcovado & Drake Inn $ These simple yet well-appointed rooms are set in two houses on the edge of town, in a quiet location with a restaurant and easy parking spots.

Rancho Corcovado Lodge $$ This beachfront hotel has ocean views, comfortable beds, air-conditioning and a delicious included breakfast.

Rancho Quemado

Rancho Verde $ Colorful cabin homestay with home-cooked locally sourced meals in the heart of Rancho Quemado.

Cabinas Laguna del Valle $ Confortable cabins hosted by the founder of Rancho Quemado. On-site meals and nature trails are available.

Los Planes

Naguala Jungle Lodge $ Rustic, rural ecolodge 7km from Agujitas; access to waterfall hikes, cabins and a yoga hut.

Puerto Jiménez

MAP p405

Hotel Hoja de Oro Corcovado $ Cute and cozy locally owned hotel in the town center; walkable to beaches, shops and restaurants.

Anluka House $ Very homey and clean set of apartments fitting up to four people, with equipped kitchens, washing machines, strong wi-fi and a quiet location in the heart of Puerto Jiménez.

Cabinas Jiménez $$$ Family-owned waterfront cabins and suites in the heart of Puerto Jiménez.

Iguana Lodge $$$ Upscale beachside ecolodge at the blissful Playa Platanares to the east of town, featuring a pool and satisfying restaurant.

Dos Brazos de Río Tigre

Bolita Hostel $ Fantastic solar-powered budget option with cabins and dorms set inside a wild forest with four waterfalls and 17km of trails. Note, it's a clothing-optional hostel, you need to hike for 30 minutes to reach it and carry in all your food to cook.

Los Mineros Guesthouse $ Orange-hued A-frame cabins with shared toilets and simple en-suite doubles set around a lush garden in the former bar, brothel and jail of Dos Brazos' miners. Host Suzana cooks for guests on request.

Amazonita Ecolodge $$ Family run ecolodge tucked at the end of the road in Dos Brazos, with charming wooden cabins, beds with mosquito nets and a jungle location.

Bosque del Río Tigre $$$ Sustainable ecolodge in Dos Brazos dedicated to birdwatching experiences. The cozy river-facing main house has four en-suite doubles. Also offers activities packages.

Matapalo

Encanta la Vida $$ Immersed in the forest and frequented by wildlife, this resort has a swimming pool, nice cabins and an inviting common area with a restaurant fitted with swings.

Lapa Ríos $$$ Where celebrities stay in the Osa. This all-inclusive luxury resort in the mountains overlooks Matapalo.

Pavones

Cabinas Mira Olas $ Welcoming cabins set around a tropical orchard backed by jungle that's a 10-minute walk from the town center and beach.

Cabinas & Café de la Suerte $ Three colorful cabins with brightly painted walls. The upstairs rooms share the hammock-hung terrace, while the downstairs room has a secluded garden corner, just 50m from the beach.

La Ponderosa Beach & Jungle Resort $$ Family-friendly beachfront hotel located outside of town, with a pool, restaurant and hiking trails.

Carate/Corcovado La Leona Station

Corcovado $ Set on a beautiful beach 1km away from the entrance to the park's La Leona sector, this hostel has cheap rooms, a campsite and offers meals, all surrounded by peaceful nature and breathtaking coastal views.

La Leona Eco-Lodge $$$ Right by La Leona, the 16 fully screened forest-green tents with beds are nestled between palm trees, with decks facing the beach that allow for frequent wildlife sightings.

GENEVIEVE VALLEE/ALAMY

Dantica Cloud Forest Lodge

TOOLKIT

The chapters in this section cover the most important topics you'll need to know about in Costa Rica. They're full of nuts-and-bolts information and valuable insights to help you understand and navigate Costa Rica and get the most out of your trip.

Catarata de Río Celeste (p194)

GALYNA ANDRUSHKO/SHUTTERSTOCK

Arriving

Costa Rica has two international airports: Aeropuerto Internacional Juan Santamaría (SJO) in Alajuela, 17km northwest of San José; and Daniel Oduber Quirós International Airport (LIR), also known as Guanacaste Airport, in Liberia on the Península de Nicoya. You'll find ATMs, food, convenience shops, currency exchanges and taxis, shuttles and buses at both airports.

Departure Tax

Visitors need to pay a US$29 departure tax when leaving Costa Rica on an outbound international flight. While many airlines will include the cost in the ticket price, budget airlines will not, and you'll need to pay it at the counter.

Visa

Most nationalities get a visa on arrival, good for a stay of up to 90 days.

Entry Requirements

You may or may not be asked for proof of onward travel or a return ticket when you arrive in Costa Rica or before you board the plane to Costa Rica. You also may be asked for details about your accomodations.

Wi-Fi

You can access free wi-fi at both the Liberia and San José airports.

Public Transport from Airport to City Center

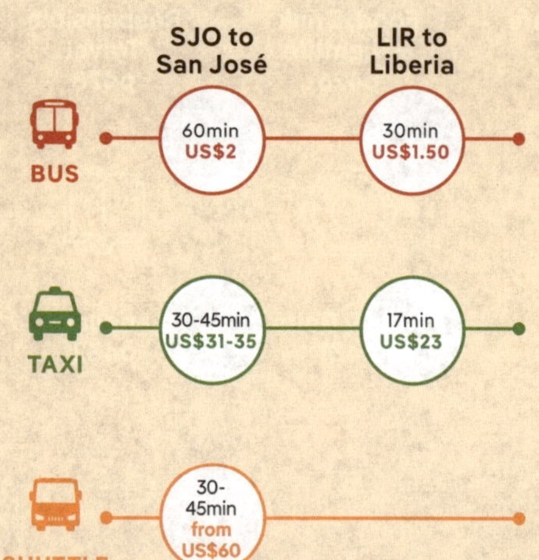

CROSSING BY LAND

Costa Rica has land border crossings with Panama and Nicaragua. The Sixaola border crossing (p172), the most popular option between Panama and Costa Rica, is open 8am to 5pm Panama time (one hour ahead of Costa Rica). You'll need to pay US$8 to leave Costa Rica, US$3 upon entering Panama, and need proof of US$500 or more in a bank account, an onward ticket from Panama and a photocopy of your passport. The Peñas Blancas border crossing (p217) between Costa Rica and Nicaragua – the only official one between these two countries – is open from 6am to midnight. You'll pay US$8 to leave Costa Rica and US$14 to enter Nicaragua.

Getting Around

Renting a car is by far the best and fastest way to see remote areas of the country, but there are networks of buses, shuttles and smaller planes that connect key places.

TRAVEL COSTS

4WD vehicle rental
From US$250/500 low/high season

Gas
Approx US$1.12 per liter

Bicycle rental
From US$10 per day

Shared shuttle
Around US$60

Public Bus

Buses are an effective and cheap way to get around, but services can be spotty in remote areas. Most local buses charge between US$1 and US$2 per fare, but it can go up to US$20 depending on the type of bus and distance. Check **The Bus Schedule** *(thebusschedule.com)*, **BusMaps** *(busmaps.com/en/costa-rica)* and **Yo Viajo** *(yoviajocr.com)*, or download the BusBud app to check routes and fares.

Tourist Shuttle

An alternative to public buses, tourist shuttle services run between many popular beaches. Depending on where you're staying, you may also be able to get an airport shuttle into town from either international airport. Major shuttle companies include **Tropical Tours** *(tropicaltourshuttles.com)*, **Interbus** *(interbusonline.com)*, **EasyRide** *(easyridecostarica.com)* and **Monkey Ride** *(monkeyridecr.com)*.

TIP

Avoid driving at night if possible. Driving after dark can be extremely precarious due to lack of lighting leading to poor visibility, and wildlife on the road.

ROAD CONDITIONS

Many roads between major areas are paved, well-maintained and passable, but driving can be tricky in some parts of the country, especially during the rainy season. On the Península de Nicoya, many roads between Playa Ostional and Santa Teresa are flooded out or muddy at certain times of the year. Having a 4WD will serve you well, and always give yourself ample time to get to your destination.

DRIVING ESSENTIALS

Drive on the right side

Driving age is 18

Speed limit is 90km/h

.05

Alcohol limit is .05mg

Internal Flights

Flying is a convenient and quick way to get around the country. Tickets start around US$140 and can be booked online with **Costa Rica Green Airways** *(costaricagreenair.com)*, **Macaw Airlines** *(macawairlines.com)* and **Sansa** *(flysansa.com)*. Flights often sell out and only run a few times per day so book in advance.

Driving

Renting a car will give you the most flexibility, but you'll need to take a few things into account. First, insurance is mandatory and many packages only cover damage that you do to other cars, not your rental. Many car rental places will request that you purchase additional insurance. Waze *(waze.com)* is an excellent navigational tool which is very useful rural areas.

Hiring a Driver

Hiring a driver to take you around Costa Rica will cost you between US$75 and US$300 depending on the distance, and difficulty of the drive. Negotiate the price in advance and check whether all tolls are included or not in that price. If you're traveling to an area that's easy to get to by shuttle or bus, it will be cheaper to opt for one of those options instead.

Money

CURRENCY: COLÓN (₡), US DOLLAR ($)

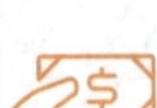

Cash is King

Many places accept cash and charge extra for credit card payments, sometimes up to 13%. At local markets, guesthouses, and for meals at *sodas*, cards might not be accepted. At high-end restaurants and resorts, you'll be able to use credit cards.

Tipping Culture

Tips are appreciated but not required in Costa Rica. Many people in the tourist sector have come to expect them as part of their payment, so it's a kind gesture and a good way to reward excellent service.

ATMs

LAFISE banks let you take out the equivalent of US$400 per day, while ScotiaBank and Banco Nacional de Costa Rica let you withdraw the equivalent of US$500 per day. Smaller towns might not have ATMs, or their ATM could be broken – always has some extra cash on you just in case.

HOW MUCH FOR A...

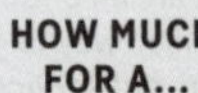

National park admission (general)
US$15-20

Bioluminescence or snorkeling excursion
US$70-100

Two-hour guided hike in the Central Valley
US$30-50

Ziplining tour
US$100-150

HOW TO... Conserve Your Colones

Budgeting tips for travel in Costa Rica including using public transportation or renting a bike rather than relying on taxis. Get accommodation with a kitchen and cook your own meals rather than eating out. Go to *sodas* and enjoy local food. Take advantage of the free beaches and rainforest wanders. And consider staying in hostels rather than hotels.

US DOLLARS

You can pay in US$ in a lot of places. However, if you do, expect to get any change in colones.

A RAINBOW OF CURRENCY

Costa Rican money is super colorful, making it easy to spot what denomination of currency you're using at a glance. The 20,000 colón bill (worth roughly US$40) is orange and features a hummingbird; the 10,000 bill is green with a sloth; and the 5000 bill is yellow with a monkey. The 2000 bill is blue with a shark, and the 1000 bill is red with a deer. Also in circulation are large, round 500 colones coins and smaller 100 colones coins.

Accommodations

High-End Hostels

In Costa Rica, the hostel experience has become competitive, with higher-end spots that feature co-working spaces, pools, gyms, spa services and excursions, along with dorm beds and private rooms. These hostels strike a fantastic balance between being backpacker-friendly and also providing that resort experience and cool, instant community. There are still humbler hostels available for those that don't want all the bells and whistles.

Repurposed Modes of Transportation

Places like the 727 Jungle Plane of Manuel Antonio and Hospedaje Combi Dream Bird hotel in Playas del Coco have taken traditional modes of transportation and transformed them into quirky and clever places to stay. These types of accommodations tend to sell out quickly, especially during the high season, so book early.

Ecolodges

Ecolodges combine a natural feel, proximity to wildlife and modern amenities for a complete experience. Often, they're set back from the main drag and serve up spectacular views and good facilities. Since they tend to be remote, you'll often need a good vehicle to get there. Rates will vary depending on the amenities and location.

Glamping

Glamorous camping pairs the great outdoors with top amenities and unique, ultra-fancy tents that come with features like private rooms and balconies. Like ecolodges, glamping experiences can vary from the slightly upscale to the downright decadent, with the most opulent tents featuring infinity pools, hot tubs and showers in the midst of the forest.

HOW MUCH FOR A NIGHT IN...

Hostel dorm
US$20-45

Guesthouse
US$90-160

Resort
US$220-500

Yoga Resorts & Relaxing Villas

Costa Rica is packed with high-end yoga resorts with on-site restaurants, spa services and opulent rooms, especially in places like Nosara on the Península de Nicoya. You can also find lower-end, but still relaxing options in places like Uvita, where the Art Villas overlook the Central Pacific Coast and offer yoga classes and meditation.

BEACH CAMPING

While you can still pull up to some of Costa Rica's beaches and pitch your tent, options are more limited than they used to be. Many beaches have signage prohibiting camping, and the general rule is to stay behind the tree line before setting up your gear if you're allowed to be there. Other options are campgrounds like **Don Trino** (p313) and **Eco Camping Papagayo** (p276), which offer basic amenities, some accommodations and a friendly community to share your rustic alfresco adventure with.

CLOCKWISE FROM TOP LEFT: CHIZHEVSKAYA EKATERINA/SHUTTERSTOCK, PIXEL-SHOT/SHUTTERSTOCK, GIVAGA/SHUTTERSTOCK, PHOTOLINC/SHUTTERSTOC, THAWORNNURAK/SHUTTERSTOCK

Family Travel

Costa Rica has a family-centric culture and plenty of activities for all ages, making it the ideal spot for your vacation. Many beaches balance the party and surf vibe with a family-friendly atmosphere, like Playa Samara, where you and your kids can connect with a community of local and international visitors. The national parks are family-friendly, too, and often offer discounts.

Discounted or Free Admission

Many activities and excursions offer discounts for kids under 12, and young children often get in for free. Under 12s also enjoy 25% off domestic airfare, although they generally pay the full bus fare. You can find specific rate information in the regional chapters of this book or on official websites. If you don't see a discount listed, always ask.

Driving & Riding with Children

When renting a car in Costa Rica, make sure to reserve your car seat in advance. Children under 12 use car seats or booster seats. Rental agencies will have these, but they are in high demand. Taxis usually don't have car seats. If you're hiring a driver, let them know that you have children so they can make the proper arrangements in advance.

BEST FOR FAMILIES

Bajos del Toro (p111)
A miniature cloud forest and dinosaur theme park in the Central Valley.

Parque Nacional Manuel Antonio (p334)
See capuchin monkeys, sloths and iguanas in this Central Pacific Coast park.

Playa Sámara (p291)
A family-friendly beach with a vibrant community.

Río Celeste (p194)
Hiking and child-friendly rafting in beautiful nature.

Monteverde (p186)
Monkey bridges and ziplining through the canopy.

Orosí Valley (p122)
Hiking, hot springs and a family-friendly coffee plantation and farm.

Airports & Border Crossings

While not guaranteed, families are often given expedited service at both air and land crossings. You'll also find family bathrooms and changing tables in all of the major airports in Costa Rica.

Family-Friendly Accomodations

Most hotels, hostels and bed and breakfasts are family-friendly, but you'll want to ask about specific needs, like cribs, in advance. You can also inquire about things like quiet hours and get a general sense of the vibe beforehand.

ESSENTIALS FOR THE KIDS

Families who land in San José can pick up any essentials they might have forgotten at City Mall in Alajuela. It's only about 15 minutes from the airport, has Spanish and English signage and is a great place to get everything from strollers to sunscreen.

Sunscreen does tend to be more expensive in Costa Rica, so bring your own, especially if you prefer a specific brand. You can buy beach toys at most major supermarkets, but floaties are a bit harder to find, so it's best to pack these in your luggage from home.

Health & Safe Travel

RESPECTING ANIMALS

Observing Costa Rica's abundant wildlife safely and respectfully is important. Do not feed or physically interact with a wild animal. Selfies with wild animals are illegal in Costa Rica. You should also keep your eyes peeled for snakes and insects, both of which can deliver painful stings and bites. Protect yourself from mosquitoes especially while trekking in the forest – malaria is not common, but dengue and chikungunya are.

Hiking Safely

Know your limitations when hiking, stay on marked trails and tell someone when you're leaving and when you're expected back. Having a fully charged phone battery, extra water and a snack for the road are smart plays too. Avoid hiking at night unless you're with a guided tour group in a well-traversed area.

Mind the Beach Signs

Always read and mind the beach signage, which will let you know if there are rip tides in the area. These signs also indicate the presence of marine animals or crocodiles. Don't take your chances with an unfriendly ocean, but if you find yourself swept away in a riptide, you should swim parallel to the shore and return once the rip is gone.

PETTY THEFT

Petty theft and pickpocketing is common in popular tourist destinations and party beaches. Keep your belongings in a zipped pocket or purse.

SWIM SAFETY FLAGS

Green flag Calm seas.

Yellow flag Swim with caution.

Red flag You can swim, but the conditions are difficult and may contain rip tides.

Purple flag Indicates the presence of marine life.

Double red flag No swimming under any circumstances. Do not enter the water.

Road Safety

Driving can be challenging or even dangerous in some parts of Costa Rica. Flooded roads, muddy conditions and unmarked routes are common, especially during the rainy season and in some of the more remote parts of the country. Invest in a 4WD, don't take unnecessary risks and avoid driving at night if you can help it. Also, give yourself extra time to get around.

FEARSOME FER-DE-LANCE

The fer-de-lance, or *barba amarilla* snake, is one of the most venomous in Costa Rica – avoid it at all costs. Fer-de-lance snakes belong to the viper family and are mainly found on the rainforest floor. These snakes, which can stretch as long as 2m, have brown and gray bodies with black diamonds on their heads.

CLOCKWISE FROM TOP LEFT: ANDREY BOYARSKIY/SHUTTERSTOCK, PHILIPPE CLEMENT/SHUTTERSTOCK

Food, Drink & Nightlife

When to Eat

Breakfast (6:30 to 10am) *Gallo pinto* (rice and beans) with eggs, avocado, plantains, cheese and coffee or juice.

Lunch (noon to 2:30pm) *Gallo pinto* with fish, meat or chicken and salad, sometimes served as a meal deal with a beverage.

Dinner (6:30 to 9pm) Dinner times vary depending on where you are, and the foods are similar to those that you'd expect at lunch.

Where to Eat

Sodas are the cheapest and most authentic places to eat and usually offer meal combinations. The atmosphere is very local, the menu might be exclusively in Spanish and the portions are significant. There are international dining options, too, from pizza chains to fusion restaurants, and some higher-end dining in places like Nosara and Manuel Antonio, where the service is top-notch and the menus varied. These upmarket choices have prices on par with what you'll find in the United States.

MENU DECODER

Platos fuertos Main courses
Arroz Rice
Frijoles Beans
Carne Beef
Cerdo Pork
Cordero Lamb
Huevos Eggs
Pan Bread
Pescado Fish
Camarón Shrimp
Pollo Chicken
Queso Cheese
Vegetariano/a Vegetarian
Vegano/a Vegan
Fresa Strawberry
Nepollo Cabbage
Papa Potato
Papas fritas French fries
Elote Corn
Melón Melon
Baya Berry
Plátanos Plantains
Aguacate Avocado
Piña Pineapple
Sandía Watermelon
Bebidas Drinks
Agua Water
Batido Smoothie
Café con leche Coffee with milk
Café con azúcar Coffee with sugar
Cerveza Beer
Vino Wine
Jugo Juice
Jugo de naranja Orange juice
Leche Milk
Té Tea
Dulces Desserts
Arroz con leche Rice pudding
Helado Ice cream

HOW TO... Enjoy a Fresh Coconut

You'll find vendors selling fresh, ice-cold coconuts all across Costa Rica. Generally, you'll select your coconut and the vendor will chop one end with a machete, exposing the opaque white flesh inside; that's easy to poke a straw through and start enjoying the coconut water below. Straws are usually provided; if not, you can simply poke through the flesh and sip directly from the coconut.

Once you've consumed all of the coconut water, you can remove the white flesh with either a straw or a spoon to enjoy it. Don't scrape too far down because you might end up getting some rind on your spoon. Instead, glide the straw or spoon over the inside of the coconut gently. Coconuts vary in cost, but you usually won't pay more than a few US dollars for this frosty treat.

CLOCKWISE FROM TOP LEFT: ADISA/SHUTTERSTOCK, KARLA FERRO/SHUTTERSTOCK

HOW MUCH FOR A...

Coffee
US$2-5

Batido
US$3-5

Casado
US$8-12

Main course at midrange restaurant
US$13-20

Imperial or Pilsen
US$2-4

Craft beer
US$8

Cocktail
US$8-10

Churchill
US$5

HOW TO... Order a Batido

Costa Rica's *batidos*, or smoothies, are refreshing, hydrating and absolutely delicious. When you order one (which might also be called a *refresco* or a *jugo natural*) – which are available everywhere – you have three big decisions:

¿Con qué fruta? (With which fruit?) Usually, your server will offer three to six fruit options, sometimes including banana, papaya, mango, *piña* (pineapple), *maracuyá* (passion fruit) and *sandía* (watermelon). There's bound to be at least one tropical fruit that you don't recognize, which is part of the fun.

¿Con leche or con agua? (With milk or with water?) Blending the fruit with milk makes it more like a milkshake (obviously), while blending with water makes it more like a juice. It's all a question of personal taste, but it's worth noting that some more acidic fruits, like pineapple, do not mix well with milk.

¿Con azúcar añadida? (With sugar added?) Actually, they don't usually ask. Unless you request otherwise, sugar is usually added. Depending on the sweetness of your fruit and the sweetness of your tooth, you may wish to request your *batido sin azúcar* (without sugar).

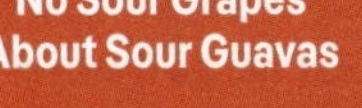

No Sour Grapes About Sour Guavas

Cas (sour guava) is a uniquely Costa Rican fruit that is too tart to eat. But blended with water and ice and plenty of sugar, it makes a refreshing drink.

SNACK LIKE A LOCAL

While out and about you'll find a variety of street eats perfect for satisfying your sweet, salty or savory tooth. *Churchills* (snow cones) are concoctions of ice cream, condensed milk, shaved ice and syrup, and you'll find them all around. *Elote* (roasted corn) is an excellent snack served piping hot and available at roadside stands and near popular attractions. *Ceviche* (marinated seafood) and chips are available on most beaches and are a great way to take the edge off your hunger. Ice-cold *pipa* (coconut water) is the way to quench your thirst and get some electrolytes at the same time. You'll also find churros, long tubes of fried dough covered in sugar and served with either caramel or chocolate sauce, and tamales, corn pudding with meat or vegetables cooked in banana leaves.

Other popular street foods include *chicharrones*, crispy strips of pork belly, and *empanadas*, half-moon-shaped pastries that can be savory or sweet. These snacks, often much less expensive than anything you'll find in a restaurant and even cheaper than *soda* fare, are ready in a flash. Many are portable, making them excellent for hiking or trekking.

You'll also find great food at night or weekend markets and food trucks. If you're craving something healthier, pop by the farmers market and pick up some super ripe fruit to enjoy on the go.

Responsible Travel

Climate Change & Travel

It's impossible to ignore the impact we have when traveling; Lonely Planet urges all travelers to engage with their travel carbon footprint, which will mainly come from air travel. While there often isn't an alternative, travelers can look to minimize the number of flights they take, opt for newer aircrafts and use cleaner ground transport, such as trains. One proposed solution – purchasing carbon offsets – unfortunately does not cancel out the impact of individual flights. While most destinations will depend on air travel for the foreseeable future, for now, pursuing ground-based travel where possible is the best course of action.

The **UN Carbon Offset Calculator** shows how flying impacts a household's emissions.

The **ICAO's carbon emissions calculator** allows visitors to analyse the CO2 generated by point-to-point journeys.

Respect Nature

Hiking in the cloud forest or rainforest and visiting beaches are two excellent ways to fully appreciate the country. Stick to the golden rule when you're visiting; leave nothing behind and stay on marked trails so as to not harm the ecosystem. Avoid making fires on beaches.

Be Careful with Wildlife

Sea turtle mass nesting and wildlife tours are popular in Costa Rica, and it's essential that these non-human residents of the country are properly respected. Do not interact with the sea turtles, or use flash photography on them, and avoid feeding any wildlife that you might meet along the way.

Consider Cycling or Public Transportation

Minimize your carbon footprint by using the power of your own two feet or opting for public transportation to get around. You'll gain a new appreciation for the country, get an excellent workout and avoid contributing to pollution.

Learn About Local Foods

Visit the Central Valley and learn about where Costa Rican food comes from. Much of the country's fruit hails from this area, and it's also an excellent place to visit a coffee plantation. You can discover the coffee harvesting process from bean to cup and patronize a local business at the same time.

Go to Animal Sanctuaries

Animal sanctuaries like **Monkey Farm** and **Rescate** provide a safe haven for injured animals and also focus heavily on conservation efforts. These organizations are a great place to spend your tourist dollars, and you'll enjoy a unique experience at the same time.

Support Local Businesses & Tours

Local tour companies and businesses rely on tourist dollars to stay afloat, so skip the bigger tour agencies and consider using smaller shops on arrival. If you're interested in surfing, there are plenty of instructors right on the beach who can give you a great deal and really appreciate the patronage.

National parks and many private reserves enforce a strict 'carry in–carry out' policy and do not allow visitors to bring in disposable packaging, including disposable bottles.

Costa Rica's tourist shuttles offer a convenient and affordable way to get around. Best of all, the shared transportation produces fewer carbon emissions, so it's better for the environment.

VOLUNTEERING RESOURCES

cloudbridge.org
Contribute to reforestation and conservation efforts.

sibusanctuary.org/visit-sibu
Help rehabilitate animals and build monkey bridges for safe passage.

reservaplayatortuga.org
Learn about sea turtle conservation and help protect vulnerable animals.

Accessible Travel

Accessibility is becoming more of a priority in Costa Rica with many outdoor destinations working to cater to those with different abilities. Beaches on the Nicoya Peninsula are also wheelchair-accessible, and you can rent beach wheelchairs on-site.

National Parks

Parque Nacional Manuel Antonio and Parque Nacional Cahuita have upgraded most of their major trails and walkways to be wheelchair-accessible, but there are still parts of these parks that are not.

Airport

The San José and Guanacaste international airports have wheelchair-accessible ramps and offer assistance for people disembarking from airplanes. Reserve two days in advance to secure your wheelchair. There is also Braille signage throughout these airports.

Accommodations

The Costa Rica Accessible Tourism Association has a list. Phone ahead to ensure that accommodations have what you need. Newer hotels will likely have amenities and infrastructure that caters to people of all needs.

RESOURCES

Costa Rica Accessible Tourism Association *(costaricaturismo accesible.com)* This NGO is an excellent resource and has a directory of hotels, restaurants, beaches and excursions that are fully accessible.

Serendipity Adventures *(serendipity adventures.com)* Organizes customized and accessible tours for both older people and travelers with disabilities.

Il Viaggio Travel Costa Rica *(ilviaggiocr.com)* Offers custom tours for travelers with disabilities

ON THE MOVE

Contact the **Association of Costa Rican Special Taxis** (+506-396-8986) to order a taxi that can accommodate your needs. Some rental companies at the international airports offer vehicles suited for all people, but be sure to reserve in advance.

Medications

Bring information from your healthcare professional about refilling medicines while you're in Costa Rica. You might be able to get your medication over the counter. If not, pharmacies can order it for you.

Visually Impaired Access

Trails in Parque Nacional Santa Rosa have QR codes that provide access to an audio description. In Parque Nacional Carara there's plenty of Braille signage.

ACCESSIBLE SIGHTS & ACTIVITIES

Museo del Jade (p58) • **Playa Pochote** (p309) • **Jardín Botánico Lankester** (p119) • **Jaguar Centro de Rescate** (p167) • **Parque Nacional Manuel Antonio** (p334) • **Reserva Biológica Bosque Nuboso Monteverde** (p182)

Costa Rica's major cities have paved sidewalks and generally smooth conditions, but you'll find rougher roads and pavements in the more rural regions. Some spots don't have sidewalks, and the roads have uneven places and potholes.

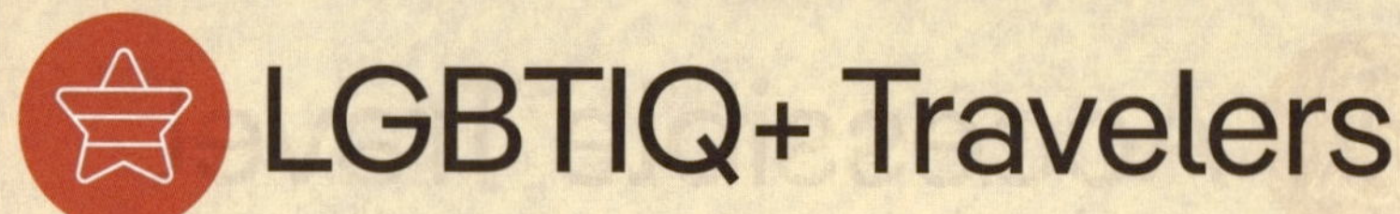

LGBTIQ+ Travelers

Costa Rica, in general, tends to be fairly LGBTIQ+ friendly, at least in more tourist-centric areas, but openly trangender folks are not as visible, and harassment can and does happen, even in popular beach communities. There are a few key destinations, like Manuel Antonio, that prioritize inclusivity and provide a safe and welcoming environment for all LGBTIQ+ travelers.

Progressive Rights

Costa Rica is the most progressive Central American country on LGBTIQ+ rights. Following some legal battles in 2020, same-sex marriages became legal. Same-sex couples are also recognized under immigration rights statutes and can adopt children.

While transgender visibility is lagging, transgender people do have legal protections, including the right to have legal paperwork reflect their gender. Transgender people also have hormone replacement therapy covered under Costa Rican healthcare, and there is anti-hate crime legislation on the books that protect LGBTIQ+ Costa Ricans.

SAN JOSÉ

The capital is home to Central America's most thriving LGBTIQ+ scene. Among the many gay gay bars and clubs are **La Avispa** *(The Wasp; @laavispacr)*, a lesbian dance club, and **Club Teatro** *(@el.teatro.cr)*, renowned for its drag performances. **Zona Rosa** is an excellent lesbian and gay sports bar, and **Sauna Oráculo** *(bargayoraculo.wixsite.com/oraculo)* is a gay men's sauna, club, and bar.

Manuel Antonio

Manuel Antonio, on Costa Rica's Central Pacific Coast, is a gorgeous destination with beautiful beaches, a top national park and regular LGBTIQ+ events, including beach parties and sailing expeditions. For more information on what's going on see *gaymanuelantonio.com* and the local LGBTIQ+ magazine Playita *(gaytourscr.com/playita-magazine)*.

COSTA RICA PRIDE CELEBRATIONS

Head to San José in June for the **Marcha de la Diversidad** (Diversity March) which goes from the Parque Central to the Estadio Nacional, with additional rallies and events at the Plaza de la Cultura. In the same month Tamarindo holds its **Tamarindo Beach Pride** *(@tamarindopridecr)*. In July it's time for Manuel Antonio's fun and festive **Orgullo en la Playa** (Pride on the Beach).

RESOURCES

The **Center for Research & Promotion of Human Rights in Central America** *(cipacdh.org)* is Costa Rica's premier LGBTIQ+ rights organization.
LGBTIQ+ dedicated travel agencies and tour organisers include **Gaycations Costa Rica** *(gaycationscostarica.com)*, **Gay Tours Costa Rica** *(gaytourscr.com)* and **Costa Rica Gay Traveler** *(costaricagaytraveler.com)*.

Best Hotels in Manuel Antonio

Manuel Antonio's top hotels and resorts that cater specifically to LGBTIQ+ clientele include **Oasis Diverse Adult Retreat**, with premier amenities, a waterfall, pool and gym; and **Hotel Villa Roca**, with plenty of outdoor space and a fantastic infinity pool.

 NITO/SHUTTERSTOCK

Nuts & Bolts

OPENING HOURS

Hours of operation vary across the country. The Central Valley tends to rise earlier and shut down right after sunset, whereas the bigger beach party towns will stay lively well after dark. Below are the most common hours of operation, but may vary depending on the season and where you are.

National parks 8am to 3pm or 4pm

Museums 9am to 4pm, closed one day of the week, generally Monday

Restaurants & Bars 7am to 9pm, but varies greatly depending on the region and type of food. Bars are open later.

Banks 9am to 3pm Monday to Friday with the exception of public holidays. Some banks are open Saturdays.

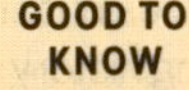

GOOD TO KNOW

Time zone
GMT minus 6

Country calling code
506

Emergency number
911

Population
5.18 million

Toilets

It's not a good idea to flush toilet paper in Costa Rica. Instead, you'll find a small bin next to the toilet where you can put your roll.

Smoking Rules

Smoking is banned in parks, outdoor restaurants and many other spaces in Costa Rica. Generally, you'll see a designated smoking area, but some hotels might not allow it on the premises. Always ask.

Electricity

110V/60Hz

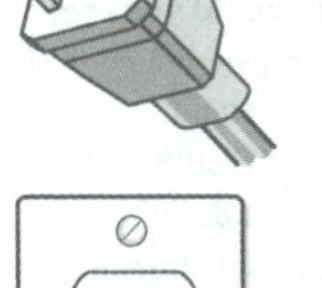

Type A
120V/60Hz

Type B
120V/60Hz

PUBLIC HOLIDAYS

Banks, public offices and many stores close for *días feriados* (national holidays).

New Year's Day January 1

Semana Santa (Holy Week) Thursday and Friday before Easter Sunday – many businesses shut down for the whole week

Día de Juan Santamaría April 11

Labor Day May 1

Día de Guanacaste July 15

Día de la Madre (Mother's Day) August 15 – coincides with the annual Catholic Feast of the Assumption

Independence Day September 15

Día de las Culturas (Indigenous Peoples' Day) October 12

Christmas Day December 25 – Christmas Eve is an unofficial holiday and many businesses also close during the week between Christmas and New Year

Tap Water

Tap water is completely safe in Costa Rica, and you can drink it and consume ice made from it without worry.

Language

Spanish is the national language of Costa Rica, and knowing some very basic phrases is not only courteous but also essential, particularly when navigating rural areas. That said, a long history of North American tourists has made English the country's unofficial second language.

Basics

Hello. Hola. *o·la*
Goodbye. Adiós. *a·dyos*
Yes. Sí. *see*
No. No. *No*
Please. Por favor. *por fa·vor*
Thank you. Gracias. *gra·syas*
Excuse me. Con permiso. *kon per·mee·so*
Sorry. Perdón. *per·don*
What's your name? ¿Cómo se llama usted?. *ko·mo se ya·ma oo·ste*
My name is ... Me llamo ... *me ya·mo ...*
Do you speak English? ¿Habla inglés? *a·bla een·gles*
I don't understand. Yo no entiendo. *yo no en·tyen·do*

Directions

Where's ...?
¿Adónde está ...? *a·don·de es·ta ...*
What's the address?
¿Cuál es la dirección? *kwal es la dee·rek·syon*
Could you please write it down?
¿Podría escribirlo? *po·dree·a es·kree·beer·lo*
Can you show me (on the map)?
¿Me puede enseñar (en el mapa)? *me pwe·de en·se·nyar (en el ma·pa)*

Signs

Abierto Open
Cerrado Closed
Entrada Entrance
Salida Exit
Servicios/Baños Toilets

Time

What time is it? ¿Qué hora es? *ke o·ra es*
It's (10) o'clock. Son (las diez). *son (las dyes)*
It's half past (one). Es (la una) y media. *es (la oo·na) ee me·dya*
morning mañana. *ma·nya·na*
afternoon tarde. *tar·de*
evening noche. *no·che*
yesterday ayer. *a·yer*
today hoy. *oy*
tomorrow mañana. *ma·nya·na*

Emergencies

Help! ¡Socorro! *so·ko·ro*
Go away! ¡Váyase! *va·ya·se*
I'm ill. Estoy enfermo/a. *es·toy per·dee·do/a* (m/f)
Call ...! ¡Llame a ...! *ya·me a ...*
a doctor un doctor. *oon dok·tor*
the police la policía. *la po·lee·see·a*

Eating & Drinking

Can I see the menu, please?
¿Puedo ver el menú, por favor? *pwe·do ver el me·noo, por fa·vor*
What would you recommend?
¿Qué me recomienda? *ke me re·ko·myen·da*
Cheers! ¡Salud! *sa·lood*
That was delicious.
¡Estuvo delicioso! *es·too·vo de·lee·syo·so*
The bill, please. La cuenta, por favor. *la kwen·ta por fa·vor*

NUMBERS

1 **uno** *oo·no*
2 **dos** *dos*
3 **tres** *tres*
4 **cuatro** *kwa·tro*
5 **cinco** *seen·ko*
6 **seis** *seys*
7 **siete** *sye·te*
8 **ocho** *o·cho*
9 **nueve** *nwe·ve*
10 **diez** *dyes*

DONATIONS TO ENGLISH

Numerous – you may recognise armada, aficionado, embargo, fiesta, machismo, patio and plaza.

DISTINCTIVE SOUNDS

Note that *kh* is a throaty sound (like the 'ch' in the Scottish loch), *v* and *b* are like a soft English 'v' (between a 'v' and a 'b'), and *r* is strongly rolled.

To Lisp or Not to Lisp

If you're familiar with the sound of European Spanish, you'll notice that Latin Americans don't 'lisp' – ie the European Spanish *th* is pronounced as *s* in Costa Rica and elsewhere in Latin America.

Tico Vocab

The abundance of diminutives formed by adding *-tico* (·tee·ko) and *-tica* (·tee·ka) to the ends of masculine and feminine words respectively – a cutesy way of saying 'small' or expressing affection – has earned Costa Ricans the nickname 'Ticos'.

Where the @!*# is it?

Spanish-language and English-language keyboard layouts differ because the two alphabets aren't quite the same. This shouldn't generally be a problem, but for one pesky – all too useful in the age of email – key. The @ ('at') symbol – in Spanish this symbol is called *la arroa* (la a·ro·a) – isn't necessarily labeled on keyboards or may not be accessed by simply pressing the keys you're used to. Try the F2 key, use an ALT code – or ask for help:

Where's the @ key? *¿Dónde está la arroa?* (don·de es·ta la a·ro·a)

The Host with the Most

If you're invited to share a meal in a Costa Rican home, your solicitous hosts will ply you with food and drink. Remember that politeness is highly valued in their culture, so be sure to extol the virtues of your hosts' cooking. This phrase should do the trick:

The food is very good! *La comida está muy rica !* (la ko·mee·da es·ta mooy ree·ka)

SPANISH AROUND THE WORLD

Though it's a distinct variety of Spanish, Costa Rican does share many similarities with its Latin American siblings which set it apart from the mother language, Castilian Spanish. Costa Rican Spanish was influenced by the southern Spanish dialect of Andalucía, from where the first Spanish conquistadors sailed to the New World.

THE COSTA RICA

STORYBOOK

Our writers delve deep into different aspects of Costa Rican life

Horse riding, Sarapiquí Valley (p248)
JOHN COLETTI/GETTY IMAGES

A HISTORY OF COSTA RICA IN 15 PLACES

From mysterious spheres and ancient civilizations in the Central Valley to the more recent history forged in the fires of Volcán Arenal and the torch carried by Juan Santamaría to fend off the *filibusteros*, these 15 places tell the story of Costa Rican resistance, a commitment to conservation and how the past shaped the Costa Rica of today. By Elizabeth Lavis

COSTA RICA IS the fcountry famous for not having an army, opting to spend what would be its military budget on conservation efforts and education. This sets it apart from many other countries in Central America and shapes much of the modern Costa Rican ethos and national identity.

Like its neighbors, Costa Rica's early history was shaped by its pre-Columbian civilizations, and we can trace their influence in a variety of ancient relics left behind. This indigenous history dates back to 10,000 BCE, well before Christopher Columbus claimed to have discovered the *costa rica* (rich coast) in 1502. The Spanish conquest decimated the indigenous population and subjugated its people until independence in 1821, but the fight was far from over. William Walker and the *filibusteros* from the US arrived in 1856, and Costa Rica experienced a tumultuous civil war in 1948.

The intervening years between then and now have been largely peaceful and focused on preserving the country's vast national treasures, from jungles and beaches to a glorious array of different fruits and vegetables as well as coffee, which is distributed throughout the world.

1. Sierpe

ANCIENT DIQUÍS SPHERES

Finca 6 is a short drive from the southern Costa Rican city of Sierpe, a UNESCO World Heritage Site featuring spheres created by the Diquís civilization between 300 BCE and 1500 CE. Nobody knows where these spheres came from, but they seem to be arranged intentionally, and many are 'in-situ,' meaning they're anchored in the earth. The spheres align with the sun between April and August, which may indicate that they had a spiritual significance for their creators. You can see similar spheres in San José's Museo Nacional de Costa Rica and Bahía Drake.

For more, see page 402

2. Turrialba

MYSTERIOUS JUNGLE RUINS

The mysterious ruins of Monumento Nacional Guayabo, just outside the Central Valley town of Turrialba, have puzzled archaeologists ever since they were discovered. They belonged to an advanced civilization that created aqueducts, sophisticated burial systems and roads, but vanished around 1400 CE, well before the Spanish arrived. These people left no written record of who they were or why they established themselves so deep in the jungle.

Visitors can walk through the ruins, see the giant mounds that once were foundations for homes, and marvel at the drawer tombs, a unique way of burying people in the hard earth.

For more, see page 133

3. Térraba

BRÖRÁN CULTURE AND CACAO

Térraba is a sustainable agricultural community in lower Puntarenas, home to the Brörán people, or Teribe. Since pre-Columbian times, the Brörán have revered and respected cacao for its health and spiritual properties. At farms such as El Descanso Térraba, visitors can take a cacao tour and learn about the importance and history of the fruit and its myriad health benefits, like anti-inflammation and antioxidants. The Brörán people are also known for their rich oral tradition and are one of the primary indigenous peoples of Costa Rica.

For more, see page 387

4. Parque Nacional Carara

THE HUETAR PEOPLE'S RIVER OF LIZARDS

One of the best spots for birdwatching in Costa Rica, Parque Nacional Carara is home to 360 different bird species and 1400 types of plants. It's renowned for unique ecosystems including the only transition forest on the Central Pacific Coast, and was once the home of the Huetar indigenous group. The Huetar were the most influential and mighty people in Costa Rica, spanning the Central Pacific Coast and through the Central Valley. Parque Nacional Carara means 'river of lizards' in Huetar language, a nod to the nearby crocodile-infested Río Tárcoles.

For more, see page 326

Basílica de Nuestra Señora de Los Ángeles (p114), Cartago

5. Cartago

THE TORCH OF INDEPENDENCE

The colonial-era capital of Costa Rica, Cartago is the oldest city in the country (founded in 1563) and a central player in its struggle for independence, as well as the site of the Basílica de Nuestra Señora de Los Ángeles, where you can find the miraculous *La Negrita*. According to legend, *La Negrita* (or the Black Virgin) can't be moved from the spot. Pilgrims travel from San José to Cartago annually for the Romería, a journey to celebrate the statue. Additionally, on September 15, the torch of independence returns to Cartago, and there's a massive celebration in Plaza Mayor.

For more, see page 113

6. Alajuela

COSTA RICA'S FAVORITE SON

Juan Santamaría of Alajuela has achieved almost mythical status in Costa Rica thanks to his efforts against the army of US mercenary William Walker in 1856. The drummer boy set fire to Walker's stronghold, dying while delivering a crushing blow to the enemy. Visit the Museo Histórico Cultural Juan Santamaría for information on the *filibusteros* from the US and the Costa Rican resistance, and Parque Juan Santamaría to see a bronze statue of young Santamaría and his legendary torch. Other famous parks include Parque Calián Vargas, named after a union organizer, and Parque General Tomás Guardia, named after one of Costa Rica's early presidents.

For more, see page 104

7. Santa Rosa

RAPID AND DECISIVE VICTORY

When William Walker and his band of marauders arrived in Santa Rosa, Guanacaste, they were met with a rapid response from the Costa Rica militia. This militia, encouraged by then-president Juan Rafael Mora Porras, had one mission: to beat the invaders back. The 1856 Battle of Santa Rosa was over in 14 minutes, and the enemy retreated north to Nicaragua. This decisive and triumphant victory is immortalized at the Museo Histórico Casona de Santa Rosa, on the site of the infamous battle. Visitors can learn about the Filibuster War and see historical relics and artwork.

For more, see page 214

8. Sarapiquí Valley

NATURAL BARRICADE AGAINST THE FILIBUSTERS

The town of Sardinal, Sarapiquí, was another pivotal flashpoint in the war between Costa Ricans and the *filibusteros*, and the Río Sarapiquí provided an invaluable tool against William Walker and his men by creating a natural barrier between Sarapiquí and the interior of Costa Rica. The invaders were successfully thwarted and slowed down at the Río Sarapiquí, buying the Costa Ricans more time to amass a resistance. This river was also essential to the coffee trade, sending beans to Puerto Limón for distribution in Europe.

For more, see page 250

9. Puerto Limón

THE LEGACY OF MARCUS GARVEY

Puerto Limón's legacy is rooted in the brave resistance of Marcus Garvey, who worked as a timekeeper for the United Fruit Company from 1910 to 1912 and stood up to the banana giant to combat racism and workers' rights violations in the city. Garvey also started the Black Star Line, designed with the purpose of uniting formerly enslaved people with their ancestral homes in Africa, and the Universal Negro Improvement Association. Puerto Limón has its own cuisine, which is a combination of Caribbean and Costa Rican flavors, and has deep ties to calypso music.

For more, see page 151

10. Monteverde

THE QUAKERS' CLOUD FOREST

Monteverde's history is entwined with a group of 44 pacifist Quakers who left the United States in the early 1950s in protest at their country's involvement in the Korean War. They moved to the misty cloud forests of Costa Rica, a country with no military, and settled on 1400 hectares of land in the northwest near Santa Elena. They created a private reserve to protect the land, originally called 'the Watershed Property,' and it eventually became Reserva Biológica Bosque Nuboso Monteverde, an area that's still protected today.

For more, see page 182

11. Cahuita

A CALYPSO LEGEND

While calypso music is nearly universally beloved on the Caribbean Coast, the town of Cahuita is in a league of its own. Walter Ferguson (1919–2023), the 'King of Calypso,' hailed from this sleepy seaside village. Locally, Ferguson was known as Segundo or Mr Gavitt, and he famously fused folk music from the Central Valley with the more complex and newer calypso from places like Limón. His style was thoroughly unique and reflected the Costa Rican experience like no other. Every July, Cahuita hosts the Walter Ferguson International Calypso Festival, and you can hear his music at popular bars such as Coco's in downtown Cahuita.

For more, see page 158

Casona de Santa Rosa (p212)

El Avión, Manuel Antonio (p331)

12. La Fortuna

TRAGEDY TURNED TOURISM

The popular tourist town of La Fortuna stands in the shadow of mighty Volcán Arenal, which hasn't bubbled up with deadly fire in have a century. On July 29, 1968, this volcano rained down lava, ash and huge rocks on two nearby villages. It continued sparking until 2010, leading curious visitors to flock to La Fortuna - which was spared in the blast - to see the spectacle and marvel at the mighty volcano. La Fortuna, once called El Borio, and other smaller towns on Arenal's eastern side avoided the volcano's wrath, inspiring the new name (literally 'the fortune').

For more, see page 231

13. Cachí Dam

A HYDROELECTIC POWERHOUSE

The Cachí Dam in Orosí Valley, built in the 1970s, is one of the thinnest double-arch dams on the planet and one of the first hydroelectric projects in Costa Rica. Lago de Cachí, the artificial lake at the base of the dam, is a fabulous area to hike and cycle around, and visitors can drive over the structure itself. The dam provides plenty of hydroelectric power and also wards off flooding. It's part of a series of such projects in the Central Valley aimed at thwarting flooding and providing fresh drinking water to the area's inhabitants.

For more, see page 126

14. Parque Nacional Manuel Antonio

AN ICONIC NATIONAL PARK

While Parque Nacional Manuel Antonio is not the country's first national park (that honor goes to Parque Nacional Volcán Poás), it's an enduring symbol of the country's commitment to biodiversity and conservation, as well as one of the most beautiful parks in the country. It was established in 1972 in an effort to protect this vast stretch of Central Pacific coastline from deforestation and development. Today, it's a mixture of ocean and forest, laced with trails and home to 109 different types of animals.

For more, see page 334

15. El Avión, Manuel Antonio

A CIA SCANDAL TURNED BAR

In the 1980s, the United States was involved in a secret weapons-for-hostages exchange with Iran, which supported the Nicaraguan Contras. This was done without Congressional sanctioning but with the full blessing of the Reagan administration. Unbeknownst to Costa Rican authorities, Nicaraguan guerillas set up secret airstrips deep in the jungle to fly weapons to the neighboring Contras. This scheme came to light when one of the aircraft was shot down, and Iran–Contra and the United States' involvement in it was exposed. Today, you can visit Manuel Antonio and have a beer in that very airplane at El Avión, more commonly known as 'Contra bar.'

For more, see page 331

MEET THE COSTA RICANS

In this Q&A, David Rodriguez Barrón tells our writer Marco Ferrarese about the slow journeys that helped him discover the essence and the heart of his beloved country.

What makes Costa Rica such an interesting place to visit?
Costa Rica is all about cool variety. You can see and feel the changes every 20km – no wonder it's considered one of the most biodiverse countries in the world! Its lush vegetation, varied landscapes, rivers, beaches, jungles, forests and volcanoes are definitely a playground for adventure-seekers.

I traversed the whole country in bikepacking mode over 4200km and covered the main cycling routes in Aventuras Con Proposito *(@aventurasconproposito)*, and I walked from the Caribbean Sea to the Pacific Ocean for 280km on El Camino de Costa Rica. Every pedal or step gives you wonderful recharging sensations and the feeling of being at one with Mother Nature.

What is in your opinion the biggest misconception about Costa Rica?
I'd say the biggest misconception about my country is that some people think we are an island (like Puerto Rico). Jokes aside, to me, people tend to think that there's only beautiful nature around here, when on the other hand we are an important technology hub with plenty of human talent in industries such as software development, medical devices and even financial services.

What do you think visitors should do to be respectful guests in Costa Rica?
I think that Costa Ricans don't take criticism about serious local issues very well – avoid making comments on our politics, religion, soccer, economy etc. Also, bargaining is not a customary thing to do here, and is not well accepted. Lastly, we don't have a very direct way of communicating issues and are wary of receiving feedback – if you do so, Ticos feel it's rude.

What have your journeys on bicycle and foot taught you about yourself and your country?
I worked for 22 years as a top executive in the largest beverage and dairy companies in Costa Rica. Work was always demanding, but I also had a desire to help socially, so I joined the Asociación Mar a Mar, which is the destination management organization for El Camino de Costa Rica – now a widely recognized 280km through-hike that crosses the country from one coast to the other – which seeks to promote sustainable rural development. That social aspect inspired me to do it, and to also decide to create bikepacking routes to help people travel all around Costa Rica.

When it comes to myself, I learned that if you prepare thoughtfully, age is not a limitation for any physical challenge – I completed all these adventures when I was already 47 years old.

And as for Costa Rica, well, thanks to those journeys, my motherland stepped up a notch inside my heart. Besides beautiful nature, every corner – rural or urban – was filled with the warm, lovely and respectful people that make this country incredible.

CLOCKWISE FROM TOP LEFT: JONATHAN GREGSON/LONELY PLANET, JONATHAN GREGSON/LONELY PLANET, CAVAN IMAGES/ALAMY, JONATHAN GREGSON/LONELY PLANET

A MIXED NATION

Costa Rica's population is made up of 83.4% white and mestizo, 7% Black, 2.4% Amerindian, 0.2% Chinese and 7% other ethnic groups such as Afro-Caribbean, most of whom live in small communities on the Caribbean Coast – a third of Puerto Limón's population is Afro-Caribbean.

TRAVERSING COSTA RICA

David grew up in San José and first started cycling and swimming to get fit when he was 10 years old. At 16, he was scouted for the Juegos Deportivos Nacionales (National Sports Games). Educated in Georgia, USA, he became an industrial engineer, working for 22 years in product management at Dos Pinos, the largest dairy company in Central America, and managing 1300 employees. Still, he kept cycling, and in 2014, he was one of the first Ticos to open a Strava account.

During the COVID-19 pandemic, David logged nearly 13,000km. In 2021, he quit his job to take a sabbatical, and set three goals for that year. First, to climb Chirripó, the highest peak in Costa Rica. Second, to walk across the country from the Caribbean to the Pacific Coast. And third, to bike around his homeland. Back then, he would have never imagined what adventures that last resolution would throw at him.

A COMMITMENT TO CONSERVATION

Costa Rica's optimistic carbon-neutral path and conservation efforts are an inspiration for every nation. By Elizabeth Lavis

COSTA RICA'S NAME literally means 'rich coast' in Spanish, and the honorific is apt. Its coastline is indeed rich, as is its gently mountainous, fertile interior farmland and prominent stratovolcanoes with their majestic craters and lakes.

In the 1990s, the country sat at a pivotal crossroads. Nearly half of its forest cover had vanished due to deforestation and overdevelopment, and it was rapidly facing down what so many other tropical countries were all too familiar with: the prospect of irreversible environmental damage.

Reversing the Past

The rapid disintegration of Costa Rica's lush forests was linked to its boom in agricultural exports. Bananas, one of its primary crops during this time, take up a lot of land and contribute to deforestation due to the sheer size of the plantations and the mixture of pesticides used to create uniform, unblemished fruit. In 1968, the first conservation legislation, called Ley Forestal de Costa Rica, was introduced and became an important precedent for the laws that would follow in the 1990s. The 1960s and '70s were also important years

Ceiba (kapok) trees (p22)

for creating protected areas and natural parks, an initiative headed by naturalist Mario Boza. As with the Ley Forestal de Costa Rica, Boza's idea for a sprawling system of national parks would be built upon in later decades.

Turning it Around

Costa Rica decided not to let deforestation win; instead, it took steps to stop and reverse it. The country began implementing a series of initiatives and incentives like the Payment for Environmental Services, which gives farmers money for their conservation and restoration efforts, and a total deforestation ban, both in 1997. The country has also created more national parks and preserved areas, as well as expanded existing ones. Currently, 25% of the land is protected, and there are plenty of Marine Protection Areas right off Costa Rica's shores.

The country continues to focus heavily on wildlife conservation, including vulnerable populations like jaguars and sea turtles. Breeding programs in the Central Valley help increase the number of scarlet macaws in the Península de Nicoya. In Playa Ostional, which experiences one of the largest turtle *arribadas* (mass nestings) on the planet, the street lamps emit a rich red color, which is less jarring to the nesting turtles than bright white lights.

Turtle on Playa Ostional (p293)

FROM LEFT: SERGE GOUJON/SHUTTERSTOCK, FERTNIG/GETTY IMAGES

Ecotourism

Costa Rica's dreamy shores and lush jungle draw visitors from all over the world, and the country has been successful in marrying its desirability as a tourist hotspot with conservation efforts. Ecotourism is a significant part of the economy, making up 8% of the GDP. Much of this ecotourism focuses on ultra-local or rural experiences, which put money directly back into the pockets of local people and creates a healthy economic environment for Costa Ricans. More local, authentic encounters also lay the groundwork for a more enjoyable vacation.

Challenges Ahead

Costa Rica has ambitious goals that it's projected to reach, including being completely carbon-neutral by 2050, but there are still challenges ahead. Old agricultural habits die hard, and encouraging farmers to embrace sustainability is difficult work. Incentives for regenerative and sustainable farming are certainly helping.

It also needs to find an effective way to balance its ever-rising tourist demands and the international community that flocks to its shores with its desire to maintain a conservationist and ecofriendly stance. There are several creative ways of tackling this problem. Animal rescue sites all across the country work with local officials to create safe passage for wildlife across busy thoroughfares, and the law maintains that beaches are public property, so the mega-resorts are not allowed to build right up to the shore.

Famously, Costa Rica doesn't have a military, opting instead to focus on healthcare, education and conservation. The population grows up with a deep understanding of how precious their 'rich coast' is, and will likely carry on the tradition of their ancestors with more innovative efforts and initiatives moving forward.

FIGHTING THE FILIBUSTEROS

Costa Ricans are peace-loving people, famously scrapping their military in favor of conservation efforts, healthcare and education, but make no mistake: they are warriors who will fiercely defend their homeland if called on to do so. By Elizabeth Lavis

IN 1855, NOT many years after winning independence from Spain, Costa Rica faced a threat in the form of mercenaries whose aims were to enslave the population and exploit the land. Fueled by imperialistic ideas of Manifest Destiny, William Walker and his band of mercenaries descended upon Nicaragua and quickly made their way into Costa Rica. Having just shaken off the yoke of Spain, the locals were understandably alarmed and answered President Juan Rafael Mora Porras' call to take up arms and defend their country. The National Campaign, which took place between 1856 and 1857, was a rapid recruitment of Costa Rican fighters, plus alliances with other Central American nations to fend off the likes of William Walker and other opportunistic invaders.

William Walker's Imperialist Dream

During the era of Manifest Destiny, people like Willian Walker were emboldened to set their sights on countries south of the United States' border and generally softly sanctioned in their endeavors despite the first Neutrality Act of 1794 that made it a crime for individual people to

Juan Santamaría monument (p104), Alajuela

go to war with another country. Walker's ambitions included invading and conquering several Central American nations and enslaving their citizens. He successfully invaded Baja California (Mexico) and then Nicaragua. He overthrew the government of Nicaragua and declared himself president between 1856 and 1857. Walker's expansionist aims eventually led him to invade Costa Rica, where he met a mighty resistance in the National Campaign both on Costa Rican and Nicaraguan soil.

The National Campaign in Action

President Mora Porras' swift response to the invader's threat worked, delivering Walker and his *filibusteros* (p214) several blistering defeats. At the Battle of Santa Rosa in 1856, Costa Ricans fended off the enemy in an impressive 14 minutes, confronting Walker's 300 soldiers with a unified force of 10,000 Costa Ricans.

At the Second Battle of Rivas, in neighboring Nicaragua, Walker's men faced Costa Rican National Campaign again and its most famous hero, Juan Santamaría. A drummer boy from Alajuela in Costa Rica's Central Valley, Santamaría lit fire to the hostel where Walker's men were resting, killing them all but tragically dying in the process. Santamaría was only 24 years old, and his cropped spiked hair earned him the nickname *el erizo*, meaning 'hedgehog.' His final request was that someone care for his mother if he perished in the battle.

Statue of Mora Porras, San José (p53)

FROM LEFT: HECTOR SEGURA/SHUTTERSTOCK, RAINER LESNIEWSKI/SHUTTERSTOCK

Juan Santamaría's Enduring Legacy

Santamaría's bold act killed 26 of Walker's men, and while his brave sacrifice didn't end the Filibuster War, it did change the trajectory of history. Santamaría showed the resolute strength of Costa Rica, and may have deterred more would-be invaders from testing their luck and attempting to subjugate the population.

Twenty-nine years after his death, Santamaria got the recognition he deserved in a national newspaper article entitled 'Un Héroe Anónimo' (An Anonymous Hero), a call to arms and response to the Guatemalan dictator Justo Rufino Barrios Auyón's threat to unite Central America forcibly. Referencing the Filibuster War and Santamaría's sacrifice, the article's intent was to fire up the population and remind them of past glories under the National Campaign.

Santamaría's star rose in the following years. He had a steamship named after him, and there is a park in his native Alajuela that bears his name. When you fly into San José, you land at the Juan Santamaría International Airport. April 11 is Juan Santamaría Day, commemorating the day he set the hostel ablaze and deterred the *filibusteros* from intruding on Costa Rica in the future.

Today, visitors can spend some time in Alajuela, right outside the airport, and visit the Museo Histórico Cultural Juan Santamaría to learn about Alajuela's most famous son and other brave members of the National Campaign who kept Costa Rica free.

INDEX

Map Pages **000**

Map Pages **000**

'San José's vibrant, pulsing culture and rapidly growing culinary and coffee scenes (p82) are undeniable and exciting to witness.'

CASSANDRA BROOKLYN

'The Río Sarapiquí (p248) is a defining symbol of Costa Rica's unwavering commitment to sustainable tourism. The mighty river houses swimming holes, white-water rapids, hidden birding spots and waterfalls galore.'

CHRISTA JIMENEZ

FROM LEFT: JOHN COLETTI/GETTY IMAGES, JOHN COLETTI/GETTY IMAGES

THIS BOOK

Destination Editor Jen Ruiz

Production Editor Jeremy Toynbee

Book Designer Dominic Allen

Cartographer Val Kremenchutskaya

Coordinating Editor Brana Vladisavljevic

Assisting Editors Anne Mulvaney, Clifton Wilkinson

Cover Researcher Kat Marsh

Thanks James Appleton, Alison Killilea, Kate Mathews, Darren O'Connell, Charlotte Orr

Paper in this book is certified against the Forest Stewardship Council™ standards. FSC™ promotes environmentally responsible, socially beneficial and economically viable management of the world's forests.

Published by Lonely Planet Global Limited
CRN 554153
16th edition – Oct 2025
ISBN 978 1 83758 394 2

10 9 8 7 6 5 4 3 2 1
Printed in China